AF842577

Global Innovation Index 2023

Innovation in the face of uncertainty

16th Edition

Soumitra Dutta, Bruno Lanvin,
Lorena Rivera León and Sacha Wunsch-Vincent

Editors

WIPO
WORLD
INTELLECTUAL PROPERTY
ORGANIZATION

This work is licensed under Creative Commons Attribution 4.0 International.

The user is allowed to reproduce, distribute, adapt, translate and publicly perform this publication, including for commercial purposes, without explicit permission, provided that the content is accompanied by an acknowledgement that WIPO is the source and that it is clearly indicated if changes were made to the original content.

Suggested citation: World Intellectual Property Organization (WIPO) (2023). *Global Innovation Index 2023: Innovation in the face of uncertainty.* Geneva: WIPO. DOI:10.34667/tind.48220

Adaptation/translation/derivatives should not carry any official emblem or logo, unless they have been approved and validated by WIPO. Please contact us via the WIPO website to obtain permission.

For any derivative work, please include the following disclaimer: "The Secretariat of WIPO assumes no liability or responsibility with regard to the transformation or translation of the original content."

When content published by WIPO, such as images, graphics, trademarks or logos, is attributed to a third party, the user of such content is solely responsible for clearing the rights with the right holder(s).

To view a copy of this license, please visit https://creativecommons.org/licenses/by/4.0

Any dispute arising under this license that cannot be settled amicably shall be referred to arbitration in accordance with Arbitration Rules of the United Nations Commission on International Trade Law (UNCITRAL) then in force. The parties shall be bound by any arbitration award rendered as a result of such arbitration as the final adjudication of such a dispute.

The designations employed and the presentation of material throughout this publication do not imply the expression of any opinion whatsoever on the part of WIPO concerning the legal status of any country, territory or area or of its authorities, or concerning the delimitation of its frontiers or boundaries.

This publication is not intended to reflect the views of the Member States or the WIPO Secretariat.

The mention of specific companies or products of manufacturers does not imply that they are endorsed or recommended by WIPO in preference to others of a similar nature that are not mentioned.

© WIPO, 2023

First published 2023

World Intellectual Property Organization
34, chemin des Colombettes, P.O. Box 18
CH-1211 Geneva 20, Switzerland

wipo.int

ISBN: 978-92-805-3320-0 (print)
ISBN: 978-92-805-3321-7 (online)
ISSN: 2263-3693 (print)
ISSN: 2788-6972 (online)

Attribution 4.0 International (CC BY 4.0)

Cover: Unsplash / Kevin Turcios, Google Deepmind, Simon Lee, Javier Miranda, Marek Piwnicki

WIPO Publication No. 2000EN/23

General enquiries relating to the GII, including from students, academics, journalists and others, may be sent to gii@wipo.int.

GII-related communications from Member States relating to innovation performance, the state of their economy's innovation metrics or related GII assistance requests should be directed to the Assistant Director General, IP and Innovation Ecosystems Sector, World Intellectual Property Organization, 34, chemin des Colombettes, CH-1211 Geneva 20, Switzerland (ies@wipo.int) and the GII Team at WIPO (gii@wipo.int).

Contents

List of figures and tables

Index to Economy profiles

Foreword

© Emmanuel Berrod/WIPO

Daren Tang, Director General,
World Intellectual Property Organization (WIPO)

Welcome to the 16th edition of WIPO's Global Innovation Index (GII), where we take the pulse of global innovation and reveal the innovative performance of 132 countries, as well as the world's top 100 science and technology clusters.

In 2023, we find the innovation environment mixed, with significant opportunities and sizeable challenges on the horizon.

On the one hand, ground-breaking technological progress continues unabated. As identified in last year's GII, two promising innovation waves are making their presence felt across economies and societies: a digital innovation wave, built on artificial intelligence (AI), supercomputing and automation, and a deep science innovation wave, based on biotechnologies and nanotechnologies.

Many of the key indicators of technological progress are trending positively. Computing power continues to increase in line with Moore's Law. Green supercomputing is becoming more efficient. Renewable energy is increasingly affordable. And the cost of genome sequencing continues to decline. Spurred on by the scale of the possibilities before us, top corporate R&D expenditure exceeded USD 1 trillion for the first time last year, with ICT firms the primary drivers.

On the other hand, anemic growth and high inflation, coupled with the lingering effects of the pandemic, are hampering global innovation. After a remarkable boom in 2021, innovation finance fell back dramatically last year, with the value of venture capital (VC) investments declining by 40 percent. While it is important to stress that, at USD 380 billion, deal value in 2022 is higher than at any point over the past decade (apart from the 2021 boom), the overall VC outlook remains uncertain.

A key challenge is converting the potential of novel innovation waves into tangible benefits that flow to everyone, everywhere. Technology adoption might be growing – more people have access to the internet, safe sanitation and drive electric vehicles than ever before – but take-up is not yet fast enough. For a second consecutive year, the GII finds that the socio-economic impact of innovation has stalled.

In this polarized innovation environment, supporting countries at all stages of development to grasp opportunities and strengthen innovation ecosystems continues to be a key objective for WIPO. While it is encouraging that many middle-income and emerging economies are climbing the GII ranks, with 21 countries overperforming on innovation relative to their level of development this year, it is still too early to determine whether the pandemic will have a lasting impact on innovation, especially in the Global South.

What we know for sure is that the data, trends and approaches featured in this year's report shine new light on global innovation performance. Whether you are from the private or public sector, are a policymaker, diplomat, researcher, investor, innovator or creator, we hope that the information contained in these pages enables you to draw informed conclusions and acts as a powerful tool for pro-innovation policymaking the world over.

Despite all the uncertainties we are currently facing, future advances in AI, energy, medicine and transport are in sight. WIPO will continue to support all Member States in their pursuit of innovation-led growth to promote job creation, development and opportunities so that new breakthroughs and discoveries can reach everyone and work for us all.

Acknowledgments

The *Global Innovation Index 2023* was prepared under the general direction of Daren Tang, Director General, in WIPO's IP and Innovation Ecosystems Sector led by Marco Alemán, Assistant Director General, and in the Department of Economics and Data Analytics led by Carsten Fink, Chief Economist.

The report and rankings are produced by a core team managed by Sacha Wunsch-Vincent, Head of Section, comprising Vanessa Behrens, Project Manager, Davide Bonaglia, Fellow, Lorena Rivera León, Economist and Jeff Slee, Data Scientist, from the WIPO Composite Indicator Research Section responsible for the GII, and the following consultant: William Becker, in a personal capacity.

Soumitra Dutta (Oxford University and Portulans Institute), Bruno Lanvin (Institut Européen d'Administration des Affaires, INSEAD, International Institute for Management Development, IMD and Portulans Institute), Lorena Rivera León (WIPO) and Sacha Wunsch-Vincent (WIPO) serve as co-editors of the GII.

The following WIPO colleagues provided substantive inputs to the GII elaboration or dissemination: Kyle Bergquist, Ryan Lamb, Bruno Le Feuvre and Hao Zhou, from the Statistics and Data Analytics Division, as well as colleagues from the External Relations Division, the Information and Digital Outreach Division, the IP and Innovation Ecosystems Sector, the Language Division, the News and Media Division, the Printing Plant, the Regional and National Development Sector, the WIPO Office in New York, and WIPO's External Offices.

A special thank you goes to our partners at the Portulans Institute, in particular, Rafael Escalona Reynoso, Mariam Chaduneli and Sylvie Antal for their contributions. We also thank the GII's Advisory Board and the GII Data Collaborators for their participation, as well as to the Competence Centre on Composite Indicators and Scoreboards (COIN) team from the European Commission's Joint Research Centre – led my Michaela Saisana – that conducted the statistical audit. Sincere appreciation is extended to Giovanni Anelli (CERN), Cristina Draghici (ISO) and Silvia Montoya (UNESCO), who participated as representatives of their respective organizations during the GII Advisory Board meeting, contributing significantly to the discussions and outcomes. The report was edited by Richard Cook, Andy Platts and James Cooke at Book Now Ltd. The GII interactive data website was developed by Pere Rovira and Victor Pascual at OneTandem.

We are grateful to the following individuals and institutions for their collaboration with data requests, without whom the Index would not be what it is:

BloombergNEF: Evelina Stoikou

Brand Finance: Annie Brown, Artur Bryzghalov, David Haigh, Bethany Johnson, Thulith Perera and Binuri Ranasinghe

CB Insights: Carson Armstrong, Matthew Rados and Aaron Winkler

Centre for Science and Technology Studies (CWTS), Leiden University: Robert Tijssen and Alfredo Yegros

Clarivate Analytics: Bastien Blondin and Joseph Brightbill

data.ai: Donny Kristianto and Lexi Sydow

European Commission Joint Research Centre: Begoña Cabeza Martínez, Jaime Lagüera González, Ana Rita Neves, Panagiotis Ravanos, Michaela Saisana, Oscar Smallenbroek and Carlos Jorge Tacao Moura from COIN; and Nicola Grassano, Hector Hernández and Elisabeth Nindl

European Organization for Nuclear Research (CERN): Giovanni Anelli and Manuela Cirilli

GitHub: Peter Cihon, Mike Linksvayer and Kevin Xu

Global Entrepreneurship Monitor (GEM): Niels Bosma, Alicia Coduras and Aileen Ionescu-Somers

Growth Lab at Harvard University: Sebastián Bustos, Timothy Paul Cheston and Annie White

International Atomic Energy Agency (IAEA): Mauro Carrara, Gerd Hinterleitner, Josephine Nkhula and Egor Titovich

International Energy Agency (IEA): Taylor Morrison, Julian Prime and Roberta Quadrelli

International Federation of Robotics: Susanne Bieller and Nina Kutzbach

International Labour Organization (ILO): Yves Perardel

International Monetary Fund (IMF): Andrea Quevedo and Kazuko Shirono

International Organization for Standardization (ISO): Laurent Charlet and Cristina Draghici

International Telecommunication Union (ITU): Thierry Geiger, Esperanza Magpantay, Nathan Menthon, Martin Schaaper and Daniel Vertesy

LUISS Guido Carli University: Filippo Bontadini, Massimiliano Iommi and Cecilia Jona-Lasinio

Moody's Analytics: Santhosh Metri, Petra Steiner and Ann Van Nieuwenhove

National Institutes of Health (NIH): Kris Wetterstrand

Omdia: David Hancock

Organisation for Economic Co-operation and Development (OECD): Fernando Galindo-Rueda, Tue Halgreen, Corinne Heckmann, Miyako Ikeda and Fabien Verger

PricewaterhouseCoopers (PwC): Arshiya Ghosh and Shruti Kumar

QS Quacquarelli Symonds Ltd: Andrew Macfarlane and Samuel Wong

Refinitiv, an LSEG business

S&P Global, Market Intelligence: Mohsen Bonakdarpour and Karen Campbell

SCImago: Félix de Moya Anegón

Siemens: Maurizio Conti

The Conference Board: Klaas de Vries

Trade Data Monitor LLC: C. Donald Brasher Jr., John Miller, Maria Vretenicic and Altan Yurdakul

TU Wien: Karl Rupp

UNESCO Institute for Statistics (UIS): Talal El Hourani, Saïd Ould Ahmedou Voffal, Rohan Pathirage and José Pessoa

United Nations Commodity Trade Statistics Database

United Nations Department of Economic and Social Affairs (UNDESA)

United Nations Industrial Development Organization (UNIDO): Fernando Cantu Bazaldua and Vladimir Lukic

United Nations International Children's Emergency Fund (UNICEF): Tom Slaymaker

World Bank: Jean-François Arvis and Christina Wiederer; Hibret Belete Maemir, Filip Jolevski, Nona Karalashvili, Frédéric Meunier and Jorge Luis Rodríguez Meza; Hiroko Maeda and Umar Serajuddin

World Economic Forum: Roberto Crotti, Attilio Di Battista, Philipp Grosskurth and Ricky Li

World Federation of Exchanges: Mihaela Croitoru

World Health Organization (WHO): Richard Johnston

World Trade Organization (WTO): Shradha Bhatia, Barbara D'Andrea Adrian and Florian Eberth; Janvier Usanase and Dayong Yu

Yale University: Sebastián Block and Martin Wolf

ZookNIC Inc: Matthew Zook

Advisory Board

Since 2011, the Advisory Board has played a valued role in advising on the strategic direction of the Global Innovation Index (GII). Its mission is to emphasize the critical role innovation plays in economic and social development and to assist in the dissemination of GII findings relevant to each of the world's economies and regions. Comprising international policymakers, thought-leaders and corporate executives, Advisory Board members are selected from diverse geographical and institutional backgrounds and serve in a personal capacity. We express our appreciation to all Advisory Board members for their continued support and collaboration.

Advisory Board members

Clare Akamanzi
Chief Executive Officer, Rwanda Development Board, Rwanda

Robert D. Atkinson
President, Information Technology and Innovation Foundation (ITIF), United States

Audrey Azoulay
Director-General, United Nations Educational, Scientific and Cultural Organization (UNESCO)

Doreen Bogdan-Martin
Secretary-General, International Telecommunication Union (ITU)

Amy L. Burke
Program Director, Science, Technology, and Innovation Analysis, National Center for Science and Engineering Statistics (NCSES), National Science Foundation (NSF), United States

María Fernanda Garza
Chair, International Chamber of Commerce (ICC), Mexico

Fabiola Gianotti
Director-General, European Organization for Nuclear Research (CERN)

John Kao
Chair, Institute for Large Scale Innovation, and former Harvard Business School Professor, United States

Victor Zhixiang Liang
Senior Vice President, Baidu, China

Raghunath Anant Mashelkar
President, Global Research Alliance; National Research Professor, National Chemical Laboratory; former Director-General, Council of Scientific & Industrial Research (CSIR), and former Chair, National Innovation Foundation, India

Philippe Kuhutama Mawoko
Professor, Université du Kwango, Democratic Republic of the Congo, and former Executive Secretary, African Observatory for Science, Technology and Innovation (AOSTI), African Union Commission

Ken Moore
Chief Innovation Officer, Mastercard

Sergio Mujica
Secretary-General, International Organization for Standardization (ISO)

Monika Schnitzer
Member, German Council of Economic Experts, and Professor, Ludwig-Maximilians-University (LMU) Munich, Germany

Heizo Takenaka
Professor Emeritus, Keio University, Japan; former Minister of State for Economic and Fiscal Policy, and Member of the World Economic Forum Board of Trustees

Blanca Treviño
President, Softtek, Mexico

Pedro Wongtschowski
Coordinator, Brazilian Entrepreneurial Movement for Innovation (MEI), Brazilian National Confederation of Industry (CNI), Brazil

The GII Partners

Preface

Soumitra Dutta and **Bruno Lanvin**
Co-editors of the
Global Innovation Index
Co-founders of the
Portulans Institute

The 2023 edition of the Global Innovation Index (GII) amplifies the narrative begun in the preceding 2022 report, diving deeper into the future of innovation-driven growth and the influence of frontier technologies on productivity. As we write this preface, the world is in a state of uncertainty marked by significant events, such as the remnants of the global pandemic, the armed conflict in Ukraine, economic volatility and the meteoric rise of transformative technologies like AI.

Amidst these challenges, we find ourselves reflecting on a crucial question: "Is our long-term vision at risk?" Present circumstances might tempt us into focusing resources on areas that promise immediate returns, such as energy and AI. However, drawing on a global network of partners, the GII underscores the necessity of continuing to endorse a wider lens on innovation, one that fosters greater international collaboration instead of narrow innovation endeavors. A retreat from such global cooperation could foster a competitive environment that prioritizes individual gains, obstructs collective problem-solving, widens disparities and hampers universal growth. In contrast, strong international collaboration, evidenced by our diverse and inclusive network, promotes a pooling of resources, knowledge and expertise for the general good.

In the midst of this complex global landscape, we remain steadfast in our belief in the immense value of precise data and comprehensive measurements – the foundation upon which the GII is built. Understanding the societal and economic implications of our actions equips us with the insights needed to make informed decisions. A commitment to consistent, long-term strategies over sporadic actions is vital on this uncertain journey. This is precisely where the GII delivers immense value. The GII is not simply a measuring tool; it is a key instrument that empowers stakeholders across public and private sectors by allowing them to gauge the impact of their policies and strategies, thereby enabling informed decision-making to drive and enhance shared progress.

Published by the World Intellectual Property Organization (WIPO) in partnership with the Portulans Institute, the GII is widely regarded as an authoritative and trusted indicator of global innovation. Throughout this important journey, we have been grateful for the unwavering support of our Corporate Network partners, namely, the Brazilian National Confederation of Industry (CNI, Brazil) and the Confederation of Indian Industry (CII, India), as well as our Academic Network partners. This global network, comprising organizations drawn from 13 countries, enriches the GII annual report with valuable insights from both industry and academia, enabling us to cultivate a holistic vision of innovation occurring at all levels.

As co-editors of the GII, we are profoundly appreciative of WIPO and its dedicated team of professionals, guided foremost by the efforts of Director General Daren Tang and Assistant Director General Marco Alemán. Since 2021, their unwavering dedication and meticulous leadership have honed the GII into the trusted tool that it is today.

Corporate network

Chandrajit Banerjee, Director General, Confederation of Indian Industry (CII)

Advancing innovative, inclusive and collaborative growth

Technology and innovation are powerful drivers of economic growth. R&D investments are critical in supporting innovation. But it is also essential that we harness the cumulative strengths of the global innovation ecosystem, in order to nurture opportunities for social development and enhance creative, inclusive and collaborative growth.

2023 is a momentous year for India. It not only marks 75 years of Independence, but also the country's G20 Presidency, when for the first time it will convene the G20 Leaders' Summit. During its Presidency, India aspires to promote universal collaboration under the theme "Vasudhaiva Kutumbakam," that is, "One Earth · One Family · One Future." The Confederation of Indian Industry (CII) has been designated as the B20 India Secretariat, the G20 business engagement group. The theme for B20 India is RAISE, which stands for responsible, accelerated, innovative, sustainable, equitable businesses. Under this banner, the CII is working toward nurturing innovation as a movement, not only across India but around the globe, instilling innovative business practices through a heightened focus on technological development, R&D, automation and artificial intelligence, digital transformation and data-enabled business models for greater efficiency and competitiveness.

The WIPO Global Innovation Index (GII) is a key enabler of this growth narrative. The GII captures the innovation capabilities of 132 economies worldwide, and over the years, has evolved into an invaluable benchmarking tool encouraging nations to leverage innovation for economic prosperity and social development. Over time, too, India has been consistently enhancing its innovation performance, and fostering continued improvement in its knowledge inputs and outputs. A founding knowledge partner of the GII, the CII is proud to be an integral part of India's inspiring journey toward becoming an innovation-driven knowledge economy.

I congratulate the team responsible for this the 2023 edition of the GII, which continues to serve as an important guide for exploring the multi-dimensional layers of innovation driving inclusive and collaborative growth around the globe.

Robson Braga de Andrade, President, Brazilian National Confederation of Industry (CNI)

Innovation-driven growth and the importance of effective public policies

Effective innovation policies can only be designed with the aid of solid economic, scientific and social indicators. Entrepreneurial Mobilization for Innovation (MEI), coordinated by the Brazilian National Confederation of Industry (CNI), is a group of approximately 500 business leaders promoting Brazil's innovation agenda, working in close partnership with academia and government institutions. Over the past 15 years, MEI has supported companies and government with information and policy proposals aimed at increasing funding and modernizing the regulatory framework for science, technology and innovation (STI) in Brazil.

Brazil's position in the Global Innovation Index (GII) has improved over recent years, moving up from 62nd in 2020 to rank 54th in 2022. Nevertheless, Brazil has much untapped potential for further improving its innovation ecosystem. In 2021, Brazil ranked 14th for scientific production. Despite such a positive showing, Brazil's R&D investment accounted for just 1.14 percent of GDP in 2020, whereas leading economies normally invest over 3 percent of GDP in R&D.

To achieve the goal of better integrating its scientific and business sectors, and consequently promoting greater innovation, Brazil requires public policies that are modern and up-to-date. The GII has a critical role to play in understanding Brazil's strengths and weaknesses in each and every STI dimension. An analysis of the country's performance and the evolution of its GII indicators over time ought to be the starting point for a revision of Brazil's STI policy and long-term strategy. The GII's business-related indicators, for instance, are a useful guide for companies defining innovation strategies. The CNI and MEI are aware of the importance of measuring innovation for enabling effective policies, achieving solid performance in STI activities, and promoting social and economic development. For this reason, our continued partnership with the GII is a valuable asset for the Brazilian innovation ecosystem and one to be celebrated.

Corporate Network partners

For the last 15 years, Corporate Network partners have actively supported the GII. Comprising firms, private sector entities and industry associations, they have been at the forefront of innovation and competitiveness within their respective nations and regions. Corporate Network partners support the Portulans Institute and are an invaluable source of information enabling the GII to measure the heartbeat of innovation across each and every one of the world's sectors and regions.

As of 2023, the GII Corporate Network comprises the Confederation of Indian Industry (the longest-standing corporate partner since 2008) and the Brazilian National Confederation of Industry (a partner since 2017).

Brazilian National Confederation of Industry (CNI)
Robson Braga de Andrade, President; Gianna Sagazio, Innovation Director; Tatiana Farah de Mello Cauville, Innovation Executive Manager; Marcos Arcuri, Industrial Development Specialist.

Confederation of Indian Industry (CII)
Chandrajit Banerjee, Director General; S. Raghupathy, Principal Adviser; Ashish Mohan, Executive Director, Technology, Innovation, R&D and IPR; Namita Bahl, Director, Technology, Innovation and R&D; Divya Arya, Deputy Director, Technology, Innovation and R&D.

PORTULANS INSTITUTE

CII Confederation of Indian Industry

CNI Brazilian National Confederation of Industry
THE FUTURE OF INDUSTRY

Academic Network partners

Created in 2011, the GII Academic Network involves top universities, their students and academic staff in GII research and facilitates the dissemination of GII findings within the academic community. The Portulans Institute hosts the network, which currently includes 12 universities actively promoting discourse and encouraging initiatives related to innovation. We express appreciation to all partners in the Academic Network for their invaluable assistance.

Brazil: University of São Paulo (USP), School of Economics, Management, Accounting and Actuarial Sciences; Moacir de Miranda Oliveira Júnior, Full Professor, Business Administration Department

China: Peking University, Office of Science and Technology Development; Weihao Yao, Director

Colombia: Universidad de los Andes, School of Management; Veneta Stefanova Andonova Zuleta, Dean, and Carolina Dávila Aranda, International Office Director

Egypt: The American University in Cairo (AUC), School of Business; Sherif Kamel, Dean, and Nagla Rizk, Professor and Director, Access to Knowledge for Development Center

France: Institut Européen d'Administration des Affaires (INSEAD); Bruno Lanvin, Distinguished Fellow

Mexico: Tecnológico de Monterrey, EGADE Business School; Osmar Zavaleta-Vázquez, Associate Dean of Research, and José Ernesto Amorós, Professor and Research Group Leader, Entrepreneurship & Innovation

Nigeria: Lagos Business School Pan-Atlantic University (LBS); Chris Ogbechie, Dean, and Olayinka David-West, Associate Dean

Russian Federation: National Research University Higher School of Economics (HSE University), Institute for Statistical Studies and Economics of Knowledge; Leonid Gokhberg, First Vice-Rector and Director

South Africa: University of Johannesburg, College of Business and Economics; Erika Kraemer-Mbula, Professor of Economics

United Kingdom: University of Oxford, Saïd Business School; Soumitra Dutta, Dean

United States of America: Cornell SC Johnson College of Business; Ravi Kanbur, Professor, Charles H. Dyson School of Applied Economics and Management

Viet Nam: VinUniversity; Rohit Verma, Founding Provost

GII 2023 at a glance

The Global Innovation Index 2023 captures the innovation ecosystem performance of 132 economies and tracks the most recent global innovation trends.

WIPO
WORLD
INTELLECTUAL PROPERTY
ORGANIZATION

Global leaders in innovation, 2023

Top three innovation economies by region

Latin America and the Caribbean
1. Brazil ↑
2. Chile ↓
3. Mexico

Northern America
1. United States
2. Canada

Sub-Saharan Africa*
1. South Africa
2. Botswana
3. Senegal ☆

Europe
1. Switzerland
2. Sweden
3. United Kingdom

Northern Africa and Western Asia†
1. Israel
2. United Arab Emirates
3. Türkiye

Central and Southern Asia
1. India
2. Iran (Islamic Republic of)
3. Kazakhstan ☆

South East Asia, East Asia, and Oceania
1. Singapore ↑
2. Republic of Korea ↓
3. China

☆ Indicates a new entrant into the top three in 2023.

↑↓ Indicates movement in ranking (up or down) within the top three, relative to 2022.

* Top three in Sub-Saharan Africa (SSA) – excluding island economies. The top five within the region, including all economies, comprise Mauritius (1st), South Africa (2nd), Botswana (3rd), Cabo Verde (4th) and Senegal (5th).

† Top three in Northern Africa and Western Asia (NAWA) – excluding island economies. The top four within the region, including all economies, comprise Israel (1st), Cyprus (2nd), United Arab Emirates (3rd) and Türkiye (4th).

Top three innovation economies by income group

High-income
1. Switzerland
2. Sweden ↑
3. United States ↓

Upper middle-income
1. China
2. Malaysia ↑
3. Bulgaria ↓

Lower middle-income
1. India
2. Viet Nam
3. Ukraine ☆

Low-income
1. Rwanda
2. Madagascar
3. Togo ☆

Source: Global Innovation Index Database, WIPO, 2023.

Notes: World Bank Income Group Classification (July 2022). Year-on-year changes in GII rank are influenced by performance and methodological considerations. Some economy data are incomplete (see Appendix I).

Global Innovation Index 2023 rankings

GII rank	Economy	Score	Income group rank	Region rank
1	Switzerland	67.6	1	1
2	Sweden	64.2	2	2
3	United States	63.5	3	1
4	United Kingdom	62.4	4	3
5	Singapore	61.5	5	1
6	Finland	61.2	6	4
7	Netherlands (Kingdom of the)	60.4	7	5
8	Germany	58.8	8	6
9	Denmark	58.7	9	7
10	Republic of Korea	58.6	10	2
11	France	56.0	11	8
12	China	55.3	1	3
13	Japan	54.6	12	4
14	Israel	54.3	13	1
15	Canada	53.8	14	2
16	Estonia	53.4	15	9
17	Hong Kong, China	53.3	16	5
18	Austria	53.2	17	10
19	Norway	50.7	18	11
20	Iceland	50.7	19	12
21	Luxembourg	50.6	20	13
22	Ireland	50.4	21	14
23	Belgium	49.9	22	15
24	Australia	49.7	23	6
25	Malta	49.1	24	16
26	Italy	46.6	25	17
27	New Zealand	46.6	26	7
28	Cyprus	46.3	27	2
29	Spain	45.9	28	18
30	Portugal	44.9	29	19
31	Czech Republic	44.8	30	20
32	United Arab Emirates	43.2	31	3
33	Slovenia	42.2	32	21
34	Lithuania	42.0	33	22
35	Hungary	41.3	34	23
36	Malaysia	40.9	2	8
37	Latvia	39.7	35	24
38	Bulgaria	39.0	3	25
39	Türkiye	38.6	4	4
40	India	38.1	1	1
41	Poland	37.7	36	26
42	Greece	37.5	37	27
43	Thailand	37.1	5	9
44	Croatia	37.1	38	28
45	Slovakia	36.2	39	29
46	Viet Nam	36.0	2	10
47	Romania	34.7	40	30
48	Saudi Arabia	34.5	41	5
49	Brazil	33.6	6	1
50	Qatar	33.4	42	6
51	Russian Federation	33.3	7	31
52	Chile	33.3	43	2
53	Serbia	33.1	8	32
54	North Macedonia	33.0	9	33
55	Ukraine	32.8	3	34
56	Philippines	32.2	4	11
57	Mauritius	32.1	10	1
58	Mexico	31.0	11	3
59	South Africa	30.4	12	2
60	Republic of Moldova	30.3	13	35
61	Indonesia	30.3	5	12
62	Iran (Islamic Republic of)	30.1	6	2
63	Uruguay	30.0	44	4
64	Kuwait	29.9	45	7
65	Georgia	29.9	14	8
66	Colombia	29.4	15	5

GII rank	Economy	Score	Income group rank	Region rank
67	Bahrain	29.1	46	9
68	Mongolia	28.8	7	13
69	Oman	28.4	47	10
70	Morocco	28.4	8	11
71	Jordan	28.2	16	12
72	Armenia	28.0	17	13
73	Argentina	28.0	18	6
74	Costa Rica	27.9	19	7
75	Montenegro	27.8	20	36
76	Peru	27.7	21	8
77	Bosnia and Herzegovina	27.1	22	37
78	Jamaica	27.1	23	9
79	Tunisia	26.9	9	14
80	Belarus	26.8	24	38
81	Kazakhstan	26.7	25	3
82	Uzbekistan	26.2	10	4
83	Albania	25.4	26	39
84	Panama	25.3	48	10
85	Botswana	24.6	27	3
86	Egypt	24.2	11	15
87	Brunei Darussalam	23.5	49	14
88	Pakistan	23.3	12	5
89	Azerbaijan	23.3	28	16
90	Sri Lanka	23.3	13	6
91	Cabo Verde	23.3	14	4
92	Lebanon	23.2	15	17
93	Senegal	22.5	16	5
94	Dominican Republic	22.4	29	11
95	El Salvador	21.8	17	12
96	Namibia	21.8	30	6
97	Bolivia (Plurinational State of)	21.4	18	13
98	Paraguay	21.4	31	14
99	Ghana	21.3	19	7
100	Kenya	21.2	20	8
101	Cambodia	20.8	21	15
102	Trinidad and Tobago	20.7	50	15
103	Rwanda	20.6	1	9
104	Ecuador	20.5	32	16
105	Bangladesh	20.2	22	7
106	Kyrgyzstan	20.2	23	8
107	Madagascar	19.1	2	10
108	Nepal	18.8	24	9
109	Nigeria	18.4	25	11
110	Lao People's Democratic Republic	18.3	26	16
111	Tajikistan	18.3	27	10
112	Côte d'Ivoire	18.2	28	12
113	United Republic of Tanzania	17.4	29	13
114	Togo	16.9	3	14
115	Nicaragua	16.9	30	17
116	Honduras	16.7	31	18
117	Zimbabwe	16.5	32	15
118	Zambia	16.4	4	16
119	Algeria	16.1	33	18
120	Benin	16.0	34	17
121	Uganda	16.0	5	18
122	Guatemala	15.8	33	19
123	Cameroon	15.3	35	19
124	Burkina Faso	14.5	6	20
125	Ethiopia	14.3	7	21
126	Mozambique	13.6	8	22
127	Mauritania	13.5	36	23
128	Guinea	13.3	9	24
129	Mali	12.9	10	25
130	Burundi	12.5	11	26
131	Niger	12.4	12	27
132	Angola	10.3	37	28

Source: Global Innovation Index Database, WIPO, 2023.

Note: For an explanation of classifications, see Economy profiles, endnote 1.

- High-income
- Upper middle-income
- Lower middle-income
- Low-income

- Europe
- Northern America
- Latin America and the Caribbean

- South East Asia, East Asia, and Oceania
- Northern Africa and Western Asia
- Sub-Saharan Africa
- Central and Southern Asia

Innovation performance at different income levels, 2023

	High-income group	Upper middle-income group	Lower middle-income group	Low-income group
Performance above expectation for level of development	Switzerland Sweden United States United Kingdom Finland Netherlands (Kingdom of the) Germany Denmark Republic of Korea France Japan Israel Canada Estonia	China Thailand Brazil North Macedonia South Africa Republic of Moldova Jordan Jamaica	India Viet Nam Ukraine Philippines Indonesia Mongolia Morocco Tunisia Uzbekistan Pakistan Senegal	Rwanda Madagascar Burundi
Performance in line with level of development	Singapore Hong Kong, China Austria Norway Iceland Belgium Australia Malta Italy New Zealand Cyprus Spain Portugal Czech Republic Slovenia Lithuania Hungary Latvia Greece Croatia Chile	Malaysia Bulgaria Türkiye Serbia Mauritius Mexico Georgia Colombia Armenia Peru Bosnia and Herzegovina Albania Namibia	Iran (Islamic Republic of) Egypt Sri Lanka Cabo Verde Lebanon El Salvador Bolivia (Plurinational State of) Ghana Kenya Cambodia Bangladesh Kyrgyzstan Nepal Nigeria Tajikistan United Republic of Tanzania Zimbabwe	Togo Zambia Uganda Burkina Faso Mozambique Niger
All other economies	Luxembourg Ireland United Arab Emirates Poland Slovakia Romania Saudi Arabia Qatar Uruguay Kuwait Bahrain Oman Panama Brunei Darussalam Trinidad and Tobago	Russian Federation Argentina Costa Rica Montenegro Belarus Kazakhstan Botswana Azerbaijan Dominican Republic Paraguay Ecuador Guatemala	Lao People's Democratic Republic Côte d'Ivoire Nicaragua Honduras Algeria Benin Cameroon Mauritania Angola	Ethiopia Guinea Mali

Source: Global Innovation Index Database, WIPO, 2023.

Key takeaways

The GII 2023 tracks global innovation trends against a background of uncertainty caused by slow economic recovery from the COVID-19 pandemic, high interest rates and geopolitical conflict, but with the promise of Digital Age and Deep Science innovation waves and technological progress.

Results of the Global Innovation Tracker 2023

1. Innovation investments showed a mixed performance in 2022 within a context of many challenges and a downturn in innovation finance. The outlook for 2023 and 2024 is uncertain.

After a boom in 2021, investments in innovation showed a mixed performance in 2022. Scientific publications, R&D, venture capital (VC) deals and patents continued to increase to higher than ever. However, growth rates were lower than the exceptional increases seen in 2021. In addition, the value of VC investment declined and international patent filings stagnated in 2022.

- Scientific publications grew moderately in 2022 by 1.5 percent to around 2 million articles, as health- and COVID-related research, which caused a boom in 2021, slowed.
- Global R&D grew strongly at a rate of 5.2 percent in 2021 – close to pre-pandemic growth in 2019; business R&D grew strongly by 7 percent – a rate unseen since 2014. Data for 2022 are not yet available.
- Global government R&D budgets are expected to have grown in real terms in 2022. Significant increases in real 2022 budgets were planned for Japan and the Republic of Korea, and a smaller one for Germany, making up for cuts in R&D budgets in 2022 by other top R&D spending governments such the United States.
- Worldwide R&D expenditure by the highest R&D spending corporations reached USD 1.1 trillion in 2022 – a historic high. Top corporate R&D spenders increased expenditure nominally by around 7.4 percent in 2022 (down from 15 percent growth in 2021). Yet, it is hard to assess whether this nominal growth compensated for surging inflation. On a positive note, the ratio of R&D expenditure to revenue is on par with 2021 and at pre-pandemic level – meaning corporations are just as R&D-intensive as ever.
- Reflecting a deteriorating climate for risk finance, the value of VC investments declined sharply in 2022 from an exceptionally high level in 2021. Nevertheless, the number of VC deals still grew healthily in 2022 by close to 17.6 percent – reflecting activity that remained strong in the first half of the year. Asia Pacific is now, for the first time, on par with Northern America in terms of deal activity. However, total VC value fell sharply in 2022 by close to 40 percent. The only region not to see a decline in dollars invested was Africa, albeit at low levels. All in all, the VC outlook for 2023 and 2024 is uncertain, with tighter monetary conditions likely to continue impacting innovation finance.
- International patent filings stagnated in 2022 (0.3 percent growth), recording the slowest rate of increase since 2009, but still achieving a record of around 280,000 filings.

2. Technological progress is rampant, without many setbacks; technology adoption is growing, but the socioeconomic impact remains weak

- Indicators of *technological progress* in the fields of information technology, health and energy continue to show progress – the Digital Age and Deep Science innovation waves outlined in GII 2022 are well underway. Supercomputers are becoming faster and more energy efficient. The cost of genome sequencing and low-emission energy technologies, such as wind and solar power, are decreasing. Due to the price volatility of required inputs, the cost of electric batteries rose sharply in 2022, although the long-term trend is still downward. Having peaked in 2020, drug approvals in the United States fell in 2022 for the second year in a row.
- With one exception, *technology adoption* is developing positively: safe sanitation, connectivity, robots and electric vehicles are now more widespread, even though penetration for some technologies remains low (e.g., electric vehicles). The adoption of radiotherapy for cancer treatment also remains inadequate in many countries.
- The *socioeconomic impact* of innovation continues to be at a low point for the second year in a row, in part due to the short-term impact of COVID-19. Labor productivity is currently at a standstill. Life expectancy fell for a second consecutive year, while the increase in healthy

life expectancy slowed. Carbon dioxide emissions rose strongly in 2021, but less so in 2022. Although the first four months of 2023 point to only a modest rise, CO_2 emissions continue to increase. If this trend persists, there is no global reduction in CO_2 emissions on the horizon.

Global Innovation Tracker Dashboard

Science and innovation investment	Scientific publications	R&D investments	Venture capital deal numbers	Venture capital deal values	International patent filings
Technological progress	Computing power	Costs of renewable energy	Electric battery price	Cost of genome sequencing	Drug approvals
Technology adoption	Safe sanitation	Connectivity	Robots	Electric vehicles	Cancer radiotherapy
Socioeconomic impact	Labor productivity		Life expectancy		Carbon dioxide emissions

Results of the Global Innovation Index 2023 rankings

The GII 2023 is unique in incorporating a significant amount of data from the pandemic and post-pandemic years. Country-specific policy responses to the pandemic, including differences in lockdowns, but also more recently the effects of armed conflict, have inevitably had a multifaceted effect on the innovation rankings that requires close scrutiny.

3. Switzerland, Sweden, the United States, the United Kingdom and Singapore lead; China, Türkiye, India, Viet Nam, the Philippines, Indonesia and the Islamic Republic of Iran are the middle-income economies making most headway in innovation over the last decade

- Switzerland – for a 13th year – ranks first in the GII 2023. Sweden is now 2nd and the United States 3rd, followed by the United Kingdom (4th) and Singapore (5th), which enters the top 5.
- Finland (6th) moves closer to the top 5, and every other Nordic (Denmark 9th and Sweden) and Baltic (Estonia, 16th, Lithuania 34th and Latvia 37th) economy is also on an upward trend, except for Iceland, which stays stable at 20th position.
- China – still the sole middle-income economy within the GII top 30, having entered the top echelon in 2014 – is ranked 12th in GII2023, while Japan is 13th.
- Israel (14th) makes it into the top 15.
- Saudi Arabia (48th), Brazil (49th) and Qatar (50th) make it into the top 50, and South Africa (59th) into the top 60.
- Indonesia (61st) joins China, Türkiye (39th), India (40th), Viet Nam (46th), the Philippines (56th), and the Islamic Republic of Iran (62nd) in the group of middle-income economies within the GII top 65. This is the group that has climbed the GII rankings fastest over the last decade.
- Outside the top 65 but within the top 100, the following middle- and low-income countries have progressed the most – by more than 20 ranks – within the last decade: Morocco (70th), Uzbekistan (82nd), Egypt (86th) and Pakistan (88th).
- In the last four years, and since the pandemic started, Mauritius (57th), Indonesia, Saudi Arabia, Brazil and Pakistan have risen the most in rank (in order of rank progression).

4. The United States, Singapore and Israel are scoring best in particular innovation indicators

- The United States continues to lead in terms of the number of GII innovation indicators in which it ranks top globally (13 out of 80 indicators).
- Singapore (11 out of 80) and Israel (9 out of 80) follow.
- Select middle- and low-income economies excel in various domains. Relative to other countries and their GDP or population, Mozambique ranks 1st in Gross capital formation, Cambodia and Nepal in Loans from microfinance institutions, Mauritius in Venture capital investors, and the Islamic Republic of Iran in Trademarks.

5. Regional GII leaders are Switzerland, the United States, Brazil, India, Singapore, Israel and Mauritius; India and Rwanda lead their income groups.

- In South East Asia, East Asia and Oceania, Singapore, the Republic of Korea (10th) and China lead.
- In Northern Africa and Western Asia, Israel leads and is followed by Cyprus (28th), the United Arab Emirates (UAE) (32nd) and Türkiye.

- In Latin America and the Caribbean, Brazil leads for the first time, followed by Chile (52nd) and Mexico (58th).
- In Central and Southern Asia, India continues to lead, and the Islamic Republic of Iran (62nd) and Kazakhstan (81st, a newcomer to the region's top 3) come next.
- In Sub-Saharan Africa, Mauritius (57th) is followed by South Africa (59th), Botswana (85th), Cabo verde (91st) and Senegal (93rd).
- India leads the lower middle-income group, followed by Viet Nam and Ukraine (55th). Ukraine is a newcomer to this income group's top 3, based on data that mostly predate 2022.
- Rwanda (103rd) leads the low-income group, followed by Madagascar (107th) and Togo (114th), a newcomer to this income group's top 3.

6. Several developing economies are performing above expectation on innovation relative to their level of economic development

- A total of 21 economies outperform on innovation relative to level of development, the majority located in Sub-Saharan Africa and South East Asia, East Asia, and Oceania.
- India, the Republic of Moldova (60th) and Viet Nam continue as record holders by being innovation overperformers for a 13th consecutive year.
- Indonesia, Uzbekistan and Pakistan keep their overperformer status for a second consecutive year, Brazil for a third.
- There are two notable comebacks in 2023, namely, Senegal and North Macedonia (54th).
- Conversely, 37 economies performed below expectation on innovation, the majority from Latin America and the Caribbean (11), followed by Sub-Saharan Africa (9), Northern Africa and Western Asia (8) and Europe (6).

Results of the global top 100 S&T cluster ranking

7. The world's five biggest science and technology clusters are all located in East Asia; Tokyo–Yokohama is the biggest S&T cluster globally, Cambridge the most S&T-intensive

- Tokyo–Yokohama (Japan) continues to lead, followed by Shenzhen–Hong Kong–Guangzhou (China and Hong Kong, China), Seoul (Republic of Korea) and then China's Beijing and Shanghai–Suzhou clusters.
- Cambridge in the United Kingdom and San Jose–San Francisco, CA, in the United States are the two most S&T-intensive clusters relative to population density. Oxford (United Kingdom), Eindhoven (Kingdom of the Netherlands) and Boston–Cambridge, MA (United States) follow. In Germany, Munich makes the top 10 most S&T-intensive clusters globally.
- For a first time, China tops the list of countries with the highest number of clusters among the top 100, having 24 in total. The United States follows, with 21 clusters, then Germany with nine.
- São Paulo (Brazil); Bengaluru, Delhi, Chennai and Mumbai (India); Tehran (Islamic Republic of Iran); Istanbul and Ankara (Türkiye); and Moscow (Russian Federation) are the only middle-income economy clusters outside China. Chennai and Bengaluru (India) see the biggest jump in ranking among this income group.

Top S&T cluster by economy or cross-border region ranked among the top 100, 2023

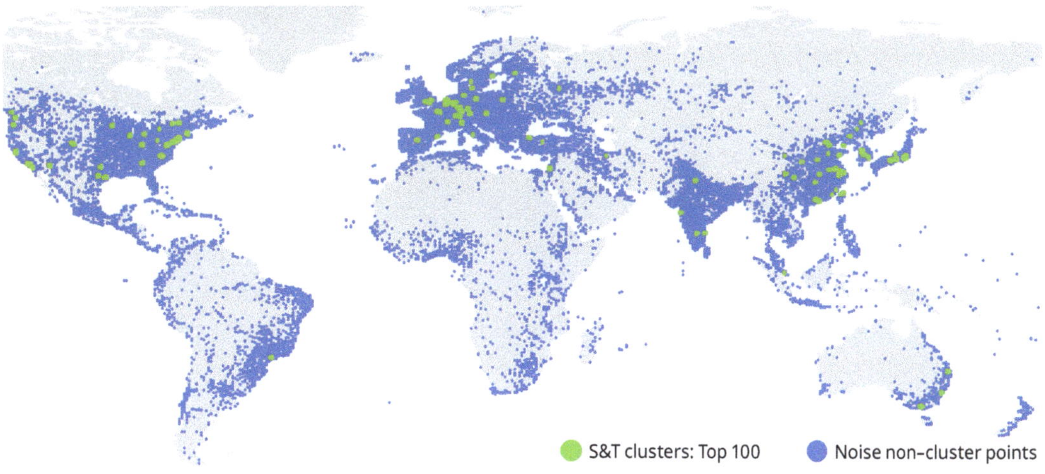

Global Innovation Tracker

What is the current state of innovation?
How rapidly is technology progressing and being embraced?
What are the resulting societal impacts?

Global Innovation Tracker Dashboard

Science and innovation investment

	Scientific publications	R&D investments		Venture capital		International patent filings
		Global total	Top corporate R&D spenders	Deal numbers	Deal values	
Short term	1.5% 2021 → 2022	5.2% 2020 → 2021	7.4% 2021 → 2022	17.6% 2021 → 2022	−37.8% 2021 → 2022	0.3% 2021 → 2022
Long term (annual growth)	4.9% 2012 → 2022	4.8% 2011 → 2021	n.a.	9.9% 2012 → 2022	20.6% 2012 → 2022	3.6% 2012 → 2022

Technological progress

	Computing power		Costs of renewable energy		Electric battery price	Cost of genome sequencing	Drug approvals
	Moore's Law	Green supercomputers	Solar photovoltaic	Wind			
Short term	54.6% 2021 → 2022	54.3% 2021 → 2022	−12.8% 2020 → 2021	−13.2% 2020 → 2021	7.1% 2021 → 2022	−23.3%* 2021 → 2022	−26.0% 2021 → 2022
Long term (annual growth)	43.7% 2012 → 2022	35.4% 2013 → 2022	−17.0% 2011 → 2021	−9.6% 2011 → 2021	−15.3% 2012 → 2022	−22.3%* 2012 → 2022	−0.5% 2012 → 2022

Technology adoption

	Safe sanitation	Connectivity		Robots	Electric vehicles	Cancer radiotherapy
		Fixed broadband	Mobile broadband			
Short term	1.4% 2021 → 2022	4.8% 2021 → 2022	6.0% 2021 → 2022	14.6% 2020 → 2021	59.9% 2021 → 2022	−1.4% 2020 → 2022
Long term (annual growth)	2.4% 2012 → 2022	6.7% 2012 → 2022	14.8% 2012 → 2022	11.7% 2011 → 2021	63.5% 2012 → 2022	−1.3% 2012 → 2022
Penetration	57 of 100 inhabitants in 2022 (45 in 2012)	17.6 per 100 inhabitants in 2022 (16.8 in 2021)	86.9 per 100 inhabitants in 2022 (82.0 in 2021)	n.a.	2.1 of 100 cars in 2022 (1.3 in 2021)	20.9 of 100 countries in 2022 (21.5 in 2020)

Socioeconomic impact

	Labor productivity	Life expectancy	Carbon dioxide emissions	
Short term	0.0% 2021 → 2022	−1.3% 2020 → 2021	5.3% 2020 → 2021	1.7%* 2021 → 2022
Long term (annual growth)	2.2% 2012 → 2022	0.0% 2011 → 2021		0.7% 2011 → 2021

Notes: See Data notes at the end of this section for a definition of indicators and their data sources. Long-term annual growth refers to the compound annual growth rate (CAGR) over the indicated period. Historical data may have been updated and could differ from last year's Global Innovation Tracker. Estimates or incomplete data are indicated by an asterisk (*). n.a. indicates not available.

What is the global state of innovation? Is innovation slowing down or accelerating? How is innovation navigating through the global turbulence caused by elevated inflation, rising interest rates and geopolitical conflict in the immediate aftermath of the COVID-19 pandemic?

The Global Innovation Tracker 2023 addresses these crucial questions. It takes the pulse of four key stages in the innovation cycle: (1) science and innovation investment; (2) technological progress; (3) technology adoption; and (4) the socioeconomic impact of innovation.

The main findings this year are as follows:

1. ***Science and innovation investment*** showed a mixed performance in 2022 in the context of many challenges, and a downturn in innovation finance. Scientific publications continued to increase in number, albeit at a slower rate. Global government R&D budgets are expected to grow in real terms in 2022, while R&D expenditure by top corporate spenders rose substantially. But it is unclear whether this can compensate for surging inflation. International patent filings, in turn, stagnated while venture capital investments declined sharply in value in 2022, following extraordinarily high levels in 2021, reflecting a deteriorating climate for risk finance.

2. Strong ***technological progress*** in the fields of information technology, health, mobility and energy continue to deliver new breakthroughs opening up new opportunities for global development. Computing power is historically strong, while the costs of renewable energy and genome sequencing costs are continuing to fall.

3. An observed increase in ***technology adoption*** is gradually making access to safe sanitation and connectivity more widespread. Electric vehicle (EV) uptake is booming, and the desire for greater automation has increased robot installation. However, for the majority of innovation indicators, overall penetration rates remain medium-to-low, and the availability of radiotherapy for cancer treatment continues to be inadequate in many countries.

4. The ***socioeconomic impact*** of innovation remains low. The COVID-19 crisis triggered volatility in labor productivity – which is currently at a standstill – and life expectancy fell for a second consecutive year (with healthy life expectancy continuing to increase, but more slowly). Carbon dioxide emissions continued to grow in 2022, albeit at a lower rate than the post-pandemic surge of 2021 – but with no global reductions in sight.

Science and innovation investment

The innovation environment is full of novel opportunities but also significant challenges. On the one hand, disruption to economies and to life has been more erratic and persistent over the last three years than is normally the case with the business cycle. This has included supply chain disruption, widespread and abnormally high inflation and armed conflict, all of which have weighed on economic recovery and innovation.

On the other hand, innovation continues unabated, partly due to the new Digital Age and the Deep Science innovation waves described in last year's GII 2022 Special theme. Developments in fields as diverse as artificial intelligence, quantum computing, genome sequencing, several green technologies and robotics show a new, possibly groundbreaking dynamic.

Economic growth is projected to slow but remain positive in 2023.[1] Persistent efforts in innovation investment will be key for a recovery and to promote productivity growth, making use of novel innovation opportunities.

Scientific publications

Scientific publications increased substantially throughout the COVID-19 pandemic, with exceptional growth in 2020 (+8.6 percent) and 2021 (8.3 percent). This was driven by a surge in COVID-19- and more generally health-related research, for which early access versions were often published in order to speed up the dissemination of research findings. At the same time, research grants were effectively redirected away from those areas less closely associated with the virus.[2]

In 2022, COVID-19- and health-related research levelled out once again, with the number of scientific articles published not increasing noticeably between 2021 and 2022 (+1.5 percent growth). As well as health, the fields of environmental and energy research are also continuing to grow. Environmental sciences claimed second place in publications, with a solid 10.5 percent growth on 2022. Publications in the energy and fuels field secured ninth spot, with a strong growth rate of 13.2 percent. The field of public, environmental and occupational health grew by 13.4 percent from 2021 to 2022 to rank in 10th position (having been stuck around 17th position prior to the pandemic). Another noteworthy trend is the ascent of India in terms of publication output (ranking fourth in 2022), overtaking the United Kingdom (fifth) and close behind Germany (third).

Research and development (R&D)

Total R&D expenditures

The most recently available data show that global R&D investment grew strongly in 2021 at a rate of 5.2 percent (in real terms), up from 3.2 percent in 2020. This is close to the pre-pandemic growth rate of around 6 percent in 2019. In turn, business R&D expenditure – the most significant component of total global R&D – grew by 7 percent in 2021, the highest growth rate observed since 2014 (see Figure 1).

The five economies that spent the most on R&D all experienced significant R&D growth in 2021. In order of R&D budget, they were the United States (+5.6 percent), followed by China (+9.8 percent), Japan (+3.6 percent), Germany (+2.7 percent) and the Republic of Korea (+7.1 percent).[3]

Even excluding the sizeable contributions made by the United States and China, global R&D still experienced a 2.7 percent increase in 2021. This is a notable change from 2020, when these two countries were single-handedly responsible for avoiding a global decline in R&D that year. Again, excluding the United States and China, business R&D witnessed a 4.1 percent growth in 2021, compared to a decline of 1.7 percent in 2020 (see Figure 1).

Data for 2021 data are, however, not yet available for a majority of the large R&D spenders among middle-income economies. Consequently, the effect of the pandemic on low- and middle-income economy R&D budgets remains largely unknown.

That said, relative to what they were pre-pandemic, high-income, upper middle-income and low-income economies have R&D expenditures that are already above pre-pandemic levels. Moreover, most of the world's regions have either returned to or have surpassed pre-pandemic levels, with the exception of Latin America and the Central and Southern Asia region.

Figure 1 GDP growth and total and business R&D growth rates, 2007–2024

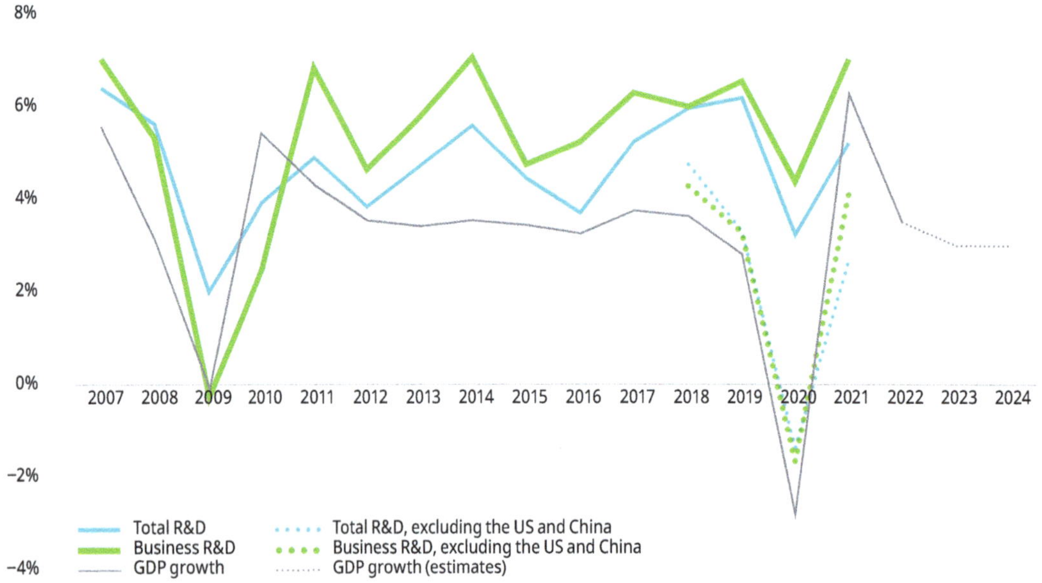

Source: WIPO estimates, based on the UNESCO Institute for Statistics database, Organisation for Economic Co- operation and Development (OECD) Main Science and Technology Indicators (March 2022), Eurostat, Ibero-American and Inter-American Network of Science and Technology Indicators (RICYT), China Statistical Yearbook 2022, and the International Monetary Fund's World Economic Outlook Update, July 2023.

To get a sense of what to expect for 2022 and 2023, one must look first at governments' planned R&D budgets and then at company data on R&D expenditure, the latter already partially covering the first quarter of 2023, depending on how the financial year is defined.

Government R&D budget, 2020–2022

Government R&D budget allocations grew robustly in 2020 for the majority of mostly high-income countries, who are also the biggest R&D spenders.[4] This positive outcome can be attributed to government efforts to support R&D expenditures as a counter-cyclical measure; a strategy that effectively sustained 2020 R&D growth.

In 2021, however, government R&D budgets diverged, with declines seen in Japan (−10.9 percent) and the United States (−8.8 percent), the two biggest R&D spenders covered. Declines were also observed in other major economies in 2021. This can be explained by a downward re-adjustment to governments' health R&D budgets in selected high-income economies.[5] Meanwhile, other major economies continued to ramp up their R&D budgets, namely, the Republic of Korea (+10.2 percent), Türkiye (+9.6 percent), Germany (+5.6 percent in 2021) and France (+2.5 percent). Data for China are unavailable; however, official Chinese statistics show an increase in government funding of 6 percent in 2020 and 10 percent in 2021.[6]

For those economies that have already disclosed their planned 2022 R&D budgets, the outlook is mixed. Significant increases in real 2022 R&D budget appropriations are planned for Japan (+15.2 percent) and the Republic of Korea (+6.5 percent), with a smaller increase planned for Germany (+1.0 percent). The United States (−1.8 percent), on the other hand, foresees a decrease. However, this is more than outweighed by the increases planned in Japan and the Republic of Korea. In sum, the total global government R&D budget is expected to grow in real terms in 2022.

Top corporate R&D spenders, 2022–2023

On the corporate side, 2022–2023 R&D data are available for around 1,700 of the top 2,500 biggest corporate R&D spenders worldwide.[7] In 2022, for the first time ever, corporate R&D expenditure worldwide exceeded the trillion dollar mark (USD 1.1 trillion in private R&D), representing a nominal R&D spending growth of around 7.4 percent for the year (see Table 1).[8] Although far under 2021's exceptional growth rate, which stood at close to 15 percent driven by high corporate revenue growth (21 percent), corporate R&D growth in 2022 is fully in line with pre-pandemic levels of around 7–8 percent a year.

Table 1 R&D and revenue growth rates for top global corporate R&D spenders, 2018–2022

	R&D		Revenue		R&D intensity
Year	Billions USD	Growth (%)	Billions USD	Growth (%)	Growth (%)
2018	774		19,770		3.9
2019	840	8.6	19,746	−0.1	4.3
2020	905	7.7	18,795	−4.8	4.8
2021	1,040	14.9	22,809	21.4	4.6
2022	1,117	7.4	24,613	7.9	4.5

Source: WIPO, based on Bureau van Dijk (BvD) Orbis database. Revenue is in current USD.

The nearly 7.5 percent nominal growth, in 2022, in top corporate R&D spend was primarily driven by software and ICT services, ICT hardware and pharma, with software and ICT services recording exceptionally strong R&D spending growth (roughly 19 percent). The seven industry sectors attracting the greatest R&D investment, in 2022, were: ICT hardware and electrical equipment (1st); software and ICT services (2nd for the first time ever); pharmaceuticals and biotechnology (3rd, overtaken by software and ICT services), automobiles (4th), construction and industrial metals (5th), industrial engineering and transportation (6th), and travel, leisure and personal goods (7th) (see Figure 2).

Figure 2 R&D expenditure and revenue totals of top global corporate R&D spenders, by industry and year, 2018–2022

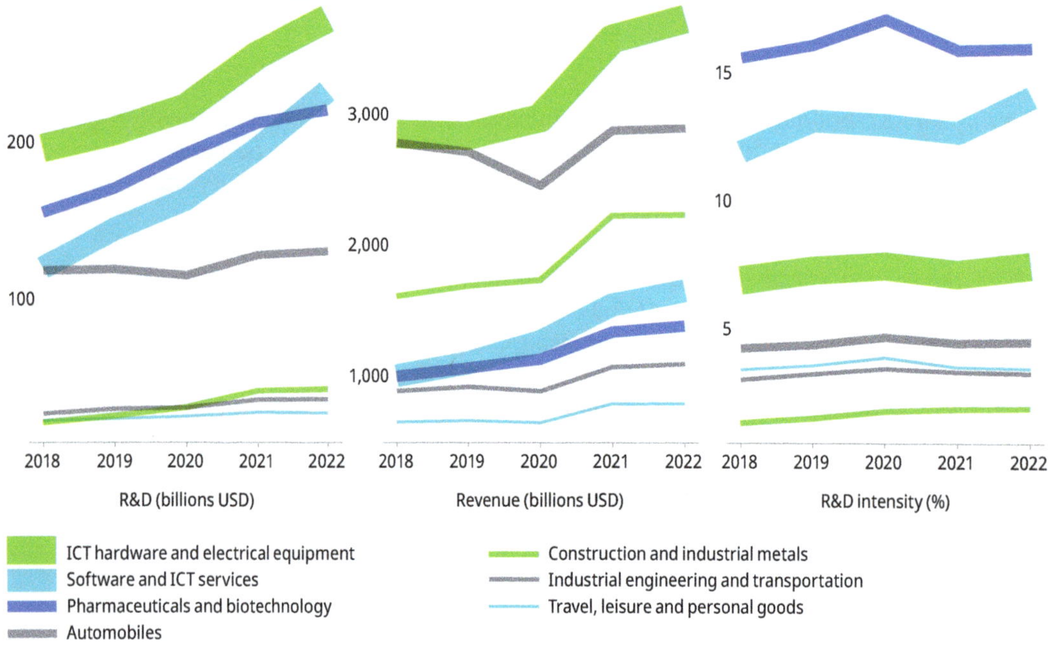

Source: WIPO, based on BvD Orbis database.

Mirroring an earlier finding, the number of firms increasing R&D in 2022 declined relative to an exceptional year in 2021. The one exception is the travel, leisure and personal goods sector. In 2022, more firms in this sector increased their R&D budget than in 2021.

Ranked by R&D intensity in 2022, pharma (15.9 percent), followed by software and ICT services (14.1 percent), lead by a wide margin from ICT hardware (7.4 percent) in third and automobiles (4.5 percent) in fourth place.

Figure 3 presents the nominal percentage change in R&D expenditure in 2022 for the top 15 firms within the top seven industries. The vertical lines indicate the annual mean by industry. Relative to 2022, a majority of the top 15 R&D companies increased R&D spending. This is most apparent in ICT hardware and in software and ICT services, but also in most other categories. The exception to this is seen in pharmaceuticals and biotechnology, as well as industrial engineering and transportation, where each had more than three companies among the top 15 per sector that recorded a decline.

- Mirroring recent news of how artificial intelligence drives and is fed by such companies, the ICT hardware sector saw graphic card and chipmakers Nvidia, SK Hynix and Mediatek record the most impressive R&D growth in 2022, pushing Apple from third into fourth spot.
- In the field of software and ICT services, Meta (formerly Facebook) maintained its lead in terms of R&D growth (+36.4 percent), the number two slot taken by Uber (+36.2 percent), which had experienced a decline in 2021, followed by Alphabet (formerly Google; +25.1 percent).
- The field of automobiles looked more positive in 2022 than in 2021, with General Motors, Volkswagen and Robert Bosch leading in expenditure, and with a majority of the top 15 R&D-spending firms increasing investment.
- In the field of travel, leisure and personal goods, Roblox (a gaming platform) claimed top spot, followed by Unity Software (a game engine company). Airbnb also returned to positive R&D spending.[9]

Figure 3 Corporate R&D expenditure, selected top R&D spenders worldwide, annual R&D expenditure, 2021 compared to 2022

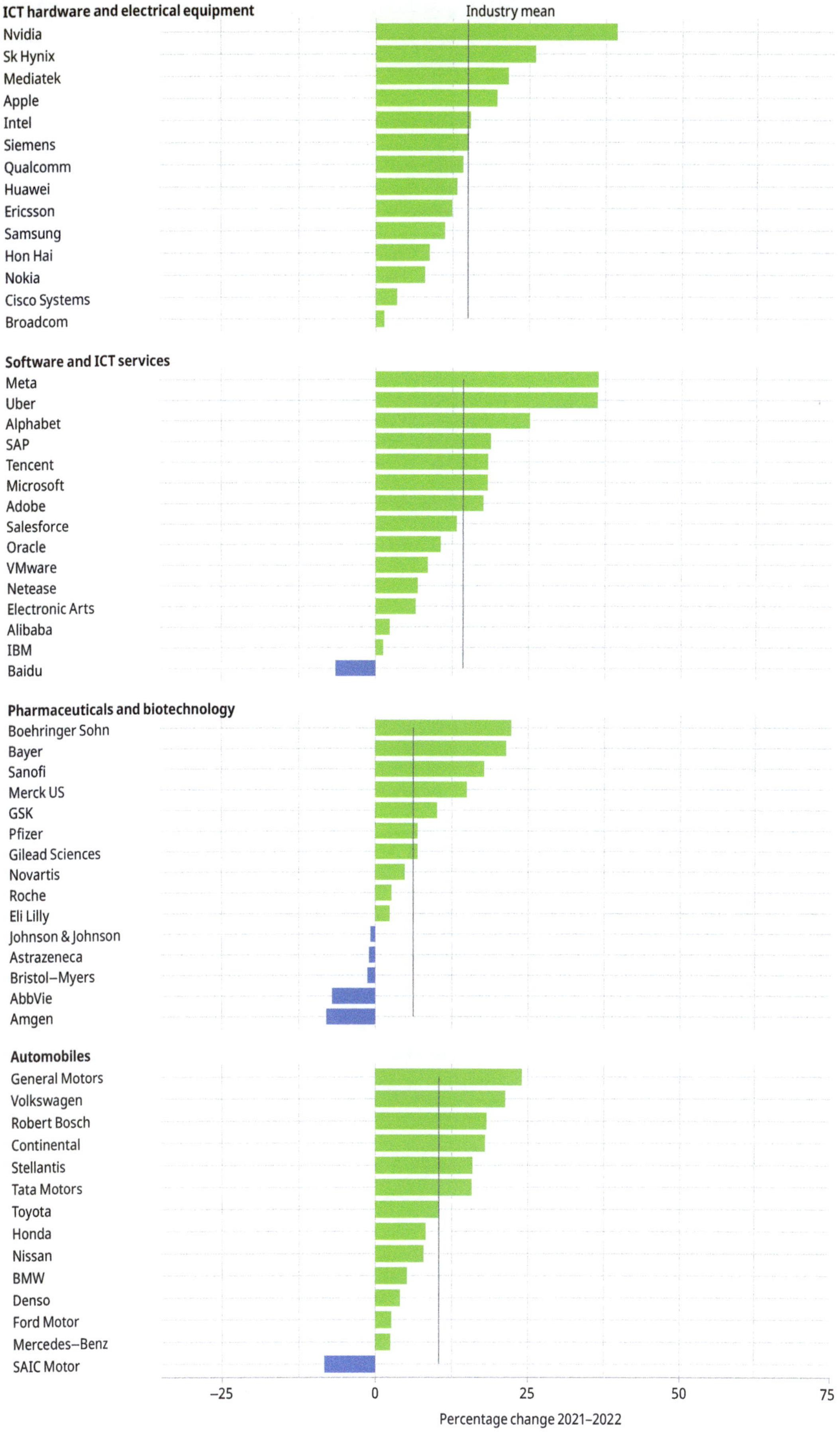

Figure 3 Continued

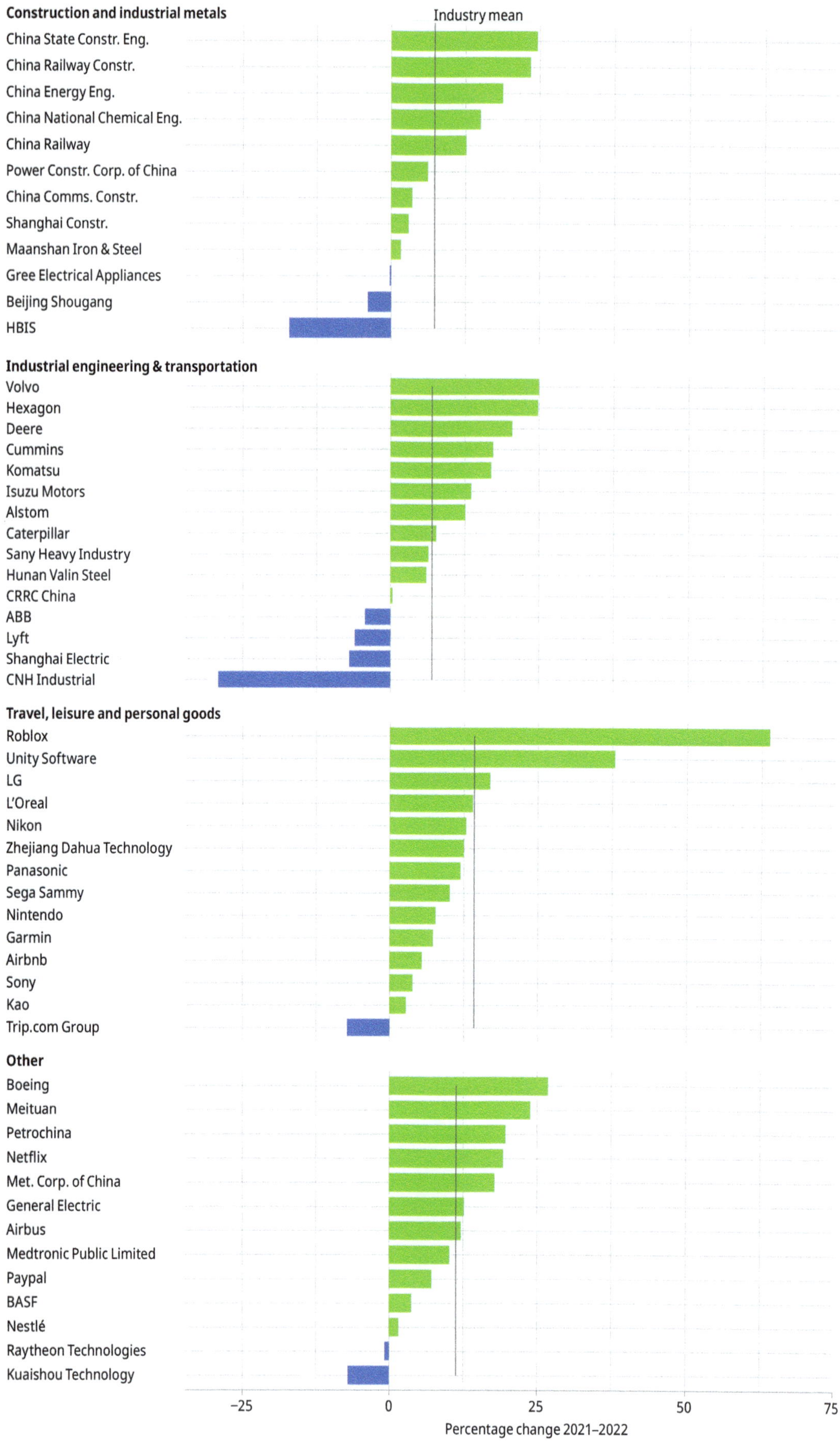

Source: WIPO, based on BvD Orbis database.

It is important to acknowledge that data presented in Figure 3 primarily focus on top R&D performers, often referred to as "R&D superfirms." A comprehensive evaluation of corporate R&D performance for 2022 would require additional data, including information from small and medium-sized enterprises that may have found innovation finance challenging in an environment where R&D is becoming both costlier and riskier.

Venture capital

After a phenomenal growth in 2021 (at a magnitude last seen just prior to the bursting of the so-called "dotcom bubble"), tighter monetary conditions in 2022 raised fears of a steep drop in venture capital (VC) investment, particularly a possible discontinuation of the VC influx that had benefitted previously underserved regions in 2021.[10] The observed outcome in 2022 contains a nuanced combination of results, but it cannot be claimed that the feared crash materialized. Whereas deals concluded showed a healthy growth of 17.6 percent (see Dashboard) to over 23,000 deals in 2022, the total amount of money invested in VCs went in the opposite direction and was cut back sharply by 37.8 percent (see Figure 4). The fall in VC value, combined with a growth in number of deals concluded, resulted in the average deal value halving from USD 31 million in 2021 to USD 16 million in 2022.

In 2022, for the first time in history, VC deal activity in the Asia Pacific region was on par with Northern America. Deals made per quarter in the Asia Pacific region have more than doubled in the space of two years, from around 1,000 deals in 2020 to approximately 2,200 in 2022. Regional differences show Africa leading, with a 46.6 percent growth in VC deals between 2021 and 2022 (albeit from low absolute levels of from 307 to 450 deals), closely followed by Latin America, with 44.0 percent growth (also from low absolute levels of from 327 to 471) and then Europe, with 39.3 percent (from 3,340 to 4,651). Africa and Latin America were the only two regions to experience a growth in VC deals above 40 percent; something that has occurred only rarely since the bursting of the dotcom bubble.

The amount invested in VC decreased from USD 610 billion in 2021 down to USD 380 billion in 2022. This decline is reminiscent of the financial crisis of 2009, marking a significant drop in VC value. One factor contributing to this decline is a notable increase in inflation, surpassing levels seen in several decades. Higher inflation negatively impacts the valuation of VC firms by necessitating a higher discount rate for future expected cash flows. The lower valuation, as a consequence, restricts the amount of financing VC firms are able to secure. Tighter monetary policy and higher interested rates further compound this effect.

The one continent not to see a decline in money invested was Africa, which remained unchanged from the previous year. Other regions, however, experienced a marked collapse in VC investment: −25 percent in Europe, −40 percent in Northern America and the Asian Pacific region, while Latin America experienced the largest VC deal value drop of −63 percent.

That said, it must be borne in mind that 2021 was an exceptional VC boom year difficult to exceed. This, in combination with elevated inflation in 2022, means that the number of deals and value invested in 2022 is after all rather impressive, being still higher than any other year within the last decade, apart from 2021.

Figure 4 Number of venture capital deals and deal value, 2012–2022

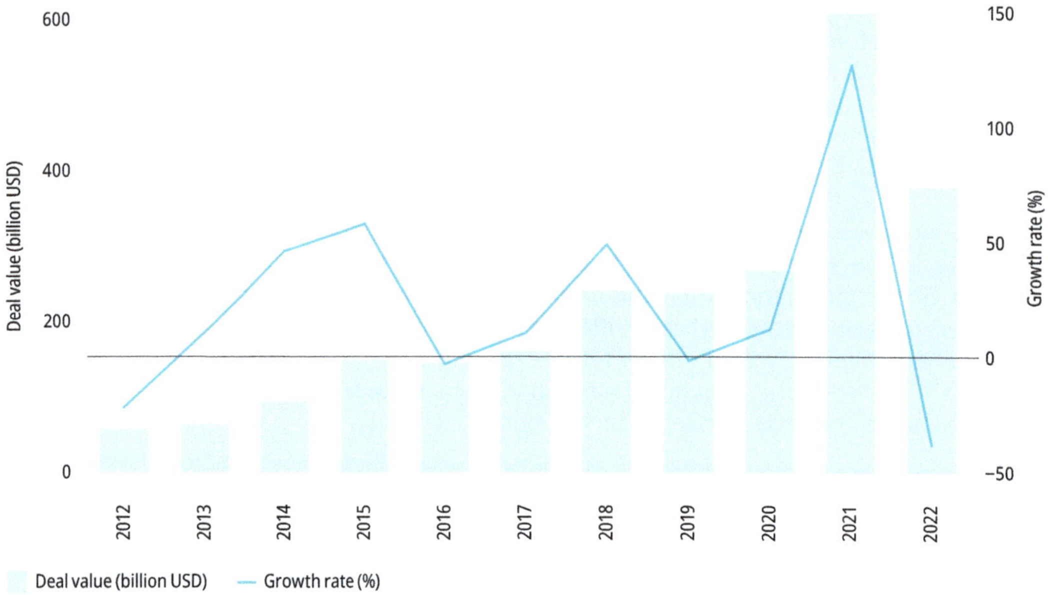

Source: WIPO, based on data by Refinitiv Eikon (private equity screener), accessed April 6, 2023.

International patent filings

Recent economic and political headwinds have impeded international patent filings, with growth throughout 2021 of 0.8 percent that was yet more sluggish in 2022 (0.3 percent), representing the slowest rate of increase since the decline in PCT applications seen in 2009.[11] Overall, this only slightly positive growth nevertheless led to the highest number of PCT filings ever recorded for a single year in 2022 (278,100). In both 2021 and 2022, Asia was the dominant force behind PCT filings, accounting for 54.7 percent of all PCT applications filed in 2022, with China, Japan and the Republic of Korea the strongest Asian international patent filers. In contrast, international patent filings from selected advanced economies, such as the United States (–0.6 percent) and the United Kingdom (–1.7 percent), underwent a decline. The marked slowdown in PCT filing growth from China – the largest filer – continued through 2022, but avoided a decline (0.6 percent growth).[12]

Technological progress

Technological progress continues to shape our world, offering opportunities as well as challenges. Enhanced computing power is playing an increasingly important role in the creation of breakthrough technologies. While supercomputers are becoming faster and more energy-efficient, the cost of producing advanced chips is becoming increasingly expensive, limiting participation in the technological chip race. DNA sequencing costs have dramatically decreased, surpassing what could be expected according to Moore's Law regarding microchip transistor count. Although the falling cost of solar and wind electricity generation has made low-emission technologies commercially competitive, higher material costs (leading to a first-ever increase in electric battery prices) may impact future progress.

Computing power

Breakthroughs in various fields, such as neuroscience, genetics, climate prediction, materials science, astrophysics, energy research and vaccine development, increasingly depend on the availability of supercomputers. Enhanced computing power is vital for the next wave of innovation-driven growth (see discussion of the Digital Age wave in last year's GII 2022 Special theme).

Moore's Law

Thanks to technological progress, Moore's Law predicts that the speed and capability of computer chips (measured by number of transistors per chip) will double every 18–24 months. This prediction has held roughly true for more than five decades since the 1970s, and the resultant increase in computer power over time has been an engine driving technological and social change.

Does Moore's Law still hold true, and will it continue to be up to the task of driving future growth? Experts are concerned that this may not be the case and that Moore's Law could soon run out of steam.[13]

The good news is that – at least for the time being – Moore's Law is holding up well, and considerably better than was expected in the 2022 Edition of the Global Innovation Tracker. Transistor counts for the decade spanning 2012 to 2022 increased annually by 44 percent, doubling every two years. Personal computer transistor counts increased by 62 percent from 2020 to 2022, doubling in under two years.

A transition to new technology yielding higher transistor density with enhanced energy efficiency is behind this success.[14] Renewed efforts by a few countries to produce new generations of chips, as well as recent advances made by graphic card producers, might well serve to sustain Moore's Law into the future as a key driver of future growth.

That said, it is also evident that fulfilling Moore's Law has become increasingly expensive. Factories designed to produce advanced chips cost more than USD 20 billion each, and fewer and fewer countries and firms possess either the know-how or the financial resources required to continue participating in what has become a technological chip race.[15]

Green supercomputing

Higher-powered computer performance has been increasing exponentially since 2019. Today, the most recent exascale computers are capable of operating at 1,000,000,000,000,000,000 FLOPS (10 to the power of 18). By way of comparison, humans are capable of computing at around 1 FLOP or operation per second, roughly equivalent to one simple mathematical addition. The fastest known supercomputer, the Frontier system in the United States, reached a top speed of more than one exascale in March 2022, followed by Fugaku in Japan and LUMI in Finland. Exascale computers are known to exist in China, too, but are not yet officially recorded in the publicly available data used here.

Speed, however, is not the only important performance metric for supercomputers. The Global Innovation Tracker asks how efficient are the greenest supercomputers, that is to say, how many Gigaflops can they perform per Watt of energy consumed? This is a key question, as a supercomputer consumes vast amounts of energy, similar to what is needed to power a small city.

The performance of energy-efficient (green) supercomputers more than doubled from 2021 to 2022 (54.3 percent, see Dashboard). This is above the longer-term performance trend between 2013 and 2022 (35.4 percent). Figure 5 shows the performance of the greenest supercomputers, as well as the performance of the 50th greenest supercomputer, highlighting the significant differences that exist even among the best of the best.

Figure 5 Performance of the most efficient supercomputers, 2013–2022

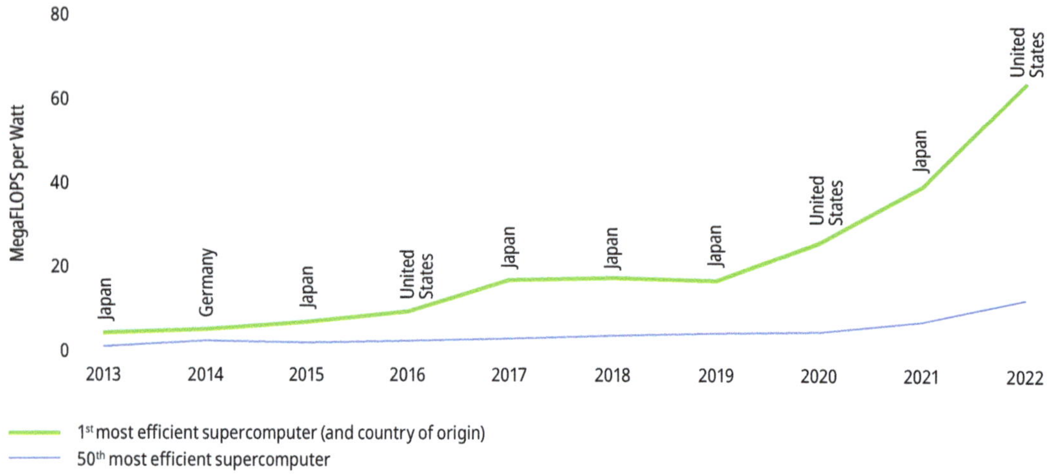

Notes: One MegaFLOP is equivalent to 1,000,000 FLOPS. Excludes China, because data are unavailable.
Source: TOP500 and TOPGreen500 Database. www.top500.org/statistics.

The greenest known supercomputer is Henri from the United States, followed by Frontier TDS, also from the United States, while third is France's Adastra (see Table 2). Regrettably, but with some exceptions, few of the fastest supercomputers are also the greenest.

Table 2 Top fastest and top most efficient (green) supercomputers, 2022

Rank: Green supercomputers	Rank: Supercomputers	Name	Country
1	405	Henri	United States
2	32	Frontier TDS	United States
3	11	Adastra	France
4	15	Setonix – GPU	Australia
5	68	Dardel GPU	Sweden

Source: TOP500.[16]
Note: Data for China are unavailable.

Costs of renewable energy

The falling cost of renewable energy is key to countering climate change and the resultant environmental challenges. Both solar and wind electricity generation costs fell by around 13 percent between 2020 and 2021 (see Dashboard). This means that 70 percent (96 percent) of the solar (wind) generation capacity newly installed in 2021 is cheaper and thus more competitive than the cheapest fossil fuel-fired new generation option (see Figure 6). This makes it possible to target cost-saving incentives at encouraging the adoption of low-emission technologies, instead of relying on regulation or taxation to deter high-emission activities. However, despite this notably positive progress, the decrease in cost recorded in 2021 may not continue into the future, owing to rises in associated material costs that are yet to be passed onto customers.[17] Even though, at present, the exceptionally high price of fossil fuels far outweighs increases in material commodity prices, the future is uncertain, not least because of geopolitical volatility and its unpredictable effect on fossil fuel prices.

Figure 6 Share of newly-installed renewable power generation capacity that is cheaper than the cheapest fossil fuel-fired option, 2016–2021

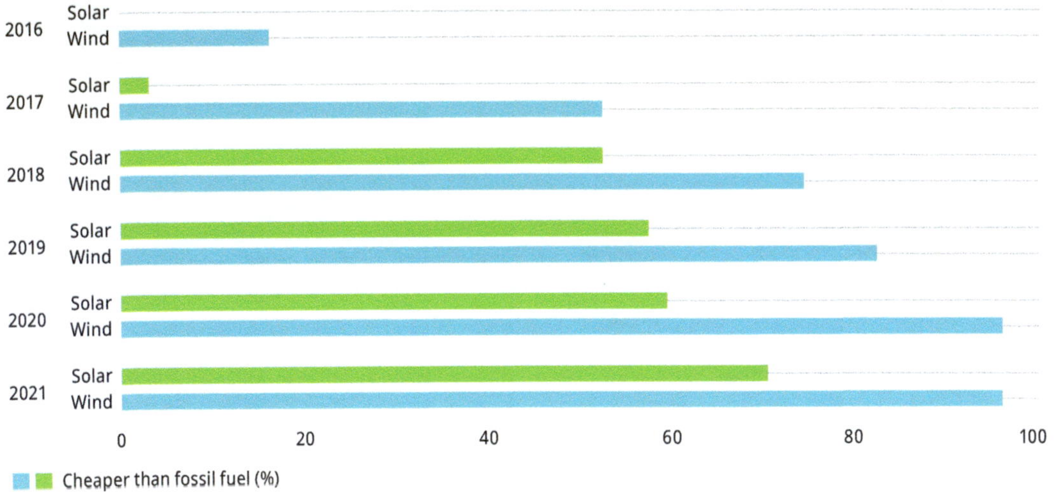

Source: IRENA Renewable Cost Database.

Notes: "Cheaper than fossil fuel" represents the capacity share of newly added solar and wind projects with a lower (levelized) cost of electricity generation than the cheapest fossil fuel-fired new generation option, at USD 54/MWh for a CCGT in the United States.

Electric battery price

Technological progress has persistently driven down the cost of lithium-ion batteries for over a decade, making EVs increasingly affordable. However, following more than a decade of decreasing prices, the rising cost of raw materials and battery components, coupled with soaring inflation, resulted in a first ever increase in the cost of a lithium-ion battery pack, up 7.1 percent in 2022 compared to the year before (i.e., from USD 141 to USD 151/kWh). Indeed, prices could have risen even further, if not for the greater use of alternative low-cost battery materials like lithium-ion phosphate in the production process and a continued reduction in the use of expensive cobalt.

Battery prices are projected to remain at a similar level next year, contrary to significant declines in the past. However, starting in 2024, as lithium prices ease and additional extraction and refining capacity becomes available, battery prices are projected to resume a downward trajectory. The day that battery packs fall to a price of USD 100/kWh (relative to USD 151/kWh today) is thought to be the day that EVs will be no different in purchase price to petrol and diesel powered vehicles. Ambitious policy programs that emphasize the strengthening of domestic supply chains and encourage reshoring of electric battery and EV production have contributed to increased local supply.

Cost of genome sequencing

Part of the ongoing Deep Science innovation wave (see GII 2022 Special theme), future medical innovation is particularly dependent on advances in genetics and stem cell research. In turn, DNA sequencing plays a crucial role in understanding the human genome, which has numerous potential applications in health care, including in the rapid diagnosis of complex diseases and the fight against new viruses such as COVID-19.

The cost and time involved in sequencing a human or other organism's genome are important factors in the success of DNA sequencing technology. The cost of sequencing an entire genome has decreased dramatically over the years, based on estimates valid for the United States. As shown in Figure 7, it has fallen from approximately USD 100 million in 2001 to just over USD 500 in 2022. This rapid decrease in cost, driven by advancements in next-generation DNA sequencing methods, far outpaces the progress expected from Moore's Law, highlighting the remarkable technological progress that has been made in the field.

Figure 7 Cost of sequencing DNA of one human genome, 2001–2022 (USD)

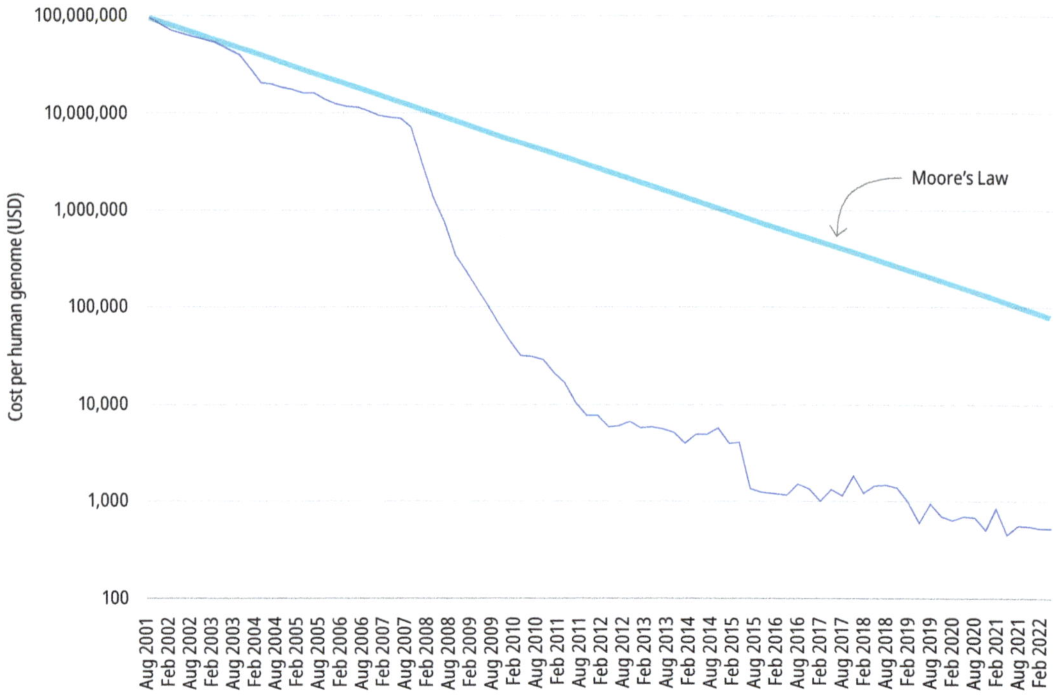

Source: National Human Genome Research Institute (NHGRI), US National Institute of Health.[18]

Going forward, it will be intriguing to further evaluate whether the cost of human sequencing can be reduced even further to below USD 500, with the advent of new sequencing technologies, and made accessible to the general public, especially in health care settings.

New, forward-looking metrics will also be required in order to assess the speed and cost of more advanced DNA sequencing techniques in the future. Emerging long-read DNA sequencing technologies provide for more accurate identification of complex structural variations, but they are more expensive and require different metrics to track progress.[19]

Finally, the pricing and accessibility of DNA sequencing outside of the United States, and particularly in low- and middle-income nations, will be a key metric of success that needs to be developed further.

Drug approvals

Drug approvals provide an insight into the cutting-edge pharmaceutical treatments being introduced to the market. In the United States – which boasts the world's biggest drugs market – there were 37 approvals in 2022, marking a 26 percent decline from 2021. Looking at the 10-year trend shows a slight average annual decline of 0.5 percent over the period.

What can we gather from these numbers? On the one hand, the 37 approvals in 2022 indicates a significant decrease in the number of new drugs entering the market compared to the previous five years. This challenges the optimism surrounding scientific advancements such as mRNA and CRISPR technology, which were expected to stimulate a wave of new pharmaceutical treatments. On the other hand, historical data show that annual drug approval numbers are prone to fluctuation. The 10-year downward trend overall is largely the result of a short-term increase in 2012 and a short-term decrease in 2022. The coming years will reveal whether the decline observed in 2022 was an anomaly or indicative of a more fundamental drop in drug approvals.

The global state of technology adoption reveals both progress and challenges in addressing pressing global issues. Access to safe sanitation has improved, but over 40 percent of the world's population continues to lack safe sanitation. Industrial robot installation has surged, driven by supply chain disruption and automation efforts, leading to increased efficiency and reshoring. Electric vehicle sales are booming, with positive ripple effects on battery production. Meanwhile, the availability of radiotherapy for cancer treatment remains inadequate in many countries, likely owing to financial constraints, lack of trained personnel and infrastructural challenges. Overall, technology penetration rates are still medium-to-low, with the exception of mobile broadband.

Safe sanitation

In an effort to track the adoption of health-related innovations, the Global Innovation Tracker now includes data on the availability of safe sanitation. Safe sanitation refers to that proportion of the population that uses an improved sanitation facility that is not shared and is safe. This indicator shows important progress over the last two decades, with a notable improvement of 1.4 percent between 2021 and 2022 (compared to 2.4 percent over 2012–2022). Progress has been quickest in Central and Southern Asia (+6.6 percent over 2012–2022) driven by a strong growth in availability of safe sanitation in India and East and South East Asia (+4.6 percent) attributable to progress in China.

In 2022, 57 percent of the world's population (4.5 billion people) had access to safe sanitation. A decade earlier, it was still only 45 percent, and in 2000 it stood at 32 percent. Since 2012, 1.3 billion people have gained access to safe sanitation across all regions, and 2.5 billion since 2000.[20] That said, there is still a long way to go. A little under half of the global population of 3.5 billion people still lacks safe sanitation. To reach the Sustainable Development Goal target of universal coverage by 2030, the annual rate of progress would need to increase to 7.4 percent from 2022 onward, up from 2.4 percent over the last decade. Disaggregated data also reveal significant disparities in access to safe sanitation both between and within countries. The situation remains dire in rural areas, where coverage is lower (46 percent) than in urban areas (65 percent), and in some of the world's regions, such as sub-Saharan Africa, only just under a quarter of people (24 percent) have safe sanitation.

Connectivity

In 2022, fixed broadband subscriptions grew by 4.8 percent, while mobile broadband subscriptions grew by 6 percent, both below the 10-year average. Mobile broadband adoption is more widespread, with 87 subscriptions per 100 inhabitants.[21] In contrast, fixed broadband subscriptions stood at only 17.6 per 100 inhabitants, though these are typically shared within households and therefore cover more people. Penetration rates for fixed broadband - which is often necessary for more advanced applications - remained poor in low-income economies. Connectivity to 5th generation mobile networks (5G) could help make up for lagging fixed broadband subscriptions rates. This new standard allows for faster, more reliable data transmission, and better suits the operation of connected machines, objects and devices (the Internet of Things), and thereby serves as an enabler unlocking the full potential of the digital era.

In 2021, according to estimates, 19 percent of the world's population was covered by 5G. Europe had the highest rollout at 52 percent, followed by Latin America and North America with 38 percent and the Asia-Pacific region at 16 percent. High infrastructure costs, device affordability, and regulatory and adoption barriers remain the primary obstacles to 5G deployment and could foster a digital divide.[22]

Robots and automatization

The number of industrial robots currently in operation grew by 14.6 percent between 2020 and 2021 (see Dashboard) to 3.4 million robots. Major supply chain disruption due to the COVID-19 pandemic and other disruptions to global trade have driven increased automation and reshoring efforts – together boosting new robot installations to a record high of 0.5 million in 2021, representing a growth rate of 31.4 percent on 2020. Robots have also become less complicated to operate, owing to their programming being increasingly intuitive to non-experts, thanks to advancements in user-friendly interfaces and sensor technologies.[23]

The top five markets for industrial robots are China, which leads with 52 percent of new installations, followed by Japan (9 percent), the United States (7 percent), the Republic of Korea (6 percent) and Germany (5 percent). Combined, these five countries represented 78 percent of new robot installations globally, in 2022.[24]

Electric vehicles

Demand for EVs is booming. In just two years, the market share of EV sales worldwide surged from 4 percent in 2020 to 14 percent in 2022. Sales of EVs surpassed 10 million units, marking a remarkable 55 percent increase between 2021 and 2022, while traditional car sales slumped by 3 percent.[25] This was despite the first ever observed increase in electric battery pack prices in 2022 (see Technological progress section above). Moreover, cars are just the first wave: electric buses and trucks will follow soon, while electric three-wheelers are already booming in major markets such as India, where over half of its three-wheeler registrations in 2022 were electric.

Encouraging EV trends are generating positive ripple effects for battery production and supply chains. Ambitious policy programs that put an emphasis on strengthening domestic supply chains and encourage reshoring – such as the European Union's (EU) Net Zero Industry Act and the United States' Inflation Reduction Act – have sparked significant planned investment by major EV and battery makers. To maximize the environmental benefits from EV transition, it is crucial to simultaneously address not only the sources of the electricity used to charge EVs, but raw material extraction and battery disposal.[26]

Nevertheless, at present, out of every car on the world's roads (in 2022) only 2.1 percent are electric (see Dashboard). This represents an EV stock of 26 million, half of which is in China (13.8 million). Europe maintained its position as the second largest market for electric cars worldwide, in 2022, accounting for 30 percent of global stock. EVs remain the fastest growing indicator (+59.9 percent and more than five times the stock in 2018, see Dashboard) in the Global Innovation Tracker this year, and further growth can be expected, regardless of uncertainty concerning how attractive traditional petrol or diesel vehicles will continue to be in the future.

Cancer radiotherapy

To better capture the adoption of health-related innovations, the 2023 Global Innovation Tracker includes data on the availability of cancer therapy equipment. A significant measure in the field of radiation oncology and medical physics is the total number of linear accelerators (LINACs) – devices for delivering high-energy x-rays or electrons to cancers for a therapeutic or palliative purpose – per cancer case requiring radiotherapy.

This metric can be regarded as a measure of the accessibility of cancer treatment infrastructure at the global level. International Atomic Energy Agency (IAEA) and DIrectory of RAdiotherapy Centres (DIRAC) data show cancer therapy has become less widely available, declining by −1.4 percent in the short term (2020–2022) and by −1.3 percent over the last decade (2012–2022). This suggests there has been an increase in cases of cancer requiring radiotherapy without an adequate corresponding increase in the number of LINACs, potentially leading to longer waiting times for patients or the need to travel abroad in order to access treatment.

In addition, there has been little improvement in the number of countries meeting minimum radiotherapy resource requirements over the last two years. Only 20.9 percent of countries worldwide met the minimum requirement in 2022 (see Dashboard). This stagnation in technological penetration is likely due to a variety of factors, including financial constraint, lack of trained personnel, infrastructural challenges and lack of awareness of the clinical role played by radiotherapy in the management of cancer.

Socioeconomic impact

The socioeconomic impact of innovation remains low. Labor productivity has come to a standstill, life expectancy continues to fall (including a slowdown in life expectancy improvement), and carbon dioxide emissions have returned to pre-pandemic levels. This is likely to be a rebound from the profound impact that COVID-19 has had on all three of these indicators. While life expectancy is sure to start increasing again in the future, developments in labor productivity and carbon dioxide emissions are less certain.

Labor productivity

Economists and policymakers around the world have been worrying about low productivity growth and how to revive the broken link between innovation and productivity – the theme of last year's GII 2022, What is the future of innovation-driven growth? – for a number of years. The year 2020 saw a sharp increase in global labor productivity (almost 4 percent). Yet this productivity spike was short-lived. One reason for the strong productivity growth rates seen early on in the pandemic (i.e., 2020) is that it was the less productive, in-person service activities that were most effected by lockdowns. This artificially raised the aggregate economy productivity level rather than it being a result of underlying technological progress. Consequently, hopes for a productivity revival were dashed again when employment readjusted and output per hour worked declined once again in 2021 to about 1 percent growth, and then down to zero in 2022 – the lowest growth rate seen in decades.

It is also notable how related economic data have fluctuated wildly in the past. In addition to volatile output and employment data (mostly due to lockdowns), changes in inflation, as well as geopolitical tensions, have also influenced productivity measures. Forecasts for 2023 foresee a modest uptick in productivity to about 1 percent, dampened in particular by negative productivity readings in Europe and the United States.[27] Prospects for 2024 and beyond look better, but are highly uncertain. Whether the Digital Age and Deep Science innovation waves outlined in the GII 2022 will reverse this productivity crisis continues to be a matter of debate. Only the next one to two decades will tell.[28]

Life expectancy

Nowadays, life expectancy is around 20 years longer than it was in 1960 (51 years). However, COVID-19 contributed to the first observed drop in life expectancy in 2020, and it continued to fall in 2021. This meant that life expectancy was nearly two years lower in 2021 (71 years) compared to pre-pandemic levels (73 years in 2019).

Examining well-being in aging and the role of innovation also involves reviewing the development of healthy life expectancy – an important measure of what people aspire to.[29] On average, healthy life stops about nine years before death. Figure 8 illustrates the relatively constant difference between the two concepts.

Figure 8 Life expectancy and healthy life expectancy, 2000–2019

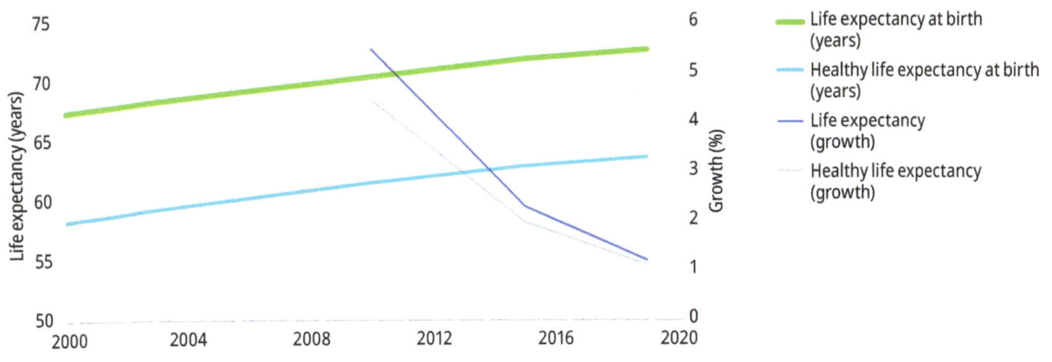

Source: World Health Organization (WHO) Global Health Observatory Database.

Figure 9 Years of life beyond 60

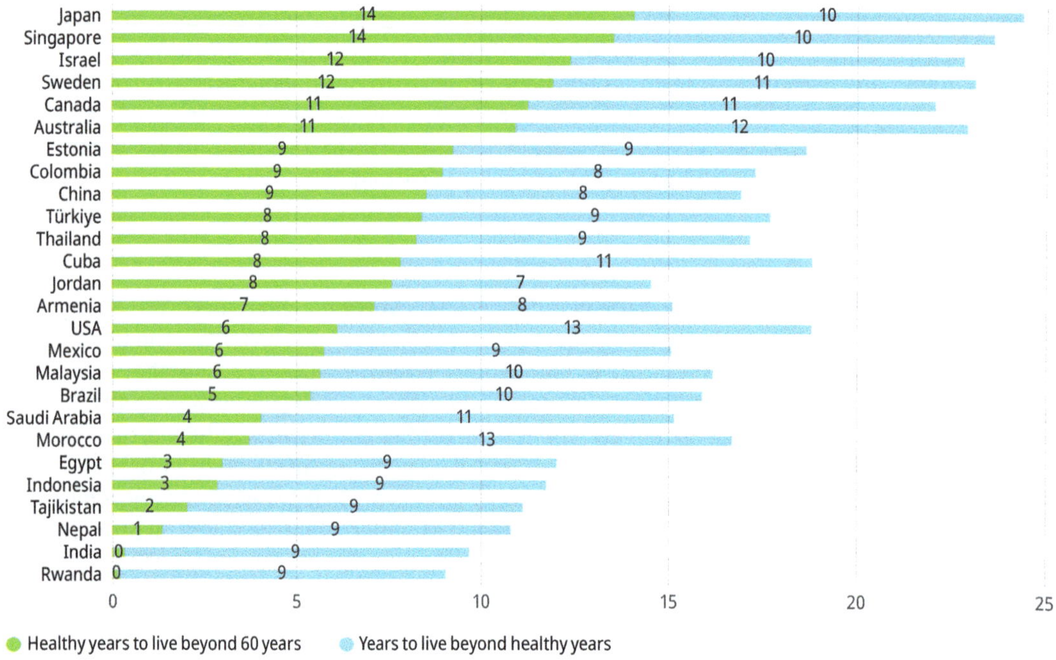

Source: World Health Organization (WHO) Global Health Observatory Database.

Healthy life expectancy beyond 60 years of age is longest in Japan, with an additional 14 years of healthy living plus a further 10 years of less healthy living (see Figure 9). Some 30 countries (out of 183 covered) enjoy more than 10 years of healthy living beyond 60 years of age, while some 55 countries have a life expectancy of under 60 years.

Carbon dioxide emissions

Strict lockdowns and travel restrictions resulted in a significant reduction in global carbon dioxide (CO_2) emissions in 2020. Unfortunately, 2021 witnessed a notable rebound, with emissions increasing by 5.3 percent, more than reversing the pandemic-induced decline.

In 2022, the growth of CO_2 emissions slowed again to 1.7 percent growth over 2021 – which is still higher than the 10-year trend of 0.7 percent (see Dashboard). Comparing the first five months of 2023 to those of 2022, the increase in CO_2 emissions appears very modest, with a 0.3 percent growth, but data are provisional and growth is still positive with no global reductions of CO_2 emissions in sight.[30]

Conclusion

The GII's Global Innovation Tracker provides a data-driven perspective on the latest innovation trends and impacts. The main findings of the 2023 edition are as follows:

- After a boom in 2021, investments in science and innovation showed a more mixed performance in 2022. Scientific publications, R&D and venture capital deals continued to increase and are at historically high levels. Novel innovation waves offer unseen possibilities, and leading innovation nations and innovation-intensive firms are ramping up their innovation efforts. But growth was lower than the exceptional rates seen in 2021. In fact, the value of VC investment has declined, possibly foreshadowing how tighter monetary conditions might come to affect innovation finance, and making the outlook for 2023 and 2024 uncertain.
- A topical question is whether the pandemic and subsequent economic downturn will have lasting negative impacts on less mature innovation systems in middle- and low-income economies, as well as on emerging firms and start-ups. The 2021 and 2022 data necessary to answer this critical question is not as yet available in most cases.

- Judging from data available to the GII, technology adoption is growing. Yet penetration often remains low. As outlined in preceding GII reports, fostering adoption in some sectors, such as agri-food, green or medical innovations, poses a significant challenge. Novel, demand-led innovation approaches, plus new regulatory set-ups and other fresh efforts are required.
- Measures of the socioeconomic impact of innovation suggest weak, if not declining, progress in recent years. To a large extent, this reflects the impact of the COVID-19 pandemic. How strongly they will rebound, as once the impact of the pandemic recedes, remains an open question.

Notes

1 IMF, 2023.

2 Massimo and Verginer, 2022.

3 Among middle-income economies, next to China, Türkiye and Serbia registered unprecedented growth in R&D in 2021, with GERD increasing by 15.6 percent and 18.1 percent, respectively. Other middle-income economies that increased their total R&D in 2021 include Kazakhstan (+7.8 percent), Armenia (+4 percent), Egypt (+2.9 percent) and Uzbekistan (+2 percent).

4 Government R&D budget indicators for the OECD area present the amounts that governments agree to allocate to R&D as part of their budgetary processes, rather than actual expenditure reported by R&D performers. Notably, economies like Japan witnessed an impressive surge of 59 percent in 2020 in real terms, while Australia experienced a noteworthy increase of 18 percent. The Republic of Korea and the United Kingdom also demonstrated strong growth rates of 15 percent and 8 percent between 2019 and 2020, respectively, and the United States 12 percent.

5 OECD, 2023 notes that "data for 2021 indicate that the decline R&D budgets was principally explained by the readjustment to health R&D. This year marks the return to growth in undirected R&D funding (general university funds and other funding for the general advancement of knowledge)."

6 China Statistical Yearbook 2022, Table 20-1, Basic statistics on Scientific and Technological activities, www.stats.gov.cn/sj/ndsj/2022/indexeh.htm.

7 Grassano *et al.*, 2022.

8 Care should be taken when looking at nominal growth rates, as they have not yet been adjusted for inflation. Growth in R&D intensities can in that sense be more informative, as inflation is cancelled out.

9 Airbnb is also no longer considered in the Software and ICT services category but handled in Travel, leisure and personal goods in the 2023 June version of the BvD Orbis database.

10 See WIPO's GII Innovation Insight on "Growth in venture capital financing will decline in 2022 relative to the 2021 boom, but remains at historic levels," December 14, 2022. Available at: www.wipo.int/global_innovation_index/en/news/2022/news_0008.html (figures have been updated).

11 For assessments of how IP filings fared during this and previous crises see, WIPO, 2010; WIPO, 2022; and Fink *et al.*, 2022.

12 WIPO, 2023b.

13 Rotman, 2020.

14 Pollie, 2021; Wang *et al.*, 2023.

15 www.intel.com/content/dam/www/central-libraries/us/en/documents/what-does-it-take-to-build-a-fab.pdf and https://techcrunch.com/2022/03/15/intel-plans-to-build-a-19-billion-chip-plant-in-germany.

16 Available here: www.top500.org/statistics. The authors of TOP500 are Erich Strohmaier, Jack Dongarra, Horst Simon and Martin Meuer.

17 IRENA, 2022. Between January 2019 and May 2022, aluminum costs – which can account for as much as 10 percent of solar photovoltaic modules' costs – rose by 50 percent, while copper, which is used extensively in all electric power generation technology, experience a 55 percent price increase. Furthermore, iron ore prices increased by 87 percent in the same period, and the steel contained within it is an important component of wind turbine towers.

18 For full definitions, see www.genome.gov/about-genomics/fact-sheets/DNA-Sequencing-Costs-Data.

19 To sequence a large stretch of DNA using NGS (next-generation sequencing), such as a human genome, the strands have to be fragmented and amplified: https://frontlinegenomics.com/long-read-sequencing-vs-short-read-sequencing.

20 UNICEF and WHO, 2023; United Nations Children's Fund (UNICEF) and World Health Organization, 2019.

21 An individual may have more than one mobile broadband subscription.

22 International Telecommunication Union, 2022.

23 https://ifr.org/ifr-press-releases/news/top-5-robot-trends-2023.

24 Müller, 2022.

25 IEA, 2023.

26 www.nytimes.com/2021/03/02/climate/electric-vehicles-environment.html.

27 www.conference-board.org/data/economydatabase.

28 This topic was also discussed in the context of the GII 2022 theme in the webinar series "Exploring the Future of Innovation-driven Growth and the Role of Intellectual Property: U.S. Industry Experiences," co-organized by WIPO and the Intellectual Property Owners Association (IPO), January 18, 2023, see www.wipo.int/global_innovation_index/en/news/2023/news_0003.html and "Exploring the Future of Innovation-driven Growth and the Role of Intellectual Property: European Industry Experiences," WIPO and BusinessEurope, April 5, 2023, www.wipo.int/export/sites/www/global_innovation_index/en/docs/businesseurope-workshop.pdf.

29 Healthy life expectancy refers to the average number of years that a person can expect to live in "full health" by taking into account years lived in less than full health, because of disease and/or injury, see www.who.int/data/gho/data/indicators/indicator-details/GHO/gho-ghe-hale-healthy-life-expectancy-at-birth. See also "Do you really want to live to be 100?," by Sarah O'Connor, *Financial Times*, December 6, 2022.

30 Carbon Monitor, https://carbonmonitor.org, accessed June 15, 2023.

Data notes

Scientific publications captures the number of peer-reviewed articles published in the Social Sciences Citation Index (SSCI) and Science Citation Index Expanded (SCIE), excluding early access articles. Source: Web of Science (Clarivate), https://apps.webofknowledge.com.

R&D investments captures R&D expenditures worldwide in PPP-adjusted constant 2015 prices. The 2021 values were calculated using available real data of gross expenditure on R&D (GERD) and business enterprise expenditure on R&D (BERD) at the country level from the UNESCO Institute for Statistics (UIS) online database; the OECD's Main Science and Technology Indicators (MSTI) database (March 2023 update); Eurostat and the Ibero-American and Inter-American Network of Science and Technology Indicators (RICYT). For those countries for which data were unavailable for 2021, the 2021 data were estimated using the last observation carried forward (LOCF) method. The R&D section also includes data on government budget allocations for R&D between 2019 and 2022 sourced from the Joint OECD–Eurostat data collection on resources devoted to R&D, April 2023, with figures in current US dollars. Data for the top global R&D spenders, in turn, are derived using the top spenders compiled in the European Commission's 2022 EU Industrial R&D Investment Scoreboard as a starting point and WIPO calculations facilitated by the Bureau van Dijk (BvD) Orbis database, with all figures in current US dollars.

Venture capital (VC) deals refers to the absolute number of VC deals received by companies located in a region. VC value refers to the total amount of current US dollars invested – via venture capital – into companies located in a region. Source: Refinitiv Eikon data on private equity and venture capital, www.refinitiv.com/en/products/eikon-trading-software/private-equity-data.

International patent filings refers to the total number of patent applications filed through the WIPO-administered Patent Cooperation Treaty. Source: WIPO IP Statistics Data Center, www.wipo.int/ipstats.

Microchip transistor count (Moore's Law) refers to the number of transistors to be found on the most advanced, commercially available microchips in a given year. Source: Karl Rupp, https://github.com/karlrupp/microprocessor-trend-data.

Green supercomputers consists of a Green500 list of the most powerful, commercially available computer systems known, which are at the same time the most energy-efficient in terms of calculation capacity per energy invested (Gflops/Watts). Source: TOP500, www.top500.org/lists/green500.

Cost of renewable energy captures the global weighted average levelized cost of electricity (LCOE) generation of solar photovoltaics and onshore wind. Source: International Renewable Energy Agency (IRENA), www.irena.org/Publications/2022/Jul/Renewable-Power-Generation-Costs-in-2021.

Electric battery price refers to the average lithium-ion battery price (in 2022 USD, including the cell, module and pack), weighted by power capacity (MWh), across all sectors. Source: BloombergNEF (BNEF), https://about.bnef.com/blog/lithium-ion-battery-pack-prices-rise-for-first-time-to-an-average-of-151-kwh.

Cost of genome sequencing refers to the cost of sequencing the DNA of one human genome (in USD). Source: National Human Genome Research Institute (NHGRI), US National Institute of Health, Wetterstrand KA. DNA sequencing costs: data from the NHGRI Genome Sequencing Program (GSP), www.genome.gov/sequencingcostsdata.

Drug approvals refers to the number of new drugs approved by the U.S. Food & Drug Administration (FDA). Data include both small molecule drugs and biologics. Source: FDA, www.fda.gov/media/135307/download.

Safe sanitation refers to that proportion of the population that has access to a sanitation facility not shared with other households and where excreta are safely disposed of *in situ* or removed and treated off-site, including flush/pour toilets connected to piped sewerage systems; septic tanks or pit latrines; pit latrines with slabs; and composting toilets. Source: WHO/UNICEF Joint Monitoring Programme for Water Supply, Sanitation and Hygiene (JMP), https://washdata.org.

Broadband penetration is equivalent to the number of fixed and (active) mobile broadband subscriptions, respectively, per 100 inhabitants. Source: International Telecommunication Union (ITU) World Telecommunication/ICT Indicators database, www.itu.int/en/ITU-D/Statistics/Pages/facts.

Robots is a measure of the number of robots currently deployed in industrial automation applications (also known as the operational stock of industrial robots). The stock is calculated assuming an average service life of 12 years with immediate withdrawal from service at the end of this period. Source: International Federation of Robotics (IFR), https://ifr.org/img/worldrobotics/Executive_Summary_WR_Industrial_Robots_2022.pdf.

Electric vehicles (EVs) stock share is the percentage of passenger cars worldwide that are battery electric vehicles (BEVs) or plug-in hybrid electric vehicles (PHEVs). Source: International Energy Agency (IEA), www.iea.org/articles/global-ev-data-explorer.

Cancer radiotherapy refers to the total number of linear accelerators per cancer cases requiring radiotherapy. Linear accelerators (LINACs) are devices for delivering high-energy x-rays or electrons to cancers for a therapeutic purpose. A higher ratio indicates a better-equipped health care system. Penetration rate refers to the number of countries that meet minimal radiotherapy resource requirements worldwide, based on a rough assumption that one in every two cancer cases requires radiotherapy and that one machine is needed for every 500 patients requiring radiotherapy. Source: Special tabulations by International Atomic Energy Agency's (IAEA) DIrectory of RAdiotherapy Centres (DIRAC) for the GII based on IAEA DIRAC (https://dirac.iaea.org) and IARC GLOBOCAN (https://gco.iarc.fr) databases.

Labor productivity refers to the world total of output per hour worked, as estimated by The Conference Board. Source: The Conference Board Total Economy Database™, April 2023, https://conference-board.org/data/economydatabase.

Life expectancy refers to the number of years a newborn infant could be expected to live, if patterns of mortality prevailing at the time of birth were to stay the same throughout its life. Source: World Development Indicators, https://databank.worldbank.org/source/world-development-indicators.

Carbon dioxide emissions refers to fossil emissions, excluding carbonation, for the world, measured in billion tonnes of CO_2 per year. Source: Global Carbon Project (2022). Supplemental data of Global Carbon Budget 2022 (Version 1.0), https://doi.org/10.18160/gcp-2022.

References

Fink, C., R. Lamb, B. Le Feuvre and H. Zhou (2022). How the COVID-19 crisis affected international intellectual property filings. In Fink, C., Y. Ménière, A. Toole and R. Veugelers. *Resilience and Ingenuity: Global Innovation Responses to Covid-19*. Center for European Policy Research. Available at: https://cepr.org/publications/books-and-reports/resilience-and-ingenuity-global-innovation-responses-covid-19.

Grassano, N., H. Hernandez Guevara, P. Fako, E. Nindl, A. Georgakaki, E. Ince, L. Napolitano, F. Rentocchini and A. Tübke (2022). *The 2022 EU Industrial R&D Investment Scoreboard*. Luxembourg: Publications Office of the European Union. Available at: https://iri.jrc.ec.europa.eu/scoreboard/2022-eu-industrial-rd-investment-scoreboard.

IEA (2023). *Global EV Outlook 2023: Catching Up with Climate Ambitions*. International Energy Agency. Available at: www.iea.org/reports/global-ev-outlook-2023.

IMF (2023). World Economic Outlook: A Rocky Recovery, April 2023. Washington, DC: International Monetary Fund. Available at: www.imf.org/en/Publications/WEO/Issues/2023/04/11/world-economic-outlook-april-2023.

International Telecommunication Union (2022). *Measuring Digital Development: Facts and Figures 2022*. Available at www.itu.int/itu-d/reports/statistics/facts-figures-2022.

IRENA (2022). *Renewable Power Generation Costs in 2021*. International Renewable Energy Agency, Abu Dhabi. Available at: www.irena.org/publications/2022/Jul/Renewable-Power-Generation-Costs-in-2021.

Massimo, R. and L. Verginer (2022). The impact of the COVID-19 pandemic on scientific research in the life sciences. *PLoS ONE*, 17(2), e0263001. Available at: https://doi.org/10.1371/journal.pone.0263001.

Müller, C. (2022). *World Robotics 2022 – Industrial Robots*. Frankfurt am Main: IFR Statistical Department, VDMA Services GmbH.

OECD (Organisation for Economic Co-operation and Development) (2023). *OECD Main Science and Technology Indicators: Highlights – March 2023*. OECD Directorate for Science, Technology and Innovation. Available at: www.oecd.org/sti/msti2023.pdf.

Pollie, R. (2021). Nanosheet chips poised to rescue Moore's Law. *Engineering*, 7(12), 1655–1656. Available at: https://doi.org/10.1016/j.eng.2021.11.008.

Rotman, D. (2020). We're not prepared for the end of Moore's Law: It has fueled prosperity of the last 50 years – But the end is now in sight. *MIT Technology Review*. Available at: www.technologyreview.com/2020/02/24/905789/were-not-prepared-for-the-end-of-moores-law.

UNICEF (United Nations Children's Fund) and WHO (World Health Organization) (2019). *Progress on Household Drinking Water, Sanitation and Hygiene 2000–2017: Special Focus on Inequalities*. Available at: https://data.unicef.org/wp-content/uploads/2019/06/JMP-2019-FINAL-high-res_compressed.pdf.

UNICEF and WHO (2023). *Progress on Household Drinking Water, Sanitation and Hygiene 2000–2022: Special Focus on Gender*. Available at: https://data.unicef.org/resources/jmp-report-2023.

Wang, X., L. Chi, W. Yuning, F. Shun, S. Dongming and C. Huiming (2023). Three-dimensional transistors and integration based on low-dimensional materials for the post-Moore's law era. *Materials Today*, 63, 170–187, ISSN 1369-7021. Available at: https://doi.org/10.1016/j.mattod.2022.11.023.

WIPO (2010). Special theme: The impact of the economic crisis and recovery on innovation. In *World Intellectual Property Indicators 2010*. Geneva: World Intellectual Property Organization. Available at: www.wipo.int/edocs/pubdocs/en/intproperty/941/wipo_pub_941_2010.pdf.

WIPO (2022). *World Intellectual Property Indicators 2022*. Geneva: World Intellectual Property Organization. Available at: www.wipo.int/publications/en/details.jsp?id=4632.

WIPO (2023a). *Madrid Yearly Review 2023: International Registration of Marks*. Geneva: World Intellectual Property Organization. Available at: www.wipo.int/publications/en/details.jsp?id=4660&plang=EN.

WIPO (2023b). *Patent Cooperation Treaty Yearly Review 2023: The International Patent System*. Geneva: World Intellectual Property Organization. Available at: www.wipo.int/edocs/pubdocs/en/wipo-pub-901-2023-en-patent-cooperation-treaty-yearly-review-2023.pdf.

GII 2023 results

The GII unveils the world's innovation leaders, gauging the innovation performance of 132 economies.

Figure 10 Key global innovation changers 2023

The GII dynamo: The top 15 innovators, 2020–2023

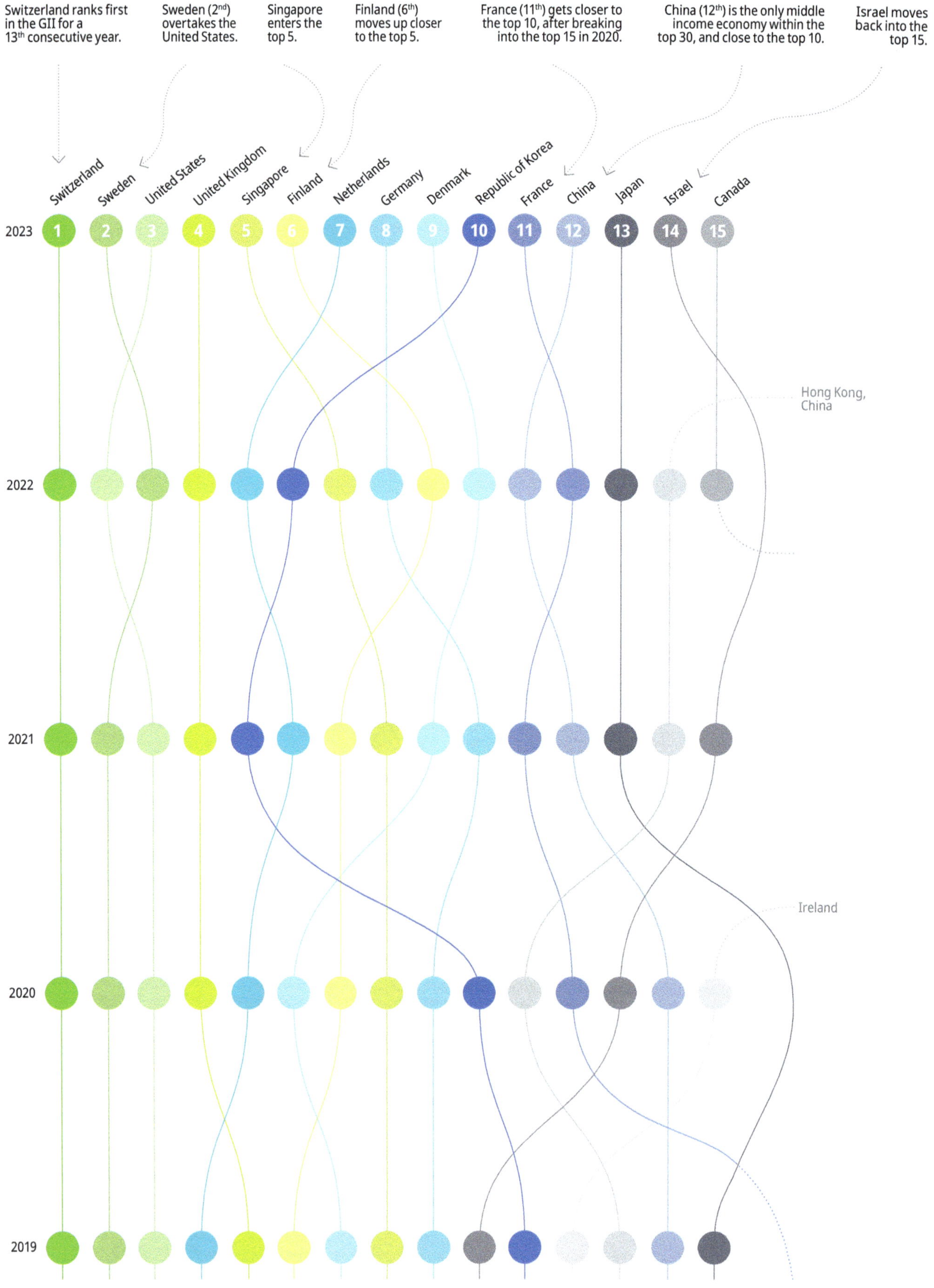

Source: Global Innovation Index Database, WIPO, 2023.

Note: Year-on-year comparisons of GII rankings need to take into account changes to the GII model that have occurred over time, as well as data availability.

Figure 10 Continued

Breaking barriers: Economies soaring to new heights in innovation, 2023

Top 70
Georgia (65th), **Bahrain** (67th), **Mongolia** (68th) and **Oman** (69th) join the top 70.

Top 60
North Macedonia (54th) and **South Africa** (59th) make it into the top 60.

Top 50
Saudi Arabia (48th), **Brazil** (49th) and **Qatar** (50th) make it into to the top 50.

Top 40
Latvia (37th) makes it into top 40.

Top 30
Portugal (30th) joins the top 30.

Top 20
Norway (19th) makes it into the top 20 in 2023.

Top climbers of the decade, 2013–2023

	2023	2013
Iran (Islamic Republic of)	62nd — Top 70	113th — Other
Indonesia	61st — Top 60	85th — Top 90
Philippines	56th — Top 60	90th — Top 90
Viet Nam	46th — Top 50	76th — Top 80
India	40th — Top 40	66th — Top 70
Türkiye	39th — Top 40	68th — Top 70
China	12th — Top 15	35th — Top 40

Group of middle-income economies within the GII top 65, which climbed fastest in the ranks over the last decade.

Standout economies' 4-year innovation surge, 2019–2023

88th Pakistan

61st Indonesia

57th Mauritius

49th Brazil

48th Saudi Arabia

In the last four years, and since the start of the pandemic, Mauritius, Indonesia, Saudi Arabia, Brazil and Pakistan ascended the most (in order of their rank progression).

Source: Global Innovation Index Database, WIPO, 2023.
Note: Year-on-year comparisons of GII rankings need to take into account changes to the GII model that have occurred over time, as well as data availability.

This section presents the highlights of the *Global Innovation Index 2023* (GII) ranking, including a discussion on the top ranked economies by income group and world region, as well as identifying those economies overperforming on innovation relative to level of development.

Appendix I provides details on how to interpret the results, cautioning against a strict year-on-year comparison of GII rankings.

It is important to note that the GII 2023 is unique, because it incorporates a significant amount of data from the pandemic and post-pandemic years. Approximately 88 percent of the data points used to construct the GII 2023 rankings cover the 2020–2023 period. Specifically, a majority of the data points are from 2021 (34 percent) and 2022 data (35 percent). This extensive use of COVID-19 pandemic-era data, together with the associated country-specific policy responses, including differences in lockdown and reopening periods, as well as the more recent impacts of armed conflict in Ukraine, has multifaceted effects on the rankings, so also the related country-specific swings in gross domestic product (GDP) – the scaling factor for a number of variables. These factors need to be considered carefully when evaluating GII 2023 rank shifts.

Innovation leaders in 2023

Switzerland continues to be the uncontested innovation world champion, Singapore makes the top five, and Indonesia joins China, Türkiye, India, the Islamic Republic of Iran and Viet Nam as most impressive innovation climbers of the last decade

For a 13th consecutive year, Switzerland ranks first in the GII (Figure 10). It is the global leader in innovation outputs, ranking first in both Knowledge and technology outputs and Creative outputs. Sweden overtakes the United States (US) to climb to second position. Sweden leads in Business sophistication (1st), Infrastructure (2nd) and Human capital and research (3rd). It holds top positions for its Researchers (1st) and its Knowledge-intensive employment (3rd). The United States continues to head the league table of scoring best in the world in 13 of the 80 GII 2023 innovation indicators (Box 1). It is number one in the world in indicators that include Global corporate R&D investors, Venture capital received, the quality of its universities, the combined valuation of its unicorn companies (a new GII indicator – Box 3), software spending and the value of corporate Intangible asset intensity.

Singapore enters the top five, and takes the leading position among South East Asia, East Asia and Oceania (SEAO) region economies. Finland (6th) gets closer to the top five, gaining three ranks this year. It comes top worldwide in Infrastructure (1st).

Denmark (9th) and the Republic of Korea (10th) remain in the top 10. France (11th) gets closer, improving one rank this year, while Japan remains strong as the 13th most innovative economy. Israel re-enters the top 15, reaching 14th place.

After a rapid ascent, gaining 23 positions over the last decade, China ranks 12th this year, dropping one rank relative to 2022.[1] China remains the sole middle-income economy to secure a position among the top 30, retaining 3rd place in the SEAO region and top spot in the upper middle-income group (see Figure 11 and Table 3). Belgium (23rd) re-enters the top 25, climbing three ranks.

All eight Nordic and Baltic economies improved their ranking this year, except for Iceland, which stays at 20th spot. Estonia gains two ranks and edges the top 15, at 16th place. Norway (19th) re-enters the top 20. Lithuania (34th) and Latvia (37th) make the largest improvements, gaining five and four ranks respectively, with Latvia re-entering the top 40.

Apart from China, there are only four other middle-income economies among the top 40 economies, namely, Malaysia (36th), Bulgaria (38th), Türkiye (39th) and India (40th).

The United Arab Emirates stabilizes at 32nd place, close to the top 30. Saudi Arabia (48th) and Qatar (50th) make it into the top 50. Middle East economies Bahrain (67th), Oman (69th), Jordan (71st) and Egypt (86th) also experience notable improvements in their innovation ranking –

with Bahrain and Oman entering the top 70, and Jordan just outside. In sum, these are some systematic and positive innovation rank developments in the Middle East.

Brazil (49th) makes it into the top 50 in 2023, following a gradual ascent over recent years, overtaking Chile (52nd) as the most innovative economy in Latin America and the Caribbean. Uruguay (63rd) and El Salvador (95th) are the only two other economies within the region that improve their ranking in 2023.

Thailand (43rd) and Viet Nam (46th) consolidate their positions in the top 50, while the Philippines (56th) gets closer. Viet Nam and the Philippines continue marching forward, after a setback in 2022, gaining two and three ranks, respectively. Indonesia (61st) moves rapidly toward the top 60, following a rise over recent years. Together with China, India, the Islamic Republic of Iran (62nd), the Philippines, Türkiye and Viet Nam, Indonesia joins the group of middle-income economies within the GII top 65 that climbed fastest in the GII ranking over the last decade.

In the last four years, and since the start of the pandemic, Mauritius (57th), Indonesia, Saudi Arabia, Brazil and Pakistan ascended most in the GII, in order of their rank progression.

In Central and Southern Asia, Kazakhstan (81st) and Uzbekistan (82nd) are close to the top 80, while Pakistan (88th) follows closely, the latter overperforming on innovation once again in 2023.

Nine out of the 26 economies from Sub-Saharan Africa (SSA) covered this year improve their ranking. South Africa (59th) enters the top 60. Rwanda (103rd and low-income group leader) continues moving ahead. Senegal (93rd) and Nigeria (109th) take two of the biggest leaps forward. Excluding island economies, Senegal becomes the region's third most innovative economy in 2023 (see Figure 11).

Figure 11 Global innovation leaders in 2023

Top three innovation economies by region

Europe	Northern America	Latin America and the Caribbean	Central and Southern Asia
1. Switzerland	1. United States	1. Brazil ↑	1. India
2. Sweden	2. Canada	2. Chile ↓	2. Iran (Islamic Republic of)
3. United Kingdom		3. Mexico	3. Kazakhstan ☆

South East Asia, East Asia, and Oceania	Northern Africa and Western Asia†	Sub-Saharan Africa*
1. Singapore ↑	1. Israel	1. South Africa
2. Republic of Korea ↓	2. United Arab Emirates	2. Botswana
3. China	3. Türkiye	3. Senegal ☆

Top three innovation economies by income group

High-income	Upper middle-income	Lower middle-income	Low-income group
1. Switzerland	1. China	1. India	1. Rwanda
2. Sweden ↑	2. Malaysia ↑	2. Viet Nam	2. Madagascar
3. United States ↓	3. Bulgaria ↓	3. Ukraine ☆	3. Togo ☆

☆ Indicates a new entrant into the top three in 2023.

↑↓ Indicates movement in ranking (up or down) within the top three, relative to 2022.

* Top three in Sub-Saharan Africa (SSA) – excluding island economies. The top five within the region, including all economies, comprise Mauritius (1st), South Africa (2nd), Botswana (3rd), Cabo Verde (4th) and Senegal (5th).

† Top three in Northern Africa and Western Asia (NAWA) – excluding island economies. The top four within the region, including all economies, comprise Israel (1st), Cyprus (2nd), United Arab Emirates (3rd) and Türkiye (4th).

Source: Global Innovation Index Database, WIPO, 2023.

Notes: World Bank Income Group Classification (July 2022). Year-on-year GII rank changes are influenced by performance and methodological considerations; some economy data are incomplete (see Appendix I).

Box 1 GII innovation indicators - 2023 trailblazers

The United States continues to lead in terms of number of GII innovation indicators for which it ranks top globally, ranking 1st in the world on 13 out of 80 indicators in 2023.

Singapore follows the United States globally and is number one worldwide on 11 indicators, the same amount as in 2022, including leading in Operational stability for businesses, Government effectiveness, ICT access, Logistics performance, Venture capital received, High-tech manufacturing, and GitHub commits. Israel follows in 3rd place, leading in nine innovation indicators, including R&D expenditure, University–industry R&D collaboration, PCT patents and ICT services exports. Switzerland and Hong Kong, China, tie jointly in 4th place, attaining top ranking in Patent families and High-tech imports, respectively. They are followed by Japan in 6th place, leading in Production and export complexity.

In addition to the top winners globally, there are middle- and low-income economies excelling in various domains. Relative to other countries and to its GDP or population, Namibia ranks 1st in Expenditure on education, Mozambique in Gross capital formation, and Cambodia and Nepal in Loans from microfinance institutions. Relatively, Mauritius leads globally in Venture capital investors, the Islamic Republic of Iran in Trademarks and Mongolia in Trademarks, as well as Industrial designs.

Box Table 1 Economies with the most GII indicators ranked top, 2023

	Innovation indicators that economies score best in worldwide		
Economy	Inputs	Outputs	Total
United States	6	7	13
Singapore	8	3	11
Israel	6	3	9
Switzerland	4	4	8
Hong Kong, China	5	3	8
Japan	4	3	7
China	2	4	6
Iceland	2	4	6
Malta	3	3	6
Finland	3	2	5
Estonia	4	1	5
Luxembourg	4	1	5

Source: Global Innovation Index Database, WIPO, 2023.
Note: The GII methodology allows multiple economies to rank 1st on any one indicator; see Economy profiles and Appendix I.

Mongolia (68th) and Egypt (86th) both improve their position by three places, while Senegal (93rd) gains six places.

Beyond the top 100, Rwanda (103rd), Nepal (108th), Nigeria (109th) and Togo (114th) have progressed the most in the rankings, increasing between two and eight positions this year. Rwanda performs exceptionally well in Institutions (33rd) and holds top ranks in Labor productivity growth (2nd), Policies for doing business (11th), Graduates in science and engineering (15th) and Venture capital recipients (20th). Rwanda also maintains 1st position among the low-income group, while Madagascar (107th) and Togo (114th) claim 2nd and 3rd position, respectively (Table 3).

Table 3 Top 10 economies by income group (rank)

Rank	Global Innovation Index 2023
High-income economies (48 in total)	
1	Switzerland (1)
2	Sweden (2)
3	United States (3)
4	United Kingdom (4)
5	Singapore (5)
6	Finland (6)
7	Netherlands (Kingdom of the) (7)
8	Germany (8)
9	Denmark (9)
10	Republic of Korea (10)
Lower middle-income economies (37 in total)	
1	India (40)
2	Viet Nam (46)
3	Ukraine (55)
4	Philippines (56)
5	Indonesia (61)
6	Iran (Islamic Republic of) (62)
7	Mongolia (68)
8	Morocco (70)
9	Tunisia (79)
10	Uzbekistan (82)

Rank	Global Innovation Index 2023
Upper middle-income economies (36 in total)	
1	China (12)
2	Malaysia (36)
3	Bulgaria (38)
4	Türkiye (39)
5	Thailand (43)
6	Brazil (49)
7	Russian Federation (51)
8	Serbia (53)
9	North Macedonia (54)
10	Mauritius (57)
Low-income economies (12 in total)	
1	Rwanda (103)
2	Madagascar (107)
3	Togo (114)
4	Zambia (118)
5	Uganda (121)
6	Burkina Faso (124)
7	Ethiopia (125)
8	Mozambique (126)
9	Guinea (128)
10	Mali (129)

Source: Global Innovation Index Database, WIPO, 2023.

Box 2 outlines important 'dos and don'ts', when using the GII to improve an economy's innovation performance.

Box 2 **How to best use the Global Innovation Index (GII) and what not to do?**

For many years, governments around the world have successfully used the Global Innovation Index (GII) to improve their economy's innovation performance and shape evidence-based innovation policies. A survey carried out by WIPO in 2022 showed 70 percent of WIPO member states were using the GII to improve innovation ecosystems and metrics, as well as it being a benchmark for national innovation policies or economic strategies. It is heartening to see that the GII is being used by a wide range of economies, from low- to high-income, across every one of the world's regions.

One major benefit of the GII is that it puts evidence and metrics at the core of conceiving, deploying and evaluating innovation policies. A first step brings together statisticians, innovation actors and policymakers in order to understand a country's innovation performance, based on the GII metrics. In a second step, the policy discussion turns to leveraging domestic innovation opportunities, while at the same time overcoming country-specific weaknesses. Both steps are an exercise in coordination among different public and private innovation actors, as well as between government entities. In select countries, the GII has facilitated just such a dialogue across innovation actors and government entities.

Some dos:

- Ensure innovation is embedded as a key priority in a country's pathway to national development and progress, possibly formulated within a clear innovation policy.
- Establish a cross-ministerial task force to pursue innovation policy matters through a "whole of government approach," ideally reporting to the top tier of government, for instance, the Prime Minister's Office.
- Ensure any innovation policy task force consults with innovation actors from both the private and public sectors, including start-ups, research universities and innovation clusters. The private sector, in particular, is key, as is broad representation from manufacturing, services and traditional industries, as well as diverse entrepreneurial strands.
- Ensure any national intellectual property (IP) policy is aligned with or even integrated into innovation policy.
- Ensure those targets or actions that are part of an innovation policy are quantifiable and can be evaluated.

Some don'ts:

- Do not set over-ambitious and therefore unrealistic GII ranking targets. GII rankings rarely increase in leaps and bounds from one year to the next, particularly at the top.
- Do not expect policy changes to result in immediate improved GII indicator performance. There are important lags between the formulation of innovation policy and its execution and impact. The latest available innovation data is also rarely current, often lagging by several years.
- Do not treat the GII as a mathematical exercise, that is, by attempting to collect or focus on specific indicators simply to climb the rankings. A country's GII rank alone is only a partial reflection of a national innovation ecosystem and related progress. Moreover, the GII framework changes regularly. Do not therefore over focus on year-on-year changes within the GII, because these are influenced by relative performance vis-à-vis other countries, together with other methodological considerations (see Appendix I). Setting objectives for a period of years - for example, three to five years - and then reviewing combined progress over several years is a more appropriate way of using the GII.

With this in mind, the GII has become a catalyst for the national collection of innovation indicators. Economies have an interest in ensuring the GII can rely on the complete and updated innovation metrics they provide. As detailed in Appendix III, the vast majority of GII data is not collected by the World Intellectual Property Organization (WIPO) itself directly from its member states. Instead, WIPO uses data submitted by economies to those organizations globally responsible for a particular data collection (e.g., the UNESCO Institute for Statistics for data relating to R&D). The sole exception is the intellectual property data WIPO collects annually from members states.[2] For all other data sets, the GII team is able to help countries identify missing and outdated data (marked clearly in the economy profiles and briefs) and advise data collectors on how to remedy the situation.

Finally, a new trend is the interest being expressed by countries in building sub-national innovation indices at the regional or city level that mirror the GII framework or comprise selected GII indicators (WIPO, 2023a). WIPO has pledged to support this work in two ways: (i) by organizing workshops on the exchange of best practice, and (ii) providing a background study on sub-national innovation indices.[3] Member states are welcome to join this effort.

Innovation overperformers

Several middle- and low-income economies are performing above expectation on innovation relative to their level of economic development

In the GII 2023, 21 economies are performing above expectation relative to their level of development - these are the GII innovation overperformers (Figure 12 and Table 4).

India, the Republic of Moldova and Viet Nam continue to be record holders by being innovation overperformers for a 13th consecutive year. The Republic of Moldova (60th) scores above its income level in Human capital and research (67th), as well as both output pillars - Knowledge and technology outputs (60th) and Creative outputs (42nd). The Philippines (56th) and Morocco (70th) keep their innovation overperformer status for a fifth time.

There are also two notable comebacks this year, namely, Senegal (93rd) and North Macedonia (54th). In addition, Indonesia (61st), Uzbekistan (82nd) and Pakistan (88th) keep their overperformer status for a second and Brazil (49th) for a third consecutive year.

From a regional perspective, this year there is an equal number of innovation overperformers in South East Asia, East Asia, and Oceania, and Sub-Saharan Africa, each region having five innovation overperformers. Tying in 3rd place, with three overperforming economies each, are Europe, Central and Southern Asia, and Northern Africa and Western Asia. In 6th place is Latin America and the Caribbean, with two innovation overperformers.

Conversely, 37 economies are performing below expectation on innovation, the majority from Latin America and the Caribbean (11) and Sub-Saharan Africa (9). Among the high-income group, three are Eastern European economies, namely, Poland (41st), Slovakia (45th) and Romania (47th).

In the upper middle-income group, the six underperformers are Latin American and Caribbean economies Argentina (73rd), Costa Rica (74th), the Dominican Republic (94th), Paraguay (98th), Ecuador (104th) and Guatemala (122nd). All six of these economies also drop down the GII ranking in 2023. In the lower middle-income group, nine economies are performing below expectation for their level of development, including Sub-Saharan African economies Côte d'Ivoire (112th), Benin (120th), Cameroon (123rd), Mauritania (127th) and Angola (132nd).

Relative to 2022, 23 economies have switched performance groups. Seven economies have raised their performance status from below expectation to matching expectation, namely, Lithuania (34th), Greece (42nd), Egypt (86th), El Salvador (95th), Namibia (96th), Nigeria (109th) and Zambia (118th).

Figure 12 Innovation overperformers, relative to their economic development

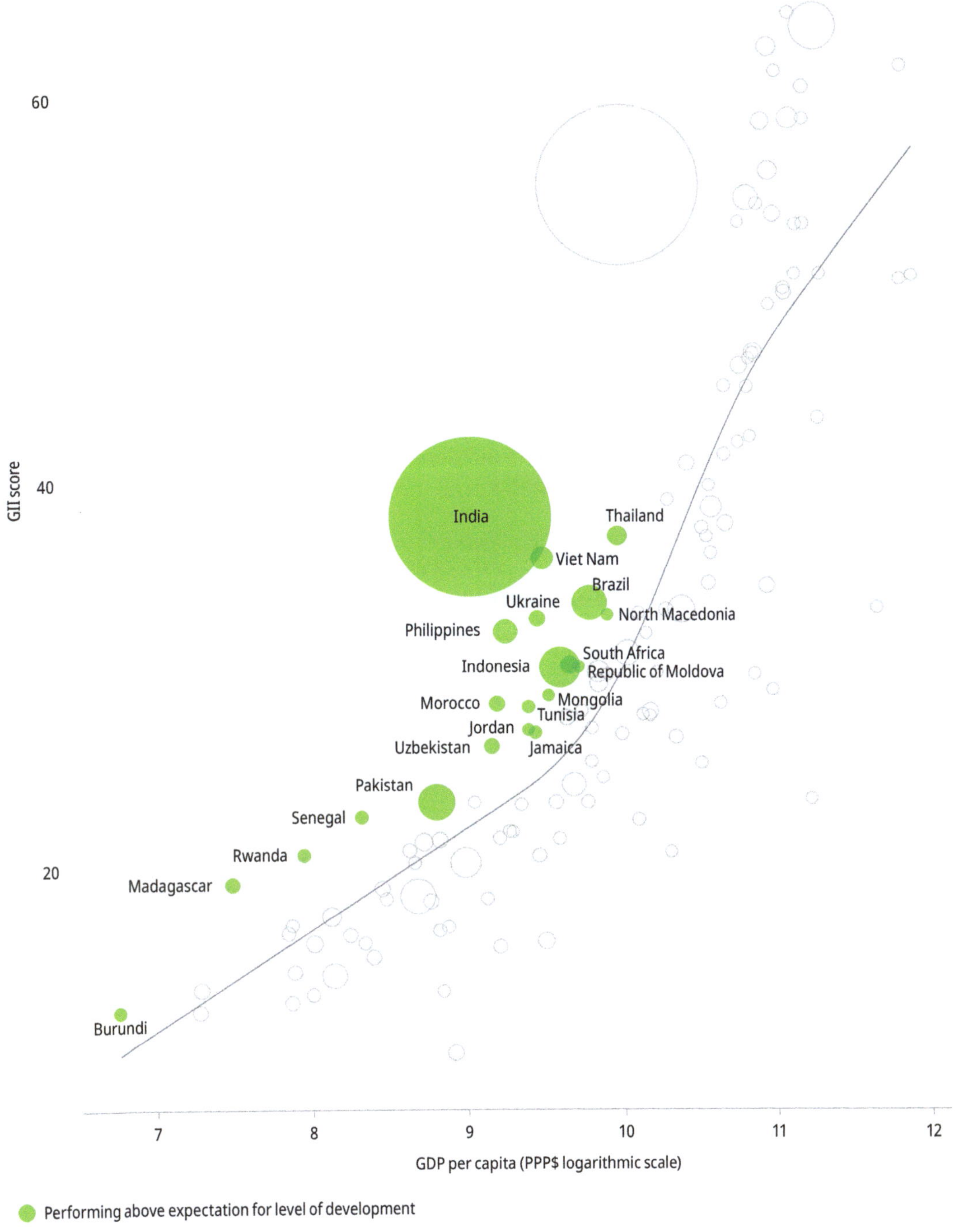

Source: Global Innovation Index Database, WIPO, 2023.

Note: Bubbles sized according to population. The cubic spline trendline shows the expected level of innovation performance at different levels of GDP per capita for all economies covered in the GII 2023.

Table 4 Innovation overperformers in 2023: Income group, region and years as an innovation overperformer

Economy	Income group	Region	Years as an innovation overperformer (total)
India	Lower middle-income	Central and Southern Asia	2011–2023 (13)
Republic of Moldova	Upper middle-income	Europe	2011–2023 (13)
Viet Nam	Lower middle-income	South East Asia, East Asia, and Oceania	2011–2023 (13)
Mongolia	Lower middle-income	South East Asia, East Asia, and Oceania	2011–2015, 2018–2023 (11)
Rwanda	Low-income	Sub-Saharan Africa	2012, 2014–2023 (11)
Ukraine	Lower middle-income	Europe	2012, 2014–2023 (11)
Thailand	Upper middle-income	South East Asia, East Asia, and Oceania	2011, 2014–2015, 2018–2023 (9)
Jordan	Upper middle-income	Northern Africa and Western Asia	2011–2015, 2022–2023 (7)
Madagascar	Low-income	Sub-Saharan Africa	2016–2018, 2020–2023 (7)
Senegal	Lower middle-income	Sub-Saharan Africa	2012–2015, 2017, 2023 (6)
South Africa	Upper middle-income	Sub-Saharan Africa	2018–2023 (6)
Morocco	Lower middle-income	Northern Africa and Western Asia	2015, 2020–2023 (5)
Philippines	Lower middle-income	South East Asia, East Asia, and Oceania	2019, 2020–2023 (5)
Tunisia	Lower middle-income	Northern Africa and Western Asia	2018, 2020–2023 (5)
Burundi	Low-income	Sub-Saharan Africa	2017, 2019, 2022–2023 (4)
Brazil	Upper middle-income	Latin America and the Caribbean	2021–2023 (3)
Jamaica	Upper middle-income	Latin America and the Caribbean	2020, 2022–2023 (3)
North Macedonia	Upper middle-income	Europe	2019–2020, 2023 (3)
Indonesia	Lower middle-income	South East Asia, East Asia, and Oceania	2022–2023 (2)
Pakistan	Lower middle-income	Central and Southern Asia	2022–2023 (2)
Uzbekistan	Lower middle-income	Central and Southern Asia	2022–2023 (2)

Source: Global Innovation Index Database, WIPO, 2023.

Notes: Income group classification follows the World Bank Income Group Classification (July, 2022). Geographical regions correspond to the United Nations publication on standard country or area codes for statistical use (M49).

Converting innovation investment into tangible innovation output

Several middle-income economies are more efficient at translating innovation inputs into outputs than their high-income counterparts

Among high-income economies, Switzerland leads (1st) in producing higher levels of outputs compared to Sweden (2nd), the United States (3rd) and Finland (6th), while Germany (8th) produces similar output levels to the United States and the Kingdom of the Netherlands (7th), but with lower input levels (Figure 13).

Among upper middle-income group economies, China (12th) also shines, producing levels of outputs comparable to high-income economies like Singapore (5th), Denmark (9th) and France (11th), but with fewer inputs. Türkiye (39th) does likewise relative to New Zealand (27th) and Hungary (35th).

Among the lower-middle income group, Morocco (70th) and Pakistan (88th) are efficient innovators, while Madagascar (107th) stands out among the low-income group.

However, certain economies, including the United Arab Emirates (32nd), Saudi Arabia (48th), Qatar (50th), Serbia (53rd), Bahrain (67th), Peru (76th), and Cabo Verde (91st), struggle to translate inputs into outputs, affecting their overall innovation performance.

This year, Canada (15th), Norway (19th) and Uzbekistan (82nd) have improved in converting inputs into outputs, no longer underperforming on this metric.

Figure 13 Innovation input to output performance, 2023

Source: Global Innovation Index Database, WIPO, 2023.

Table 5 Heatmap: GII 2023 rankings overall and by innovation pillar, 2023

Country/economy	Overall GII	Institutions	Human capital and research	Infrastructure	Market sophistication	Business sophistication	Knowledge and technology outputs	Creative outputs
Switzerland	1	2	6	4	7	5	1	1
Sweden	2	18	3	2	10	1	3	8
United States	3	16	12	25	1	2	2	12
United Kingdom	4	24	8	6	3	13	7	2
Singapore	5	1	2	8	6	3	10	18
Finland	6	3	5	1	12	4	4	16
Netherlands (Kingdom of the)	7	6	13	14	15	8	8	9
Germany	8	22	4	23	14	16	9	7
Denmark	9	5	9	3	21	12	12	10
Republic of Korea	10	32	1	11	23	9	11	5
France	11	27	17	22	9	17	16	6
China	12	43	22	27	13	20	6	14
Japan	13	21	18	13	8	11	13	25
Israel	14	40	20	36	11	6	5	33
Canada	15	14	10	30	4	18	19	22
Estonia	16	11	34	5	5	25	20	15
Hong Kong, China	17	8	15	9	2	28	51	3
Austria	18	13	11	12	39	19	17	13
Norway	19	4	19	7	29	22	28	23
Iceland	20	9	24	10	32	15	25	20
Luxembourg	21	7	31	31	35	7	38	11
Ireland	22	15	28	18	51	14	14	26
Belgium	23	30	14	44	26	10	15	30
Australia	24	17	7	19	17	24	30	24
Malta	25	34	39	17	43	21	36	4
Italy	26	52	33	21	40	33	18	21
New Zealand	27	12	21	29	31	29	39	28
Cyprus	28	41	38	32	38	31	23	17
Spain	29	46	27	16	33	32	24	29
Portugal	30	35	23	45	42	34	32	19
Czech Republic	31	36	30	24	82	27	21	32
United Arab Emirates	32	10	16	15	25	23	59	50
Slovenia	33	38	25	20	68	26	27	48
Lithuania	34	19	42	43	34	35	29	41
Hungary	35	47	36	42	64	30	26	38
Malaysia	36	29	32	51	18	36	37	47
Latvia	37	39	43	33	61	37	49	31
Bulgaria	38	66	66	28	60	42	34	34
Türkiye	39	105	41	50	36	46	44	27
India	40	56	48	84	20	57	22	49
Poland	41	76	40	47	67	41	40	35
Greece	42	63	29	38	66	62	43	39
Thailand	43	85	74	49	22	43	42	44
Croatia	44	72	44	26	48	53	33	52
Slovakia	45	65	53	41	72	47	31	56
Viet Nam	46	54	71	70	49	49	48	36
Romania	47	74	75	34	75	51	35	58
Saudi Arabia	48	45	35	48	28	45	68	66
Brazil	49	99	56	58	50	39	52	46
Qatar	50	23	54	39	44	73	82	65
Russian Federation	51	110	26	72	56	44	54	53
Chile	52	49	58	52	47	55	58	59
Serbia	53	57	51	35	41	68	41	92
North Macedonia	54	75	78	40	30	60	53	69
Ukraine	55	100	47	77	104	48	45	37
Philippines	56	79	88	86	55	38	46	60
Mauritius	57	26	64	74	24	91	90	57
Mexico	58	111	63	65	57	79	57	45
South Africa	59	88	84	68	45	61	56	63
Republic of Moldova	60	96	67	75	76	101	60	42
Indonesia	61	70	85	69	37	77	61	68
Iran (Islamic Republic of)	62	131	60	97	19	117	55	43
Uruguay	63	31	83	57	86	59	66	78
Kuwait	64	86	55	46	62	103	73	64
Georgia	65	25	69	80	77	58	72	81
Colombia	66	78	81	60	73	40	62	80

1th quartile (best performers, ranks 1st to 33rd) 2rd quartile (ranks 34th to 66th) 3nd quartile (ranks 67th to 99th) 4st quartile (ranks 100th to 132nd)

Table 5 Continued

Country/economy	Overall GII	Institutions	Human capital and research	Infrastructure	Market sophistication	Business sophistication	Knowledge and technology outputs	Creative outputs
Bahrain	67	28	77	37	78	92	74	98
Mongolia	68	80	65	81	101	67	88	40
Oman	69	62	52	61	74	95	75	79
Morocco	70	83	86	94	80	107	65	55
Jordan	71	51	82	87	53	70	76	75
Armenia	72	69	92	79	89	94	67	61
Argentina	73	123	70	66	92	54	79	51
Costa Rica	74	48	79	62	90	63	70	89
Montenegro	75	82	62	56	54	66	80	85
Peru	76	81	50	63	52	52	101	74
Bosnia and Herzegovina	77	104	68	67	27	106	64	91
Jamaica	78	53	91	91	109	69	92	54
Tunisia	79	107	46	89	98	119	50	72
Belarus	80	128	37	71	99	74	47	88
Kazakhstan	81	61	59	59	87	75	83	90
Uzbekistan	82	55	89	73	69	78	78	93
Albania	83	60	96	53	93	50	91	87
Panama	84	77	103	55	102	124	87	67
Botswana	85	37	73	85	70	56	117	106
Egypt	86	103	95	90	88	100	77	73
Brunei Darussalam	87	20	57	54	105	80	126	127
Pakistan	88	113	117	120	97	72	69	70
Azerbaijan	89	42	87	95	85	64	114	100
Sri Lanka	90	124	110	82	106	71	71	83
Cabo Verde	91	44	97	64	96	65	98	108
Lebanon	92	125	72	96	46	76	86	96
Senegal	93	59	107	98	81	122	63	113
Dominican Republic	94	67	109	76	91	86	95	94
El Salvador	95	101	106	99	95	85	94	77
Namibia	96	50	76	100	84	99	123	104
Bolivia (Plurinational State of)	97	132	61	104	16	81	106	102
Paraguay	98	112	129	83	79	87	109	76
Ghana	99	93	105	105	117	83	111	71
Kenya	100	84	118	107	108	84	81	95
Cambodia	101	87	101	108	59	125	93	103
Trinidad and Tobago	102	68	45	88	124	113	103	109
Rwanda	103	33	94	101	115	109	100	117
Ecuador	104	109	98	78	103	90	102	99
Bangladesh	105	108	125	93	100	126	89	82
Kyrgyzstan	106	122	49	92	71	114	96	116
Madagascar	107	121	102	131	113	123	121	62
Nepal	108	114	123	110	63	89	110	101
Nigeria	109	115	80	123	127	82	124	84
Lao People's Democratic Republic	110	95	115	109	65	102	97	124
Tajikistan	111	90	99	122	94	110	85	123
Côte d'Ivoire	112	71	128	106	123	96	118	97
United Republic of Tanzania	113	73	126	115	83	105	119	120
Togo	114	102	111	117	111	131	108	105
Nicaragua	115	127	120	113	58	97	122	111
Honduras	116	126	90	112	107	104	107	114
Zimbabwe	117	130	104	119	121	112	113	86
Zambia	118	119	93	111	110	98	130	112
Algeria	119	97	113	102	125	120	128	107
Benin	120	58	114	114	118	111	116	129
Uganda	121	64	124	116	128	118	105	122
Guatemala	122	120	122	118	112	93	99	119
Cameroon	123	91	112	130	129	88	104	118
Burkina Faso	124	92	108	121	116	128	112	130
Ethiopia	125	116	131	132	114	130	84	126
Mozambique	126	129	116	103	122	129	127	115
Mauritania	127	89	119	124	130	108	115	131
Guinea	128	98	132	127	132	127	125	110
Mali	129	117	121	128	126	115	120	128
Burundi	130	106	100	126	131	121	131	125
Niger	131	94	130	125	120	116	129	132
Angola	132	118	127	129	119	132	132	121

1th quartile (best performers, ranks 1st to 33rd) 2rd quartile (ranks 34th to 66th) 3nd quartile (ranks 67th to 99th) 4st quartile (ranks 100th to 132nd)

Source: Global Innovation Index Database, WIPO, 2023.

Box 3 Who leads on unicorns?

A unicorn company is a privately held startup valued at over USD 1 billion.[4] Unicorn companies exhibit rapid growth. They often disrupt industries by introducing innovative products, services or business models that have the potential to reshape entire sectors.

This 2023 edition of the GII includes a new indicator showing the combined valuation of a country's unicorn companies (6.2.2 Unicorn valuation, % GDP; see Appendix III).

According to CBInsights' Tracker of Unicorn companies, as of April 2023, there were 1,206 unicorn companies located in 50 different countries globally.[5] According to a simple count, only five economies host 80 percent of all the world's unicorns, namely, the United States (54 percent), China (14 percent), India (6 percent), the United Kingdom (4 percent) and Germany (2 percent). Out of a total unicorn valuation of USD 3.8 trillion in 2023, US unicorns account of USD 2 trillion – a huge lead – followed by China at USD 736 billion and India at USD 193 billion.

Of the top 25 most valuable unicorn companies and their origin, China comes first, with ByteDance (1st, artificial intelligence), followed by SHEIN (3rd, e-commerce) and Xiaohongshu (12th, e-commerce). The United States follows, with SpaceX (2nd, space and telecommunications), Stripe (4th, fintech) and Epic Games (7th, videogames). Australia has Canva (5th, graphic design and software) and Indonesia has J&T Express (13th, logistics and delivery).

In the GII, the cumulative value of unicorns is scaled by GDP. After scaling, five economies tie in first place, namely, Estonia, Israel, Lithuania, Senegal and the United States. Estonia leads with Bolt (auto and transportation), Israel with Wiz (cybersecurity), Lithuania has Vinted (e-commerce) and Senegal leads with Wave (fintech). These five top hubs for unicorns are followed by Hong Kong, China (6th), the United Kingdom (7th), Singapore (8th), India (9th) and Finland (10th).

Plotting an economy's level of development against the cumulative value of its unicorn companies shows whether it is overperforming relative to level of development. In the figure below, most economies in the upper-right quadrant are in the high-income group. The lower-right quadrant also contains high-income economies – largely European – but with a lower concentration of unicorn companies.

Box Figure 1 Unicorn valuation by level of economic development, 2023

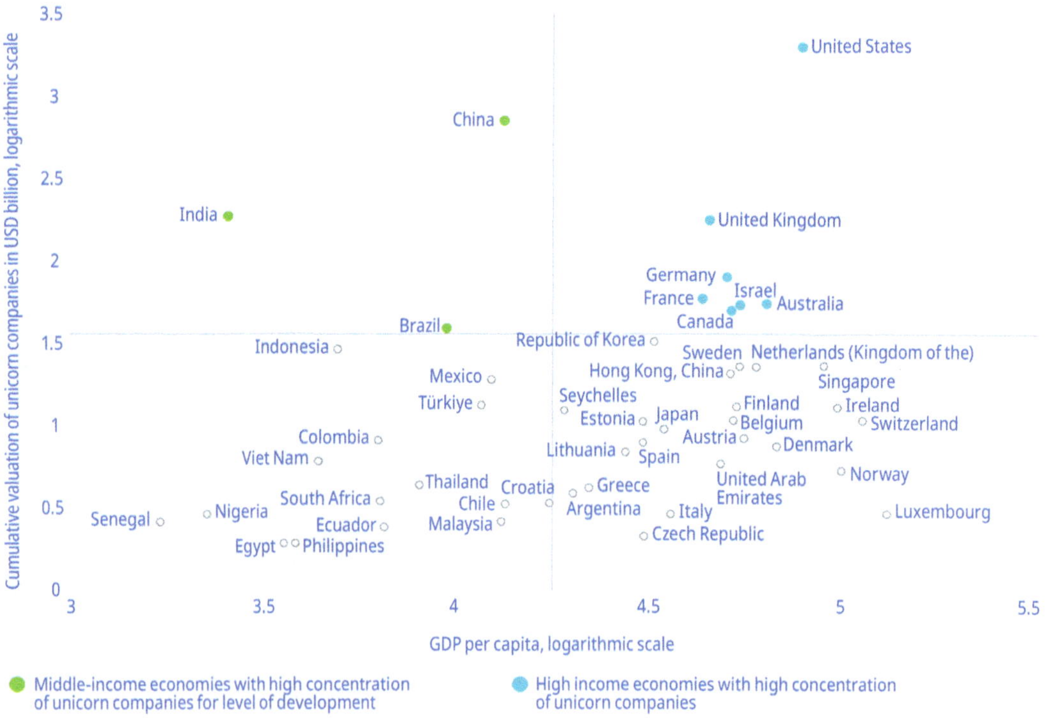

Source: Authors, based on CBInsights, 2023 and IMF World Economic Outlook, April 2023.

The economies in the left-hand quadrants are the most interesting cases. Upper-left, middle-income economies China, India and Brazil shine, having a high concentration of unicorn companies relative to their level of development. Lower left are those middle- and low-income economies hosting unicorn companies, even when their valuation is relatively lower. Latin American economies are the most represented, comprising Argentina, Chile, Colombia, Ecuador and Mexico, with leading unicorns Kavak (Mexico, e-commerce), Rappi (Colombia, supply chain) and Uala (Argentina, fintech).

Innovation leaders (top 25) demonstrate balanced and strong performance across all seven pillars. They include France (11th), Japan (13th), Canada (15th), Norway (19th), Iceland (20th) and Australia (24th) (Table 5). Some lower-ranked economies excel in specific innovation pillars, such as Georgia and Rwanda in Institutions (25th and 33rd, respectively), Trinidad and Tobago in Human capital and research (45th), Croatia (44th) in Infrastructure (26th), and Malaysia and Thailand in Market sophistication (18th and 22nd, respectively). India and Slovakia excel in Knowledge and technology outputs (22nd and 31st, respectively), while Türkiye and Latvia shine in Creative outputs (27th and 31st, respectively). These examples showcase the diverse strengths of economies vibrant in innovation, which can be nurtured to enhance their overall rankings.

Innovation across the world's regions

South East Asia, East Asia, and Oceania continues to narrow the gap with Europe, while Central and Southern Asia is getting closer to Latin America and the Caribbean

For yet another year, there are no changes in the rankings of the world's regions, based on an unweighted average GII score of all economies within a region. Northern America and Europe continue to lead, followed by South East Asia, East Asia, and Oceania (SEAO). Northern Africa and Western Asia, Latin America and the Caribbean, Central and Southern Asia, and Sub-Saharan Africa, follow more distantly. However, this year, the distance dividing economies in the SEAO region from those in Europe is on average no more than four GII score points, while economies in Central and Southern Asia are narrowing the gap between them and those in Latin America and the Caribbean.

Northern America
Largely driven by the United States, Northern America, comprising the United States and Canada, is the most innovative world region. Canada performs best in Market sophistication (4th), Human capital and research (10th) and Institutions (14th). It continues to lead in indicators Venture capital recipients (1st), the impact of its scientific publications (H-Index, 4th) and Software spending (5th).

Europe
Europe still hosts the highest number of innovation leaders among the top 25 – 16 in total, one more than in 2022. Out of 39 European economies covered, 19 move up the rankings this year (seven more than last year), namely, Sweden (2nd), Finland (6th), Denmark (9th), France (11th), Estonia (16th), Norway (19th), Ireland (22nd), Belgium (23rd), Italy (26th), Portugal (30th), Lithuania (34th), Latvia (37th), Greece (42nd), Slovakia (45th), Romania (47th), Serbia (53rd), North Macedonia (54th), Ukraine (55th) and Albania (83rd).

Among economies improving, France excels in Intangible assets (3rd), Global brands (4th), Industrial designs (8th) and Global corporate R&D investors (9th). Top companies like LVMH, L'Oreal and Christian Dior are contributing to its success. Belgium is performing well in R&D expenditure (6th), Researchers (8th) and University-industry R&D collaboration (9th). Serbia approaches the top 50 with a strong performance in FDI inflows (11th) and Labor productivity growth (14th).

This year, the Nordic and Baltic economies have made notable progress.

South East Asia, East Asia, and Oceania
The difference in GII scores between the South East Asia, East Asia, and Oceania (SEAO) region and Europe continues to diminish. Six SEAO economies are world innovation leaders, namely, Singapore (5th), the Republic of Korea (10th), China (12th), Japan (13th), Hong Kong, China (17th) and Australia (24th). These six economies continue to lead in key innovation indicators. China leads globally (1st) in Labor productivity growth, Japan in Production and export complexity, the Republic of Korea in PCT patents, Australia in School life expectancy, Hong Kong, China in Global brand value and Singapore in Venture capital received.

Eight economies within the SEAO region improve their rankings this year, with Indonesia (61st) making the greatest advance. Indonesia makes marked improvements in innovation outputs, notably in Knowledge creation and Online creativity. It excels in ICT-related indicators and ranks among the top 10 globally for University–industry R&D collaboration (5th), State of cluster development (5th), Entrepreneurship policies and culture (5th) and Finance for startups and scaleups (8th).

Mongolia (68th), Brunei Darussalam (87th) and the Lao People's Democratic Republic (110th) also move up the rankings.

Central and Southern Asia

Within Central and Southern Asia, India continues to lead, maintaining its 40th position overall. India leads the lower middle-income group (Table 3), performing strongly in every innovation pillar except for Infrastructure. It holds top ranking within the Central and Southern Asia region for Human capital and research (48th), Business sophistication (57th) and Knowledge and technology outputs (22nd). Strong indicators include ICT services exports (5th), Venture capital received (6th), Graduates in science and engineering (11th) and Global corporate R&D investors (13th).

The Islamic Republic of Iran is 2nd within the region once again, at 62nd position. It is the regional leader in Market sophistication (19th) and Creative outputs (43rd). It performs well in Intangible assets (13th), ranks 1st globally in Trademarks (1st) and in the top 15 worldwide in Graduates in science and engineering (3rd), Market capitalization (5th) and Industrial designs (11th).

Kazakhstan (81st) takes over 3rd position within the region, gaining two ranks and displacing Uzbekistan to 4th, which retains its 82nd position overall. Only Kazakhstan and Nepal (108th) within the region go up the rankings. Kazakhstan tops in Infrastructure (59th), thanks to its good performance in Government's online service (8th) and E-participation (15th).

Northern Africa and Western Asia

In Northern Africa and Western Asia, Israel (14th) has made significant progress this year and consistently leads the region as a whole. Israel stands out in various areas, holding top position in Market sophistication (11th), Business sophistication (6th) and Knowledge and technology outputs (5th). Furthermore, it distinguishes itself globally as the one country that allocates over 5 percent of GDP to R&D, with a remarkable expenditure of 5.6 percent in 2021.

Saudi Arabia (48th) enters the top 50, leading globally in ICT access (7th), ICT use (10th) and Policies for doing business (16th). It also excels for its Global corporate R&D investors (16th) and for its Global brand value (18th), thanks to leaders Aramco (oil and gas), stc (telecoms) and Al-Rajhi Bank (banking). Oman also takes a big leap forward this year by achieving 69th place, and ranks among the top 10 worldwide in Graduates in science and engineering (2nd) and Government funding per pupil (9th).

An additional seven economies within the region move up the ranking, including notable improvers Georgia (65th), Bahrain (67th), Jordan (71st) and Armenia (72nd).

Latin America and the Caribbean

In Latin America and the Caribbean, Brazil (49th) holds top position, followed by Chile (52nd), while Mexico maintains 3rd place at 58th. Uruguay (63rd) and El Salvador (95th) are the only other countries within the region to have improved their position this year.

Uruguay is the regional leader in Institutions (31st), Peru leads in Human capital and research (50th), Chile in Infrastructure (52nd), Brazil is top of the region for Business sophistication (39th) and Knowledge and technology outputs (52nd), while Mexico tops in Creative outputs (45th).

Brazil (49th) climbs up five ranks this year, improving notably in the Innovation Outputs Sub-Index (49th). It ranks 22nd globally for the valuation of its 16 unicorn companies, representing 1.9 percent of its GDP in 2023, thanks to leaders QuintoAndar (e-commerce), C6 Bank (fintech) and Creditas (fintech) (Box 3). It also improves in Intangible assets (31st), ranking 13th worldwide for its Trademarks, and in Global brand value (39th), thanks to its leading banking brands, Itaú, Bradesco and Banco do Brasil. It ranks among the top 15 globally for Government's online service (14th) and E-participation (11th).

Uruguay leads in the top 10 for Policies for doing business (4th), ICT services imports (5th) and exports (7th), and Operational stability for businesses (10th). El Salvador can point to its ranking for Firms offering formal training (15th) and Trademarks (20th).

This year, Brazil and Jamaica continue to perform above expectation for their level of development (Table 4). Conversely, the performance status of Costa Rica (74th) has declined, no longer meeting expectation but instead performing below expectation for its level of development.

Sub-Saharan Africa

In Sub-Saharan Africa, only Mauritius (57th) and South Africa (59th) rank among the top 60, with South Africa entering this group having gained two ranks since last year. Six of the region's other economies rank within the top 100 globally, namely, Botswana (85th), Cabo Verde (91st) – making a comeback to the GII in 2023 – Senegal (93rd), Namibia (96th), Ghana (99th) and Kenya (100th). Nine of the region's economies move up the GII ranking, including South Africa, Senegal, Rwanda (103rd), Togo (114th) and Mauritania (127th).

Botswana (85th) continues moving ahead, gaining one rank and retaining 2nd position within the region. South Africa (59th) – moving ahead by two ranks and entering the top 60 – Madagascar (107th) and Burundi (130th) are also innovation overperformers this year. Other notable improvers within the region are Nigeria (109th), Togo (114th), Benin (120th) and Guinea (128th).

Mauritius ranks highest within the region in Institutions (26th), Human capital and research (64th), Market sophistication (24th) and Creative outputs (57th). It leads worldwide in Venture capital investors (1st) and ranks 5th in Venture capital received. Cabo Verde leads the region in Infrastructure (64th) and performs well in indicators Gross capital formation (3rd), Expenditure on education (13th) and FDI inflows (17th). Botswana tops in Business sophistication (56th), and performs well in Loans from microfinance institutions (12th).

South Africa heads the region in Knowledge and technology outputs (56th), thanks to its good performance in Software spending (28th), Patents by origin (34th), PCT patents (40th) and for the valuation of its two unicorn companies (37th), Promasidor Holdings (consumer and retail) and Cell C (mobile and telecommunications).

Finally, Senegal gains six ranks this year, improving notably in Knowledge and technology outputs (63rd). It ranks 1st in the world for the valuation of its unicorn company Wave (fintech), sharing top place with high-income economies Estonia, Israel, Lithuania and the United States. It also performs well in Gross capital formation (8th), Loans from microfinance institutions (10th), FDI inflows (13th) and Venture capital received (19th).

Box 4 Innovation as the driver of the United Nations Sustainable Development Goals

The 2030 Agenda for Sustainable Development, with its 17 Sustainable Development Goals (SDGs), has set an ambitious agenda. While technology and innovation are a recognized key facilitator in achieving all related targets, innovation is a specific policy target in its own right. SDG 9 specifically targets innovation-related goals, in particular target 9.5, which promotes increasing R&D expenditure as a proportion of GDP (9.5.1), and increasing the number of researchers per million inhabitants (9.5.2), both of which are also important GII indicators.[6]

In this context, the GII has been recognized an authoritative benchmark for measuring innovation within the 2019 and 2021 UN General Assembly resolutions on Science, Technology and Innovation for Sustainable Development. Events such as the eighth annual Multi-Stakeholder Forum on Science, Technology and Innovation for the SDGs (STI Forum) held this year in May 2023 concern the role that can be played by innovation in accelerating the post-pandemic recovery.[7]

Looking forward, around the time of the GII launch in September 2023, an SDG Summit is due to be convened during the High-Level Week of the UN General Assembly marking the mid-way point in the agenda – which has seven more years to run – and to accelerate action during the lead up to 2030.[8]

Conclusion

Several key insights emerge from this year's GII report.

- The global innovation landscape is changing at this time of pandemic and recovery and geopolitical upheaval, not only within the group of leading innovation economies, but more widely. As a result, some of the changes in GII rank this year may partly reflect short rather than longer term trends. The most notable changes to the innovation landscape are as follows:
  - There has been a shift within this year's top 20 innovators, with Sweden, Singapore, Finland, Denmark, France and Israel (in order of their ranking) moving up the ranking, and generally a strong showing by the Nordic and Baltic countries.
  - There is a mixed picture for leading emerging economies, with Indonesia rising fast over recent years, the Philippines and Viet Nam progressing again and India stable, but with China, Türkiye and the Islamic Republic of Iran falling back slightly, possibly in part due to recent COVID-19 induced effects.
  - India, the Republic of Moldova and Viet Nam have overperformed on innovation relative to development for a 13th year in a row, with Indonesia, Uzbekistan and Pakistan maintaining the overperformer status they first achieved in 2022, and Brazil overperforming on innovation relative to development for a third consecutive year.
  - There are some systematically positive innovation ranking developments in the Middle East, with the United Arab Emirates (UAE) close to the top 30, and Saudi Arabia, Qatar, Bahrain, Oman and other neighboring countries progressing up the rankings.
  - Mauritius and South Africa are leading Sub-Sahara Africa, with solid positions in the GII top 60, and a total of five economies within the region overperforming on innovation, with Rwanda having done so for the longest.
- Similar to last year, and excepting those economies just mentioned, more middle- and low-income economies would benefit from more a systematic and gradual improvement to the set-up and performance of their innovation ecosystem.
- Today, more than ever, pandemic impacts, downward pressure on risk capital, high interest rates and high debt levels, together with the effects of disruption to global supply chains on nascent innovation systems in middle- and low-income economies, all need close monitoring. This is to preserve the many positive changes that have come about over the last two decades in terms of getting innovation systems and policies onto the agenda of developing countries' policymakers, legislators and innovation actors. Closely monitoring the evolution of innovation is key also in the SDG context (see Box 4).

Future editions of the GII will continue to track developments closely – and innovation impacts, in particular – with the aim of fostering a better understanding of innovation and its measurement. Future editions will tell us which of the GII performance changes at the country or regional level listed above are transitory and which longer term in nature.

Notes

1 It is difficult to determine whether this decline has been caused directly by the COVID-19 pandemic. However, it is worth noting that approximately 93 percent of the data points used for China in this year's model span the period from 2020 to 2023.

2 See www.wipo.int/ipstats.

3 The study reviews the applicability of the GII framework to the development of sub-national innovation metrics. It analyses the existing sub-national innovation indices of WIPO Member States who have pioneered this field. It also determines which future innovation metrics are applicable to the measurement of innovation at the sub-national level, particularly those exploiting "big data" and new computational methods. See WIPO (2023a).

4 Aileen Lee, a venture capitalist, coined the term in 2013. See: https://techcrunch.com/2013/11/02/welcome-to-the-unicorn-club.

5 www.cbinsights.com/research-unicorn-companies.

6 https://sdgs.un.org/goals/goal9.

7 https://sdgs.un.org/tfm/STIForum2023. See also the WIPO side event on the "The future of innovation-driven growth: Will the novel Digital Age and Deep Science waves drive a global revival?," on May 3, 2023, organized by WIPO, Oxford University Said Business School, the Brazilian National Confederation of Industry (CNI) and the Permanent Mission of Brazil to the United Nations, https://sdgs.un.org/sites/default/files/2023-05/Innovation-Driven%20Growth.pdf.

8 For more on the role of intellectual property in achieving SDGs, see WIPO (2023b) and www.wipo.int/sdgs.

Reference

WIPO (2023a, forthcoming). *Enabling Innovation Measurement at the Sub-National Level: A WIPO Toolkit*. Authors: Gaétan de Rassenfosse (EPFL) and Sacha Wunsch-Vincent (WIPO). Geneva: WIPO, Department for Economics and Data Analytics.

WIPO (2023b), *Intellectual Property Offices and Sustainable Innovation: Implementing the SDGs in National Intellectual Property Systems*. Geneva: World Intellectual Property Organization. Available at: www.wipo.int/edocs/pubdocs/en/wipo-pub-rn2023-10-en-intellectual-property-offices-and-sustainable-innovation.pdf.

Cluster ranking

The GII reveals the world's top 100 science and technology (S&T) clusters and identifies the most S&T-intensive top global clusters.

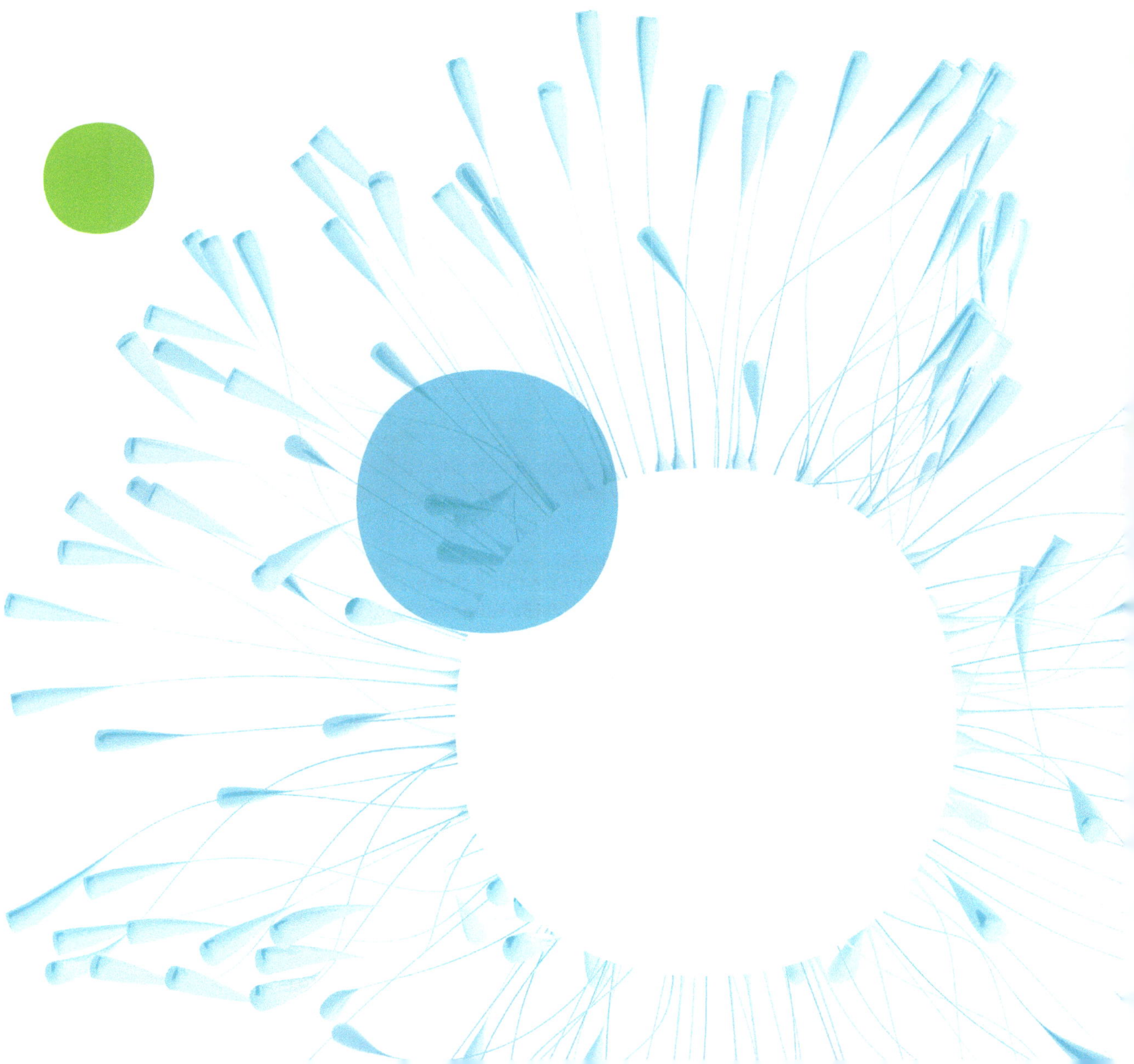

The GII 2023 top 100 science and technology clusters

Recognizing that innovation output at the local level is equally as important as output at the national level, the Global Innovation Index (GII) continues to chart the world's largest top 100 science and technology (S&T) clusters (see Map 1). These are the geographical areas around the world where the highest density of inventors and scientific authors are located (see Appendix IV for details on the methodological adjustment employed).

For a second time, the GII 2023 also presents S&T clusters beyond the top 100, shedding light on clusters not normally highlighted within this section.

Tokyo–Yokohama and four other Asian clusters lead the top 100 S&T clusters

Among the top 100, Tokyo–Yokohama (Japan) is the top performing cluster, followed by Shenzhen–Hong Kong–Guangzhou (China and Hong Kong, China), Seoul (Republic of Korea), Beijing (China) and Shanghai–Suzhou (China).

Seoul (Republic of Korea) climbs one place to third in the rankings overtaking Beijing (China) in fourth, in 2023.[1]

Shanghai–Suzhou (China) rises one place to enter the top 5, primarily owing to a strong growth in PCT filings. San Jose–San Francisco, CA (United States) follows in sixth position.[2]

The four remaining top 10 clusters are unchanged on the previous year, with the exception of San Diego, CA, which climbs two places from 11th to 9th with New York City, NY dropping a place to 10th and Paris two places to 12th.

Map 1 Top 100 clusters worldwide, 2023

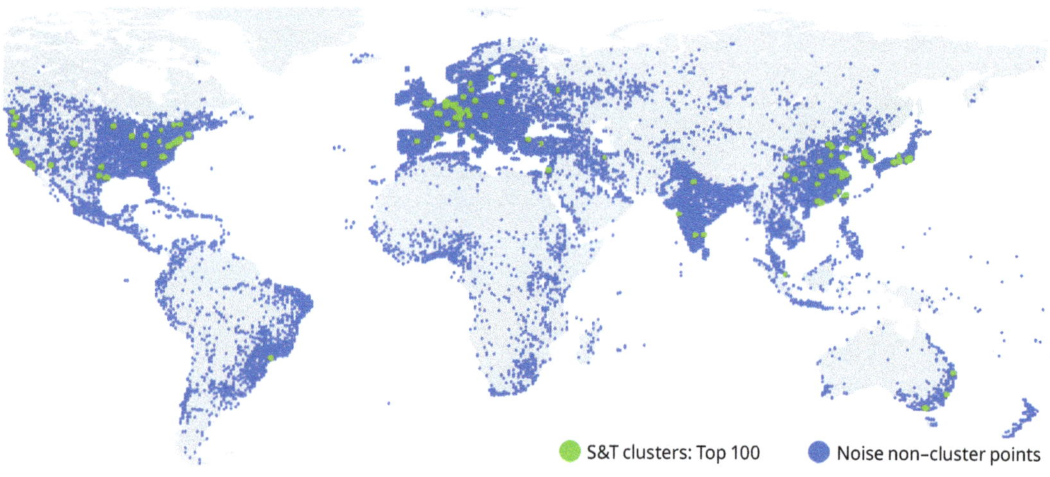

Source: WIPO Statistics Database, May 2023.
Note: Noise refers to all inventor/author locations not classified in a cluster.

The highest climbers in the ranking are three clusters in China, namely, Zhenjiang (+15 positions), Hefei (+13) and Wuxi (+13). Following significant growth, Wuxi and Zhenjiang, together with another Chinese cluster, Fuzhou (+8 positions) enter the top 100 for the first time.

It is clusters in China that have recorded the largest increases in S&T output in 2023, the median increase equating to +12.1 percent, with that economy hosting the two fastest growing clusters globally – Hefei (+21.6 percent) and Qingdao (+19.4 percent).[3]

Clusters located in other middle-income economies besides China also experienced strong S&T output growth, four of which were in India, namely, Chennai (+10.3), Bengaluru (+7.9 percent), Mumbai (+7.1 percent) and Delhi (+5.4 percent).

High-income economy clusters generally grew at a slower pace than clusters in middle-income economies, with 26 out of the 67 high-income clusters actually experiencing negative net S&T

output for the period. That said, there are some notable exceptions to this trend among high-income economy clusters. In addition to San Diego, CA (+7.5 percent) and Seoul (+6.4 percent) already highlighted, Daejeon (Republic of Korea, +7.8 percent), Denver, CO (United States, +4.4 percent), Rome (Italy, +4.0 percent) and Milan (Italy, +3.7 percent) all experienced strong S&T output in comparison to other high-income clusters.

The top S&T clusters for each economy or cross-border region are shown in Table 6. The leading clusters per country remain unchanged from last year, except for Munich overtaking Cologne to become the leading German S&T cluster.

The cluster around Singapore now encapsulates Johor Bahru, Malaysia, which lies to the north of Singapore, with a significant amount of daily commuting occurring from Malaysia to Singapore.

Table 6 Top S&T cluster by economy or cross-border region ranked among the top 100, 2023

Rank	Cluster name	Economy	Top applicant	Top organization
1	Tokyo–Yokohama	JP	Mitsubishi Electric	University of Tokyo
2	Shenzhen–Hong Kong–Guangzhou	CN/HK	Huawei	Sun Yat Sen University
3	Seoul	KR	Samsung Electronics	Seoul National University
4	Beijing	CN	BOE Technology	Tsinghua University
6	San Jose–San Francisco, CA	US	Google	Stanford University
12	Paris	FR	PSA Automobiles	Sorbonne Universite
20	London	GB	Nicoventures Trading	University College London
22	Munich	DE	BMW	Technical University of Munich
26	Amsterdam–Rotterdam	NL	TNO	Utrecht University
27	Taipei–Hsinchu	TW*	Hewlett-Packard	National Taiwan University
30	Tel Aviv–Jerusalem	IL	Yeda Research and Development	Hebrew University of Jerusalem
31	Moscow	RU	Samsung Electronics	Lomonosov Moscow State University
33	Singapore	SG/MY	A*Star	National University of Singapore
34	Tehran	IR	Ghanbari, Ahmad	University of Tehran
38	Stockholm	SE	LM Ericsson	Karolinska Institutet
42	Melbourne	AU	Monash University	University of Melbourne
48	Madrid	ES	LM Ericsson	Complutense University of Madrid
49	Zürich	CH	ETH Zurich	ETH Zürich
50	Milan	IT	Pirelli Tyre	University of Milan
51	Brussels–Antwerp	BE	Agfa	KU Leuven
52	Toronto, ON	CA	DH Technologies Development	University of Toronto
56	Bengaluru	IN	Samsung Electronics	IISC – Bangalore
59	Istanbul	TR	Sanovel Ilac Sanayi Ve Ticaret A.S.	Istanbul University
61	Copenhagen	DK	Novo Nordisk	University of Copenhagen
72	São Paulo	BR	Braskem	Universidade de São Paulo
73	Helsinki	FI	Nokia	University of Helsinki
76	Vienna	AT	Technische Universitat Wien	Medical University of Vienna
90	Warsaw	PL	Samsung Electronics	University of Warsaw
97	Basel	CH/DE/FR	DSM IP Assets	University of Basel

Source: WIPO Statistics Database, May 2023.

Notes: Tables in this section use ISO alpha-2 country codes, with the following additions: TW* = Taiwan, Province of China; IISC – Bangalore = Indian Institute of Science – Bangalore; TNO = Nederlandse Organisatie voor Toegepast Natuurwetenschappelijk Onderzoek. Economy labels were assigned to a cluster, when at least 1 percent of a cluster's output occurred in a given economy.

China overtook the United States in number of top 100 S&T clusters

In 2023, as in previous years, the top 100 S&T clusters are concentrated in three regions, namely, Northern America, Europe and Asia, and more specifically in two countries: China and the United States (see Map 1).

For the first time, in 2023, China is the economy that has the most clusters (24) ranked among the top 100, overtaking the United States with 21 clusters unchanged on the year (see Table 7). Germany follows, with nine clusters in the top 100, with Munich now that economy's number one cluster followed by Cologne and Stuttgart. Japan has four clusters in the top 100, with Tokyo-Yokohama (1st) and Osaka-Kobe-Kyoto (7th) ranking among the top 10 clusters. France has three clusters in the top 100.

Map 2 Top S&T clusters, East Asia, India, Türkiye and Israel, 2023

(a) East Asia

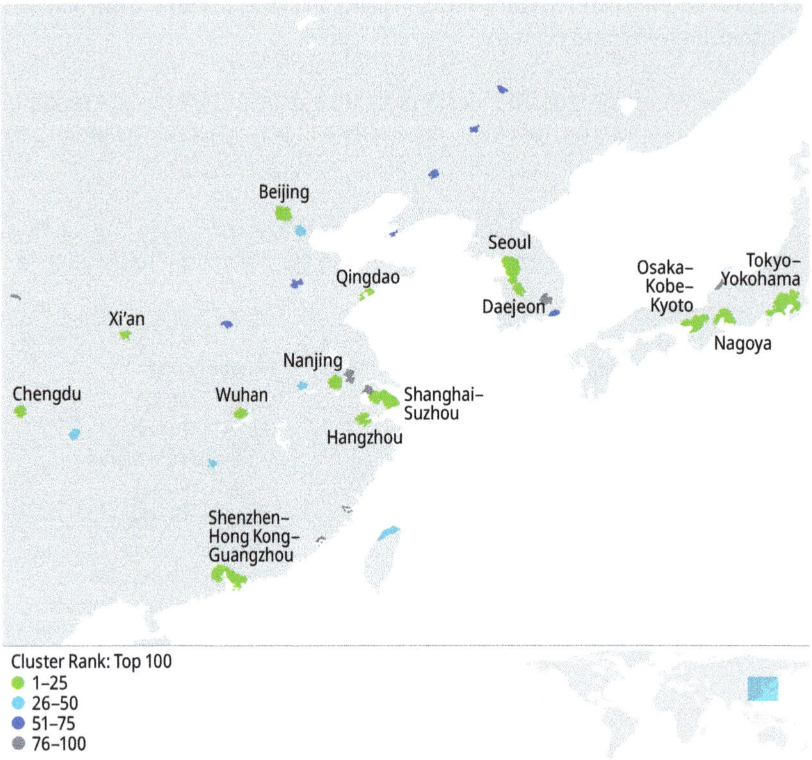

(b) India

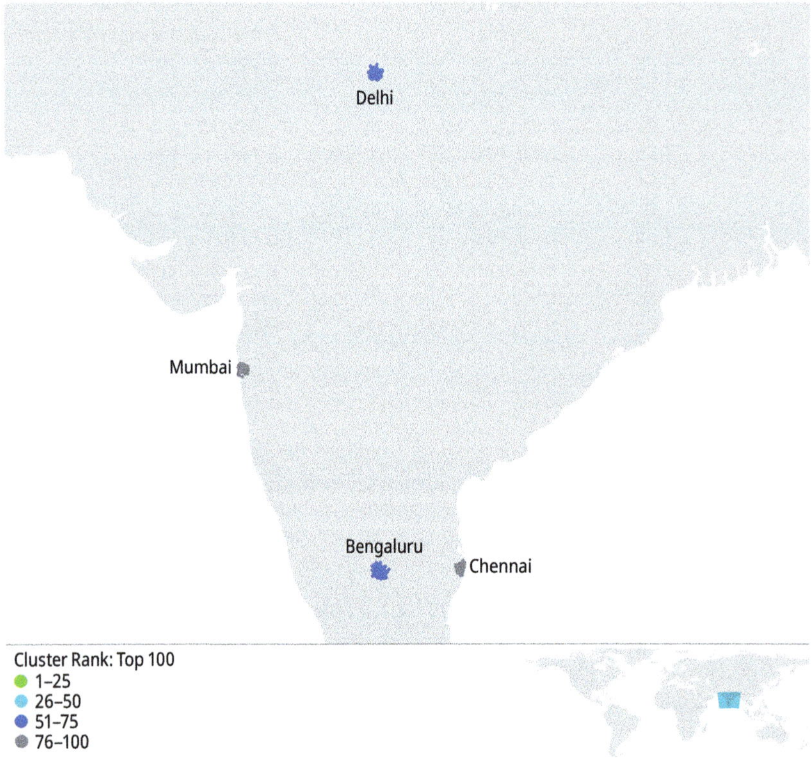

Map 2 Continued

(c) Türkiye and Israel

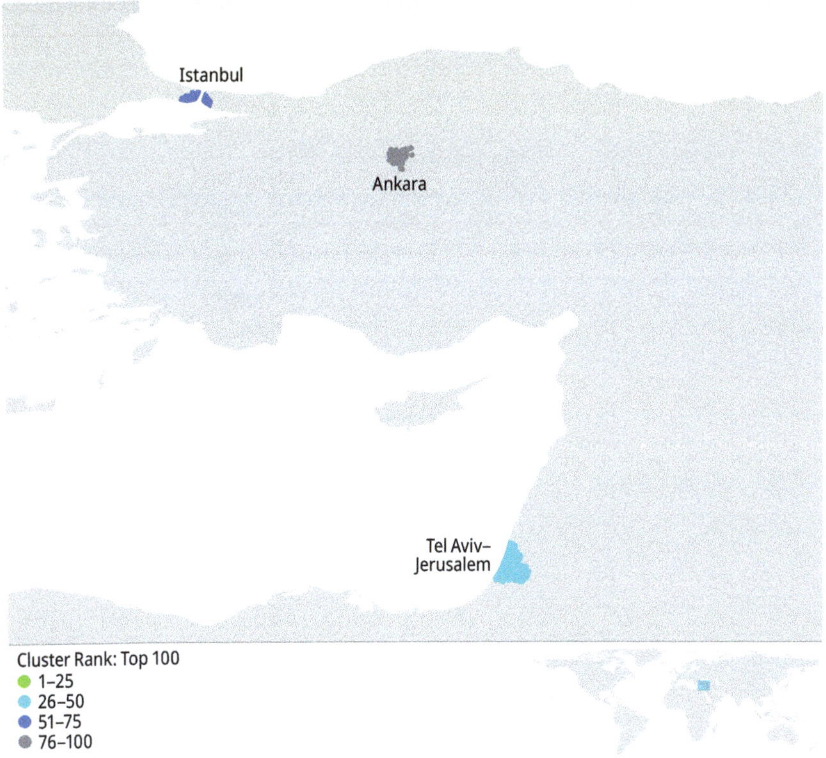

Source: WIPO Statistics Database, May 2023.

With the exception of China, only five middle-income economies have clusters among the top 100:

- Brazil (1 cluster), with São Paulo, is the sole top 100 S&T cluster in Latin America;
- India (4), with Bengaluru, Delhi, Chennai and Mumbai;
- Islamic Republic of Iran (1), with Tehran;
- Russian Federation (1), with Moscow; and
- Türkiye (2), with Istanbul and Ankara.[4]

The two Indian clusters Chennai and Bengaluru experienced the biggest increases in density of inventors and scientific authors.

Table 7 Economies with three or more top 100 S&T clusters, 2023

Economy	Economy name	Top 100 clusters
CN	China	24
US	United States	21
DE	Germany	9
JP	Japan	4
CA	Canada	4
IN	India	4
KR	Republic of Korea	4
FR	France	3
GB	United Kingdom	3
AU	Australia	3

Source: WIPO Statistics Database, May 2023.

Beyond the top 100, Bangkok, Buenos Aires, Cairo, Kuala Lumpur and Mexico City are top middle-income economy S&T clusters

Based on the same parameters applied to produce the top 100 ranking S&T clusters globally, the GII 2023 has been able to identify clusters beyond the top 100. In all, 137 additional clusters were identified beyond the top 100, including 24 clusters based in the United States, 16 in China and 11 in each of France and the United Kingdom.

Table 8 identifies top S&T clusters in economies not covered previously in the top 100, including Portugal and Saudi Arabia, which each had two clusters. Two economies not previously identified as having an S&T cluster are Pakistan at Islamabad, mainly driven by academic publications by Quaid-i-Azam University, and Slovenia at Ljubljana, mainly driven by publications by the University of Ljubljana.

Table 8 Top S&T clusters in extended ranking, economies not covered by the top 100 S&T clusters, 2023

Economy	Economy name	Clusters beyond top 100	Cluster name(s)
PT	Portugal	2	Lisbon and Porto
SA	Saudi Arabia	2	Dammam and Riyadh
AR	Argentina	1	Buenos Aires
CL	Chile	1	Santiago
CZ	Czech Republic	1	Prague
EG	Egypt	1	Cairo
GR	Greece	1	Athens
HU	Hungary	1	Budapest
IE	Ireland	1	Dublin
MO	Macao, China	1	Macau
MX	Mexico	1	Mexico City
NZ	New Zealand	1	Auckland
NO	Norway	1	Oslo
PK	Pakistan	1	Islamabad
RO	Romania	1	Bucharest
RS	Serbia	1	Belgrade
SI	Slovenia	1	Ljubljana
TH	Thailand	1	Bangkok

Source: WIPO Statistics Database, May 2023.

Middle-income economies, Argentina, Egypt, Mexico, Pakistan, Serbia and Thailand all host a top S&T cluster in the extended list, namely, Buenos Aires, Cairo, Mexico City, Islamabad, Belgrade and Bangkok, respectively.

S&T intensity of the top 100 clusters: Europe and the United States occupy the top 5 spots, with Cambridge (United Kingdom) and San Jose–San Francisco, CA (United States) out in the lead

Since 2020, the GII has also presented the top 100 clusters ranked by S&T intensity, that is, the sum of their patent and scientific publication shares divided by population. This work draws on geospatial imagery in order to estimate the underlying population level (see Appendix IV).

Cambridge in the United Kingdom and San Jose–San Francisco, CA, in the United States were found to be the two most S&T-intensive clusters, followed by Oxford (United Kingdom), Eindhoven (Kingdom of the Netherlands) and Boston–Cambridge, MA (United States) (see Table 9). The most intensive S&T clusters are primarily located in Europe and the United States (see Map 3).

Map 3 European and North American S&T clusters by intensity, 2023

(a) Europe

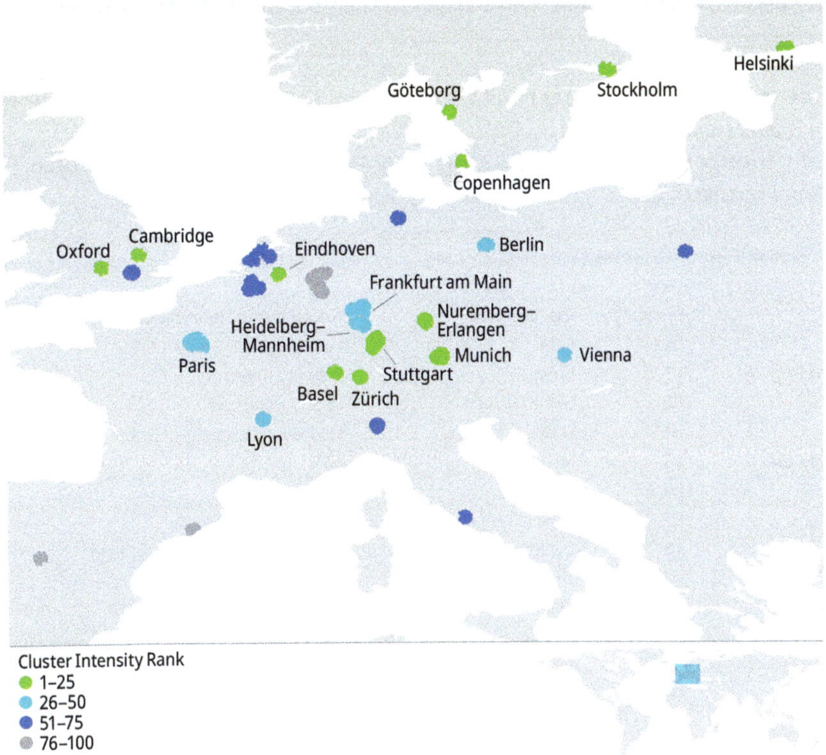

(b) North America

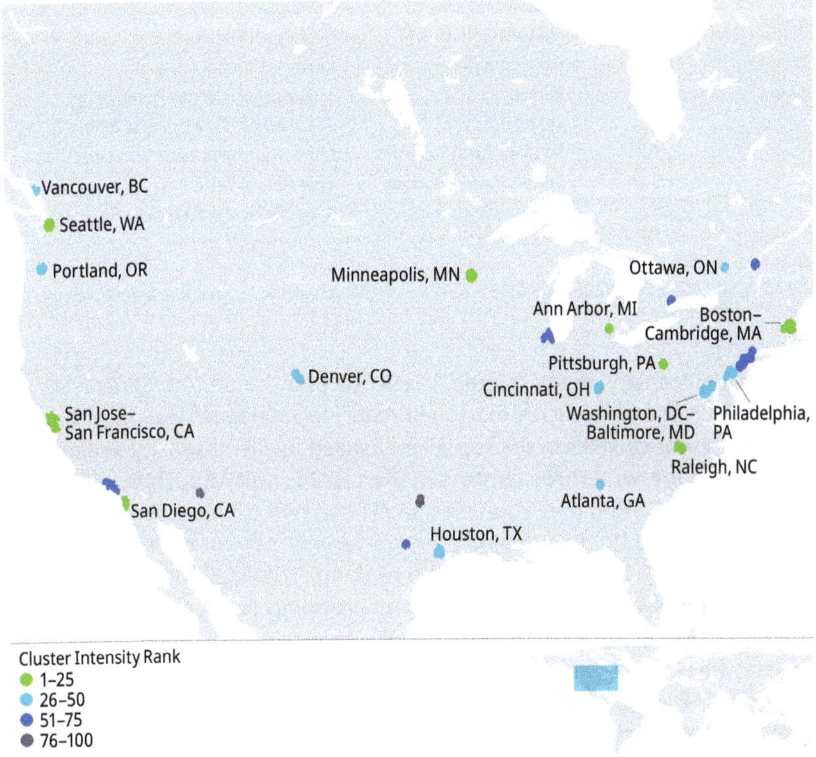

Source: WIPO Statistics Database, May 2023.

Daejeon (Republic of Korea) is the highest-ranking Asian S&T cluster by intensity.

Only three clusters were in the global top 10 and simultaneously in the top 10 for intensity, all in the United States, namely, San Jose–San Francisco, CA, Boston–Cambridge, MA and San Diego, CA.

Cambridge produced the most SCIE articles per capita, at just over 37,000 per one million people (see Appendix Table 4). It was closely followed by Oxford and Ann Arbor, MI (United States). Eindhoven leads on PCT filings per inhabitant, producing roughly 7,700 per one million people, followed by San Jose–San Francisco, CA.

Table 9 Top 25 S&T clusters by S&T intensity, 2023

Rank per-capita[a]	Cluster name	Economy	Top Applicant	Top scientific organization
1	Cambridge	GB	ARM	Cambridge University
2	San Jose–San Francisco, CA	US	Google	Stanford University
3	Oxford	GB	Oxford University	Oxford University
4	Eindhoven	NL	Philips Electronics	Eindhoven University of Tech.
5	Boston–Cambridge, MA	US	MIT	MIT
6	Daejeon	KR	LG Chem	KAIST
7	Ann Arbor, MI	US	University of Michigan	University of Michigan
8	San Diego, CA	US	Qualcomm	University of California San Diego
9	Seattle, WA	US	Microsoft	University of Washington Seattle
10	Munich	DE	BMW	Technical University of Munich
11	Kanazawa	JP	Fujitsu	Kanazawa University
12	Raleigh, NC	US	Duke University	Duke University
13	Göteborg	SE	LM Ericsson	University of Gothenburg
14	Beijing	CN	BOE Technology	Tsinghua University
15	Stockholm	SE	LM Ericsson	Karolinska Institutet
16	Helsinki	FI	Nokia	University of Helsinki
17	Zürich	CH	ETH Zürich	ETH Zürich
18	Tokyo–Yokohama	JP	Mitsubishi Electric	University of Tokyo
19	Basel	CH/DE/FR	DSM IP Assets	University of Basel
20	Copenhagen	DK	Novo Nordisk	University of Copenhagen
21	Nuremberg–Erlangen	DE	Siemens	University of Erlangen Nuremberg
22	Stuttgart	DE	Robert Bosch	Eberhard Karls University of Tubingen
23	Minneapolis, MN	US	3M Innovative Properties	University of Minnesota Twin Cities
24	Pittsburgh, PA	US	University of Pittsburgh	University of Pittsburgh
25	Seoul	KR	Samsung Electronics	Seoul National University

Source: WIPO Statistics Database, May 2023.

Notes: [a] Per capita figures refer to 1,000,000 of population. KAIST = Korea Advanced Institute of Science & Technology; MIT = Massachusetts Institute of Technology.

Seen through a lens focused on intensity, many clusters in Europe and the United States are seen to exhibit S&T activity that is more intensive than their Asian counterparts (see Map 3 and Table 9). The United States has eight clusters in the top 25 measured by S&T intensity. Following behind the United States is Germany, with three clusters in the top 25 (with Munich moving up rapidly to 10th spot), while the following four countries each have two clusters: the United Kingdom (with Cambridge and Oxford holding two of the top 3 rankings by intensity), Japan (with Kanazawa and Tokyo–Yokohama both improving their ranking), the Republic of Korea (with Seoul entering into the top 25) and Sweden (with Lund–Malmö dropping out of the top 25).

Clusters located in China show a relatively weaker performance, with regards to S&T intensity. However, there is one exception: Beijing. With a population estimated at almost 20 million, Beijing ranks 14th by intensity, mid-way between the smaller metropolises of Göteborg (13th) and Stockholm (15th) located in Sweden. Apart from Beijing, there is no other S&T cluster located in China or any other middle-income economy that ranks among the top 25 most intensive clusters globally.

India, however, does make it into the top 100 by S&T intensity for four clusters: Bengaluru, Chennai, Delhi and Mumbai.

Endnotes

1 Seoul's improvement in ranking was primarily due to its merging with Cheonan-si, a city just to the south of Seoul whose patent and scientific publication density reached the clustering threshold for the first time this year.

2 See Appendix Table 3, noting that, relative to population, US cluster San Jose–San Francisco, CA, ranks second in the world, see section S&T intensity of the top 100 clusters

3 Net S&T output refers to a change in combined output of both components (PCT filings and SCIE articles) over time.

4 Istanbul deserves a closer look, as it underwent a steep decline in ranking. This decline was primarily driven by a large area to its southeast failing to meet density criteria and therefore no longer within the cluster boundary of Istanbul. When controlling for the cluster's boundaries, Istanbul had positive growth in both PCT filings and SCIE articles.

Reference

Bergquist, K. and C. Fink (2020). The top 100 science and technology clusters. In Dutta, S., B. Lanvin and S. Wunsch-Vincent (eds), *The Global Innovation Index 2020: Who Will Finance Innovation?* Ithaca, NY, Fontainebleau and Geneva: Cornell University, INSEAD and WIPO.

GII 2023 Economy profiles

The following tables provide detailed profiles for 132 economies.

Framework of the Global Innovation Index 2023

Source: Global Innovation Index Database, WIPO, 2023.

How to read the Economy profiles

The following tables provide detailed profiles for each of the 132 economies in the *Global Innovation Index 2023*. They are composed of four sections.

1 At the top is the overall Global Innovation Index (GII) rank for each economy.

2 Next are the key metrics for each profile which provide the specific context for that particular economy: namely, its Innovation Input and Output Sub-Index rankings, the income group to which the economy belongs, its geographical region,[1] population in millions,[2] GDP in billion USD purchasing power parity (PPP), and, lastly, GDP per capita in USD PPP.[3]

Because economies may either drop in or out of the GII, and due to adjustments made to the GII framework every year and other technical factors unrelated to actual performance (missing data, updates of data, and so on), the GII rankings are not directly comparable between one year and another. Appendix I provides further details.

The Innovation Input Sub-Index rank is computed based on a simple average of the scores in the first five pillars, while the Innovation Output Sub-Index rank is computed based on a simple average of the scores in the last two pillars. Scores are normalized values falling within the 0–100 range.

3 Pillars are identified by an illustrative icon, sub-pillars by two-digit and indicators by three-digit numbers. For example, under the pillar Institutions 🏛 is the sub-pillar 1.3, Business environment, under which is indicator 1.3.2, Entrepreneurship policies and culture.

The GII 2023 includes 80 indicators in total and three types of data. Composite (or index) indicators are identified with an asterisk (*), survey questions with a dagger (†). The remaining indicators are all hard data series.

As far as possible, we have provided the (scaled/unscaled) value of the indicators rather than the score. Indicators based on survey responses (five indicators) or an index (11 indicators) are always reported as scores, while nine of the 64 hard data indicators are likewise reported as scores. This means that, overall, 55 out of 80 indicators are reported as values in the economy profiles.

When data are either unavailable or out of date, "n/a" is used, with a cutoff year of 2013. To the right of an indicator name, a clock symbol ⏲ is used when the available economy data are older than the base year. For information on data exceptions and limitations and a detailed explanation of the GII framework, see Appendix I. For further details on indicator sources and definitions, see Appendix III.

4 On the far right of each column, the strengths of an economy are indicated by a solid circle ● and weaknesses by a hollow circle ○. The strengths of an economy within its income group are indicated by a solid diamond ◆ and weaknesses by a hollow diamond ◇. The exceptions to this are the top 25 high-income economies, whose strengths and weaknesses are instead computed within the top 25 group.[4]

Rankings of 1, 2 and 3 are highlighted as an economy's strengths, except in particular instances at the sub-pillar level, when the desired data minimum coverage (DMC) is unmet for that sub-pillar. For the remaining indicators, the strengths and weaknesses of a specific economy are based on the percentage of economies whose scores fall either above or below its own score (i.e., percentile ranks) and where the data is no older than the indicator mode minus 5 years. In practice, this means that for indicators with a data year mode of 2022, an economy's data year must date from 2017 or be more recent in order to classify as a strength or weakness.

For any given economy, strengths ● are those scores with percentile ranks greater than the 10th largest percentile rank among the 80 indicators for that economy.

For that same economy, weaknesses ○ are those scores with percentile ranks lower than the 10th smallest percentile rank among the 80 indicators for that economy.

Similarly, for any given economy, income group strengths ◆ are those scores above the income group average plus the standard deviation within that group.

For that same economy, income group weaknesses ◇ are those scores below the income group average minus the standard deviation within that group.

In addition, economies with a sub-pillar that does not meet the DMC requirement will show the score for that sub-pillar within square brackets. Those with more than one such sub-pillar also include the ranks for that pillar within square brackets. For these pillars and sub-pillars, neither strengths nor weaknesses are signaled.

A complete explanation of the methodology for the calculation of strengths and weaknesses is available in Appendix I.

Notes

1 Economies are classified according to the World Bank Income Group Classification (July 2022, see https://unstats.un.org/unsd/methodology/m49). Geographical regions correspond to the United Nations' publication on standard country or area codes for statistical use (M49), as follows: EUR = Europe; NAC = Northern America; LCN = Latin America and the Caribbean; CSA = Central and Southern Asia; SEAO = South East Asia, East Asia, and Oceania; NAWA = Northern Africa and Western Asia; SSA = Sub-Saharan Africa.

2 Data are from the United Nations, Department of Economic and Social Affairs, Population Division, World Population Prospects: 2022 Revision.

3 Data for GDP and GDP per capita are from the International Monetary Fund's World Economic Outlook Database: October 2022 edition.

4 As the only economy in the top 25 that does not fall within the high-income group, China's income group strengths and weaknesses are computed within the non-top 25 group.

Albania

GII 2023 rank

83

Output rank	Input rank	Income	Region	Population (mn)	GDP, PPP$ (bn)	GDP per capita, PPP$
94	73	Upper middle	EUR	2.8	51.2	17,858

			Score/ Value	Rank	
	Institutions		**51.9**	**60**	
1.1	**Institutional environment**		**44.7**	**68**	
1.1.1	Operational stability for businesses*		52.8	65	
1.1.2	Government effectiveness*		36.7	70	
1.2	**Regulatory environment**		**57.1**	**80**	
1.2.1	Regulatory quality*		47.1	60	
1.2.2	Rule of law*		32.2	79	
1.2.3	Cost of redundancy dismissal		20.8	92	
1.3	**Business environment**		**54.0**	**[49]**	
1.3.1	Policies for doing business†		54.0	52	
1.3.2	Entrepreneurship policies and culture†		n/a	n/a	
	Human capital and research		**21.5**	**96**	
2.1	**Education**		**41.9**	**92**	
2.1.1	Expenditure on education, % GDP	⊙	3.3	97	
2.1.2	Government funding/pupil, secondary, % GDP/cap		9.8	91	○ ◇
2.1.3	School life expectancy, years		14.3	67	
2.1.4	PISA scales in reading, maths and science		419.8	56	
2.1.5	Pupil-teacher ratio, secondary		10.1	33	
2.2	**Tertiary education**		**22.6**	**83**	
2.2.1	Tertiary enrolment, % gross		56.7	58	
2.2.2	Graduates in science and engineering, %		18.5	85	
2.2.3	Tertiary inbound mobility, %		1.7	81	
2.3	**Research and development (R&D)**		**0.0**	**[119]**	
2.3.1	Researchers, FTE/mn pop.		n/a	n/a	
2.3.2	Gross expenditure on R&D, % GDP		n/a	n/a	
2.3.3	Global corporate R&D investors, top 3, mn USD		0.0	40	○ ◇
2.3.4	QS university ranking, top 3*		0.0	71	○ ◇
	Infrastructure		**45.4**	**53**	
3.1	**Information and communication technologies (ICTs)**		**75.9**	**47**	
3.1.1	ICT access*		78.9	76	
3.1.2	ICT use*		69.1	76	
3.1.3	Government's online service*		79.9	33	●
3.1.4	E-participation*		75.6	22	●
3.2	**General infrastructure**		**20.5**	**90**	
3.2.1	Electricity output, GWh/mn pop.		3,186.3	63	
3.2.2	Logistics performance*		18.2	89	○ ◇
3.2.3	Gross capital formation, % GDP		28.5	29	●
3.3	**Ecological sustainability**		**39.7**	**32**	●
3.3.1	GDP/unit of energy use		17.1	15	● ◆
3.3.2	Environmental performance*		47.8	48	
3.3.3	ISO 14001 environment/bn PPP$ GDP		3.6	27	●
	Market sophistication		**25.0**	**93**	◇
4.1	**Credit**		**9.6**	**114**	◇
4.1.1	Finance for startups and scaleups†		n/a	n/a	
4.1.2	Domestic credit to private sector, % GDP		38.0	86	
4.1.3	Loans from microfinance institutions, % GDP		0.5	37	
4.2	**Investment**		**2.9**	**[93]**	
4.2.1	Market capitalization, % GDP		n/a	n/a	
4.2.2	Venture capital (VC) investors, deals/bn PPP$ GDP		n/a	n/a	
4.2.3	VC recipients, deals/bn PPP$ GDP	⊙	0.0	78	
4.2.4	VC received, value, % GDP	⊙	0.0	93	○
4.3	**Trade, diversification and market scale**		**62.6**	**48**	
4.3.1	Applied tariff rate, weighted avg., %		1.1	12	●
4.3.2	Domestic industry diversification		93.9	35	
4.3.3	Domestic market scale, bn PPP$		51.2	106	

			Score/ Value	Rank	
	Business sophistication		**32.1**	**50**	
5.1	**Knowledge workers**		**41.8**	**[45]**	
5.1.1	Knowledge-intensive employment, %	⊙	18.4	78	
5.1.2	Firms offering formal training, %		46.2	24	●
5.1.3	GERD performed by business, % GDP		n/a	n/a	
5.1.4	GERD financed by business, %		n/a	n/a	
5.1.5	Females employed w/advanced degrees, %	⊙	12.9	59	
5.2	**Innovation linkages**		**25.3**	**52**	
5.2.1	University-industry R&D collaboration†		61.8	33	◆
5.2.2	State of cluster development†		34.0	85	
5.2.3	GERD financed by abroad, % GDP		n/a	n/a	
5.2.4	Joint venture/strategic alliance deals/bn PPP$ GDP		0.0	82	
5.2.5	Patent families/bn PPP$ GDP		0.0	64	
5.3	**Knowledge absorption**		**29.2**	**81**	
5.3.1	Intellectual property payments, % total trade		0.7	59	
5.3.2	High-tech imports, % total trade	⊙	4.2	124	○ ◇
5.3.3	ICT services imports, % total trade		1.1	79	
5.3.4	FDI net inflows, % GDP		7.2	12	● ◆
5.3.5	Research talent, % in businesses		n/a	n/a	
	Knowledge and technology outputs		**14.8**	**91**	
6.1	**Knowledge creation**		**5.6**	**109**	
6.1.1	Patents by origin/bn PPP$ GDP		0.6	76	
6.1.2	PCT patents by origin/bn PPP$ GDP		0.1	65	
6.1.3	Utility models by origin/bn PPP$ GDP		0.0	63	
6.1.4	Scientific and technical articles/bn PPP$ GDP		6.4	99	
6.1.5	Citable documents H-index		2.9	121	○
6.2	**Knowledge impact**		**20.3**	**103**	
6.2.1	Labor productivity growth, %		2.2	29	●
6.2.2	Unicorn valuation, % GDP		0.0	48	○ ◇
6.2.3	Software spending, % GDP		0.1	86	
6.2.4	High-tech manufacturing, %		5.3	101	○ ◇
6.3	**Knowledge diffusion**		**18.6**	**80**	
6.3.1	Intellectual property receipts, % total trade		0.3	34	◆
6.3.2	Production and export complexity		48.0	73	
6.3.3	High-tech exports, % total trade	⊙	0.1	123	○ ◇
6.3.4	ICT services exports, % total trade		1.7	64	
6.3.5	ISO 9001 quality/bn PPP$ GDP		8.1	34	
	Creative outputs		**16.5**	**87**	
7.1	**Intangible assets**		**16.2**	**95**	
7.1.1	Intangible asset intensity, top 15, %		n/a	n/a	
7.1.2	Trademarks by origin/bn PPP$ GDP		39.7	58	
7.1.3	Global brand value, top 5,000, % GDP		0.0	74	○ ◇
7.1.4	Industrial designs by origin/bn PPP$ GDP		1.2	61	
7.2	**Creative goods and services**		**15.4**	**58**	
7.2.1	Cultural and creative services exports, % total trade		1.4	21	● ◆
7.2.2	National feature films/mn pop. 15–69		2.9	40	
7.2.3	Entertainment and media market/th pop. 15–69		n/a	n/a	
7.2.4	Creative goods exports, % total trade	⊙	0.0	114	
7.3	**Online creativity**		**18.3**	**76**	
7.3.1	Generic top-level domains (TLDs)/th pop. 15–69		7.7	48	
7.3.2	Country-code TLDs/th pop. 15–69		3.8	62	
7.3.3	GitHub commits/mn pop. 15–69		6.0	67	
7.3.4	Mobile app creation/bn PPP$ GDP		55.6	94	

NOTES: ● indicates a strength; ○ a weakness; ◆ an income group strength; ◇ an income group weakness; * an index; † a survey question. ⊙ is used when the available economy data are older than the base year; see appendices for details, including the year of the data, at wipo.int/gii-ranking. Square brackets [ ] indicate that the data minimum coverage (DMC) requirements were not met at the sub-pillar or pillar level.

GII 2023 rank

Algeria **119**

Output rank	Input rank	Income	Region	Population (mn)	GDP, PPP$ (bn)	GDP per capita, PPP$
116	118	Lower middle	NAWA	44.9	600.7	13,324

			Score/Value	Rank	
	Institutions		**38.7**	**97**	
1.1	**Institutional environment**		**27.2**	**106**	
1.1.1	Operational stability for businesses*		34.7	111	
1.1.2	Government effectiveness*		19.6	106	
1.2	**Regulatory environment**		**47.6**	**106**	
1.2.1	Regulatory quality*		11.7	130	○◇
1.2.2	Rule of law*		15.8	110	
1.2.3	Cost of redundancy dismissal		17.3	71	●
1.3	**Business environment**		**41.3**	**[79]**	
1.3.1	Policies for doing business†	◷	41.3	82	
1.3.2	Entrepreneurship policies and culture†		n/a	n/a	

			Score/Value	Rank	
	Human capital and research		**16.0**	**113**	
2.1	**Education**		**11.3**	**[132]**	
2.1.1	Expenditure on education, % GDP		n/a	n/a	
2.1.2	Government funding/pupil, secondary, % GDP/cap		n/a	n/a	
2.1.3	School life expectancy, years		n/a	n/a	
2.1.4	PISA scales in reading, maths and science	◷	361.7	77	○
2.1.5	Pupil-teacher ratio, secondary		n/a	n/a	
2.2	**Tertiary education**		**32.1**	**60**	●◆
2.2.1	Tertiary enrolment, % gross		53.7	64	●◆
2.2.2	Graduates in science and engineering, %		30.1	19	●
2.2.3	Tertiary inbound mobility, %		0.6	98	
2.3	**Research and development (R&D)**		**4.5**	**78**	
2.3.1	Researchers, FTE/mn pop.	◷	819.3	56	●
2.3.2	Gross expenditure on R&D, % GDP	◷	0.5	58	●
2.3.3	Global corporate R&D investors, top 3, mn USD		0.0	40	○◇
2.3.4	QS university ranking, top 3*		0.0	71	○◇

			Score/Value	Rank	
	Infrastructure		**27.6**	**102**	
3.1	**Information and communication technologies (ICTs)**		**47.7**	**102**	
3.1.1	ICT access*		72.2	86	
3.1.2	ICT use*		66.7	78	
3.1.3	Government's online service*		30.8	121	
3.1.4	E-participation*		20.9	122	
3.2	**General infrastructure**		**22.7**	**79**	
3.2.1	Electricity output, GWh/mn pop.	◷	1,805.2	87	
3.2.2	Logistics performance*		18.2	89	
3.2.3	Gross capital formation, % GDP		36.8	11	●
3.3	**Ecological sustainability**		**12.4**	**117**	
3.3.1	GDP/unit of energy use		8.1	87	
3.3.2	Environmental performance*		18.1	113	
3.3.3	ISO 14001 environment/bn PPP$ GDP		0.3	103	

			Score/Value	Rank	
	Market sophistication		**13.9**	**125**	◇
4.1	**Credit**		**9.6**	**[115]**	
4.1.1	Finance for startups and scaleups†		n/a	n/a	
4.1.2	Domestic credit to private sector, % GDP		29.7	97	
4.1.3	Loans from microfinance institutions, % GDP		n/a	n/a	
4.2	**Investment**		**1.8**	**104**	
4.2.1	Market capitalization, % GDP	◷	0.2	78	○◇
4.2.2	Venture capital (VC) investors, deals/bn PPP$ GDP		n/a	n/a	
4.2.3	VC recipients, deals/bn PPP$ GDP		0.0	101	○◇
4.2.4	VC received, value, % GDP		0.0	63	
4.3	**Trade, diversification and market scale**		**30.2**	**115**	
4.3.1	Applied tariff rate, weighted avg., %		10.2	118	
4.3.2	Domestic industry diversification	◷	43.5	106	◇
4.3.3	Domestic market scale, bn PPP$		600.7	40	●

			Score/Value	Rank	
	Business sophistication		**16.6**	**120**	◇
5.1	**Knowledge workers**		**14.9**	**113**	
5.1.1	Knowledge-intensive employment, %	◷	17.9	81	
5.1.2	Firms offering formal training, %		n/a	n/a	
5.1.3	GERD performed by business, % GDP	◷	0.0	76	
5.1.4	GERD financed by business, %	◷	6.7	80	
5.1.5	Females employed w/advanced degrees, %	◷	8.1	83	
5.2	**Innovation linkages**		**14.3**	**101**	
5.2.1	University-industry R&D collaboration†	◷	28.9	98	
5.2.2	State of cluster development†	◷	41.5	64	●
5.2.3	GERD financed by abroad, % GDP	◷	0.0	95	
5.2.4	Joint venture/strategic alliance deals/bn PPP$ GDP		0.0	121	
5.2.5	Patent families/bn PPP$ GDP		0.0	93	
5.3	**Knowledge absorption**		**20.4**	**128**	◇
5.3.1	Intellectual property payments, % total trade		0.3	79	
5.3.2	High-tech imports, % total trade	◷	8.9	53	●
5.3.3	ICT services imports, % total trade		0.4	115	
5.3.4	FDI net inflows, % GDP		0.7	105	
5.3.5	Research talent, % in businesses	◷	0.5	81	◇

			Score/Value	Rank	
	Knowledge and technology outputs		**9.5**	**128**	◇
6.1	**Knowledge creation**		**8.8**	**86**	
6.1.1	Patents by origin/bn PPP$ GDP		0.5	80	
6.1.2	PCT patents by origin/bn PPP$ GDP		0.0	81	
6.1.3	Utility models by origin/bn PPP$ GDP		n/a	n/a	
6.1.4	Scientific and technical articles/bn PPP$ GDP		7.9	86	
6.1.5	Citable documents H-index		10.7	73	
6.2	**Knowledge impact**		**11.9**	**126**	◇
6.2.1	Labor productivity growth, %		-0.0	97	
6.2.2	Unicorn valuation, % GDP		0.0	48	○◇
6.2.3	Software spending, % GDP		0.0	128	○◇
6.2.4	High-tech manufacturing, %	◷	4.1	104	◇
6.3	**Knowledge diffusion**		**7.6**	**120**	
6.3.1	Intellectual property receipts, % total trade		0.0	101	
6.3.2	Production and export complexity		34.1	104	
6.3.3	High-tech exports, % total trade	◷	0.0	131	○
6.3.4	ICT services exports, % total trade		0.2	121	
6.3.5	ISO 9001 quality/bn PPP$ GDP		1.0	106	

			Score/Value	Rank	
	Creative outputs		**9.9**	**107**	
7.1	**Intangible assets**		**13.5**	**102**	
7.1.1	Intangible asset intensity, top 15, %		n/a	n/a	
7.1.2	Trademarks by origin/bn PPP$ GDP		20.8	90	
7.1.3	Global brand value, top 5,000, % GDP		0.0	74	○◇
7.1.4	Industrial designs by origin/bn PPP$ GDP		1.6	48	●
7.2	**Creative goods and services**		**0.2**	**128**	
7.2.1	Cultural and creative services exports, % total trade		0.0	102	
7.2.2	National feature films/mn pop. 15–69		0.1	79	○
7.2.3	Entertainment and media market/th pop. 15–69		0.2	58	
7.2.4	Creative goods exports, % total trade	◷	0.0	124	
7.3	**Online creativity**		**12.5**	**106**	
7.3.1	Generic top-level domains (TLDs)/th pop. 15–69		0.5	110	
7.3.2	Country-code TLDs/th pop. 15–69		0.1	116	
7.3.3	GitHub commits/mn pop. 15–69		0.9	115	
7.3.4	Mobile app creation/bn PPP$ GDP		48.5	102	

NOTES: ● indicates a strength; ○ a weakness; ◆ an income group strength; ◇ an income group weakness; * an index; † a survey question. ◷ is used when the available economy data are older than the base year; see appendices for details, including the year of the data, at wipo.int/gii-ranking. Square brackets [ ] indicate that the data minimum coverage (DMC) requirements were not met at the sub-pillar or pillar level.

Angola

GII 2023 rank

132

Output rank	Input rank	Income	Region	Population (mn)	GDP, PPP$ (bn)	GDP per capita, PPP$
132	132	Lower middle	SSA	35.6	245.4	7,455

			Score/ Value	Rank	
	Institutions		**31.8**	**118**	
1.1	**Institutional environment**		**23.2**	**118**	
1.1.1	Operational stability for businesses*		38.9	96	●
1.1.2	Government effectiveness*		7.5	128	◇
1.2	**Regulatory environment**		**49.4**	**101**	●
1.2.1	Regulatory quality*		24.9	111	
1.2.2	Rule of law*		11.8	119	
1.2.3	Cost of redundancy dismissal		17.9	77	●
1.3	**Business environment**		**22.9**	**114**	
1.3.1	Policies for doing business†		31.2	104	●
1.3.2	Entrepreneurship policies and culture†		14.6	73	◇
	Human capital and research		**11.0**	**127**	◇
2.1	**Education**		**26.2**	**[124]**	
2.1.1	Expenditure on education, % GDP		2.1	116	◇
2.1.2	Government funding/pupil, secondary, % GDP/cap		n/a	n/a	
2.1.3	School life expectancy, years		n/a	n/a	
2.1.4	PISA scales in reading, maths and science		n/a	n/a	
2.1.5	Pupil–teacher ratio, secondary	⊙	26.8	114	◇
2.2	**Tertiary education**		**6.6**	**118**	◇
2.2.1	Tertiary enrolment, % gross	⊙	10.6	112	
2.2.2	Graduates in science and engineering, %	⊙	12.0	105	◇
2.2.3	Tertiary inbound mobility, %		n/a	n/a	
2.3	**Research and development (R&D)**		**0.1**	**116**	
2.3.1	Researchers, FTE/mn pop.	⊙	18.8	105	
2.3.2	Gross expenditure on R&D, % GDP	⊙	0.0	111	◇
2.3.3	Global corporate R&D investors, top 3, mn USD		0.0	40	○◇
2.3.4	QS university ranking, top 3*		0.0	71	○◇
	Infrastructure		**16.1**	**129**	◇
3.1	**Information and communication technologies (ICTs)**		**23.4**	**126**	◇
3.1.1	ICT access*		14.3	128	◇
3.1.2	ICT use*		22.7	124	◇
3.1.3	Government's online service*		41.6	106	●
3.1.4	E-participation*		15.1	128	◇
3.2	**General infrastructure**		**6.6**	**130**	◇
3.2.1	Electricity output, GWh/mn pop.	⊙	498.4	111	
3.2.2	Logistics performance*		0.0	111	○◇
3.2.3	Gross capital formation, % GDP		22.6	78	●
3.3	**Ecological sustainability**		**18.2**	**89**	●
3.3.1	GDP/unit of energy use		14.0	32	●
3.3.2	Environmental performance*		19.7	109	
3.3.3	ISO 14001 environment/bn PPP$ GDP		0.1	128	
	Market sophistication		**16.6**	**119**	
4.1	**Credit**		**7.9**	**119**	
4.1.1	Finance for startups and scaleups†		20.8	79	◇
4.1.2	Domestic credit to private sector, % GDP		12.9	125	◇
4.1.3	Loans from microfinance institutions, % GDP	⊙	0.0	56	
4.2	**Investment**		**n/a**	**[n/a]**	
4.2.1	Market capitalization, % GDP		n/a	n/a	
4.2.2	Venture capital (VC) investors, deals/bn PPP$ GDP		n/a	n/a	
4.2.3	VC recipients, deals/bn PPP$ GDP		n/a	n/a	
4.2.4	VC received, value, % GDP		n/a	n/a	
4.3	**Trade, diversification and market scale**		**25.3**	**120**	◇
4.3.1	Applied tariff rate, weighted avg., %		9.2	113	
4.3.2	Domestic industry diversification		30.3	110	◇
4.3.3	Domestic market scale, bn PPP$		245.4	64	●

			Score/ Value	Rank	
	Business sophistication		**8.5**	**132**	○◇
5.1	**Knowledge workers**		**5.7**	**[127]**	
5.1.1	Knowledge-intensive employment, %	⊙	7.5	113	
5.1.2	Firms offering formal training, %		n/a	n/a	
5.1.3	GERD performed by business, % GDP		n/a	n/a	
5.1.4	GERD financed by business, %		n/a	n/a	
5.1.5	Females employed w/advanced degrees, %	⊙	1.3	113	
5.2	**Innovation linkages**		**0.7**	**132**	○◇
5.2.1	University–industry R&D collaboration†		0.0	129	○◇
5.2.2	State of cluster development†		1.6	128	○◇
5.2.3	GERD financed by abroad, % GDP		n/a	n/a	
5.2.4	Joint venture/strategic alliance deals/bn PPP$ GDP		0.0	119	
5.2.5	Patent families/bn PPP$ GDP		0.0	95	○◇
5.3	**Knowledge absorption**		**19.0**	**131**	○◇
5.3.1	Intellectual property payments, % total trade		0.5	66	●
5.3.2	High-tech imports, % total trade		3.8	125	
5.3.3	ICT services imports, % total trade		0.3	123	
5.3.4	FDI net inflows, % GDP		−5.3	129	◇
5.3.5	Research talent, % in businesses		n/a	n/a	
	Knowledge and technology outputs		**1.6**	**132**	○◇
6.1	**Knowledge creation**		**0.4**	**132**	○◇
6.1.1	Patents by origin/bn PPP$ GDP	⊙	0.0	130	
6.1.2	PCT patents by origin/bn PPP$ GDP		0.0	101	○◇
6.1.3	Utility models by origin/bn PPP$ GDP	⊙	0.0	65	●
6.1.4	Scientific and technical articles/bn PPP$ GDP		0.6	131	○◇
6.1.5	Citable documents H-index		1.0	129	◇
6.2	**Knowledge impact**		**3.3**	**131**	○◇
6.2.1	Labor productivity growth, %		−3.9	130	○◇
6.2.2	Unicorn valuation, % GDP		0.0	48	○◇
6.2.3	Software spending, % GDP		n/a	n/a	
6.2.4	High-tech manufacturing, %		3.0	108	◇
6.3	**Knowledge diffusion**		**1.1**	**131**	○◇
6.3.1	Intellectual property receipts, % total trade		0.0	105	
6.3.2	Production and export complexity		0.0	120	○◇
6.3.3	High-tech exports, % total trade		0.2	110	
6.3.4	ICT services exports, % total trade		0.1	126	
6.3.5	ISO 9001 quality/bn PPP$ GDP		0.5	121	
	Creative outputs		**6.1**	**[121]**	
7.1	**Intangible assets**		**7.1**	**[112]**	
7.1.1	Intangible asset intensity, top 15, %		n/a	n/a	
7.1.2	Trademarks by origin/bn PPP$ GDP	⊙	12.0	106	●
7.1.3	Global brand value, top 5,000, % GDP		n/a	n/a	
7.1.4	Industrial designs by origin/bn PPP$ GDP		n/a	n/a	
7.2	**Creative goods and services**		**0.1**	**[131]**	
7.2.1	Cultural and creative services exports, % total trade		n/a	n/a	
7.2.2	National feature films/mn pop. 15–69		n/a	n/a	
7.2.3	Entertainment and media market/th pop. 15–69		n/a	n/a	
7.2.4	Creative goods exports, % total trade		0.0	127	
7.3	**Online creativity**		**9.9**	**115**	
7.3.1	Generic top-level domains (TLDs)/th pop. 15–69		0.0	130	
7.3.2	Country-code TLDs/th pop. 15–69		0.1	117	
7.3.3	GitHub commits/mn pop. 15–69		0.2	126	
7.3.4	Mobile app creation/bn PPP$ GDP		39.3	113	◇

NOTES: ● indicates a strength; ○ a weakness; ◆ an income group strength; ◇ an income group weakness; * an index; † a survey question. ⊙ is used when the available economy data are older than the base year; see appendices for details, including the year of the data, at wipo.int/gii-ranking. Square brackets [ ] indicate that the data minimum coverage (DMC) requirements were not met at the sub-pillar or pillar level.

Argentina

GII 2023 rank

73

Output rank	Input rank	Income	Region	Population (mn)	GDP, PPP$ (bn)	GDP per capita, PPP$
59	84	Upper middle	LCN	45.5	1,207.2	26,074

			Score/ Value	Rank	
	Institutions		**30.9**	**123**	○◇
1.1	**Institutional environment**		**36.0**	**89**	
1.1.1	Operational stability for businesses*		45.1	81	
1.1.2	Government effectiveness*		26.9	92	
1.2	**Regulatory environment**		**40.9**	**118**	○◇
1.2.1	Regulatory quality*		26.1	106	◇
1.2.2	Rule of law*		26.2	91	
1.2.3	Cost of redundancy dismissal		30.3	119	○◇
1.3	**Business environment**		**15.8**	**126**	○◇
1.3.1	Policies for doing business†		0.0	129	○◇
1.3.2	Entrepreneurship policies and culture†		31.7	56	
	Human capital and research		**30.0**	**70**	
2.1	**Education**		**43.7**	**84**	
2.1.1	Expenditure on education, % GDP	⊙	5.1	40	
2.1.2	Government funding/pupil, secondary, % GDP/cap		17.6	63	
2.1.3	School life expectancy, years		18.1	13	●◆
2.1.4	PISA scales in reading, maths and science		395.0	69	○
2.1.5	Pupil–teacher ratio, secondary		n/a	n/a	
2.2	**Tertiary education**		**29.6**	**69**	
2.2.1	Tertiary enrolment, % gross		99.2	5	●◆
2.2.2	Graduates in science and engineering, %		14.1	101	○◇
2.2.3	Tertiary inbound mobility, %		3.5	60	
2.3	**Research and development (R&D)**		**16.5**	**48**	
2.3.1	Researchers, FTE/mn pop.	⊙	1,232.0	50	
2.3.2	Gross expenditure on R&D, % GDP	⊙	0.5	59	
2.3.3	Global corporate R&D investors, top 3, mn USD		0.0	40	○◇
2.3.4	QS university ranking, top 3*		44.3	29	●◆
	Infrastructure		**39.9**	**66**	
3.1	**Information and communication technologies (ICTs)**		**74.8**	**50**	
3.1.1	ICT access*		86.1	45	
3.1.2	ICT use*		70.4	70	
3.1.3	Government's online service*		78.9	38	
3.1.4	E-participation*		64.0	51	
3.2	**General infrastructure**		**21.1**	**87**	
3.2.1	Electricity output, GWh/mn pop.		3,290.0	62	
3.2.2	Logistics performance*		31.8	71	
3.2.3	Gross capital formation, % GDP		20.9	89	
3.3	**Ecological sustainability**		**23.6**	**67**	
3.3.1	GDP/unit of energy use		10.4	61	
3.3.2	Environmental performance*		37.6	68	
3.3.3	ISO 14001 environment/bn PPP$ GDP		1.2	59	
	Market sophistication		**25.2**	**92**	◇
4.1	**Credit**		**14.7**	**101**	
4.1.1	Finance for startups and scaleups†		25.3	75	○
4.1.2	Domestic credit to private sector, % GDP	⊙	16.0	116	○◇
4.1.3	Loans from microfinance institutions, % GDP		n/a	n/a	
4.2	**Investment**		**4.2**	**85**	
4.2.1	Market capitalization, % GDP	⊙	11.5	69	○
4.2.2	Venture capital (VC) investors, deals/bn PPP$ GDP		0.0	83	○
4.2.3	VC recipients, deals/bn PPP$ GDP		0.0	83	
4.2.4	VC received, value, % GDP		0.0	59	
4.3	**Trade, diversification and market scale**		**56.8**	**74**	
4.3.1	Applied tariff rate, weighted avg., %		6.9	101	◇
4.3.2	Domestic industry diversification		88.9	53	
4.3.3	Domestic market scale, bn PPP$		1,207.2	28	●

			Score/ Value	Rank	
	Business sophistication		**30.3**	**54**	
5.1	**Knowledge workers**		**34.3**	**61**	
5.1.1	Knowledge-intensive employment, %	⊙	25.3	54	
5.1.2	Firms offering formal training, %	⊙	40.2	33	
5.1.3	GERD performed by business, % GDP	⊙	0.2	54	
5.1.4	GERD financed by business, %		23.4	63	
5.1.5	Females employed w/advanced degrees, %	⊙	16.3	45	
5.2	**Innovation linkages**		**15.4**	**95**	
5.2.1	University–industry R&D collaboration†		33.5	89	
5.2.2	State of cluster development†		26.8	102	
5.2.3	GERD financed by abroad, % GDP		0.1	42	
5.2.4	Joint venture/strategic alliance deals/bn PPP$ GDP		0.0	101	
5.2.5	Patent families/bn PPP$ GDP		0.1	63	
5.3	**Knowledge absorption**		**41.1**	**40**	
5.3.1	Intellectual property payments, % total trade		2.1	12	●◆
5.3.2	High-tech imports, % total trade		11.7	22	●
5.3.3	ICT services imports, % total trade		2.2	30	●◆
5.3.4	FDI net inflows, % GDP		1.4	92	
5.3.5	Research talent, % in businesses	⊙	10.6	60	
	Knowledge and technology outputs		**19.2**	**79**	
6.1	**Knowledge creation**		**13.0**	**70**	
6.1.1	Patents by origin/bn PPP$ GDP		0.4	87	
6.1.2	PCT patents by origin/bn PPP$ GDP		n/a	n/a	
6.1.3	Utility models by origin/bn PPP$ GDP		0.1	50	
6.1.4	Scientific and technical articles/bn PPP$ GDP		7.1	92	
6.1.5	Citable documents H-index		28.0	36	
6.2	**Knowledge impact**		**23.8**	**82**	
6.2.1	Labor productivity growth, %		-1.8	124	○◇
6.2.2	Unicorn valuation, % GDP		0.4	41	
6.2.3	Software spending, % GDP		0.3	47	
6.2.4	High-tech manufacturing, %		28.1	45	
6.3	**Knowledge diffusion**		**20.9**	**70**	
6.3.1	Intellectual property receipts, % total trade		0.4	31	◆
6.3.2	Production and export complexity		47.8	74	
6.3.3	High-tech exports, % total trade		0.6	86	
6.3.4	ICT services exports, % total trade		2.7	47	
6.3.5	ISO 9001 quality/bn PPP$ GDP		5.5	51	
	Creative outputs		**30.3**	**51**	
7.1	**Intangible assets**		**39.7**	**42**	
7.1.1	Intangible asset intensity, top 15, %		69.0	21	
7.1.2	Trademarks by origin/bn PPP$ GDP		64.7	31	●
7.1.3	Global brand value, top 5,000, % GDP		1.1	54	
7.1.4	Industrial designs by origin/bn PPP$ GDP		1.4	57	
7.2	**Creative goods and services**		**18.2**	**52**	
7.2.1	Cultural and creative services exports, % total trade		1.1	23	●◆
7.2.2	National feature films/mn pop. 15–69		6.9	13	●◆
7.2.3	Entertainment and media market/th pop. 15–69		3.4	47	◇
7.2.4	Creative goods exports, % total trade		0.2	76	
7.3	**Online creativity**		**23.4**	**56**	
7.3.1	Generic top-level domains (TLDs)/th pop. 15–69		3.4	64	
7.3.2	Country-code TLDs/th pop. 15–69		6.4	49	
7.3.3	GitHub commits/mn pop. 15–69		14.8	48	
7.3.4	Mobile app creation/bn PPP$ GDP		68.9	57	

NOTES: ● indicates a strength; ○ a weakness; ◆ an income group strength; ◇ an income group weakness; * an index; † a survey question. ⊙ is used when the available economy data are older than the base year; see appendices for details, including the year of the data, at wipo.int/gii-ranking. Square brackets [ ] indicate that the data minimum coverage (DMC) requirements were not met at the sub-pillar or pillar level.

Armenia

GII 2023 rank

72

Output rank	Input rank	Income	Region	Population (mn)	GDP, PPP$ (bn)	GDP per capita, PPP$
62	83	Upper middle	NAWA	2.8	49.8	16,798

			Score/ Value	Rank	
	Institutions		**49.1**	**69**	
1.1	**Institutional environment**		**35.8**	**90**	
1.1.1	Operational stability for businesses*		41.7	87	
1.1.2	Government effectiveness*		29.9	87	
1.2	**Regulatory environment**		**65.7**	**59**	
1.2.1	Regulatory quality*		45.9	64	
1.2.2	Rule of law*		36.9	69	
1.2.3	Cost of redundancy dismissal		13.0	41	
1.3	**Business environment**		**45.9**	**65**	
1.3.1	Policies for doing business†		40.3	83	
1.3.2	Entrepreneurship policies and culture†	⊙	51.6	34	
	Human capital and research		**22.7**	**92**	
2.1	**Education**		**41.6**	**93**	
2.1.1	Expenditure on education, % GDP		2.8	111	◇
2.1.2	Government funding/pupil, secondary, % GDP/cap		13.2	81	
2.1.3	School life expectancy, years		13.5	78	
2.1.4	PISA scales in reading, maths and science		n/a	n/a	
2.1.5	Pupil–teacher ratio, secondary		11.1	43	●
2.2	**Tertiary education**		**25.3**	**79**	
2.2.1	Tertiary enrolment, % gross		55.4	60	
2.2.2	Graduates in science and engineering, %		17.7	88	
2.2.3	Tertiary inbound mobility, %		5.9	43	
2.3	**Research and development (R&D)**		**1.2**	**99**	
2.3.1	Researchers, FTE/mn pop.		n/a	n/a	
2.3.2	Gross expenditure on R&D, % GDP		0.2	88	
2.3.3	Global corporate R&D investors, top 3, mn USD		0.0	40	○◇
2.3.4	QS university ranking, top 3*		0.0	71	○◇
	Infrastructure		**36.6**	**79**	
3.1	**Information and communication technologies (ICTs)**		**72.8**	**58**	
3.1.1	ICT access*		91.6	18	●◆
3.1.2	ICT use*		73.4	65	
3.1.3	Government's online service*		69.3	63	
3.1.4	E-participation*		57.0	64	
3.2	**General infrastructure**		**13.3**	**114**	◇
3.2.1	Electricity output, GWh/mn pop.		2,584.2	72	
3.2.2	Logistics performance*		18.2	89	○◇
3.2.3	Gross capital formation, % GDP		17.1	115	○
3.3	**Ecological sustainability**		**23.6**	**68**	
3.3.1	GDP/unit of energy use		9.2	79	
3.3.2	Environmental performance*		49.8	45	●
3.3.3	ISO 14001 environment/bn PPP$ GDP		0.1	125	○
	Market sophistication		**27.5**	**89**	
4.1	**Credit**		**29.6**	**67**	
4.1.1	Finance for startups and scaleups†	⊙	32.9	65	
4.1.2	Domestic credit to private sector, % GDP		72.2	50	
4.1.3	Loans from microfinance institutions, % GDP		n/a	n/a	
4.2	**Investment**		**2.5**	**[97]**	
4.2.1	Market capitalization, % GDP		n/a	n/a	
4.2.2	Venture capital (VC) investors, deals/bn PPP$ GDP		0.0	63	
4.2.3	VC recipients, deals/bn PPP$ GDP		n/a	n/a	
4.2.4	VC received, value, % GDP		n/a	n/a	
4.3	**Trade, diversification and market scale**		**50.4**	**85**	
4.3.1	Applied tariff rate, weighted avg., %		3.1	74	
4.3.2	Domestic industry diversification		70.2	93	◇
4.3.3	Domestic market scale, bn PPP$		49.8	107	

			Score/ Value	Rank	
	Business sophistication		**22.7**	**94**	
5.1	**Knowledge workers**		**32.4**	**65**	
5.1.1	Knowledge-intensive employment, %	⊙	18.7	77	
5.1.2	Firms offering formal training, %		27.5	60	
5.1.3	GERD performed by business, % GDP		n/a	n/a	
5.1.4	GERD financed by business, %	⊙	16.7	71	
5.1.5	Females employed w/advanced degrees, %	⊙	16.4	44	●
5.2	**Innovation linkages**		**11.2**	**115**	◇
5.2.1	University–industry R&D collaboration†		28.6	100	
5.2.2	State of cluster development†		21.2	111	◇
5.2.3	GERD financed by abroad, % GDP	⊙	0.0	73	
5.2.4	Joint venture/strategic alliance deals/bn PPP$ GDP	⊙	0.0	107	
5.2.5	Patent families/bn PPP$ GDP		0.1	57	
5.3	**Knowledge absorption**		**24.6**	**107**	◇
5.3.1	Intellectual property payments, % total trade		0.0	118	○◇
5.3.2	High-tech imports, % total trade		7.9	73	
5.3.3	ICT services imports, % total trade		0.8	94	
5.3.4	FDI net inflows, % GDP		1.3	95	
5.3.5	Research talent, % in businesses		n/a	n/a	
	Knowledge and technology outputs		**22.6**	**67**	
6.1	**Knowledge creation**		**18.7**	**59**	
6.1.1	Patents by origin/bn PPP$ GDP		1.0	59	
6.1.2	PCT patents by origin/bn PPP$ GDP		0.1	53	
6.1.3	Utility models by origin/bn PPP$ GDP		1.4	16	●
6.1.4	Scientific and technical articles/bn PPP$ GDP		15.2	49	
6.1.5	Citable documents H-index		10.3	76	
6.2	**Knowledge impact**		**25.5**	**70**	
6.2.1	Labor productivity growth, %		3.2	13	●◆
6.2.2	Unicorn valuation, % GDP		0.0	48	○◇
6.2.3	Software spending, % GDP		0.2	58	
6.2.4	High-tech manufacturing, %		5.6	100	○◇
6.3	**Knowledge diffusion**		**23.6**	**61**	
6.3.1	Intellectual property receipts, % total trade		0.0	114	○◇
6.3.2	Production and export complexity		47.4	76	
6.3.3	High-tech exports, % total trade		0.7	79	
6.3.4	ICT services exports, % total trade		7.0	9	●◆
6.3.5	ISO 9001 quality/bn PPP$ GDP		1.1	105	
	Creative outputs		**26.1**	**61**	
7.1	**Intangible assets**		**31.3**	**68**	
7.1.1	Intangible asset intensity, top 15, %		n/a	n/a	
7.1.2	Trademarks by origin/bn PPP$ GDP		97.5	16	●◆
7.1.3	Global brand value, top 5,000, % GDP		0.0	74	○◇
7.1.4	Industrial designs by origin/bn PPP$ GDP		1.8	45	
7.2	**Creative goods and services**		**14.0**	**[60]**	
7.2.1	Cultural and creative services exports, % total trade		0.5	52	
7.2.2	National feature films/mn pop. 15–69		n/a	n/a	
7.2.3	Entertainment and media market/th pop. 15–69		n/a	n/a	
7.2.4	Creative goods exports, % total trade		1.5	35	●
7.3	**Online creativity**		**28.0**	**42**	●
7.3.1	Generic top-level domains (TLDs)/th pop. 15–69		3.8	61	
7.3.2	Country-code TLDs/th pop. 15–69		6.1	52	
7.3.3	GitHub commits/mn pop. 15–69		29.4	35	●◆
7.3.4	Mobile app creation/bn PPP$ GDP		72.6	43	●

NOTES: ● indicates a strength; ○ a weakness; ◆ an income group strength; ◇ an income group weakness; * an index; † a survey question. ⊙ is used when the available economy data are older than the base year; see appendices for details, including the year of the data, at wipo.int/gii-ranking. Square brackets [ ] indicate that the data minimum coverage (DMC) requirements were not met at the sub-pillar or pillar level.

GII 2023 rank

Australia

24

Output rank	Input rank	Income	Region	Population (mn)	GDP, PPP$ (bn)	GDP per capita, PPP$
30	16	High	SEAO	26.2	1,615.3	62,192

		Score/Value	Rank
Institutions		**75.6**	**17**
1.1	**Institutional environment**	**77.8**	**14**
1.1.1	Operational stability for businesses*	77.1	14
1.1.2	Government effectiveness*	78.5	13
1.2	**Regulatory environment**	**90.7**	**10**
1.2.1	Regulatory quality*	89.8	4 ●
1.2.2	Rule of law*	88.8	12
1.2.3	Cost of redundancy dismissal	12.0	39
1.3	**Business environment**	**58.4**	**37**
1.3.1	Policies for doing business†	69.3	27
1.3.2	Entrepreneurship policies and culture† ⏲	47.6	37
Human capital and research		**59.5**	**7 ●**
2.1	**Education**	**59.2**	**40**
2.1.1	Expenditure on education, % GDP ⏲	5.1	35
2.1.2	Government funding/pupil, secondary, % GDP/cap	17.0	67 ○◇
2.1.3	School life expectancy, years	21.1	1 ●◆
2.1.4	PISA scales in reading, maths and science	499.0	20
2.1.5	Pupil–teacher ratio, secondary	n/a	n/a
2.2	**Tertiary education**	**59.2**	**4 ●◆**
2.2.1	Tertiary enrolment, % gross	114.2	3 ●◆
2.2.2	Graduates in science and engineering, %	20.6	68 ○
2.2.3	Tertiary inbound mobility, %	26.0	5 ●◆
2.3	**Research and development (R&D)**	**60.0**	**16**
2.3.1	Researchers, FTE/mn pop.	n/a	n/a
2.3.2	Gross expenditure on R&D, % GDP ⏲	1.8	21
2.3.3	Global corporate R&D investors, top 3, mn USD	65.5	18
2.3.4	QS university ranking, top 3*	82.2	6 ●
Infrastructure		**58.8**	**19**
3.1	**Information and communication technologies (ICTs)**	**91.8**	**9**
3.1.1	ICT access*	82.3	66 ◇
3.1.2	ICT use*	92.7	14
3.1.3	Government's online service*	93.1	7 ●
3.1.4	E-participation*	98.8	2 ●◆
3.2	**General infrastructure**	**47.9**	**23**
3.2.1	Electricity output, GWh/mn pop.	10,300.7	14
3.2.2	Logistics performance*	72.7	18
3.2.3	Gross capital formation, % GDP	23.2	72
3.3	**Ecological sustainability**	**36.7**	**38**
3.3.1	GDP/unit of energy use	9.7	74 ○
3.3.2	Environmental performance*	69.8	17
3.3.3	ISO 14001 environment/bn PPP$ GDP	2.4	37
Market sophistication		**53.7**	**17**
4.1	**Credit**	**57.3**	**21**
4.1.1	Finance for startups and scaleups† ⏲	60.6	32
4.1.2	Domestic credit to private sector, % GDP	142.4	12
4.1.3	Loans from microfinance institutions, % GDP	n/a	n/a
4.2	**Investment**	**29.5**	**24**
4.2.1	Market capitalization, % GDP	108.3	13
4.2.2	Venture capital (VC) investors, deals/bn PPP$ GDP	0.3	21
4.2.3	VC recipients, deals/bn PPP$ GDP	0.1	18
4.2.4	VC received, value, % GDP	0.0	32
4.3	**Trade, diversification and market scale**	**74.3**	**15**
4.3.1	Applied tariff rate, weighted avg., %	0.7	7 ●
4.3.2	Domestic industry diversification	92.8	41
4.3.3	Domestic market scale, bn PPP$	1,615.3	19

		Score/Value	Rank
Business sophistication		**50.7**	**24 ◇**
5.1	**Knowledge workers**	**63.6**	**[15]**
5.1.1	Knowledge-intensive employment, % ⏲	51.5	8
5.1.2	Firms offering formal training, %	n/a	n/a
5.1.3	GERD performed by business, % GDP ⏲	0.9	24
5.1.4	GERD financed by business, %	n/a	n/a
5.1.5	Females employed w/advanced degrees, % ⏲	28.7	6 ●
5.2	**Innovation linkages**	**52.3**	**18**
5.2.1	University–industry R&D collaboration†	70.2	24
5.2.2	State of cluster development†	64.6	30
5.2.3	GERD financed by abroad, % GDP	n/a	n/a
5.2.4	Joint venture/strategic alliance deals/bn PPP$ GDP	0.2	11
5.2.5	Patent families/bn PPP$ GDP	1.0	27 ◇
5.3	**Knowledge absorption**	**36.2**	**54 ◇**
5.3.1	Intellectual property payments, % total trade	1.2	30
5.3.2	High-tech imports, % total trade	11.0	25
5.3.3	ICT services imports, % total trade	1.1	82 ○◇
5.3.4	FDI net inflows, % GDP	1.8	79 ○
5.3.5	Research talent, % in businesses	n/a	n/a
Knowledge and technology outputs		**34.9**	**30 ◇**
6.1	**Knowledge creation**	**45.8**	**17**
6.1.1	Patents by origin/bn PPP$ GDP	2.0	35 ◇
6.1.2	PCT patents by origin/bn PPP$ GDP	1.1	27 ◇
6.1.3	Utility models by origin/bn PPP$ GDP	1.2	21
6.1.4	Scientific and technical articles/bn PPP$ GDP	39.3	9
6.1.5	Citable documents H-index	69.6	7 ●
6.2	**Knowledge impact**	**38.4**	**34**
6.2.1	Labor productivity growth, %	0.5	81 ○
6.2.2	Unicorn valuation, % GDP	3.1	14
6.2.3	Software spending, % GDP	0.2	67 ◇
6.2.4	High-tech manufacturing, %	25.1	50 ◇
6.3	**Knowledge diffusion**	**20.5**	**72 ◇**
6.3.1	Intellectual property receipts, % total trade	0.3	32 ◇
6.3.2	Production and export complexity	41.5	90 ○◇
6.3.3	High-tech exports, % total trade	1.8	62 ◇
6.3.4	ICT services exports, % total trade	1.3	76 ○
6.3.5	ISO 9001 quality/bn PPP$ GDP	5.8	49
Creative outputs		**44.6**	**24**
7.1	**Intangible assets**	**46.8**	**33**
7.1.1	Intangible asset intensity, top 15, %	66.9	24
7.1.2	Trademarks by origin/bn PPP$ GDP	66.9	29
7.1.3	Global brand value, top 5,000, % GDP	7.6	27
7.1.4	Industrial designs by origin/bn PPP$ GDP	1.8	46
7.2	**Creative goods and services**	**20.9**	**47 ◇**
7.2.1	Cultural and creative services exports, % total trade	0.3	65 ○
7.2.2	National feature films/mn pop. 15–69	1.2	58 ○◇
7.2.3	Entertainment and media market/th pop. 15–69	62.7	8
7.2.4	Creative goods exports, % total trade	0.6	58
7.3	**Online creativity**	**64.0**	**12**
7.3.1	Generic top-level domains (TLDs)/th pop. 15–69	67.7	11
7.3.2	Country-code TLDs/th pop. 15–69	67.2	10
7.3.3	GitHub commits/mn pop. 15–69	47.5	22
7.3.4	Mobile app creation/bn PPP$ GDP	73.5	37

NOTES: ● indicates a strength; ○ a weakness; ◆ an income group strength; ◇ an income group weakness; * an index; † a survey question. ⏲ is used when the available economy data are older than the base year; see appendices for details, including the year of the data, at wipo.int/gii-ranking. Square brackets [ ] indicate that the data minimum coverage (DMC) requirements were not met at the sub-pillar or pillar level.

Austria

GII 2023 rank

18

Output rank	Input rank	Income	Region	Population (mn)	GDP, PPP$ (bn)	GDP per capita, PPP$
15	18	High	EUR	8.9	599.5	66,680

		Score/Value	Rank	
	Institutions	**78.5**	**13**	
1.1	**Institutional environment**	**76.2**	**15**	
1.1.1	Operational stability for businesses*	72.2	22	
1.1.2	Government effectiveness*	80.1	11	
1.2	**Regulatory environment**	**92.3**	**6**	●
1.2.1	Regulatory quality*	77.1	20	
1.2.2	Rule of law*	92.1	7	●
1.2.3	Cost of redundancy dismissal	8.0	1	●
1.3	**Business environment**	**66.9**	**25**	
1.3.1	Policies for doing business†	82.4	6	●
1.3.2	Entrepreneurship policies and culture†	51.5	35	○
	Human capital and research	**58.0**	**11**	
2.1	**Education**	**62.0**	**24**	
2.1.1	Expenditure on education, % GDP ⊙	5.2	30	
2.1.2	Government funding/pupil, secondary, % GDP/cap	25.4	18	
2.1.3	School life expectancy, years	16.0	37	
2.1.4	PISA scales in reading, maths and science	491.0	27	
2.1.5	Pupil–teacher ratio, secondary	9.4	23	
2.2	**Tertiary education**	**55.6**	**5**	● ◆
2.2.1	Tertiary enrolment, % gross	87.2	15	
2.2.2	Graduates in science and engineering, %	30.6	16	◆
2.2.3	Tertiary inbound mobility, %	18.0	10	
2.3	**Research and development (R&D)**	**56.3**	**17**	
2.3.1	Researchers, FTE/mn pop.	6,163.0	9	
2.3.2	Gross expenditure on R&D, % GDP	3.2	8	●
2.3.3	Global corporate R&D investors, top 3, mn USD	59.2	25	
2.3.4	QS university ranking, top 3*	44.7	27	
	Infrastructure	**60.4**	**12**	
3.1	**Information and communication technologies (ICTs)**	**86.3**	**17**	
3.1.1	ICT access*	88.4	31	
3.1.2	ICT use*	93.1	13	
3.1.3	Government's online service*	87.0	19	
3.1.4	E-participation*	76.7	21	
3.2	**General infrastructure**	**49.8**	**18**	
3.2.1	Electricity output, GWh/mn pop.	7,480.7	23	
3.2.2	Logistics performance*	86.4	7	
3.2.3	Gross capital formation, % GDP	27.1	36	
3.3	**Ecological sustainability**	**45.0**	**26**	
3.3.1	GDP/unit of energy use	13.7	33	
3.3.2	Environmental performance*	80.7	8	●
3.3.3	ISO 14001 environment/bn PPP$ GDP	2.6	34	
	Market sophistication	**44.4**	**39**	◇
4.1	**Credit**	**47.9**	**32**	
4.1.1	Finance for startups and scaleups†	61.3	31	
4.1.2	Domestic credit to private sector, % GDP	92.8	32	
4.1.3	Loans from microfinance institutions, % GDP	n/a	n/a	
4.2	**Investment**	**17.8**	**41**	○ ◇
4.2.1	Market capitalization, % GDP	28.7	48	○ ◇
4.2.2	Venture capital (VC) investors, deals/bn PPP$ GDP	0.3	23	
4.2.3	VC recipients, deals/bn PPP$ GDP	0.1	33	
4.2.4	VC received, value, % GDP	0.0	35	◇
4.3	**Trade, diversification and market scale**	**67.5**	**24**	
4.3.1	Applied tariff rate, weighted avg., %	1.5	20	
4.3.2	Domestic industry diversification	99.4	3	●
4.3.3	Domestic market scale, bn PPP$	599.5	41	

		Score/Value	Rank	
	Business sophistication	**55.7**	**19**	
5.1	**Knowledge workers**	**54.0**	**25**	◇
5.1.1	Knowledge-intensive employment, %	44.3	24	
5.1.2	Firms offering formal training, %	42.6	29	
5.1.3	GERD performed by business, % GDP	2.2	7	●
5.1.4	GERD financed by business, %	50.6	27	
5.1.5	Females employed w/advanced degrees, %	13.4	56	○ ◇
5.2	**Innovation linkages**	**63.6**	**9**	●
5.2.1	University–industry R&D collaboration†	68.3	26	
5.2.2	State of cluster development†	81.1	10	
5.2.3	GERD financed by abroad, % GDP	0.5	5	● ◆
5.2.4	Joint venture/strategic alliance deals/bn PPP$ GDP	0.0	36	◇
5.2.5	Patent families/bn PPP$ GDP	3.5	11	
5.3	**Knowledge absorption**	**49.5**	**22**	
5.3.1	Intellectual property payments, % total trade	0.7	52	○
5.3.2	High-tech imports, % total trade	9.1	50	○
5.3.3	ICT services imports, % total trade	3.4	11	
5.3.4	FDI net inflows, % GDP	−1.0	125	○
5.3.5	Research talent, % in businesses	63.3	9	
	Knowledge and technology outputs	**45.3**	**17**	
6.1	**Knowledge creation**	**45.2**	**18**	
6.1.1	Patents by origin/bn PPP$ GDP	7.8	11	
6.1.2	PCT patents by origin/bn PPP$ GDP	2.4	12	
6.1.3	Utility models by origin/bn PPP$ GDP	0.5	31	○
6.1.4	Scientific and technical articles/bn PPP$ GDP	29.5	23	
6.1.5	Citable documents H-index	44.4	18	
6.2	**Knowledge impact**	**48.9**	**19**	
6.2.1	Labor productivity growth, %	0.2	93	○
6.2.2	Unicorn valuation, % GDP	1.6	27	
6.2.3	Software spending, % GDP	0.7	8	●
6.2.4	High-tech manufacturing, %	45.7	19	
6.3	**Knowledge diffusion**	**41.9**	**30**	
6.3.1	Intellectual property receipts, % total trade	0.6	26	◇
6.3.2	Production and export complexity	88.1	7	●
6.3.3	High-tech exports, % total trade	7.9	23	
6.3.4	ICT services exports, % total trade	3.6	31	
6.3.5	ISO 9001 quality/bn PPP$ GDP	7.1	40	
	Creative outputs	**48.9**	**13**	
7.1	**Intangible assets**	**50.1**	**25**	
7.1.1	Intangible asset intensity, top 15, %	53.0	46	○ ◇
7.1.2	Trademarks by origin/bn PPP$ GDP	58.2	39	
7.1.3	Global brand value, top 5,000, % GDP	7.5	29	
7.1.4	Industrial designs by origin/bn PPP$ GDP	5.9	17	
7.2	**Creative goods and services**	**37.3**	**17**	
7.2.1	Cultural and creative services exports, % total trade	1.1	24	
7.2.2	National feature films/mn pop. 15–69	7.7	11	
7.2.3	Entertainment and media market/th pop. 15–69	63.2	7	
7.2.4	Creative goods exports, % total trade	1.2	42	
7.3	**Online creativity**	**58.0**	**15**	
7.3.1	Generic top-level domains (TLDs)/th pop. 15–69	42.1	18	
7.3.2	Country-code TLDs/th pop. 15–69	68.2	9	●
7.3.3	GitHub commits/mn pop. 15–69	50.7	20	
7.3.4	Mobile app creation/bn PPP$ GDP	71.0	48	○

NOTES: ● indicates a strength; ○ a weakness; ◆ an income group strength; ◇ an income group weakness; * an index; † a survey question. ⊙ is used when the available economy data are older than the base year; see appendices for details, including the year of the data, at wipo.int/gii-ranking. Square brackets [ ] indicate that the data minimum coverage (DMC) requirements were not met at the sub-pillar or pillar level.

GII 2023 rank

Azerbaijan

89

Output rank	Input rank	Income	Region	Population (mn)	GDP, PPP$ (bn)	GDP per capita, PPP$
104	76	Upper middle	NAWA	10.4	178.7	17,448

			Score/ Value	Rank	
	Institutions		**61.2**	**42**	●◆
1.1	**Institutional environment**		**49.6**	**54**	●
1.1.1	Operational stability for businesses*		55.6	56	
1.1.2	Government effectiveness*		43.6	58	●
1.2	**Regulatory environment**		**60.1**	**71**	
1.2.1	Regulatory quality*		40.6	74	
1.2.2	Rule of law*		22.6	98	
1.2.3	Cost of redundancy dismissal		13.7	51	●
1.3	**Business environment**		**73.9**	**[17]**	
1.3.1	Policies for doing business†	⊙	73.9	22	●◆
1.3.2	Entrepreneurship policies and culture†		n/a	n/a	

			Score/ Value	Rank	
	Human capital and research		**25.5**	**87**	
2.1	**Education**		**46.8**	**76**	
2.1.1	Expenditure on education, % GDP		3.5	89	
2.1.2	Government funding/pupil, secondary, % GDP/cap		23.6	28	●
2.1.3	School life expectancy, years		13.5	77	
2.1.4	PISA scales in reading, maths and science		402.2	65	
2.1.5	Pupil–teacher ratio, secondary		8.5	17	●
2.2	**Tertiary education**		**24.3**	**82**	
2.2.1	Tertiary enrolment, % gross		38.2	79	
2.2.2	Graduates in science and engineering, %		24.2	47	●
2.2.3	Tertiary inbound mobility, %		2.3	75	
2.3	**Research and development (R&D)**		**5.4**	**73**	
2.3.1	Researchers, FTE/mn pop.		1,741.1	44	●
2.3.2	Gross expenditure on R&D, % GDP		0.2	87	
2.3.3	Global corporate R&D investors, top 3, mn USD		0.0	40	○◇
2.3.4	QS university ranking, top 3*		0.0	71	○◇

			Score/ Value	Rank	
	Infrastructure		**29.5**	**95**	◇
3.1	**Information and communication technologies (ICTs)**		**60.3**	**81**	
3.1.1	ICT access*		81.0	71	
3.1.2	ICT use*		65.8	81	
3.1.3	Government's online service*		57.1	81	
3.1.4	E-participation*		37.2	91	◇
3.2	**General infrastructure**		**9.2**	**125**	○◇
3.2.1	Electricity output, GWh/mn pop.		2,749.1	67	
3.2.2	Logistics performance*		n/a	n/a	
3.2.3	Gross capital formation, % GDP		14.6	122	○◇
3.3	**Ecological sustainability**		**19.0**	**84**	
3.3.1	GDP/unit of energy use		9.0	81	
3.3.2	Environmental performance*		33.4	77	
3.3.3	ISO 14001 environment/bn PPP$ GDP		0.5	83	

			Score/ Value	Rank	
	Market sophistication		**28.8**	**[85]**	
4.1	**Credit**		**8.1**	**[117]**	
4.1.1	Finance for startups and scaleups†		n/a	n/a	
4.1.2	Domestic credit to private sector, % GDP		26.0	106	◇
4.1.3	Loans from microfinance institutions, % GDP		n/a	n/a	
4.2	**Investment**		**n/a**	**[n/a]**	
4.2.1	Market capitalization, % GDP		n/a	n/a	
4.2.2	Venture capital (VC) investors, deals/bn PPP$ GDP		n/a	n/a	
4.2.3	VC recipients, deals/bn PPP$ GDP		n/a	n/a	
4.2.4	VC received, value, % GDP		n/a	n/a	
4.3	**Trade, diversification and market scale**		**49.5**	**88**	
4.3.1	Applied tariff rate, weighted avg., %		5.9	96	◇
4.3.2	Domestic industry diversification		83.1	68	
4.3.3	Domestic market scale, bn PPP$		178.7	74	

			Score/ Value	Rank	
	Business sophistication		**28.4**	**64**	
5.1	**Knowledge workers**		**31.0**	**66**	
5.1.1	Knowledge-intensive employment, %	⊙	23.2	62	
5.1.2	Firms offering formal training, %		33.9	48	
5.1.3	GERD performed by business, % GDP	⊙	0.0	89	○
5.1.4	GERD financed by business, %	⊙	30.8	57	
5.1.5	Females employed w/advanced degrees, %	⊙	13.5	55	●
5.2	**Innovation linkages**		**27.6**	**48**	●
5.2.1	University–industry R&D collaboration†	⊙	69.2	25	●◆
5.2.2	State of cluster development†	⊙	66.9	28	●◆
5.2.3	GERD financed by abroad, % GDP	⊙	0.0	96	○◇
5.2.4	Joint venture/strategic alliance deals/bn PPP$ GDP		0.0	115	○
5.2.5	Patent families/bn PPP$ GDP		0.0	95	○◇
5.3	**Knowledge absorption**		**26.7**	**[97]**	
5.3.1	Intellectual property payments, % total trade		n/a	n/a	
5.3.2	High-tech imports, % total trade		4.9	117	
5.3.3	ICT services imports, % total trade		0.4	114	◇
5.3.4	FDI net inflows, % GDP		0.4	118	◇
5.3.5	Research talent, % in businesses		n/a	n/a	

			Score/ Value	Rank	
	Knowledge and technology outputs		**11.3**	**114**	◇
6.1	**Knowledge creation**		**6.4**	**103**	
6.1.1	Patents by origin/bn PPP$ GDP		0.9	63	
6.1.2	PCT patents by origin/bn PPP$ GDP		0.0	87	
6.1.3	Utility models by origin/bn PPP$ GDP		0.2	49	
6.1.4	Scientific and technical articles/bn PPP$ GDP		4.1	112	
6.1.5	Citable documents H-index		5.9	95	
6.2	**Knowledge impact**		**18.3**	**112**	
6.2.1	Labor productivity growth, %		1.0	62	
6.2.2	Unicorn valuation, % GDP		0.0	48	○◇
6.2.3	Software spending, % GDP		0.1	102	◇
6.2.4	High-tech manufacturing, %		12.3	85	
6.3	**Knowledge diffusion**		**9.2**	**110**	◇
6.3.1	Intellectual property receipts, % total trade		n/a	n/a	
6.3.2	Production and export complexity		26.5	114	○◇
6.3.3	High-tech exports, % total trade		0.1	118	◇
6.3.4	ICT services exports, % total trade		0.5	104	
6.3.5	ISO 9001 quality/bn PPP$ GDP		1.7	91	

			Score/ Value	Rank	
	Creative outputs		**12.6**	**100**	◇
7.1	**Intangible assets**		**16.0**	**[96]**	
7.1.1	Intangible asset intensity, top 15, %		n/a	n/a	
7.1.2	Trademarks by origin/bn PPP$ GDP		35.2	66	
7.1.3	Global brand value, top 5,000, % GDP		n/a	n/a	
7.1.4	Industrial designs by origin/bn PPP$ GDP		0.4	88	
7.2	**Creative goods and services**		**3.0**	**97**	
7.2.1	Cultural and creative services exports, % total trade		0.1	83	
7.2.2	National feature films/mn pop. 15–69		1.1	60	
7.2.3	Entertainment and media market/th pop. 15–69		n/a	n/a	
7.2.4	Creative goods exports, % total trade		0.0	121	○
7.3	**Online creativity**		**15.4**	**94**	
7.3.1	Generic top-level domains (TLDs)/th pop. 15–69		1.0	98	
7.3.2	Country-code TLDs/th pop. 15–69		1.6	76	
7.3.3	GitHub commits/mn pop. 15–69		4.0	76	
7.3.4	Mobile app creation/bn PPP$ GDP		54.8	97	

NOTES: ● indicates a strength; ○ a weakness; ◆ an income group strength; ◇ an income group weakness; * an index; † a survey question. ⊙ is used when the available economy data are older than the base year; see appendices for details, including the year of the data, at wipo.int/gii-ranking. Square brackets [ ] indicate that the data minimum coverage (DMC) requirements were not met at the sub-pillar or pillar level.

GII 2023 rank

Bahrain

67

Output rank	Input rank	Income	Region	Population (mn)	GDP, PPP$ (bn)	GDP per capita, PPP$
86	47	High	NAWA	1.5	87.9	57,921

			Score/ Value	Rank	
Institutions			**69.2**	**28**	●
1.1	**Institutional environment**		**54.7**	**45**	◇
1.1.1	Operational stability for businesses*		52.8	65	◇
1.1.2	Government effectiveness*		56.5	40	
1.2	**Regulatory environment**		**73.9**	**36**	
1.2.1	Regulatory quality*		64.1	36	
1.2.2	Rule of law*		53.5	43	◇
1.2.3	Cost of redundancy dismissal		13.6	49	
1.3	**Business environment**		**79.1**	**[7]**	
1.3.1	Policies for doing business†		79.1	10	●
1.3.2	Entrepreneurship policies and culture†		n/a	n/a	
Human capital and research			**28.1**	**77**	◇
2.1	**Education**		**47.8**	**74**	◇
2.1.1	Expenditure on education, % GDP	⊙	2.3	115	○ ◇
2.1.2	Government funding/pupil, secondary, % GDP/cap	⊙	17.4	64	
2.1.3	School life expectancy, years	⊙	16.3	29	●
2.1.4	PISA scales in reading, maths and science		n/a	n/a	
2.1.5	Pupil–teacher ratio, secondary	⊙	10.4	35	
2.2	**Tertiary education**		**30.6**	**63**	◇
2.2.1	Tertiary enrolment, % gross		64.5	49	
2.2.2	Graduates in science and engineering, %		15.8	96	◇
2.2.3	Tertiary inbound mobility, %		11.7	21	●
2.3	**Research and development (R&D)**		**5.8**	**71**	◇
2.3.1	Researchers, FTE/mn pop.	⊙	369.0	76	
2.3.2	Gross expenditure on R&D, % GDP	⊙	0.1	104	
2.3.3	Global corporate R&D investors, top 3, mn USD		0.0	40	○ ◇
2.3.4	QS university ranking, top 3*		18.0	55	
Infrastructure			**53.8**	**37**	
3.1	**Information and communication technologies (ICTs)**		**75.0**	**48**	
3.1.1	ICT access*		98.6	3	● ◆
3.1.2	ICT use*		85.9	34	●
3.1.3	Government's online service*		72.6	54	
3.1.4	E-participation*		43.0	86	◇
3.2	**General infrastructure**		**65.8**	**2**	● ◆
3.2.1	Electricity output, GWh/mn pop.	⊙	19,600.5	1	● ◆
3.2.2	Logistics performance*		63.6	33	
3.2.3	Gross capital formation, % GDP		32.6	17	● ◆
3.3	**Ecological sustainability**		**20.5**	**79**	◇
3.3.1	GDP/unit of energy use		4.2	122	○ ◇
3.3.2	Environmental performance*		39.2	66	◇
3.3.3	ISO 14001 environment/bn PPP$ GDP		2.2	42	
Market sophistication			**31.7**	**78**	◇
4.1	**Credit**		**27.0**	**[72]**	
4.1.1	Finance for startups and scaleups†		n/a	n/a	
4.1.2	Domestic credit to private sector, % GDP	⊙	73.9	47	
4.1.3	Loans from microfinance institutions, % GDP		n/a	n/a	
4.2	**Investment**		**15.1**	**46**	
4.2.1	Market capitalization, % GDP		66.1	26	
4.2.2	Venture capital (VC) investors, deals/bn PPP$ GDP		0.1	33	
4.2.3	VC recipients, deals/bn PPP$ GDP		0.0	52	
4.2.4	VC received, value, % GDP		0.0	38	
4.3	**Trade, diversification and market scale**		**52.9**	**81**	
4.3.1	Applied tariff rate, weighted avg., %		2.0	61	
4.3.2	Domestic industry diversification	⊙	69.9	94	◇
4.3.3	Domestic market scale, bn PPP$		87.9	91	

			Score/ Value	Rank	
Business sophistication			**22.9**	**92**	◇
5.1	**Knowledge workers**		**19.5**	**[100]**	
5.1.1	Knowledge-intensive employment, %	⊙	21.9	68	
5.1.2	Firms offering formal training, %		n/a	n/a	
5.1.3	GERD performed by business, % GDP	⊙	0.0	80	
5.1.4	GERD financed by business, %	⊙	21.8	65	
5.1.5	Females employed w/advanced degrees, %		n/a	n/a	
5.2	**Innovation linkages**		**27.6**	**49**	
5.2.1	University–industry R&D collaboration†		33.3	91	◇
5.2.2	State of cluster development†		61.2	36	
5.2.3	GERD financed by abroad, % GDP	⊙	0.0	71	
5.2.4	Joint venture/strategic alliance deals/bn PPP$ GDP		0.1	16	●
5.2.5	Patent families/bn PPP$ GDP		0.0	75	
5.3	**Knowledge absorption**		**21.5**	**122**	○ ◇
5.3.1	Intellectual property payments, % total trade		n/a	n/a	
5.3.2	High-tech imports, % total trade	⊙	4.7	118	○
5.3.3	ICT services imports, % total trade		0.5	107	◇
5.3.4	FDI net inflows, % GDP		3.8	36	
5.3.5	Research talent, % in businesses	⊙	0.4	82	
Knowledge and technology outputs			**20.9**	**74**	◇
6.1	**Knowledge creation**		**5.0**	**113**	◇
6.1.1	Patents by origin/bn PPP$ GDP		0.1	123	○ ◇
6.1.2	PCT patents by origin/bn PPP$ GDP		0.1	64	
6.1.3	Utility models by origin/bn PPP$ GDP		n/a	n/a	
6.1.4	Scientific and technical articles/bn PPP$ GDP		6.7	95	◇
6.1.5	Citable documents H-index		5.0	103	◇
6.2	**Knowledge impact**		**26.2**	**68**	◇
6.2.1	Labor productivity growth, %		2.3	26	● ◆
6.2.2	Unicorn valuation, % GDP		0.0	48	○ ◇
6.2.3	Software spending, % GDP		0.3	45	
6.2.4	High-tech manufacturing, %	⊙	9.8	93	◇
6.3	**Knowledge diffusion**		**31.6**	**49**	
6.3.1	Intellectual property receipts, % total trade		n/a	n/a	
6.3.2	Production and export complexity		54.8	56	◇
6.3.3	High-tech exports, % total trade	⊙	1.4	68	◇
6.3.4	ICT services exports, % total trade		4.2	26	●
6.3.5	ISO 9001 quality/bn PPP$ GDP		6.6	43	
Creative outputs			**13.3**	**98**	◇
7.1	**Intangible assets**		**15.2**	**97**	◇
7.1.1	Intangible asset intensity, top 15, %		-7.1	71	◇
7.1.2	Trademarks by origin/bn PPP$ GDP		5.1	122	○ ◇
7.1.3	Global brand value, top 5,000, % GDP		1.2	53	
7.1.4	Industrial designs by origin/bn PPP$ GDP		0.1	111	○ ◇
7.2	**Creative goods and services**		**5.5**	**[86]**	
7.2.1	Cultural and creative services exports, % total trade		n/a	n/a	
7.2.2	National feature films/mn pop. 15–69		n/a	n/a	
7.2.3	Entertainment and media market/th pop. 15–69		3.5	46	◇
7.2.4	Creative goods exports, % total trade	⊙	0.6	57	
7.3	**Online creativity**		**17.3**	**83**	◇
7.3.1	Generic top-level domains (TLDs)/th pop. 15–69		5.5	56	
7.3.2	Country-code TLDs/th pop. 15–69		1.4	81	◇
7.3.3	GitHub commits/mn pop. 15–69		6.2	66	◇
7.3.4	Mobile app creation/bn PPP$ GDP		56.1	92	◇

NOTES: ● indicates a strength; ○ a weakness; ◆ an income group strength; ◇ an income group weakness; * an index; † a survey question. ⊙ is used when the available economy data are older than the base year; see appendices for details, including the year of the data, at wipo.int/gii-ranking. Square brackets [ ] indicate that the data minimum coverage (DMC) requirements were not met at the sub-pillar or pillar level.

Bangladesh

GII 2023 rank

105

Output rank	Input rank	Income	Region	Population (mn)	GDP, PPP$ (bn)	GDP per capita, PPP$
89	114	Lower middle	CSA	171.2	1,345.7	7,985

			Score/Value	Rank
Institutions			**35.7**	**108**
1.1	**Institutional environment**		**26.7**	**109**
1.1.1	Operational stability for businesses*		34.0	112
1.1.2	Government effectiveness*		19.4	108
1.2	**Regulatory environment**		**37.7**	**122**
1.2.1	Regulatory quality*		20.2	118
1.2.2	Rule of law*		21.8	102
1.2.3	Cost of redundancy dismissal		31.0	121
1.3	**Business environment**		**42.6**	**[76]**
1.3.1	Policies for doing business†		42.6	79
1.3.2	Entrepreneurship policies and culture†		n/a	n/a
Human capital and research			**11.4**	**125** ◇
2.1	**Education**		**19.1**	**128** ○◇
2.1.1	Expenditure on education, % GDP		1.8	122 ○◇
2.1.2	Government funding/pupil, secondary, % GDP/cap		6.5	96 ○◇
2.1.3	School life expectancy, years		12.4	90
2.1.4	PISA scales in reading, maths and science		n/a	n/a
2.1.5	Pupil-teacher ratio, secondary		33.1	123 ○◇
2.2	**Tertiary education**		**10.3**	**111**
2.2.1	Tertiary enrolment, % gross		25.1	92
2.2.2	Graduates in science and engineering, %		11.1	108 ○◇
2.2.3	Tertiary inbound mobility, %		n/a	n/a
2.3	**Research and development (R&D)**		**4.9**	**[76]**
2.3.1	Researchers, FTE/mn pop.		n/a	n/a
2.3.2	Gross expenditure on R&D, % GDP		n/a	n/a
2.3.3	Global corporate R&D investors, top 3, mn USD		0.0	40 ○◇
2.3.4	QS university ranking, top 3*		9.8	66 ●
Infrastructure			**30.5**	**93**
3.1	**Information and communication technologies (ICTs)**		**55.1**	**90**
3.1.1	ICT access*		63.0	95
3.1.2	ICT use*		44.7	109
3.1.3	Government's online service*		61.5	74
3.1.4	E-participation*		51.2	74
3.2	**General infrastructure**		**19.2**	**93**
3.2.1	Electricity output, GWh/mn pop.	⊙	514.7	110
3.2.2	Logistics performance*		22.7	82
3.2.3	Gross capital formation, % GDP		31.7	19 ●
3.3	**Ecological sustainability**		**17.3**	**96**
3.3.1	GDP/unit of energy use		17.1	14 ●◆
3.3.2	Environmental performance*		7.1	129 ○◇
3.3.3	ISO 14001 environment/bn PPP$ GDP		0.2	115
Market sophistication			**23.7**	**100**
4.1	**Credit**		**22.4**	**86**
4.1.1	Finance for startups and scaleups†		n/a	n/a
4.1.2	Domestic credit to private sector, % GDP		39.2	83
4.1.3	Loans from microfinance institutions, % GDP		2.7	14 ●
4.2	**Investment**		**3.1**	**92**
4.2.1	Market capitalization, % GDP		22.1	57
4.2.2	Venture capital (VC) investors, deals/bn PPP$ GDP		0.0	94 ○◇
4.2.3	VC recipients, deals/bn PPP$ GDP		0.0	88
4.2.4	VC received, value, % GDP		0.0	78
4.3	**Trade, diversification and market scale**		**45.7**	**96**
4.3.1	Applied tariff rate, weighted avg., %		11.0	123 ◇
4.3.2	Domestic industry diversification	⊙	79.3	79
4.3.3	Domestic market scale, bn PPP$		1,345.7	24 ●

			Score/Value	Rank
Business sophistication			**15.9**	**126** ◇
5.1	**Knowledge workers**		**11.4**	**[119]**
5.1.1	Knowledge-intensive employment, %	⊙	8.3	110
5.1.2	Firms offering formal training, %	⊙	21.9	73
5.1.3	GERD performed by business, % GDP		n/a	n/a
5.1.4	GERD financed by business, %		n/a	n/a
5.1.5	Females employed w/advanced degrees, %	⊙	1.3	114
5.2	**Innovation linkages**		**14.4**	**100**
5.2.1	University-industry R&D collaboration†		21.6	115
5.2.2	State of cluster development†		34.1	84
5.2.3	GERD financed by abroad, % GDP		n/a	n/a
5.2.4	Joint venture/strategic alliance deals/bn PPP$ GDP		0.0	117
5.2.5	Patent families/bn PPP$ GDP		0.0	95 ○◇
5.3	**Knowledge absorption**		**21.9**	**120**
5.3.1	Intellectual property payments, % total trade		0.1	99
5.3.2	High-tech imports, % total trade	⊙	8.1	67
5.3.3	ICT services imports, % total trade		0.2	130 ○◇
5.3.4	FDI net inflows, % GDP		0.5	114
5.3.5	Research talent, % in businesses		n/a	n/a
Knowledge and technology outputs			**15.2**	**89**
6.1	**Knowledge creation**		**7.5**	**[95]**
6.1.1	Patents by origin/bn PPP$ GDP		0.1	120
6.1.2	PCT patents by origin/bn PPP$ GDP		n/a	n/a
6.1.3	Utility models by origin/bn PPP$ GDP		n/a	n/a
6.1.4	Scientific and technical articles/bn PPP$ GDP		4.4	111
6.1.5	Citable documents H-index		13.5	63 ●
6.2	**Knowledge impact**		**27.4**	**62** ●
6.2.1	Labor productivity growth, %		4.5	7 ●◆
6.2.2	Unicorn valuation, % GDP		0.0	48 ○◇
6.2.3	Software spending, % GDP		0.2	75
6.2.4	High-tech manufacturing, %	⊙	6.5	99
6.3	**Knowledge diffusion**		**10.7**	**106**
6.3.1	Intellectual property receipts, % total trade		0.0	96
6.3.2	Production and export complexity		40.0	92
6.3.3	High-tech exports, % total trade	⊙	0.2	104
6.3.4	ICT services exports, % total trade		0.9	90
6.3.5	ISO 9001 quality/bn PPP$ GDP		0.6	117
Creative outputs			**18.6**	**82**
7.1	**Intangible assets**		**28.0**	**73**
7.1.1	Intangible asset intensity, top 15, %		61.2	36 ●
7.1.2	Trademarks by origin/bn PPP$ GDP		9.2	112
7.1.3	Global brand value, top 5,000, % GDP		0.4	68
7.1.4	Industrial designs by origin/bn PPP$ GDP		1.1	63 ●
7.2	**Creative goods and services**		**1.7**	**[108]**
7.2.1	Cultural and creative services exports, % total trade		0.1	79
7.2.2	National feature films/mn pop. 15–69		n/a	n/a
7.2.3	Entertainment and media market/th pop. 15–69		n/a	n/a
7.2.4	Creative goods exports, % total trade	⊙	0.1	104
7.3	**Online creativity**		**16.8**	**87**
7.3.1	Generic top-level domains (TLDs)/th pop. 15–69		0.4	114
7.3.2	Country-code TLDs/th pop. 15–69		0.1	126
7.3.3	GitHub commits/mn pop. 15–69		2.2	98
7.3.4	Mobile app creation/bn PPP$ GDP		64.4	67

NOTES: ● indicates a strength; ○ a weakness; ◆ an income group strength; ◇ an income group weakness; * an index; † a survey question. ⊙ is used when the available economy data are older than the base year; see appendices for details, including the year of the data, at wipo.int/gii-ranking. Square brackets [ ] indicate that the data minimum coverage (DMC) requirements were not met at the sub-pillar or pillar level.

GII 2023 rank

Belarus **80**

Output rank	Input rank	Income	Region	Population (mn)	GDP, PPP$ (bn)	GDP per capita, PPP$
66	88	Upper middle	EUR	9.5	202.0	21,709

			Score/ Value	Rank	
Institutions			**24.3**	**128**	○◇
1.1	**Institutional environment**		**25.4**	**110**	◇
1.1.1	Operational stability for businesses*		35.4	108	◇
1.1.2	Government effectiveness*		15.5	117	◇
1.2	**Regulatory environment**		**42.9**	**115**	◇
1.2.1	Regulatory quality*		18.2	121	○◇
1.2.2	Rule of law*		7.5	126	○◇
1.2.3	Cost of redundancy dismissal		21.7	96	
1.3	**Business environment**		**4.5**	**[130]**	
1.3.1	Policies for doing business†		n/a	n/a	
1.3.2	Entrepreneurship policies and culture†	⊙	4.5	82	○◇
Human capital and research			**39.9**	**37**	◆
2.1	**Education**		**61.6**	**26**	●◆
2.1.1	Expenditure on education, % GDP		4.7	45	
2.1.2	Government funding/pupil, secondary, % GDP/cap		n/a	n/a	
2.1.3	School life expectancy, years		15.1	47	
2.1.4	PISA scales in reading, maths and science		472.3	36	◆
2.1.5	Pupil–teacher ratio, secondary		9.4	24	●
2.2	**Tertiary education**		**48.1**	**13**	●◆
2.2.1	Tertiary enrolment, % gross		82.2	22	●◆
2.2.2	Graduates in science and engineering, %		34.6	9	●◆
2.2.3	Tertiary inbound mobility, %		6.5	38	
2.3	**Research and development (R&D)**		**10.1**	**59**	
2.3.1	Researchers, FTE/mn pop.		1,417.7	49	
2.3.2	Gross expenditure on R&D, % GDP		0.5	62	
2.3.3	Global corporate R&D investors, top 3, mn USD		0.0	40	○◇
2.3.4	QS university ranking, top 3*		17.6	56	
Infrastructure			**38.7**	**71**	
3.1	**Information and communication technologies (ICTs)**		**66.8**	**74**	
3.1.1	ICT access*		90.0	22	●◆
3.1.2	ICT use*		87.2	28	●◆
3.1.3	Government's online service*		48.1	94	◇
3.1.4	E-participation*		41.9	87	
3.2	**General infrastructure**		**22.6**	**81**	
3.2.1	Electricity output, GWh/mn pop.	⊙	4,109.8	54	
3.2.2	Logistics performance*		27.3	76	
3.2.3	Gross capital formation, % GDP		23.8	68	
3.3	**Ecological sustainability**		**26.6**	**59**	
3.3.1	GDP/unit of energy use		7.1	97	
3.3.2	Environmental performance*		50.2	44	
3.3.3	ISO 14001 environment/bn PPP$ GDP		2.0	45	
Market sophistication			**23.8**	**99**	◇
4.1	**Credit**		**8.9**	**116**	◇
4.1.1	Finance for startups and scaleups†	⊙	15.9	81	○◇
4.1.2	Domestic credit to private sector, % GDP		32.5	92	
4.1.3	Loans from microfinance institutions, % GDP		0.0	54	
4.2	**Investment**		**0.7**	**109**	○
4.2.1	Market capitalization, % GDP	⊙	1.4	77	○
4.2.2	Venture capital (VC) investors, deals/bn PPP$ GDP	⊙	0.0	90	○
4.2.3	VC recipients, deals/bn PPP$ GDP		0.0	90	
4.2.4	VC received, value, % GDP		0.0	96	○
4.3	**Trade, diversification and market scale**		**61.9**	**50**	
4.3.1	Applied tariff rate, weighted avg., %		1.8	56	
4.3.2	Domestic industry diversification		92.8	40	
4.3.3	Domestic market scale, bn PPP$		202.0	69	

			Score/ Value	Rank	
Business sophistication			**26.3**	**74**	
5.1	**Knowledge workers**		**46.2**	**38**	◆
5.1.1	Knowledge-intensive employment, %	⊙	41.7	27	●◆
5.1.2	Firms offering formal training, %	⊙	31.5	54	
5.1.3	GERD performed by business, % GDP	⊙	0.4	43	
5.1.4	GERD financed by business, %	⊙	45.0	35	
5.1.5	Females employed w/advanced degrees, %	⊙	20.9	30	◆
5.2	**Innovation linkages**		**6.0**	**[127]**	
5.2.1	University–industry R&D collaboration†		n/a	n/a	
5.2.2	State of cluster development†		n/a	n/a	
5.2.3	GERD financed by abroad, % GDP	⊙	0.1	41	
5.2.4	Joint venture/strategic alliance deals/bn PPP$ GDP	⊙	0.0	105	
5.2.5	Patent families/bn PPP$ GDP		0.1	56	
5.3	**Knowledge absorption**		**26.7**	**95**	
5.3.1	Intellectual property payments, % total trade		0.5	69	
5.3.2	High-tech imports, % total trade		4.7	119	
5.3.3	ICT services imports, % total trade		1.0	86	
5.3.4	FDI net inflows, % GDP		2.0	70	
5.3.5	Research talent, % in businesses		n/a	n/a	
Knowledge and technology outputs			**29.9**	**47**	
6.1	**Knowledge creation**		**16.7**	**60**	
6.1.1	Patents by origin/bn PPP$ GDP		1.8	37	
6.1.2	PCT patents by origin/bn PPP$ GDP		0.1	66	
6.1.3	Utility models by origin/bn PPP$ GDP		1.5	12	●
6.1.4	Scientific and technical articles/bn PPP$ GDP		5.8	103	
6.1.5	Citable documents H-index		10.2	78	
6.2	**Knowledge impact**		**23.1**	**88**	
6.2.1	Labor productivity growth, %		0.9	66	
6.2.2	Unicorn valuation, % GDP		0.0	48	○◇
6.2.3	Software spending, % GDP		0.0	111	◇
6.2.4	High-tech manufacturing, %		29.5	40	
6.3	**Knowledge diffusion**		**49.9**	**18**	●◆
6.3.1	Intellectual property receipts, % total trade		0.3	38	◆
6.3.2	Production and export complexity		70.0	31	◆
6.3.3	High-tech exports, % total trade		1.8	63	
6.3.4	ICT services exports, % total trade		6.8	10	●◆
6.3.5	ISO 9001 quality/bn PPP$ GDP		34.6	2	●◆
Creative outputs			**16.3**	**88**	
7.1	**Intangible assets**		**12.8**	**103**	
7.1.1	Intangible asset intensity, top 15, %		n/a	n/a	
7.1.2	Trademarks by origin/bn PPP$ GDP		22.7	88	
7.1.3	Global brand value, top 5,000, % GDP		0.0	74	○◇
7.1.4	Industrial designs by origin/bn PPP$ GDP		1.4	58	
7.2	**Creative goods and services**		**9.2**	**[71]**	
7.2.1	Cultural and creative services exports, % total trade		0.4	61	
7.2.2	National feature films/mn pop. 15–69		n/a	n/a	
7.2.3	Entertainment and media market/th pop. 15–69		n/a	n/a	
7.2.4	Creative goods exports, % total trade		0.9	48	
7.3	**Online creativity**		**30.3**	**40**	◆
7.3.1	Generic top-level domains (TLDs)/th pop. 15–69		2.0	84	
7.3.2	Country-code TLDs/th pop. 15–69		6.6	48	
7.3.3	GitHub commits/mn pop. 15–69		24.2	39	◆
7.3.4	Mobile app creation/bn PPP$ GDP		88.4	2	●◆

NOTES: ● indicates a strength; ○ a weakness; ◆ an income group strength; ◇ an income group weakness; * an index; † a survey question. ⊙ is used when the available economy data are older than the base year; see appendices for details, including the year of the data, at wipo.int/gii-ranking. Square brackets [ ] indicate that the data minimum coverage (DMC) requirements were not met at the sub-pillar or pillar level.

Belgium

GII 2023 rank **23**

Output rank	Input rank	Income	Region	Population (mn)	GDP, PPP$ (bn)	GDP per capita, PPP$
22	23	High	EUR	11.7	723.1	62,065

			Score/ Value	Rank	
Institutions			**68.3**	**30**	
1.1	**Institutional environment**		**68.6**	**29**	
1.1.1	Operational stability for businesses*		69.4	29	
1.1.2	Government effectiveness*		67.8	27	◇
1.2	**Regulatory environment**		**77.3**	**31**	
1.2.1	Regulatory quality*		76.9	22	
1.2.2	Rule of law*		78.6	21	
1.2.3	Cost of redundancy dismissal		19.7	85	○
1.3	**Business environment**		**58.9**	**35**	
1.3.1	Policies for doing business†		66.1	31	
1.3.2	Entrepreneurship policies and culture†	⊙	51.6	33	
Human capital and research			**55.4**	**14**	
2.1	**Education**		**69.6**	**6**	● ◆
2.1.1	Expenditure on education, % GDP	⊙	6.3	15	
2.1.2	Government funding/pupil, secondary, % GDP/cap		23.3	29	
2.1.3	School life expectancy, years		19.4	6	● ◆
2.1.4	PISA scales in reading, maths and science		499.9	19	
2.1.5	Pupil–teacher ratio, secondary		8.7	19	◆
2.2	**Tertiary education**		**34.9**	**48**	
2.2.1	Tertiary enrolment, % gross		80.9	23	
2.2.2	Graduates in science and engineering, %		17.6	89	○ ◇
2.2.3	Tertiary inbound mobility, %		10.4	24	
2.3	**Research and development (R&D)**		**61.6**	**13**	
2.3.1	Researchers, FTE/mn pop.		6,604.4	8	●
2.3.2	Gross expenditure on R&D, % GDP		3.2	6	●
2.3.3	Global corporate R&D investors, top 3, mn USD		65.4	19	
2.3.4	QS university ranking, top 3*		54.6	17	
Infrastructure			**51.6**	**44**	◇
3.1	**Information and communication technologies (ICTs)**		**70.9**	**64**	○ ◇
3.1.1	ICT access*		84.7	53	
3.1.2	ICT use*		88.8	24	
3.1.3	Government's online service*		65.7	67	○ ◇
3.1.4	E-participation*		44.2	83	○ ◇
3.2	**General infrastructure**		**50.3**	**17**	
3.2.1	Electricity output, GWh/mn pop.		8,560.7	16	
3.2.2	Logistics performance*		86.4	7	
3.2.3	Gross capital formation, % GDP		24.6	60	○
3.3	**Ecological sustainability**		**33.8**	**41**	
3.3.1	GDP/unit of energy use		10.1	66	○
3.3.2	Environmental performance*		66.6	21	
3.3.3	ISO 14001 environment/bn PPP$ GDP		1.6	55	
Market sophistication			**47.9**	**26**	
4.1	**Credit**		**56.0**	**23**	
4.1.1	Finance for startups and scaleups†	⊙	84.4	4	
4.1.2	Domestic credit to private sector, % GDP		75.3	45	◇
4.1.3	Loans from microfinance institutions, % GDP		n/a	n/a	
4.2	**Investment**		**22.5**	**32**	◇
4.2.1	Market capitalization, % GDP	⊙	75.2	22	
4.2.2	Venture capital (VC) investors, deals/bn PPP$ GDP		0.3	20	
4.2.3	VC recipients, deals/bn PPP$ GDP		0.1	31	
4.2.4	VC received, value, % GDP		0.0	36	◇
4.3	**Trade, diversification and market scale**		**65.2**	**27**	
4.3.1	Applied tariff rate, weighted avg., %		1.5	20	
4.3.2	Domestic industry diversification		89.8	49	
4.3.3	Domestic market scale, bn PPP$		723.1	36	

			Score/ Value	Rank	
Business sophistication			**60.8**	**10**	●
5.1	**Knowledge workers**		**74.2**	**4**	● ◆
5.1.1	Knowledge-intensive employment, %		49.2	12	
5.1.2	Firms offering formal training, %		57.8	10	
5.1.3	GERD performed by business, % GDP		2.4	5	●
5.1.4	GERD financed by business, %	⊙	64.3	8	●
5.1.5	Females employed w/advanced degrees, %		28.3	7	●
5.2	**Innovation linkages**		**61.0**	**13**	
5.2.1	University–industry R&D collaboration†		85.1	9	●
5.2.2	State of cluster development†		74.0	19	
5.2.3	GERD financed by abroad, % GDP	⊙	0.5	6	● ◆
5.2.4	Joint venture/strategic alliance deals/bn PPP$ GDP		0.1	25	
5.2.5	Patent families/bn PPP$ GDP		2.5	15	
5.3	**Knowledge absorption**		**47.3**	**29**	
5.3.1	Intellectual property payments, % total trade		0.7	55	
5.3.2	High-tech imports, % total trade		9.2	47	
5.3.3	ICT services imports, % total trade		2.9	20	
5.3.4	FDI net inflows, % GDP		−1.5	127	○
5.3.5	Research talent, % in businesses		64.3	8	
Knowledge and technology outputs			**46.8**	**15**	
6.1	**Knowledge creation**		**50.1**	**13**	
6.1.1	Patents by origin/bn PPP$ GDP		5.0	17	
6.1.2	PCT patents by origin/bn PPP$ GDP		1.8	17	
6.1.3	Utility models by origin/bn PPP$ GDP		n/a	n/a	
6.1.4	Scientific and technical articles/bn PPP$ GDP		30.4	20	
6.1.5	Citable documents H-index		54.1	14	
6.2	**Knowledge impact**		**49.1**	**18**	
6.2.1	Labor productivity growth, %		0.2	95	○
6.2.2	Unicorn valuation, % GDP		1.7	26	
6.2.3	Software spending, % GDP		0.7	10	●
6.2.4	High-tech manufacturing, %		45.9	18	
6.3	**Knowledge diffusion**		**41.1**	**33**	
6.3.1	Intellectual property receipts, % total trade		0.9	23	
6.3.2	Production and export complexity		76.3	22	
6.3.3	High-tech exports, % total trade		11.9	13	
6.3.4	ICT services exports, % total trade		3.5	33	
6.3.5	ISO 9001 quality/bn PPP$ GDP		4.3	60	
Creative outputs			**39.4**	**30**	◇
7.1	**Intangible assets**		**39.3**	**44**	◇
7.1.1	Intangible asset intensity, top 15, %		62.1	34	
7.1.2	Trademarks by origin/bn PPP$ GDP		34.3	70	○
7.1.3	Global brand value, top 5,000, % GDP		4.8	35	◇
7.1.4	Industrial designs by origin/bn PPP$ GDP		2.2	40	
7.2	**Creative goods and services**		**27.0**	**36**	◇
7.2.1	Cultural and creative services exports, % total trade		1.3	22	
7.2.2	National feature films/mn pop. 15–69		3.4	37	
7.2.3	Entertainment and media market/th pop. 15–69		50.5	17	
7.2.4	Creative goods exports, % total trade		0.9	47	
7.3	**Online creativity**		**52.0**	**22**	
7.3.1	Generic top-level domains (TLDs)/th pop. 15–69		24.7	26	◇
7.3.2	Country-code TLDs/th pop. 15–69		63.7	13	
7.3.3	GitHub commits/mn pop. 15–69		57.9	15	
7.3.4	Mobile app creation/bn PPP$ GDP		61.9	76	○ ◇

NOTES: ● indicates a strength; ○ a weakness; ◆ an income group strength; ◇ an income group weakness; * an index; † a survey question. ⊙ is used when the available economy data are older than the base year; see appendices for details, including the year of the data, at wipo.int/gii-ranking. Square brackets [ ] indicate that the data minimum coverage (DMC) requirements were not met at the sub-pillar or pillar level.

GII 2023 rank

Benin

120

Output rank	Input rank	Income	Region	Population (mn)	GDP, PPP$ (bn)	GDP per capita, PPP$
128	108	Lower middle	SSA	13.4	53.7	4,183

		Score/Value	Rank
	Institutions	**52.2**	**58 ●◆**
1.1	**Institutional environment**	**36.4**	**88**
1.1.1	Operational stability for businesses*	41.7	87
1.1.2	Government effectiveness*	31.0	85 ●
1.2	**Regulatory environment**	**59.7**	**74 ●**
1.2.1	Regulatory quality*	30.9	95
1.2.2	Rule of law*	22.3	100
1.2.3	Cost of redundancy dismissal	11.6	38 ●
1.3	**Business environment**	**60.6**	**[32]**
1.3.1	Policies for doing business†	60.6	38 ●◆
1.3.2	Entrepreneurship policies and culture†	n/a	n/a
	Human capital and research	**15.2**	**114**
2.1	**Education**	**31.1**	**119**
2.1.1	Expenditure on education, % GDP	3.2	103
2.1.2	Government funding/pupil, secondary, % GDP/cap ⊙	8.2	95
2.1.3	School life expectancy, years	10.8	100
2.1.4	PISA scales in reading, maths and science	n/a	n/a
2.1.5	Pupil–teacher ratio, secondary	18.1	91
2.2	**Tertiary education**	**14.4**	**104**
2.2.1	Tertiary enrolment, % gross	11.1	111
2.2.2	Graduates in science and engineering, %	19.7	74
2.2.3	Tertiary inbound mobility, %	3.0	66 ●
2.3	**Research and development (R&D)**	**0.0**	**[119]**
2.3.1	Researchers, FTE/mn pop.	n/a	n/a
2.3.2	Gross expenditure on R&D, % GDP	n/a	n/a
2.3.3	Global corporate R&D investors, top 3, mn USD	0.0	40 ○◇
2.3.4	QS university ranking, top 3*	0.0	71 ○◇
	Infrastructure	**22.7**	**114**
3.1	**Information and communication technologies (ICTs)**	**35.8**	**114**
3.1.1	ICT access*	32.6	121 ◇
3.1.2	ICT use*	30.6	116 ◇
3.1.3	Government's online service*	47.4	96
3.1.4	E-participation*	32.6	100
3.2	**General infrastructure**	**21.4**	**83 ●**
3.2.1	Electricity output, GWh/mn pop. ⊙	81.7	123 ○◇
3.2.2	Logistics performance*	36.4	65 ●
3.2.3	Gross capital formation, % GDP	28.6	28 ●
3.3	**Ecological sustainability**	**11.0**	**124 ◇**
3.3.1	GDP/unit of energy use	7.1	96
3.3.2	Environmental performance*	18.1	113
3.3.3	ISO 14001 environment/bn PPP$ GDP	0.1	123
	Market sophistication	**16.7**	**118**
4.1	**Credit**	**14.7**	**102**
4.1.1	Finance for startups and scaleups†	n/a	n/a
4.1.2	Domestic credit to private sector, % GDP	15.5	117
4.1.3	Loans from microfinance institutions, % GDP	2.2	18 ●
4.2	**Investment**	**n/a**	**[n/a]**
4.2.1	Market capitalization, % GDP	n/a	n/a
4.2.2	Venture capital (VC) investors, deals/bn PPP$ GDP	n/a	n/a
4.2.3	VC recipients, deals/bn PPP$ GDP	n/a	n/a
4.2.4	VC received, value, % GDP	n/a	n/a
4.3	**Trade, diversification and market scale**	**18.6**	**127 ◇**
4.3.1	Applied tariff rate, weighted avg., %	9.9	117
4.3.2	Domestic industry diversification	n/a	n/a
4.3.3	Domestic market scale, bn PPP$	53.7	104

		Score/Value	Rank
	Business sophistication	**19.4**	**[111]**
5.1	**Knowledge workers**	**9.2**	**[123]**
5.1.1	Knowledge-intensive employment, % ⊙	6.1	117 ◇
5.1.2	Firms offering formal training, % ⊙	20.0	81
5.1.3	GERD performed by business, % GDP	n/a	n/a
5.1.4	GERD financed by business, %	n/a	n/a
5.1.5	Females employed w/advanced degrees, % ⊙	1.2	115
5.2	**Innovation linkages**	**14.5**	**[97]**
5.2.1	University–industry R&D collaboration†	26.8	102
5.2.2	State of cluster development†	16.6	117
5.2.3	GERD financed by abroad, % GDP	n/a	n/a
5.2.4	Joint venture/strategic alliance deals/bn PPP$ GDP	n/a	n/a
5.2.5	Patent families/bn PPP$ GDP	0.0	95 ○◇
5.3	**Knowledge absorption**	**34.6**	**58 ●**
5.3.1	Intellectual property payments, % total trade	0.0	114 ◇
5.3.2	High-tech imports, % total trade	3.8	126
5.3.3	ICT services imports, % total trade	3.4	12 ●◆
5.3.4	FDI net inflows, % GDP	1.5	87
5.3.5	Research talent, % in businesses	n/a	n/a
	Knowledge and technology outputs	**11.0**	**116**
6.1	**Knowledge creation**	**5.4**	**111**
6.1.1	Patents by origin/bn PPP$ GDP	0.2	99
6.1.2	PCT patents by origin/bn PPP$ GDP	0.0	90
6.1.3	Utility models by origin/bn PPP$ GDP	0.0	75 ○◇
6.1.4	Scientific and technical articles/bn PPP$ GDP	9.3	79 ●
6.1.5	Citable documents H-index	4.6	108
6.2	**Knowledge impact**	**26.9**	**64 ●**
6.2.1	Labor productivity growth, %	3.5	9 ●◆
6.2.2	Unicorn valuation, % GDP	0.0	48 ○◇
6.2.3	Software spending, % GDP	0.1	104
6.2.4	High-tech manufacturing, %	n/a	n/a
6.3	**Knowledge diffusion**	**0.8**	**132 ○◇**
6.3.1	Intellectual property receipts, % total trade	0.0	108
6.3.2	Production and export complexity	n/a	n/a
6.3.3	High-tech exports, % total trade	0.0	127
6.3.4	ICT services exports, % total trade	0.0	132 ○◇
6.3.5	ISO 9001 quality/bn PPP$ GDP	0.9	111
	Creative outputs	**2.6**	**129 ○◇**
7.1	**Intangible assets**	**1.5**	**129 ○◇**
7.1.1	Intangible asset intensity, top 15, %	n/a	n/a
7.1.2	Trademarks by origin/bn PPP$ GDP	4.0	127 ○
7.1.3	Global brand value, top 5,000, % GDP	0.0	74 ○◇
7.1.4	Industrial designs by origin/bn PPP$ GDP	0.1	112
7.2	**Creative goods and services**	**0.1**	**[130]**
7.2.1	Cultural and creative services exports, % total trade	0.0	111 ○◇
7.2.2	National feature films/mn pop. 15–69	n/a	n/a
7.2.3	Entertainment and media market/th pop. 15–69	n/a	n/a
7.2.4	Creative goods exports, % total trade	0.0	122
7.3	**Online creativity**	**7.1**	**120 ◇**
7.3.1	Generic top-level domains (TLDs)/th pop. 15–69	0.6	105
7.3.2	Country-code TLDs/th pop. 15–69	0.1	124
7.3.3	GitHub commits/mn pop. 15–69	0.8	117
7.3.4	Mobile app creation/bn PPP$ GDP	26.9	119 ◇

NOTES: ● indicates a strength; ○ a weakness; ◆ an income group strength; ◇ an income group weakness; * an index; † a survey question. ⊙ is used when the available economy data are older than the base year; see appendices for details, including the year of the data, at wipo.int/gii-ranking. Square brackets [ ] indicate that the data minimum coverage (DMC) requirements were not met at the sub-pillar or pillar level.

GII 2023 rank

Bolivia (Plurinational State of) **97**

Output rank	Input rank	Income	Region	Population (mn)	GDP, PPP$ (bn)	GDP per capita, PPP$
101	91	Lower middle	LCN	12.2	118.8	9,933

			Score/ Value	Rank	
	Institutions		**12.3**	**132**	○◇
1.1	**Institutional environment**		**22.2**	**120**	
1.1.1	Operational stability for businesses*		27.8	120	
1.1.2	Government effectiveness*		16.5	113	
1.2	**Regulatory environment**		**8.9**	**132**	○◇
1.2.1	Regulatory quality*		12.2	129	○◇
1.2.2	Rule of law*		5.6	128	○◇
1.2.3	Cost of redundancy dismissal		n/a	n/a	
1.3	**Business environment**		**5.7**	**[129]**	
1.3.1	Policies for doing business†		5.7	127	○◇
1.3.2	Entrepreneurship policies and culture†		n/a	n/a	
	Human capital and research		**32.5**	**[61]**	
2.1	**Education**		**65.0**	**[15]**	
2.1.1	Expenditure on education, % GDP	⊙	8.4	2	●◆
2.1.2	Government funding/pupil, secondary, % GDP/cap		24.1	25	●
2.1.3	School life expectancy, years		n/a	n/a	
2.1.4	PISA scales in reading, maths and science		n/a	n/a	
2.1.5	Pupil-teacher ratio, secondary		18.7	95	
2.2	**Tertiary education**		**n/a**	**[n/a]**	
2.2.1	Tertiary enrolment, % gross		n/a	n/a	
2.2.2	Graduates in science and engineering, %		n/a	n/a	
2.2.3	Tertiary inbound mobility, %		n/a	n/a	
2.3	**Research and development (R&D)**		**0.0**	**[119]**	
2.3.1	Researchers, FTE/mn pop.		n/a	n/a	
2.3.2	Gross expenditure on R&D, % GDP		n/a	n/a	
2.3.3	Global corporate R&D investors, top 3, mn USD		0.0	40	○◇
2.3.4	QS university ranking, top 3*		0.0	71	○◇
	Infrastructure		**27.0**	**104**	
3.1	**Information and communication technologies (ICTs)**		**50.2**	**99**	
3.1.1	ICT access*		62.5	96	
3.1.2	ICT use*		61.0	91	
3.1.3	Government's online service*		46.9	97	
3.1.4	E-participation*		30.2	104	
3.2	**General infrastructure**		**9.4**	**124**	○
3.2.1	Electricity output, GWh/mn pop.		911.9	101	
3.2.2	Logistics performance*		13.6	103	○
3.2.3	Gross capital formation, % GDP		18.0	112	◇
3.3	**Ecological sustainability**		**21.4**	**76**	
3.3.1	GDP/unit of energy use		10.5	60	●
3.3.2	Environmental performance*		35.9	73	◆
3.3.3	ISO 14001 environment/bn PPP$ GDP		0.5	80	
	Market sophistication		**55.3**	**16**	●◆
4.1	**Credit**		**63.0**	**14**	●◆
4.1.1	Finance for startups and scaleups†		n/a	n/a	
4.1.2	Domestic credit to private sector, % GDP	⊙	71.2	51	●
4.1.3	Loans from microfinance institutions, % GDP		16.8	1	●◆
4.2	**Investment**		**n/a**	**[n/a]**	
4.2.1	Market capitalization, % GDP		n/a	n/a	
4.2.2	Venture capital (VC) investors, deals/bn PPP$ GDP		n/a	n/a	
4.2.3	VC recipients, deals/bn PPP$ GDP		n/a	n/a	
4.2.4	VC received, value, % GDP		n/a	n/a	
4.3	**Trade, diversification and market scale**		**47.6**	**91**	
4.3.1	Applied tariff rate, weighted avg., %		5.2	91	
4.3.2	Domestic industry diversification	⊙	73.9	90	
4.3.3	Domestic market scale, bn PPP$		118.8	85	

			Score/ Value	Rank	
	Business sophistication		**25.1**	**81**	
5.1	**Knowledge workers**		**40.2**	**[47]**	
5.1.1	Knowledge-intensive employment, %	⊙	13.9	92	
5.1.2	Firms offering formal training, %	⊙	49.9	20	●◆
5.1.3	GERD performed by business, % GDP		n/a	n/a	
5.1.4	GERD financed by business, %		n/a	n/a	
5.1.5	Females employed w/advanced degrees, %	⊙	11.9	64	●
5.2	**Innovation linkages**		**8.1**	**124**	○◇
5.2.1	University-industry R&D collaboration†		12.3	123	○◇
5.2.2	State of cluster development†		17.9	115	
5.2.3	GERD financed by abroad, % GDP		n/a	n/a	
5.2.4	Joint venture/strategic alliance deals/bn PPP$ GDP		0.0	112	
5.2.5	Patent families/bn PPP$ GDP		0.0	95	○◇
5.3	**Knowledge absorption**		**27.0**	**93**	
5.3.1	Intellectual property payments, % total trade		0.5	71	
5.3.2	High-tech imports, % total trade		7.4	77	
5.3.3	ICT services imports, % total trade		0.9	92	
5.3.4	FDI net inflows, % GDP		−0.7	124	○◇
5.3.5	Research talent, % in businesses		n/a	n/a	
	Knowledge and technology outputs		**12.7**	**106**	
6.1	**Knowledge creation**		**6.1**	**105**	
6.1.1	Patents by origin/bn PPP$ GDP	⊙	0.6	72	
6.1.2	PCT patents by origin/bn PPP$ GDP		n/a	n/a	
6.1.3	Utility models by origin/bn PPP$ GDP	⊙	0.1	54	
6.1.4	Scientific and technical articles/bn PPP$ GDP		2.5	119	
6.1.5	Citable documents H-index		6.6	92	
6.2	**Knowledge impact**		**21.2**	**98**	
6.2.1	Labor productivity growth, %		0.3	88	
6.2.2	Unicorn valuation, % GDP		0.0	48	○◇
6.2.3	Software spending, % GDP		0.3	50	●
6.2.4	High-tech manufacturing, %	⊙	10.6	87	
6.3	**Knowledge diffusion**		**10.9**	**103**	
6.3.1	Intellectual property receipts, % total trade		0.1	69	
6.3.2	Production and export complexity		33.7	105	
6.3.3	High-tech exports, % total trade		0.4	90	
6.3.4	ICT services exports, % total trade		0.5	102	
6.3.5	ISO 9001 quality/bn PPP$ GDP		2.3	84	
	Creative outputs		**12.2**	**102**	
7.1	**Intangible assets**		**14.2**	**[100]**	
7.1.1	Intangible asset intensity, top 15, %		n/a	n/a	
7.1.2	Trademarks by origin/bn PPP$ GDP	⊙	37.0	62	●
7.1.3	Global brand value, top 5,000, % GDP		n/a	n/a	
7.1.4	Industrial designs by origin/bn PPP$ GDP	⊙	0.2	108	
7.2	**Creative goods and services**		**9.0**	**72**	
7.2.1	Cultural and creative services exports, % total trade		0.0	95	
7.2.2	National feature films/mn pop. 15–69		0.8	67	
7.2.3	Entertainment and media market/th pop. 15–69		n/a	n/a	
7.2.4	Creative goods exports, % total trade		1.9	26	●
7.3	**Online creativity**		**11.4**	**111**	
7.3.1	Generic top-level domains (TLDs)/th pop. 15–69		1.9	88	
7.3.2	Country-code TLDs/th pop. 15–69		0.5	99	
7.3.3	GitHub commits/mn pop. 15–69		3.0	90	
7.3.4	Mobile app creation/bn PPP$ GDP		40.4	112	◇

NOTES: ● indicates a strength; ○ a weakness; ◆ an income group strength; ◇ an income group weakness; * an index; † a survey question. ⊙ is used when the available economy data are older than the base year; see appendices for details, including the year of the data, at wipo.int/gii-ranking. Square brackets [ ] indicate that the data minimum coverage (DMC) requirements were not met at the sub-pillar or pillar level.

GII 2023 rank

Bosnia and Herzegovina 77

Output rank	Input rank	Income	Region	Population (mn)	GDP, PPP$ (bn)	GDP per capita, PPP$
80	75	Upper middle	EUR	3.2	62.2	17,899

			Score/ Value	Rank	
	Institutions		**36.5**	**104**	
1.1	**Institutional environment**		**24.8**	**113**	○◇
1.1.1	Operational stability for businesses*		41.7	87	
1.1.2	Government effectiveness*		8.0	127	○◇
1.2	**Regulatory environment**		**66.0**	**56**	
1.2.1	Regulatory quality*		37.5	81	
1.2.2	Rule of law*		31.6	80	
1.2.3	Cost of redundancy dismissal		9.2	24	●◆
1.3	**Business environment**		**18.7**	**120**	○◇
1.3.1	Policies for doing business†		11.2	126	○◇
1.3.2	Entrepreneurship policies and culture†	⊙	26.1	66	
	Human capital and research		**30.5**	**68**	
2.1	**Education**		**61.3**	**[28]**	
2.1.1	Expenditure on education, % GDP		n/a	n/a	
2.1.2	Government funding/pupil, secondary, % GDP/cap	⊙	33.5	5	●◆
2.1.3	School life expectancy, years		n/a	n/a	
2.1.4	PISA scales in reading, maths and science		402.6	63	
2.1.5	Pupil–teacher ratio, secondary		8.3	13	●◆
2.2	**Tertiary education**		**28.2**	**73**	
2.2.1	Tertiary enrolment, % gross		39.2	78	
2.2.2	Graduates in science and engineering, %		24.0	50	
2.2.3	Tertiary inbound mobility, %		6.6	37	●
2.3	**Research and development (R&D)**		**1.9**	**90**	
2.3.1	Researchers, FTE/mn pop.		447.2	72	
2.3.2	Gross expenditure on R&D, % GDP		0.2	89	
2.3.3	Global corporate R&D investors, top 3, mn USD		0.0	40	○◇
2.3.4	QS university ranking, top 3*		0.0	71	○◇
	Infrastructure		**39.5**	**67**	
3.1	**Information and communication technologies (ICTs)**		**59.5**	**83**	
3.1.1	ICT access*		78.7	77	
3.1.2	ICT use*		63.5	87	
3.1.3	Government's online service*		43.6	102	◇
3.1.4	E-participation*		52.3	71	
3.2	**General infrastructure**		**28.6**	**58**	
3.2.1	Electricity output, GWh/mn pop.		5,639.0	38	●◆
3.2.2	Logistics performance*		40.9	60	
3.2.3	Gross capital formation, % GDP		21.8	83	
3.3	**Ecological sustainability**		**30.3**	**53**	
3.3.1	GDP/unit of energy use		6.4	104	○◇
3.3.2	Environmental performance*		34.7	75	
3.3.3	ISO 14001 environment/bn PPP$ GDP		5.6	17	●
	Market sophistication		**47.9**	**27**	●◆
4.1	**Credit**		**35.9**	**50**	
4.1.1	Finance for startups and scaleups†	⊙	50.8	44	
4.1.2	Domestic credit to private sector, % GDP		58.5	63	
4.1.3	Loans from microfinance institutions, % GDP		n/a	n/a	
4.2	**Investment**		**n/a**	**[n/a]**	
4.2.1	Market capitalization, % GDP		n/a	n/a	
4.2.2	Venture capital (VC) investors, deals/bn PPP$ GDP		n/a	n/a	
4.2.3	VC recipients, deals/bn PPP$ GDP		n/a	n/a	
4.2.4	VC received, value, % GDP		n/a	n/a	
4.3	**Trade, diversification and market scale**		**59.9**	**56**	
4.3.1	Applied tariff rate, weighted avg., %		2.9	72	
4.3.2	Domestic industry diversification		96.9	18	●◆
4.3.3	Domestic market scale, bn PPP$		62.2	100	

			Score/ Value	Rank	
	Business sophistication		**20.5**	**106**	◇
5.1	**Knowledge workers**		**30.9**	**67**	
5.1.1	Knowledge-intensive employment, %		25.2	55	
5.1.2	Firms offering formal training, %		37.9	39	
5.1.3	GERD performed by business, % GDP	⊙	0.1	64	
5.1.4	GERD financed by business, %		29.4	59	
5.1.5	Females employed w/advanced degrees, %		10.7	71	
5.2	**Innovation linkages**		**9.8**	**119**	○◇
5.2.1	University–industry R&D collaboration†		11.0	126	○◇
5.2.2	State of cluster development†		31.2	90	
5.2.3	GERD financed by abroad, % GDP		0.0	74	
5.2.4	Joint venture/strategic alliance deals/bn PPP$ GDP	⊙	0.0	79	
5.2.5	Patent families/bn PPP$ GDP		0.0	81	
5.3	**Knowledge absorption**		**20.7**	**127**	○◇
5.3.1	Intellectual property payments, % total trade		0.2	95	◇
5.3.2	High-tech imports, % total trade		6.0	103	
5.3.3	ICT services imports, % total trade		0.5	108	◇
5.3.4	FDI net inflows, % GDP		2.4	65	
5.3.5	Research talent, % in businesses	⊙	9.7	62	
	Knowledge and technology outputs		**23.1**	**64**	
6.1	**Knowledge creation**		**11.2**	**79**	
6.1.1	Patents by origin/bn PPP$ GDP		0.9	61	
6.1.2	PCT patents by origin/bn PPP$ GDP		0.1	68	
6.1.3	Utility models by origin/bn PPP$ GDP		n/a	n/a	
6.1.4	Scientific and technical articles/bn PPP$ GDP		11.8	66	
6.1.5	Citable documents H-index		5.5	98	
6.2	**Knowledge impact**		**21.0**	**100**	
6.2.1	Labor productivity growth, %		1.5	45	●
6.2.2	Unicorn valuation, % GDP		0.0	48	○◇
6.2.3	Software spending, % GDP		0.1	98	
6.2.4	High-tech manufacturing, %		16.6	73	
6.3	**Knowledge diffusion**		**37.1**	**37**	●◆
6.3.1	Intellectual property receipts, % total trade		0.1	50	
6.3.2	Production and export complexity		67.2	36	●
6.3.3	High-tech exports, % total trade		2.9	48	
6.3.4	ICT services exports, % total trade		2.2	54	
6.3.5	ISO 9001 quality/bn PPP$ GDP		23.4	6	●◆
	Creative outputs		**15.6**	**91**	
7.1	**Intangible assets**		**17.5**	**91**	
7.1.1	Intangible asset intensity, top 15, %		-27.9	76	○
7.1.2	Trademarks by origin/bn PPP$ GDP		17.9	96	◇
7.1.3	Global brand value, top 5,000, % GDP		0.0	74	○◇
7.1.4	Industrial designs by origin/bn PPP$ GDP		0.9	73	
7.2	**Creative goods and services**		**12.1**	**63**	
7.2.1	Cultural and creative services exports, % total trade		0.4	60	
7.2.2	National feature films/mn pop. 15–69		3.7	35	◆
7.2.3	Entertainment and media market/th pop. 15–69		n/a	n/a	
7.2.4	Creative goods exports, % total trade		0.4	68	
7.3	**Online creativity**		**15.2**	**96**	
7.3.1	Generic top-level domains (TLDs)/th pop. 15–69		3.4	66	
7.3.2	Country-code TLDs/th pop. 15–69		3.3	63	
7.3.3	GitHub commits/mn pop. 15–69		7.0	61	
7.3.4	Mobile app creation/bn PPP$ GDP		47.2	105	○◇

NOTES: ● indicates a strength; ○ a weakness; ◆ an income group strength; ◇ an income group weakness; * an index; † a survey question. ⊙ is used when the available economy data are older than the base year; see appendices for details, including the year of the data, at wipo.int/gii-ranking. Square brackets [ ] indicate that the data minimum coverage (DMC) requirements were not met at the sub-pillar or pillar level.

Botswana

GII 2023 rank

85

Output rank	Input rank	Income	Region	Population (mn)	GDP, PPP$ (bn)	GDP per capita, PPP$
110	61	Upper middle	SSA	2.6	47.0	19,199

			Score/ Value	Rank	
	Institutions		**63.5**	**37**	◆
1.1	**Institutional environment**		**58.0**	**42**	◆
1.1.1	Operational stability for businesses*		69.4	29	●◆
1.1.2	Government effectiveness*		46.5	51	
1.2	**Regulatory environment**		**65.8**	**58**	
1.2.1	Regulatory quality*		58.0	44	◆
1.2.2	Rule of law*		53.8	42	◆
1.2.3	Cost of redundancy dismissal		20.3	88	
1.3	**Business environment**		**66.8**	**26**	●◆
1.3.1	Policies for doing business†		75.3	17	●◆
1.3.2	Entrepreneurship policies and culture†	⊙	58.3	25	
	Human capital and research		**29.7**	**73**	
2.1	**Education**		**68.9**	**[9]**	
2.1.1	Expenditure on education, % GDP	⊙	8.1	3	●◆
2.1.2	Government funding/pupil, secondary, % GDP/cap		n/a	n/a	
2.1.3	School life expectancy, years		12.1	92	◇
2.1.4	PISA scales in reading, maths and science		n/a	n/a	
2.1.5	Pupil–teacher ratio, secondary		11.5	46	
2.2	**Tertiary education**		**17.2**	**96**	
2.2.1	Tertiary enrolment, % gross		24.7	94	◇
2.2.2	Graduates in science and engineering, %		19.7	71	
2.2.3	Tertiary inbound mobility, %		2.5	72	
2.3	**Research and development (R&D)**		**2.9**	**88**	
2.3.1	Researchers, FTE/mn pop.	⊙	185.2	83	
2.3.2	Gross expenditure on R&D, % GDP	⊙	0.6	57	
2.3.3	Global corporate R&D investors, top 3, mn USD		0.0	40	○◇
2.3.4	QS university ranking, top 3*		0.0	71	○◇
	Infrastructure		**34.2**	**85**	
3.1	**Information and communication technologies (ICTs)**		**45.6**	**105**	◇
3.1.1	ICT access*		82.0	69	
3.1.2	ICT use*		65.4	85	
3.1.3	Government's online service*		19.8	129	○◇
3.1.4	E-participation*		15.1	128	○◇
3.2	**General infrastructure**		**24.3**	**76**	
3.2.1	Electricity output, GWh/mn pop.	⊙	926.9	100	◇
3.2.2	Logistics performance*		45.5	56	
3.2.3	Gross capital formation, % GDP		25.8	45	
3.3	**Ecological sustainability**		**32.8**	**44**	
3.3.1	GDP/unit of energy use		14.3	29	●
3.3.2	Environmental performance*		59.5	33	●◆
3.3.3	ISO 14001 environment/bn PPP$ GDP		0.5	82	
	Market sophistication		**33.7**	**70**	
4.1	**Credit**		**38.2**	**44**	
4.1.1	Finance for startups and scaleups†	⊙	66.2	24	
4.1.2	Domestic credit to private sector, % GDP		39.8	81	
4.1.3	Loans from microfinance institutions, % GDP	⊙	3.0	12	●
4.2	**Investment**		**3.2**	**[90]**	
4.2.1	Market capitalization, % GDP		n/a	n/a	
4.2.2	Venture capital (VC) investors, deals/bn PPP$ GDP		n/a	n/a	
4.2.3	VC recipients, deals/bn PPP$ GDP	⊙	0.0	75	
4.2.4	VC received, value, % GDP	⊙	0.0	92	
4.3	**Trade, diversification and market scale**		**59.8**	**57**	
4.3.1	Applied tariff rate, weighted avg., %		0.8	8	●◆
4.3.2	Domestic industry diversification		83.6	67	
4.3.3	Domestic market scale, bn PPP$		47.0	112	

			Score/ Value	Rank	
	Business sophistication		**29.6**	**56**	
5.1	**Knowledge workers**		**28.8**	**74**	
5.1.1	Knowledge-intensive employment, %		23.3	61	
5.1.2	Firms offering formal training, %		n/a	n/a	
5.1.3	GERD performed by business, % GDP	⊙	0.1	63	
5.1.4	GERD financed by business, %	⊙	17.7	70	
5.1.5	Females employed w/advanced degrees, %		17.9	40	
5.2	**Innovation linkages**		**29.2**	**42**	◆
5.2.1	University–industry R&D collaboration†		57.4	39	
5.2.2	State of cluster development†		62.9	35	●◆
5.2.3	GERD financed by abroad, % GDP	⊙	0.1	33	
5.2.4	Joint venture/strategic alliance deals/bn PPP$ GDP		0.0	62	
5.2.5	Patent families/bn PPP$ GDP		0.0	95	○◇
5.3	**Knowledge absorption**		**30.7**	**77**	
5.3.1	Intellectual property payments, % total trade		0.8	51	
5.3.2	High-tech imports, % total trade		5.3	111	
5.3.3	ICT services imports, % total trade		3.0	16	●◆
5.3.4	FDI net inflows, % GDP		0.4	120	◇
5.3.5	Research talent, % in businesses	⊙	1.0	79	
	Knowledge and technology outputs		**11.0**	**117**	◇
6.1	**Knowledge creation**		**5.9**	**108**	
6.1.1	Patents by origin/bn PPP$ GDP		0.1	116	
6.1.2	PCT patents by origin/bn PPP$ GDP		0.0	101	○◇
6.1.3	Utility models by origin/bn PPP$ GDP		0.1	51	
6.1.4	Scientific and technical articles/bn PPP$ GDP		10.1	73	
6.1.5	Citable documents H-index		5.2	100	
6.2	**Knowledge impact**		**18.9**	**111**	
6.2.1	Labor productivity growth, %		−0.6	113	
6.2.2	Unicorn valuation, % GDP		0.0	48	○◇
6.2.3	Software spending, % GDP		0.1	90	
6.2.4	High-tech manufacturing, %		22.1	58	
6.3	**Knowledge diffusion**		**8.3**	**114**	◇
6.3.1	Intellectual property receipts, % total trade		0.0	90	
6.3.2	Production and export complexity		32.3	109	◇
6.3.3	High-tech exports, % total trade		0.3	101	
6.3.4	ICT services exports, % total trade		0.2	118	
6.3.5	ISO 9001 quality/bn PPP$ GDP		0.5	120	
	Creative outputs		**11.1**	**106**	◇
7.1	**Intangible assets**		**19.1**	**88**	
7.1.1	Intangible asset intensity, top 15, %		1.8	70	
7.1.2	Trademarks by origin/bn PPP$ GDP	⊙	18.2	95	◇
7.1.3	Global brand value, top 5,000, % GDP		0.0	74	○◇
7.1.4	Industrial designs by origin/bn PPP$ GDP		0.4	87	
7.2	**Creative goods and services**		**1.9**	**[104]**	
7.2.1	Cultural and creative services exports, % total trade		0.1	84	
7.2.2	National feature films/mn pop. 15–69		n/a	n/a	
7.2.3	Entertainment and media market/th pop. 15–69		n/a	n/a	
7.2.4	Creative goods exports, % total trade		0.1	92	
7.3	**Online creativity**		**4.5**	**122**	◇
7.3.1	Generic top-level domains (TLDs)/th pop. 15–69		1.1	95	
7.3.2	Country-code TLDs/th pop. 15–69		1.9	73	
7.3.3	GitHub commits/mn pop. 15–69		1.3	109	
7.3.4	Mobile app creation/bn PPP$ GDP		13.5	122	○◇

NOTES: ● indicates a strength; ○ a weakness; ◆ an income group strength; ◇ an income group weakness; * an index; † a survey question. ⊙ is used when the available economy data are older than the base year; see appendices for details, including the year of the data, at wipo.int/gii-ranking. Square brackets [ ] indicate that the data minimum coverage (DMC) requirements were not met at the sub-pillar or pillar level.

Brazil

GII 2023 rank

49

Output rank	Input rank	Income	Region	Population (mn)	GDP, PPP$ (bn)	GDP per capita, PPP$
49	59	Upper middle	LCN	215.3	3,782.8	17,684

			Score/Value	Rank
Institutions			**38.5**	**99**
1.1	**Institutional environment**		**34.9**	**91**
1.1.1	Operational stability for businesses*		45.8	79
1.1.2	Government effectiveness*		24.0	98
1.2	**Regulatory environment**		**60.3**	**70**
1.2.1	Regulatory quality*		39.2	79
1.2.2	Rule of law*		31.5	81
1.2.3	Cost of redundancy dismissal		15.4	62
1.3	**Business environment**		**20.2**	**118** ○◇
1.3.1	Policies for doing business†		31.7	103 ○
1.3.2	Entrepreneurship policies and culture†		8.7	79 ○◇
Human capital and research			**33.5**	**56**
2.1	**Education**		**50.0**	**68**
2.1.1	Expenditure on education, % GDP	⊙	6.0	19 ●
2.1.2	Government funding/pupil, secondary, % GDP/cap		21.4	44
2.1.3	School life expectancy, years		15.1	49
2.1.4	PISA scales in reading, maths and science		400.0	68 ○
2.1.5	Pupil–teacher ratio, secondary		16.3	84
2.2	**Tertiary education**		**19.8**	**90**
2.2.1	Tertiary enrolment, % gross		54.6	63
2.2.2	Graduates in science and engineering, %		17.5	90 ○
2.2.3	Tertiary inbound mobility, %		0.2	107 ○◇
2.3	**Research and development (R&D)**		**30.8**	**35** ◆
2.3.1	Researchers, FTE/mn pop.	⊙	887.7	54
2.3.2	Gross expenditure on R&D, % GDP	⊙	1.2	34 ◆
2.3.3	Global corporate R&D investors, top 3, mn USD		48.9	34 ◆
2.3.4	QS university ranking, top 3*		44.1	30 ●◆
Infrastructure			**43.5**	**58**
3.1	**Information and communication technologies (ICTs)**		**81.0**	**36** ◆
3.1.1	ICT access*		72.9	84
3.1.2	ICT use*		73.1	66
3.1.3	Government's online service*		88.5	14 ●◆
3.1.4	E-participation*		89.5	11 ●◆
3.2	**General infrastructure**		**25.6**	**70**
3.2.1	Electricity output, GWh/mn pop.		3,065.9	66
3.2.2	Logistics performance*		50.0	50
3.2.3	Gross capital formation, % GDP		18.8	104 ○
3.3	**Ecological sustainability**		**23.9**	**65**
3.3.1	GDP/unit of energy use		10.2	63
3.3.2	Environmental performance*		41.9	60
3.3.3	ISO 14001 environment/bn PPP$ GDP		0.9	69
Market sophistication			**38.1**	**50**
4.1	**Credit**		**24.1**	**80**
4.1.1	Finance for startups and scaleups†		46.6	51
4.1.2	Domestic credit to private sector, % GDP		70.0	52
4.1.3	Loans from microfinance institutions, % GDP		0.0	55 ○
4.2	**Investment**		**16.9**	**44**
4.2.1	Market capitalization, % GDP		59.8	30
4.2.2	Venture capital (VC) investors, deals/bn PPP$ GDP		0.1	53
4.2.3	VC recipients, deals/bn PPP$ GDP		0.0	46
4.2.4	VC received, value, % GDP		0.0	27
4.3	**Trade, diversification and market scale**		**73.3**	**18** ●
4.3.1	Applied tariff rate, weighted avg., %		8.4	107 ○◇
4.3.2	Domestic industry diversification		93.1	39
4.3.3	Domestic market scale, bn PPP$		3,782.8	8 ●◆

			Score/Value	Rank
Business sophistication			**37.6**	**39** ◆
5.1	**Knowledge workers**		**44.9**	**[41]**
5.1.1	Knowledge-intensive employment, %		23.9	60
5.1.2	Firms offering formal training, %		n/a	n/a
5.1.3	GERD performed by business, % GDP		n/a	n/a
5.1.4	GERD financed by business, %		43.2	39
5.1.5	Females employed w/advanced degrees, %		14.5	52
5.2	**Innovation linkages**		**23.3**	**60**
5.2.1	University–industry R&D collaboration†		38.2	78
5.2.2	State of cluster development†		47.5	50
5.2.3	GERD financed by abroad, % GDP		n/a	n/a
5.2.4	Joint venture/strategic alliance deals/bn PPP$ GDP		0.0	77
5.2.5	Patent families/bn PPP$ GDP		0.1	53
5.3	**Knowledge absorption**		**44.7**	**32** ◆
5.3.1	Intellectual property payments, % total trade		1.8	17 ●◆
5.3.2	High-tech imports, % total trade		13.5	19 ●
5.3.3	ICT services imports, % total trade		2.1	34
5.3.4	FDI net inflows, % GDP		3.1	45
5.3.5	Research talent, % in businesses	⊙	26.1	50
Knowledge and technology outputs			**26.8**	**52**
6.1	**Knowledge creation**		**21.2**	**53**
6.1.1	Patents by origin/bn PPP$ GDP		1.4	49
6.1.2	PCT patents by origin/bn PPP$ GDP		0.1	51
6.1.3	Utility models by origin/bn PPP$ GDP		0.7	26
6.1.4	Scientific and technical articles/bn PPP$ GDP		12.8	61
6.1.5	Citable documents H-index		39.4	23 ●◆
6.2	**Knowledge impact**		**37.4**	**37** ◆
6.2.1	Labor productivity growth, %		−0.1	100 ○
6.2.2	Unicorn valuation, % GDP		1.9	22 ●◆
6.2.3	Software spending, % GDP		0.3	44
6.2.4	High-tech manufacturing, %		35.6	33
6.3	**Knowledge diffusion**		**22.0**	**67**
6.3.1	Intellectual property receipts, % total trade		0.2	41
6.3.2	Production and export complexity		53.2	59
6.3.3	High-tech exports, % total trade		2.1	58
6.3.4	ICT services exports, % total trade		1.1	86
6.3.5	ISO 9001 quality/bn PPP$ GDP		4.8	56
Creative outputs			**31.2**	**46**
7.1	**Intangible assets**		**47.4**	**31**
7.1.1	Intangible asset intensity, top 15, %		64.1	30
7.1.2	Trademarks by origin/bn PPP$ GDP		100.9	13 ●◆
7.1.3	Global brand value, top 5,000, % GDP		3.6	39
7.1.4	Industrial designs by origin/bn PPP$ GDP		1.3	60
7.2	**Creative goods and services**		**5.6**	**85**
7.2.1	Cultural and creative services exports, % total trade		0.5	53
7.2.2	National feature films/mn pop. 15–69		0.8	63 ○
7.2.3	Entertainment and media market/th pop. 15–69		5.4	41
7.2.4	Creative goods exports, % total trade		0.2	80
7.3	**Online creativity**		**24.6**	**52**
7.3.1	Generic top-level domains (TLDs)/th pop. 15–69		1.8	89
7.3.2	Country-code TLDs/th pop. 15–69		9.3	42
7.3.3	GitHub commits/mn pop. 15–69		14.1	49
7.3.4	Mobile app creation/bn PPP$ GDP		73.2	40

NOTES: ● indicates a strength; ○ a weakness; ◆ an income group strength; ◇ an income group weakness; * an index; † a survey question. ⊙ is used when the available economy data are older than the base year; see appendices for details, including the year of the data, at wipo.int/gii-ranking. Square brackets [ ] indicate that the data minimum coverage (DMC) requirements were not met at the sub-pillar or pillar level.

Brunei Darussalam

GII 2023 rank **87**

Output rank	Input rank	Income	Region	Population (mn)	GDP, PPP$ (bn)	GDP per capita, PPP$
125	53	High	SEAO	0.4	31.9	74,196

			Score/ Value	Rank	
	Institutions		**72.9**	**20**	●
1.1	**Institutional environment**		**84.3**	**6**	●◆
1.1.1	Operational stability for businesses*		91.7	3	●◆
1.1.2	Government effectiveness*		76.9	15	●
1.2	**Regulatory environment**		**83.4**	**20**	●
1.2.1	Regulatory quality*		67.9	31	●
1.2.2	Rule of law*		65.8	32	●
1.2.3	Cost of redundancy dismissal		8.0	1	●◆
1.3	**Business environment**		**50.9**	**[52]**	
1.3.1	Policies for doing business†	⊙	50.9	59	
1.3.2	Entrepreneurship policies and culture†		n/a	n/a	
	Human capital and research		**33.2**	**57**	◇
2.1	**Education**		**52.2**	**63**	
2.1.1	Expenditure on education, % GDP	⊙	4.4	56	
2.1.2	Government funding/pupil, secondary, % GDP/cap	⊙	24.0	26	
2.1.3	School life expectancy, years		14.0	72	◇
2.1.4	PISA scales in reading, maths and science		423.1	53	◇
2.1.5	Pupil–teacher ratio, secondary		7.2	3	●◆
2.2	**Tertiary education**		**37.9**	**39**	
2.2.1	Tertiary enrolment, % gross		32.0	86	◇
2.2.2	Graduates in science and engineering, %		38.4	4	●◆
2.2.3	Tertiary inbound mobility, %		3.7	59	
2.3	**Research and development (R&D)**		**9.5**	**63**	◇
2.3.1	Researchers, FTE/mn pop.		n/a	n/a	
2.3.2	Gross expenditure on R&D, % GDP	⊙	0.3	80	◇
2.3.3	Global corporate R&D investors, top 3, mn USD		0.0	40	○◇
2.3.4	QS university ranking, top 3*		23.5	46	
	Infrastructure		**45.2**	**54**	◇
3.1	**Information and communication technologies (ICTs)**		**65.5**	**75**	◇
3.1.1	ICT access*		76.6	81	◇
3.1.2	ICT use*		84.6	41	
3.1.3	Government's online service*		54.4	86	◇
3.1.4	E-participation*		46.5	80	◇
3.2	**General infrastructure**		**48.3**	**20**	●
3.2.1	Electricity output, GWh/mn pop.	⊙	13,135.0	10	●
3.2.2	Logistics performance*		n/a	n/a	
3.2.3	Gross capital formation, % GDP		30.0	25	●◆
3.3	**Ecological sustainability**		**21.8**	**75**	◇
3.3.1	GDP/unit of energy use		6.9	99	
3.3.2	Environmental performance*		45.4	55	
3.3.3	ISO 14001 environment/bn PPP$ GDP		0.8	70	◇
	Market sophistication		**22.7**	**[105]**	
4.1	**Credit**		**13.5**	**[104]**	
4.1.1	Finance for startups and scaleups†		n/a	n/a	
4.1.2	Domestic credit to private sector, % GDP		39.7	82	◇
4.1.3	Loans from microfinance institutions, % GDP		n/a	n/a	
4.2	**Investment**		**4.3**	**[84]**	
4.2.1	Market capitalization, % GDP		n/a	n/a	
4.2.2	Venture capital (VC) investors, deals/bn PPP$ GDP		0.1	47	
4.2.3	VC recipients, deals/bn PPP$ GDP		n/a	n/a	
4.2.4	VC received, value, % GDP		n/a	n/a	
4.3	**Trade, diversification and market scale**		**50.2**	**86**	◇
4.3.1	Applied tariff rate, weighted avg., %		0.0	2	●◆
4.3.2	Domestic industry diversification		n/a	n/a	
4.3.3	Domestic market scale, bn PPP$		31.9	124	○

			Score/ Value	Rank	
	Business sophistication		**25.3**	**80**	◇
5.1	**Knowledge workers**		**30.7**	**[68]**	
5.1.1	Knowledge-intensive employment, %	⊙	33.5	43	
5.1.2	Firms offering formal training, %		n/a	n/a	
5.1.3	GERD performed by business, % GDP		n/a	n/a	
5.1.4	GERD financed by business, %	⊙	0.0	98	○◇
5.1.5	Females employed w/advanced degrees, %	⊙	13.0	58	◇
5.2	**Innovation linkages**		**21.4**	**66**	◇
5.2.1	University–industry R&D collaboration†	⊙	53.5	47	
5.2.2	State of cluster development†	⊙	41.7	63	
5.2.3	GERD financed by abroad, % GDP	⊙	0.0	91	◇
5.2.4	Joint venture/strategic alliance deals/bn PPP$ GDP	⊙	0.0	43	
5.2.5	Patent families/bn PPP$ GDP		0.0	68	
5.3	**Knowledge absorption**		**23.7**	**111**	◇
5.3.1	Intellectual property payments, % total trade		0.2	93	◇
5.3.2	High-tech imports, % total trade		2.8	130	○◇
5.3.3	ICT services imports, % total trade		1.1	80	
5.3.4	FDI net inflows, % GDP		3.0	47	
5.3.5	Research talent, % in businesses		n/a	n/a	
	Knowledge and technology outputs		**9.8**	**126**	○◇
6.1	**Knowledge creation**		**8.7**	**89**	◇
6.1.1	Patents by origin/bn PPP$ GDP		0.1	118	◇
6.1.2	PCT patents by origin/bn PPP$ GDP		0.0	101	○◇
6.1.3	Utility models by origin/bn PPP$ GDP		n/a	n/a	
6.1.4	Scientific and technical articles/bn PPP$ GDP		15.1	50	
6.1.5	Citable documents H-index		4.3	110	◇
6.2	**Knowledge impact**		**17.1**	**116**	◇
6.2.1	Labor productivity growth, %		−1.7	121	◇
6.2.2	Unicorn valuation, % GDP		0.0	48	○◇
6.2.3	Software spending, % GDP		0.2	62	
6.2.4	High-tech manufacturing, %		n/a	n/a	
6.3	**Knowledge diffusion**		**3.5**	**128**	○◇
6.3.1	Intellectual property receipts, % total trade		0.0	114	○◇
6.3.2	Production and export complexity		n/a	n/a	
6.3.3	High-tech exports, % total trade		0.3	98	◇
6.3.4	ICT services exports, % total trade		0.0	129	○◇
6.3.5	ISO 9001 quality/bn PPP$ GDP		2.9	76	
	Creative outputs		**4.4**	**[127]**	
7.1	**Intangible assets**		**1.5**	**[128]**	
7.1.1	Intangible asset intensity, top 15, %		n/a	n/a	
7.1.2	Trademarks by origin/bn PPP$ GDP		6.0	118	◇
7.1.3	Global brand value, top 5,000, % GDP		n/a	n/a	
7.1.4	Industrial designs by origin/bn PPP$ GDP		0.0	120	○◇
7.2	**Creative goods and services**		**0.2**	**[129]**	
7.2.1	Cultural and creative services exports, % total trade		0.0	109	○◇
7.2.2	National feature films/mn pop. 15–69		n/a	n/a	
7.2.3	Entertainment and media market/th pop. 15–69		n/a	n/a	
7.2.4	Creative goods exports, % total trade		0.0	116	
7.3	**Online creativity**		**14.4**	**101**	◇
7.3.1	Generic top-level domains (TLDs)/th pop. 15–69		8.1	46	
7.3.2	Country-code TLDs/th pop. 15–69		1.1	86	◇
7.3.3	GitHub commits/mn pop. 15–69		4.3	74	◇
7.3.4	Mobile app creation/bn PPP$ GDP		43.9	109	◇

NOTES: ● indicates a strength; ○ a weakness; ◆ an income group strength; ◇ an income group weakness; * an index; † a survey question. ⊙ is used when the available economy data are older than the base year; see appendices for details, including the year of the data, at wipo.int/gii-ranking. Square brackets [ ] indicate that the data minimum coverage (DMC) requirements were not met at the sub-pillar or pillar level.

GII 2023 rank

Bulgaria

38

Output rank	Input rank	Income	Region	Population (mn)	GDP, PPP$ (bn)	GDP per capita, PPP$
34	45	Upper middle	EUR	6.8	198.3	29,178

			Score/ Value	Rank	
	Institutions		**49.5**	**66**	
1.1	**Institutional environment**		**43.2**	**73**	
1.1.1	Operational stability for businesses*		53.5	64	
1.1.2	Government effectiveness*		32.9	80	
1.2	**Regulatory environment**		**72.4**	**39**	◆
1.2.1	Regulatory quality*		53.7	49	
1.2.2	Rule of law*		38.4	63	
1.2.3	Cost of redundancy dismissal		8.6	16	● ◆
1.3	**Business environment**		**33.0**	**94**	○
1.3.1	Policies for doing business†		38.5	90	○
1.3.2	Entrepreneurship policies and culture†	⊙	27.5	63	○
	Human capital and research		**31.1**	**66**	
2.1	**Education**		**48.8**	**71**	
2.1.1	Expenditure on education, % GDP	⊙	4.2	65	
2.1.2	Government funding/pupil, secondary, % GDP/cap		23.2	30	
2.1.3	School life expectancy, years		13.6	73	
2.1.4	PISA scales in reading, maths and science		426.7	50	
2.1.5	Pupil–teacher ratio, secondary		11.7	51	
2.2	**Tertiary education**		**33.2**	**58**	
2.2.1	Tertiary enrolment, % gross		75.4	27	
2.2.2	Graduates in science and engineering, %		19.5	76	○
2.2.3	Tertiary inbound mobility, %		7.8	34	◆
2.3	**Research and development (R&D)**		**11.3**	**57**	
2.3.1	Researchers, FTE/mn pop.		2,346.5	37	◆
2.3.2	Gross expenditure on R&D, % GDP		0.8	47	
2.3.3	Global corporate R&D investors, top 3, mn USD		0.0	40	○ ◇
2.3.4	QS university ranking, top 3*		7.4	69	
	Infrastructure		**56.2**	**28**	◆
3.1	**Information and communication technologies (ICTs)**		**78.1**	**43**	
3.1.1	ICT access*		89.5	24	●
3.1.2	ICT use*		82.0	53	
3.1.3	Government's online service*		67.9	64	
3.1.4	E-participation*		73.3	29	
3.2	**General infrastructure**		**32.5**	**48**	
3.2.1	Electricity output, GWh/mn pop.		6,856.1	29	◆
3.2.2	Logistics performance*		50.0	50	
3.2.3	Gross capital formation, % GDP		19.6	101	○
3.3	**Ecological sustainability**		**57.8**	**8**	● ◆
3.3.1	GDP/unit of energy use		8.2	86	○
3.3.2	Environmental performance*		55.9	35	◆
3.3.3	ISO 14001 environment/bn PPP$ GDP		12.7	1	● ◆
	Market sophistication		**36.7**	**60**	
4.1	**Credit**		**40.0**	**42**	
4.1.1	Finance for startups and scaleups†	⊙	61.8	29	
4.1.2	Domestic credit to private sector, % GDP		51.5	72	
4.1.3	Loans from microfinance institutions, % GDP		n/a	n/a	
4.2	**Investment**		**6.4**	**68**	
4.2.1	Market capitalization, % GDP		24.2	53	○
4.2.2	Venture capital (VC) investors, deals/bn PPP$ GDP		0.1	43	
4.2.3	VC recipients, deals/bn PPP$ GDP		0.0	56	
4.2.4	VC received, value, % GDP		0.0	75	○
4.3	**Trade, diversification and market scale**		**63.8**	**35**	
4.3.1	Applied tariff rate, weighted avg., %		1.5	20	
4.3.2	Domestic industry diversification		96.9	19	● ◆
4.3.3	Domestic market scale, bn PPP$		198.3	70	

		Score/ Value	Rank	
	Business sophistication	**36.0**	**42**	◆
5.1	**Knowledge workers**	**37.3**	**54**	
5.1.1	Knowledge-intensive employment, %	32.6	45	◆
5.1.2	Firms offering formal training, %	20.0	81	○
5.1.3	GERD performed by business, % GDP	0.5	39	
5.1.4	GERD financed by business, %	35.4	53	
5.1.5	Females employed w/advanced degrees, %	20.1	33	◆
5.2	**Innovation linkages**	**33.0**	**38**	◆
5.2.1	University–industry R&D collaboration†	48.0	53	
5.2.2	State of cluster development†	47.6	49	
5.2.3	GERD financed by abroad, % GDP	0.3	10	● ◆
5.2.4	Joint venture/strategic alliance deals/bn PPP$ GDP	0.0	47	
5.2.5	Patent families/bn PPP$ GDP	0.3	41	
5.3	**Knowledge absorption**	**37.6**	**52**	
5.3.1	Intellectual property payments, % total trade	0.6	64	
5.3.2	High-tech imports, % total trade	8.0	70	
5.3.3	ICT services imports, % total trade	1.3	67	
5.3.4	FDI net inflows, % GDP	3.6	37	
5.3.5	Research talent, % in businesses	49.8	25	◆
	Knowledge and technology outputs	**33.9**	**34**	◆
6.1	**Knowledge creation**	**18.7**	**58**	
6.1.1	Patents by origin/bn PPP$ GDP	1.2	54	
6.1.2	PCT patents by origin/bn PPP$ GDP	0.2	47	
6.1.3	Utility models by origin/bn PPP$ GDP	1.2	20	
6.1.4	Scientific and technical articles/bn PPP$ GDP	13.1	59	
6.1.5	Citable documents H-index	16.2	53	
6.2	**Knowledge impact**	**30.0**	**57**	
6.2.1	Labor productivity growth, %	2.9	20	●
6.2.2	Unicorn valuation, % GDP	0.0	48	○ ◇
6.2.3	Software spending, % GDP	0.2	74	
6.2.4	High-tech manufacturing, %	25.3	49	
6.3	**Knowledge diffusion**	**52.9**	**12**	● ◆
6.3.1	Intellectual property receipts, % total trade	0.4	29	◆
6.3.2	Production and export complexity	65.8	39	
6.3.3	High-tech exports, % total trade	5.2	35	
6.3.4	ICT services exports, % total trade	5.4	19	● ◆
6.3.5	ISO 9001 quality/bn PPP$ GDP	37.4	1	● ◆
	Creative outputs	**38.2**	**34**	◆
7.1	**Intangible assets**	**47.6**	**30**	◆
7.1.1	Intangible asset intensity, top 15, %	71.6	17	
7.1.2	Trademarks by origin/bn PPP$ GDP	78.0	19	●
7.1.3	Global brand value, top 5,000, % GDP	0.0	74	○ ◇
7.1.4	Industrial designs by origin/bn PPP$ GDP	4.7	23	◆
7.2	**Creative goods and services**	**24.7**	**42**	◆
7.2.1	Cultural and creative services exports, % total trade	1.7	16	● ◆
7.2.2	National feature films/mn pop. 15–69	4.1	33	◆
7.2.3	Entertainment and media market/th pop. 15–69	n/a	n/a	
7.2.4	Creative goods exports, % total trade	1.0	46	
7.3	**Online creativity**	**33.0**	**36**	◆
7.3.1	Generic top-level domains (TLDs)/th pop. 15–69	28.4	24	● ◆
7.3.2	Country-code TLDs/th pop. 15–69	4.6	57	
7.3.3	GitHub commits/mn pop. 15–69	27.9	36	◆
7.3.4	Mobile app creation/bn PPP$ GDP	71.2	46	

NOTES: ● indicates a strength; ○ a weakness; ◆ an income group strength; ◇ an income group weakness; * an index; † a survey question. ⊙ is used when the available economy data are older than the base year; see appendices for details, including the year of the data, at wipo.int/gii-ranking. Square brackets [ ] indicate that the data minimum coverage (DMC) requirements were not met at the sub-pillar or pillar level.

GII 2023 rank

Burkina Faso

124

Output rank	Input rank	Income	Region	Population (mn)	GDP, PPP$ (bn)	GDP per capita, PPP$
127	119	Low	SSA	22.7	58.8	2,656

			Score/ Value	Rank
	Institutions		**41.2**	**92**
1.1	**Institutional environment**		**17.4**	**125**
1.1.1	Operational stability for businesses*		18.1	125
1.1.2	Government effectiveness*		16.7	111
1.2	**Regulatory environment**		**61.8**	**67 ●**
1.2.1	Regulatory quality*		30.0	97
1.2.2	Rule of law*		26.9	89
1.2.3	Cost of redundancy dismissal		10.5	33 ●
1.3	**Business environment**		**44.6**	**71 ●**
1.3.1	Policies for doing business†	⊙	45.7	71 ●
1.3.2	Entrepreneurship policies and culture†	⊙	43.5	42 ●◆
	Human capital and research		**17.8**	**108**
2.1	**Education**		**37.9**	**105**
2.1.1	Expenditure on education, % GDP		5.2	29 ●
2.1.2	Government funding/pupil, secondary, % GDP/cap	⊙	16.2	70
2.1.3	School life expectancy, years		9.1	106
2.1.4	PISA scales in reading, maths and science		n/a	n/a
2.1.5	Pupil–teacher ratio, secondary		20.1	97
2.2	**Tertiary education**		**14.1**	**105**
2.2.1	Tertiary enrolment, % gross		9.5	116
2.2.2	Graduates in science and engineering, %		20.7	66
2.2.3	Tertiary inbound mobility, %		1.9	78
2.3	**Research and development (R&D)**		**1.4**	**94**
2.3.1	Researchers, FTE/mn pop.		n/a	n/a
2.3.2	Gross expenditure on R&D, % GDP		0.3	84
2.3.3	Global corporate R&D investors, top 3, mn USD		0.0	40 ○◇
2.3.4	QS university ranking, top 3*		0.0	71 ○◇
	Infrastructure		**19.7**	**121**
3.1	**Information and communication technologies (ICTs)**		**27.8**	**123**
3.1.1	ICT access*		36.9	120
3.1.2	ICT use*		22.8	123
3.1.3	Government's online service*		30.7	122
3.1.4	E-participation*		20.9	122
3.2	**General infrastructure**		**17.1**	**100**
3.2.1	Electricity output, GWh/mn pop.		n/a	n/a
3.2.2	Logistics performance*		9.1	106 ◇
3.2.3	Gross capital formation, % GDP		27.3	35 ●
3.3	**Ecological sustainability**		**14.1**	**108**
3.3.1	GDP/unit of energy use		n/a	n/a
3.3.2	Environmental performance*		28.1	91
3.3.3	ISO 14001 environment/bn PPP$ GDP		0.1	129 ○◇
	Market sophistication		**17.6**	**116**
4.1	**Credit**		**20.3**	**92 ◆**
4.1.1	Finance for startups and scaleups†	⊙	21.8	78
4.1.2	Domestic credit to private sector, % GDP		28.3	99 ◆
4.1.3	Loans from microfinance institutions, % GDP		2.6	15 ●◆
4.2	**Investment**		**5.0**	**[77]**
4.2.1	Market capitalization, % GDP		n/a	n/a
4.2.2	Venture capital (VC) investors, deals/bn PPP$ GDP		n/a	n/a
4.2.3	VC recipients, deals/bn PPP$ GDP	⊙	0.0	51 ●
4.2.4	VC received, value, % GDP	⊙	0.0	100 ○◇
4.3	**Trade, diversification and market scale**		**27.5**	**117**
4.3.1	Applied tariff rate, weighted avg., %		7.2	102
4.3.2	Domestic industry diversification		n/a	n/a
4.3.3	Domestic market scale, bn PPP$		58.8	102

			Score/ Value	Rank
	Business sophistication		**14.8**	**128**
5.1	**Knowledge workers**		**9.7**	**[122]**
5.1.1	Knowledge-intensive employment, %	⊙	13.3	97 ◆
5.1.2	Firms offering formal training, %		n/a	n/a
5.1.3	GERD performed by business, % GDP		n/a	n/a
5.1.4	GERD financed by business, %		n/a	n/a
5.1.5	Females employed w/advanced degrees, %	⊙	0.8	120
5.2	**Innovation linkages**		**6.0**	**128 ◇**
5.2.1	University–industry R&D collaboration†	⊙	16.7	120 ◇
5.2.2	State of cluster development†	⊙	0.0	129 ○◇
5.2.3	GERD financed by abroad, % GDP	⊙	0.0	55 ●
5.2.4	Joint venture/strategic alliance deals/bn PPP$ GDP	⊙	0.0	110 ◇
5.2.5	Patent families/bn PPP$ GDP		n/a	n/a
5.3	**Knowledge absorption**		**28.8**	**84**
5.3.1	Intellectual property payments, % total trade		0.0	113
5.3.2	High-tech imports, % total trade		4.4	121
5.3.3	ICT services imports, % total trade		2.2	29 ●◆
5.3.4	FDI net inflows, % GDP		0.4	119
5.3.5	Research talent, % in businesses		n/a	n/a
	Knowledge and technology outputs		**11.6**	**112**
6.1	**Knowledge creation**		**5.1**	**112**
6.1.1	Patents by origin/bn PPP$ GDP		0.1	113
6.1.2	PCT patents by origin/bn PPP$ GDP		0.0	101 ○◇
6.1.3	Utility models by origin/bn PPP$ GDP	⊙	0.0	75 ○◇
6.1.4	Scientific and technical articles/bn PPP$ GDP		9.9	74
6.1.5	Citable documents H-index		5.1	101
6.2	**Knowledge impact**		**19.8**	**105**
6.2.1	Labor productivity growth, %		1.4	49 ●
6.2.2	Unicorn valuation, % GDP		0.0	48 ○◇
6.2.3	Software spending, % GDP		0.0	115
6.2.4	High-tech manufacturing, %		n/a	n/a
6.3	**Knowledge diffusion**		**9.7**	**109**
6.3.1	Intellectual property receipts, % total trade		0.0	89
6.3.2	Production and export complexity		37.5	97
6.3.3	High-tech exports, % total trade		0.1	125
6.3.4	ICT services exports, % total trade		1.0	87
6.3.5	ISO 9001 quality/bn PPP$ GDP		0.5	122
	Creative outputs		**2.0**	**130 ○**
7.1	**Intangible assets**		**3.1**	**124**
7.1.1	Intangible asset intensity, top 15, %		n/a	n/a
7.1.2	Trademarks by origin/bn PPP$ GDP		6.7	116
7.1.3	Global brand value, top 5,000, % GDP		0.0	74 ○◇
7.1.4	Industrial designs by origin/bn PPP$ GDP		0.2	104
7.2	**Creative goods and services**		**1.9**	**[106]**
7.2.1	Cultural and creative services exports, % total trade		0.2	73
7.2.2	National feature films/mn pop. 15–69		n/a	n/a
7.2.3	Entertainment and media market/th pop. 15–69		n/a	n/a
7.2.4	Creative goods exports, % total trade		0.0	126
7.3	**Online creativity**		**0.1**	**132 ○◇**
7.3.1	Generic top-level domains (TLDs)/th pop. 15–69		0.1	127
7.3.2	Country-code TLDs/th pop. 15–69		0.0	128
7.3.3	GitHub commits/mn pop. 15–69		0.1	130 ○
7.3.4	Mobile app creation/bn PPP$ GDP		n/a	n/a

NOTES: ● indicates a strength; ○ a weakness; ◆ an income group strength; ◇ an income group weakness; * an index; † a survey question. ⊙ is used when the available economy data are older than the base year; see appendices for details, including the year of the data, at wipo.int/gii-ranking. Square brackets [ ] indicate that the data minimum coverage (DMC) requirements were not met at the sub-pillar or pillar level.

Burundi

GII 2023 rank

130

Output rank	Input rank	Income	Region	Population (mn)	GDP, PPP$ (bn)	GDP per capita, PPP$
130	126	Low	SSA	12.9	10.9	865

			Score/Value	Rank	
	Institutions		**36.3**	**106**	
1.1	**Institutional environment**		**13.2**	**128**	
1.1.1	Operational stability for businesses*		26.4	122	
1.1.2	Government effectiveness*		0.0	132	○ ◇
1.2	**Regulatory environment**		**46.8**	**109**	
1.2.1	Regulatory quality*		16.6	126	◇
1.2.2	Rule of law*		1.8	131	◇
1.2.3	Cost of redundancy dismissal		15.9	66	●
1.3	**Business environment**		**49.0**	**[57]**	
1.3.1	Policies for doing business†	⊙	49.0	62	●
1.3.2	Entrepreneurship policies and culture†		n/a	n/a	
	Human capital and research		**20.7**	**100**	
2.1	**Education**		**46.3**	**79**	◆
2.1.1	Expenditure on education, % GDP	⊙	5.1	39	●
2.1.2	Government funding/pupil, secondary, % GDP/cap	⊙	32.8	6	
2.1.3	School life expectancy, years	⊙	10.8	99	
2.1.4	PISA scales in reading, maths and science		n/a	n/a	
2.1.5	Pupil–teacher ratio, secondary		24.9	110	
2.2	**Tertiary education**		**14.9**	**103**	
2.2.1	Tertiary enrolment, % gross		6.0	122	
2.2.2	Graduates in science and engineering, %	⊙	19.7	73	
2.2.3	Tertiary inbound mobility, %	⊙	4.8	51	● ◆
2.3	**Research and development (R&D)**		**0.9**	**101**	
2.3.1	Researchers, FTE/mn pop.	⊙	23.4	103	
2.3.2	Gross expenditure on R&D, % GDP	⊙	0.2	86	
2.3.3	Global corporate R&D investors, top 3, mn USD		0.0	40	○ ◇
2.3.4	QS university ranking, top 3*		0.0	71	○ ◇
	Infrastructure		**17.0**	**126**	
3.1	**Information and communication technologies (ICTs)**		**17.4**	**130**	◇
3.1.1	ICT access*		10.3	130	◇
3.1.2	ICT use*		0.0	132	○ ◇
3.1.3	Government's online service*		26.8	127	
3.1.4	E-participation*		32.6	100	
3.2	**General infrastructure**		**22.1**	**[82]**	
3.2.1	Electricity output, GWh/mn pop.		n/a	n/a	
3.2.2	Logistics performance*		n/a	n/a	
3.2.3	Gross capital formation, % GDP		25.4	50	●
3.3	**Ecological sustainability**		**11.6**	**122**	
3.3.1	GDP/unit of energy use		n/a	n/a	
3.3.2	Environmental performance*		19.7	109	
3.3.3	ISO 14001 environment/bn PPP$ GDP		0.5	84	◆
	Market sophistication		**7.3**	**131**	◇
4.1	**Credit**		**5.6**	**123**	
4.1.1	Finance for startups and scaleups†		n/a	n/a	
4.1.2	Domestic credit to private sector, % GDP		23.6	112	
4.1.3	Loans from microfinance institutions, % GDP	⊙	0.3	41	
4.2	**Investment**		**n/a**	**[n/a]**	
4.2.1	Market capitalization, % GDP		n/a	n/a	
4.2.2	Venture capital (VC) investors, deals/bn PPP$ GDP		n/a	n/a	
4.2.3	VC recipients, deals/bn PPP$ GDP		n/a	n/a	
4.2.4	VC received, value, % GDP		n/a	n/a	
4.3	**Trade, diversification and market scale**		**9.0**	**131**	◇
4.3.1	Applied tariff rate, weighted avg., %		11.3	124	
4.3.2	Domestic industry diversification	⊙	0.0	111	
4.3.3	Domestic market scale, bn PPP$		10.9	131	

			Score/Value	Rank	
	Business sophistication		**16.5**	**121**	
5.1	**Knowledge workers**		**10.0**	**121**	
5.1.1	Knowledge-intensive employment, %	⊙	2.7	126	○ ◇
5.1.2	Firms offering formal training, %	⊙	32.0	50	●
5.1.3	GERD performed by business, % GDP	⊙	0.0	81	
5.1.4	GERD financed by business, %	⊙	8.8	76	◆
5.1.5	Females employed w/advanced degrees, %	⊙	0.7	122	
5.2	**Innovation linkages**		**14.4**	**99**	
5.2.1	University–industry R&D collaboration†	⊙	31.5	93	
5.2.2	State of cluster development†	⊙	26.1	103	
5.2.3	GERD financed by abroad, % GDP	⊙	0.0	96	○ ◇
5.2.4	Joint venture/strategic alliance deals/bn PPP$ GDP		n/a	n/a	
5.2.5	Patent families/bn PPP$ GDP		0.0	95	○ ◇
5.3	**Knowledge absorption**		**25.2**	**102**	
5.3.1	Intellectual property payments, % total trade		0.0	117	
5.3.2	High-tech imports, % total trade		9.8	41	● ◆
5.3.3	ICT services imports, % total trade		1.8	41	●
5.3.4	FDI net inflows, % GDP		0.2	121	
5.3.5	Research talent, % in businesses	⊙	1.5	77	
	Knowledge and technology outputs		**5.8**	**131**	◇
6.1	**Knowledge creation**		**6.7**	**102**	
6.1.1	Patents by origin/bn PPP$ GDP	⊙	0.2	96	
6.1.2	PCT patents by origin/bn PPP$ GDP		n/a	n/a	
6.1.3	Utility models by origin/bn PPP$ GDP	⊙	0.3	37	●
6.1.4	Scientific and technical articles/bn PPP$ GDP		7.1	93	
6.1.5	Citable documents H-index		1.0	129	◇
6.2	**Knowledge impact**		**8.2**	**129**	◇
6.2.1	Labor productivity growth, %		−2.2	128	◇
6.2.2	Unicorn valuation, % GDP		0.0	48	○ ◇
6.2.3	Software spending, % GDP		0.1	100	◆
6.2.4	High-tech manufacturing, %	⊙	3.9	105	
6.3	**Knowledge diffusion**		**2.6**	**130**	◇
6.3.1	Intellectual property receipts, % total trade		0.0	107	
6.3.2	Production and export complexity		n/a	n/a	
6.3.3	High-tech exports, % total trade		0.1	117	
6.3.4	ICT services exports, % total trade		0.6	100	
6.3.5	ISO 9001 quality/bn PPP$ GDP		1.4	97	◆
	Creative outputs		**4.9**	**125**	
7.1	**Intangible assets**		**2.7**	**125**	
7.1.1	Intangible asset intensity, top 15, %		n/a	n/a	
7.1.2	Trademarks by origin/bn PPP$ GDP	⊙	4.6	124	
7.1.3	Global brand value, top 5,000, % GDP		0.0	74	○ ◇
7.1.4	Industrial designs by origin/bn PPP$ GDP	⊙	0.2	102	
7.2	**Creative goods and services**		**2.4**	**[101]**	
7.2.1	Cultural and creative services exports, % total trade		0.2	72	
7.2.2	National feature films/mn pop. 15–69		n/a	n/a	
7.2.3	Entertainment and media market/th pop. 15–69		n/a	n/a	
7.2.4	Creative goods exports, % total trade		0.1	106	
7.3	**Online creativity**		**11.6**	**110**	
7.3.1	Generic top-level domains (TLDs)/th pop. 15–69		0.1	128	
7.3.2	Country-code TLDs/th pop. 15–69		0.1	120	
7.3.3	GitHub commits/mn pop. 15–69		0.2	128	
7.3.4	Mobile app creation/bn PPP$ GDP		46.2	107	

NOTES: ● indicates a strength; ○ a weakness; ◆ an income group strength; ◇ an income group weakness; * an index; † a survey question. ⊙ is used when the available economy data are older than the base year; see appendices for details, including the year of the data, at wipo.int/gii-ranking. Square brackets [ ] indicate that the data minimum coverage (DMC) requirements were not met at the sub-pillar or pillar level.

GII 2023 rank

Cabo Verde

91

Output rank	Input rank	Income	Region	Population (mn)	GDP, PPP$ (bn)	GDP per capita, PPP$
106	74	Lower middle	SSA	0.6	4.8	8,460

			Score/ Value	Rank	
	Institutions		**59.7**	**44**	●◆
1.1	**Institutional environment**		**51.3**	**52**	◆
1.1.1	Operational stability for businesses*		64.6	37	●◆
1.1.2	Government effectiveness*		37.9	67	◆
1.2	**Regulatory environment**		**65.5**	**60**	◆
1.2.1	Regulatory quality*		49.2	57	◆
1.2.2	Rule of law*		50.0	50	●◆
1.2.3	Cost of redundancy dismissal		17.4	75	
1.3	**Business environment**		**62.2**	**[30]**	
1.3.1	Policies for doing business†		62.2	35	●◆
1.3.2	Entrepreneurship policies and culture†		n/a	n/a	
	Human capital and research		**21.3**	**97**	
2.1	**Education**		**51.1**	**66**	
2.1.1	Expenditure on education, % GDP		6.5	13	●◆
2.1.2	Government funding/pupil, secondary, % GDP/cap		16.1	71	
2.1.3	School life expectancy, years	⊙	12.7	88	
2.1.4	PISA scales in reading, maths and science		n/a	n/a	
2.1.5	Pupil–teacher ratio, secondary	⊙	15.3	79	
2.2	**Tertiary education**		**12.5**	**106**	
2.2.1	Tertiary enrolment, % gross	⊙	23.6	96	
2.2.2	Graduates in science and engineering, %	⊙	16.1	94	
2.2.3	Tertiary inbound mobility, %	⊙	1.4	83	
2.3	**Research and development (R&D)**		**0.4**	**112**	
2.3.1	Researchers, FTE/mn pop.	⊙	123.5	88	
2.3.2	Gross expenditure on R&D, % GDP		n/a	n/a	
2.3.3	Global corporate R&D investors, top 3, mn USD		0.0	40	○◇
2.3.4	QS university ranking, top 3*		0.0	71	○◇
	Infrastructure		**41.1**	**64**	◆
3.1	**Information and communication technologies (ICTs)**		**48.6**	**101**	
3.1.1	ICT access*		68.6	91	
3.1.2	ICT use*		58.3	96	
3.1.3	Government's online service*		44.4	99	
3.1.4	E-participation*		23.3	115	
3.2	**General infrastructure**		**53.7**	**[11]**	
3.2.1	Electricity output, GWh/mn pop.		n/a	n/a	
3.2.2	Logistics performance*		n/a	n/a	
3.2.3	Gross capital formation, % GDP		44.7	3	●◆
3.3	**Ecological sustainability**		**21.1**	**78**	
3.3.1	GDP/unit of energy use		n/a	n/a	
3.3.2	Environmental performance*		39.0	67	◆
3.3.3	ISO 14001 environment/bn PPP$ GDP		0.5	88	
	Market sophistication		**24.7**	**[96]**	
4.1	**Credit**		**26.7**	**[73]**	
4.1.1	Finance for startups and scaleups†		n/a	n/a	
4.1.2	Domestic credit to private sector, % GDP		73.2	48	●
4.1.3	Loans from microfinance institutions, % GDP		n/a	n/a	
4.2	**Investment**		**n/a**	**[n/a]**	
4.2.1	Market capitalization, % GDP		n/a	n/a	
4.2.2	Venture capital (VC) investors, deals/bn PPP$ GDP		n/a	n/a	
4.2.3	VC recipients, deals/bn PPP$ GDP		n/a	n/a	
4.2.4	VC received, value, % GDP		n/a	n/a	
4.3	**Trade, diversification and market scale**		**22.7**	**124**	◇
4.3.1	Applied tariff rate, weighted avg., %		12.2	128	○◇
4.3.2	Domestic industry diversification	⊙	47.0	105	○◇
4.3.3	Domestic market scale, bn PPP$		4.8	132	○◇

			Score/ Value	Rank	
	Business sophistication		**28.4**	**[65]**	
5.1	**Knowledge workers**		**23.8**	**[82]**	
5.1.1	Knowledge-intensive employment, %	⊙	17.1	84	
5.1.2	Firms offering formal training, %		n/a	n/a	
5.1.3	GERD performed by business, % GDP		n/a	n/a	
5.1.4	GERD financed by business, %		n/a	n/a	
5.1.5	Females employed w/advanced degrees, %	⊙	7.6	86	
5.2	**Innovation linkages**		**23.1**	**[63]**	
5.2.1	University–industry R&D collaboration†		35.5	85	
5.2.2	State of cluster development†		33.8	86	
5.2.3	GERD financed by abroad, % GDP		n/a	n/a	
5.2.4	Joint venture/strategic alliance deals/bn PPP$ GDP		n/a	n/a	
5.2.5	Patent families/bn PPP$ GDP		0.0	95	○◇
5.3	**Knowledge absorption**		**38.2**	**50**	●◆
5.3.1	Intellectual property payments, % total trade		0.5	68	
5.3.2	High-tech imports, % total trade	⊙	6.8	91	
5.3.3	ICT services imports, % total trade		2.7	24	●◆
5.3.4	FDI net inflows, % GDP		5.2	17	●
5.3.5	Research talent, % in businesses		n/a	n/a	
	Knowledge and technology outputs		**13.8**	**98**	
6.1	**Knowledge creation**		**9.2**	**[84]**	
6.1.1	Patents by origin/bn PPP$ GDP		0.2	94	
6.1.2	PCT patents by origin/bn PPP$ GDP		n/a	n/a	
6.1.3	Utility models by origin/bn PPP$ GDP		n/a	n/a	
6.1.4	Scientific and technical articles/bn PPP$ GDP		12.0	64	
6.1.5	Citable documents H-index		0.0	132	○◇
6.2	**Knowledge impact**		**25.2**	**72**	
6.2.1	Labor productivity growth, %		2.2	30	●
6.2.2	Unicorn valuation, % GDP		0.0	48	○◇
6.2.3	Software spending, % GDP		0.3	53	
6.2.4	High-tech manufacturing, %	⊙	10.0	92	
6.3	**Knowledge diffusion**		**7.1**	**121**	
6.3.1	Intellectual property receipts, % total trade		0.0	97	
6.3.2	Production and export complexity		n/a	n/a	
6.3.3	High-tech exports, % total trade	⊙	0.0	132	○◇
6.3.4	ICT services exports, % total trade		1.2	82	
6.3.5	ISO 9001 quality/bn PPP$ GDP		7.4	36	●◆
	Creative outputs		**9.2**	**[108]**	
7.1	**Intangible assets**		**14.5**	**[99]**	
7.1.1	Intangible asset intensity, top 15, %		n/a	n/a	
7.1.2	Trademarks by origin/bn PPP$ GDP		15.0	99	
7.1.3	Global brand value, top 5,000, % GDP		n/a	n/a	
7.1.4	Industrial designs by origin/bn PPP$ GDP	⊙	1.0	67	
7.2	**Creative goods and services**		**5.7**	**[84]**	
7.2.1	Cultural and creative services exports, % total trade		0.6	50	
7.2.2	National feature films/mn pop. 15–69		n/a	n/a	
7.2.3	Entertainment and media market/th pop. 15–69		n/a	n/a	
7.2.4	Creative goods exports, % total trade	⊙	0.0	130	○
7.3	**Online creativity**		**2.3**	**124**	◇
7.3.1	Generic top-level domains (TLDs)/th pop. 15–69		2.1	81	
7.3.2	Country-code TLDs/th pop. 15–69		2.3	69	
7.3.3	GitHub commits/mn pop. 15–69		2.4	97	
7.3.4	Mobile app creation/bn PPP$ GDP		n/a	n/a	

NOTES: ● indicates a strength; ○ a weakness; ◆ an income group strength; ◇ an income group weakness; * an index; † a survey question. ⊙ is used when the available economy data are older than the base year; see appendices for details, including the year of the data, at wipo.int/gii-ranking. Square brackets [ ] indicate that the data minimum coverage (DMC) requirements were not met at the sub-pillar or pillar level.

GII 2023 rank

Cambodia **101**

Output rank	Input rank	Income	Region	Population (mn)	GDP, PPP$ (bn)	GDP per capita, PPP$
100	97	Lower middle	SEAO	16.8	89.3	5,583

		Score/ Value	Rank
	Institutions	**44.2**	**87**
1.1	**Institutional environment**	**41.4**	**74**
1.1.1	Operational stability for businesses*	57.6	53 ●◆
1.1.2	Government effectiveness*	25.1	96
1.2	**Regulatory environment**	**48.4**	**104**
1.2.1	Regulatory quality*	25.4	110
1.2.2	Rule of law*	13.4	116
1.2.3	Cost of redundancy dismissal	19.4	84
1.3	**Business environment**	**42.8**	**[74]**
1.3.1	Policies for doing business†	42.8	78
1.3.2	Entrepreneurship policies and culture†	n/a	n/a

		Score/ Value	Rank
	Human capital and research	**20.5**	**101**
2.1	**Education**	**45.2**	**[81]**
2.1.1	Expenditure on education, % GDP	1.7	124 ○◇
2.1.2	Government funding/pupil, secondary, % GDP/cap	n/a	n/a
2.1.3	School life expectancy, years	n/a	n/a
2.1.4	PISA scales in reading, maths and science	n/a	n/a
2.1.5	Pupil–teacher ratio, secondary	9.9	31 ●◆
2.2	**Tertiary education**	**15.9**	**100**
2.2.1	Tertiary enrolment, % gross	13.0	107
2.2.2	Graduates in science and engineering, % ⊙	23.2	53
2.2.3	Tertiary inbound mobility, %	0.3	106 ○
2.3	**Research and development (R&D)**	**0.5**	**109**
2.3.1	Researchers, FTE/mn pop. ⊙	30.4	99
2.3.2	Gross expenditure on R&D, % GDP ⊙	0.1	102
2.3.3	Global corporate R&D investors, top 3, mn USD	0.0	40 ○◇
2.3.4	QS university ranking, top 3*	0.0	71 ○◇

		Score/ Value	Rank
	Infrastructure	**25.1**	**108**
3.1	**Information and communication technologies (ICTs)**	**49.9**	**100**
3.1.1	ICT access*	70.5	89
3.1.2	ICT use*	66.5	79
3.1.3	Government's online service*	35.7	116
3.1.4	E-participation*	26.7	106
3.2	**General infrastructure**	**12.6**	**117**
3.2.1	Electricity output, GWh/mn pop. ⊙	537.1	109
3.2.2	Logistics performance*	13.6	103 ○
3.2.3	Gross capital formation, % GDP	25.0	54 ●
3.3	**Ecological sustainability**	**12.7**	**115**
3.3.1	GDP/unit of energy use	7.9	88
3.3.2	Environmental performance*	19.0	112
3.3.3	ISO 14001 environment/bn PPP$ GDP	0.4	95

		Score/ Value	Rank
	Market sophistication	**36.7**	**59 ●**
4.1	**Credit**	**76.5**	**3 ●◆**
4.1.1	Finance for startups and scaleups†	n/a	n/a
4.1.2	Domestic credit to private sector, % GDP	139.6	13 ●◆
4.1.3	Loans from microfinance institutions, % GDP	28.7	1 ●◆
4.2	**Investment**	**2.9**	**94**
4.2.1	Market capitalization, % GDP	n/a	n/a
4.2.2	Venture capital (VC) investors, deals/bn PPP$ GDP	0.0	75
4.2.3	VC recipients, deals/bn PPP$ GDP	0.0	71
4.2.4	VC received, value, % GDP	0.0	89
4.3	**Trade, diversification and market scale**	**30.8**	**114**
4.3.1	Applied tariff rate, weighted avg., %	6.2	98
4.3.2	Domestic industry diversification	n/a	n/a
4.3.3	Domestic market scale, bn PPP$	89.3	90

		Score/ Value	Rank
	Business sophistication	**16.2**	**125 ○◇**
5.1	**Knowledge workers**	**11.6**	**118 ◇**
5.1.1	Knowledge-intensive employment, % ⊙	5.9	118 ○◇
5.1.2	Firms offering formal training, % ⊙	22.2	71
5.1.3	GERD performed by business, % GDP ⊙	0.0	83
5.1.4	GERD financed by business, % ⊙	19.4	67
5.1.5	Females employed w/advanced degrees, % ⊙	2.1	108
5.2	**Innovation linkages**	**15.6**	**94**
5.2.1	University–industry R&D collaboration†	26.2	103
5.2.2	State of cluster development†	37.4	82
5.2.3	GERD financed by abroad, % GDP ⊙	0.0	52 ◆
5.2.4	Joint venture/strategic alliance deals/bn PPP$ GDP	0.0	57 ●
5.2.5	Patent families/bn PPP$ GDP	0.0	86
5.3	**Knowledge absorption**	**21.3**	**124 ○**
5.3.1	Intellectual property payments, % total trade	0.1	102
5.3.2	High-tech imports, % total trade	4.6	120
5.3.3	ICT services imports, % total trade	0.7	99
5.3.4	FDI net inflows, % GDP	13.5	9 ●◆
5.3.5	Research talent, % in businesses ⊙	4.3	71

		Score/ Value	Rank
	Knowledge and technology outputs	**14.6**	**93**
6.1	**Knowledge creation**	**3.3**	**120**
6.1.1	Patents by origin/bn PPP$ GDP ⊙	0.0	129 ○
6.1.2	PCT patents by origin/bn PPP$ GDP	0.0	101 ○◇
6.1.3	Utility models by origin/bn PPP$ GDP	n/a	n/a
6.1.4	Scientific and technical articles/bn PPP$ GDP	4.5	110
6.1.5	Citable documents H-index	5.1	101
6.2	**Knowledge impact**	**23.6**	**87**
6.2.1	Labor productivity growth, %	2.6	22 ●
6.2.2	Unicorn valuation, % GDP	0.0	48 ○◇
6.2.3	Software spending, % GDP	0.0	114 ◇
6.2.4	High-tech manufacturing, %	n/a	n/a
6.3	**Knowledge diffusion**	**16.9**	**89**
6.3.1	Intellectual property receipts, % total trade	0.0	79
6.3.2	Production and export complexity	48.3	72
6.3.3	High-tech exports, % total trade	1.7	65
6.3.4	ICT services exports, % total trade	0.3	109
6.3.5	ISO 9001 quality/bn PPP$ GDP	2.6	78

		Score/ Value	Rank
	Creative outputs	**11.6**	**103**
7.1	**Intangible assets**	**10.7**	**106**
7.1.1	Intangible asset intensity, top 15, %	n/a	n/a
7.1.2	Trademarks by origin/bn PPP$ GDP ⊙	39.5	59
7.1.3	Global brand value, top 5,000, % GDP	0.0	74 ○◇
7.1.4	Industrial designs by origin/bn PPP$ GDP ⊙	0.3	99
7.2	**Creative goods and services**	**6.7**	**[79]**
7.2.1	Cultural and creative services exports, % total trade	n/a	n/a
7.2.2	National feature films/mn pop. 15–69	n/a	n/a
7.2.3	Entertainment and media market/th pop. 15–69	n/a	n/a
7.2.4	Creative goods exports, % total trade	0.6	60 ●
7.3	**Online creativity**	**18.3**	**77**
7.3.1	Generic top-level domains (TLDs)/th pop. 15–69	0.8	101
7.3.2	Country-code TLDs/th pop. 15–69	0.1	123
7.3.3	GitHub commits/mn pop. 15–69	1.7	103
7.3.4	Mobile app creation/bn PPP$ GDP	70.4	54 ●

NOTES: ● indicates a strength; ○ a weakness; ◆ an income group strength; ◇ an income group weakness; * an index; † a survey question. ⊙ is used when the available economy data are older than the base year; see appendices for details, including the year of the data, at wipo.int/gii-ranking. Square brackets [ ] indicate that the data minimum coverage (DMC) requirements were not met at the sub-pillar or pillar level.

Cameroon

GII 2023 rank **123**

Output rank	Input rank	Income	Region	Population (mn)	GDP, PPP$ (bn)	GDP per capita, PPP$
117	123	Lower middle	SSA	27.9	123.3	4,419

			Score/Value	Rank	
	Institutions		**41.3**	**91**	
1.1	**Institutional environment**		**21.6**	**122**	
1.1.1	Operational stability for businesses*		30.6	117	
1.1.2	Government effectiveness*		12.6	123	
1.2	**Regulatory environment**		**44.7**	**111**	
1.2.1	Regulatory quality*		18.2	122	
1.2.2	Rule of law*		7.6	125	◇
1.2.3	Cost of redundancy dismissal		19.9	86	
1.3	**Business environment**		**57.5**	**40**	●
1.3.1	Policies for doing business†		47.5	64	●
1.3.2	Entrepreneurship policies and culture†	⊙	67.6	16	
	Human capital and research		**16.2**	**[112]**	
2.1	**Education**		**41.5**	**[95]**	
2.1.1	Expenditure on education, % GDP		2.8	110	
2.1.2	Government funding/pupil, secondary, % GDP/cap		n/a	n/a	
2.1.3	School life expectancy, years	⊙	12.1	94	
2.1.4	PISA scales in reading, maths and science		n/a	n/a	
2.1.5	Pupil–teacher ratio, secondary		17.5	88	
2.2	**Tertiary education**		**7.0**	**117**	◇
2.2.1	Tertiary enrolment, % gross	⊙	14.3	106	
2.2.2	Graduates in science and engineering, %		n/a	n/a	
2.2.3	Tertiary inbound mobility, %	⊙	2.8	70	
2.3	**Research and development (R&D)**		**0.0**	**[119]**	
2.3.1	Researchers, FTE/mn pop.		n/a	n/a	
2.3.2	Gross expenditure on R&D, % GDP		n/a	n/a	
2.3.3	Global corporate R&D investors, top 3, mn USD		0.0	40	○◇
2.3.4	QS university ranking, top 3*		0.0	71	○◇
	Infrastructure		**15.0**	**130**	○◇
3.1	**Information and communication technologies (ICTs)**		**27.2**	**124**	◇
3.1.1	ICT access*		10.6	129	○◇
3.1.2	ICT use*		38.9	110	
3.1.3	Government's online service*		32.8	118	
3.1.4	E-participation*		26.7	106	
3.2	**General infrastructure**		**4.2**	**131**	○◇
3.2.1	Electricity output, GWh/mn pop.	⊙	339.4	115	
3.2.2	Logistics performance*		0.0	111	○◇
3.2.3	Gross capital formation, % GDP		18.6	105	
3.3	**Ecological sustainability**		**13.4**	**112**	
3.3.1	GDP/unit of energy use		9.2	80	
3.3.2	Environmental performance*		19.2	111	
3.3.3	ISO 14001 environment/bn PPP$ GDP		0.1	122	
	Market sophistication		**9.0**	**129**	○◇
4.1	**Credit**		**23.5**	**84**	
4.1.1	Finance for startups and scaleups†	⊙	54.5	39	
4.1.2	Domestic credit to private sector, % GDP	⊙	14.7	120	
4.1.3	Loans from microfinance institutions, % GDP	⊙	1.0	27	●
4.2	**Investment**		**2.1**	**101**	
4.2.1	Market capitalization, % GDP		n/a	n/a	
4.2.2	Venture capital (VC) investors, deals/bn PPP$ GDP	⊙	0.0	77	
4.2.3	VC recipients, deals/bn PPP$ GDP		0.0	85	
4.2.4	VC received, value, % GDP		0.0	82	
4.3	**Trade, diversification and market scale**		**1.3**	**132**	○◇
4.3.1	Applied tariff rate, weighted avg., %	⊙	15.5	132	○◇
4.3.2	Domestic industry diversification		n/a	n/a	
4.3.3	Domestic market scale, bn PPP$		123.3	84	

			Score/Value	Rank	
	Business sophistication		**23.2**	**88**	
5.1	**Knowledge workers**		**21.5**	**[93]**	
5.1.1	Knowledge-intensive employment, %	⊙	10.9	104	
5.1.2	Firms offering formal training, %	⊙	37.6	40	●
5.1.3	GERD performed by business, % GDP		n/a	n/a	
5.1.4	GERD financed by business, %		n/a	n/a	
5.1.5	Females employed w/advanced degrees, %	⊙	2.0	110	
5.2	**Innovation linkages**		**19.8**	**74**	
5.2.1	University–industry R&D collaboration†		46.6	58	●
5.2.2	State of cluster development†		31.2	91	
5.2.3	GERD financed by abroad, % GDP		n/a	n/a	
5.2.4	Joint venture/strategic alliance deals/bn PPP$ GDP		0.0	118	
5.2.5	Patent families/bn PPP$ GDP		0.0	95	○◇
5.3	**Knowledge absorption**		**28.3**	**86**	
5.3.1	Intellectual property payments, % total trade		0.0	109	
5.3.2	High-tech imports, % total trade	⊙	6.1	101	
5.3.3	ICT services imports, % total trade		1.7	50	●
5.3.4	FDI net inflows, % GDP		2.1	69	●
5.3.5	Research talent, % in businesses		n/a	n/a	
	Knowledge and technology outputs		**12.9**	**104**	
6.1	**Knowledge creation**		**8.7**	**90**	
6.1.1	Patents by origin/bn PPP$ GDP		0.6	75	
6.1.2	PCT patents by origin/bn PPP$ GDP		0.0	80	
6.1.3	Utility models by origin/bn PPP$ GDP		0.0	75	○◇
6.1.4	Scientific and technical articles/bn PPP$ GDP		12.8	62	●
6.1.5	Citable documents H-index		7.8	87	
6.2	**Knowledge impact**		**21.2**	**99**	
6.2.1	Labor productivity growth, %		0.8	72	
6.2.2	Unicorn valuation, % GDP		0.0	48	○◇
6.2.3	Software spending, % GDP		0.1	85	
6.2.4	High-tech manufacturing, %		n/a	n/a	
6.3	**Knowledge diffusion**		**8.7**	**113**	
6.3.1	Intellectual property receipts, % total trade		0.0	78	
6.3.2	Production and export complexity		18.6	117	○◇
6.3.3	High-tech exports, % total trade	⊙	0.2	107	
6.3.4	ICT services exports, % total trade		2.3	51	●
6.3.5	ISO 9001 quality/bn PPP$ GDP		0.7	115	
	Creative outputs		**6.4**	**118**	◇
7.1	**Intangible assets**		**3.9**	**121**	◇
7.1.1	Intangible asset intensity, top 15, %		n/a	n/a	
7.1.2	Trademarks by origin/bn PPP$ GDP		7.0	115	
7.1.3	Global brand value, top 5,000, % GDP		0.0	74	○◇
7.1.4	Industrial designs by origin/bn PPP$ GDP		0.3	94	
7.2	**Creative goods and services**		**3.4**	**[92]**	
7.2.1	Cultural and creative services exports, % total trade		0.3	64	
7.2.2	National feature films/mn pop. 15–69		n/a	n/a	
7.2.3	Entertainment and media market/th pop. 15–69		n/a	n/a	
7.2.4	Creative goods exports, % total trade	⊙	0.0	123	
7.3	**Online creativity**		**14.5**	**100**	
7.3.1	Generic top-level domains (TLDs)/th pop. 15–69		0.2	118	
7.3.2	Country-code TLDs/th pop. 15–69		0.9	92	
7.3.3	GitHub commits/mn pop. 15–69		1.3	111	
7.3.4	Mobile app creation/bn PPP$ GDP		55.5	95	

NOTES: ● indicates a strength; ○ a weakness; ◆ an income group strength; ◇ an income group weakness; * an index; † a survey question. ⊙ is used when the available economy data are older than the base year; see appendices for details, including the year of the data, at wipo.int/gii-ranking. Square brackets [ ] indicate that the data minimum coverage (DMC) requirements were not met at the sub-pillar or pillar level.

Canada

GII 2023 rank

15

Output rank	Input rank	Income	Region	Population (mn)	GDP, PPP$ (bn)	GDP per capita, PPP$
20	9	High	NAC	38.5	2,240.4	57,827

		Score/Value	Rank	
	Institutions	**78.0**	**14**	
1.1	**Institutional environment**	**78.4**	**13**	
1.1.1	Operational stability for businesses*	75.7	15	
1.1.2	Government effectiveness*	81.0	10	●
1.2	**Regulatory environment**	**90.9**	**9**	●
1.2.1	Regulatory quality*	84.1	12	
1.2.2	Rule of law*	87.4	13	
1.2.3	Cost of redundancy dismissal	10.0	29	
1.3	**Business environment**	**64.8**	**28**	
1.3.1	Policies for doing business†	68.8	28	
1.3.2	Entrepreneurship policies and culture†	60.8	23	

		Score/Value	Rank	
	Human capital and research	**58.1**	**10**	●
2.1	**Education**	**68.7**	**10**	●
2.1.1	Expenditure on education, % GDP	⊙ 4.8	44	
2.1.2	Government funding/pupil, secondary, % GDP/cap	n/a	n/a	
2.1.3	School life expectancy, years	16.6	22	
2.1.4	PISA scales in reading, maths and science	516.7	7	
2.1.5	Pupil–teacher ratio, secondary	9.6	25	
2.2	**Tertiary education**	**49.4**	**10**	
2.2.1	Tertiary enrolment, % gross	79.5	26	
2.2.2	Graduates in science and engineering, %	25.7	42	
2.2.3	Tertiary inbound mobility, %	18.2	8	●
2.3	**Research and development (R&D)**	**56.0**	**18**	
2.3.1	Researchers, FTE/mn pop.	⊙ 4,860.5	19	
2.3.2	Gross expenditure on R&D, % GDP	1.6	25	
2.3.3	Global corporate R&D investors, top 3, mn USD	64.9	20	
2.3.4	QS university ranking, top 3*	81.2	7	●

		Score/Value	Rank	
	Infrastructure	**56.0**	**30**	◇
3.1	**Information and communication technologies (ICTs)**	**82.3**	**31**	
3.1.1	ICT access*	79.5	73	○◇
3.1.2	ICT use*	83.6	48	◇
3.1.3	Government's online service*	83.5	27	
3.1.4	E-participation*	82.6	14	
3.2	**General infrastructure**	**63.6**	**5**	●◆
3.2.1	Electricity output, GWh/mn pop.	16,810.1	6	●◆
3.2.2	Logistics performance*	86.4	7	
3.2.3	Gross capital formation, % GDP	23.3	70	○
3.3	**Ecological sustainability**	**22.2**	**73**	○◇
3.3.1	GDP/unit of energy use	5.9	107	○◇
3.3.2	Environmental performance*	52.7	42	
3.3.3	ISO 14001 environment/bn PPP$ GDP	0.4	91	○◇

		Score/Value	Rank	
	Market sophistication	**68.1**	**4**	●◆
4.1	**Credit**	**64.8**	**[10]**	
4.1.1	Finance for startups and scaleups†	64.8	26	
4.1.2	Domestic credit to private sector, % GDP	n/a	n/a	
4.1.3	Loans from microfinance institutions, % GDP	n/a	n/a	
4.2	**Investment**	**60.7**	**9**	
4.2.1	Market capitalization, % GDP	137.0	8	
4.2.2	Venture capital (VC) investors, deals/bn PPP$ GDP	0.5	12	
4.2.3	VC recipients, deals/bn PPP$ GDP	0.4	1	●◆
4.2.4	VC received, value, % GDP	0.0	10	
4.3	**Trade, diversification and market scale**	**78.8**	**13**	
4.3.1	Applied tariff rate, weighted avg., %	1.5	47	
4.3.2	Domestic industry diversification	97.8	11	
4.3.3	Domestic market scale, bn PPP$	2,240.4	15	

		Score/Value	Rank	
	Business sophistication	**56.0**	**18**	
5.1	**Knowledge workers**	**50.7**	**28**	◇
5.1.1	Knowledge-intensive employment, %	⊙ 43.7	25	
5.1.2	Firms offering formal training, %	n/a	n/a	
5.1.3	GERD performed by business, % GDP	0.9	28	
5.1.4	GERD financed by business, %	44.1	37	◇
5.1.5	Females employed w/advanced degrees, %	20.0	35	
5.2	**Innovation linkages**	**65.7**	**6**	●
5.2.1	University–industry R&D collaboration†	85.8	7	●
5.2.2	State of cluster development†	77.5	15	
5.2.3	GERD financed by abroad, % GDP	0.2	28	
5.2.4	Joint venture/strategic alliance deals/bn PPP$ GDP	0.3	1	●◆
5.2.5	Patent families/bn PPP$ GDP	2.0	19	
5.3	**Knowledge absorption**	**51.6**	**16**	
5.3.1	Intellectual property payments, % total trade	2.6	10	
5.3.2	High-tech imports, % total trade	10.3	32	
5.3.3	ICT services imports, % total trade	1.4	63	○◇
5.3.4	FDI net inflows, % GDP	2.6	58	○
5.3.5	Research talent, % in businesses	⊙ 60.5	14	

		Score/Value	Rank	
	Knowledge and technology outputs	**43.9**	**19**	
6.1	**Knowledge creation**	**49.0**	**16**	
6.1.1	Patents by origin/bn PPP$ GDP	2.3	32	
6.1.2	PCT patents by origin/bn PPP$ GDP	1.2	24	◇
6.1.3	Utility models by origin/bn PPP$ GDP	n/a	n/a	
6.1.4	Scientific and technical articles/bn PPP$ GDP	30.3	21	
6.1.5	Citable documents H-index	80.0	4	●◆
6.2	**Knowledge impact**	**47.8**	**21**	
6.2.1	Labor productivity growth, %	0.2	94	○
6.2.2	Unicorn valuation, % GDP	2.2	17	
6.2.3	Software spending, % GDP	0.7	5	●
6.2.4	High-tech manufacturing, %	34.7	34	
6.3	**Knowledge diffusion**	**34.9**	**41**	
6.3.1	Intellectual property receipts, % total trade	1.3	18	
6.3.2	Production and export complexity	64.4	43	◇
6.3.3	High-tech exports, % total trade	5.8	33	
6.3.4	ICT services exports, % total trade	2.1	55	
6.3.5	ISO 9001 quality/bn PPP$ GDP	2.7	77	○◇

		Score/Value	Rank	
	Creative outputs	**44.7**	**22**	
7.1	**Intangible assets**	**39.6**	**43**	◇
7.1.1	Intangible asset intensity, top 15, %	67.6	23	
7.1.2	Trademarks by origin/bn PPP$ GDP	32.8	71	○
7.1.3	Global brand value, top 5,000, % GDP	11.4	15	
7.1.4	Industrial designs by origin/bn PPP$ GDP	0.4	91	○◇
7.2	**Creative goods and services**	**32.3**	**23**	
7.2.1	Cultural and creative services exports, % total trade	1.5	20	
7.2.2	National feature films/mn pop. 15–69	4.3	30	
7.2.3	Entertainment and media market/th pop. 15–69	62.2	9	
7.2.4	Creative goods exports, % total trade	0.8	53	
7.3	**Online creativity**	**67.4**	**10**	●
7.3.1	Generic top-level domains (TLDs)/th pop. 15–69	99.0	3	●◆
7.3.2	Country-code TLDs/th pop. 15–69	35.8	19	
7.3.3	GitHub commits/mn pop. 15–69	61.7	12	
7.3.4	Mobile app creation/bn PPP$ GDP	73.0	41	

NOTES: ● indicates a strength; ○ a weakness; ◆ an income group strength; ◇ an income group weakness; * an index; † a survey question. ⊙ is used when the available economy data are older than the base year; see appendices for details, including the year of the data, at wipo.int/gii-ranking. Square brackets [ ] indicate that the data minimum coverage (DMC) requirements were not met at the sub-pillar or pillar level.

GII 2023 rank

Chile

52

Output rank	Input rank	Income	Region	Population (mn)	GDP, PPP$ (bn)	GDP per capita, PPP$
56	48	High	LCN	19.6	575.5	28,888

			Score/Value	Rank	
	Institutions		**56.7**	**49**	
1.1	**Institutional environment**		**56.5**	**43**	
1.1.1	Operational stability for businesses*		59.0	48	
1.1.2	Government effectiveness*		54.0	43	
1.2	**Regulatory environment**		**64.1**	**62**	◇
1.2.1	Regulatory quality*		66.8	32	
1.2.2	Rule of law*		66.5	31	
1.2.3	Cost of redundancy dismissal		27.4	111	○◇
1.3	**Business environment**		**49.4**	**55**	
1.3.1	Policies for doing business†		46.8	65	
1.3.2	Entrepreneurship policies and culture†		51.9	31	
	Human capital and research		**33.0**	**58**	◇
2.1	**Education**		**52.8**	**62**	
2.1.1	Expenditure on education, % GDP	⊙	5.6	22	●
2.1.2	Government funding/pupil, secondary, % GDP/cap		19.9	55	
2.1.3	School life expectancy, years		16.6	24	●
2.1.4	PISA scales in reading, maths and science		437.8	46	◇
2.1.5	Pupil–teacher ratio, secondary		17.7	90	○◇
2.2	**Tertiary education**		**32.7**	**59**	
2.2.1	Tertiary enrolment, % gross		91.7	12	●
2.2.2	Graduates in science and engineering, %		21.4	63	
2.2.3	Tertiary inbound mobility, %		1.1	87	○◇
2.3	**Research and development (R&D)**		**13.6**	**51**	◇
2.3.1	Researchers, FTE/mn pop.	⊙	512.0	70	◇
2.3.2	Gross expenditure on R&D, % GDP	⊙	0.3	72	◇
2.3.3	Global corporate R&D investors, top 3, mn USD		0.0	40	○◇
2.3.4	QS university ranking, top 3*		43.2	31	
	Infrastructure		**46.4**	**52**	◇
3.1	**Information and communication technologies (ICTs)**		**80.9**	**38**	
3.1.1	ICT access*		88.0	33	
3.1.2	ICT use*		85.8	36	
3.1.3	Government's online service*		81.0	30	●
3.1.4	E-participation*		68.6	43	
3.2	**General infrastructure**		**28.2**	**59**	◇
3.2.1	Electricity output, GWh/mn pop.		4,372.6	52	
3.2.2	Logistics performance*		40.9	60	◇
3.2.3	Gross capital formation, % GDP		25.1	53	
3.3	**Ecological sustainability**		**30.2**	**54**	
3.3.1	GDP/unit of energy use		12.2	45	
3.3.2	Environmental performance*		47.1	51	
3.3.3	ISO 14001 environment/bn PPP$ GDP		1.9	51	
	Market sophistication		**38.9**	**47**	
4.1	**Credit**		**40.0**	**41**	
4.1.1	Finance for startups and scaleups†		33.0	64	○◇
4.1.2	Domestic credit to private sector, % GDP		124.6	19	●
4.1.3	Loans from microfinance institutions, % GDP		n/a	n/a	
4.2	**Investment**		**13.9**	**47**	
4.2.1	Market capitalization, % GDP		77.0	21	
4.2.2	Venture capital (VC) investors, deals/bn PPP$ GDP		0.1	49	
4.2.3	VC recipients, deals/bn PPP$ GDP		0.0	55	
4.2.4	VC received, value, % GDP		0.0	44	
4.3	**Trade, diversification and market scale**		**62.9**	**47**	
4.3.1	Applied tariff rate, weighted avg., %		0.4	5	●
4.3.2	Domestic industry diversification	⊙	79.1	80	○
4.3.3	Domestic market scale, bn PPP$		575.5	44	

			Score/Value	Rank	
	Business sophistication		**29.8**	**55**	◇
5.1	**Knowledge workers**		**33.2**	**64**	◇
5.1.1	Knowledge-intensive employment, %		31.9	48	
5.1.2	Firms offering formal training, %		n/a	n/a	
5.1.3	GERD performed by business, % GDP	⊙	0.1	61	◇
5.1.4	GERD financed by business, %		34.7	55	
5.1.5	Females employed w/advanced degrees, %		12.4	61	◇
5.2	**Innovation linkages**		**17.5**	**88**	◇
5.2.1	University–industry R&D collaboration†		35.7	83	◇
5.2.2	State of cluster development†		37.8	80	◇
5.2.3	GERD financed by abroad, % GDP		0.0	78	○◇
5.2.4	Joint venture/strategic alliance deals/bn PPP$ GDP		0.0	53	
5.2.5	Patent families/bn PPP$ GDP		0.2	43	
5.3	**Knowledge absorption**		**38.7**	**48**	
5.3.1	Intellectual property payments, % total trade		2.0	14	●
5.3.2	High-tech imports, % total trade		10.0	38	
5.3.3	ICT services imports, % total trade		0.9	90	
5.3.4	FDI net inflows, % GDP		4.4	25	●
5.3.5	Research talent, % in businesses	⊙	26.6	48	
	Knowledge and technology outputs		**24.3**	**58**	◇
6.1	**Knowledge creation**		**16.6**	**61**	
6.1.1	Patents by origin/bn PPP$ GDP		0.8	68	
6.1.2	PCT patents by origin/bn PPP$ GDP		0.3	36	
6.1.3	Utility models by origin/bn PPP$ GDP		0.2	47	
6.1.4	Scientific and technical articles/bn PPP$ GDP		17.0	43	
6.1.5	Citable documents H-index		25.0	38	
6.2	**Knowledge impact**		**38.6**	**33**	
6.2.1	Labor productivity growth, %		1.9	37	
6.2.2	Unicorn valuation, % GDP		0.7	36	
6.2.3	Software spending, % GDP		0.5	21	●
6.2.4	High-tech manufacturing, %	⊙	23.9	55	
6.3	**Knowledge diffusion**		**17.7**	**84**	◇
6.3.1	Intellectual property receipts, % total trade		0.1	70	
6.3.2	Production and export complexity		47.4	75	◇
6.3.3	High-tech exports, % total trade		1.3	70	◇
6.3.4	ICT services exports, % total trade		0.6	99	○
6.3.5	ISO 9001 quality/bn PPP$ GDP		5.5	52	
	Creative outputs		**26.8**	**59**	
7.1	**Intangible assets**		**39.2**	**46**	
7.1.1	Intangible asset intensity, top 15, %		42.2	60	○
7.1.2	Trademarks by origin/bn PPP$ GDP		101.6	10	●◆
7.1.3	Global brand value, top 5,000, % GDP		3.4	41	
7.1.4	Industrial designs by origin/bn PPP$ GDP		0.1	115	○◇
7.2	**Creative goods and services**		**6.6**	**80**	◇
7.2.1	Cultural and creative services exports, % total trade		0.2	70	
7.2.2	National feature films/mn pop. 15–69		1.3	57	◇
7.2.3	Entertainment and media market/th pop. 15–69		12.6	30	◇
7.2.4	Creative goods exports, % total trade		0.1	90	
7.3	**Online creativity**		**22.3**	**59**	◇
7.3.1	Generic top-level domains (TLDs)/th pop. 15–69		2.3	77	◇
7.3.2	Country-code TLDs/th pop. 15–69		14.8	32	
7.3.3	GitHub commits/mn pop. 15–69		8.2	57	◇
7.3.4	Mobile app creation/bn PPP$ GDP		63.7	71	

NOTES: ● indicates a strength; ○ a weakness; ◆ an income group strength; ◇ an income group weakness; * an index; † a survey question. ⊙ is used when the available economy data are older than the base year; see appendices for details, including the year of the data, at wipo.int/gii-ranking. Square brackets [ ] indicate that the data minimum coverage (DMC) requirements were not met at the sub-pillar or pillar level.

GII 2023 rank

China

12

Output rank	Input rank	Income	Region	Population (mn)	GDP, PPP$ (bn)	GDP per capita, PPP$
8	25	Upper middle	SEAO	1,425.9	30,074.4	21,291

		Score/Value	Rank	
	Institutions	**60.2**	**43**	◆
1.1	**Institutional environment**	**56.4**	**44**	◆
1.1.1	Operational stability for businesses*	52.8	65	
1.1.2	Government effectiveness*	60.0	37	◆
1.2	**Regulatory environment**	**49.5**	**100**	○
1.2.1	Regulatory quality*	34.0	89	○
1.2.2	Rule of law*	40.8	62	
1.2.3	Cost of redundancy dismissal	27.4	111	○◇
1.3	**Business environment**	**74.9**	**14**	◆
1.3.1	Policies for doing business†	74.4	21	◆
1.3.2	Entrepreneurship policies and culture†	75.4	10	◆
	Human capital and research	**49.8**	**22**	◆
2.1	**Education**	**68.5**	**[11]**	
2.1.1	Expenditure on education, % GDP	⊙ 3.5	88	○
2.1.2	Government funding/pupil, secondary, % GDP/cap	n/a	n/a	
2.1.3	School life expectancy, years	n/a	n/a	
2.1.4	PISA scales in reading, maths and science	579.0	1	●◆
2.1.5	Pupil–teacher ratio, secondary	13.3	62	
2.2	**Tertiary education**	**20.6**	**88**	○
2.2.1	Tertiary enrolment, % gross	63.6	50	
2.2.2	Graduates in science and engineering, %	n/a	n/a	
2.2.3	Tertiary inbound mobility, %	0.4	101	○◇
2.3	**Research and development (R&D)**	**60.3**	**15**	◆
2.3.1	Researchers, FTE/mn pop.	⊙ 1,584.9	48	
2.3.2	Gross expenditure on R&D, % GDP	⊙ 2.4	14	◆
2.3.3	Global corporate R&D investors, top 3, mn USD	92.9	2	●◆
2.3.4	QS university ranking, top 3*	88.8	3	●◆
	Infrastructure	**56.4**	**27**	◆
3.1	**Information and communication technologies (ICTs)**	**86.0**	**18**	◆
3.1.1	ICT access*	82.7	64	
3.1.2	ICT use*	87.7	26	◆
3.1.3	Government's online service*	87.6	15	◆
3.1.4	E-participation*	86.0	13	◆
3.2	**General infrastructure**	**52.4**	**13**	◆
3.2.1	Electricity output, GWh/mn pop.	6,019.0	32	◆
3.2.2	Logistics performance*	72.7	18	◆
3.2.3	Gross capital formation, % GDP	44.8	2	●◆
3.3	**Ecological sustainability**	**30.7**	**50**	
3.3.1	GDP/unit of energy use	6.8	100	○◇
3.3.2	Environmental performance*	16.1	118	○◇
3.3.3	ISO 14001 environment/bn PPP$ GDP	8.0	10	◆
	Market sophistication	**56.7**	**13**	◆
4.1	**Credit**	**50.0**	**28**	◆
4.1.1	Finance for startups and scaleups†	70.5	16	◆
4.1.2	Domestic credit to private sector, % GDP	182.9	4	◆
4.1.3	Loans from microfinance institutions, % GDP	0.8	32	
4.2	**Investment**	**25.3**	**27**	
4.2.1	Market capitalization, % GDP	62.8	28	
4.2.2	Venture capital (VC) investors, deals/bn PPP$ GDP	0.1	36	
4.2.3	VC recipients, deals/bn PPP$ GDP	0.1	27	◆
4.2.4	VC received, value, % GDP	0.0	18	◆
4.3	**Trade, diversification and market scale**	**94.6**	**3**	●◆
4.3.1	Applied tariff rate, weighted avg., %	2.5	66	
4.3.2	Domestic industry diversification	⊙ 99.8	2	●◆
4.3.3	Domestic market scale, bn PPP$	30,074.4	1	●◆

		Score/Value	Rank	
	Business sophistication	**54.1**	**20**	◆
5.1	**Knowledge workers**	**66.1**	**[12]**	
5.1.1	Knowledge-intensive employment, %	n/a	n/a	
5.1.2	Firms offering formal training, %	n/a	n/a	
5.1.3	GERD performed by business, % GDP	⊙ 1.8	13	◆
5.1.4	GERD financed by business, %	77.5	3	●◆
5.1.5	Females employed w/advanced degrees, %	n/a	n/a	
5.2	**Innovation linkages**	**43.8**	**27**	◆
5.2.1	University–industry R&D collaboration†	86.8	6	◆
5.2.2	State of cluster development†	91.4	2	●◆
5.2.3	GERD financed by abroad, % GDP	0.0	76	○
5.2.4	Joint venture/strategic alliance deals/bn PPP$ GDP	0.0	70	
5.2.5	Patent families/bn PPP$ GDP	1.7	23	◆
5.3	**Knowledge absorption**	**52.5**	**14**	◆
5.3.1	Intellectual property payments, % total trade	1.4	24	
5.3.2	High-tech imports, % total trade	22.6	6	◆
5.3.3	ICT services imports, % total trade	1.2	76	
5.3.4	FDI net inflows, % GDP	1.6	82	○
5.3.5	Research talent, % in businesses	⊙ 58.5	17	◆
	Knowledge and technology outputs	**61.5**	**6**	◆
6.1	**Knowledge creation**	**71.9**	**3**	●◆
6.1.1	Patents by origin/bn PPP$ GDP	52.4	2	●◆
6.1.2	PCT patents by origin/bn PPP$ GDP	2.3	14	◆
6.1.3	Utility models by origin/bn PPP$ GDP	104.6	1	●◆
6.1.4	Scientific and technical articles/bn PPP$ GDP	21.9	32	◆
6.1.5	Citable documents H-index	66.1	11	◆
6.2	**Knowledge impact**	**65.5**	**3**	●◆
6.2.1	Labor productivity growth, %	6.0	1	●◆
6.2.2	Unicorn valuation, % GDP	3.8	12	◆
6.2.3	Software spending, % GDP	0.4	27	◆
6.2.4	High-tech manufacturing, %	⊙ 48.5	13	◆
6.3	**Knowledge diffusion**	**47.2**	**20**	◆
6.3.1	Intellectual property receipts, % total trade	0.3	33	◆
6.3.2	Production and export complexity	79.8	17	◆
6.3.3	High-tech exports, % total trade	28.0	5	◆
6.3.4	ICT services exports, % total trade	2.3	52	
6.3.5	ISO 9001 quality/bn PPP$ GDP	15.7	19	
	Creative outputs	**48.9**	**14**	◆
7.1	**Intangible assets**	**80.5**	**1**	●◆
7.1.1	Intangible asset intensity, top 15, %	75.7	11	
7.1.2	Trademarks by origin/bn PPP$ GDP	337.9	1	●◆
7.1.3	Global brand value, top 5,000, % GDP	9.4	20	◆
7.1.4	Industrial designs by origin/bn PPP$ GDP	28.9	2	●◆
7.2	**Creative goods and services**	**31.4**	**28**	◆
7.2.1	Cultural and creative services exports, % total trade	0.6	51	
7.2.2	National feature films/mn pop. 15–69	0.5	69	○
7.2.3	Entertainment and media market/th pop. 15–69	11.1	32	◆
7.2.4	Creative goods exports, % total trade	11.3	1	●◆
7.3	**Online creativity**	**3.1**	**123**	○◇
7.3.1	Generic top-level domains (TLDs)/th pop. 15–69	2.8	74	
7.3.2	Country-code TLDs/th pop. 15–69	5.0	56	
7.3.3	GitHub commits/mn pop. 15–69	1.4	107	○
7.3.4	Mobile app creation/bn PPP$ GDP	n/a	n/a	

NOTES: ● indicates a strength; ○ a weakness; ◆ an income group strength; ◇ an income group weakness; * an index; † a survey question. ⊙ is used when the available economy data are older than the base year; see appendices for details, including the year of the data, at wipo.int/gii-ranking. Square brackets [ ] indicate that the data minimum coverage (DMC) requirements were not met at the sub-pillar or pillar level.

Colombia

GII 2023 rank

66

Output rank	Input rank	Income	Region	Population (mn)	GDP, PPP$ (bn)	GDP per capita, PPP$
71	**63**	**Upper middle**	**LCN**	**51.9**	**964.7**	**18,693**

			Score/Value	Rank	
	Institutions		**46.7**	**78**	
1.1	**Institutional environment**		**39.0**	**81**	
1.1.1	Operational stability for businesses*		41.7	87	
1.1.2	Government effectiveness*		36.3	71	
1.2	**Regulatory environment**		**60.0**	**72**	
1.2.1	Regulatory quality*		47.8	58	
1.2.2	Rule of law*		26.5	90	
1.2.3	Cost of redundancy dismissal		16.7	68	
1.3	**Business environment**		**41.0**	**83**	
1.3.1	Policies for doing business†		40.1	84	
1.3.2	Entrepreneurship policies and culture†		41.9	47	
	Human capital and research		**27.0**	**81**	
2.1	**Education**		**43.8**	**83**	
2.1.1	Expenditure on education, % GDP	⊙	5.2	28	
2.1.2	Government funding/pupil, secondary, % GDP/cap		23.1	33	
2.1.3	School life expectancy, years		14.8	58	
2.1.4	PISA scales in reading, maths and science		405.5	62	○
2.1.5	Pupil–teacher ratio, secondary		26.2	113	○ ◇
2.2	**Tertiary education**		**26.5**	**76**	
2.2.1	Tertiary enrolment, % gross		57.1	57	
2.2.2	Graduates in science and engineering, %		23.9	51	
2.2.3	Tertiary inbound mobility, %		0.2	109	○ ◇
2.3	**Research and development (R&D)**		**10.7**	**58**	
2.3.1	Researchers, FTE/mn pop.	⊙	88.0	92	○ ◇
2.3.2	Gross expenditure on R&D, % GDP	⊙	0.3	78	
2.3.3	Global corporate R&D investors, top 3, mn USD		0.0	40	○ ◇
2.3.4	QS university ranking, top 3*		37.1	35	
	Infrastructure		**43.1**	**60**	
3.1	**Information and communication technologies (ICTs)**		**71.5**	**62**	
3.1.1	ICT access*		79.9	72	
3.1.2	ICT use*		63.8	86	
3.1.3	Government's online service*		71.5	59	
3.1.4	E-participation*		70.9	37	
3.2	**General infrastructure**		**19.3**	**92**	
3.2.1	Electricity output, GWh/mn pop.		1,642.1	89	
3.2.2	Logistics performance*		36.4	65	
3.2.3	Gross capital formation, % GDP		20.0	98	
3.3	**Ecological sustainability**		**38.5**	**36**	
3.3.1	GDP/unit of energy use		17.9	13	● ◆
3.3.2	Environmental performance*		39.8	63	
3.3.3	ISO 14001 environment/bn PPP$ GDP		3.8	25	●
	Market sophistication		**33.4**	**73**	
4.1	**Credit**		**23.8**	**81**	
4.1.1	Finance for startups and scaleups†		28.3	73	○
4.1.2	Domestic credit to private sector, % GDP		54.3	68	
4.1.3	Loans from microfinance institutions, % GDP		n/a	n/a	
4.2	**Investment**		**12.8**	**49**	
4.2.1	Market capitalization, % GDP		37.1	42	
4.2.2	Venture capital (VC) investors, deals/bn PPP$ GDP		0.0	84	○
4.2.3	VC recipients, deals/bn PPP$ GDP		0.0	60	
4.2.4	VC received, value, % GDP		0.0	28	
4.3	**Trade, diversification and market scale**		**63.5**	**39**	
4.3.1	Applied tariff rate, weighted avg., %		2.4	65	
4.3.2	Domestic industry diversification		85.5	63	
4.3.3	Domestic market scale, bn PPP$		964.7	31	

			Score/Value	Rank	
	Business sophistication		**37.3**	**40**	◆
5.1	**Knowledge workers**		**48.1**	**34**	◆
5.1.1	Knowledge-intensive employment, %		24.2	58	
5.1.2	Firms offering formal training, %	⊙	63.0	6	● ◆
5.1.3	GERD performed by business, % GDP	⊙	0.1	57	
5.1.4	GERD financed by business, %		53.4	22	● ◆
5.1.5	Females employed w/advanced degrees, %		16.3	46	
5.2	**Innovation linkages**		**19.9**	**72**	
5.2.1	University–industry R&D collaboration†		47.7	55	
5.2.2	State of cluster development†		44.2	58	
5.2.3	GERD financed by abroad, % GDP		0.0	66	
5.2.4	Joint venture/strategic alliance deals/bn PPP$ GDP		0.0	89	
5.2.5	Patent families/bn PPP$ GDP		0.1	59	
5.3	**Knowledge absorption**		**43.9**	**33**	◆
5.3.1	Intellectual property payments, % total trade		2.4	11	● ◆
5.3.2	High-tech imports, % total trade		17.5	12	● ◆
5.3.3	ICT services imports, % total trade		1.9	39	
5.3.4	FDI net inflows, % GDP		3.4	40	
5.3.5	Research talent, % in businesses	⊙	2.5	75	○
	Knowledge and technology outputs		**23.7**	**62**	
6.1	**Knowledge creation**		**9.7**	**81**	
6.1.1	Patents by origin/bn PPP$ GDP		0.5	79	
6.1.2	PCT patents by origin/bn PPP$ GDP		0.1	56	
6.1.3	Utility models by origin/bn PPP$ GDP		0.2	46	
6.1.4	Scientific and technical articles/bn PPP$ GDP		6.9	94	
6.1.5	Citable documents H-index		19.3	46	
6.2	**Knowledge impact**		**37.3**	**38**	◆
6.2.1	Labor productivity growth, %		3.1	15	●
6.2.2	Unicorn valuation, % GDP		2.0	20	● ◆
6.2.3	Software spending, % GDP		0.2	79	
6.2.4	High-tech manufacturing, %		20.9	61	
6.3	**Knowledge diffusion**		**24.0**	**60**	
6.3.1	Intellectual property receipts, % total trade		0.2	43	
6.3.2	Production and export complexity		51.3	63	
6.3.3	High-tech exports, % total trade		1.3	69	
6.3.4	ICT services exports, % total trade		1.1	85	
6.3.5	ISO 9001 quality/bn PPP$ GDP		12.3	21	●
	Creative outputs		**19.1**	**80**	
7.1	**Intangible assets**		**23.0**	**80**	
7.1.1	Intangible asset intensity, top 15, %		−19.0	74	○
7.1.2	Trademarks by origin/bn PPP$ GDP		40.1	57	
7.1.3	Global brand value, top 5,000, % GDP		2.3	45	
7.1.4	Industrial designs by origin/bn PPP$ GDP		0.6	80	
7.2	**Creative goods and services**		**5.8**	**83**	
7.2.1	Cultural and creative services exports, % total trade		0.5	55	
7.2.2	National feature films/mn pop. 15–69		0.8	64	○
7.2.3	Entertainment and media market/th pop. 15–69		5.8	40	
7.2.4	Creative goods exports, % total trade		0.3	72	
7.3	**Online creativity**		**24.7**	**51**	
7.3.1	Generic top-level domains (TLDs)/th pop. 15–69		3.1	67	
7.3.2	Country-code TLDs/th pop. 15–69		25.3	28	● ◆
7.3.3	GitHub commits/mn pop. 15–69		7.1	60	
7.3.4	Mobile app creation/bn PPP$ GDP		63.4	72	

NOTES: ● indicates a strength; ○ a weakness; ◆ an income group strength; ◇ an income group weakness; * an index; † a survey question. ⊙ is used when the available economy data are older than the base year; see appendices for details, including the year of the data, at wipo.int/gii-ranking. Square brackets [ ] indicate that the data minimum coverage (DMC) requirements were not met at the sub-pillar or pillar level.

Costa Rica

GII 2023 rank

74

Output rank	Input rank	Income	Region	Population (mn)	GDP, PPP$ (bn)	GDP per capita, PPP$
81	66	Upper middle	LCN	5.2	129.9	24,837

			Score/Value	Rank	
	Institutions		**57.9**	**48**	
1.1	**Institutional environment**		**49.0**	**55**	
1.1.1	Operational stability for businesses*		54.2	62	
1.1.2	Government effectiveness*		43.8	56	
1.2	**Regulatory environment**		**66.1**	**55**	
1.2.1	Regulatory quality*		53.9	48	
1.2.2	Rule of law*		53.0	44	◆
1.2.3	Cost of redundancy dismissal		18.7	79	
1.3	**Business environment**		**58.7**	**[36]**	
1.3.1	Policies for doing business†		58.7	42	
1.3.2	Entrepreneurship policies and culture†		n/a	n/a	

			Score/Value	Rank	
	Human capital and research		**27.9**	**79**	
2.1	**Education**		**58.3**	**44**	
2.1.1	Expenditure on education, % GDP	⊙	6.7	9	● ◆
2.1.2	Government funding/pupil, secondary, % GDP/cap		25.1	21	●
2.1.3	School life expectancy, years	⊙	16.5	27	● ◆
2.1.4	PISA scales in reading, maths and science		414.8	59	
2.1.5	Pupil–teacher ratio, secondary		12.8	59	
2.2	**Tertiary education**		**19.8**	**91**	
2.2.1	Tertiary enrolment, % gross	⊙	57.7	56	
2.2.2	Graduates in science and engineering, %		15.9	95	○
2.2.3	Tertiary inbound mobility, %	⊙	1.2	86	
2.3	**Research and development (R&D)**		**5.5**	**72**	
2.3.1	Researchers, FTE/mn pop.	⊙	345.0	78	
2.3.2	Gross expenditure on R&D, % GDP	⊙	0.4	68	
2.3.3	Global corporate R&D investors, top 3, mn USD		0.0	40	○ ◇
2.3.4	QS university ranking, top 3*		12.1	62	

			Score/Value	Rank	
	Infrastructure		**42.0**	**62**	
3.1	**Information and communication technologies (ICTs)**		**69.9**	**65**	
3.1.1	ICT access*		86.3	44	
3.1.2	ICT use*		73.9	64	
3.1.3	Government's online service*		64.8	70	
3.1.4	E-participation*		54.7	66	
3.2	**General infrastructure**		**21.1**	**86**	
3.2.1	Electricity output, GWh/mn pop.		2,464.6	76	
3.2.2	Logistics performance*		36.4	65	
3.2.3	Gross capital formation, % GDP		20.8	93	
3.3	**Ecological sustainability**		**35.0**	**40**	
3.3.1	GDP/unit of energy use		19.3	9	● ◆
3.3.2	Environmental performance*		46.4	53	
3.3.3	ISO 14001 environment/bn PPP$ GDP		1.1	63	

			Score/Value	Rank	
	Market sophistication		**27.2**	**90**	
4.1	**Credit**		**21.7**	**[88]**	
4.1.1	Finance for startups and scaleups†		n/a	n/a	
4.1.2	Domestic credit to private sector, % GDP		60.4	58	
4.1.3	Loans from microfinance institutions, % GDP		n/a	n/a	
4.2	**Investment**		**2.4**	**99**	○
4.2.1	Market capitalization, % GDP		3.4	76	○
4.2.2	Venture capital (VC) investors, deals/bn PPP$ GDP		0.0	62	
4.2.3	VC recipients, deals/bn PPP$ GDP		0.0	81	○
4.2.4	VC received, value, % GDP		0.0	84	○
4.3	**Trade, diversification and market scale**		**57.5**	**69**	
4.3.1	Applied tariff rate, weighted avg., %		1.5	48	
4.3.2	Domestic industry diversification		79.5	78	
4.3.3	Domestic market scale, bn PPP$		129.9	82	

			Score/Value	Rank	
	Business sophistication		**28.7**	**63**	
5.1	**Knowledge workers**		**18.5**	**104**	◇
5.1.1	Knowledge-intensive employment, %		21.4	72	
5.1.2	Firms offering formal training, %		n/a	n/a	
5.1.3	GERD performed by business, % GDP	⊙	0.1	58	
5.1.4	GERD financed by business, %	⊙	2.3	86	○ ◇
5.1.5	Females employed w/advanced degrees, %		11.8	65	
5.2	**Innovation linkages**		**19.9**	**73**	
5.2.1	University–industry R&D collaboration†		39.9	73	
5.2.2	State of cluster development†		52.8	43	
5.2.3	GERD financed by abroad, % GDP	⊙	0.0	67	
5.2.4	Joint venture/strategic alliance deals/bn PPP$ GDP	⊙	0.0	88	
5.2.5	Patent families/bn PPP$ GDP		0.0	74	
5.3	**Knowledge absorption**		**47.6**	**28**	● ◆
5.3.1	Intellectual property payments, % total trade		3.0	8	● ◆
5.3.2	High-tech imports, % total trade		8.3	64	
5.3.3	ICT services imports, % total trade		1.3	65	
5.3.4	FDI net inflows, % GDP		4.4	26	●
5.3.5	Research talent, % in businesses		n/a	n/a	

			Score/Value	Rank	
	Knowledge and technology outputs		**21.7**	**70**	
6.1	**Knowledge creation**		**5.4**	**110**	○
6.1.1	Patents by origin/bn PPP$ GDP		0.1	108	○
6.1.2	PCT patents by origin/bn PPP$ GDP		0.0	85	
6.1.3	Utility models by origin/bn PPP$ GDP		0.1	62	
6.1.4	Scientific and technical articles/bn PPP$ GDP		6.6	96	
6.1.5	Citable documents H-index		10.5	75	
6.2	**Knowledge impact**		**25.9**	**69**	
6.2.1	Labor productivity growth, %		1.4	47	
6.2.2	Unicorn valuation, % GDP		0.0	48	○ ◇
6.2.3	Software spending, % GDP		0.3	32	● ◆
6.2.4	High-tech manufacturing, %		13.0	83	
6.3	**Knowledge diffusion**		**33.8**	**44**	
6.3.1	Intellectual property receipts, % total trade		0.0	80	
6.3.2	Production and export complexity		58.9	48	
6.3.3	High-tech exports, % total trade		6.3	30	●
6.3.4	ICT services exports, % total trade		6.4	15	● ◆
6.3.5	ISO 9001 quality/bn PPP$ GDP		3.1	73	

			Score/Value	Rank	
	Creative outputs		**16.2**	**89**	
7.1	**Intangible assets**		**17.5**	**92**	
7.1.1	Intangible asset intensity, top 15, %		n/a	n/a	
7.1.2	Trademarks by origin/bn PPP$ GDP		76.0	21	●
7.1.3	Global brand value, top 5,000, % GDP		0.0	74	○ ◇
7.1.4	Industrial designs by origin/bn PPP$ GDP		0.1	116	○
7.2	**Creative goods and services**		**8.4**	**74**	
7.2.1	Cultural and creative services exports, % total trade		0.6	47	
7.2.2	National feature films/mn pop. 15–69		1.6	51	
7.2.3	Entertainment and media market/th pop. 15–69		n/a	n/a	
7.2.4	Creative goods exports, % total trade		0.2	77	
7.3	**Online creativity**		**21.7**	**60**	
7.3.1	Generic top-level domains (TLDs)/th pop. 15–69		12.8	38	◆
7.3.2	Country-code TLDs/th pop. 15–69		1.4	83	
7.3.3	GitHub commits/mn pop. 15–69		11.2	53	
7.3.4	Mobile app creation/bn PPP$ GDP		61.4	77	

NOTES: ● indicates a strength; ○ a weakness; ◆ an income group strength; ◇ an income group weakness; * an index; † a survey question. ⊙ is used when the available economy data are older than the base year; see appendices for details, including the year of the data, at wipo.int/gii-ranking. Square brackets [ ] indicate that the data minimum coverage (DMC) requirements were not met at the sub-pillar or pillar level.

Côte d'Ivoire

GII 2023 rank

112

Output rank	Input rank	Income	Region	Population (mn)	GDP, PPP$ (bn)	GDP per capita, PPP$
102	112	Lower middle	SSA	28.2	181.5	6,397

		Score/Value	Rank
	Institutions	**48.1**	**71**
1.1	**Institutional environment**	**36.8**	**86**
1.1.1	Operational stability for businesses*	50.7	70 ●
1.1.2	Government effectiveness*	22.9	100
1.2	**Regulatory environment**	**59.1**	**75**
1.2.1	Regulatory quality*	35.4	86
1.2.2	Rule of law*	21.2	103
1.2.3	Cost of redundancy dismissal	13.1	47 ●
1.3	**Business environment**	**48.4**	**[60]**
1.3.1	Policies for doing business†	48.4	63 ●
1.3.2	Entrepreneurship policies and culture†	n/a	n/a

		Score/Value	Rank
	Human capital and research	**10.5**	**128 ○◇**
2.1	**Education**	**26.1**	**125 ○**
2.1.1	Expenditure on education, % GDP	3.5	92
2.1.2	Government funding/pupil, secondary, % GDP/cap	10.8	89
2.1.3	School life expectancy, years	10.7	101
2.1.4	PISA scales in reading, maths and science	n/a	n/a
2.1.5	Pupil–teacher ratio, secondary	29.3	119 ○◇
2.2	**Tertiary education**	**5.0**	**121 ○◇**
2.2.1	Tertiary enrolment, % gross	9.9	115
2.2.2	Graduates in science and engineering, %	n/a	n/a
2.2.3	Tertiary inbound mobility, %	2.4	73
2.3	**Research and development (R&D)**	**0.4**	**113**
2.3.1	Researchers, FTE/mn pop.	n/a	n/a
2.3.2	Gross expenditure on R&D, % GDP ⊙	0.1	107 ○
2.3.3	Global corporate R&D investors, top 3, mn USD	0.0	40 ○◇
2.3.4	QS university ranking, top 3*	0.0	71 ○◇

		Score/Value	Rank
	Infrastructure	**25.9**	**106**
3.1	**Information and communication technologies (ICTs)**	**46.0**	**104**
3.1.1	ICT access*	51.0	106
3.1.2	ICT use*	47.0	106
3.1.3	Government's online service*	49.9	91
3.1.4	E-participation*	36.0	93
3.2	**General infrastructure**	**12.7**	**116**
3.2.1	Electricity output, GWh/mn pop. ⊙	426.5	113
3.2.2	Logistics performance*	n/a	n/a
3.2.3	Gross capital formation, % GDP	26.2	43 ●
3.3	**Ecological sustainability**	**18.8**	**85**
3.3.1	GDP/unit of energy use	12.9	38 ●
3.3.2	Environmental performance*	23.6	100
3.3.3	ISO 14001 environment/bn PPP$ GDP	0.3	106

		Score/Value	Rank
	Market sophistication	**14.0**	**123 ○◇**
4.1	**Credit**	**10.5**	**110**
4.1.1	Finance for startups and scaleups†	n/a	n/a
4.1.2	Domestic credit to private sector, % GDP	21.1	114
4.1.3	Loans from microfinance institutions, % GDP	1.3	23 ●
4.2	**Investment**	**4.1**	**86**
4.2.1	Market capitalization, % GDP	13.5	67
4.2.2	Venture capital (VC) investors, deals/bn PPP$ GDP	0.0	66
4.2.3	VC recipients, deals/bn PPP$ GDP	0.0	65
4.2.4	VC received, value, % GDP	0.0	79
4.3	**Trade, diversification and market scale**	**27.2**	**118**
4.3.1	Applied tariff rate, weighted avg., %	7.6	104
4.3.2	Domestic industry diversification	n/a	n/a
4.3.3	Domestic market scale, bn PPP$	181.5	73

		Score/Value	Rank
	Business sophistication	**22.1**	**96**
5.1	**Knowledge workers**	**17.5**	**[107]**
5.1.1	Knowledge-intensive employment, % ⊙	7.1	115
5.1.2	Firms offering formal training, % ⊙	35.5	46 ●
5.1.3	GERD performed by business, % GDP	n/a	n/a
5.1.4	GERD financed by business, %	n/a	n/a
5.1.5	Females employed w/advanced degrees, % ⊙	1.2	116
5.2	**Innovation linkages**	**20.9**	**68 ●**
5.2.1	University-industry R&D collaboration†	42.0	71
5.2.2	State of cluster development†	39.9	71
5.2.3	GERD financed by abroad, % GDP	n/a	n/a
5.2.4	Joint venture/strategic alliance deals/bn PPP$ GDP	0.0	116
5.2.5	Patent families/bn PPP$ GDP	0.0	95 ○◇
5.3	**Knowledge absorption**	**28.0**	**88**
5.3.1	Intellectual property payments, % total trade	0.1	103
5.3.2	High-tech imports, % total trade ⊙	5.7	106
5.3.3	ICT services imports, % total trade	1.7	51 ●
5.3.4	FDI net inflows, % GDP	1.5	88
5.3.5	Research talent, % in businesses	n/a	n/a

		Score/Value	Rank
	Knowledge and technology outputs	**11.0**	**118**
6.1	**Knowledge creation**	**2.9**	**122**
6.1.1	Patents by origin/bn PPP$ GDP	0.3	91
6.1.2	PCT patents by origin/bn PPP$ GDP	0.0	96
6.1.3	Utility models by origin/bn PPP$ GDP	0.0	75 ○◇
6.1.4	Scientific and technical articles/bn PPP$ GDP	2.4	120
6.1.5	Citable documents H-index	5.5	98
6.2	**Knowledge impact**	**21.2**	**97**
6.2.1	Labor productivity growth, %	1.9	34 ●
6.2.2	Unicorn valuation, % GDP	0.0	48 ○◇
6.2.3	Software spending, % GDP	0.0	123 ○◇
6.2.4	High-tech manufacturing, %	n/a	n/a
6.3	**Knowledge diffusion**	**8.8**	**112**
6.3.1	Intellectual property receipts, % total trade	0.0	99
6.3.2	Production and export complexity	24.2	116 ○◇
6.3.3	High-tech exports, % total trade ⊙	0.4	91
6.3.4	ICT services exports, % total trade	0.9	91
6.3.5	ISO 9001 quality/bn PPP$ GDP	1.5	93

		Score/Value	Rank
	Creative outputs	**13.6**	**97**
7.1	**Intangible assets**	**22.2**	**81**
7.1.1	Intangible asset intensity, top 15, %	35.9	65
7.1.2	Trademarks by origin/bn PPP$ GDP	7.2	114
7.1.3	Global brand value, top 5,000, % GDP	0.5	62 ●
7.1.4	Industrial designs by origin/bn PPP$ GDP	0.5	81
7.2	**Creative goods and services**	**0.4**	**[125]**
7.2.1	Cultural and creative services exports, % total trade	0.0	93
7.2.2	National feature films/mn pop. 15–69	n/a	n/a
7.2.3	Entertainment and media market/th pop. 15–69	n/a	n/a
7.2.4	Creative goods exports, % total trade ⊙	0.0	119
7.3	**Online creativity**	**9.4**	**118**
7.3.1	Generic top-level domains (TLDs)/th pop. 15–69	0.5	112
7.3.2	Country-code TLDs/th pop. 15–69	0.3	108
7.3.3	GitHub commits/mn pop. 15–69	0.4	123 ○
7.3.4	Mobile app creation/bn PPP$ GDP	36.4	115 ◇

NOTES: ● indicates a strength; ○ a weakness; ◆ an income group strength; ◇ an income group weakness; * an index; † a survey question. ⊙ is used when the available economy data are older than the base year; see appendices for details, including the year of the data, at wipo.int/gii-ranking. Square brackets [ ] indicate that the data minimum coverage (DMC) requirements were not met at the sub-pillar or pillar level.

Croatia

GII 2023 rank

44

Output rank	Input rank	Income	Region	Population (mn)	GDP, PPP$ (bn)	GDP per capita, PPP$
44	43	High	EUR	4.0	150.4	37,550

		Score/ Value	Rank	
Institutions		**48.0**	**72**	◇
1.1	**Institutional environment**	**61.3**	**40**	
1.1.1	Operational stability for businesses*	69.4	29	
1.1.2	Government effectiveness*	53.1	44	
1.2	**Regulatory environment**	**68.9**	**46**	
1.2.1	Regulatory quality*	55.1	46	◇
1.2.2	Rule of law*	48.6	51	◇
1.2.3	Cost of redundancy dismissal	15.1	61	
1.3	**Business environment**	**13.8**	**127**	○◇
1.3.1	Policies for doing business† ⓒ	26.5	112	○◇
1.3.2	Entrepreneurship policies and culture†	1.0	84	○◇

		Score/ Value	Rank	
Human capital and research		**36.6**	**44**	
2.1	**Education**	**61.0**	**30**	
2.1.1	Expenditure on education, % GDP ⓒ	3.9	76	
2.1.2	Government funding/pupil, secondary, % GDP/cap	n/a	n/a	
2.1.3	School life expectancy, years	15.1	52	
2.1.4	PISA scales in reading, maths and science	471.9	37	
2.1.5	Pupil–teacher ratio, secondary	6.1	1	●◆
2.2	**Tertiary education**	**35.9**	**42**	
2.2.1	Tertiary enrolment, % gross	68.1	44	
2.2.2	Graduates in science and engineering, %	28.5	26	
2.2.3	Tertiary inbound mobility, %	3.0	67	
2.3	**Research and development (R&D)**	**12.8**	**52**	◇
2.3.1	Researchers, FTE/mn pop.	2,355.6	36	
2.3.2	Gross expenditure on R&D, % GDP	1.2	33	
2.3.3	Global corporate R&D investors, top 3, mn USD	0.0	40	○◇
2.3.4	QS university ranking, top 3*	4.6	70	◇

		Score/ Value	Rank	
Infrastructure		**56.7**	**26**	
3.1	**Information and communication technologies (ICTs)**	**81.1**	**34**	
3.1.1	ICT access*	86.4	43	
3.1.2	ICT use*	85.5	37	
3.1.3	Government's online service*	79.1	36	
3.1.4	E-participation*	73.3	29	
3.2	**General infrastructure**	**30.0**	**55**	◇
3.2.1	Electricity output, GWh/mn pop.	3,890.7	57	
3.2.2	Logistics performance*	54.5	42	
3.2.3	Gross capital formation, % GDP	21.4	85	○
3.3	**Ecological sustainability**	**59.0**	**5**	●◆
3.3.1	GDP/unit of energy use	12.5	41	
3.3.2	Environmental performance*	70.0	16	●
3.3.3	ISO 14001 environment/bn PPP$ GDP	9.8	5	●◆

		Score/ Value	Rank	
Market sophistication		**38.8**	**48**	
4.1	**Credit**	**33.7**	**57**	
4.1.1	Finance for startups and scaleups†	46.0	52	
4.1.2	Domestic credit to private sector, % GDP	59.5	62	
4.1.3	Loans from microfinance institutions, % GDP	n/a	n/a	
4.2	**Investment**	**19.6**	**36**	
4.2.1	Market capitalization, % GDP	35.9	43	
4.2.2	Venture capital (VC) investors, deals/bn PPP$ GDP	0.0	81	○
4.2.3	VC recipients, deals/bn PPP$ GDP	0.0	54	
4.2.4	VC received, value, % GDP	0.0	14	●
4.3	**Trade, diversification and market scale**	**63.2**	**41**	
4.3.1	Applied tariff rate, weighted avg., %	1.5	20	
4.3.2	Domestic industry diversification	96.2	24	
4.3.3	Domestic market scale, bn PPP$	150.4	78	

		Score/ Value	Rank	
Business sophistication		**30.6**	**53**	◇
5.1	**Knowledge workers**	**39.3**	**49**	
5.1.1	Knowledge-intensive employment, %	35.2	41	
5.1.2	Firms offering formal training, %	26.2	64	○◇
5.1.3	GERD performed by business, % GDP	0.6	36	
5.1.4	GERD financed by business, %	37.6	50	
5.1.5	Females employed w/advanced degrees, %	17.8	41	
5.2	**Innovation linkages**	**16.6**	**91**	○◇
5.2.1	University–industry R&D collaboration† ⓒ	22.0	113	○◇
5.2.2	State of cluster development† ⓒ	8.4	125	○◇
5.2.3	GERD financed by abroad, % GDP	0.3	13	●
5.2.4	Joint venture/strategic alliance deals/bn PPP$ GDP	0.0	68	
5.2.5	Patent families/bn PPP$ GDP	0.1	49	
5.3	**Knowledge absorption**	**35.9**	**55**	
5.3.1	Intellectual property payments, % total trade	1.1	34	
5.3.2	High-tech imports, % total trade	7.2	83	
5.3.3	ICT services imports, % total trade	1.7	46	
5.3.4	FDI net inflows, % GDP	5.1	19	●
5.3.5	Research talent, % in businesses	26.4	49	

		Score/ Value	Rank	
Knowledge and technology outputs		**34.0**	**33**	
6.1	**Knowledge creation**	**20.1**	**54**	
6.1.1	Patents by origin/bn PPP$ GDP	0.8	67	
6.1.2	PCT patents by origin/bn PPP$ GDP	0.1	55	
6.1.3	Utility models by origin/bn PPP$ GDP	0.2	43	
6.1.4	Scientific and technical articles/bn PPP$ GDP	31.5	18	●
6.1.5	Citable documents H-index	18.0	49	
6.2	**Knowledge impact**	**41.9**	**25**	
6.2.1	Labor productivity growth, %	1.7	40	
6.2.2	Unicorn valuation, % GDP	4.1	11	●◆
6.2.3	Software spending, % GDP	0.0	108	○◇
6.2.4	High-tech manufacturing, %	26.2	48	
6.3	**Knowledge diffusion**	**40.1**	**35**	
6.3.1	Intellectual property receipts, % total trade	0.3	40	
6.3.2	Production and export complexity	69.3	32	
6.3.3	High-tech exports, % total trade	3.7	42	
6.3.4	ICT services exports, % total trade	3.5	35	
6.3.5	ISO 9001 quality/bn PPP$ GDP	21.4	8	●◆

		Score/ Value	Rank	
Creative outputs		**30.0**	**52**	
7.1	**Intangible assets**	**34.3**	**56**	
7.1.1	Intangible asset intensity, top 15, %	37.3	64	○
7.1.2	Trademarks by origin/bn PPP$ GDP	32.1	73	
7.1.3	Global brand value, top 5,000, % GDP	0.2	71	◇
7.1.4	Industrial designs by origin/bn PPP$ GDP	3.6	28	
7.2	**Creative goods and services**	**19.6**	**50**	
7.2.1	Cultural and creative services exports, % total trade	1.7	15	●
7.2.2	National feature films/mn pop. 15–69	2.1	47	◇
7.2.3	Entertainment and media market/th pop. 15–69	n/a	n/a	
7.2.4	Creative goods exports, % total trade	0.9	49	
7.3	**Online creativity**	**31.9**	**38**	
7.3.1	Generic top-level domains (TLDs)/th pop. 15–69	17.7	32	
7.3.2	Country-code TLDs/th pop. 15–69	12.8	37	
7.3.3	GitHub commits/mn pop. 15–69	26.3	38	
7.3.4	Mobile app creation/bn PPP$ GDP	70.8	50	

NOTES: ● indicates a strength; ○ a weakness; ◆ an income group strength; ◇ an income group weakness; * an index; † a survey question. ⓒ is used when the available economy data are older than the base year; see appendices for details, including the year of the data, at wipo.int/gii-ranking. Square brackets [ ] indicate that the data minimum coverage (DMC) requirements were not met at the sub-pillar or pillar level.

GII 2023 rank

Cyprus **28**

Output rank	Input rank	Income	Region	Population (mn)	GDP, PPP$ (bn)	GDP per capita, PPP$
21	**33**	**High**	**NAWA**	**1.3**	**44.8**	**49,504**

		Score/Value	Rank	
	Institutions	**61.8**	**41**	
1.1	**Institutional environment**	**61.9**	**39**	
1.1.1	Operational stability for businesses*	66.7	36	
1.1.2	Government effectiveness*	57.1	39	
1.2	**Regulatory environment**	**80.7**	**27**	
1.2.1	Regulatory quality*	64.4	35	
1.2.2	Rule of law*	58.4	39	
1.2.3	Cost of redundancy dismissal	8.0	1	● ◆
1.3	**Business environment**	**42.8**	**75**	
1.3.1	Policies for doing business†	56.2	48	
1.3.2	Entrepreneurship policies and culture†	29.4	58	
	Human capital and research	**39.8**	**38**	
2.1	**Education**	**62.5**	**22**	
2.1.1	Expenditure on education, % GDP ⊙	5.2	31	
2.1.2	Government funding/pupil, secondary, % GDP/cap	34.9	4	● ◆
2.1.3	School life expectancy, years	15.8	42	
2.1.4	PISA scales in reading, maths and science	438.0	45	◇
2.1.5	Pupil–teacher ratio, secondary	7.7	7	● ◆
2.2	**Tertiary education**	**48.3**	**12**	
2.2.1	Tertiary enrolment, % gross	92.9	10	
2.2.2	Graduates in science and engineering, %	13.1	103	○ ◇
2.2.3	Tertiary inbound mobility, %	27.2	4	● ◆
2.3	**Research and development (R&D)**	**8.5**	**66**	◇
2.3.1	Researchers, FTE/mn pop.	1,813.6	43	
2.3.2	Gross expenditure on R&D, % GDP	0.9	45	
2.3.3	Global corporate R&D investors, top 3, mn USD	0.0	40	○ ◇
2.3.4	QS university ranking, top 3*	0.0	71	○ ◇
	Infrastructure	**55.5**	**32**	
3.1	**Information and communication technologies (ICTs)**	**83.0**	**28**	
3.1.1	ICT access*	97.6	6	● ◆
3.1.2	ICT use*	84.3	42	
3.1.3	Government's online service*	75.6	46	
3.1.4	E-participation*	74.4	25	
3.2	**General infrastructure**	**30.2**	**54**	◇
3.2.1	Electricity output, GWh/mn pop.	5,856.2	34	
3.2.2	Logistics performance*	50.0	50	◇
3.2.3	Gross capital formation, % GDP	18.5	107	○ ◇
3.3	**Ecological sustainability**	**53.3**	**14**	
3.3.1	GDP/unit of energy use	15.1	25	
3.3.2	Environmental performance*	66.3	22	
3.3.3	ISO 14001 environment/bn PPP$ GDP	7.2	12	◆
	Market sophistication	**44.5**	**38**	
4.1	**Credit**	**37.2**	**45**	
4.1.1	Finance for startups and scaleups†	33.6	62	◇
4.1.2	Domestic credit to private sector, % GDP	108.8	24	
4.1.3	Loans from microfinance institutions, % GDP	n/a	n/a	
4.2	**Investment**	**39.1**	**15**	
4.2.1	Market capitalization, % GDP	16.1	64	○
4.2.2	Venture capital (VC) investors, deals/bn PPP$ GDP	1.6	4	● ◆
4.2.3	VC recipients, deals/bn PPP$ GDP	0.2	10	
4.2.4	VC received, value, % GDP	0.0	33	
4.3	**Trade, diversification and market scale**	**57.3**	**70**	
4.3.1	Applied tariff rate, weighted avg., %	1.5	20	
4.3.2	Domestic industry diversification	80.8	72	
4.3.3	Domestic market scale, bn PPP$	44.8	113	○

		Score/Value	Rank	
	Business sophistication	**43.9**	**31**	
5.1	**Knowledge workers**	**49.7**	**31**	
5.1.1	Knowledge-intensive employment, %	38.4	33	
5.1.2	Firms offering formal training, %	39.7	35	
5.1.3	GERD performed by business, % GDP	0.4	44	
5.1.4	GERD financed by business, %	38.0	47	
5.1.5	Females employed w/advanced degrees, %	26.7	13	
5.2	**Innovation linkages**	**36.4**	**32**	
5.2.1	University–industry R&D collaboration†	39.4	75	
5.2.2	State of cluster development†	47.3	51	
5.2.3	GERD financed by abroad, % GDP	0.2	22	
5.2.4	Joint venture/strategic alliance deals/bn PPP$ GDP	0.1	17	
5.2.5	Patent families/bn PPP$ GDP	1.4	24	
5.3	**Knowledge absorption**	**45.7**	**31**	
5.3.1	Intellectual property payments, % total trade	1.2	29	
5.3.2	High-tech imports, % total trade	4.3	122	○ ◇
5.3.3	ICT services imports, % total trade	13.9	1	● ◆
5.3.4	FDI net inflows, % GDP	–5.9	130	○ ◇
5.3.5	Research talent, % in businesses	35.4	38	
	Knowledge and technology outputs	**39.5**	**23**	
6.1	**Knowledge creation**	**36.0**	**26**	
6.1.1	Patents by origin/bn PPP$ GDP	1.1	55	
6.1.2	PCT patents by origin/bn PPP$ GDP	1.2	23	
6.1.3	Utility models by origin/bn PPP$ GDP	n/a	n/a	
6.1.4	Scientific and technical articles/bn PPP$ GDP	42.7	4	● ◆
6.1.5	Citable documents H-index	13.4	64	
6.2	**Knowledge impact**	**23.0**	**89**	◇
6.2.1	Labor productivity growth, %	1.4	51	
6.2.2	Unicorn valuation, % GDP	0.0	48	○ ◇
6.2.3	Software spending, % GDP	0.2	81	◇
6.2.4	High-tech manufacturing, %	17.7	68	◇
6.3	**Knowledge diffusion**	**59.4**	**5**	● ◆
6.3.1	Intellectual property receipts, % total trade	2.5	12	
6.3.2	Production and export complexity	61.4	45	
6.3.3	High-tech exports, % total trade	0.9	74	◇
6.3.4	ICT services exports, % total trade	17.6	1	● ◆
6.3.5	ISO 9001 quality/bn PPP$ GDP	19.1	14	◆
	Creative outputs	**47.5**	**17**	
7.1	**Intangible assets**	**52.9**	**18**	
7.1.1	Intangible asset intensity, top 15, %	40.5	61	
7.1.2	Trademarks by origin/bn PPP$ GDP	110.6	8	◆
7.1.3	Global brand value, top 5,000, % GDP	0.0	74	○ ◇
7.1.4	Industrial designs by origin/bn PPP$ GDP	8.5	12	◆
7.2	**Creative goods and services**	**27.4**	**35**	
7.2.1	Cultural and creative services exports, % total trade	2.6	9	◆
7.2.2	National feature films/mn pop. 15–69	4.3	28	
7.2.3	Entertainment and media market/th pop. 15–69	n/a	n/a	
7.2.4	Creative goods exports, % total trade	0.2	79	
7.3	**Online creativity**	**56.6**	**17**	
7.3.1	Generic top-level domains (TLDs)/th pop. 15–69	79.0	8	● ◆
7.3.2	Country-code TLDs/th pop. 15–69	7.8	45	
7.3.3	GitHub commits/mn pop. 15–69	39.6	26	
7.3.4	Mobile app creation/bn PPP$ GDP	100.0	1	● ◆

NOTES: ● indicates a strength; ○ a weakness; ◆ an income group strength; ◇ an income group weakness; * an index; † a survey question. ⊙ is used when the available economy data are older than the base year; see appendices for details, including the year of the data, at wipo.int/gii-ranking. Square brackets [ ] indicate that the data minimum coverage (DMC) requirements were not met at the sub-pillar or pillar level.

Czech Republic

GII 2023 rank

31

Output rank	Input rank	Income	Region	Population (mn)	GDP, PPP$ (bn)	GDP per capita, PPP$
27	34	High	EUR	10.5	514.7	48,919

			Score/ Value	Rank
	Institutions		**63.7**	**36**
1.1	**Institutional environment**		**69.8**	**23**
1.1.1	Operational stability for businesses*		72.2	22
1.1.2	Government effectiveness*		67.4	29
1.2	**Regulatory environment**		**75.3**	**34**
1.2.1	Regulatory quality*		77.1	21
1.2.2	Rule of law*		72.7	25
1.2.3	Cost of redundancy dismissal		20.2	87 ○
1.3	**Business environment**		**45.9**	**[66]**
1.3.1	Policies for doing business†		45.9	69 ○
1.3.2	Entrepreneurship policies and culture†		n/a	n/a
	Human capital and research		**44.6**	**30**
2.1	**Education**		**60.7**	**32**
2.1.1	Expenditure on education, % GDP	⦸	4.5	53
2.1.2	Government funding/pupil, secondary, % GDP/cap		27.1	13
2.1.3	School life expectancy, years		16.3	30
2.1.4	PISA scales in reading, maths and science		495.5	23
2.1.5	Pupil–teacher ratio, secondary	⦸	11.5	48
2.2	**Tertiary education**		**44.1**	**23**
2.2.1	Tertiary enrolment, % gross		68.1	45
2.2.2	Graduates in science and engineering, %		25.9	40
2.2.3	Tertiary inbound mobility, %		15.0	13
2.3	**Research and development (R&D)**		**28.9**	**36**
2.3.1	Researchers, FTE/mn pop.		4,581.3	22
2.3.2	Gross expenditure on R&D, % GDP		2.0	19
2.3.3	Global corporate R&D investors, top 3, mn USD		0.0	40 ○◇
2.3.4	QS university ranking, top 3*		32.5	39
	Infrastructure		**56.8**	**24**
3.1	**Information and communication technologies (ICTs)**		**73.3**	**56**
3.1.1	ICT access*		84.9	50
3.1.2	ICT use*		85.5	38
3.1.3	Government's online service*		63.5	72 ○◇
3.1.4	E-participation*		59.3	57
3.2	**General infrastructure**		**41.7**	**30**
3.2.1	Electricity output, GWh/mn pop.		7,824.6	22
3.2.2	Logistics performance*		54.5	42
3.2.3	Gross capital formation, % GDP		30.7	23 ◆
3.3	**Ecological sustainability**		**55.5**	**12 ●◆**
3.3.1	GDP/unit of energy use		9.4	77 ○
3.3.2	Environmental performance*		69.5	19
3.3.3	ISO 14001 environment/bn PPP$ GDP		9.7	6 ●◆
	Market sophistication		**30.4**	**82 ○◇**
4.1	**Credit**		**18.8**	**[94]**
4.1.1	Finance for startups and scaleups†		n/a	n/a
4.1.2	Domestic credit to private sector, % GDP		53.1	70 ○
4.1.3	Loans from microfinance institutions, % GDP		n/a	n/a
4.2	**Investment**		**7.3**	**64 ○**
4.2.1	Market capitalization, % GDP		10.6	70 ○◇
4.2.2	Venture capital (VC) investors, deals/bn PPP$ GDP		0.1	44
4.2.3	VC recipients, deals/bn PPP$ GDP		0.0	61 ○
4.2.4	VC received, value, % GDP		0.0	49
4.3	**Trade, diversification and market scale**		**65.2**	**28**
4.3.1	Applied tariff rate, weighted avg., %		1.5	20
4.3.2	Domestic industry diversification		94.0	34
4.3.3	Domestic market scale, bn PPP$		514.7	47

		Score/ Value	Rank
	Business sophistication	**47.2**	**27**
5.1	**Knowledge workers**	**45.9**	**39**
5.1.1	Knowledge-intensive employment, %	40.0	30
5.1.2	Firms offering formal training, %	43.6	27
5.1.3	GERD performed by business, % GDP	1.3	19
5.1.4	GERD financed by business, %	36.1	52 ○
5.1.5	Females employed w/advanced degrees, %	13.9	54
5.2	**Innovation linkages**	**45.8**	**25**
5.2.1	University–industry R&D collaboration†	72.4	23
5.2.2	State of cluster development†	41.4	66
5.2.3	GERD financed by abroad, % GDP	0.6	1 ●◆
5.2.4	Joint venture/strategic alliance deals/bn PPP$ GDP	0.0	80 ○
5.2.5	Patent families/bn PPP$ GDP	0.5	32
5.3	**Knowledge absorption**	**49.9**	**19**
5.3.1	Intellectual property payments, % total trade	0.8	48
5.3.2	High-tech imports, % total trade	21.2	7 ●◆
5.3.3	ICT services imports, % total trade	1.7	53
5.3.4	FDI net inflows, % GDP	3.5	39
5.3.5	Research talent, % in businesses	53.3	20
	Knowledge and technology outputs	**43.5**	**21**
6.1	**Knowledge creation**	**35.0**	**27**
6.1.1	Patents by origin/bn PPP$ GDP	1.6	44
6.1.2	PCT patents by origin/bn PPP$ GDP	0.5	33
6.1.3	Utility models by origin/bn PPP$ GDP	2.2	7 ●◆
6.1.4	Scientific and technical articles/bn PPP$ GDP	27.7	26
6.1.5	Citable documents H-index	30.7	32
6.2	**Knowledge impact**	**41.5**	**27**
6.2.1	Labor productivity growth, %	0.9	67
6.2.2	Unicorn valuation, % GDP	0.4	40
6.2.3	Software spending, % GDP	0.3	34
6.2.4	High-tech manufacturing, %	59.7	4 ●◆
6.3	**Knowledge diffusion**	**54.0**	**11 ●**
6.3.1	Intellectual property receipts, % total trade	0.4	28
6.3.2	Production and export complexity	89.8	6 ●◆
6.3.3	High-tech exports, % total trade	20.7	7 ●◆
6.3.4	ICT services exports, % total trade	3.1	39
6.3.5	ISO 9001 quality/bn PPP$ GDP	24.4	4 ●◆
	Creative outputs	**38.7**	**32**
7.1	**Intangible assets**	**28.4**	**71 ○**
7.1.1	Intangible asset intensity, top 15, %	n/a	n/a
7.1.2	Trademarks by origin/bn PPP$ GDP	61.7	37
7.1.3	Global brand value, top 5,000, % GDP	1.6	47
7.1.4	Industrial designs by origin/bn PPP$ GDP	2.9	34
7.2	**Creative goods and services**	**45.1**	**8 ●◆**
7.2.1	Cultural and creative services exports, % total trade	0.6	45
7.2.2	National feature films/mn pop. 15–69	6.3	16
7.2.3	Entertainment and media market/th pop. 15–69	27.2	25
7.2.4	Creative goods exports, % total trade	10.9	1 ●◆
7.3	**Online creativity**	**53.1**	**20**
7.3.1	Generic top-level domains (TLDs)/th pop. 15–69	20.6	30
7.3.2	Country-code TLDs/th pop. 15–69	59.1	16
7.3.3	GitHub commits/mn pop. 15–69	58.0	14 ●
7.3.4	Mobile app creation/bn PPP$ GDP	74.8	26

NOTES: ● indicates a strength; ○ a weakness; ◆ an income group strength; ◇ an income group weakness; * an index; † a survey question. ⦸ is used when the available economy data are older than the base year; see appendices for details, including the year of the data, at wipo.int/gii-ranking. Square brackets [ ] indicate that the data minimum coverage (DMC) requirements were not met at the sub-pillar or pillar level.

GII 2023 rank

Denmark 9

Output rank	Input rank	Income	Region	Population (mn)	GDP, PPP$ (bn)	GDP per capita, PPP$
10	7	High	EUR	5.9	411.0	69,845

		Score/Value	Rank
	Institutions	**83.9**	**5 ●**
1.1	**Institutional environment**	**88.7**	**2 ●◆**
1.1.1	Operational stability for businesses*	85.4	6 ◆
1.1.2	Government effectiveness*	92.1	3 ●◆
1.2	**Regulatory environment**	**85.7**	**17**
1.2.1	Regulatory quality*	89.0	5 ●
1.2.2	Rule of law*	96.4	3 ●◆
1.2.3	Cost of redundancy dismissal	18.8	81 ○
1.3	**Business environment**	**77.2**	**[12]**
1.3.1	Policies for doing business†	77.2	14
1.3.2	Entrepreneurship policies and culture†	n/a	n/a
	Human capital and research	**58.1**	**9**
2.1	**Education**	**69.2**	**7**
2.1.1	Expenditure on education, % GDP ⊙	6.9	7 ◆
2.1.2	Government funding/pupil, secondary, % GDP/cap	22.4	37
2.1.3	School life expectancy, years	18.7	10
2.1.4	PISA scales in reading, maths and science	501.1	17
2.1.5	Pupil–teacher ratio, secondary	10.1	32
2.2	**Tertiary education**	**40.4**	**34**
2.2.1	Tertiary enrolment, % gross	82.8	20
2.2.2	Graduates in science and engineering, %	23.0	55 ○
2.2.3	Tertiary inbound mobility, %	10.2	26
2.3	**Research and development (R&D)**	**64.5**	**10**
2.3.1	Researchers, FTE/mn pop.	7,708.3	4 ●◆
2.3.2	Gross expenditure on R&D, % GDP	2.8	12
2.3.3	Global corporate R&D investors, top 3, mn USD	70.1	14
2.3.4	QS university ranking, top 3*	57.6	16
	Infrastructure	**65.6**	**3 ●◆**
3.1	**Information and communication technologies (ICTs)**	**94.2**	**7 ◆**
3.1.1	ICT access*	90.9	20
3.1.2	ICT use*	99.6	2 ●◆
3.1.3	Government's online service*	97.8	4 ●◆
3.1.4	E-participation*	88.4	12
3.2	**General infrastructure**	**46.6**	**25**
3.2.1	Electricity output, GWh/mn pop.	5,644.0	36
3.2.2	Logistics performance*	90.9	3 ●◆
3.2.3	Gross capital formation, % GDP	24.2	63 ○
3.3	**Ecological sustainability**	**56.2**	**10 ◆**
3.3.1	GDP/unit of energy use	18.6	10
3.3.2	Environmental performance*	100.0	1 ●◆
3.3.3	ISO 14001 environment/bn PPP$ GDP	2.6	35
	Market sophistication	**52.8**	**21**
4.1	**Credit**	**62.5**	**[15]**
4.1.1	Finance for startups and scaleups†	n/a	n/a
4.1.2	Domestic credit to private sector, % GDP	163.7	8
4.1.3	Loans from microfinance institutions, % GDP	n/a	n/a
4.2	**Investment**	**33.0**	**21**
4.2.1	Market capitalization, % GDP	n/a	n/a
4.2.2	Venture capital (VC) investors, deals/bn PPP$ GDP	0.4	14
4.2.3	VC recipients, deals/bn PPP$ GDP	0.2	14
4.2.4	VC received, value, % GDP	0.0	26
4.3	**Trade, diversification and market scale**	**63.0**	**44**
4.3.1	Applied tariff rate, weighted avg., %	1.5	20
4.3.2	Domestic industry diversification	89.7	50 ○
4.3.3	Domestic market scale, bn PPP$	411.0	51

		Score/Value	Rank
	Business sophistication	**59.0**	**12**
5.1	**Knowledge workers**	**63.1**	**17**
5.1.1	Knowledge-intensive employment, %	48.9	13
5.1.2	Firms offering formal training, %	40.6	32
5.1.3	GERD performed by business, % GDP	1.7	14
5.1.4	GERD financed by business, % ⊙	59.6	15
5.1.5	Females employed w/advanced degrees, %	25.3	18
5.2	**Innovation linkages**	**64.0**	**8**
5.2.1	University–industry R&D collaboration†	81.5	13
5.2.2	State of cluster development†	69.0	25
5.2.3	GERD financed by abroad, % GDP ⊙	0.2	27
5.2.4	Joint venture/strategic alliance deals/bn PPP$ GDP	0.1	15
5.2.5	Patent families/bn PPP$ GDP	4.9	8 ◆
5.3	**Knowledge absorption**	**49.8**	**21**
5.3.1	Intellectual property payments, % total trade	0.8	49 ○
5.3.2	High-tech imports, % total trade	6.5	100 ○
5.3.3	ICT services imports, % total trade	4.1	7 ◆
5.3.4	FDI net inflows, % GDP	1.0	97 ○
5.3.5	Research talent, % in businesses	56.2	18
	Knowledge and technology outputs	**51.3**	**12**
6.1	**Knowledge creation**	**59.6**	**11**
6.1.1	Patents by origin/bn PPP$ GDP	9.9	9
6.1.2	PCT patents by origin/bn PPP$ GDP	3.6	7
6.1.3	Utility models by origin/bn PPP$ GDP	0.2	42 ○
6.1.4	Scientific and technical articles/bn PPP$ GDP	47.9	2 ●◆
6.1.5	Citable documents H-index	51.5	15
6.2	**Knowledge impact**	**48.1**	**20**
6.2.1	Labor productivity growth, %	0.4	83 ○
6.2.2	Unicorn valuation, % GDP	1.7	25
6.2.3	Software spending, % GDP	0.5	22
6.2.4	High-tech manufacturing, %	50.5	10
6.3	**Knowledge diffusion**	**46.2**	**22**
6.3.1	Intellectual property receipts, % total trade	2.3	13
6.3.2	Production and export complexity	76.0	23
6.3.3	High-tech exports, % total trade	5.5	34
6.3.4	ICT services exports, % total trade	3.5	34
6.3.5	ISO 9001 quality/bn PPP$ GDP	6.0	48
	Creative outputs	**55.9**	**10**
7.1	**Intangible assets**	**55.6**	**15**
7.1.1	Intangible asset intensity, top 15, %	85.7	3 ●◆
7.1.2	Trademarks by origin/bn PPP$ GDP	31.3	75 ○
7.1.3	Global brand value, top 5,000, % GDP	14.2	9
7.1.4	Industrial designs by origin/bn PPP$ GDP	5.8	18
7.2	**Creative goods and services**	**37.9**	**16**
7.2.1	Cultural and creative services exports, % total trade	0.9	34
7.2.2	National feature films/mn pop. 15–69	5.7	20
7.2.3	Entertainment and media market/th pop. 15–69	77.8	3 ●
7.2.4	Creative goods exports, % total trade	1.6	32
7.3	**Online creativity**	**74.5**	**4 ●**
7.3.1	Generic top-level domains (TLDs)/th pop. 15–69	56.8	14
7.3.2	Country-code TLDs/th pop. 15–69	100.0	1 ●◆
7.3.3	GitHub commits/mn pop. 15–69	64.7	9
7.3.4	Mobile app creation/bn PPP$ GDP	76.4	16

NOTES: ● indicates a strength; ○ a weakness; ◆ an income group strength; ◇ an income group weakness; * an index; † a survey question. ⊙ is used when the available economy data are older than the base year; see appendices for details, including the year of the data, at wipo.int/gii-ranking. Square brackets [ ] indicate that the data minimum coverage (DMC) requirements were not met at the sub-pillar or pillar level.

GII 2023 rank

Dominican Republic

94

Output rank	Input rank	Income	Region	Population (mn)	GDP, PPP$ (bn)	GDP per capita, PPP$
96	89	Upper middle	LCN	11.2	256.4	24,120

			Score/ Value	Rank	
	Institutions		**49.3**	**67**	
1.1	**Institutional environment**		**47.3**	**59**	
1.1.1	Operational stability for businesses*		56.9	55	●
1.1.2	Government effectiveness*		37.6	68	
1.2	**Regulatory environment**		**52.3**	**93**	
1.2.1	Regulatory quality*		44.4	67	
1.2.2	Rule of law*		36.9	70	
1.2.3	Cost of redundancy dismissal		26.2	107	
1.3	**Business environment**		**48.4**	**61**	
1.3.1	Policies for doing business†		58.8	41	●
1.3.2	Entrepreneurship policies and culture†	⊙	37.9	50	
	Human capital and research		**17.5**	**109**	◇
2.1	**Education**		**35.8**	**110**	◇
2.1.1	Expenditure on education, % GDP		3.7	80	
2.1.2	Government funding/pupil, secondary, % GDP/cap		13.6	80	
2.1.3	School life expectancy, years	⊙	14.2	70	
2.1.4	PISA scales in reading, maths and science		334.1	79	○ ◇
2.1.5	Pupil–teacher ratio, secondary		13.5	66	
2.2	**Tertiary education**		**16.6**	**97**	◇
2.2.1	Tertiary enrolment, % gross	⊙	59.9	53	●
2.2.2	Graduates in science and engineering, %	⊙	11.6	106	◇
2.2.3	Tertiary inbound mobility, %	⊙	1.7	80	
2.3	**Research and development (R&D)**		**0.0**	**[119]**	
2.3.1	Researchers, FTE/mn pop.		n/a	n/a	
2.3.2	Gross expenditure on R&D, % GDP		n/a	n/a	
2.3.3	Global corporate R&D investors, top 3, mn USD		0.0	40	○ ◇
2.3.4	QS university ranking, top 3*		0.0	71	○ ◇
	Infrastructure		**37.0**	**76**	
3.1	**Information and communication technologies (ICTs)**		**58.2**	**85**	
3.1.1	ICT access*		61.6	97	◇
3.1.2	ICT use*		69.3	74	
3.1.3	Government's online service*		57.8	79	
3.1.4	E-participation*		44.2	83	
3.2	**General infrastructure**		**20.8**	**88**	
3.2.1	Electricity output, GWh/mn pop.	⊙	1,533.0	91	◇
3.2.2	Logistics performance*		22.7	82	
3.2.3	Gross capital formation, % GDP		31.5	20	● ◆
3.3	**Ecological sustainability**		**31.9**	**49**	●
3.3.1	GDP/unit of energy use		21.2	7	● ◆
3.3.2	Environmental performance*		39.5	65	
3.3.3	ISO 14001 environment/bn PPP$ GDP		0.1	120	
	Market sophistication		**25.3**	**91**	◇
4.1	**Credit**		**10.5**	**111**	◇
4.1.1	Finance for startups and scaleups†	⊙	11.1	83	○ ◇
4.1.2	Domestic credit to private sector, % GDP		30.5	95	
4.1.3	Loans from microfinance institutions, % GDP		n/a	n/a	
4.2	**Investment**		**n/a**	**[n/a]**	
4.2.1	Market capitalization, % GDP		n/a	n/a	
4.2.2	Venture capital (VC) investors, deals/bn PPP$ GDP		n/a	n/a	
4.2.3	VC recipients, deals/bn PPP$ GDP		n/a	n/a	
4.2.4	VC received, value, % GDP		n/a	n/a	
4.3	**Trade, diversification and market scale**		**40.1**	**103**	◇
4.3.1	Applied tariff rate, weighted avg., %		3.9	81	
4.3.2	Domestic industry diversification		n/a	n/a	
4.3.3	Domestic market scale, bn PPP$		256.4	62	

			Score/ Value	Rank	
	Business sophistication		**23.7**	**86**	
5.1	**Knowledge workers**		**25.0**	**[78]**	
5.1.1	Knowledge-intensive employment, %	⊙	15.2	88	◇
5.1.2	Firms offering formal training, %	⊙	23.4	70	
5.1.3	GERD performed by business, % GDP		n/a	n/a	
5.1.4	GERD financed by business, %		n/a	n/a	
5.1.5	Females employed w/advanced degrees, %	⊙	9.6	77	
5.2	**Innovation linkages**		**19.2**	**78**	
5.2.1	University–industry R&D collaboration†		31.1	94	
5.2.2	State of cluster development†		43.9	59	
5.2.3	GERD financed by abroad, % GDP		n/a	n/a	
5.2.4	Joint venture/strategic alliance deals/bn PPP$ GDP		0.0	123	○
5.2.5	Patent families/bn PPP$ GDP		0.0	65	
5.3	**Knowledge absorption**		**26.9**	**94**	
5.3.1	Intellectual property payments, % total trade		0.4	78	
5.3.2	High-tech imports, % total trade		8.9	52	●
5.3.3	ICT services imports, % total trade		0.4	112	◇
5.3.4	FDI net inflows, % GDP		3.3	42	●
5.3.5	Research talent, % in businesses		n/a	n/a	
	Knowledge and technology outputs		**14.4**	**95**	
6.1	**Knowledge creation**		**1.0**	**130**	○ ◇
6.1.1	Patents by origin/bn PPP$ GDP		0.0	126	○
6.1.2	PCT patents by origin/bn PPP$ GDP		0.0	84	
6.1.3	Utility models by origin/bn PPP$ GDP		0.0	66	
6.1.4	Scientific and technical articles/bn PPP$ GDP		0.8	130	○ ◇
6.1.5	Citable documents H-index		2.4	123	
6.2	**Knowledge impact**		**24.4**	**76**	
6.2.1	Labor productivity growth, %		3.0	16	●
6.2.2	Unicorn valuation, % GDP		0.0	48	○ ◇
6.2.3	Software spending, % GDP		0.0	122	◇
6.2.4	High-tech manufacturing, %		n/a	n/a	
6.3	**Knowledge diffusion**		**17.7**	**85**	
6.3.1	Intellectual property receipts, % total trade		0.0	114	○ ◇
6.3.2	Production and export complexity		52.2	61	
6.3.3	High-tech exports, % total trade		2.4	53	●
6.3.4	ICT services exports, % total trade		0.3	114	
6.3.5	ISO 9001 quality/bn PPP$ GDP		1.0	107	
	Creative outputs		**14.1**	**94**	
7.1	**Intangible assets**		**9.8**	**108**	◇
7.1.1	Intangible asset intensity, top 15, %		n/a	n/a	
7.1.2	Trademarks by origin/bn PPP$ GDP		43.1	53	●
7.1.3	Global brand value, top 5,000, % GDP		0.2	70	
7.1.4	Industrial designs by origin/bn PPP$ GDP		0.0	119	○ ◇
7.2	**Creative goods and services**		**22.3**	**[46]**	
7.2.1	Cultural and creative services exports, % total trade		n/a	n/a	
7.2.2	National feature films/mn pop. 15–69		2.1	46	
7.2.3	Entertainment and media market/th pop. 15–69		n/a	n/a	
7.2.4	Creative goods exports, % total trade		2.7	21	●
7.3	**Online creativity**		**14.6**	**99**	
7.3.1	Generic top-level domains (TLDs)/th pop. 15–69		2.7	76	
7.3.2	Country-code TLDs/th pop. 15–69		1.4	79	
7.3.3	GitHub commits/mn pop. 15–69		3.2	87	
7.3.4	Mobile app creation/bn PPP$ GDP		51.0	101	

NOTES: ● indicates a strength; ○ a weakness; ◆ an income group strength; ◇ an income group weakness; * an index; † a survey question. ⊙ is used when the available economy data are older than the base year; see appendices for details, including the year of the data, at wipo.int/gii-ranking. Square brackets [ ] indicate that the data minimum coverage (DMC) requirements were not met at the sub-pillar or pillar level.

Ecuador

GII 2023 rank

104

Output rank	Input rank	Income	Region	Population (mn)	GDP, PPP$ (bn)	GDP per capita, PPP$
99	98	Upper middle	LCN	18.0	229.8	12,763

			Score/ Value	Rank	
Institutions			**35.1**	**109**	◇
1.1	**Institutional environment**		**33.9**	**95**	
1.1.1	Operational stability for businesses*		36.8	107	◇
1.1.2	Government effectiveness*		31.0	86	
1.2	**Regulatory environment**		**39.9**	**120**	○◇
1.2.1	Regulatory quality*		23.9	112	◇
1.2.2	Rule of law*		29.8	83	
1.2.3	Cost of redundancy dismissal		31.8	122	○◇
1.3	**Business environment**		**31.7**	**96**	
1.3.1	Policies for doing business†		26.0	113	
1.3.2	Entrepreneurship policies and culture†	⊙	37.3	52	
Human capital and research			**21.3**	**98**	◇
2.1	**Education**		**36.5**	**109**	◇
2.1.1	Expenditure on education, % GDP		3.7	83	
2.1.2	Government funding/pupil, secondary, % GDP/cap		6.0	99	○◇
2.1.3	School life expectancy, years		14.8	59	
2.1.4	PISA scales in reading, maths and science		n/a	n/a	
2.1.5	Pupil–teacher ratio, secondary		21.0	102	◇
2.2	**Tertiary education**		**22.1**	**85**	
2.2.1	Tertiary enrolment, % gross		52.6	67	
2.2.2	Graduates in science and engineering, %		19.7	72	
2.2.3	Tertiary inbound mobility, %		1.0	89	
2.3	**Research and development (R&D)**		**5.3**	**74**	
2.3.1	Researchers, FTE/mn pop.	⊙	399.5	74	
2.3.2	Gross expenditure on R&D, % GDP	⊙	0.4	65	
2.3.3	Global corporate R&D investors, top 3, mn USD		0.0	40	○◇
2.3.4	QS university ranking, top 3*		9.5	68	
Infrastructure			**36.8**	**78**	
3.1	**Information and communication technologies (ICTs)**		**65.3**	**76**	
3.1.1	ICT access*		58.9	99	◇
3.1.2	ICT use*		58.6	95	
3.1.3	Government's online service*		74.0	50	●
3.1.4	E-participation*		69.8	41	●
3.2	**General infrastructure**		**17.0**	**102**	
3.2.1	Electricity output, GWh/mn pop.		1,807.9	86	
3.2.2	Logistics performance*		n/a	n/a	
3.2.3	Gross capital formation, % GDP		27.1	37	●
3.3	**Ecological sustainability**		**28.0**	**57**	
3.3.1	GDP/unit of energy use		12.5	40	●
3.3.2	Environmental performance*		46.8	52	
3.3.3	ISO 14001 environment/bn PPP$ GDP		1.0	65	
Market sophistication			**23.3**	**103**	◇
4.1	**Credit**		**22.5**	**85**	
4.1.1	Finance for startups and scaleups†	⊙	31.3	68	
4.1.2	Domestic credit to private sector, % GDP		47.4	75	
4.1.3	Loans from microfinance institutions, % GDP	⊙	1.7	19	●
4.2	**Investment**		**2.7**	**[96]**	
4.2.1	Market capitalization, % GDP		n/a	n/a	
4.2.2	Venture capital (VC) investors, deals/bn PPP$ GDP		n/a	n/a	
4.2.3	VC recipients, deals/bn PPP$ GDP	⊙	0.0	96	○
4.2.4	VC received, value, % GDP	⊙	0.0	66	
4.3	**Trade, diversification and market scale**		**44.8**	**97**	◇
4.3.1	Applied tariff rate, weighted avg., %		6.2	98	◇
4.3.2	Domestic industry diversification		69.7	95	◇
4.3.3	Domestic market scale, bn PPP$		229.8	65	

			Score/ Value	Rank	
Business sophistication			**23.2**	**90**	
5.1	**Knowledge workers**		**29.5**	**72**	
5.1.1	Knowledge-intensive employment, %		12.5	100	◇
5.1.2	Firms offering formal training, %	⊙	73.7	1	●◆
5.1.3	GERD performed by business, % GDP	⊙	0.2	56	
5.1.4	GERD financed by business, %	⊙	0.2	97	
5.1.5	Females employed w/advanced degrees, %		8.6	81	
5.2	**Innovation linkages**		**11.3**	**114**	◇
5.2.1	University–industry R&D collaboration†		30.9	96	
5.2.2	State of cluster development†		21.2	112	◇
5.2.3	GERD financed by abroad, % GDP	⊙	0.0	64	
5.2.4	Joint venture/strategic alliance deals/bn PPP$ GDP		0.0	124	○
5.2.5	Patent families/bn PPP$ GDP		0.0	80	
5.3	**Knowledge absorption**		**28.7**	**85**	
5.3.1	Intellectual property payments, % total trade		0.6	61	
5.3.2	High-tech imports, % total trade		9.7	42	●
5.3.3	ICT services imports, % total trade		0.6	106	
5.3.4	FDI net inflows, % GDP		0.9	101	
5.3.5	Research talent, % in businesses		n/a	n/a	
Knowledge and technology outputs			**13.4**	**102**	
6.1	**Knowledge creation**		**6.9**	**99**	
6.1.1	Patents by origin/bn PPP$ GDP		0.2	104	
6.1.2	PCT patents by origin/bn PPP$ GDP		0.0	83	
6.1.3	Utility models by origin/bn PPP$ GDP		0.1	56	
6.1.4	Scientific and technical articles/bn PPP$ GDP		9.8	75	
6.1.5	Citable documents H-index		9.5	83	
6.2	**Knowledge impact**		**22.5**	**91**	
6.2.1	Labor productivity growth, %		−0.8	115	○◇
6.2.2	Unicorn valuation, % GDP		1.2	32	●◆
6.2.3	Software spending, % GDP		0.2	69	
6.2.4	High-tech manufacturing, %		10.3	89	
6.3	**Knowledge diffusion**		**10.9**	**104**	◇
6.3.1	Intellectual property receipts, % total trade		0.0	91	
6.3.2	Production and export complexity		29.5	113	○◇
6.3.3	High-tech exports, % total trade		0.3	102	
6.3.4	ICT services exports, % total trade		0.3	108	
6.3.5	ISO 9001 quality/bn PPP$ GDP		6.0	47	●
Creative outputs			**12.9**	**99**	◇
7.1	**Intangible assets**		**17.7**	**90**	
7.1.1	Intangible asset intensity, top 15, %		n/a	n/a	
7.1.2	Trademarks by origin/bn PPP$ GDP		66.9	28	●
7.1.3	Global brand value, top 5,000, % GDP		0.0	74	○◇
7.1.4	Industrial designs by origin/bn PPP$ GDP		0.4	90	
7.2	**Creative goods and services**		**0.3**	**[127]**	
7.2.1	Cultural and creative services exports, % total trade		0.0	101	○
7.2.2	National feature films/mn pop. 15–69		n/a	n/a	
7.2.3	Entertainment and media market/th pop. 15–69		n/a	n/a	
7.2.4	Creative goods exports, % total trade		0.0	115	
7.3	**Online creativity**		**15.8**	**92**	
7.3.1	Generic top-level domains (TLDs)/th pop. 15–69		2.1	80	
7.3.2	Country-code TLDs/th pop. 15–69		1.2	85	
7.3.3	GitHub commits/mn pop. 15–69		3.9	80	
7.3.4	Mobile app creation/bn PPP$ GDP		56.0	93	

NOTES: ● indicates a strength; ○ a weakness; ◆ an income group strength; ◇ an income group weakness; * an index; † a survey question. ⊙ is used when the available economy data are older than the base year; see appendices for details, including the year of the data, at wipo.int/gii-ranking. Square brackets [ ] indicate that the data minimum coverage (DMC) requirements were not met at the sub-pillar or pillar level.

GII 2023 rank

Egypt

86

Output rank	Input rank	Income	Region	Population (mn)	GDP, PPP$ (bn)	GDP per capita, PPP$
74	99	Lower middle	NAWA	111.0	1,662.0	15,959

Institutions

			Score/Value	Rank	
	Institutions		**36.6**	**103**	
1.1	**Institutional environment**		**31.9**	**98**	
1.1.1	Operational stability for businesses*		38.9	96	
1.1.2	Government effectiveness*		24.8	97	
1.2	**Regulatory environment**		**36.8**	**124**	○
1.2.1	Regulatory quality*		29.0	99	
1.2.2	Rule of law*		32.5	76	
1.2.3	Cost of redundancy dismissal		36.8	125	○ ◇
1.3	**Business environment**		**41.2**	**81**	
1.3.1	Policies for doing business†		53.7	53	
1.3.2	Entrepreneurship policies and culture†		28.7	62	

Human capital and research

			Score/Value	Rank	
	Human capital and research		**21.9**	**95**	
2.1	**Education**		**42.1**	**91**	
2.1.1	Expenditure on education, % GDP	⊙	3.9	75	
2.1.2	Government funding/pupil, secondary, % GDP/cap		12.5	86	
2.1.3	School life expectancy, years	⊙	13.6	75	
2.1.4	PISA scales in reading, maths and science		n/a	n/a	
2.1.5	Pupil–teacher ratio, secondary	⊙	15.8	81	
2.2	**Tertiary education**		**11.7**	**109**	
2.2.1	Tertiary enrolment, % gross		42.7	76	
2.2.2	Graduates in science and engineering, %	⊙	11.2	107	○ ◇
2.2.3	Tertiary inbound mobility, %		0.9	90	
2.3	**Research and development (R&D)**		**11.8**	**55**	
2.3.1	Researchers, FTE/mn pop.		854.3	55	
2.3.2	Gross expenditure on R&D, % GDP		1.0	42	● ◆
2.3.3	Global corporate R&D investors, top 3, mn USD		0.0	40	○ ◇
2.3.4	QS university ranking, top 3*		21.5	49	● ◆

Infrastructure

			Score/Value	Rank	
	Infrastructure		**31.9**	**90**	
3.1	**Information and communication technologies (ICTs)**		**53.7**	**92**	
3.1.1	ICT access*		73.3	83	
3.1.2	ICT use*		55.1	99	
3.1.3	Government's online service*		52.8	87	
3.1.4	E-participation*		33.7	97	
3.2	**General infrastructure**		**18.3**	**98**	
3.2.1	Electricity output, GWh/mn pop.	⊙	1,875.3	84	
3.2.2	Logistics performance*		45.5	56	◆
3.2.3	Gross capital formation, % GDP		11.8	126	○ ◇
3.3	**Ecological sustainability**		**23.7**	**66**	◆
3.3.1	GDP/unit of energy use		15.2	24	● ◆
3.3.2	Environmental performance*		28.1	91	
3.3.3	ISO 14001 environment/bn PPP$ GDP		0.7	76	

Market sophistication

			Score/Value	Rank	
	Market sophistication		**27.6**	**88**	
4.1	**Credit**		**20.6**	**91**	
4.1.1	Finance for startups and scaleups†		48.1	50	
4.1.2	Domestic credit to private sector, % GDP		27.1	104	
4.1.3	Loans from microfinance institutions, % GDP		0.4	39	
4.2	**Investment**		**7.7**	**59**	
4.2.1	Market capitalization, % GDP		14.2	66	
4.2.2	Venture capital (VC) investors, deals/bn PPP$ GDP		0.0	68	
4.2.3	VC recipients, deals/bn PPP$ GDP		0.0	45	
4.2.4	VC received, value, % GDP		0.0	50	
4.3	**Trade, diversification and market scale**		**54.7**	**76**	
4.3.1	Applied tariff rate, weighted avg., %	⊙	10.4	120	○
4.3.2	Domestic industry diversification	⊙	95.8	25	● ◆
4.3.3	Domestic market scale, bn PPP$		1,662.0	18	● ◆

Business sophistication

			Score/Value	Rank	
	Business sophistication		**21.4**	**100**	
5.1	**Knowledge workers**		**11.3**	**120**	○ ◇
5.1.1	Knowledge-intensive employment, %	⊙	22.8	65	
5.1.2	Firms offering formal training, %		7.9	95	○ ◇
5.1.3	GERD performed by business, % GDP	⊙	0.0	77	
5.1.4	GERD financed by business, %	⊙	3.9	84	◇
5.1.5	Females employed w/advanced degrees, %	⊙	5.7	92	
5.2	**Innovation linkages**		**27.6**	**47**	● ◆
5.2.1	University–industry R&D collaboration†		50.7	50	
5.2.2	State of cluster development†		83.5	7	● ◆
5.2.3	GERD financed by abroad, % GDP	⊙	0.0	85	
5.2.4	Joint venture/strategic alliance deals/bn PPP$ GDP		0.0	99	
5.2.5	Patent families/bn PPP$ GDP		0.0	90	
5.3	**Knowledge absorption**		**25.3**	**101**	
5.3.1	Intellectual property payments, % total trade		0.5	73	
5.3.2	High-tech imports, % total trade		7.4	75	
5.3.3	ICT services imports, % total trade		1.2	72	
5.3.4	FDI net inflows, % GDP		1.9	73	
5.3.5	Research talent, % in businesses	⊙	6.3	66	

Knowledge and technology outputs

			Score/Value	Rank	
	Knowledge and technology outputs		**19.9**	**77**	
6.1	**Knowledge creation**		**12.2**	**73**	
6.1.1	Patents by origin/bn PPP$ GDP		0.6	73	
6.1.2	PCT patents by origin/bn PPP$ GDP		0.0	79	
6.1.3	Utility models by origin/bn PPP$ GDP		0.0	74	○
6.1.4	Scientific and technical articles/bn PPP$ GDP		15.7	47	●
6.1.5	Citable documents H-index		19.2	47	● ◆
6.2	**Knowledge impact**		**31.1**	**53**	
6.2.1	Labor productivity growth, %		3.3	12	●
6.2.2	Unicorn valuation, % GDP		0.2	45	●
6.2.3	Software spending, % GDP		0.2	72	
6.2.4	High-tech manufacturing, %	⊙	22.6	57	
6.3	**Knowledge diffusion**		**16.2**	**90**	
6.3.1	Intellectual property receipts, % total trade		0.0	106	
6.3.2	Production and export complexity		50.6	68	
6.3.3	High-tech exports, % total trade		0.7	81	
6.3.4	ICT services exports, % total trade		1.7	65	
6.3.5	ISO 9001 quality/bn PPP$ GDP		1.6	92	

Creative outputs

			Score/Value	Rank	
	Creative outputs		**21.2**	**73**	
7.1	**Intangible assets**		**31.3**	**66**	
7.1.1	Intangible asset intensity, top 15, %		47.8	51	
7.1.2	Trademarks by origin/bn PPP$ GDP		29.7	77	
7.1.3	Global brand value, top 5,000, % GDP		0.6	61	
7.1.4	Industrial designs by origin/bn PPP$ GDP		1.5	51	
7.2	**Creative goods and services**		**6.7**	**78**	
7.2.1	Cultural and creative services exports, % total trade		n/a	n/a	
7.2.2	National feature films/mn pop. 15–69		0.4	74	○
7.2.3	Entertainment and media market/th pop. 15–69		1.2	54	○
7.2.4	Creative goods exports, % total trade		1.4	38	●
7.3	**Online creativity**		**15.6**	**93**	
7.3.1	Generic top-level domains (TLDs)/th pop. 15–69		1.2	94	
7.3.2	Country-code TLDs/th pop. 15–69		0.0	129	○
7.3.3	GitHub commits/mn pop. 15–69		2.5	95	
7.3.4	Mobile app creation/bn PPP$ GDP		58.7	87	

NOTES: ● indicates a strength; ○ a weakness; ◆ an income group strength; ◇ an income group weakness; * an index; † a survey question. ⊙ is used when the available economy data are older than the base year; see appendices for details, including the year of the data, at wipo.int/gii-ranking. Square brackets [ ] indicate that the data minimum coverage (DMC) requirements were not met at the sub-pillar or pillar level.

GII 2023 rank

El Salvador **95**

Output rank	Input rank	Income	Region	Population (mn)	GDP, PPP$ (bn)	GDP per capita, PPP$
90	102	Lower middle	LCN	6.3	69.3	10,576

		Score/Value	Rank	
	Institutions	**37.8**	**101**	
1.1	**Institutional environment**	**37.7**	**83**	
1.1.1	Operational stability for businesses*	47.2	75	
1.1.2	Government effectiveness*	28.1	90	
1.2	**Regulatory environment**	**47.3**	**107**	
1.2.1	Regulatory quality*	33.2	91	
1.2.2	Rule of law*	14.9	111	
1.2.3	Cost of redundancy dismissal	22.9	99	
1.3	**Business environment**	**28.4**	**104**	
1.3.1	Policies for doing business†	17.9	122	○◇
1.3.2	Entrepreneurship policies and culture† ⊙	38.8	49	

		Score/Value	Rank	
	Human capital and research	**18.3**	**106**	
2.1	**Education**	**35.4**	**111**	
2.1.1	Expenditure on education, % GDP	4.6	51	●
2.1.2	Government funding/pupil, secondary, % GDP/cap	13.1	82	
2.1.3	School life expectancy, years ⊙	12.5	89	
2.1.4	PISA scales in reading, maths and science	n/a	n/a	
2.1.5	Pupil–teacher ratio, secondary ⊙	27.6	117	◇
2.2	**Tertiary education**	**18.5**	**94**	
2.2.1	Tertiary enrolment, % gross ⊙	29.9	88	
2.2.2	Graduates in science and engineering, % ⊙	21.8	62	
2.2.3	Tertiary inbound mobility, % ⊙	0.4	102	
2.3	**Research and development (R&D)**	**0.9**	**102**	
2.3.1	Researchers, FTE/mn pop. ⊙	73.0	93	
2.3.2	Gross expenditure on R&D, % GDP ⊙	0.2	94	
2.3.3	Global corporate R&D investors, top 3, mn USD	0.0	40	○◇
2.3.4	QS university ranking, top 3*	0.0	71	○◇

		Score/Value	Rank	
	Infrastructure	**28.8**	**99**	
3.1	**Information and communication technologies (ICTs)**	**47.7**	**103**	
3.1.1	ICT access*	59.7	98	
3.1.2	ICT use*	56.1	97	
3.1.3	Government's online service*	41.1	108	
3.1.4	E-participation*	33.7	97	
3.2	**General infrastructure**	**16.5**	**104**	
3.2.1	Electricity output, GWh/mn pop. ⊙	974.4	97	
3.2.2	Logistics performance*	27.3	76	
3.2.3	Gross capital formation, % GDP	22.6	77	
3.3	**Ecological sustainability**	**22.3**	**72**	◆
3.3.1	GDP/unit of energy use	11.7	50	●
3.3.2	Environmental performance*	37.1	71	◆
3.3.3	ISO 14001 environment/bn PPP$ GDP	0.3	102	

		Score/Value	Rank	
	Market sophistication	**24.8**	**95**	
4.1	**Credit**	**27.8**	**69**	
4.1.1	Finance for startups and scaleups† ⊙	31.6	67	
4.1.2	Domestic credit to private sector, % GDP	66.3	55	●
4.1.3	Loans from microfinance institutions, % GDP	n/a	n/a	
4.2	**Investment**	**2.0**	**[103]**	
4.2.1	Market capitalization, % GDP	n/a	n/a	
4.2.2	Venture capital (VC) investors, deals/bn PPP$ GDP	0.0	72	
4.2.3	VC recipients, deals/bn PPP$ GDP	n/a	n/a	
4.2.4	VC received, value, % GDP	n/a	n/a	
4.3	**Trade, diversification and market scale**	**44.5**	**98**	
4.3.1	Applied tariff rate, weighted avg., %	1.9	59	◆
4.3.2	Domestic industry diversification	n/a	n/a	
4.3.3	Domestic market scale, bn PPP$	69.3	98	

		Score/Value	Rank	
	Business sophistication	**23.8**	**85**	
5.1	**Knowledge workers**	**29.9**	**69**	
5.1.1	Knowledge-intensive employment, %	14.8	90	
5.1.2	Firms offering formal training, % ⊙	53.8	15	●◆
5.1.3	GERD performed by business, % GDP ⊙	0.1	70	
5.1.4	GERD financed by business, %	35.1	54	
5.1.5	Females employed w/advanced degrees, %	4.9	94	
5.2	**Innovation linkages**	**8.4**	**122**	◇
5.2.1	University-industry R&D collaboration†	22.5	112	
5.2.2	State of cluster development†	13.8	122	○◇
5.2.3	GERD financed by abroad, % GDP ⊙	0.0	70	
5.2.4	Joint venture/strategic alliance deals/bn PPP$ GDP ⊙	0.0	91	
5.2.5	Patent families/bn PPP$ GDP	0.0	95	○◇
5.3	**Knowledge absorption**	**33.3**	**65**	
5.3.1	Intellectual property payments, % total trade	1.0	38	●◆
5.3.2	High-tech imports, % total trade	10.8	30	●
5.3.3	ICT services imports, % total trade	0.7	98	
5.3.4	FDI net inflows, % GDP	2.3	67	
5.3.5	Research talent, % in businesses	n/a	n/a	

		Score/Value	Rank	
	Knowledge and technology outputs	**14.6**	**94**	
6.1	**Knowledge creation**	**1.3**	**128**	○◇
6.1.1	Patents by origin/bn PPP$ GDP	0.0	125	○
6.1.2	PCT patents by origin/bn PPP$ GDP	0.0	101	○◇
6.1.3	Utility models by origin/bn PPP$ GDP ⊙	0.1	58	
6.1.4	Scientific and technical articles/bn PPP$ GDP	1.4	128	○
6.1.5	Citable documents H-index	2.2	126	○
6.2	**Knowledge impact**	**19.1**	**109**	
6.2.1	Labor productivity growth, %	1.0	65	
6.2.2	Unicorn valuation, % GDP	0.0	48	○◇
6.2.3	Software spending, % GDP	0.0	107	
6.2.4	High-tech manufacturing, %	n/a	n/a	
6.3	**Knowledge diffusion**	**23.4**	**62**	
6.3.1	Intellectual property receipts, % total trade	0.0	93	
6.3.2	Production and export complexity	53.0	60	
6.3.3	High-tech exports, % total trade	2.9	47	●
6.3.4	ICT services exports, % total trade	2.7	48	●
6.3.5	ISO 9001 quality/bn PPP$ GDP	2.9	75	

		Score/Value	Rank	
	Creative outputs	**19.2**	**[77]**	
7.1	**Intangible assets**	**28.8**	**[69]**	
7.1.1	Intangible asset intensity, top 15, %	n/a	n/a	
7.1.2	Trademarks by origin/bn PPP$ GDP	77.5	20	●◆
7.1.3	Global brand value, top 5,000, % GDP	n/a	n/a	
7.1.4	Industrial designs by origin/bn PPP$ GDP	0.3	100	
7.2	**Creative goods and services**	**4.0**	**[91]**	
7.2.1	Cultural and creative services exports, % total trade ⊙	0.0	105	○
7.2.2	National feature films/mn pop. 15–69	n/a	n/a	
7.2.3	Entertainment and media market/th pop. 15–69	n/a	n/a	
7.2.4	Creative goods exports, % total trade	0.7	54	●
7.3	**Online creativity**	**15.2**	**97**	
7.3.1	Generic top-level domains (TLDs)/th pop. 15–69	2.8	75	
7.3.2	Country-code TLDs/th pop. 15–69	0.6	97	
7.3.3	GitHub commits/mn pop. 15–69	3.8	82	
7.3.4	Mobile app creation/bn PPP$ GDP	53.7	98	

NOTES: ● indicates a strength; ○ a weakness; ◆ an income group strength; ◇ an income group weakness; * an index; † a survey question. ⊙ is used when the available economy data are older than the base year; see appendices for details, including the year of the data, at wipo.int/gii-ranking. Square brackets [ ] indicate that the data minimum coverage (DMC) requirements were not met at the sub-pillar or pillar level.

GII 2023 rank

Estonia

16

Output rank	Input rank	Income	Region	Population (mn)	GDP, PPP$ (bn)	GDP per capita, PPP$
16	14	High	EUR	1.3	61.4	46,126

			Score/Value	Rank	
	Institutions		**78.6**	**11**	
1.1	**Institutional environment**		**75.3**	**17**	
1.1.1	Operational stability for businesses*		75.7	15	
1.1.2	Government effectiveness*		74.9	19	
1.2	**Regulatory environment**		**86.2**	**16**	
1.2.1	Regulatory quality*		82.6	15	
1.2.2	Rule of law*		81.5	18	
1.2.3	Cost of redundancy dismissal		12.9	40	
1.3	**Business environment**		**74.3**	**16**	
1.3.1	Policies for doing business†		60.7	37	
1.3.2	Entrepreneurship policies and culture†	⊙	88.0	3	● ◆
	Human capital and research		**42.9**	**34**	◇
2.1	**Education**		**62.5**	**21**	
2.1.1	Expenditure on education, % GDP	⊙	5.3	26	
2.1.2	Government funding/pupil, secondary, % GDP/cap		20.3	51	○
2.1.3	School life expectancy, years		16.0	39	
2.1.4	PISA scales in reading, maths and science		525.5	4	●
2.1.5	Pupil–teacher ratio, secondary		9.8	29	
2.2	**Tertiary education**		**43.4**	**24**	
2.2.1	Tertiary enrolment, % gross	⊙	69.0	43	
2.2.2	Graduates in science and engineering, %		27.5	31	
2.2.3	Tertiary inbound mobility, %		12.3	20	
2.3	**Research and development (R&D)**		**22.7**	**42**	◇
2.3.1	Researchers, FTE/mn pop.		4,037.4	27	
2.3.2	Gross expenditure on R&D, % GDP		1.8	22	
2.3.3	Global corporate R&D investors, top 3, mn USD		0.0	40	○ ◇
2.3.4	QS university ranking, top 3*		17.6	56	◇
	Infrastructure		**64.3**	**5**	●
3.1	**Information and communication technologies (ICTs)**		**95.6**	**2**	● ◆
3.1.1	ICT access*		90.0	23	
3.1.2	ICT use*		94.8	12	
3.1.3	Government's online service*		100.0	1	● ◆
3.1.4	E-participation*		97.7	3	● ◆
3.2	**General infrastructure**		**40.1**	**33**	
3.2.1	Electricity output, GWh/mn pop.		5,500.4	40	
3.2.2	Logistics performance*		68.2	25	◇
3.2.3	Gross capital formation, % GDP		26.6	41	
3.3	**Ecological sustainability**		**57.2**	**9**	◆
3.3.1	GDP/unit of energy use		9.5	76	○
3.3.2	Environmental performance*		72.0	14	
3.3.3	ISO 14001 environment/bn PPP$ GDP		10.0	4	● ◆
	Market sophistication		**67.6**	**5**	● ◆
4.1	**Credit**		**50.8**	**27**	
4.1.1	Finance for startups and scaleups†	⊙	76.0	11	
4.1.2	Domestic credit to private sector, % GDP		63.4	57	◇
4.1.3	Loans from microfinance institutions, % GDP		4.6	8	◆
4.2	**Investment**		**89.2**	**2**	● ◆
4.2.1	Market capitalization, % GDP		n/a	n/a	
4.2.2	Venture capital (VC) investors, deals/bn PPP$ GDP		1.3	5	◆
4.2.3	VC recipients, deals/bn PPP$ GDP		0.7	1	● ◆
4.2.4	VC received, value, % GDP		0.0	1	● ◆
4.3	**Trade, diversification and market scale**		**62.9**	**46**	
4.3.1	Applied tariff rate, weighted avg., %		1.5	20	
4.3.2	Domestic industry diversification		97.0	17	
4.3.3	Domestic market scale, bn PPP$		61.4	101	○

			Score/Value	Rank	
	Business sophistication		**49.2**	**25**	◇
5.1	**Knowledge workers**		**58.8**	**22**	
5.1.1	Knowledge-intensive employment, %		46.8	17	
5.1.2	Firms offering formal training, %		40.7	31	
5.1.3	GERD performed by business, % GDP		1.0	23	
5.1.4	GERD financed by business, %		50.1	29	
5.1.5	Females employed w/advanced degrees, %		28.1	8	
5.2	**Innovation linkages**		**37.3**	**30**	◇
5.2.1	University–industry R&D collaboration†		54.1	44	◇
5.2.2	State of cluster development†		41.9	62	○ ◇
5.2.3	GERD financed by abroad, % GDP		0.2	19	
5.2.4	Joint venture/strategic alliance deals/bn PPP$ GDP		0.1	18	
5.2.5	Patent families/bn PPP$ GDP		0.9	28	◇
5.3	**Knowledge absorption**		**51.5**	**17**	
5.3.1	Intellectual property payments, % total trade		0.3	87	○ ◇
5.3.2	High-tech imports, % total trade		8.4	60	○
5.3.3	ICT services imports, % total trade		10.0	1	● ◆
5.3.4	FDI net inflows, % GDP		13.7	8	
5.3.5	Research talent, % in businesses		43.2	33	◇
	Knowledge and technology outputs		**43.7**	**20**	
6.1	**Knowledge creation**		**28.4**	**34**	◇
6.1.1	Patents by origin/bn PPP$ GDP		1.7	41	◇
6.1.2	PCT patents by origin/bn PPP$ GDP		0.6	30	◇
6.1.3	Utility models by origin/bn PPP$ GDP		0.6	30	
6.1.4	Scientific and technical articles/bn PPP$ GDP		36.3	13	
6.1.5	Citable documents H-index		18.5	48	◇
6.2	**Knowledge impact**		**52.4**	**10**	
6.2.1	Labor productivity growth, %		1.9	35	
6.2.2	Unicorn valuation, % GDP		23.8	1	● ◆
6.2.3	Software spending, % GDP		0.1	89	○ ◇
6.2.4	High-tech manufacturing, %		29.9	37	
6.3	**Knowledge diffusion**		**50.3**	**17**	
6.3.1	Intellectual property receipts, % total trade		0.5	27	◇
6.3.2	Production and export complexity		73.2	27	
6.3.3	High-tech exports, % total trade		9.7	18	
6.3.4	ICT services exports, % total trade		7.2	8	
6.3.5	ISO 9001 quality/bn PPP$ GDP		17.9	16	◆
	Creative outputs		**48.8**	**15**	
7.1	**Intangible assets**		**48.3**	**29**	
7.1.1	Intangible asset intensity, top 15, %		46.9	53	○ ◇
7.1.2	Trademarks by origin/bn PPP$ GDP		104.1	9	◆
7.1.3	Global brand value, top 5,000, % GDP		0.0	74	○ ◇
7.1.4	Industrial designs by origin/bn PPP$ GDP		4.2	24	
7.2	**Creative goods and services**		**47.2**	**7**	◆
7.2.1	Cultural and creative services exports, % total trade		2.1	11	
7.2.2	National feature films/mn pop. 15–69		13.1	3	● ◆
7.2.3	Entertainment and media market/th pop. 15–69		n/a	n/a	
7.2.4	Creative goods exports, % total trade		1.3	40	
7.3	**Online creativity**		**51.3**	**23**	
7.3.1	Generic top-level domains (TLDs)/th pop. 15–69		13.1	37	◇
7.3.2	Country-code TLDs/th pop. 15–69		50.1	17	
7.3.3	GitHub commits/mn pop. 15–69		58.1	13	
7.3.4	Mobile app creation/bn PPP$ GDP		83.9	6	◆

NOTES: ● indicates a strength; ○ a weakness; ◆ an income group strength; ◇ an income group weakness; * an index; † a survey question. ⊙ is used when the available economy data are older than the base year; see appendices for details, including the year of the data, at wipo.int/gii-ranking. Square brackets [ ] indicate that the data minimum coverage (DMC) requirements were not met at the sub-pillar or pillar level.

Ethiopia

GII 2023 rank

125

Output rank	Input rank	Income	Region	Population (mn)	GDP, PPP$ (bn)	GDP per capita, PPP$
109	130	Low	SSA	123.4	347.8	3,434

			Score/Value	Rank	
Institutions			**32.7**	**116**	
1.1	**Institutional environment**		**18.6**	**123**	
1.1.1	Operational stability for businesses*		17.4	126	◇
1.1.2	Government effectiveness*		19.8	103	
1.2	**Regulatory environment**		**49.0**	**103**	
1.2.1	Regulatory quality*		18.0	123	
1.2.2	Rule of law*		22.0	101	
1.2.3	Cost of redundancy dismissal		19.1	83	
1.3	**Business environment**		**30.5**	**[99]**	
1.3.1	Policies for doing business†	⏲	30.5	105	
1.3.2	Entrepreneurship policies and culture†		n/a	n/a	
Human capital and research			**8.0**	**[131]**	
2.1	**Education**		**18.6**	**[130]**	
2.1.1	Expenditure on education, % GDP		3.7	82	
2.1.2	Government funding/pupil, secondary, % GDP/cap	⏲	17.0	66	
2.1.3	School life expectancy, years		n/a	n/a	
2.1.4	PISA scales in reading, maths and science		n/a	n/a	
2.1.5	Pupil–teacher ratio, secondary	⏲	43.7	124	◇
2.2	**Tertiary education**		**4.1**	**[123]**	
2.2.1	Tertiary enrolment, % gross	⏲	10.4	113	
2.2.2	Graduates in science and engineering, %		n/a	n/a	
2.2.3	Tertiary inbound mobility, %		n/a	n/a	
2.3	**Research and development (R&D)**		**1.4**	**96**	
2.3.1	Researchers, FTE/mn pop.	⏲	90.5	90	◆
2.3.2	Gross expenditure on R&D, % GDP	⏲	0.3	81	
2.3.3	Global corporate R&D investors, top 3, mn USD		0.0	40	○◇
2.3.4	QS university ranking, top 3*		0.0	71	○◇
Infrastructure			**12.1**	**132**	○◇
3.1	**Information and communication technologies (ICTs)**		**17.0**	**132**	○◇
3.1.1	ICT access*		9.9	131	○◇
3.1.2	ICT use*		9.8	131	○◇
3.1.3	Government's online service*		30.7	122	
3.1.4	E-participation*		17.4	125	◇
3.2	**General infrastructure**		**8.8**	**126**	
3.2.1	Electricity output, GWh/mn pop.	⏲	134.8	119	
3.2.2	Logistics performance*		n/a	n/a	
3.2.3	Gross capital formation, % GDP		22.2	79	
3.3	**Ecological sustainability**		**10.5**	**125**	
3.3.1	GDP/unit of energy use		5.5	114	
3.3.2	Environmental performance*		21.9	103	
3.3.3	ISO 14001 environment/bn PPP$ GDP		0.1	131	○◇
Market sophistication			**19.8**	**114**	
4.1	**Credit**		**n/a**	**[n/a]**	
4.1.1	Finance for startups and scaleups†		n/a	n/a	
4.1.2	Domestic credit to private sector, % GDP		n/a	n/a	
4.1.3	Loans from microfinance institutions, % GDP		n/a	n/a	
4.2	**Investment**		**0.4**	**111**	○◇
4.2.1	Market capitalization, % GDP		n/a	n/a	
4.2.2	Venture capital (VC) investors, deals/bn PPP$ GDP		0.0	93	◇
4.2.3	VC recipients, deals/bn PPP$ GDP		0.0	95	◇
4.2.4	VC received, value, % GDP		0.0	98	
4.3	**Trade, diversification and market scale**		**39.3**	**105**	◆
4.3.1	Applied tariff rate, weighted avg., %	⏲	12.1	127	◇
4.3.2	Domestic industry diversification	⏲	88.9	52	
4.3.3	Domestic market scale, bn PPP$		347.8	55	●◆

			Score/Value	Rank	
Business sophistication			**14.7**	**130**	
5.1	**Knowledge workers**		**5.0**	**128**	◇
5.1.1	Knowledge-intensive employment, %	⏲	4.4	121	
5.1.2	Firms offering formal training, %	⏲	20.8	77	
5.1.3	GERD performed by business, % GDP	⏲	0.0	86	
5.1.4	GERD financed by business, %	⏲	1.5	90	
5.1.5	Females employed w/advanced degrees, %	⏲	0.3	126	
5.2	**Innovation linkages**		**12.8**	**108**	
5.2.1	University–industry R&D collaboration†	⏲	33.4	90	
5.2.2	State of cluster development†	⏲	19.1	114	
5.2.3	GERD financed by abroad, % GDP	⏲	0.1	48	●
5.2.4	Joint venture/strategic alliance deals/bn PPP$ GDP		0.0	106	
5.2.5	Patent families/bn PPP$ GDP		0.0	95	○◇
5.3	**Knowledge absorption**		**26.2**	**100**	
5.3.1	Intellectual property payments, % total trade		0.0	111	
5.3.2	High-tech imports, % total trade		9.8	40	●◆
5.3.3	ICT services imports, % total trade		1.8	43	●
5.3.4	FDI net inflows, % GDP		2.9	48	●
5.3.5	Research talent, % in businesses	⏲	2.2	76	
Knowledge and technology outputs			**17.9**	**84**	◆
6.1	**Knowledge creation**		**19.2**	**56**	●◆
6.1.1	Patents by origin/bn PPP$ GDP	⏲	0.0	127	◇
6.1.2	PCT patents by origin/bn PPP$ GDP		n/a	n/a	
6.1.3	Utility models by origin/bn PPP$ GDP	⏲	1.3	19	●◆
6.1.4	Scientific and technical articles/bn PPP$ GDP		18.1	40	●◆
6.1.5	Citable documents H-index		9.7	81	◆
6.2	**Knowledge impact**		**24.1**	**79**	◆
6.2.1	Labor productivity growth, %		4.0	8	●◆
6.2.2	Unicorn valuation, % GDP		0.0	48	○◇
6.2.3	Software spending, % GDP		0.0	130	○◇
6.2.4	High-tech manufacturing, %	⏲	13.5	81	
6.3	**Knowledge diffusion**		**10.2**	**108**	
6.3.1	Intellectual property receipts, % total trade		0.0	112	
6.3.2	Production and export complexity		37.8	96	
6.3.3	High-tech exports, % total trade		0.2	112	
6.3.4	ICT services exports, % total trade		1.2	81	
6.3.5	ISO 9001 quality/bn PPP$ GDP		0.3	129	◇
Creative outputs			**4.5**	**[126]**	
7.1	**Intangible assets**		**2.1**	**[127]**	
7.1.1	Intangible asset intensity, top 15, %		n/a	n/a	
7.1.2	Trademarks by origin/bn PPP$ GDP	⏲	5.5	120	
7.1.3	Global brand value, top 5,000, % GDP		0.4	66	●◆
7.1.4	Industrial designs by origin/bn PPP$ GDP		n/a	n/a	
7.2	**Creative goods and services**		**0.4**	**[126]**	
7.2.1	Cultural and creative services exports, % total trade		0.0	104	
7.2.2	National feature films/mn pop. 15–69		n/a	n/a	
7.2.3	Entertainment and media market/th pop. 15–69		n/a	n/a	
7.2.4	Creative goods exports, % total trade		0.1	108	
7.3	**Online creativity**		**13.6**	**103**	◆
7.3.1	Generic top-level domains (TLDs)/th pop. 15–69		0.0	131	○
7.3.2	Country-code TLDs/th pop. 15–69		0.0	132	○◇
7.3.3	GitHub commits/mn pop. 15–69		1.2	113	
7.3.4	Mobile app creation/bn PPP$ GDP		53.3	99	

NOTES: ● indicates a strength; ○ a weakness; ◆ an income group strength; ◇ an income group weakness; * an index; † a survey question. ⏲ is used when the available economy data are older than the base year; see appendices for details, including the year of the data, at wipo.int/gii-ranking. Square brackets [ ] indicate that the data minimum coverage (DMC) requirements were not met at the sub-pillar or pillar level.

Finland

GII 2023 rank

6

Output rank	Input rank	Income	Region	Population (mn)	GDP, PPP$ (bn)	GDP per capita, PPP$
9	5	High	EUR	5.5	324.8	58,659

			Score/Value	Rank
	Institutions		**85.4**	**3 ●◆**
1.1	**Institutional environment**		**84.0**	**8**
1.1.1	Operational stability for businesses*		77.1	13
1.1.2	Government effectiveness*		90.9	4 ●◆
1.2	**Regulatory environment**		**95.7**	**2 ●◆**
1.2.1	Regulatory quality*		91.4	3 ●
1.2.2	Rule of law*		100.0	1 ●◆
1.2.3	Cost of redundancy dismissal		10.1	31
1.3	**Business environment**		**76.6**	**13**
1.3.1	Policies for doing business†		79.6	8
1.3.2	Entrepreneurship policies and culture†	ⓢ	73.6	12
	Human capital and research		**60.0**	**5**
2.1	**Education**		**69.2**	**8**
2.1.1	Expenditure on education, % GDP	ⓢ	6.4	14
2.1.2	Government funding/pupil, secondary, % GDP/cap		24.2	24
2.1.3	School life expectancy, years		19.1	7 ◆
2.1.4	PISA scales in reading, maths and science		516.4	8
2.1.5	Pupil–teacher ratio, secondary		12.6	58 ○
2.2	**Tertiary education**		**46.0**	**19**
2.2.1	Tertiary enrolment, % gross		95.0	7
2.2.2	Graduates in science and engineering, %		27.9	28
2.2.3	Tertiary inbound mobility, %		8.0	32
2.3	**Research and development (R&D)**		**64.7**	**9**
2.3.1	Researchers, FTE/mn pop.		7,870.6	3 ●◆
2.3.2	Gross expenditure on R&D, % GDP		3.0	10
2.3.3	Global corporate R&D investors, top 3, mn USD		73.2	11
2.3.4	QS university ranking, top 3*		50.5	18
	Infrastructure		**69.2**	**1 ●◆**
3.1	**Information and communication technologies (ICTs)**		**94.7**	**4 ●◆**
3.1.1	ICT access*		89.1	28
3.1.2	ICT use*		96.1	7
3.1.3	Government's online service*		98.2	2 ●◆
3.1.4	E-participation*		95.3	6
3.2	**General infrastructure**		**60.5**	**7 ◆**
3.2.1	Electricity output, GWh/mn pop.		12,939.4	11
3.2.2	Logistics performance*		95.5	2 ●◆
3.2.3	Gross capital formation, % GDP		24.1	66 ○
3.3	**Ecological sustainability**		**52.4**	**18**
3.3.1	GDP/unit of energy use		7.7	89 ○
3.3.2	Environmental performance*		97.6	3 ●◆
3.3.3	ISO 14001 environment/bn PPP$ GDP		5.5	19 ◆
	Market sophistication		**58.7**	**12**
4.1	**Credit**		**68.7**	**6**
4.1.1	Finance for startups and scaleups†	ⓢ	100.0	1 ●◆
4.1.2	Domestic credit to private sector, % GDP		100.2	30
4.1.3	Loans from microfinance institutions, % GDP		n/a	n/a
4.2	**Investment**		**42.3**	**14**
4.2.1	Market capitalization, % GDP		n/a	n/a
4.2.2	Venture capital (VC) investors, deals/bn PPP$ GDP		0.3	19
4.2.3	VC recipients, deals/bn PPP$ GDP		0.2	9
4.2.4	VC received, value, % GDP		0.0	15
4.3	**Trade, diversification and market scale**		**65.0**	**29**
4.3.1	Applied tariff rate, weighted avg., %		1.5	20 ○
4.3.2	Domestic industry diversification	ⓢ	97.6	13
4.3.3	Domestic market scale, bn PPP$		324.8	57 ○

			Score/Value	Rank
	Business sophistication		**65.8**	**4 ●**
5.1	**Knowledge workers**		**66.6**	**11**
5.1.1	Knowledge-intensive employment, %		47.4	15
5.1.2	Firms offering formal training, %		50.2	19
5.1.3	GERD performed by business, % GDP		2.1	11
5.1.4	GERD financed by business, %		56.0	20
5.1.5	Females employed w/advanced degrees, %		26.4	15
5.2	**Innovation linkages**		**74.2**	**5 ◆**
5.2.1	University–industry R&D collaboration†		81.5	14
5.2.2	State of cluster development†		69.2	23
5.2.3	GERD financed by abroad, % GDP		0.4	7 ◆
5.2.4	Joint venture/strategic alliance deals/bn PPP$ GDP		0.2	12
5.2.5	Patent families/bn PPP$ GDP		6.1	1 ●◆
5.3	**Knowledge absorption**		**56.6**	**7**
5.3.1	Intellectual property payments, % total trade		1.0	36
5.3.2	High-tech imports, % total trade		7.4	78 ○
5.3.3	ICT services imports, % total trade		4.8	4 ●◆
5.3.4	FDI net inflows, % GDP		4.3	28
5.3.5	Research talent, % in businesses		62.0	10
	Knowledge and technology outputs		**61.6**	**4 ●◆**
6.1	**Knowledge creation**		**61.3**	**7**
6.1.1	Patents by origin/bn PPP$ GDP		12.3	6
6.1.2	PCT patents by origin/bn PPP$ GDP		5.4	1 ●◆
6.1.3	Utility models by origin/bn PPP$ GDP		0.8	24
6.1.4	Scientific and technical articles/bn PPP$ GDP		42.5	5 ◆
6.1.5	Citable documents H-index		43.0	19
6.2	**Knowledge impact**		**55.5**	**8**
6.2.1	Labor productivity growth, %		−0.5	108 ○
6.2.2	Unicorn valuation, % GDP		4.4	10
6.2.3	Software spending, % GDP		0.6	14
6.2.4	High-tech manufacturing, %	ⓢ	38.1	28
6.3	**Knowledge diffusion**		**68.1**	**1 ●◆**
6.3.1	Intellectual property receipts, % total trade		3.2	8
6.3.2	Production and export complexity		81.9	14
6.3.3	High-tech exports, % total trade		4.7	39
6.3.4	ICT services exports, % total trade		13.0	1 ●◆
6.3.5	ISO 9001 quality/bn PPP$ GDP		9.8	29
	Creative outputs		**47.5**	**16**
7.1	**Intangible assets**		**50.1**	**26**
7.1.1	Intangible asset intensity, top 15, %		73.0	14
7.1.2	Trademarks by origin/bn PPP$ GDP		38.4	60 ○
7.1.3	Global brand value, top 5,000, % GDP		11.8	13
7.1.4	Industrial designs by origin/bn PPP$ GDP		3.6	29
7.2	**Creative goods and services**		**31.0**	**30**
7.2.1	Cultural and creative services exports, % total trade		0.5	54 ○
7.2.2	National feature films/mn pop. 15–69		8.0	9
7.2.3	Entertainment and media market/th pop. 15–69		56.1	12
7.2.4	Creative goods exports, % total trade		0.6	59 ○
7.3	**Online creativity**		**58.9**	**14**
7.3.1	Generic top-level domains (TLDs)/th pop. 15–69		33.8	21
7.3.2	Country-code TLDs/th pop. 15–69		42.4	18
7.3.3	GitHub commits/mn pop. 15–69		78.2	7
7.3.4	Mobile app creation/bn PPP$ GDP		81.1	9

NOTES: ● indicates a strength; ○ a weakness; ◆ an income group strength; ◇ an income group weakness; * an index; † a survey question. ⓢ is used when the available economy data are older than the base year; see appendices for details, including the year of the data, at wipo.int/gii-ranking. Square brackets [ ] indicate that the data minimum coverage (DMC) requirements were not met at the sub-pillar or pillar level.

France

GII 2023 rank **11**

Output rank	Input rank	Income	Region	Population (mn)	GDP, PPP$ (bn)	GDP per capita, PPP$
11	17	High	EUR	64.6	3,688.3	56,200

		Score/Value	Rank
	Institutions	**70.0**	**27**
1.1	**Institutional environment**	**66.4**	**34** ◇
1.1.1	Operational stability for businesses*	61.1	43 ◇
1.1.2	Government effectiveness*	71.7	25
1.2	**Regulatory environment**	**83.0**	**22**
1.2.1	Regulatory quality*	74.2	24
1.2.2	Rule of law*	77.5	22
1.2.3	Cost of redundancy dismissal	13.0	41
1.3	**Business environment**	**60.6**	**33**
1.3.1	Policies for doing business†	58.9	40 ◇
1.3.2	Entrepreneurship policies and culture†	62.3	20
	Human capital and research	**54.0**	**17**
2.1	**Education**	**60.3**	**35**
2.1.1	Expenditure on education, % GDP ⊙	5.4	25
2.1.2	Government funding/pupil, secondary, % GDP/cap	25.1	19
2.1.3	School life expectancy, years	15.9	41 ○
2.1.4	PISA scales in reading, maths and science	493.7	25
2.1.5	Pupil–teacher ratio, secondary ⊙	13.4	64 ○
2.2	**Tertiary education**	**39.2**	**35**
2.2.1	Tertiary enrolment, % gross	69.3	41
2.2.2	Graduates in science and engineering, %	25.9	39
2.2.3	Tertiary inbound mobility, %	9.2	28
2.3	**Research and development (R&D)**	**62.5**	**12**
2.3.1	Researchers, FTE/mn pop.	5,025.4	18
2.3.2	Gross expenditure on R&D, % GDP	2.2	17
2.3.3	Global corporate R&D investors, top 3, mn USD	80.4	9 ●
2.3.4	QS university ranking, top 3*	77.9	9 ●
	Infrastructure	**57.2**	**22**
3.1	**Information and communication technologies (ICTs)**	**84.1**	**23**
3.1.1	ICT access*	83.7	60 ○
3.1.2	ICT use*	95.6	9 ●
3.1.3	Government's online service*	86.4	20
3.1.4	E-participation*	70.9	37
3.2	**General infrastructure**	**48.1**	**22**
3.2.1	Electricity output, GWh/mn pop.	8,069.8	18
3.2.2	Logistics performance*	81.8	13
3.2.3	Gross capital formation, % GDP	24.9	56 ○
3.3	**Ecological sustainability**	**39.3**	**33**
3.3.1	GDP/unit of energy use	12.2	46 ○
3.3.2	Environmental performance*	73.9	12
3.3.3	ISO 14001 environment/bn PPP$ GDP	1.9	48 ○
	Market sophistication	**60.7**	**9** ●
4.1	**Credit**	**58.1**	**19**
4.1.1	Finance for startups and scaleups†	70.3	17
4.1.2	Domestic credit to private sector, % GDP	122.0	20
4.1.3	Loans from microfinance institutions, % GDP	n/a	n/a
4.2	**Investment**	**35.4**	**18**
4.2.1	Market capitalization, % GDP ⊙	92.7	18
4.2.2	Venture capital (VC) investors, deals/bn PPP$ GDP	0.3	24
4.2.3	VC recipients, deals/bn PPP$ GDP	0.2	12
4.2.4	VC received, value, % GDP	0.0	17
4.3	**Trade, diversification and market scale**	**88.5**	**8** ●◆
4.3.1	Applied tariff rate, weighted avg., %	1.5	20
4.3.2	Domestic industry diversification	95.7	27
4.3.3	Domestic market scale, bn PPP$	3,688.3	10 ●◆

		Score/Value	Rank
	Business sophistication	**56.1**	**17**
5.1	**Knowledge workers**	**69.1**	**7** ●
5.1.1	Knowledge-intensive employment, %	47.7	14
5.1.2	Firms offering formal training, %	67.9	2 ●◆
5.1.3	GERD performed by business, % GDP	1.5	17
5.1.4	GERD financed by business, %	56.8	19
5.1.5	Females employed w/advanced degrees, %	25.3	19
5.2	**Innovation linkages**	**47.3**	**23** ◇
5.2.1	University–industry R&D collaboration†	58.6	38 ◇
5.2.2	State of cluster development†	69.2	24
5.2.3	GERD financed by abroad, % GDP	0.2	23
5.2.4	Joint venture/strategic alliance deals/bn PPP$ GDP	0.1	24
5.2.5	Patent families/bn PPP$ GDP	2.9	13
5.3	**Knowledge absorption**	**51.9**	**15**
5.3.1	Intellectual property payments, % total trade	1.4	23
5.3.2	High-tech imports, % total trade	9.4	44
5.3.3	ICT services imports, % total trade	3.0	17
5.3.4	FDI net inflows, % GDP	1.8	80 ○
5.3.5	Research talent, % in businesses	61.8	11
	Knowledge and technology outputs	**46.7**	**16**
6.1	**Knowledge creation**	**43.7**	**21**
6.1.1	Patents by origin/bn PPP$ GDP	7.2	12
6.1.2	PCT patents by origin/bn PPP$ GDP	2.1	15
6.1.3	Utility models by origin/bn PPP$ GDP	0.1	53 ○
6.1.4	Scientific and technical articles/bn PPP$ GDP	18.6	39
6.1.5	Citable documents H-index	77.9	5 ●
6.2	**Knowledge impact**	**51.2**	**12**
6.2.1	Labor productivity growth, %	−0.3	105 ○
6.2.2	Unicorn valuation, % GDP	2.1	18
6.2.3	Software spending, % GDP	0.7	7 ●
6.2.4	High-tech manufacturing, %	48.8	12
6.3	**Knowledge diffusion**	**45.3**	**23**
6.3.1	Intellectual property receipts, % total trade	1.7	14
6.3.2	Production and export complexity	79.5	18
6.3.3	High-tech exports, % total trade	10.4	17
6.3.4	ICT services exports, % total trade	2.4	50 ○
6.3.5	ISO 9001 quality/bn PPP$ GDP	6.6	44
	Creative outputs	**58.2**	**6** ●
7.1	**Intangible assets**	**74.9**	**3** ●◆
7.1.1	Intangible asset intensity, top 15, %	88.0	2 ●◆
7.1.2	Trademarks by origin/bn PPP$ GDP	97.6	15
7.1.3	Global brand value, top 5,000, % GDP	18.4	4 ●
7.1.4	Industrial designs by origin/bn PPP$ GDP	11.0	8 ●◆
7.2	**Creative goods and services**	**33.1**	**22**
7.2.1	Cultural and creative services exports, % total trade	1.1	25
7.2.2	National feature films/mn pop. 15–69	6.1	17
7.2.3	Entertainment and media market/th pop. 15–69	51.6	15
7.2.4	Creative goods exports, % total trade	1.6	31
7.3	**Online creativity**	**49.9**	**26**
7.3.1	Generic top-level domains (TLDs)/th pop. 15–69	49.3	16
7.3.2	Country-code TLDs/th pop. 15–69	27.2	26
7.3.3	GitHub commits/mn pop. 15–69	46.8	23
7.3.4	Mobile app creation/bn PPP$ GDP	76.4	17

NOTES: ● indicates a strength; ○ a weakness; ◆ an income group strength; ◇ an income group weakness; * an index; † a survey question. ⊙ is used when the available economy data are older than the base year; see appendices for details, including the year of the data, at wipo.int/gii-ranking. Square brackets [ ] indicate that the data minimum coverage (DMC) requirements were not met at the sub-pillar or pillar level.

Georgia

GII 2023 rank

65

Output rank	Input rank	Income	Region	Population (mn)	GDP, PPP$ (bn)	GDP per capita, PPP$
77	54	Upper middle	NAWA	3.7	73.6	19,789

			Score/Value	Rank
	Institutions		**70.6**	**25 ●◆**
1.1	**Institutional environment**		**52.4**	**51**
1.1.1	Operational stability for businesses*		50.0	71
1.1.2	Government effectiveness*		54.8	41 ◆
1.2	**Regulatory environment**		**78.0**	**30 ●◆**
1.2.1	Regulatory quality*		69.6	29 ●◆
1.2.2	Rule of law*		44.7	57
1.2.3	Cost of redundancy dismissal		8.6	16 ●◆
1.3	**Business environment**		**81.5**	**4 ●◆**
1.3.1	Policies for doing business†		70.5	25 ●◆
1.3.2	Entrepreneurship policies and culture†	⊙	92.4	2

			Score/Value	Rank
	Human capital and research		**30.2**	**69**
2.1	**Education**		**51.7**	**64**
2.1.1	Expenditure on education, % GDP		3.6	84
2.1.2	Government funding/pupil, secondary, % GDP/cap		n/a	n/a
2.1.3	School life expectancy, years		15.9	40
2.1.4	PISA scales in reading, maths and science		386.7	70 ○
2.1.5	Pupil–teacher ratio, secondary		8.0	9 ●◆
2.2	**Tertiary education**		**33.8**	**55**
2.2.1	Tertiary enrolment, % gross		72.5	30 ●
2.2.2	Graduates in science and engineering, %		19.6	75
2.2.3	Tertiary inbound mobility, %		9.1	29 ◆
2.3	**Research and development (R&D)**		**5.3**	**75**
2.3.1	Researchers, FTE/mn pop.		1,623.7	46
2.3.2	Gross expenditure on R&D, % GDP		0.3	83
2.3.3	Global corporate R&D investors, top 3, mn USD		0.0	40 ○◇
2.3.4	QS university ranking, top 3*		0.0	71 ○◇

			Score/Value	Rank
	Infrastructure		**36.2**	**80**
3.1	**Information and communication technologies (ICTs)**		**69.8**	**67**
3.1.1	ICT access*		89.3	25 ●
3.1.2	ICT use*		80.6	56
3.1.3	Government's online service*		57.0	82
3.1.4	E-participation*		52.3	71
3.2	**General infrastructure**		**19.2**	**94**
3.2.1	Electricity output, GWh/mn pop.		3,410.6	61
3.2.2	Logistics performance*		27.3	76
3.2.3	Gross capital formation, % GDP		19.8	100 ○
3.3	**Ecological sustainability**		**19.7**	**81**
3.3.1	GDP/unit of energy use		10.1	65
3.3.2	Environmental performance*		34.2	76
3.3.3	ISO 14001 environment/bn PPP$ GDP		0.3	104 ○

			Score/Value	Rank
	Market sophistication		**32.3**	**77**
4.1	**Credit**		**36.7**	**46**
4.1.1	Finance for startups and scaleups†	⊙	53.6	41
4.1.2	Domestic credit to private sector, % GDP		79.9	43
4.1.3	Loans from microfinance institutions, % GDP		2.3	17
4.2	**Investment**		**1.2**	**[106]**
4.2.1	Market capitalization, % GDP		n/a	n/a
4.2.2	Venture capital (VC) investors, deals/bn PPP$ GDP		0.0	80 ○
4.2.3	VC recipients, deals/bn PPP$ GDP		n/a	n/a
4.2.4	VC received, value, % GDP		n/a	n/a
4.3	**Trade, diversification and market scale**		**58.9**	**63**
4.3.1	Applied tariff rate, weighted avg., %		0.2	4 ●◆
4.3.2	Domestic industry diversification		76.6	83 ○◇
4.3.3	Domestic market scale, bn PPP$		73.6	94

			Score/Value	Rank
	Business sophistication		**29.4**	**58**
5.1	**Knowledge workers**		**33.3**	**63**
5.1.1	Knowledge-intensive employment, %	⊙	24.7	57
5.1.2	Firms offering formal training, %		32.0	50
5.1.3	GERD performed by business, % GDP		n/a	n/a
5.1.4	GERD financed by business, %	⊙	1.7	89 ○◇
5.1.5	Females employed w/advanced degrees, %	⊙	18.1	39
5.2	**Innovation linkages**		**24.1**	**58**
5.2.1	University–industry R&D collaboration†		56.5	41
5.2.2	State of cluster development†		52.9	41
5.2.3	GERD financed by abroad, % GDP	⊙	0.0	56
5.2.4	Joint venture/strategic alliance deals/bn PPP$ GDP		0.0	69
5.2.5	Patent families/bn PPP$ GDP		0.0	83
5.3	**Knowledge absorption**		**30.7**	**78**
5.3.1	Intellectual property payments, % total trade		0.6	65
5.3.2	High-tech imports, % total trade		7.4	76
5.3.3	ICT services imports, % total trade		1.0	88
5.3.4	FDI net inflows, % GDP		6.1	16 ●◆
5.3.5	Research talent, % in businesses		n/a	n/a

			Score/Value	Rank
	Knowledge and technology outputs		**21.4**	**72**
6.1	**Knowledge creation**		**16.2**	**62**
6.1.1	Patents by origin/bn PPP$ GDP		1.4	46
6.1.2	PCT patents by origin/bn PPP$ GDP		0.1	59
6.1.3	Utility models by origin/bn PPP$ GDP		1.0	22
6.1.4	Scientific and technical articles/bn PPP$ GDP		11.6	68
6.1.5	Citable documents H-index		10.8	72
6.2	**Knowledge impact**		**28.8**	**59**
6.2.1	Labor productivity growth, %		5.8	3 ●◆
6.2.2	Unicorn valuation, % GDP		0.0	48 ○◇
6.2.3	Software spending, % GDP		0.1	97
6.2.4	High-tech manufacturing, %		10.4	88 ○
6.3	**Knowledge diffusion**		**19.3**	**78**
6.3.1	Intellectual property receipts, % total trade		0.0	81
6.3.2	Production and export complexity		50.9	67
6.3.3	High-tech exports, % total trade		1.0	72
6.3.4	ICT services exports, % total trade		2.3	53
6.3.5	ISO 9001 quality/bn PPP$ GDP		3.6	70

			Score/Value	Rank
	Creative outputs		**18.8**	**81**
7.1	**Intangible assets**		**20.6**	**84**
7.1.1	Intangible asset intensity, top 15, %		n/a	n/a
7.1.2	Trademarks by origin/bn PPP$ GDP		45.6	51
7.1.3	Global brand value, top 5,000, % GDP		1.3	52
7.1.4	Industrial designs by origin/bn PPP$ GDP		1.6	49
7.2	**Creative goods and services**		**8.4**	**73**
7.2.1	Cultural and creative services exports, % total trade		0.2	68
7.2.2	National feature films/mn pop. 15–69	⊙	2.7	41
7.2.3	Entertainment and media market/th pop. 15–69		n/a	n/a
7.2.4	Creative goods exports, % total trade		0.3	69
7.3	**Online creativity**		**25.7**	**50**
7.3.1	Generic top-level domains (TLDs)/th pop. 15–69		2.2	79
7.3.2	Country-code TLDs/th pop. 15–69		6.4	50
7.3.3	GitHub commits/mn pop. 15–69		30.3	34 ◆
7.3.4	Mobile app creation/bn PPP$ GDP		64.0	70

NOTES: ● indicates a strength; ○ a weakness; ◆ an income group strength; ◇ an income group weakness; * an index; † a survey question. ⊙ is used when the available economy data are older than the base year; see appendices for details, including the year of the data, at wipo.int/gii-ranking. Square brackets [ ] indicate that the data minimum coverage (DMC) requirements were not met at the sub-pillar or pillar level.

GII 2023 rank

Germany 8

Output rank	Input rank	Income	Region	Population (mn)	GDP, PPP$ (bn)	GDP per capita, PPP$
6	13	High	EUR	83.4	5,316.9	63,835

		Score/Value	Rank	
	Institutions	**71.9**	**22**	
1.1	**Institutional environment**	**71.8**	**20**	
1.1.1	Operational stability for businesses*	70.1	28	
1.1.2	Government effectiveness*	73.5	22	
1.2	**Regulatory environment**	**79.4**	**29**	
1.2.1	Regulatory quality*	84.4	11	
1.2.2	Rule of law*	86.8	14	
1.2.3	Cost of redundancy dismissal	21.6	93	○◇
1.3	**Business environment**	**64.6**	**29**	
1.3.1	Policies for doing business†	75.8	15	
1.3.2	Entrepreneurship policies and culture†	53.5	29	
	Human capital and research	**61.1**	**4**	●
2.1	**Education**	**62.2**	**23**	
2.1.1	Expenditure on education, % GDP ⊙	5.1	36	
2.1.2	Government funding/pupil, secondary, % GDP/cap	24.3	23	
2.1.3	School life expectancy, years	16.9	20	
2.1.4	PISA scales in reading, maths and science	500.4	18	
2.1.5	Pupil–teacher ratio, secondary	11.5	47	○
2.2	**Tertiary education**	**51.4**	**8**	●
2.2.1	Tertiary enrolment, % gross	73.0	29	
2.2.2	Graduates in science and engineering, %	35.8	8	◆
2.2.3	Tertiary inbound mobility, %	11.2	23	
2.3	**Research and development (R&D)**	**69.6**	**7**	●
2.3.1	Researchers, FTE/mn pop.	5,538.0	14	
2.3.2	Gross expenditure on R&D, % GDP	3.1	9	
2.3.3	Global corporate R&D investors, top 3, mn USD	92.0	3	●◆
2.3.4	QS university ranking, top 3*	72.9	11	
	Infrastructure	**57.1**	**23**	
3.1	**Information and communication technologies (ICTs)**	**82.0**	**32**	
3.1.1	ICT access*	88.0	34	
3.1.2	ICT use*	91.2	19	
3.1.3	Government's online service*	76.8	44	◇
3.1.4	E-participation*	72.1	32	
3.2	**General infrastructure**	**48.3**	**21**	
3.2.1	Electricity output, GWh/mn pop.	7,102.1	27	
3.2.2	Logistics performance*	90.9	3	●◆
3.2.3	Gross capital formation, % GDP	22.7	76	○
3.3	**Ecological sustainability**	**41.2**	**30**	
3.3.1	GDP/unit of energy use	14.2	30	
3.3.2	Environmental performance*	73.7	13	
3.3.3	ISO 14001 environment/bn PPP$ GDP	1.9	50	○
	Market sophistication	**56.5**	**14**	
4.1	**Credit**	**49.3**	**30**	
4.1.1	Finance for startups and scaleups†	67.3	21	
4.1.2	Domestic credit to private sector, % GDP	84.8	37	
4.1.3	Loans from microfinance institutions, % GDP	n/a	n/a	
4.2	**Investment**	**24.9**	**28**	
4.2.1	Market capitalization, % GDP	52.3	33	○
4.2.2	Venture capital (VC) investors, deals/bn PPP$ GDP	0.2	25	
4.2.3	VC recipients, deals/bn PPP$ GDP	0.1	22	
4.2.4	VC received, value, % GDP	0.0	25	
4.3	**Trade, diversification and market scale**	**95.2**	**2**	●◆
4.3.1	Applied tariff rate, weighted avg., %	1.5	20	
4.3.2	Domestic industry diversification	95.1	29	
4.3.3	Domestic market scale, bn PPP$	5,316.9	1	●◆

		Score/Value	Rank	
	Business sophistication	**56.9**	**16**	
5.1	**Knowledge workers**	**59.0**	**21**	
5.1.1	Knowledge-intensive employment, %	46.1	20	
5.1.2	Firms offering formal training, %	44.1	25	
5.1.3	GERD performed by business, % GDP	2.1	9	
5.1.4	GERD financed by business, %	62.6	11	
5.1.5	Females employed w/advanced degrees, %	15.6	48	○◇
5.2	**Innovation linkages**	**63.1**	**10**	
5.2.1	University–industry R&D collaboration†	76.2	17	
5.2.2	State of cluster development†	82.6	9	●
5.2.3	GERD financed by abroad, % GDP	0.2	16	
5.2.4	Joint venture/strategic alliance deals/bn PPP$ GDP	0.1	26	◇
5.2.5	Patent families/bn PPP$ GDP	5.0	1	●◆
5.3	**Knowledge absorption**	**48.6**	**26**	
5.3.1	Intellectual property payments, % total trade	1.0	37	
5.3.2	High-tech imports, % total trade	10.3	33	
5.3.3	ICT services imports, % total trade	2.6	27	
5.3.4	FDI net inflows, % GDP	2.4	63	○
5.3.5	Research talent, % in businesses	60.1	15	
	Knowledge and technology outputs	**55.4**	**9**	●
6.1	**Knowledge creation**	**61.5**	**6**	●
6.1.1	Patents by origin/bn PPP$ GDP	13.5	5	●
6.1.2	PCT patents by origin/bn PPP$ GDP	3.3	10	
6.1.3	Utility models by origin/bn PPP$ GDP	1.4	15	
6.1.4	Scientific and technical articles/bn PPP$ GDP	20.5	35	
6.1.5	Citable documents H-index	86.8	3	●◆
6.2	**Knowledge impact**	**50.7**	**15**	
6.2.1	Labor productivity growth, %	−0.0	98	○
6.2.2	Unicorn valuation, % GDP	2.0	21	
6.2.3	Software spending, % GDP	0.6	15	
6.2.4	High-tech manufacturing, %	52.9	9	
6.3	**Knowledge diffusion**	**54.1**	**10**	
6.3.1	Intellectual property receipts, % total trade	2.5	11	
6.3.2	Production and export complexity	93.6	3	●◆
6.3.3	High-tech exports, % total trade	11.3	15	
6.3.4	ICT services exports, % total trade	2.1	56	○
6.3.5	ISO 9001 quality/bn PPP$ GDP	10.1	28	
	Creative outputs	**58.2**	**7**	●
7.1	**Intangible assets**	**65.5**	**7**	●
7.1.1	Intangible asset intensity, top 15, %	73.6	13	
7.1.2	Trademarks by origin/bn PPP$ GDP	69.1	24	
7.1.3	Global brand value, top 5,000, % GDP	15.6	8	●
7.1.4	Industrial designs by origin/bn PPP$ GDP	10.5	9	◆
7.2	**Creative goods and services**	**32.2**	**24**	
7.2.1	Cultural and creative services exports, % total trade	0.9	37	
7.2.2	National feature films/mn pop. 15–69	4.4	27	
7.2.3	Entertainment and media market/th pop. 15–69	56.4	11	
7.2.4	Creative goods exports, % total trade	2.2	24	
7.3	**Online creativity**	**69.4**	**8**	●
7.3.1	Generic top-level domains (TLDs)/th pop. 15–69	60.9	12	
7.3.2	Country-code TLDs/th pop. 15–69	88.6	6	●◆
7.3.3	GitHub commits/mn pop. 15–69	57.0	16	
7.3.4	Mobile app creation/bn PPP$ GDP	71.1	47	○

NOTES: ● indicates a strength; ○ a weakness; ◆ an income group strength; ◇ an income group weakness; * an index; † a survey question. ⊙ is used when the available economy data are older than the base year; see appendices for details, including the year of the data, at wipo.int/gii-ranking. Square brackets [ ] indicate that the data minimum coverage (DMC) requirements were not met at the sub-pillar or pillar level.

Ghana

GII 2023 rank **99**

Output rank	Input rank	Income	Region	Population (mn)	GDP, PPP$ (bn)	GDP per capita, PPP$
85	107	Lower middle	SSA	33.5	217.5	6,780

		Score/ Value	Rank	
	Institutions	**41.1**	**93**	
1.1	**Institutional environment**	**39.2**	**79**	
1.1.1	Operational stability for businesses*	45.8	79	
1.1.2	Government effectiveness*	32.6	81	
1.2	**Regulatory environment**	**27.2**	**128**	○ ◇
1.2.1	Regulatory quality*	36.9	82	
1.2.2	Rule of law*	37.3	67	◆
1.2.3	Cost of redundancy dismissal	49.8	127	○ ◇
1.3	**Business environment**	**56.8**	**[42]**	
1.3.1	Policies for doing business†	56.8	45	●
1.3.2	Entrepreneurship policies and culture†	n/a	n/a	

		Score/ Value	Rank	
	Human capital and research	**18.4**	**105**	
2.1	**Education**	**43.4**	**87**	
2.1.1	Expenditure on education, % GDP ⊙	3.9	78	
2.1.2	Government funding/pupil, secondary, % GDP/cap ⊙	19.5	57	
2.1.3	School life expectancy, years	12.3	91	
2.1.4	PISA scales in reading, maths and science	n/a	n/a	
2.1.5	Pupil–teacher ratio, secondary	16.1	83	
2.2	**Tertiary education**	**11.7**	**110**	
2.2.1	Tertiary enrolment, % gross	19.5	100	
2.2.2	Graduates in science and engineering, %	16.7	93	
2.2.3	Tertiary inbound mobility, %	0.9	91	
2.3	**Research and development (R&D)**	**0.3**	**114**	
2.3.1	Researchers, FTE/mn pop. ⊙	89.1	91	
2.3.2	Gross expenditure on R&D, % GDP	n/a	n/a	
2.3.3	Global corporate R&D investors, top 3, mn USD	0.0	40	○ ◇
2.3.4	QS university ranking, top 3*	0.0	71	○ ◇

		Score/ Value	Rank	
	Infrastructure	**26.8**	**105**	
3.1	**Information and communication technologies (ICTs)**	**51.2**	**98**	
3.1.1	ICT access*	58.2	100	
3.1.2	ICT use*	53.6	101	
3.1.3	Government's online service*	48.7	93	
3.1.4	E-participation*	44.2	83	
3.2	**General infrastructure**	**10.5**	**121**	
3.2.1	Electricity output, GWh/mn pop. ⊙	634.3	105	
3.2.2	Logistics performance*	18.2	89	
3.2.3	Gross capital formation, % GDP	18.0	111	◇
3.3	**Ecological sustainability**	**18.6**	**87**	
3.3.1	GDP/unit of energy use	15.3	23	● ◆
3.3.2	Environmental performance*	14.9	126	○
3.3.3	ISO 14001 environment/bn PPP$ GDP	0.4	96	

		Score/ Value	Rank	
	Market sophistication	**17.1**	**117**	
4.1	**Credit**	**2.2**	**130**	○ ◇
4.1.1	Finance for startups and scaleups†	n/a	n/a	
4.1.2	Domestic credit to private sector, % GDP	13.2	122	
4.1.3	Loans from microfinance institutions, % GDP	0.1	50	
4.2	**Investment**	**7.5**	**61**	
4.2.1	Market capitalization, % GDP	13.2	68	
4.2.2	Venture capital (VC) investors, deals/bn PPP$ GDP	0.0	57	
4.2.3	VC recipients, deals/bn PPP$ GDP	0.1	43	●
4.2.4	VC received, value, % GDP	0.0	56	
4.3	**Trade, diversification and market scale**	**41.5**	**100**	
4.3.1	Applied tariff rate, weighted avg., %	10.5	121	
4.3.2	Domestic industry diversification ⊙	88.0	56	
4.3.3	Domestic market scale, bn PPP$	217.5	66	

		Score/ Value	Rank	
	Business sophistication	**24.2**	**83**	
5.1	**Knowledge workers**	**23.1**	**[89]**	
5.1.1	Knowledge-intensive employment, % ⊙	9.6	107	
5.1.2	Firms offering formal training, % ⊙	40.1	34	
5.1.3	GERD performed by business, % GDP	n/a	n/a	
5.1.4	GERD financed by business, %	n/a	n/a	
5.1.5	Females employed w/advanced degrees, % ⊙	2.9	104	
5.2	**Innovation linkages**	**25.0**	**53**	● ◆
5.2.1	University–industry R&D collaboration†	45.2	61	
5.2.2	State of cluster development†	49.4	47	●
5.2.3	GERD financed by abroad, % GDP	n/a	n/a	
5.2.4	Joint venture/strategic alliance deals/bn PPP$ GDP	0.0	75	
5.2.5	Patent families/bn PPP$ GDP	0.0	95	○ ◇
5.3	**Knowledge absorption**	**24.6**	**106**	
5.3.1	Intellectual property payments, % total trade	0.7	56	◆
5.3.2	High-tech imports, % total trade ⊙	2.8	129	○ ◇
5.3.3	ICT services imports, % total trade	0.6	105	
5.3.4	FDI net inflows, % GDP	3.9	32	●
5.3.5	Research talent, % in businesses	n/a	n/a	

		Score/ Value	Rank	
	Knowledge and technology outputs	**11.7**	**111**	
6.1	**Knowledge creation**	**7.3**	**98**	
6.1.1	Patents by origin/bn PPP$ GDP ⊙	0.1	119	
6.1.2	PCT patents by origin/bn PPP$ GDP	0.0	101	○ ◇
6.1.3	Utility models by origin/bn PPP$ GDP ⊙	0.0	71	
6.1.4	Scientific and technical articles/bn PPP$ GDP	13.1	58	
6.1.5	Citable documents H-index	9.6	82	
6.2	**Knowledge impact**	**18.9**	**110**	
6.2.1	Labor productivity growth, %	2.0	32	●
6.2.2	Unicorn valuation, % GDP	0.0	48	○ ◇
6.2.3	Software spending, % GDP	0.0	127	○ ◇
6.2.4	High-tech manufacturing, % ⊙	11.0	86	
6.3	**Knowledge diffusion**	**9.0**	**111**	
6.3.1	Intellectual property receipts, % total trade	0.2	42	● ◆
6.3.2	Production and export complexity	31.1	111	
6.3.3	High-tech exports, % total trade ⊙	0.0	128	○
6.3.4	ICT services exports, % total trade	0.6	96	
6.3.5	ISO 9001 quality/bn PPP$ GDP	0.7	113	

		Score/ Value	Rank	
	Creative outputs	**22.6**	**71**	
7.1	**Intangible assets**	**27.4**	**74**	
7.1.1	Intangible asset intensity, top 15, %	–52.8	78	◇
7.1.2	Trademarks by origin/bn PPP$ GDP ⊙	4.8	123	
7.1.3	Global brand value, top 5,000, % GDP	n/a	n/a	
7.1.4	Industrial designs by origin/bn PPP$ GDP ⊙	5.2	20	● ◆
7.2	**Creative goods and services**	**26.3**	**[39]**	
7.2.1	Cultural and creative services exports, % total trade	2.6	8	● ◆
7.2.2	National feature films/mn pop. 15–69	n/a	n/a	
7.2.3	Entertainment and media market/th pop. 15–69	n/a	n/a	
7.2.4	Creative goods exports, % total trade ⊙	0.0	120	
7.3	**Online creativity**	**9.5**	**116**	
7.3.1	Generic top-level domains (TLDs)/th pop. 15–69	0.6	106	
7.3.2	Country-code TLDs/th pop. 15–69	0.0	127	○
7.3.3	GitHub commits/mn pop. 15–69	2.9	92	
7.3.4	Mobile app creation/bn PPP$ GDP	34.3	117	◇

NOTES: ● indicates a strength; ○ a weakness; ◆ an income group strength; ◇ an income group weakness; * an index; † a survey question. ⊙ is used when the available economy data are older than the base year; see appendices for details, including the year of the data, at wipo.int/gii-ranking. Square brackets [ ] indicate that the data minimum coverage (DMC) requirements were not met at the sub-pillar or pillar level.

GII 2023 rank

Greece

42

Output rank	Input rank	Income	Region	Population (mn)	GDP, PPP$ (bn)	GDP per capita, PPP$
41	42	High	EUR	10.4	387.8	36,466

			Score/ Value	Rank	
	Institutions		**50.9**	**63**	◇
1.1	**Institutional environment**		**53.3**	**49**	◇
1.1.1	Operational stability for businesses*		57.6	53	
1.1.2	Government effectiveness*		49.0	47	◇
1.2	**Regulatory environment**		**68.1**	**48**	
1.2.1	Regulatory quality*		53.6	50	◇
1.2.2	Rule of law*		50.0	49	◇
1.2.3	Cost of redundancy dismissal		15.9	67	
1.3	**Business environment**		**31.3**	**97**	◇
1.3.1	Policies for doing business†		42.9	77	
1.3.2	Entrepreneurship policies and culture†		19.7	69	○◇
	Human capital and research		**45.1**	**29**	
2.1	**Education**		**58.6**	**42**	
2.1.1	Expenditure on education, % GDP	⊙	3.6	86	
2.1.2	Government funding/pupil, secondary, % GDP/cap		20.1	53	
2.1.3	School life expectancy, years		20.1	3	●◆
2.1.4	PISA scales in reading, maths and science		453.5	43	
2.1.5	Pupil–teacher ratio, secondary		8.4	15	●
2.2	**Tertiary education**		**53.6**	**6**	●◆
2.2.1	Tertiary enrolment, % gross		150.9	1	●◆
2.2.2	Graduates in science and engineering, %		27.4	32	
2.2.3	Tertiary inbound mobility, %		2.8	71	
2.3	**Research and development (R&D)**		**23.1**	**41**	
2.3.1	Researchers, FTE/mn pop.		4,164.9	26	
2.3.2	Gross expenditure on R&D, % GDP		1.5	28	
2.3.3	Global corporate R&D investors, top 3, mn USD		0.0	40	○◇
2.3.4	QS university ranking, top 3*		23.2	47	
	Infrastructure		**53.7**	**38**	
3.1	**Information and communication technologies (ICTs)**		**76.9**	**44**	
3.1.1	ICT access*		85.9	48	
3.1.2	ICT use*		86.0	33	
3.1.3	Government's online service*		75.2	48	
3.1.4	E-participation*		60.5	55	
3.2	**General infrastructure**		**36.2**	**40**	
3.2.1	Electricity output, GWh/mn pop.		4,987.3	45	
3.2.2	Logistics performance*		72.7	18	●
3.2.3	Gross capital formation, % GDP		18.3	109	○◇
3.3	**Ecological sustainability**		**47.9**	**24**	●
3.3.1	GDP/unit of energy use		14.7	27	●
3.3.2	Environmental performance*		63.2	28	●
3.3.3	ISO 14001 environment/bn PPP$ GDP		5.6	18	●
	Market sophistication		**34.7**	**66**	
4.1	**Credit**		**35.7**	**51**	
4.1.1	Finance for startups and scaleups†		41.1	57	◇
4.1.2	Domestic credit to private sector, % GDP		82.3	39	
4.1.3	Loans from microfinance institutions, % GDP		n/a	n/a	
4.2	**Investment**		**5.4**	**74**	
4.2.1	Market capitalization, % GDP		23.7	55	
4.2.2	Venture capital (VC) investors, deals/bn PPP$ GDP		0.1	48	
4.2.3	VC recipients, deals/bn PPP$ GDP		0.0	86	○
4.2.4	VC received, value, % GDP		0.0	64	
4.3	**Trade, diversification and market scale**		**63.0**	**43**	
4.3.1	Applied tariff rate, weighted avg., %		1.5	20	
4.3.2	Domestic industry diversification		90.3	47	
4.3.3	Domestic market scale, bn PPP$		387.8	53	

			Score/ Value	Rank	
	Business sophistication		**28.7**	**62**	◇
5.1	**Knowledge workers**		**39.0**	**50**	
5.1.1	Knowledge-intensive employment, %		32.0	46	
5.1.2	Firms offering formal training, %	⊙	21.6	76	○◇
5.1.3	GERD performed by business, % GDP		0.7	34	
5.1.4	GERD financed by business, %		38.4	45	
5.1.5	Females employed w/advanced degrees, %		20.1	34	
5.2	**Innovation linkages**		**17.7**	**87**	◇
5.2.1	University–industry R&D collaboration†		19.9	118	○◇
5.2.2	State of cluster development†		15.5	120	○◇
5.2.3	GERD financed by abroad, % GDP		0.2	20	●
5.2.4	Joint venture/strategic alliance deals/bn PPP$ GDP		0.0	38	
5.2.5	Patent families/bn PPP$ GDP		0.3	38	
5.3	**Knowledge absorption**		**29.4**	**80**	◇
5.3.1	Intellectual property payments, % total trade		0.4	76	
5.3.2	High-tech imports, % total trade		6.5	99	○
5.3.3	ICT services imports, % total trade		1.0	85	
5.3.4	FDI net inflows, % GDP		2.3	66	
5.3.5	Research talent, % in businesses		29.8	44	
	Knowledge and technology outputs		**31.2**	**43**	
6.1	**Knowledge creation**		**25.4**	**38**	
6.1.1	Patents by origin/bn PPP$ GDP		1.7	40	
6.1.2	PCT patents by origin/bn PPP$ GDP		0.4	34	
6.1.3	Utility models by origin/bn PPP$ GDP		0.0	64	○
6.1.4	Scientific and technical articles/bn PPP$ GDP		30.6	19	●
6.1.5	Citable documents H-index		34.3	29	
6.2	**Knowledge impact**		**36.6**	**39**	
6.2.1	Labor productivity growth, %		−0.6	109	○◇
6.2.2	Unicorn valuation, % GDP		1.5	29	
6.2.3	Software spending, % GDP		0.6	13	●◆
6.2.4	High-tech manufacturing, %		17.1	71	◇
6.3	**Knowledge diffusion**		**31.6**	**50**	
6.3.1	Intellectual property receipts, % total trade		0.1	62	
6.3.2	Production and export complexity		57.7	50	
6.3.3	High-tech exports, % total trade		2.4	54	
6.3.4	ICT services exports, % total trade		1.5	70	
6.3.5	ISO 9001 quality/bn PPP$ GDP		20.6	11	●◆
	Creative outputs		**33.7**	**39**	
7.1	**Intangible assets**		**41.7**	**39**	
7.1.1	Intangible asset intensity, top 15, %		56.0	42	
7.1.2	Trademarks by origin/bn PPP$ GDP		n/a	n/a	
7.1.3	Global brand value, top 5,000, % GDP		0.7	57	
7.1.4	Industrial designs by origin/bn PPP$ GDP		3.3	31	
7.2	**Creative goods and services**		**20.7**	**48**	
7.2.1	Cultural and creative services exports, % total trade		0.8	41	
7.2.2	National feature films/mn pop. 15–69		4.8	24	
7.2.3	Entertainment and media market/th pop. 15–69		22.9	26	
7.2.4	Creative goods exports, % total trade		1.1	44	
7.3	**Online creativity**		**30.8**	**39**	
7.3.1	Generic top-level domains (TLDs)/th pop. 15–69		15.3	34	
7.3.2	Country-code TLDs/th pop. 15–69		22.2	30	
7.3.3	GitHub commits/mn pop. 15–69		21.1	42	
7.3.4	Mobile app creation/bn PPP$ GDP		64.5	66	

NOTES: ● indicates a strength; ○ a weakness; ◆ an income group strength; ◇ an income group weakness; * an index; † a survey question. ⊙ is used when the available economy data are older than the base year; see appendices for details, including the year of the data, at wipo.int/gii-ranking. Square brackets [ ] indicate that the data minimum coverage (DMC) requirements were not met at the sub-pillar or pillar level.

GII 2023 rank

Guatemala

122

Output rank	Input rank	Income	Region	Population (mn)	GDP, PPP$ (bn)	GDP per capita, PPP$
115	121	Upper middle	LCN	17.8	185.8	9,931

			Score/ Value	Rank	
	Institutions		**31.3**	**120**	◇
1.1	**Institutional environment**		**26.7**	**108**	◇
1.1.1	Operational stability for businesses*		37.5	103	
1.1.2	Government effectiveness*		16.0	115	◇
1.2	**Regulatory environment**		**41.6**	**117**	◇
1.2.1	Regulatory quality*		33.9	90	
1.2.2	Rule of law*		7.7	124	◇
1.2.3	Cost of redundancy dismissal		27.0	108	◇
1.3	**Business environment**		**25.5**	**109**	
1.3.1	Policies for doing business†		36.2	98	
1.3.2	Entrepreneurship policies and culture†		14.7	72	◇
	Human capital and research		**13.2**	**122**	◇
2.1	**Education**		**34.4**	**112**	◇
2.1.1	Expenditure on education, % GDP		3.1	105	
2.1.2	Government funding/pupil, secondary, % GDP/cap		5.4	100	○◇
2.1.3	School life expectancy, years	⊙	10.6	102	◇
2.1.4	PISA scales in reading, maths and science		n/a	n/a	
2.1.5	Pupil–teacher ratio, secondary		9.6	26	●
2.2	**Tertiary education**		**5.0**	**122**	◇
2.2.1	Tertiary enrolment, % gross	⊙	22.1	98	◇
2.2.2	Graduates in science and engineering, %	⊙	9.8	109	◇
2.2.3	Tertiary inbound mobility, %	⊙	0.2	108	◇
2.3	**Research and development (R&D)**		**0.2**	**115**	
2.3.1	Researchers, FTE/mn pop.		13.9	106	○◇
2.3.2	Gross expenditure on R&D, % GDP		0.1	110	○◇
2.3.3	Global corporate R&D investors, top 3, mn USD		0.0	40	○◇
2.3.4	QS university ranking, top 3*		0.0	71	○◇
	Infrastructure		**20.7**	**118**	◇
3.1	**Information and communication technologies (ICTs)**		**38.5**	**110**	◇
3.1.1	ICT access*		49.8	107	◇
3.1.2	ICT use*		23.6	122	◇
3.1.3	Government's online service*		49.3	92	◇
3.1.4	E-participation*		31.4	103	◇
3.2	**General infrastructure**		**10.4**	**122**	◇
3.2.1	Electricity output, GWh/mn pop.		844.5	102	◇
3.2.2	Logistics performance*		22.7	82	
3.2.3	Gross capital formation, % GDP		14.4	123	○◇
3.3	**Ecological sustainability**		**13.1**	**114**	◇
3.3.1	GDP/unit of energy use		10.0	67	
3.3.2	Environmental performance*		15.4	124	◇
3.3.3	ISO 14001 environment/bn PPP$ GDP		0.2	112	
	Market sophistication		**20.1**	**112**	◇
4.1	**Credit**		**13.0**	**106**	◇
4.1.1	Finance for startups and scaleups†		14.0	82	◇
4.1.2	Domestic credit to private sector, % GDP		35.9	89	
4.1.3	Loans from microfinance institutions, % GDP		n/a	n/a	
4.2	**Investment**		**0.6**	**[110]**	
4.2.1	Market capitalization, % GDP		n/a	n/a	
4.2.2	Venture capital (VC) investors, deals/bn PPP$ GDP		0.0	87	
4.2.3	VC recipients, deals/bn PPP$ GDP		n/a	n/a	
4.2.4	VC received, value, % GDP		n/a	n/a	
4.3	**Trade, diversification and market scale**		**46.8**	**94**	◇
4.3.1	Applied tariff rate, weighted avg., %		1.6	51	●
4.3.2	Domestic industry diversification		n/a	n/a	
4.3.3	Domestic market scale, bn PPP$		185.8	72	

			Score/ Value	Rank	
	Business sophistication		**22.9**	**93**	
5.1	**Knowledge workers**		**21.1**	**95**	◇
5.1.1	Knowledge-intensive employment, %	⊙	9.3	109	◇
5.1.2	Firms offering formal training, %	⊙	55.7	12	●◆
5.1.3	GERD performed by business, % GDP	⊙	0.0	90	○
5.1.4	GERD financed by business, %	⊙	11.1	74	
5.1.5	Females employed w/advanced degrees, %	⊙	2.7	105	◇
5.2	**Innovation linkages**		**14.4**	**98**	
5.2.1	University–industry R&D collaboration†		33.9	87	
5.2.2	State of cluster development†		37.0	83	
5.2.3	GERD financed by abroad, % GDP	⊙	0.0	94	
5.2.4	Joint venture/strategic alliance deals/bn PPP$ GDP		0.0	122	
5.2.5	Patent families/bn PPP$ GDP		0.0	95	○◇
5.3	**Knowledge absorption**		**33.1**	**68**	
5.3.1	Intellectual property payments, % total trade		1.5	22	●
5.3.2	High-tech imports, % total trade		10.8	29	●
5.3.3	ICT services imports, % total trade		1.5	59	●
5.3.4	FDI net inflows, % GDP		2.3	68	
5.3.5	Research talent, % in businesses	⊙	3.5	73	
	Knowledge and technology outputs		**13.7**	**99**	
6.1	**Knowledge creation**		**1.5**	**127**	◇
6.1.1	Patents by origin/bn PPP$ GDP		0.1	121	
6.1.2	PCT patents by origin/bn PPP$ GDP		0.0	97	
6.1.3	Utility models by origin/bn PPP$ GDP		0.0	70	
6.1.4	Scientific and technical articles/bn PPP$ GDP		1.3	129	○◇
6.1.5	Citable documents H-index		4.2	112	
6.2	**Knowledge impact**		**19.9**	**104**	
6.2.1	Labor productivity growth, %		1.5	46	●
6.2.2	Unicorn valuation, % GDP		0.0	48	○◇
6.2.3	Software spending, % GDP		0.0	125	◇
6.2.4	High-tech manufacturing, %		n/a	n/a	
6.3	**Knowledge diffusion**		**19.8**	**76**	
6.3.1	Intellectual property receipts, % total trade		0.1	59	●
6.3.2	Production and export complexity		45.4	81	
6.3.3	High-tech exports, % total trade		1.6	67	
6.3.4	ICT services exports, % total trade		3.1	40	●
6.3.5	ISO 9001 quality/bn PPP$ GDP		1.3	100	
	Creative outputs		**6.3**	**[119]**	
7.1	**Intangible assets**		**5.3**	**[119]**	
7.1.1	Intangible asset intensity, top 15, %		n/a	n/a	
7.1.2	Trademarks by origin/bn PPP$ GDP		n/a	n/a	
7.1.3	Global brand value, top 5,000, % GDP		n/a	n/a	
7.1.4	Industrial designs by origin/bn PPP$ GDP		0.2	105	
7.2	**Creative goods and services**		**2.5**	**[100]**	
7.2.1	Cultural and creative services exports, % total trade		0.1	89	
7.2.2	National feature films/mn pop. 15–69		n/a	n/a	
7.2.3	Entertainment and media market/th pop. 15–69		n/a	n/a	
7.2.4	Creative goods exports, % total trade		0.3	70	
7.3	**Online creativity**		**12.2**	**108**	◇
7.3.1	Generic top-level domains (TLDs)/th pop. 15–69		4.4	58	●
7.3.2	Country-code TLDs/th pop. 15–69		0.6	98	
7.3.3	GitHub commits/mn pop. 15–69		2.0	99	
7.3.4	Mobile app creation/bn PPP$ GDP		41.8	111	◇

NOTES: ● indicates a strength; ○ a weakness; ◆ an income group strength; ◇ an income group weakness; * an index; † a survey question. ⊙ is used when the available economy data are older than the base year; see appendices for details, including the year of the data, at wipo.int/gii-ranking. Square brackets [ ] indicate that the data minimum coverage (DMC) requirements were not met at the sub-pillar or pillar level.

Guinea

GII 2023 rank

128

Output rank	Input rank	Income	Region	Population (mn)	GDP, PPP$ (bn)	GDP per capita, PPP$
119	131	Low	SSA	13.9	43.9	2,993

			Score/Value	Rank	
	Institutions		**38.7**	**98**	●
1.1	**Institutional environment**		**23.4**	**116**	
1.1.1	Operational stability for businesses*		35.4	108	
1.1.2	Government effectiveness*		11.5	124	
1.2	**Regulatory environment**		**53.9**	**90**	●
1.2.1	Regulatory quality*		17.1	125	◇
1.2.2	Rule of law*		6.6	127	◇
1.2.3	Cost of redundancy dismissal		10.1	30	●
1.3	**Business environment**		**38.6**	**[92]**	
1.3.1	Policies for doing business†	⏲	38.6	89	●
1.3.2	Entrepreneurship policies and culture†		n/a	n/a	
	Human capital and research		**7.9**	**[132]**	
2.1	**Education**		**22.0**	**126**	◇
2.1.1	Expenditure on education, % GDP		2.1	118	◇
2.1.2	Government funding/pupil, secondary, % GDP/cap	⏲	8.4	94	◇
2.1.3	School life expectancy, years	⏲	9.0	107	
2.1.4	PISA scales in reading, maths and science		n/a	n/a	
2.1.5	Pupil–teacher ratio, secondary		22.1	105	
2.2	**Tertiary education**		**1.6**	**[126]**	
2.2.1	Tertiary enrolment, % gross		6.7	121	
2.2.2	Graduates in science and engineering, %		n/a	n/a	
2.2.3	Tertiary inbound mobility, %		n/a	n/a	
2.3	**Research and development (R&D)**		**0.0**	**[119]**	
2.3.1	Researchers, FTE/mn pop.		n/a	n/a	
2.3.2	Gross expenditure on R&D, % GDP		n/a	n/a	
2.3.3	Global corporate R&D investors, top 3, mn USD		0.0	40	○◇
2.3.4	QS university ranking, top 3*		0.0	71	○◇
	Infrastructure		**16.9**	**127**	
3.1	**Information and communication technologies (ICTs)**		**26.8**	**125**	
3.1.1	ICT access*		24.9	124	
3.1.2	ICT use*		17.4	127	
3.1.3	Government's online service*		38.3	110	
3.1.4	E-participation*		26.7	106	
3.2	**General infrastructure**		**12.9**	**115**	
3.2.1	Electricity output, GWh/mn pop.		n/a	n/a	
3.2.2	Logistics performance*		18.2	89	
3.2.3	Gross capital formation, % GDP		16.5	116	
3.3	**Ecological sustainability**		**11.1**	**123**	
3.3.1	GDP/unit of energy use		n/a	n/a	
3.3.2	Environmental performance*		21.5	105	
3.3.3	ISO 14001 environment/bn PPP$ GDP		0.2	119	
	Market sophistication		**6.9**	**132**	○◇
4.1	**Credit**		**3.0**	**128**	
4.1.1	Finance for startups and scaleups†		n/a	n/a	
4.1.2	Domestic credit to private sector, % GDP		10.0	128	○◇
4.1.3	Loans from microfinance institutions, % GDP		0.4	40	●
4.2	**Investment**		**n/a**	**[n/a]**	
4.2.1	Market capitalization, % GDP		n/a	n/a	
4.2.2	Venture capital (VC) investors, deals/bn PPP$ GDP		n/a	n/a	
4.2.3	VC recipients, deals/bn PPP$ GDP		n/a	n/a	
4.2.4	VC received, value, % GDP		n/a	n/a	
4.3	**Trade, diversification and market scale**		**10.9**	**129**	◇
4.3.1	Applied tariff rate, weighted avg., %		12.2	130	◇
4.3.2	Domestic industry diversification		n/a	n/a	
4.3.3	Domestic market scale, bn PPP$		43.9	114	

			Score/Value	Rank	
	Business sophistication		**15.6**	**127**	
5.1	**Knowledge workers**		**9.0**	**[124]**	
5.1.1	Knowledge-intensive employment, %	⏲	7.4	114	
5.1.2	Firms offering formal training, %	⏲	16.0	90	◇
5.1.3	GERD performed by business, % GDP		n/a	n/a	
5.1.4	GERD financed by business, %		n/a	n/a	
5.1.5	Females employed w/advanced degrees, %	⏲	2.2	107	
5.2	**Innovation linkages**		**20.3**	**70**	●
5.2.1	University–industry R&D collaboration†	⏲	46.3	59	●◆
5.2.2	State of cluster development†	⏲	28.6	97	●
5.2.3	GERD financed by abroad, % GDP		n/a	n/a	
5.2.4	Joint venture/strategic alliance deals/bn PPP$ GDP		0.0	66	●
5.2.5	Patent families/bn PPP$ GDP		0.0	95	○◇
5.3	**Knowledge absorption**		**17.4**	**132**	○◇
5.3.1	Intellectual property payments, % total trade		0.0	118	○◇
5.3.2	High-tech imports, % total trade	⏲	2.4	131	○◇
5.3.3	ICT services imports, % total trade		0.3	124	◇
5.3.4	FDI net inflows, % GDP		0.9	99	●
5.3.5	Research talent, % in businesses		n/a	n/a	
	Knowledge and technology outputs		**9.8**	**125**	
6.1	**Knowledge creation**		**1.8**	**125**	◇
6.1.1	Patents by origin/bn PPP$ GDP		0.1	114	
6.1.2	PCT patents by origin/bn PPP$ GDP		0.0	86	●◆
6.1.3	Utility models by origin/bn PPP$ GDP		0.0	75	○◇
6.1.4	Scientific and technical articles/bn PPP$ GDP		2.8	118	◇
6.1.5	Citable documents H-index		2.2	125	
6.2	**Knowledge impact**		**24.9**	**73**	●◆
6.2.1	Labor productivity growth, %		2.9	18	●
6.2.2	Unicorn valuation, % GDP		0.0	48	○◇
6.2.3	Software spending, % GDP		0.0	109	
6.2.4	High-tech manufacturing, %		n/a	n/a	
6.3	**Knowledge diffusion**		**2.7**	**129**	◇
6.3.1	Intellectual property receipts, % total trade		0.0	114	○◇
6.3.2	Production and export complexity		12.5	119	◇
6.3.3	High-tech exports, % total trade	⏲	0.0	130	◇
6.3.4	ICT services exports, % total trade		0.0	130	◇
6.3.5	ISO 9001 quality/bn PPP$ GDP		0.3	128	
	Creative outputs		**9.1**	**[110]**	
7.1	**Intangible assets**		**15.0**	**[98]**	
7.1.1	Intangible asset intensity, top 15, %		n/a	n/a	
7.1.2	Trademarks by origin/bn PPP$ GDP		7.6	113	
7.1.3	Global brand value, top 5,000, % GDP		n/a	n/a	
7.1.4	Industrial designs by origin/bn PPP$ GDP		1.5	53	●
7.2	**Creative goods and services**		**0.1**	**[132]**	
7.2.1	Cultural and creative services exports, % total trade		n/a	n/a	
7.2.2	National feature films/mn pop. 15–69		n/a	n/a	
7.2.3	Entertainment and media market/th pop. 15–69		n/a	n/a	
7.2.4	Creative goods exports, % total trade	⏲	0.0	128	
7.3	**Online creativity**		**6.4**	**121**	
7.3.1	Generic top-level domains (TLDs)/th pop. 15–69		0.1	126	
7.3.2	Country-code TLDs/th pop. 15–69		0.0	131	○
7.3.3	GitHub commits/mn pop. 15–69		0.0	131	○
7.3.4	Mobile app creation/bn PPP$ GDP		25.6	121	

NOTES: ● indicates a strength; ○ a weakness; ◆ an income group strength; ◇ an income group weakness; * an index; † a survey question. ⏲ is used when the available economy data are older than the base year; see appendices for details, including the year of the data, at wipo.int/gii-ranking. Square brackets [ ] indicate that the data minimum coverage (DMC) requirements were not met at the sub-pillar or pillar level.

Honduras

GII 2023 rank

116

Output rank	Input rank	Income	Region	Population (mn)	GDP, PPP$ (bn)	GDP per capita, PPP$
114	115	Lower middle	LCN	10.4	69.7	6,769

			Score/Value	Rank	
	Institutions		**26.1**	**126**	◇
1.1	**Institutional environment**		**24.6**	**115**	
1.1.1	Operational stability for businesses*		34.0	112	
1.1.2	Government effectiveness*		15.2	118	
1.2	**Regulatory environment**		**37.1**	**123**	
1.2.1	Regulatory quality*		28.6	100	
1.2.2	Rule of law*		8.3	121	◇
1.2.3	Cost of redundancy dismissal		30.3	119	
1.3	**Business environment**		**16.7**	**[125]**	
1.3.1	Policies for doing business†		16.7	123	◇
1.3.2	Entrepreneurship policies and culture†		n/a	n/a	

			Score/Value	Rank	
	Human capital and research		**23.7**	**90**	
2.1	**Education**		**58.4**	**[43]**	
2.1.1	Expenditure on education, % GDP	⊙	6.1	18	●◆
2.1.2	Government funding/pupil, secondary, % GDP/cap	⊙	20.7	47	
2.1.3	School life expectancy, years		n/a	n/a	
2.1.4	PISA scales in reading, maths and science		n/a	n/a	
2.1.5	Pupil–teacher ratio, secondary		11.6	49	●◆
2.2	**Tertiary education**		**12.0**	**108**	
2.2.1	Tertiary enrolment, % gross	⊙	25.5	91	
2.2.2	Graduates in science and engineering, %	⊙	15.7	97	
2.2.3	Tertiary inbound mobility, %	⊙	0.8	95	
2.3	**Research and development (R&D)**		**0.7**	**106**	
2.3.1	Researchers, FTE/mn pop.	⊙	189.9	82	
2.3.2	Gross expenditure on R&D, % GDP	⊙	0.1	109	
2.3.3	Global corporate R&D investors, top 3, mn USD		0.0	40	○◇
2.3.4	QS university ranking, top 3*		0.0	71	○◇

			Score/Value	Rank	
	Infrastructure		**23.5**	**112**	
3.1	**Information and communication technologies (ICTs)**		**30.2**	**119**	◇
3.1.1	ICT access*		49.3	108	
3.1.2	ICT use*		47.2	105	
3.1.3	Government's online service*		16.2	130	○◇
3.1.4	E-participation*		8.1	130	○◇
3.2	**General infrastructure**		**22.6**	**80**	
3.2.1	Electricity output, GWh/mn pop.	⊙	1,019.7	96	
3.2.2	Logistics performance*		36.4	65	
3.2.3	Gross capital formation, % GDP		28.0	32	●
3.3	**Ecological sustainability**		**17.8**	**91**	
3.3.1	GDP/unit of energy use		8.7	83	
3.3.2	Environmental performance*		29.8	88	
3.3.3	ISO 14001 environment/bn PPP$ GDP		0.6	78	

			Score/Value	Rank	
	Market sophistication		**22.2**	**[107]**	
4.1	**Credit**		**25.4**	**[77]**	
4.1.1	Finance for startups and scaleups†		n/a	n/a	
4.1.2	Domestic credit to private sector, % GDP		69.8	53	●
4.1.3	Loans from microfinance institutions, % GDP		n/a	n/a	
4.2	**Investment**		**1.3**	**[105]**	
4.2.1	Market capitalization, % GDP		n/a	n/a	
4.2.2	Venture capital (VC) investors, deals/bn PPP$ GDP		0.0	78	
4.2.3	VC recipients, deals/bn PPP$ GDP		n/a	n/a	
4.2.4	VC received, value, % GDP		n/a	n/a	
4.3	**Trade, diversification and market scale**		**40.0**	**104**	
4.3.1	Applied tariff rate, weighted avg., %		3.3	76	
4.3.2	Domestic industry diversification		n/a	n/a	
4.3.3	Domestic market scale, bn PPP$		69.7	97	

			Score/Value	Rank	
	Business sophistication		**20.8**	**104**	
5.1	**Knowledge workers**		**23.5**	**85**	
5.1.1	Knowledge-intensive employment, %	⊙	12.3	101	
5.1.2	Firms offering formal training, %	⊙	47.7	22	●◆
5.1.3	GERD performed by business, % GDP	⊙	0.0	88	
5.1.4	GERD financed by business, %	⊙	21.1	66	
5.1.5	Females employed w/advanced degrees, %	⊙	4.8	95	
5.2	**Innovation linkages**		**10.6**	**117**	
5.2.1	University–industry R&D collaboration†		24.0	106	
5.2.2	State of cluster development†		27.0	101	
5.2.3	GERD financed by abroad, % GDP	⊙	0.0	82	
5.2.4	Joint venture/strategic alliance deals/bn PPP$ GDP	⊙	0.0	120	
5.2.5	Patent families/bn PPP$ GDP		0.0	95	○◇
5.3	**Knowledge absorption**		**28.2**	**87**	
5.3.1	Intellectual property payments, % total trade		0.8	47	●◆
5.3.2	High-tech imports, % total trade		7.9	71	
5.3.3	ICT services imports, % total trade		1.6	56	●
5.3.4	FDI net inflows, % GDP		2.6	59	●
5.3.5	Research talent, % in businesses	⊙	3.4	74	

			Score/Value	Rank	
	Knowledge and technology outputs		**12.5**	**107**	
6.1	**Knowledge creation**		**1.2**	**129**	◇
6.1.1	Patents by origin/bn PPP$ GDP		0.0	132	○◇
6.1.2	PCT patents by origin/bn PPP$ GDP		0.0	95	
6.1.3	Utility models by origin/bn PPP$ GDP	⊙	0.0	75	○◇
6.1.4	Scientific and technical articles/bn PPP$ GDP		2.2	123	
6.1.5	Citable documents H-index		2.3	124	
6.2	**Knowledge impact**		**24.4**	**77**	
6.2.1	Labor productivity growth, %		0.9	71	
6.2.2	Unicorn valuation, % GDP		0.0	48	○◇
6.2.3	Software spending, % GDP		0.2	66	
6.2.4	High-tech manufacturing, %		n/a	n/a	
6.3	**Knowledge diffusion**		**11.9**	**99**	
6.3.1	Intellectual property receipts, % total trade		0.0	114	○◇
6.3.2	Production and export complexity		39.0	94	
6.3.3	High-tech exports, % total trade		0.2	108	
6.3.4	ICT services exports, % total trade		1.2	78	
6.3.5	ISO 9001 quality/bn PPP$ GDP		2.5	81	

			Score/Value	Rank	
	Creative outputs		**7.6**	**114**	
7.1	**Intangible assets**		**8.5**	**111**	
7.1.1	Intangible asset intensity, top 15, %		n/a	n/a	
7.1.2	Trademarks by origin/bn PPP$ GDP		36.4	64	●
7.1.3	Global brand value, top 5,000, % GDP		0.0	74	○◇
7.1.4	Industrial designs by origin/bn PPP$ GDP	⊙	0.1	117	
7.2	**Creative goods and services**		**1.0**	**[116]**	
7.2.1	Cultural and creative services exports, % total trade		n/a	n/a	
7.2.2	National feature films/mn pop. 15–69		n/a	n/a	
7.2.3	Entertainment and media market/th pop. 15–69		n/a	n/a	
7.2.4	Creative goods exports, % total trade		0.1	101	
7.3	**Online creativity**		**12.5**	**105**	
7.3.1	Generic top-level domains (TLDs)/th pop. 15–69		0.6	108	
7.3.2	Country-code TLDs/th pop. 15–69		0.3	104	
7.3.3	GitHub commits/mn pop. 15–69		1.6	104	
7.3.4	Mobile app creation/bn PPP$ GDP		47.6	104	

NOTES: ● indicates a strength; ○ a weakness; ◆ an income group strength; ◇ an income group weakness; * an index; † a survey question. ⊙ is used when the available economy data are older than the base year; see appendices for details, including the year of the data, at wipo.int/gii-ranking. Square brackets [ ] indicate that the data minimum coverage (DMC) requirements were not met at the sub-pillar or pillar level.

GII 2023 rank

Hong Kong, China

17

Output rank	Input rank	Income	Region	Population (mn)	GDP, PPP$ (bn)	GDP per capita, PPP$
24	8	High	SEAO	7.5	518.7	69,987

		Score/Value	Rank	
	Institutions	**81.4**	**8**	
1.1	**Institutional environment**	**74.2**	**18**	
1.1.1	Operational stability for businesses*	69.4	29	
1.1.2	Government effectiveness*	78.9	12	
1.2	**Regulatory environment**	**91.3**	**7**	
1.2.1	Regulatory quality*	83.2	13	
1.2.2	Rule of law*	82.1	17	
1.2.3	Cost of redundancy dismissal	8.0	1	●
1.3	**Business environment**	**78.7**	**9**	
1.3.1	Policies for doing business†	74.5	20	
1.3.2	Entrepreneurship policies and culture†	⊙ 82.9	6	
	Human capital and research	**54.4**	**15**	
2.1	**Education**	**63.2**	**18**	
2.1.1	Expenditure on education, % GDP	4.0	71	○
2.1.2	Government funding/pupil, secondary, % GDP/cap	26.0	16	
2.1.3	School life expectancy, years	17.1	18	
2.1.4	PISA scales in reading, maths and science	530.7	3	●◆
2.1.5	Pupil-teacher ratio, secondary	10.8	39	
2.2	**Tertiary education**	**50.6**	**9**	
2.2.1	Tertiary enrolment, % gross	88.4	13	
2.2.2	Graduates in science and engineering, %	n/a	n/a	
2.2.3	Tertiary inbound mobility, %	16.5	12	
2.3	**Research and development (R&D)**	**49.3**	**20**	
2.3.1	Researchers, FTE/mn pop.	4,553.4	23	
2.3.2	Gross expenditure on R&D, % GDP	1.0	41	◇
2.3.3	Global corporate R&D investors, top 3, mn USD	n/a	n/a	
2.3.4	QS university ranking, top 3*	83.6	4	●
	Infrastructure	**62.9**	**9**	
3.1	**Information and communication technologies (ICTs)**	**95.1**	**[3]**	
3.1.1	ICT access*	97.8	5	◆
3.1.2	ICT use*	92.5	16	
3.1.3	Government's online service*	n/a	n/a	
3.1.4	E-participation*	n/a	n/a	
3.2	**General infrastructure**	**40.1**	**32**	
3.2.1	Electricity output, GWh/mn pop.	⊙ 4,707.9	48	
3.2.2	Logistics performance*	86.4	7	
3.2.3	Gross capital formation, % GDP	18.0	110	○◇
3.3	**Ecological sustainability**	**53.6**	**13**	
3.3.1	GDP/unit of energy use	32.7	2	●◆
3.3.2	Environmental performance*	n/a	n/a	
3.3.3	ISO 14001 environment/bn PPP$ GDP	2.3	38	
	Market sophistication	**71.8**	**2**	**●◆**
4.1	**Credit**	**92.2**	**1**	**●◆**
4.1.1	Finance for startups and scaleups†	⊙ 84.3	5	
4.1.2	Domestic credit to private sector, % GDP	258.9	1	●◆
4.1.3	Loans from microfinance institutions, % GDP	n/a	n/a	
4.2	**Investment**	**64.3**	**7**	
4.2.1	Market capitalization, % GDP	1,394.2	1	●◆
4.2.2	Venture capital (VC) investors, deals/bn PPP$ GDP	1.3	6	◆
4.2.3	VC recipients, deals/bn PPP$ GDP	0.1	25	
4.2.4	VC received, value, % GDP	0.0	9	
4.3	**Trade, diversification and market scale**	**58.8**	**64**	
4.3.1	Applied tariff rate, weighted avg., %	0.0	1	●◆
4.3.2	Domestic industry diversification	65.3	100	○◇
4.3.3	Domestic market scale, bn PPP$	518.7	46	

		Score/Value	Rank	
	Business sophistication	**47.0**	**28**	**◇**
5.1	**Knowledge workers**	**45.4**	**40**	**◇**
5.1.1	Knowledge-intensive employment, %	⊙ 40.7	29	
5.1.2	Firms offering formal training, %	n/a	n/a	
5.1.3	GERD performed by business, % GDP	⊙ 0.4	46	◇
5.1.4	GERD financed by business, %	⊙ 49.2	32	
5.1.5	Females employed w/advanced degrees, %	⊙ 15.8	47	◇
5.2	**Innovation linkages**	**46.9**	**24**	**◇**
5.2.1	University-industry R&D collaboration†	74.9	18	
5.2.2	State of cluster development†	75.6	18	
5.2.3	GERD financed by abroad, % GDP	⊙ 0.0	54	◇
5.2.4	Joint venture/strategic alliance deals/bn PPP$ GDP	0.2	7	
5.2.5	Patent families/bn PPP$ GDP	0.7	29	◇
5.3	**Knowledge absorption**	**48.8**	**23**	
5.3.1	Intellectual property payments, % total trade	⊙ 0.3	84	○◇
5.3.2	High-tech imports, % total trade	59.1	1	●◆
5.3.3	ICT services imports, % total trade	⊙ 0.4	119	○◇
5.3.4	FDI net inflows, % GDP	29.1	3	●◆
5.3.5	Research talent, % in businesses	⊙ 35.6	37	◇
	Knowledge and technology outputs	**26.9**	**51**	**◇**
6.1	**Knowledge creation**	**24.5**	**[40]**	
6.1.1	Patents by origin/bn PPP$ GDP	0.8	65	◇
6.1.2	PCT patents by origin/bn PPP$ GDP	n/a	n/a	
6.1.3	Utility models by origin/bn PPP$ GDP	0.8	25	
6.1.4	Scientific and technical articles/bn PPP$ GDP	n/a	n/a	
6.1.5	Citable documents H-index	39.4	23	
6.2	**Knowledge impact**	**49.9**	**16**	
6.2.1	Labor productivity growth, %	0.5	78	○
6.2.2	Unicorn valuation, % GDP	5.3	6	◆
6.2.3	Software spending, % GDP	0.4	26	
6.2.4	High-tech manufacturing, %	20.0	63	○◇
6.3	**Knowledge diffusion**	**6.4**	**122**	**○◇**
6.3.1	Intellectual property receipts, % total trade	⊙ 0.1	53	◇
6.3.2	Production and export complexity	n/a	n/a	
6.3.3	High-tech exports, % total trade	0.1	121	○◇
6.3.4	ICT services exports, % total trade	⊙ 0.5	101	○
6.3.5	ISO 9001 quality/bn PPP$ GDP	6.2	45	
	Creative outputs	**59.2**	**3**	**●◆**
7.1	**Intangible assets**	**57.5**	**11**	
7.1.1	Intangible asset intensity, top 15, %	n/a	n/a	
7.1.2	Trademarks by origin/bn PPP$ GDP	63.8	34	
7.1.3	Global brand value, top 5,000, % GDP	27.6	1	●◆
7.1.4	Industrial designs by origin/bn PPP$ GDP	1.9	42	
7.2	**Creative goods and services**	**50.9**	**3**	**●◆**
7.2.1	Cultural and creative services exports, % total trade	0.1	86	○◇
7.2.2	National feature films/mn pop. 15–69	8.2	7	
7.2.3	Entertainment and media market/th pop. 15–69	48.8	19	
7.2.4	Creative goods exports, % total trade	12.7	1	●◆
7.3	**Online creativity**	**70.9**	**6**	
7.3.1	Generic top-level domains (TLDs)/th pop. 15–69	86.4	7	◆
7.3.2	Country-code TLDs/th pop. 15–69	11.8	40	◇
7.3.3	GitHub commits/mn pop. 15–69	100.0	1	●◆
7.3.4	Mobile app creation/bn PPP$ GDP	85.5	5	◆

NOTES: ● indicates a strength; ○ a weakness; ◆ an income group strength; ◇ an income group weakness; * an index; † a survey question. ⊙ is used when the available economy data are older than the base year; see appendices for details, including the year of the data, at wipo.int/gii-ranking. Square brackets [ ] indicate that the data minimum coverage (DMC) requirements were not met at the sub-pillar or pillar level.

GII 2023 rank

Hungary

35

Output rank	Input rank	Income	Region	Population (mn)	GDP, PPP$ (bn)	GDP per capita, PPP$
33	36	High	EUR	10.0	409.8	42,132

		Score/ Value	Rank	
	Institutions	**58.4**	**47**	
1.1	**Institutional environment**	**62.9**	**37**	
1.1.1	Operational stability for businesses*	71.5	26	
1.1.2	Government effectiveness*	54.3	42	
1.2	**Regulatory environment**	**72.2**	**40**	
1.2.1	Regulatory quality*	55.0	47	◇
1.2.2	Rule of law*	55.3	41	
1.2.3	Cost of redundancy dismissal	13.4	48	
1.3	**Business environment**	**40.2**	**85**	○
1.3.1	Policies for doing business†	43.3	75	
1.3.2	Entrepreneurship policies and culture†	37.0	53	○
	Human capital and research	**40.2**	**36**	
2.1	**Education**	**54.0**	**58**	
2.1.1	Expenditure on education, % GDP	© 4.2	64	
2.1.2	Government funding/pupil, secondary, % GDP/cap	19.1	59	
2.1.3	School life expectancy, years	15.1	51	
2.1.4	PISA scales in reading, maths and science	479.3	33	
2.1.5	Pupil–teacher ratio, secondary	10.4	36	
2.2	**Tertiary education**	**29.8**	**67**	◇
2.2.1	Tertiary enrolment, % gross	55.2	62	
2.2.2	Graduates in science and engineering, %	15.5	98	○ ◇
2.2.3	Tertiary inbound mobility, %	13.5	15	●
2.3	**Research and development (R&D)**	**36.7**	**30**	
2.3.1	Researchers, FTE/mn pop.	4,461.8	25	
2.3.2	Gross expenditure on R&D, % GDP	1.6	24	
2.3.3	Global corporate R&D investors, top 3, mn USD	51.6	30	
2.3.4	QS university ranking, top 3*	19.7	54	
	Infrastructure	**53.0**	**42**	
3.1	**Information and communication technologies (ICTs)**	**72.1**	**60**	◇
3.1.1	ICT access*	83.5	61	
3.1.2	ICT use*	83.0	50	
3.1.3	Government's online service*	72.0	56	
3.1.4	E-participation*	50.0	75	◇
3.2	**General infrastructure**	**33.6**	**45**	
3.2.1	Electricity output, GWh/mn pop.	3,720.9	59	
3.2.2	Logistics performance*	50.0	50	◇
3.2.3	Gross capital formation, % GDP	31.4	22	◆
3.3	**Ecological sustainability**	**53.3**	**15**	●
3.3.1	GDP/unit of energy use	11.5	53	
3.3.2	Environmental performance*	61.4	31	
3.3.3	ISO 14001 environment/bn PPP$ GDP	9.1	9	● ◆
	Market sophistication	**35.3**	**64**	
4.1	**Credit**	**36.2**	**47**	
4.1.1	Finance for startups and scaleups†	59.5	33	
4.1.2	Domestic credit to private sector, % GDP	37.9	87	○ ◇
4.1.3	Loans from microfinance institutions, % GDP	n/a	n/a	
4.2	**Investment**	**5.1**	**75**	○
4.2.1	Market capitalization, % GDP	18.6	61	○
4.2.2	Venture capital (VC) investors, deals/bn PPP$ GDP	0.0	59	○
4.2.3	VC recipients, deals/bn PPP$ GDP	0.0	76	○
4.2.4	VC received, value, % GDP	0.0	65	○
4.3	**Trade, diversification and market scale**	**64.5**	**32**	
4.3.1	Applied tariff rate, weighted avg., %	1.5	20	
4.3.2	Domestic industry diversification	94.3	32	
4.3.3	Domestic market scale, bn PPP$	409.8	52	

		Score/ Value	Rank	
	Business sophistication	**45.1**	**30**	
5.1	**Knowledge workers**	**47.5**	**36**	
5.1.1	Knowledge-intensive employment, %	38.7	32	
5.1.2	Firms offering formal training, %	29.3	58	
5.1.3	GERD performed by business, % GDP	1.2	20	
5.1.4	GERD financed by business, %	50.2	28	
5.1.5	Females employed w/advanced degrees, %	18.3	37	
5.2	**Innovation linkages**	**32.2**	**39**	
5.2.1	University–industry R&D collaboration†	49.0	52	
5.2.2	State of cluster development†	55.7	38	
5.2.3	GERD financed by abroad, % GDP	0.3	12	●
5.2.4	Joint venture/strategic alliance deals/bn PPP$ GDP	0.0	64	
5.2.5	Patent families/bn PPP$ GDP	0.3	37	
5.3	**Knowledge absorption**	**55.6**	**9**	●
5.3.1	Intellectual property payments, % total trade	1.1	31	
5.3.2	High-tech imports, % total trade	15.1	15	●
5.3.3	ICT services imports, % total trade	1.6	57	
5.3.4	FDI net inflows, % GDP	61.0	1	● ◆
5.3.5	Research talent, % in businesses	60.6	13	
	Knowledge and technology outputs	**38.4**	**26**	
6.1	**Knowledge creation**	**22.4**	**47**	
6.1.1	Patents by origin/bn PPP$ GDP	1.5	45	
6.1.2	PCT patents by origin/bn PPP$ GDP	0.4	35	
6.1.3	Utility models by origin/bn PPP$ GDP	0.5	32	
6.1.4	Scientific and technical articles/bn PPP$ GDP	20.0	37	
6.1.5	Citable documents H-index	29.7	33	
6.2	**Knowledge impact**	**41.8**	**26**	
6.2.1	Labor productivity growth, %	2.4	24	◆
6.2.2	Unicorn valuation, % GDP	0.0	48	○ ◇
6.2.3	Software spending, % GDP	0.3	51	
6.2.4	High-tech manufacturing, %	58.8	5	● ◆
6.3	**Knowledge diffusion**	**51.1**	**16**	●
6.3.1	Intellectual property receipts, % total trade	1.0	21	
6.3.2	Production and export complexity	84.8	9	●
6.3.3	High-tech exports, % total trade	13.3	10	● ◆
6.3.4	ICT services exports, % total trade	2.0	60	
6.3.5	ISO 9001 quality/bn PPP$ GDP	21.8	7	● ◆
	Creative outputs	**34.1**	**38**	
7.1	**Intangible assets**	**33.8**	**57**	
7.1.1	Intangible asset intensity, top 15, %	45.3	57	○
7.1.2	Trademarks by origin/bn PPP$ GDP	27.9	81	○
7.1.3	Global brand value, top 5,000, % GDP	0.8	56	
7.1.4	Industrial designs by origin/bn PPP$ GDP	2.8	35	
7.2	**Creative goods and services**	**31.4**	**27**	
7.2.1	Cultural and creative services exports, % total trade	0.8	39	
7.2.2	National feature films/mn pop. 15–69	2.4	43	
7.2.3	Entertainment and media market/th pop. 15–69	13.5	29	◇
7.2.4	Creative goods exports, % total trade	6.8	9	● ◆
7.3	**Online creativity**	**37.6**	**32**	
7.3.1	Generic top-level domains (TLDs)/th pop. 15–69	12.4	39	
7.3.2	Country-code TLDs/th pop. 15–69	35.3	20	
7.3.3	GitHub commits/mn pop. 15–69	34.9	31	
7.3.4	Mobile app creation/bn PPP$ GDP	67.7	58	

NOTES: ● indicates a strength; ○ a weakness; ◆ an income group strength; ◇ an income group weakness; * an index; † a survey question. © is used when the available economy data are older than the base year; see appendices for details, including the year of the data, at wipo.int/gii-ranking. Square brackets [ ] indicate that the data minimum coverage (DMC) requirements were not met at the sub-pillar or pillar level.

GII 2023 rank

Iceland **20**

Output rank	Input rank	Income	Region	Population (mn)	GDP, PPP$ (bn)	GDP per capita, PPP$
25	20	High	EUR	0.4	24.9	66,467

		Score/Value	Rank	
	Institutions	**80.9**	**9**	
1.1	**Institutional environment**	**84.4**	**5**	●
1.1.1	Operational stability for businesses*	86.8	4	●◆
1.1.2	Government effectiveness*	82.0	9	
1.2	**Regulatory environment**	**88.3**	**13**	
1.2.1	Regulatory quality*	81.9	16	
1.2.2	Rule of law*	91.1	9	
1.2.3	Cost of redundancy dismissal	13.0	41	
1.3	**Business environment**	**70.0**	**[23]**	
1.3.1	Policies for doing business†	70.0	26	
1.3.2	Entrepreneurship policies and culture†	n/a	n/a	
	Human capital and research	**49.0**	**24**	
2.1	**Education**	**70.5**	**5**	●◆
2.1.1	Expenditure on education, % GDP ⏲	7.6	6	◆
2.1.2	Government funding/pupil, secondary, % GDP/cap	22.3	39	
2.1.3	School life expectancy, years	19.4	5	●◆
2.1.4	PISA scales in reading, maths and science	481.4	30	
2.1.5	Pupil-teacher ratio, secondary	9.3	22	
2.2	**Tertiary education**	**34.6**	**49**	
2.2.1	Tertiary enrolment, % gross	84.3	19	
2.2.2	Graduates in science and engineering, %	18.2	87	○◇
2.2.3	Tertiary inbound mobility, %	8.5	30	
2.3	**Research and development (R&D)**	**41.9**	**25**	◇
2.3.1	Researchers, FTE/mn pop.	6,875.2	7	
2.3.2	Gross expenditure on R&D, % GDP	2.8	13	
2.3.3	Global corporate R&D investors, top 3, mn USD	45.9	36	◇
2.3.4	QS university ranking, top 3*	0.0	71	○◇
	Infrastructure	**60.8**	**10**	
3.1	**Information and communication technologies (ICTs)**	**90.1**	**13**	
3.1.1	ICT access*	95.7	8	◆
3.1.2	ICT use*	98.1	5	●◆
3.1.3	Government's online service*	87.5	16	
3.1.4	E-participation*	79.1	17	
3.2	**General infrastructure**	**62.0**	**6**	●◆
3.2.1	Electricity output, GWh/mn pop.	52,600.5	1	●◆
3.2.2	Logistics performance*	68.2	25	◇
3.2.3	Gross capital formation, % GDP	22.7	75	
3.3	**Ecological sustainability**	**30.4**	**52**	◇
3.3.1	GDP/unit of energy use	3.2	125	○◇
3.3.2	Environmental performance*	74.4	10	
3.3.3	ISO 14001 environment/bn PPP$ GDP	1.8	52	
	Market sophistication	**46.5**	**32**	◇
4.1	**Credit**	**18.6**	**95**	◇
4.1.1	Finance for startups and scaleups†	n/a	n/a	
4.1.2	Domestic credit to private sector, % GDP	100.0	31	
4.1.3	Loans from microfinance institutions, % GDP	0.0	59	○
4.2	**Investment**	**66.4**	**6**	◆
4.2.1	Market capitalization, % GDP	n/a	n/a	
4.2.2	Venture capital (VC) investors, deals/bn PPP$ GDP	0.6	10	
4.2.3	VC recipients, deals/bn PPP$ GDP	0.4	1	●◆
4.2.4	VC received, value, % GDP	0.0	11	
4.3	**Trade, diversification and market scale**	**54.4**	**79**	◇
4.3.1	Applied tariff rate, weighted avg., % ⏲	1.5	50	
4.3.2	Domestic industry diversification	72.6	91	○◇
4.3.3	Domestic market scale, bn PPP$	24.9	128	○

		Score/Value	Rank	
	Business sophistication	**57.0**	**15**	
5.1	**Knowledge workers**	**63.5**	**16**	
5.1.1	Knowledge-intensive employment, %	52.2	6	●
5.1.2	Firms offering formal training, %	n/a	n/a	
5.1.3	GERD performed by business, % GDP	2.0	12	
5.1.4	GERD financed by business, %	38.6	44	◇
5.1.5	Females employed w/advanced degrees, %	26.5	14	
5.2	**Innovation linkages**	**57.6**	**14**	
5.2.1	University-industry R&D collaboration†	63.7	30	
5.2.2	State of cluster development†	45.5	55	◇
5.2.3	GERD financed by abroad, % GDP	0.6	3	●◆
5.2.4	Joint venture/strategic alliance deals/bn PPP$ GDP	0.1	19	
5.2.5	Patent families/bn PPP$ GDP	2.3	17	
5.3	**Knowledge absorption**	**49.9**	**20**	
5.3.1	Intellectual property payments, % total trade	0.9	44	
5.3.2	High-tech imports, % total trade	9.5	43	
5.3.3	ICT services imports, % total trade	4.0	8	
5.3.4	FDI net inflows, % GDP	−2.0	128	○
5.3.5	Research talent, % in businesses	53.1	22	
	Knowledge and technology outputs	**39.2**	**25**	
6.1	**Knowledge creation**	**49.9**	**14**	
6.1.1	Patents by origin/bn PPP$ GDP	4.3	20	
6.1.2	PCT patents by origin/bn PPP$ GDP	1.6	18	
6.1.3	Utility models by origin/bn PPP$ GDP	n/a	n/a	
6.1.4	Scientific and technical articles/bn PPP$ GDP	50.8	1	●◆
6.1.5	Citable documents H-index	19.5	43	◇
6.2	**Knowledge impact**	**24.0**	**80**	◇
6.2.1	Labor productivity growth, %	0.6	76	
6.2.2	Unicorn valuation, % GDP	0.0	48	○◇
6.2.3	Software spending, % GDP	0.3	39	
6.2.4	High-tech manufacturing, %	14.1	80	○◇
6.3	**Knowledge diffusion**	**43.6**	**26**	
6.3.1	Intellectual property receipts, % total trade	3.6	1	●◆
6.3.2	Production and export complexity	n/a	n/a	
6.3.3	High-tech exports, % total trade	2.4	52	◇
6.3.4	ICT services exports, % total trade	3.9	28	
6.3.5	ISO 9001 quality/bn PPP$ GDP	4.8	54	
	Creative outputs	**45.9**	**20**	
7.1	**Intangible assets**	**33.4**	**58**	◇
7.1.1	Intangible asset intensity, top 15, %	55.0	43	◇
7.1.2	Trademarks by origin/bn PPP$ GDP	64.2	32	
7.1.3	Global brand value, top 5,000, % GDP	0.7	59	◇
7.1.4	Industrial designs by origin/bn PPP$ GDP	0.3	97	○◇
7.2	**Creative goods and services**	**36.6**	**18**	
7.2.1	Cultural and creative services exports, % total trade	0.4	62	
7.2.2	National feature films/mn pop. 15–69	37.9	1	●◆
7.2.3	Entertainment and media market/th pop. 15–69	n/a	n/a	
7.2.4	Creative goods exports, % total trade	0.2	81	
7.3	**Online creativity**	**80.0**	**3**	●◆
7.3.1	Generic top-level domains (TLDs)/th pop. 15–69	100.0	1	●◆
7.3.2	Country-code TLDs/th pop. 15–69	96.3	5	●◆
7.3.3	GitHub commits/mn pop. 15–69	64.2	10	
7.3.4	Mobile app creation/bn PPP$ GDP	59.5	83	◇

NOTES: ● indicates a strength; ○ a weakness; ◆ an income group strength; ◇ an income group weakness; * an index; † a survey question. ⏲ is used when the available economy data are older than the base year; see appendices for details, including the year of the data, at wipo.int/gii-ranking. Square brackets [ ] indicate that the data minimum coverage (DMC) requirements were not met at the sub-pillar or pillar level.

GII 2023 rank

India

40

Output rank	Input rank	Income	Region	Population (mn)	GDP, PPP$ (bn)	GDP per capita, PPP$
35	46	Lower middle	CSA	1,417.2	11,665.5	8,293

			Score/ Value	Rank	
	Institutions		53.9	56	◆
1.1	**Institutional environment**		**44.5**	**69**	◆
1.1.1	Operational stability for businesses*		44.4	82	
1.1.2	Government effectiveness*		44.5	53	◆
1.2	**Regulatory environment**		**61.7**	**68**	◆
1.2.1	Regulatory quality*		40.1	76	◆
1.2.2	Rule of law*		37.3	66	◆
1.2.3	Cost of redundancy dismissal		15.8	63	
1.3	**Business environment**		**55.6**	**47**	
1.3.1	Policies for doing business†		37.9	92	
1.3.2	Entrepreneurship policies and culture†		73.3	13	◆
	Human capital and research		35.5	48	◆
2.1	**Education**		**42.8**	**88**	
2.1.1	Expenditure on education, % GDP		4.6	49	
2.1.2	Government funding/pupil, secondary, % GDP/cap		18.0	61	
2.1.3	School life expectancy, years		12.8	86	○
2.1.4	PISA scales in reading, maths and science		n/a	n/a	
2.1.5	Pupil–teacher ratio, secondary		20.8	101	○
2.2	**Tertiary education**		**30.5**	**65**	
2.2.1	Tertiary enrolment, % gross		32.1	85	
2.2.2	Graduates in science and engineering, %		34.0	11	● ◆
2.2.3	Tertiary inbound mobility, %		0.1	110	○
2.3	**Research and development (R&D)**		**33.2**	**32**	◆
2.3.1	Researchers, FTE/mn pop.	⊙	262.3	81	○
2.3.2	Gross expenditure on R&D, % GDP	⊙	0.6	54	◆
2.3.3	Global corporate R&D investors, top 3, mn USD		70.6	13	● ◆
2.3.4	QS university ranking, top 3*		48.2	22	◆
	Infrastructure		34.3	84	
3.1	**Information and communication technologies (ICTs)**		**60.2**	**82**	
3.1.1	ICT access*		56.2	101	○
3.1.2	ICT use*		49.2	103	○
3.1.3	Government's online service*		77.2	42	◆
3.1.4	E-participation*		58.1	61	◆
3.2	**General infrastructure**		**33.1**	**46**	◆
3.2.1	Electricity output, GWh/mn pop.		1,185.0	93	
3.2.2	Logistics performance*		59.1	37	◆
3.2.3	Gross capital formation, % GDP		32.8	16	●
3.3	**Ecological sustainability**		**9.7**	**128**	○ ◇
3.3.1	GDP/unit of energy use		9.8	71	
3.3.2	Environmental performance*		0.0	131	○ ◇
3.3.3	ISO 14001 environment/bn PPP$ GDP		0.9	67	
	Market sophistication		52.9	20	◆
4.1	**Credit**		**34.0**	**56**	
4.1.1	Finance for startups and scaleups†		78.6	9	● ◆
4.1.2	Domestic credit to private sector, % GDP		54.7	67	
4.1.3	Loans from microfinance institutions, % GDP		0.3	42	
4.2	**Investment**		**38.6**	**17**	◆
4.2.1	Market capitalization, % GDP		87.5	19	
4.2.2	Venture capital (VC) investors, deals/bn PPP$ GDP		0.1	39	◆
4.2.3	VC recipients, deals/bn PPP$ GDP		0.1	24	◆
4.2.4	VC received, value, % GDP		0.0	6	● ◆
4.3	**Trade, diversification and market scale**		**85.9**	**9**	● ◆
4.3.1	Applied tariff rate, weighted avg., %		6.2	97	
4.3.2	Domestic industry diversification	⊙	97.9	10	● ◆
4.3.3	Domestic market scale, bn PPP$		11,665.5	1	● ◆

			Score/ Value	Rank	
	Business sophistication		29.6	57	◆
5.1	**Knowledge workers**		**24.4**	**81**	
5.1.1	Knowledge-intensive employment, %		13.0	99	○
5.1.2	Firms offering formal training, %	⊙	35.9	43	
5.1.3	GERD performed by business, % GDP	⊙	0.2	50	◆
5.1.4	GERD financed by business, %		40.6	41	
5.1.5	Females employed w/advanced degrees, %		2.6	106	○
5.2	**Innovation linkages**		**23.4**	**59**	
5.2.1	University–industry R&D collaboration†		44.4	66	
5.2.2	State of cluster development†		28.3	98	
5.2.3	GERD financed by abroad, % GDP		n/a	n/a	
5.2.4	Joint venture/strategic alliance deals/bn PPP$ GDP		0.0	28	◆
5.2.5	Patent families/bn PPP$ GDP		0.2	46	◆
5.3	**Knowledge absorption**		**40.9**	**41**	◆
5.3.1	Intellectual property payments, % total trade		1.4	25	◆
5.3.2	High-tech imports, % total trade		10.0	37	
5.3.3	ICT services imports, % total trade		2.1	32	◆
5.3.4	FDI net inflows, % GDP		1.9	77	
5.3.5	Research talent, % in businesses	⊙	30.7	43	◆
	Knowledge and technology outputs		39.7	22	◆
6.1	**Knowledge creation**		**23.6**	**44**	◆
6.1.1	Patents by origin/bn PPP$ GDP		2.6	28	◆
6.1.2	PCT patents by origin/bn PPP$ GDP		0.2	43	◆
6.1.3	Utility models by origin/bn PPP$ GDP		n/a	n/a	
6.1.4	Scientific and technical articles/bn PPP$ GDP		8.9	81	
6.1.5	Citable documents H-index		42.8	20	◆
6.2	**Knowledge impact**		**53.3**	**9**	● ◆
6.2.1	Labor productivity growth, %		1.6	43	
6.2.2	Unicorn valuation, % GDP		5.0	9	● ◆
6.2.3	Software spending, % GDP		0.2	56	
6.2.4	High-tech manufacturing, %	⊙	34.2	35	◆
6.3	**Knowledge diffusion**		**42.1**	**29**	◆
6.3.1	Intellectual property receipts, % total trade		0.2	45	◆
6.3.2	Production and export complexity		61.2	46	◆
6.3.3	High-tech exports, % total trade		4.0	41	◆
6.3.4	ICT services exports, % total trade		12.1	5	● ◆
6.3.5	ISO 9001 quality/bn PPP$ GDP		3.6	69	
	Creative outputs		30.3	49	◆
7.1	**Intangible assets**		**42.2**	**38**	◆
7.1.1	Intangible asset intensity, top 15, %		78.6	8	● ◆
7.1.2	Trademarks by origin/bn PPP$ GDP		42.7	54	
7.1.3	Global brand value, top 5,000, % GDP		5.5	31	◆
7.1.4	Industrial designs by origin/bn PPP$ GDP		1.7	47	
7.2	**Creative goods and services**		**16.9**	**56**	◆
7.2.1	Cultural and creative services exports, % total trade		1.7	18	◆
7.2.2	National feature films/mn pop. 15–69		1.8	49	
7.2.3	Entertainment and media market/th pop. 15–69		0.7	55	○
7.2.4	Creative goods exports, % total trade		1.8	27	
7.3	**Online creativity**		**19.8**	**66**	
7.3.1	Generic top-level domains (TLDs)/th pop. 15–69		1.0	99	
7.3.2	Country-code TLDs/th pop. 15–69		0.8	96	
7.3.3	GitHub commits/mn pop. 15–69		3.9	78	
7.3.4	Mobile app creation/bn PPP$ GDP		73.6	36	◆

NOTES: ● indicates a strength; ○ a weakness; ◆ an income group strength; ◇ an income group weakness; * an index; † a survey question. ⊙ is used when the available economy data are older than the base year; see appendices for details, including the year of the data, at wipo.int/gii-ranking. Square brackets [ ] indicate that the data minimum coverage (DMC) requirements were not met at the sub-pillar or pillar level.

GII 2023 rank

Indonesia

61

Output rank	Input rank	Income	Region	Population (mn)	GDP, PPP$ (bn)	GDP per capita, PPP$
63	64	Lower middle	SEAO	275.5	4,023.5	14,638

			Score/ Value	Rank	
	Institutions		**48.7**	**70**	
1.1	**Institutional environment**		**46.5**	**63**	◆
1.1.1	Operational stability for businesses*		45.8	78	
1.1.2	Government effectiveness*		47.2	49	◆
1.2	**Regulatory environment**		**21.5**	**129**	○◇
1.2.1	Regulatory quality*		49.8	56	◆
1.2.2	Rule of law*		33.1	74	
1.2.3	Cost of redundancy dismissal		57.8	129	○◇
1.3	**Business environment**		**78.2**	**11**	●◆
1.3.1	Policies for doing business†		72.8	24	●◆
1.3.2	Entrepreneurship policies and culture†		83.6	5	●◆
	Human capital and research		**25.8**	**85**	
2.1	**Education**		**34.3**	**113**	
2.1.1	Expenditure on education, % GDP	⊙	2.8	109	
2.1.2	Government funding/pupil, secondary, % GDP/cap	⊙	10.6	90	○
2.1.3	School life expectancy, years	⊙	13.6	74	
2.1.4	PISA scales in reading, maths and science		381.9	72	○
2.1.5	Pupil–teacher ratio, secondary	⊙	15.2	78	
2.2	**Tertiary education**		**17.4**	**95**	
2.2.1	Tertiary enrolment, % gross	⊙	36.3	81	
2.2.2	Graduates in science and engineering, %	⊙	19.4	79	
2.2.3	Tertiary inbound mobility, %	⊙	0.1	111	○◇
2.3	**Research and development (R&D)**		**25.6**	**39**	◆
2.3.1	Researchers, FTE/mn pop.	⊙	395.7	75	
2.3.2	Gross expenditure on R&D, % GDP	⊙	0.3	79	
2.3.3	Global corporate R&D investors, top 3, mn USD		53.6	28	◆
2.3.4	QS university ranking, top 3*		40.0	32	◆
	Infrastructure		**39.2**	**69**	◆
3.1	**Information and communication technologies (ICTs)**		**73.9**	**54**	◆
3.1.1	ICT access*		84.9	49	◆
3.1.2	ICT use*		65.8	80	
3.1.3	Government's online service*		74.0	51	◆
3.1.4	E-participation*		70.9	37	◆
3.2	**General infrastructure**		**25.5**	**71**	
3.2.1	Electricity output, GWh/mn pop.		1,118.4	95	
3.2.2	Logistics performance*		40.9	60	◆
3.2.3	Gross capital formation, % GDP		30.3	24	●
3.3	**Ecological sustainability**		**18.2**	**88**	
3.3.1	GDP/unit of energy use		13.5	34	
3.3.2	Environmental performance*		15.8	122	○
3.3.3	ISO 14001 environment/bn PPP$ GDP		0.8	74	
	Market sophistication		**45.0**	**37**	◆
4.1	**Credit**		**31.2**	**63**	
4.1.1	Finance for startups and scaleups†		80.4	8	●◆
4.1.2	Domestic credit to private sector, % GDP		38.7	84	
4.1.3	Loans from microfinance institutions, % GDP		0.0	58	○
4.2	**Investment**		**13.8**	**48**	
4.2.1	Market capitalization, % GDP		46.8	38	
4.2.2	Venture capital (VC) investors, deals/bn PPP$ GDP		0.0	71	
4.2.3	VC recipients, deals/bn PPP$ GDP		0.0	59	
4.2.4	VC received, value, % GDP		0.0	30	
4.3	**Trade, diversification and market scale**		**90.1**	**5**	●◆
4.3.1	Applied tariff rate, weighted avg., %		2.0	62	◆
4.3.2	Domestic industry diversification	⊙	97.1	16	●◆
4.3.3	Domestic market scale, bn PPP$		4,023.5	7	●◆

			Score/ Value	Rank	
	Business sophistication		**25.6**	**77**	
5.1	**Knowledge workers**		**8.7**	**125**	○◇
5.1.1	Knowledge-intensive employment, %		10.9	105	
5.1.2	Firms offering formal training, %	⊙	7.7	97	○◇
5.1.3	GERD performed by business, % GDP	⊙	0.0	82	○
5.1.4	GERD financed by business, %	⊙	8.0	78	
5.1.5	Females employed w/advanced degrees, %		6.3	89	
5.2	**Innovation linkages**		**35.2**	**35**	◆
5.2.1	University-industry R&D collaboration†		87.4	5	●◆
5.2.2	State of cluster development†		86.5	5	●◆
5.2.3	GERD financed by abroad, % GDP	⊙	0.0	93	○
5.2.4	Joint venture/strategic alliance deals/bn PPP$ GDP		0.0	111	
5.2.5	Patent families/bn PPP$ GDP		0.0	91	
5.3	**Knowledge absorption**		**32.9**	**70**	
5.3.1	Intellectual property payments, % total trade		0.9	46	◆
5.3.2	High-tech imports, % total trade		10.4	31	
5.3.3	ICT services imports, % total trade		2.1	35	◆
5.3.4	FDI net inflows, % GDP		1.9	72	
5.3.5	Research talent, % in businesses	⊙	7.5	63	
	Knowledge and technology outputs		**23.7**	**61**	
6.1	**Knowledge creation**		**9.5**	**82**	
6.1.1	Patents by origin/bn PPP$ GDP		0.4	85	
6.1.2	PCT patents by origin/bn PPP$ GDP		0.0	100	
6.1.3	Utility models by origin/bn PPP$ GDP		0.9	23	
6.1.4	Scientific and technical articles/bn PPP$ GDP		1.7	126	○
6.1.5	Citable documents H-index		14.8	57	
6.2	**Knowledge impact**		**41.4**	**28**	◆
6.2.1	Labor productivity growth, %		1.3	54	
6.2.2	Unicorn valuation, % GDP		2.1	19	●◆
6.2.3	Software spending, % GDP		0.4	25	◆
6.2.4	High-tech manufacturing, %	⊙	29.8	39	◆
6.3	**Knowledge diffusion**		**20.2**	**73**	
6.3.1	Intellectual property receipts, % total trade		0.0	73	
6.3.2	Production and export complexity		51.0	66	
6.3.3	High-tech exports, % total trade		3.2	45	
6.3.4	ICT services exports, % total trade		0.8	93	
6.3.5	ISO 9001 quality/bn PPP$ GDP		2.3	85	
	Creative outputs		**23.8**	**68**	
7.1	**Intangible assets**		**33.3**	**59**	
7.1.1	Intangible asset intensity, top 15, %		69.7	19	
7.1.2	Trademarks by origin/bn PPP$ GDP		25.6	83	
7.1.3	Global brand value, top 5,000, % GDP		3.2	43	◆
7.1.4	Industrial designs by origin/bn PPP$ GDP		0.8	76	
7.2	**Creative goods and services**		**9.4**	**68**	
7.2.1	Cultural and creative services exports, % total trade		0.0	98	
7.2.2	National feature films/mn pop. 15–69		0.5	70	
7.2.3	Entertainment and media market/th pop. 15–69		3.3	48	◆
7.2.4	Creative goods exports, % total trade		2.7	22	●◆
7.3	**Online creativity**		**19.0**	**71**	
7.3.1	Generic top-level domains (TLDs)/th pop. 15–69		1.7	91	
7.3.2	Country-code TLDs/th pop. 15–69		1.1	87	
7.3.3	GitHub commits/mn pop. 15–69		6.0	68	
7.3.4	Mobile app creation/bn PPP$ GDP		67.3	60	

NOTES: ● indicates a strength; ○ a weakness; ◆ an income group strength; ◇ an income group weakness; * an index; † a survey question. ⊙ is used when the available economy data are older than the base year; see appendices for details, including the year of the data, at wipo.int/gii-ranking. Square brackets [ ] indicate that the data minimum coverage (DMC) requirements were not met at the sub-pillar or pillar level.

GII 2023 rank

Iran (Islamic Republic of) 62

Output rank	Input rank	Income	Region	Population (mn)	GDP, PPP$ (bn)	GDP per capita, PPP$
48	87	Lower middle	CSA	88.6	1,599.2	18,663

			Score/ Value	Rank	
	Institutions		**20.6**	**131**	○◇
1.1	**Institutional environment**		**15.2**	**127**	○◇
1.1.1	Operational stability for businesses*		17.4	126	○◇
1.1.2	Government effectiveness*		13.1	121	
1.2	**Regulatory environment**		**38.0**	**121**	
1.2.1	Regulatory quality*		0.0	132	○◇
1.2.2	Rule of law*		12.0	118	
1.2.3	Cost of redundancy dismissal		23.1	100	
1.3	**Business environment**		**8.7**	**128**	○◇
1.3.1	Policies for doing business†	⏲	13.7	124	○◇
1.3.2	Entrepreneurship policies and culture†		3.6	83	○◇
	Human capital and research		**32.6**	**60**	◆
2.1	**Education**		**41.5**	**96**	
2.1.1	Expenditure on education, % GDP	⏲	3.2	100	
2.1.2	Government funding/pupil, secondary, % GDP/cap		16.0	72	
2.1.3	School life expectancy, years		14.6	64	◆
2.1.4	PISA scales in reading, maths and science		n/a	n/a	
2.1.5	Pupil–teacher ratio, secondary	⏲	19.0	96	
2.2	**Tertiary education**		**41.8**	**31**	●◆
2.2.1	Tertiary enrolment, % gross		58.2	55	◆
2.2.2	Graduates in science and engineering, %		39.0	3	●◆
2.2.3	Tertiary inbound mobility, %		0.8	96	
2.3	**Research and development (R&D)**		**14.5**	**49**	◆
2.3.1	Researchers, FTE/mn pop.	⏲	1,659.5	45	◆
2.3.2	Gross expenditure on R&D, % GDP	⏲	0.8	46	◆
2.3.3	Global corporate R&D investors, top 3, mn USD		0.0	40	○◇
2.3.4	QS university ranking, top 3*		27.0	44	◆
	Infrastructure		**29.3**	**97**	
3.1	**Information and communication technologies (ICTs)**		**51.2**	**97**	
3.1.1	ICT access*		77.5	80	
3.1.2	ICT use*		75.3	61	◆
3.1.3	Government's online service*		35.9	115	
3.1.4	E-participation*		16.3	127	○◇
3.2	**General infrastructure**		**25.0**	**74**	
3.2.1	Electricity output, GWh/mn pop.	⏲	3,867.6	58	◆
3.2.2	Logistics performance*		9.1	106	○
3.2.3	Gross capital formation, % GDP		40.1	9	●◆
3.3	**Ecological sustainability**		**11.8**	**120**	
3.3.1	GDP/unit of energy use		4.7	118	◇
3.3.2	Environmental performance*		26.4	95	
3.3.3	ISO 14001 environment/bn PPP$ GDP		0.2	108	
	Market sophistication		**52.9**	**19**	●◆
4.1	**Credit**		**27.7**	**70**	
4.1.1	Finance for startups and scaleups†		33.8	61	
4.1.2	Domestic credit to private sector, % GDP	⏲	60.3	59	
4.1.3	Loans from microfinance institutions, % GDP		n/a	n/a	
4.2	**Investment**		**83.3**	**[3]**	
4.2.1	Market capitalization, % GDP		221.5	5	●◆
4.2.2	Venture capital (VC) investors, deals/bn PPP$ GDP		n/a	n/a	
4.2.3	VC recipients, deals/bn PPP$ GDP		n/a	n/a	
4.2.4	VC received, value, % GDP		n/a	n/a	
4.3	**Trade, diversification and market scale**		**47.8**	**90**	
4.3.1	Applied tariff rate, weighted avg., %		12.1	126	◇
4.3.2	Domestic industry diversification	⏲	87.3	59	
4.3.3	Domestic market scale, bn PPP$		1,599.2	20	●

			Score/ Value	Rank	
	Business sophistication		**17.7**	**117**	
5.1	**Knowledge workers**		**18.8**	**[102]**	
5.1.1	Knowledge-intensive employment, %	⏲	19.9	76	
5.1.2	Firms offering formal training, %		n/a	n/a	
5.1.3	GERD performed by business, % GDP	⏲	0.2	53	
5.1.4	GERD financed by business, %		n/a	n/a	
5.1.5	Females employed w/advanced degrees, %	⏲	7.6	85	
5.2	**Innovation linkages**		**11.4**	**113**	
5.2.1	University–industry R&D collaboration†	⏲	12.2	124	○◇
5.2.2	State of cluster development†	⏲	33.1	87	
5.2.3	GERD financed by abroad, % GDP		n/a	n/a	
5.2.4	Joint venture/strategic alliance deals/bn PPP$ GDP		0.0	126	○◇
5.2.5	Patent families/bn PPP$ GDP		0.0	85	
5.3	**Knowledge absorption**		**22.9**	**116**	
5.3.1	Intellectual property payments, % total trade		0.2	89	
5.3.2	High-tech imports, % total trade	⏲	5.1	114	
5.3.3	ICT services imports, % total trade		0.7	96	
5.3.4	FDI net inflows, % GDP		0.5	112	
5.3.5	Research talent, % in businesses	⏲	19.2	54	
	Knowledge and technology outputs		**25.9**	**55**	◆
6.1	**Knowledge creation**		**32.0**	**29**	●◆
6.1.1	Patents by origin/bn PPP$ GDP		7.0	13	●◆
6.1.2	PCT patents by origin/bn PPP$ GDP		0.2	41	◆
6.1.3	Utility models by origin/bn PPP$ GDP		n/a	n/a	
6.1.4	Scientific and technical articles/bn PPP$ GDP		25.9	27	●◆
6.1.5	Citable documents H-index		23.4	40	●◆
6.2	**Knowledge impact**		**35.2**	**40**	●
6.2.1	Labor productivity growth, %		0.4	82	
6.2.2	Unicorn valuation, % GDP		0.0	48	○◇
6.2.3	Software spending, % GDP		0.6	16	●◆
6.2.4	High-tech manufacturing, %	⏲	28.6	44	◆
6.3	**Knowledge diffusion**		**10.5**	**107**	
6.3.1	Intellectual property receipts, % total trade		0.0	88	
6.3.2	Production and export complexity		44.4	84	
6.3.3	High-tech exports, % total trade	⏲	0.2	109	
6.3.4	ICT services exports, % total trade		0.2	122	
6.3.5	ISO 9001 quality/bn PPP$ GDP		1.0	108	
	Creative outputs		**33.1**	**43**	◆
7.1	**Intangible assets**		**55.7**	**13**	●◆
7.1.1	Intangible asset intensity, top 15, %		n/a	n/a	
7.1.2	Trademarks by origin/bn PPP$ GDP		349.8	1	●◆
7.1.3	Global brand value, top 5,000, % GDP		0.0	73	
7.1.4	Industrial designs by origin/bn PPP$ GDP		9.6	11	●◆
7.2	**Creative goods and services**		**4.3**	**90**	
7.2.1	Cultural and creative services exports, % total trade		0.2	74	
7.2.2	National feature films/mn pop. 15–69		1.6	52	
7.2.3	Entertainment and media market/th pop. 15–69		2.8	51	
7.2.4	Creative goods exports, % total trade	⏲	0.1	96	
7.3	**Online creativity**		**16.8**	**86**	
7.3.1	Generic top-level domains (TLDs)/th pop. 15–69		2.0	85	
7.3.2	Country-code TLDs/th pop. 15–69		6.9	47	◆
7.3.3	GitHub commits/mn pop. 15–69		1.6	105	
7.3.4	Mobile app creation/bn PPP$ GDP		56.6	91	

NOTES: ● indicates a strength; ○ a weakness; ◆ an income group strength; ◇ an income group weakness; * an index; † a survey question. ⏲ is used when the available economy data are older than the base year; see appendices for details, including the year of the data, at wipo.int/gii-ranking. Square brackets [ ] indicate that the data minimum coverage (DMC) requirements were not met at the sub-pillar or pillar level.

Ireland

GII 2023 rank

22

Output rank	Input rank	Income	Region	Population (mn)	GDP, PPP$ (bn)	GDP per capita, PPP$
18	26	High	EUR	5.0	666.3	131,034

			Score/ Value	Rank	
	Institutions		**77.4**	**15**	
1.1	**Institutional environment**		**75.6**	**16**	
1.1.1	Operational stability for businesses*		72.9	20	
1.1.2	Government effectiveness*		78.3	14	
1.2	**Regulatory environment**		**85.5**	**18**	
1.2.1	Regulatory quality*		82.6	14	
1.2.2	Rule of law*		84.5	16	
1.2.3	Cost of redundancy dismissal		14.3	55	
1.3	**Business environment**		**71.2**	**22**	
1.3.1	Policies for doing business†		78.5	12	
1.3.2	Entrepreneurship policies and culture†	⊙	63.9	19	
	Human capital and research		**45.2**	**28**	◇
2.1	**Education**		**47.2**	**75**	○◇
2.1.1	Expenditure on education, % GDP	⊙	3.3	98	○◇
2.1.2	Government funding/pupil, secondary, % GDP/cap		11.6	88	○◇
2.1.3	School life expectancy, years		18.8	9	●
2.1.4	PISA scales in reading, maths and science		504.6	10	
2.1.5	Pupil-teacher ratio, secondary		n/a	n/a	
2.2	**Tertiary education**		**41.8**	**29**	
2.2.1	Tertiary enrolment, % gross		74.7	28	
2.2.2	Graduates in science and engineering, %		26.4	36	
2.2.3	Tertiary inbound mobility, %		10.2	27	
2.3	**Research and development (R&D)**		**46.7**	**21**	
2.3.1	Researchers, FTE/mn pop.		4,592.6	21	
2.3.2	Gross expenditure on R&D, % GDP		1.1	38	◇
2.3.3	Global corporate R&D investors, top 3, mn USD		72.4	12	
2.3.4	QS university ranking, top 3*		47.9	23	
	Infrastructure		**59.2**	**18**	
3.1	**Information and communication technologies (ICTs)**		**78.3**	**42**	◇
3.1.1	ICT access*		82.4	65	◇
3.1.2	ICT use*		87.7	27	◇
3.1.3	Government's online service*		75.6	45	◇
3.1.4	E-participation*		67.4	47	◇
3.2	**General infrastructure**		**40.4**	**31**	
3.2.1	Electricity output, GWh/mn pop.		6,302.1	31	
3.2.2	Logistics performance*		68.2	25	◇
3.2.3	Gross capital formation, % GDP		24.7	59	
3.3	**Ecological sustainability**		**59.0**	**4**	●◆
3.3.1	GDP/unit of energy use		36.3	1	●◆
3.3.2	Environmental performance*		65.3	24	
3.3.3	ISO 14001 environment/bn PPP$ GDP		1.5	56	
	Market sophistication		**37.9**	**51**	◇
4.1	**Credit**		**36.1**	**48**	◇
4.1.1	Finance for startups and scaleups†	⊙	61.6	30	
4.1.2	Domestic credit to private sector, % GDP		32.4	93	○◇
4.1.3	Loans from microfinance institutions, % GDP		n/a	n/a	
4.2	**Investment**		**18.5**	**38**	◇
4.2.1	Market capitalization, % GDP	⊙	37.4	41	○◇
4.2.2	Venture capital (VC) investors, deals/bn PPP$ GDP		0.3	22	
4.2.3	VC recipients, deals/bn PPP$ GDP		0.1	28	
4.2.4	VC received, value, % GDP		0.0	42	◇
4.3	**Trade, diversification and market scale**		**59.0**	**61**	
4.3.1	Applied tariff rate, weighted avg., %		1.5	20	
4.3.2	Domestic industry diversification	⊙	72.4	92	
4.3.3	Domestic market scale, bn PPP$		666.3	39	

			Score/ Value	Rank	
	Business sophistication		**57.0**	**14**	
5.1	**Knowledge workers**		**68.3**	**8**	●
5.1.1	Knowledge-intensive employment, %		47.2	16	
5.1.2	Firms offering formal training, %		59.8	8	●
5.1.3	GERD performed by business, % GDP		0.8	29	
5.1.4	GERD financed by business, %	⊙	62.8	10	
5.1.5	Females employed w/advanced degrees, %		29.5	4	●◆
5.2	**Innovation linkages**		**48.3**	**21**	
5.2.1	University-industry R&D collaboration†		78.6	15	
5.2.2	State of cluster development†		63.6	34	
5.2.3	GERD financed by abroad, % GDP	⊙	0.2	26	
5.2.4	Joint venture/strategic alliance deals/bn PPP$ GDP		0.1	23	
5.2.5	Patent families/bn PPP$ GDP		2.3	18	
5.3	**Knowledge absorption**		**54.5**	**12**	●
5.3.1	Intellectual property payments, % total trade		20.4	1	●◆
5.3.2	High-tech imports, % total trade		6.9	88	○
5.3.3	ICT services imports, % total trade		1.7	52	
5.3.4	FDI net inflows, % GDP		4.2	29	
5.3.5	Research talent, % in businesses		45.5	31	
	Knowledge and technology outputs		**46.8**	**14**	
6.1	**Knowledge creation**		**23.9**	**43**	◇
6.1.1	Patents by origin/bn PPP$ GDP		1.8	38	◇
6.1.2	PCT patents by origin/bn PPP$ GDP		1.2	22	◇
6.1.3	Utility models by origin/bn PPP$ GDP		0.2	45	○
6.1.4	Scientific and technical articles/bn PPP$ GDP		13.6	54	◇
6.1.5	Citable documents H-index		35.5	28	
6.2	**Knowledge impact**		**51.3**	**11**	●
6.2.1	Labor productivity growth, %		−0.1	102	○
6.2.2	Unicorn valuation, % GDP		1.8	23	
6.2.3	Software spending, % GDP		0.6	17	
6.2.4	High-tech manufacturing, %	⊙	58.5	6	
6.3	**Knowledge diffusion**		**65.3**	**3**	●◆
6.3.1	Intellectual property receipts, % total trade		2.8	10	●
6.3.2	Production and export complexity		80.8	15	
6.3.3	High-tech exports, % total trade		8.7	21	
6.3.4	ICT services exports, % total trade		35.2	1	●◆
6.3.5	ISO 9001 quality/bn PPP$ GDP		3.8	65	○
	Creative outputs		**44.1**	**26**	
7.1	**Intangible assets**		**43.8**	**36**	
7.1.1	Intangible asset intensity, top 15, %		81.8	5	●
7.1.2	Trademarks by origin/bn PPP$ GDP		n/a	n/a	
7.1.3	Global brand value, top 5,000, % GDP		4.3	37	◇
7.1.4	Industrial designs by origin/bn PPP$ GDP		1.1	64	○
7.2	**Creative goods and services**		**36.0**	**20**	
7.2.1	Cultural and creative services exports, % total trade		0.9	35	
7.2.2	National feature films/mn pop. 15–69		9.5	6	●
7.2.3	Entertainment and media market/th pop. 15–69		51.8	14	
7.2.4	Creative goods exports, % total trade		1.1	45	
7.3	**Online creativity**		**52.9**	**21**	
7.3.1	Generic top-level domains (TLDs)/th pop. 15–69		56.0	15	
7.3.2	Country-code TLDs/th pop. 15–69		27.7	25	
7.3.3	GitHub commits/mn pop. 15–69		53.3	18	
7.3.4	Mobile app creation/bn PPP$ GDP		74.4	29	

NOTES: ● indicates a strength; ○ a weakness; ◆ an income group strength; ◇ an income group weakness; * an index; † a survey question. ⊙ is used when the available economy data are older than the base year; see appendices for details, including the year of the data, at wipo.int/gii-ranking. Square brackets [ ] indicate that the data minimum coverage (DMC) requirements were not met at the sub-pillar or pillar level.

Israel

GII 2023 rank

14

Output rank	Input rank	Income	Region	Population (mn)	GDP, PPP$ (bn)	GDP per capita, PPP$
13	21	High	NAWA	9.0	496.8	52,173

			Score/Value	Rank	
Institutions			**62.6**	**40**	◇
1.1	**Institutional environment**		**63.6**	**36**	◇
1.1.1	Operational stability for businesses*		54.9	61	○◇
1.1.2	Government effectiveness*		72.4	23	
1.2	**Regulatory environment**		**65.9**	**57**	◇
1.2.1	Regulatory quality*		73.5	26	
1.2.2	Rule of law*		67.3	29	◇
1.2.3	Cost of redundancy dismissal		27.4	114	○◇
1.3	**Business environment**		**58.1**	**38**	
1.3.1	Policies for doing business†		59.9	39	◇
1.3.2	Entrepreneurship policies and culture†		56.2	26	
Human capital and research			**52.5**	**20**	
2.1	**Education**		**57.3**	**48**	◇
2.1.1	Expenditure on education, % GDP	⊙	6.1	17	
2.1.2	Government funding/pupil, secondary, % GDP/cap		19.6	56	○
2.1.3	School life expectancy, years		16.1	35	
2.1.4	PISA scales in reading, maths and science		465.2	39	○◇
2.1.5	Pupil–teacher ratio, secondary		14.1	71	○◇
2.2	**Tertiary education**		**33.2**	**57**	○
2.2.1	Tertiary enrolment, % gross		61.1	52	
2.2.2	Graduates in science and engineering, %		26.9	34	
2.2.3	Tertiary inbound mobility, %		3.4	61	○◇
2.3	**Research and development (R&D)**		**66.9**	**8**	
2.3.1	Researchers, FTE/mn pop.		n/a	n/a	
2.3.2	Gross expenditure on R&D, % GDP		5.6	1	●◆
2.3.3	Global corporate R&D investors, top 3, mn USD		64.4	21	
2.3.4	QS university ranking, top 3*		36.2	36	
Infrastructure			**54.2**	**36**	◇
3.1	**Information and communication technologies (ICTs)**		**82.6**	**30**	
3.1.1	ICT access*		84.1	58	○
3.1.2	ICT use*		89.5	23	
3.1.3	Government's online service*		86.1	21	
3.1.4	E-participation*		70.9	37	
3.2	**General infrastructure**		**43.9**	**27**	
3.2.1	Electricity output, GWh/mn pop.		7,896.6	21	
3.2.2	Logistics performance*		68.2	25	◇
3.2.3	Gross capital formation, % GDP		26.1	44	
3.3	**Ecological sustainability**		**36.1**	**39**	
3.3.1	GDP/unit of energy use		17.0	16	
3.3.2	Environmental performance*		49.7	46	◇
3.3.3	ISO 14001 environment/bn PPP$ GDP		2.0	46	
Market sophistication			**59.0**	**11**	
4.1	**Credit**		**45.7**	**33**	
4.1.1	Finance for startups and scaleups†		66.8	22	
4.1.2	Domestic credit to private sector, % GDP		67.6	54	◇
4.1.3	Loans from microfinance institutions, % GDP		n/a	n/a	
4.2	**Investment**		**68.3**	**5**	●◆
4.2.1	Market capitalization, % GDP		57.4	31	
4.2.2	Venture capital (VC) investors, deals/bn PPP$ GDP		0.9	8	
4.2.3	VC recipients, deals/bn PPP$ GDP		0.7	1	●◆
4.2.4	VC received, value, % GDP		0.0	1	●◆
4.3	**Trade, diversification and market scale**		**63.1**	**42**	
4.3.1	Applied tariff rate, weighted avg., %	⊙	1.8	58	○
4.3.2	Domestic industry diversification	⊙	90.6	46	
4.3.3	Domestic market scale, bn PPP$		496.8	48	

			Score/Value	Rank	
Business sophistication			**65.1**	**6**	
5.1	**Knowledge workers**		**64.9**	**14**	
5.1.1	Knowledge-intensive employment, %	⊙	51.9	7	
5.1.2	Firms offering formal training, %	⊙	18.6	84	
5.1.3	GERD performed by business, % GDP		5.1	1	●◆
5.1.4	GERD financed by business, %		40.0	43	◇
5.1.5	Females employed w/advanced degrees, %	⊙	24.2	21	
5.2	**Innovation linkages**		**89.6**	**1**	●◆
5.2.1	University–industry R&D collaboration†		100.0	1	●◆
5.2.2	State of cluster development†		56.2	37	◇
5.2.3	GERD financed by abroad, % GDP		2.9	1	●◆
5.2.4	Joint venture/strategic alliance deals/bn PPP$ GDP		0.3	3	●◆
5.2.5	Patent families/bn PPP$ GDP		4.9	7	◆
5.3	**Knowledge absorption**		**40.8**	**42**	◇
5.3.1	Intellectual property payments, % total trade		0.9	41	
5.3.2	High-tech imports, % total trade		10.2	34	
5.3.3	ICT services imports, % total trade		2.2	28	
5.3.4	FDI net inflows, % GDP		4.8	23	
5.3.5	Research talent, % in businesses		n/a	n/a	
Knowledge and technology outputs			**61.6**	**5**	●◆
6.1	**Knowledge creation**		**60.0**	**10**	
6.1.1	Patents by origin/bn PPP$ GDP		3.6	22	
6.1.2	PCT patents by origin/bn PPP$ GDP		4.0	1	●◆
6.1.3	Utility models by origin/bn PPP$ GDP		n/a	n/a	
6.1.4	Scientific and technical articles/bn PPP$ GDP		29.5	22	
6.1.5	Citable documents H-index		46.7	16	
6.2	**Knowledge impact**		**58.4**	**5**	●
6.2.1	Labor productivity growth, %		2.4	25	◆
6.2.2	Unicorn valuation, % GDP		9.6	1	●◆
6.2.3	Software spending, % GDP		0.2	68	○◇
6.2.4	High-tech manufacturing, %	⊙	38.0	29	
6.3	**Knowledge diffusion**		**66.4**	**2**	●◆
6.3.1	Intellectual property receipts, % total trade		1.2	19	
6.3.2	Production and export complexity		76.5	21	
6.3.3	High-tech exports, % total trade		12.3	12	
6.3.4	ICT services exports, % total trade		19.2	1	●◆
6.3.5	ISO 9001 quality/bn PPP$ GDP		20.5	12	◆
Creative outputs			**38.3**	**33**	◇
7.1	**Intangible assets**		**31.9**	**65**	○◇
7.1.1	Intangible asset intensity, top 15, %		66.8	25	
7.1.2	Trademarks by origin/bn PPP$ GDP		11.6	107	○◇
7.1.3	Global brand value, top 5,000, % GDP		2.4	44	◇
7.1.4	Industrial designs by origin/bn PPP$ GDP		1.4	54	
7.2	**Creative goods and services**		**38.5**	**13**	
7.2.1	Cultural and creative services exports, % total trade		3.2	5	●◆
7.2.2	National feature films/mn pop. 15–69		5.5	21	
7.2.3	Entertainment and media market/th pop. 15–69		37.7	21	
7.2.4	Creative goods exports, % total trade		1.5	37	
7.3	**Online creativity**		**50.9**	**24**	
7.3.1	Generic top-level domains (TLDs)/th pop. 15–69		23.4	28	◇
7.3.2	Country-code TLDs/th pop. 15–69		14.5	33	◇
7.3.3	GitHub commits/mn pop. 15–69		78.7	6	
7.3.4	Mobile app creation/bn PPP$ GDP		87.2	3	●◆

NOTES: ● indicates a strength; ○ a weakness; ◆ an income group strength; ◇ an income group weakness; * an index; † a survey question. ⊙ is used when the available economy data are older than the base year; see appendices for details, including the year of the data, at wipo.int/gii-ranking. Square brackets [ ] indicate that the data minimum coverage (DMC) requirements were not met at the sub-pillar or pillar level.

Italy

GII 2023 rank

26

Output rank	Input rank	Income	Region	Population (mn)	GDP, PPP$ (bn)	GDP per capita, PPP$
19	35	High	EUR	59.0	3,022.2	51,062

		Score/ Value	Rank
	Institutions	**55.4**	**52** ◇
1.1	**Institutional environment**	**51.1**	**53** ◇
1.1.1	Operational stability for businesses*	55.6	56 ◇
1.1.2	Government effectiveness*	46.7	50 ◇
1.2	**Regulatory environment**	**76.0**	**32**
1.2.1	Regulatory quality*	56.2	45 ◇
1.2.2	Rule of law*	47.6	52 ◇
1.2.3	Cost of redundancy dismissal	8.0	1 ●◆
1.3	**Business environment**	**39.2**	**87** ○
1.3.1	Policies for doing business†	52.4	56
1.3.2	Entrepreneurship policies and culture†	26.1	65 ○◇
	Human capital and research	**43.7**	**33**
2.1	**Education**	**57.2**	**49**
2.1.1	Expenditure on education, % GDP ⦸	4.1	68
2.1.2	Government funding/pupil, secondary, % GDP/cap	23.2	31
2.1.3	School life expectancy, years	16.3	28
2.1.4	PISA scales in reading, maths and science	477.0	34
2.1.5	Pupil-teacher ratio, secondary	9.8	30
2.2	**Tertiary education**	**30.5**	**64** ◇
2.2.1	Tertiary enrolment, % gross	69.5	39
2.2.2	Graduates in science and engineering, %	22.7	58
2.2.3	Tertiary inbound mobility, %	2.9	69 ○
2.3	**Research and development (R&D)**	**43.4**	**23**
2.3.1	Researchers, FTE/mn pop.	2,920.8	32
2.3.2	Gross expenditure on R&D, % GDP	1.5	27
2.3.3	Global corporate R&D investors, top 3, mn USD	67.3	17
2.3.4	QS university ranking, top 3*	49.5	19
	Infrastructure	**57.2**	**21**
3.1	**Information and communication technologies (ICTs)**	**81.1**	**35**
3.1.1	ICT access*	82.9	62 ◇
3.1.2	ICT use*	84.0	44
3.1.3	Government's online service*	85.2	23
3.1.4	E-participation*	72.1	32
3.2	**General infrastructure**	**37.9**	**36**
3.2.1	Electricity output, GWh/mn pop.	4,818.3	46
3.2.2	Logistics performance*	72.7	18
3.2.3	Gross capital formation, % GDP	21.9	82 ○
3.3	**Ecological sustainability**	**52.8**	**17**
3.3.1	GDP/unit of energy use	15.5	22
3.3.2	Environmental performance*	65.8	23
3.3.3	ISO 14001 environment/bn PPP$ GDP	6.8	14 ●◆
	Market sophistication	**44.3**	**40**
4.1	**Credit**	**41.4**	**40**
4.1.1	Finance for startups and scaleups†	52.1	43
4.1.2	Domestic credit to private sector, % GDP	83.1	38
4.1.3	Loans from microfinance institutions, % GDP	n/a	n/a
4.2	**Investment**	**6.7**	**67** ○
4.2.1	Market capitalization, % GDP ⦸	26.3	50
4.2.2	Venture capital (VC) investors, deals/bn PPP$ GDP	0.0	64 ○
4.2.3	VC recipients, deals/bn PPP$ GDP	0.0	67 ○
4.2.4	VC received, value, % GDP	0.0	58 ○
4.3	**Trade, diversification and market scale**	**84.9**	**10** ●◆
4.3.1	Applied tariff rate, weighted avg., %	1.5	20
4.3.2	Domestic industry diversification	99.3	5 ●
4.3.3	Domestic market scale, bn PPP$	3,022.2	12 ●◆

		Score/ Value	Rank
	Business sophistication	**41.3**	**33**
5.1	**Knowledge workers**	**37.9**	**52**
5.1.1	Knowledge-intensive employment, %	35.7	40
5.1.2	Firms offering formal training, %	12.6	93 ○◇
5.1.3	GERD performed by business, % GDP	0.9	25
5.1.4	GERD financed by business, %	52.8	23
5.1.5	Females employed w/advanced degrees, %	13.9	53
5.2	**Innovation linkages**	**45.6**	**26**
5.2.1	University-industry R&D collaboration†	74.0	19
5.2.2	State of cluster development†	80.2	12 ●◆
5.2.3	GERD financed by abroad, % GDP	0.2	25
5.2.4	Joint venture/strategic alliance deals/bn PPP$ GDP	0.0	44
5.2.5	Patent families/bn PPP$ GDP	1.8	22
5.3	**Knowledge absorption**	**40.4**	**43**
5.3.1	Intellectual property payments, % total trade	0.8	50
5.3.2	High-tech imports, % total trade	8.3	65
5.3.3	ICT services imports, % total trade	2.0	36
5.3.4	FDI net inflows, % GDP	0.4	117 ○
5.3.5	Research talent, % in businesses	48.8	26
	Knowledge and technology outputs	**44.3**	**18**
6.1	**Knowledge creation**	**41.2**	**23**
6.1.1	Patents by origin/bn PPP$ GDP	5.6	15 ●
6.1.2	PCT patents by origin/bn PPP$ GDP	1.1	26
6.1.3	Utility models by origin/bn PPP$ GDP	0.7	29
6.1.4	Scientific and technical articles/bn PPP$ GDP	25.3	28
6.1.5	Citable documents H-index	68.6	8 ●◆
6.2	**Knowledge impact**	**40.5**	**29**
6.2.1	Labor productivity growth, %	0.2	89 ○
6.2.2	Unicorn valuation, % GDP	0.1	47
6.2.3	Software spending, % GDP	0.7	3 ●◆
6.2.4	High-tech manufacturing, %	38.3	27
6.3	**Knowledge diffusion**	**51.2**	**15** ●
6.3.1	Intellectual property receipts, % total trade	0.8	25
6.3.2	Production and export complexity	80.5	16
6.3.3	High-tech exports, % total trade	6.4	29
6.3.4	ICT services exports, % total trade	1.4	73
6.3.5	ISO 9001 quality/bn PPP$ GDP	34.3	3 ●◆
	Creative outputs	**45.3**	**21**
7.1	**Intangible assets**	**60.1**	**9** ●◆
7.1.1	Intangible asset intensity, top 15, %	77.6	9 ●
7.1.2	Trademarks by origin/bn PPP$ GDP	53.8	43
7.1.3	Global brand value, top 5,000, % GDP	10.0	17
7.1.4	Industrial designs by origin/bn PPP$ GDP	13.9	7 ●◆
7.2	**Creative goods and services**	**26.5**	**38**
7.2.1	Cultural and creative services exports, % total trade	0.5	57
7.2.2	National feature films/mn pop. 15–69	5.9	19
7.2.3	Entertainment and media market/th pop. 15–69	30.4	23
7.2.4	Creative goods exports, % total trade	2.4	23
7.3	**Online creativity**	**34.5**	**35**
7.3.1	Generic top-level domains (TLDs)/th pop. 15–69	27.3	25
7.3.2	Country-code TLDs/th pop. 15–69	24.9	29
7.3.3	GitHub commits/mn pop. 15–69	18.5	47
7.3.4	Mobile app creation/bn PPP$ GDP	67.4	59

NOTES: ● indicates a strength; ○ a weakness; ◆ an income group strength; ◇ an income group weakness; * an index; † a survey question. ⦸ is used when the available economy data are older than the base year; see appendices for details, including the year of the data, at wipo.int/gii-ranking. Square brackets [ ] indicate that the data minimum coverage (DMC) requirements were not met at the sub-pillar or pillar level.

Jamaica

GII 2023 rank

78

Output rank	Input rank	Income	Region	Population (mn)	GDP, PPP$ (bn)	GDP per capita, PPP$
69	82	Upper middle	LCN	2.8	32.8	11,962

			Score/ Value	Rank	
	Institutions		**55.2**	**53**	
1.1	**Institutional environment**		**54.6**	**46**	◆
1.1.1	Operational stability for businesses*		61.1	43	
1.1.2	Government effectiveness*		48.2	48	
1.2	**Regulatory environment**		**64.6**	**61**	
1.2.1	Regulatory quality*		47.2	59	
1.2.2	Rule of law*		34.8	73	
1.2.3	Cost of redundancy dismissal		14.0	53	
1.3	**Business environment**		**46.5**	**63**	
1.3.1	Policies for doing business†	⏲	55.2	51	
1.3.2	Entrepreneurship policies and culture†	⏲	37.8	51	
	Human capital and research		**23.1**	**[91]**	
2.1	**Education**		**53.9**	**[59]**	
2.1.1	Expenditure on education, % GDP	⏲	5.2	33	●
2.1.2	Government funding/pupil, secondary, % GDP/cap		27.3	12	●◆
2.1.3	School life expectancy, years		n/a	n/a	
2.1.4	PISA scales in reading, maths and science		n/a	n/a	
2.1.5	Pupil–teacher ratio, secondary		18.2	93	
2.2	**Tertiary education**		**15.5**	**[101]**	
2.2.1	Tertiary enrolment, % gross	⏲	27.1	90	◇
2.2.2	Graduates in science and engineering, %		n/a	n/a	
2.2.3	Tertiary inbound mobility, %		n/a	n/a	
2.3	**Research and development (R&D)**		**0.0**	**[119]**	
2.3.1	Researchers, FTE/mn pop.		n/a	n/a	
2.3.2	Gross expenditure on R&D, % GDP		n/a	n/a	
2.3.3	Global corporate R&D investors, top 3, mn USD		0.0	40	○◇
2.3.4	QS university ranking, top 3*		0.0	71	○◇
	Infrastructure		**31.3**	**91**	◇
3.1	**Information and communication technologies (ICTs)**		**52.6**	**95**	◇
3.1.1	ICT access*		78.4	78	
3.1.2	ICT use*		61.6	89	
3.1.3	Government's online service*		43.8	101	◇
3.1.4	E-participation*		26.7	106	○◇
3.2	**General infrastructure**		**16.6**	**103**	
3.2.1	Electricity output, GWh/mn pop.	⏲	1,459.0	92	◇
3.2.2	Logistics performance*		18.2	89	○◇
3.2.3	Gross capital formation, % GDP		26.7	39	
3.3	**Ecological sustainability**		**24.6**	**64**	
3.3.1	GDP/unit of energy use		10.8	59	
3.3.2	Environmental performance*		45.3	56	
3.3.3	ISO 14001 environment/bn PPP$ GDP		0.5	85	
	Market sophistication		**22.0**	**109**	◇
4.1	**Credit**		**25.7**	**76**	
4.1.1	Finance for startups and scaleups†	⏲	31.3	69	
4.1.2	Domestic credit to private sector, % GDP		56.3	64	
4.1.3	Loans from microfinance institutions, % GDP		n/a	n/a	
4.2	**Investment**		**17.3**	**[43]**	
4.2.1	Market capitalization, % GDP		87.0	20	●
4.2.2	Venture capital (VC) investors, deals/bn PPP$ GDP		0.0	73	
4.2.3	VC recipients, deals/bn PPP$ GDP		n/a	n/a	
4.2.4	VC received, value, % GDP		n/a	n/a	
4.3	**Trade, diversification and market scale**		**23.1**	**123**	○◇
4.3.1	Applied tariff rate, weighted avg., %		8.4	107	◇
4.3.2	Domestic industry diversification		n/a	n/a	
4.3.3	Domestic market scale, bn PPP$		32.8	122	○

			Score/ Value	Rank	
	Business sophistication		**27.7**	**69**	
5.1	**Knowledge workers**		**21.9**	**[92]**	
5.1.1	Knowledge-intensive employment, %	⏲	21.6	71	
5.1.2	Firms offering formal training, %		n/a	n/a	
5.1.3	GERD performed by business, % GDP		n/a	n/a	
5.1.4	GERD financed by business, %		n/a	n/a	
5.1.5	Females employed w/advanced degrees, %	⏲	4.1	96	◇
5.2	**Innovation linkages**		**24.7**	**56**	
5.2.1	University–industry R&D collaboration†	⏲	42.6	69	
5.2.2	State of cluster development†	⏲	37.6	81	
5.2.3	GERD financed by abroad, % GDP		n/a	n/a	
5.2.4	Joint venture/strategic alliance deals/bn PPP$ GDP		0.1	27	●◆
5.2.5	Patent families/bn PPP$ GDP		0.0	95	○◇
5.3	**Knowledge absorption**		**36.4**	**53**	
5.3.1	Intellectual property payments, % total trade		1.1	35	
5.3.2	High-tech imports, % total trade		5.3	109	
5.3.3	ICT services imports, % total trade		2.1	33	●
5.3.4	FDI net inflows, % GDP		2.8	56	
5.3.5	Research talent, % in businesses		n/a	n/a	
	Knowledge and technology outputs		**14.7**	**92**	
6.1	**Knowledge creation**		**6.3**	**104**	
6.1.1	Patents by origin/bn PPP$ GDP		0.5	78	
6.1.2	PCT patents by origin/bn PPP$ GDP		0.1	72	
6.1.3	Utility models by origin/bn PPP$ GDP		n/a	n/a	
6.1.4	Scientific and technical articles/bn PPP$ GDP		5.2	105	
6.1.5	Citable documents H-index		4.8	105	
6.2	**Knowledge impact**		**19.7**	**107**	
6.2.1	Labor productivity growth, %		−1.9	125	○◇
6.2.2	Unicorn valuation, % GDP		0.0	48	○◇
6.2.3	Software spending, % GDP		0.3	29	●◆
6.2.4	High-tech manufacturing, %		n/a	n/a	
6.3	**Knowledge diffusion**		**18.0**	**81**	
6.3.1	Intellectual property receipts, % total trade		0.1	51	
6.3.2	Production and export complexity		45.0	82	
6.3.3	High-tech exports, % total trade		0.1	114	○◇
6.3.4	ICT services exports, % total trade		4.6	21	●
6.3.5	ISO 9001 quality/bn PPP$ GDP		1.2	101	
	Creative outputs		**29.8**	**54**	
7.1	**Intangible assets**		**51.8**	**22**	●◆
7.1.1	Intangible asset intensity, top 15, %		53.4	45	
7.1.2	Trademarks by origin/bn PPP$ GDP		86.4	18	●
7.1.3	Global brand value, top 5,000, % GDP		8.1	25	●◆
7.1.4	Industrial designs by origin/bn PPP$ GDP		3.2	33	●
7.2	**Creative goods and services**		**2.1**	**103**	◇
7.2.1	Cultural and creative services exports, % total trade		0.1	77	
7.2.2	National feature films/mn pop. 15–69	⏲	0.5	71	
7.2.3	Entertainment and media market/th pop. 15–69		n/a	n/a	
7.2.4	Creative goods exports, % total trade		0.1	109	
7.3	**Online creativity**		**13.5**	**104**	
7.3.1	Generic top-level domains (TLDs)/th pop. 15–69		1.9	87	
7.3.2	Country-code TLDs/th pop. 15–69		1.1	88	
7.3.3	GitHub commits/mn pop. 15–69		3.1	89	
7.3.4	Mobile app creation/bn PPP$ GDP		47.8	103	◇

NOTES: ● indicates a strength; ○ a weakness; ◆ an income group strength; ◇ an income group weakness; * an index; † a survey question. ⏲ is used when the available economy data are older than the base year; see appendices for details, including the year of the data, at wipo.int/gii-ranking. Square brackets [ ] indicate that the data minimum coverage (DMC) requirements were not met at the sub-pillar or pillar level.

GII 2023 rank

Japan

13

Output rank	Input rank	Income	Region	Population (mn)	GDP, PPP$ (bn)	GDP per capita, PPP$
14	11	High	SEAO	124.0	6,110.0	48,813

		Score/ Value	Rank	
	Institutions	**72.3**	**21**	
1.1	**Institutional environment**	**79.7**	**11**	
1.1.1	Operational stability for businesses*	84.0	7	
1.1.2	Government effectiveness*	75.5	17	
1.2	**Regulatory environment**	**90.9**	**8**	
1.2.1	Regulatory quality*	77.8	19	
1.2.2	Rule of law*	86.0	15	
1.2.3	Cost of redundancy dismissal	8.0	1	●
1.3	**Business environment**	**46.1**	**64**	◇
1.3.1	Policies for doing business†	64.8	33	
1.3.2	Entrepreneurship policies and culture†	27.4	64	○◇

		Score/ Value	Rank	
	Human capital and research	**53.8**	**18**	
2.1	**Education**	**60.7**	**33**	
2.1.1	Expenditure on education, % GDP ⊙	3.2	104	○◇
2.1.2	Government funding/pupil, secondary, % GDP/cap	n/a	n/a	
2.1.3	School life expectancy, years	15.1	48	◇
2.1.4	PISA scales in reading, maths and science	520.0	5	
2.1.5	Pupil–teacher ratio, secondary	10.7	38	
2.2	**Tertiary education**	**29.0**	**71**	○◇
2.2.1	Tertiary enrolment, % gross	65.3	48	
2.2.2	Graduates in science and engineering, %	19.5	77	○
2.2.3	Tertiary inbound mobility, %	5.7	44	
2.3	**Research and development (R&D)**	**71.5**	**5**	●
2.3.1	Researchers, FTE/mn pop.	5,613.5	11	
2.3.2	Gross expenditure on R&D, % GDP	3.3	5	●
2.3.3	Global corporate R&D investors, top 3, mn USD	88.0	6	●
2.3.4	QS university ranking, top 3*	80.8	8	

		Score/ Value	Rank	
	Infrastructure	**60.3**	**13**	
3.1	**Information and communication technologies (ICTs)**	**90.3**	**12**	
3.1.1	ICT access*	84.6	54	
3.1.2	ICT use*	86.5	31	◇
3.1.3	Government's online service*	90.0	10	
3.1.4	E-participation*	100.0	1	●◆
3.2	**General infrastructure**	**48.3**	**19**	
3.2.1	Electricity output, GWh/mn pop.	7,964.2	20	
3.2.2	Logistics performance*	81.8	13	
3.2.3	Gross capital formation, % GDP	25.7	47	
3.3	**Ecological sustainability**	**42.3**	**28**	
3.3.1	GDP/unit of energy use	12.9	37	
3.3.2	Environmental performance*	64.9	25	
3.3.3	ISO 14001 environment/bn PPP$ GDP	3.9	24	

		Score/ Value	Rank	
	Market sophistication	**61.9**	**8**	
4.1	**Credit**	**65.8**	**8**	
4.1.1	Finance for startups and scaleups†	57.5	36	◇
4.1.2	Domestic credit to private sector, % GDP	193.5	3	●◆
4.1.3	Loans from microfinance institutions, % GDP	n/a	n/a	
4.2	**Investment**	**26.2**	**26**	
4.2.1	Market capitalization, % GDP	119.8	10	
4.2.2	Venture capital (VC) investors, deals/bn PPP$ GDP	0.2	27	
4.2.3	VC recipients, deals/bn PPP$ GDP	0.1	17	
4.2.4	VC received, value, % GDP	0.0	51	○◇
4.3	**Trade, diversification and market scale**	**93.6**	**4**	●◆
4.3.1	Applied tariff rate, weighted avg., %	2.2	63	
4.3.2	Domestic industry diversification ⊙	95.2	28	
4.3.3	Domestic market scale, bn PPP$	6,110.0	1	●◆

		Score/ Value	Rank	
	Business sophistication	**59.9**	**11**	
5.1	**Knowledge workers**	**62.9**	**18**	
5.1.1	Knowledge-intensive employment, %	20.8	73	○◇
5.1.2	Firms offering formal training, %	n/a	n/a	
5.1.3	GERD performed by business, % GDP	2.6	4	●
5.1.4	GERD financed by business, %	78.1	2	●◆
5.1.5	Females employed w/advanced degrees, % ⊙	22.9	25	
5.2	**Innovation linkages**	**50.2**	**20**	
5.2.1	University–industry R&D collaboration†	64.0	28	
5.2.2	State of cluster development†	72.3	20	
5.2.3	GERD financed by abroad, % GDP	0.0	62	○◇
5.2.4	Joint venture/strategic alliance deals/bn PPP$ GDP	0.0	42	◇
5.2.5	Patent families/bn PPP$ GDP	13.0	1	●◆
5.3	**Knowledge absorption**	**66.6**	**4**	●◆
5.3.1	Intellectual property payments, % total trade	3.2	7	
5.3.2	High-tech imports, % total trade	15.0	16	
5.3.3	ICT services imports, % total trade	2.7	23	
5.3.4	FDI net inflows, % GDP	0.9	100	○
5.3.5	Research talent, % in businesses	75.1	5	◆

		Score/ Value	Rank	
	Knowledge and technology outputs	**51.1**	**13**	
6.1	**Knowledge creation**	**59.1**	**12**	
6.1.1	Patents by origin/bn PPP$ GDP	39.7	3	●◆
6.1.2	PCT patents by origin/bn PPP$ GDP	8.2	1	●◆
6.1.3	Utility models by origin/bn PPP$ GDP	0.7	28	
6.1.4	Scientific and technical articles/bn PPP$ GDP	13.5	57	◇
6.1.5	Citable documents H-index	67.2	9	
6.2	**Knowledge impact**	**35.0**	**41**	◇
6.2.1	Labor productivity growth, %	−0.6	111	○
6.2.2	Unicorn valuation, % GDP	0.2	46	◇
6.2.3	Software spending, % GDP	0.3	42	
6.2.4	High-tech manufacturing, % ⊙	54.6	8	
6.3	**Knowledge diffusion**	**59.2**	**6**	●
6.3.1	Intellectual property receipts, % total trade	5.3	1	●◆
6.3.2	Production and export complexity	100.0	1	●◆
6.3.3	High-tech exports, % total trade	12.6	11	
6.3.4	ICT services exports, % total trade	1.1	83	○
6.3.5	ISO 9001 quality/bn PPP$ GDP	7.3	37	

		Score/ Value	Rank	
	Creative outputs	**44.1**	**25**	
7.1	**Intangible assets**	**55.7**	**14**	
7.1.1	Intangible asset intensity, top 15, %	69.0	20	
7.1.2	Trademarks by origin/bn PPP$ GDP	48.1	48	
7.1.3	Global brand value, top 5,000, % GDP	16.0	7	
7.1.4	Industrial designs by origin/bn PPP$ GDP	3.9	25	
7.2	**Creative goods and services**	**35.3**	**21**	
7.2.1	Cultural and creative services exports, % total trade	0.4	58	○
7.2.2	National feature films/mn pop. 15–69	6.1	18	
7.2.3	Entertainment and media market/th pop. 15–69	72.4	5	
7.2.4	Creative goods exports, % total trade	1.8	30	
7.3	**Online creativity**	**30.0**	**41**	◇
7.3.1	Generic top-level domains (TLDs)/th pop. 15–69	19.1	31	◇
7.3.2	Country-code TLDs/th pop. 15–69	6.4	51	◇
7.3.3	GitHub commits/mn pop. 15–69	21.9	41	◇
7.3.4	Mobile app creation/bn PPP$ GDP	72.6	42	

NOTES: ● indicates a strength; ○ a weakness; ◆ an income group strength; ◇ an income group weakness; * an index; † a survey question. ⊙ is used when the available economy data are older than the base year; see appendices for details, including the year of the data, at wipo.int/gii-ranking. Square brackets [ ] indicate that the data minimum coverage (DMC) requirements were not met at the sub-pillar or pillar level.

Jordan

GII 2023 rank

71

Output rank	Input rank	Income	Region	Population (mn)	GDP, PPP$ (bn)	GDP per capita, PPP$
76	70	Upper middle	NAWA	11.3	123.4	11,975

		Score/ Value	Rank	
	Institutions	**55.9**	**51**	
1.1	**Institutional environment**	**45.1**	**65**	
1.1.1	Operational stability for businesses*	47.2	75	
1.1.2	Government effectiveness*	43.0	59	
1.2	**Regulatory environment**	**73.0**	**37**	● ◆
1.2.1	Regulatory quality*	46.0	63	
1.2.2	Rule of law*	46.0	55	
1.2.3	Cost of redundancy dismissal	8.0	1	● ◆
1.3	**Business environment**	**49.5**	**54**	
1.3.1	Policies for doing business†	56.6	46	
1.3.2	Entrepreneurship policies and culture† ⊙	42.4	46	
	Human capital and research	**26.8**	**82**	
2.1	**Education**	**36.9**	**108**	◇
2.1.1	Expenditure on education, % GDP	3.2	102	
2.1.2	Government funding/pupil, secondary, % GDP/cap	16.9	68	
2.1.3	School life expectancy, years	10.9	98	○ ◇
2.1.4	PISA scales in reading, maths and science	416.0	58	
2.1.5	Pupil–teacher ratio, secondary	15.4	80	
2.2	**Tertiary education**	**34.9**	**47**	
2.2.1	Tertiary enrolment, % gross	34.1	84	
2.2.2	Graduates in science and engineering, %	26.9	35	●
2.2.3	Tertiary inbound mobility, %	12.3	19	● ◆
2.3	**Research and development (R&D)**	**8.7**	**65**	
2.3.1	Researchers, FTE/mn pop. ⊙	596.0	65	
2.3.2	Gross expenditure on R&D, % GDP ⊙	0.7	50	
2.3.3	Global corporate R&D investors, top 3, mn USD	0.0	40	○ ◇
2.3.4	QS university ranking, top 3*	16.3	59	
	Infrastructure	**32.5**	**87**	◇
3.1	**Information and communication technologies (ICTs)**	**58.7**	**84**	
3.1.1	ICT access*	53.4	104	◇
3.1.2	ICT use*	65.7	82	
3.1.3	Government's online service*	62.4	73	
3.1.4	E-participation*	53.5	67	
3.2	**General infrastructure**	**12.4**	**118**	○ ◇
3.2.1	Electricity output, GWh/mn pop. ⊙	2,063.1	81	
3.2.2	Logistics performance*	n/a	n/a	
3.2.3	Gross capital formation, % GDP	20.7	94	
3.3	**Ecological sustainability**	**26.3**	**60**	
3.3.1	GDP/unit of energy use	11.0	56	
3.3.2	Environmental performance*	41.9	60	
3.3.3	ISO 14001 environment/bn PPP$ GDP	1.5	58	
	Market sophistication	**37.8**	**53**	
4.1	**Credit**	**32.8**	**59**	
4.1.1	Finance for startups and scaleups† ⊙	58.1	35	
4.1.2	Domestic credit to private sector, % GDP	82.2	40	●
4.1.3	Loans from microfinance institutions, % GDP	0.8	30	
4.2	**Investment**	**23.5**	**30**	●
4.2.1	Market capitalization, % GDP	46.8	37	
4.2.2	Venture capital (VC) investors, deals/bn PPP$ GDP	0.1	37	
4.2.3	VC recipients, deals/bn PPP$ GDP	0.1	36	
4.2.4	VC received, value, % GDP	0.0	16	● ◆
4.3	**Trade, diversification and market scale**	**57.1**	**71**	
4.3.1	Applied tariff rate, weighted avg., %	4.0	83	
4.3.2	Domestic industry diversification	94.6	30	●
4.3.3	Domestic market scale, bn PPP$	123.4	83	

		Score/ Value	Rank	
	Business sophistication	**27.0**	**70**	
5.1	**Knowledge workers**	**24.6**	**[79]**	
5.1.1	Knowledge-intensive employment, % ⊙	23.0	64	
5.1.2	Firms offering formal training, %	16.9	88	○ ◇
5.1.3	GERD performed by business, % GDP	n/a	n/a	
5.1.4	GERD financed by business, %	n/a	n/a	
5.1.5	Females employed w/advanced degrees, % ⊙	8.4	82	
5.2	**Innovation linkages**	**34.1**	**37**	● ◆
5.2.1	University–industry R&D collaboration†	57.0	40	●
5.2.2	State of cluster development†	67.7	27	● ◆
5.2.3	GERD financed by abroad, % GDP	n/a	n/a	
5.2.4	Joint venture/strategic alliance deals/bn PPP$ GDP	0.0	41	
5.2.5	Patent families/bn PPP$ GDP	0.0	82	
5.3	**Knowledge absorption**	**22.3**	**119**	○ ◇
5.3.1	Intellectual property payments, % total trade	0.2	94	◇
5.3.2	High-tech imports, % total trade	7.2	82	
5.3.3	ICT services imports, % total trade	0.2	125	○ ◇
5.3.4	FDI net inflows, % GDP	1.6	86	
5.3.5	Research talent, % in businesses	n/a	n/a	
	Knowledge and technology outputs	**20.3**	**76**	
6.1	**Knowledge creation**	**21.5**	**50**	
6.1.1	Patents by origin/bn PPP$ GDP	0.2	95	
6.1.2	PCT patents by origin/bn PPP$ GDP	0.2	45	
6.1.3	Utility models by origin/bn PPP$ GDP	n/a	n/a	
6.1.4	Scientific and technical articles/bn PPP$ GDP	33.3	15	● ◆
6.1.5	Citable documents H-index	11.1	71	
6.2	**Knowledge impact**	**21.4**	**95**	
6.2.1	Labor productivity growth, %	−1.0	117	○ ◇
6.2.2	Unicorn valuation, % GDP	0.0	48	○ ◇
6.2.3	Software spending, % GDP	0.3	41	◆
6.2.4	High-tech manufacturing, %	17.7	67	
6.3	**Knowledge diffusion**	**18.0**	**82**	
6.3.1	Intellectual property receipts, % total trade	0.1	65	
6.3.2	Production and export complexity	53.9	58	
6.3.3	High-tech exports, % total trade	1.2	71	
6.3.4	ICT services exports, % total trade	0.1	125	○
6.3.5	ISO 9001 quality/bn PPP$ GDP	4.8	55	
	Creative outputs	**20.7**	**75**	
7.1	**Intangible assets**	**28.7**	**70**	
7.1.1	Intangible asset intensity, top 15, %	39.7	62	
7.1.2	Trademarks by origin/bn PPP$ GDP	28.8	80	
7.1.3	Global brand value, top 5,000, % GDP	0.9	55	
7.1.4	Industrial designs by origin/bn PPP$ GDP	1.0	68	
7.2	**Creative goods and services**	**4.4**	**88**	
7.2.1	Cultural and creative services exports, % total trade	0.0	106	○ ◇
7.2.2	National feature films/mn pop. 15–69	0.6	68	
7.2.3	Entertainment and media market/th pop. 15–69	0.2	57	○ ◇
7.2.4	Creative goods exports, % total trade	1.2	43	
7.3	**Online creativity**	**20.9**	**63**	
7.3.1	Generic top-level domains (TLDs)/th pop. 15–69	4.9	57	
7.3.2	Country-code TLDs/th pop. 15–69	0.2	113	○
7.3.3	GitHub commits/mn pop. 15–69	3.7	84	
7.3.4	Mobile app creation/bn PPP$ GDP	74.7	27	●

NOTES: ● indicates a strength; ○ a weakness; ◆ an income group strength; ◇ an income group weakness; * an index; † a survey question. ⊙ is used when the available economy data are older than the base year; see appendices for details, including the year of the data, at wipo.int/gii-ranking. Square brackets [ ] indicate that the data minimum coverage (DMC) requirements were not met at the sub-pillar or pillar level.

GII 2023 rank

Kazakhstan **81**

Output rank	Input rank	Income	Region	Population (mn)	GDP, PPP$ (bn)	GDP per capita, PPP$
87	68	Upper middle	CSA	19.4	596.7	30,827

			Score/ Value	Rank	
	Institutions		**51.9**	**61**	
1.1	**Institutional environment**		**44.3**	**72**	
1.1.1	Operational stability for businesses*		50.0	71	
1.1.2	Government effectiveness*		38.5	63	
1.2	**Regulatory environment**		**66.8**	**51**	
1.2.1	Regulatory quality*		44.4	66	
1.2.2	Rule of law*		25.5	93	
1.2.3	Cost of redundancy dismissal		8.7	18	●◆
1.3	**Business environment**		**44.7**	**70**	
1.3.1	Policies for doing business†		35.5	99	
1.3.2	Entrepreneurship policies and culture†	⊙	53.8	28	

			Score/ Value	Rank	
	Human capital and research		**32.6**	**59**	
2.1	**Education**		**51.5**	**65**	
2.1.1	Expenditure on education, % GDP		4.5	54	
2.1.2	Government funding/pupil, secondary, % GDP/cap	⊙	21.2	45	
2.1.3	School life expectancy, years		15.8	44	
2.1.4	PISA scales in reading, maths and science		402.4	64	
2.1.5	Pupil–teacher ratio, secondary		8.3	12	●◆
2.2	**Tertiary education**		**34.5**	**50**	
2.2.1	Tertiary enrolment, % gross		70.7	35	●
2.2.2	Graduates in science and engineering, %		24.1	49	
2.2.3	Tertiary inbound mobility, %		5.5	45	
2.3	**Research and development (R&D)**		**11.9**	**54**	
2.3.1	Researchers, FTE/mn pop.		629.9	64	
2.3.2	Gross expenditure on R&D, % GDP		0.1	100	○
2.3.3	Global corporate R&D investors, top 3, mn USD		0.0	40	○◇
2.3.4	QS university ranking, top 3*		39.1	33	●

			Score/ Value	Rank	
	Infrastructure		**43.1**	**59**	
3.1	**Information and communication technologies (ICTs)**		**85.2**	**21**	●◆
3.1.1	ICT access*		86.7	41	
3.1.2	ICT use*		80.9	55	
3.1.3	Government's online service*		92.7	8	●◆
3.1.4	E-participation*		80.2	15	●◆
3.2	**General infrastructure**		**26.2**	**67**	
3.2.1	Electricity output, GWh/mn pop.	⊙	5,912.2	33	●◆
3.2.2	Logistics performance*		27.3	76	
3.2.3	Gross capital formation, % GDP		24.8	57	
3.3	**Ecological sustainability**		**18.1**	**90**	
3.3.1	GDP/unit of energy use		6.9	98	◇
3.3.2	Environmental performance*		37.3	69	
3.3.3	ISO 14001 environment/bn PPP$ GDP		0.5	89	

			Score/ Value	Rank	
	Market sophistication		**27.7**	**87**	
4.1	**Credit**		**22.1**	**87**	
4.1.1	Finance for startups and scaleups†	⊙	45.6	53	
4.1.2	Domestic credit to private sector, % GDP		25.6	109	◇
4.1.3	Loans from microfinance institutions, % GDP		1.1	26	
4.2	**Investment**		**2.4**	**100**	○
4.2.1	Market capitalization, % GDP		23.9	54	
4.2.2	Venture capital (VC) investors, deals/bn PPP$ GDP		0.0	95	○◇
4.2.3	VC recipients, deals/bn PPP$ GDP		0.0	98	○
4.2.4	VC received, value, % GDP		0.0	99	○
4.3	**Trade, diversification and market scale**		**58.5**	**66**	
4.3.1	Applied tariff rate, weighted avg., %		2.0	60	
4.3.2	Domestic industry diversification	⊙	75.6	87	◇
4.3.3	Domestic market scale, bn PPP$		596.7	42	

			Score/ Value	Rank	
	Business sophistication		**26.1**	**75**	
5.1	**Knowledge workers**		**40.8**	**46**	
5.1.1	Knowledge-intensive employment, %	⊙	36.9	37	◆
5.1.2	Firms offering formal training, %		21.8	74	
5.1.3	GERD performed by business, % GDP	⊙	0.1	72	
5.1.4	GERD financed by business, %	⊙	47.4	34	
5.1.5	Females employed w/advanced degrees, %	⊙	20.7	32	●◆
5.2	**Innovation linkages**		**8.4**	**123**	○◇
5.2.1	University–industry R&D collaboration†		20.3	117	○◇
5.2.2	State of cluster development†		16.6	118	○◇
5.2.3	GERD financed by abroad, % GDP	⊙	0.0	88	○
5.2.4	Joint venture/strategic alliance deals/bn PPP$ GDP		0.0	104	
5.2.5	Patent families/bn PPP$ GDP		0.1	60	
5.3	**Knowledge absorption**		**29.0**	**83**	
5.3.1	Intellectual property payments, % total trade		0.3	82	
5.3.2	High-tech imports, % total trade	⊙	9.9	39	
5.3.3	ICT services imports, % total trade		0.8	93	
5.3.4	FDI net inflows, % GDP		2.9	51	
5.3.5	Research talent, % in businesses		n/a	n/a	

			Score/ Value	Rank	
	Knowledge and technology outputs		**18.2**	**83**	
6.1	**Knowledge creation**		**15.5**	**63**	
6.1.1	Patents by origin/bn PPP$ GDP	⊙	1.8	39	
6.1.2	PCT patents by origin/bn PPP$ GDP		0.0	78	
6.1.3	Utility models by origin/bn PPP$ GDP	⊙	1.6	10	●
6.1.4	Scientific and technical articles/bn PPP$ GDP		3.4	115	
6.1.5	Citable documents H-index		6.2	93	
6.2	**Knowledge impact**		**19.6**	**108**	
6.2.1	Labor productivity growth, %		1.6	42	
6.2.2	Unicorn valuation, % GDP		0.0	48	○◇
6.2.3	Software spending, % GDP		0.0	124	○◇
6.2.4	High-tech manufacturing, %	⊙	15.3	76	
6.3	**Knowledge diffusion**		**19.5**	**77**	
6.3.1	Intellectual property receipts, % total trade		0.0	98	◇
6.3.2	Production and export complexity		45.6	80	
6.3.3	High-tech exports, % total trade	⊙	5.1	36	●
6.3.4	ICT services exports, % total trade		0.3	111	
6.3.5	ISO 9001 quality/bn PPP$ GDP		0.9	112	

			Score/ Value	Rank	
	Creative outputs		**16.0**	**90**	
7.1	**Intangible assets**		**20.9**	**82**	
7.1.1	Intangible asset intensity, top 15, %		13.2	68	
7.1.2	Trademarks by origin/bn PPP$ GDP		24.0	85	
7.1.3	Global brand value, top 5,000, % GDP		0.3	69	
7.1.4	Industrial designs by origin/bn PPP$ GDP		0.3	98	
7.2	**Creative goods and services**		**3.3**	**93**	
7.2.1	Cultural and creative services exports, % total trade		0.1	90	
7.2.2	National feature films/mn pop. 15–69		1.0	61	
7.2.3	Entertainment and media market/th pop. 15–69		n/a	n/a	
7.2.4	Creative goods exports, % total trade	⊙	0.2	82	
7.3	**Online creativity**		**18.8**	**73**	
7.3.1	Generic top-level domains (TLDs)/th pop. 15–69		0.4	115	
7.3.2	Country-code TLDs/th pop. 15–69		4.0	59	
7.3.3	GitHub commits/mn pop. 15–69		5.7	70	
7.3.4	Mobile app creation/bn PPP$ GDP		65.3	63	

NOTES: ● indicates a strength; ○ a weakness; ◆ an income group strength; ◇ an income group weakness; * an index; † a survey question. ⊙ is used when the available economy data are older than the base year; see appendices for details, including the year of the data, at wipo.int/gii-ranking. Square brackets [ ] indicate that the data minimum coverage (DMC) requirements were not met at the sub-pillar or pillar level.

GII 2023 rank

Kenya **100**

Output rank	Input rank	Income	Region	Population (mn)	GDP, PPP$ (bn)	GDP per capita, PPP$
91	104	Lower middle	SSA	54.0	311.8	6,122

			Score/ Value	Rank	
	Institutions		**45.0**	**84**	
1.1	**Institutional environment**		**32.2**	**96**	
1.1.1	Operational stability for businesses*		36.8	104	
1.1.2	Government effectiveness*		27.6	91	
1.2	**Regulatory environment**		**57.0**	**81**	
1.2.1	Regulatory quality*		30.5	96	
1.2.2	Rule of law*		28.3	86	
1.2.3	Cost of redundancy dismissal		15.8	63	
1.3	**Business environment**		**45.8**	**[67]**	
1.3.1	Policies for doing business†		45.8	70	
1.3.2	Entrepreneurship policies and culture†		n/a	n/a	
	Human capital and research		**14.7**	**[118]**	
2.1	**Education**		**40.5**	**[98]**	
2.1.1	Expenditure on education, % GDP	⊙	5.1	37	●
2.1.2	Government funding/pupil, secondary, % GDP/cap		n/a	n/a	
2.1.3	School life expectancy, years		n/a	n/a	
2.1.4	PISA scales in reading, maths and science		n/a	n/a	
2.1.5	Pupil–teacher ratio, secondary	⊙	30.7	122	○ ◇
2.2	**Tertiary education**		**3.5**	**124**	○ ◇
2.2.1	Tertiary enrolment, % gross	⊙	10.0	114	○
2.2.2	Graduates in science and engineering, %		n/a	n/a	
2.2.3	Tertiary inbound mobility, %	⊙	1.3	85	
2.3	**Research and development (R&D)**		**0.0**	**[119]**	
2.3.1	Researchers, FTE/mn pop.		n/a	n/a	
2.3.2	Gross expenditure on R&D, % GDP		n/a	n/a	
2.3.3	Global corporate R&D investors, top 3, mn USD		0.0	40	○ ◇
2.3.4	QS university ranking, top 3*		0.0	71	○ ◇
	Infrastructure		**25.3**	**107**	
3.1	**Information and communication technologies (ICTs)**		**56.4**	**87**	
3.1.1	ICT access*		68.5	92	
3.1.2	ICT use*		35.2	111	◇
3.1.3	Government's online service*		64.9	68	◆
3.1.4	E-participation*		57.0	64	◆
3.2	**General infrastructure**		**7.0**	**129**	○ ◇
3.2.1	Electricity output, GWh/mn pop.	⊙	215.9	116	○
3.2.2	Logistics performance*		n/a	n/a	
3.2.3	Gross capital formation, % GDP		19.8	99	
3.3	**Ecological sustainability**		**12.5**	**116**	
3.3.1	GDP/unit of energy use		7.4	93	
3.3.2	Environmental performance*		20.2	106	
3.3.3	ISO 14001 environment/bn PPP$ GDP		0.3	98	
	Market sophistication		**22.1**	**108**	
4.1	**Credit**		**7.2**	**120**	○
4.1.1	Finance for startups and scaleups†		n/a	n/a	
4.1.2	Domestic credit to private sector, % GDP		32.1	94	
4.1.3	Loans from microfinance institutions, % GDP		0.3	44	
4.2	**Investment**		**21.5**	**33**	●
4.2.1	Market capitalization, % GDP		23.1	56	
4.2.2	Venture capital (VC) investors, deals/bn PPP$ GDP		0.1	42	◆
4.2.3	VC recipients, deals/bn PPP$ GDP		0.2	13	● ◆
4.2.4	VC received, value, % GDP		0.0	29	●
4.3	**Trade, diversification and market scale**		**37.5**	**109**	
4.3.1	Applied tariff rate, weighted avg., %		9.3	115	
4.3.2	Domestic industry diversification		66.1	98	○
4.3.3	Domestic market scale, bn PPP$		311.8	59	

			Score/ Value	Rank	
	Business sophistication		**24.2**	**84**	
5.1	**Knowledge workers**		**22.7**	**[91]**	
5.1.1	Knowledge-intensive employment, %	⊙	13.8	93	
5.1.2	Firms offering formal training, %	⊙	37.4	41	●
5.1.3	GERD performed by business, % GDP		n/a	n/a	
5.1.4	GERD financed by business, %		n/a	n/a	
5.1.5	Females employed w/advanced degrees, %	⊙	1.7	112	○
5.2	**Innovation linkages**		**23.2**	**62**	
5.2.1	University–industry R&D collaboration†		44.6	64	
5.2.2	State of cluster development†		41.0	69	
5.2.3	GERD financed by abroad, % GDP		n/a	n/a	
5.2.4	Joint venture/strategic alliance deals/bn PPP$ GDP		0.0	58	
5.2.5	Patent families/bn PPP$ GDP		0.0	92	
5.3	**Knowledge absorption**		**26.7**	**96**	
5.3.1	Intellectual property payments, % total trade		0.6	62	
5.3.2	High-tech imports, % total trade		8.5	59	
5.3.3	ICT services imports, % total trade		0.4	118	○
5.3.4	FDI net inflows, % GDP		0.4	115	
5.3.5	Research talent, % in businesses		n/a	n/a	
	Knowledge and technology outputs		**18.4**	**81**	
6.1	**Knowledge creation**		**11.3**	**77**	
6.1.1	Patents by origin/bn PPP$ GDP		0.6	74	
6.1.2	PCT patents by origin/bn PPP$ GDP		0.0	92	
6.1.3	Utility models by origin/bn PPP$ GDP		0.5	34	●
6.1.4	Scientific and technical articles/bn PPP$ GDP		9.4	77	
6.1.5	Citable documents H-index		16.2	53	●
6.2	**Knowledge impact**		**23.8**	**84**	
6.2.1	Labor productivity growth, %		2.5	23	●
6.2.2	Unicorn valuation, % GDP		0.0	48	○ ◇
6.2.3	Software spending, % GDP		0.1	84	
6.2.4	High-tech manufacturing, %		13.5	82	
6.3	**Knowledge diffusion**		**20.2**	**74**	
6.3.1	Intellectual property receipts, % total trade		0.4	30	● ◆
6.3.2	Production and export complexity		41.6	89	
6.3.3	High-tech exports, % total trade		0.6	85	
6.3.4	ICT services exports, % total trade		4.3	24	●
6.3.5	ISO 9001 quality/bn PPP$ GDP		1.8	90	
	Creative outputs		**14.1**	**95**	
7.1	**Intangible assets**		**18.9**	**89**	
7.1.1	Intangible asset intensity, top 15, %		−18.3	72	◇
7.1.2	Trademarks by origin/bn PPP$ GDP	⊙	21.3	89	
7.1.3	Global brand value, top 5,000, % GDP		1.8	46	●
7.1.4	Industrial designs by origin/bn PPP$ GDP		0.5	85	
7.2	**Creative goods and services**		**1.3**	**112**	
7.2.1	Cultural and creative services exports, % total trade		0.0	100	○
7.2.2	National feature films/mn pop. 15–69		n/a	n/a	
7.2.3	Entertainment and media market/th pop. 15–69		1.7	52	
7.2.4	Creative goods exports, % total trade		0.2	87	
7.3	**Online creativity**		**17.2**	**84**	
7.3.1	Generic top-level domains (TLDs)/th pop. 15–69		1.1	97	
7.3.2	Country-code TLDs/th pop. 15–69		0.9	93	
7.3.3	GitHub commits/mn pop. 15–69		7.5	59	
7.3.4	Mobile app creation/bn PPP$ GDP		59.2	84	

NOTES: ● indicates a strength; ○ a weakness; ◆ an income group strength; ◇ an income group weakness; * an index; † a survey question. ⊙ is used when the available economy data are older than the base year; see appendices for details, including the year of the data, at wipo.int/gii-ranking. Square brackets [ ] indicate that the data minimum coverage (DMC) requirements were not met at the sub-pillar or pillar level.

GII 2023 rank

Kuwait

64

Output rank	Input rank	Income	Region	Population (mn)	GDP, PPP$ (bn)	GDP per capita, PPP$
65	67	High	NAWA	4.3	248.1	51,528

			Score/Value	Rank	
	Institutions		**44.2**	**86**	◇
1.1	**Institutional environment**		**38.7**	**82**	◇
1.1.1	Operational stability for businesses*		41.7	87	◇
1.1.2	Government effectiveness*		35.7	73	◇
1.2	**Regulatory environment**		**53.6**	**91**	◇
1.2.1	Regulatory quality*		46.6	62	◇
1.2.2	Rule of law*		47.4	53	◇
1.2.3	Cost of redundancy dismissal		28.1	116	○◇
1.3	**Business environment**		**40.4**	**84**	
1.3.1	Policies for doing business†		52.0	57	
1.3.2	Entrepreneurship policies and culture†	⊙	28.8	61	
	Human capital and research		**33.6**	**[55]**	
2.1	**Education**		**60.0**	**[37]**	
2.1.1	Expenditure on education, % GDP		n/a	n/a	
2.1.2	Government funding/pupil, secondary, % GDP/cap	⊙	17.9	62	
2.1.3	School life expectancy, years	⊙	14.7	61	◇
2.1.4	PISA scales in reading, maths and science		n/a	n/a	
2.1.5	Pupil–teacher ratio, secondary	⊙	7.6	4	●◆
2.2	**Tertiary education**		**37.2**	**[40]**	
2.2.1	Tertiary enrolment, % gross		58.8	54	
2.2.2	Graduates in science and engineering, %		n/a	n/a	
2.2.3	Tertiary inbound mobility, %		n/a	n/a	
2.3	**Research and development (R&D)**		**3.7**	**81**	◇
2.3.1	Researchers, FTE/mn pop.	⊙	173.5	85	◇
2.3.2	Gross expenditure on R&D, % GDP	⊙	0.2	90	◇
2.3.3	Global corporate R&D investors, top 3, mn USD		0.0	40	○◇
2.3.4	QS university ranking, top 3*		10.1	64	
	Infrastructure		**48.5**	**46**	◇
3.1	**Information and communication technologies (ICTs)**		**74.7**	**52**	
3.1.1	ICT access*		94.5	9	●
3.1.2	ICT use*		84.2	43	●
3.1.3	Government's online service*		66.5	66	◇
3.1.4	E-participation*		53.5	67	
3.2	**General infrastructure**		**51.7**	**14**	●
3.2.1	Electricity output, GWh/mn pop.	⊙	17,504.1	4	●◆
3.2.2	Logistics performance*		50.0	50	◇
3.2.3	Gross capital formation, % GDP		21.5	84	
3.3	**Ecological sustainability**		**19.1**	**82**	◇
3.3.1	GDP/unit of energy use		4.3	121	○◇
3.3.2	Environmental performance*		39.8	63	◇
3.3.3	ISO 14001 environment/bn PPP$ GDP		1.5	57	
	Market sophistication		**35.6**	**62**	
4.1	**Credit**		**48.8**	**31**	●
4.1.1	Finance for startups and scaleups†	⊙	49.8	46	
4.1.2	Domestic credit to private sector, % GDP		126.5	18	●
4.1.3	Loans from microfinance institutions, % GDP		n/a	n/a	
4.2	**Investment**		**10.7**	**54**	
4.2.1	Market capitalization, % GDP		93.4	17	●
4.2.2	Venture capital (VC) investors, deals/bn PPP$ GDP		0.1	52	
4.2.3	VC recipients, deals/bn PPP$ GDP		0.0	89	
4.2.4	VC received, value, % GDP		0.0	73	◇
4.3	**Trade, diversification and market scale**		**47.2**	**93**	◇
4.3.1	Applied tariff rate, weighted avg., %		3.0	73	
4.3.2	Domestic industry diversification	⊙	56.0	102	○◇
4.3.3	Domestic market scale, bn PPP$		248.1	63	

			Score/Value	Rank	
	Business sophistication		**21.2**	**[103]**	
5.1	**Knowledge workers**		**16.8**	**[110]**	
5.1.1	Knowledge-intensive employment, %	⊙	22.7	66	
5.1.2	Firms offering formal training, %		n/a	n/a	
5.1.3	GERD performed by business, % GDP		n/a	n/a	
5.1.4	GERD financed by business, %	⊙	1.0	92	
5.1.5	Females employed w/advanced degrees, %		n/a	n/a	
5.2	**Innovation linkages**		**19.8**	**75**	◇
5.2.1	University–industry R&D collaboration†		35.6	84	◇
5.2.2	State of cluster development†		53.1	40	●
5.2.3	GERD financed by abroad, % GDP	⊙	0.0	96	
5.2.4	Joint venture/strategic alliance deals/bn PPP$ GDP		0.0	52	
5.2.5	Patent families/bn PPP$ GDP		0.0	76	
5.3	**Knowledge absorption**		**27.0**	**[91]**	
5.3.1	Intellectual property payments, % total trade		n/a	n/a	
5.3.2	High-tech imports, % total trade	⊙	7.1	86	
5.3.3	ICT services imports, % total trade		0.2	128	○◇
5.3.4	FDI net inflows, % GDP	⊙	−0.1	123	○
5.3.5	Research talent, % in businesses		n/a	n/a	
	Knowledge and technology outputs		**21.4**	**73**	◇
6.1	**Knowledge creation**		**6.1**	**106**	◇
6.1.1	Patents by origin/bn PPP$ GDP	⊙	0.1	117	○◇
6.1.2	PCT patents by origin/bn PPP$ GDP		0.0	91	◇
6.1.3	Utility models by origin/bn PPP$ GDP		n/a	n/a	
6.1.4	Scientific and technical articles/bn PPP$ GDP		7.1	91	◇
6.1.5	Citable documents H-index		9.4	84	◇
6.2	**Knowledge impact**		**30.7**	**55**	
6.2.1	Labor productivity growth, %		1.1	59	
6.2.2	Unicorn valuation, % GDP		0.0	48	○◇
6.2.3	Software spending, % GDP		0.5	24	●
6.2.4	High-tech manufacturing, %	⊙	20.9	62	
6.3	**Knowledge diffusion**		**27.5**	**57**	
6.3.1	Intellectual property receipts, % total trade		n/a	n/a	
6.3.2	Production and export complexity		44.0	85	◇
6.3.3	High-tech exports, % total trade	⊙	0.3	99	◇
6.3.4	ICT services exports, % total trade		6.8	11	●
6.3.5	ISO 9001 quality/bn PPP$ GDP		3.0	74	
	Creative outputs		**25.1**	**64**	◇
7.1	**Intangible assets**		**39.3**	**45**	
7.1.1	Intangible asset intensity, top 15, %		51.2	48	
7.1.2	Trademarks by origin/bn PPP$ GDP	⊙	16.4	98	◇
7.1.3	Global brand value, top 5,000, % GDP		7.9	26	●
7.1.4	Industrial designs by origin/bn PPP$ GDP		n/a	n/a	
7.2	**Creative goods and services**		**3.2**	**[94]**	
7.2.1	Cultural and creative services exports, % total trade		n/a	n/a	
7.2.2	National feature films/mn pop. 15–69		n/a	n/a	
7.2.3	Entertainment and media market/th pop. 15–69		5.4	42	◇
7.2.4	Creative goods exports, % total trade	⊙	0.1	100	
7.3	**Online creativity**		**18.6**	**75**	◇
7.3.1	Generic top-level domains (TLDs)/th pop. 15–69		8.7	45	
7.3.2	Country-code TLDs/th pop. 15–69		0.3	105	◇
7.3.3	GitHub commits/mn pop. 15–69		1.8	102	◇
7.3.4	Mobile app creation/bn PPP$ GDP		63.4	73	

NOTES: ● indicates a strength; ○ a weakness; ◆ an income group strength; ◇ an income group weakness; * an index; † a survey question. ⊙ is used when the available economy data are older than the base year; see appendices for details, including the year of the data, at wipo.int/gii-ranking. Square brackets [ ] indicate that the data minimum coverage (DMC) requirements were not met at the sub-pillar or pillar level.

Kyrgyzstan

GII 2023 rank

106

Output rank	Input rank	Income	Region	Population (mn)	GDP, PPP$ (bn)	GDP per capita, PPP$
112	94	Lower middle	CSA	6.6	39.2	5,771

			Score/Value	Rank	
	Institutions		**31.0**	**122**	
1.1	**Institutional environment**		**18.1**	**124**	◇
1.1.1	Operational stability for businesses*		19.4	123	◇
1.1.2	Government effectiveness*		16.7	112	
1.2	**Regulatory environment**		**49.6**	**99**	
1.2.1	Regulatory quality*		27.1	103	
1.2.2	Rule of law*		8.3	123	◇
1.2.3	Cost of redundancy dismissal		17.3	71	
1.3	**Business environment**		**25.4**	**[110]**	
1.3.1	Policies for doing business†		25.4	115	
1.3.2	Entrepreneurship policies and culture†		n/a	n/a	
	Human capital and research		**35.5**	**49**	●◆
2.1	**Education**		**65.3**	**[14]**	
2.1.1	Expenditure on education, % GDP	⊙	6.6	10	●◆
2.1.2	Government funding/pupil, secondary, % GDP/cap		n/a	n/a	
2.1.3	School life expectancy, years		13.6	76	
2.1.4	PISA scales in reading, maths and science		n/a	n/a	
2.1.5	Pupil–teacher ratio, secondary		12.4	55	●◆
2.2	**Tertiary education**		**40.6**	**33**	●◆
2.2.1	Tertiary enrolment, % gross		53.5	65	◆
2.2.2	Graduates in science and engineering, %		18.3	86	
2.2.3	Tertiary inbound mobility, %		23.0	6	●◆
2.3	**Research and development (R&D)**		**0.5**	**111**	
2.3.1	Researchers, FTE/mn pop.		n/a	n/a	
2.3.2	Gross expenditure on R&D, % GDP	⊙	0.1	106	
2.3.3	Global corporate R&D investors, top 3, mn USD		0.0	40	○◇
2.3.4	QS university ranking, top 3*		0.0	71	○◇
	Infrastructure		**30.9**	**92**	
3.1	**Information and communication technologies (ICTs)**		**64.4**	**78**	◆
3.1.1	ICT access*		81.8	70	◆
3.1.2	ICT use*		69.2	75	◆
3.1.3	Government's online service*		57.7	80	
3.1.4	E-participation*		48.8	78	
3.2	**General infrastructure**		**13.7**	**109**	
3.2.1	Electricity output, GWh/mn pop.	⊙	2,340.4	77	
3.2.2	Logistics performance*		9.1	106	○
3.2.3	Gross capital formation, % GDP		24.2	65	
3.3	**Ecological sustainability**		**14.5**	**105**	
3.3.1	GDP/unit of energy use		7.2	95	
3.3.2	Environmental performance*		28.5	90	
3.3.3	ISO 14001 environment/bn PPP$ GDP		0.1	126	○
	Market sophistication		**33.6**	**71**	
4.1	**Credit**		**26.4**	**75**	
4.1.1	Finance for startups and scaleups†		n/a	n/a	
4.1.2	Domestic credit to private sector, % GDP		28.3	100	
4.1.3	Loans from microfinance institutions, % GDP		3.7	9	●
4.2	**Investment**		**n/a**	**[n/a]**	
4.2.1	Market capitalization, % GDP		n/a	n/a	
4.2.2	Venture capital (VC) investors, deals/bn PPP$ GDP		n/a	n/a	
4.2.3	VC recipients, deals/bn PPP$ GDP		n/a	n/a	
4.2.4	VC received, value, % GDP		n/a	n/a	
4.3	**Trade, diversification and market scale**		**40.8**	**102**	
4.3.1	Applied tariff rate, weighted avg., %		2.3	64	◆
4.3.2	Domestic industry diversification		36.7	109	○◇
4.3.3	Domestic market scale, bn PPP$		39.2	119	

			Score/Value	Rank	
	Business sophistication		**18.5**	**114**	
5.1	**Knowledge workers**		**24.6**	**80**	
5.1.1	Knowledge-intensive employment, %	⊙	18.1	80	
5.1.2	Firms offering formal training, %		41.4	30	●
5.1.3	GERD performed by business, % GDP	⊙	0.0	78	
5.1.4	GERD financed by business, %	⊙	6.9	79	
5.1.5	Females employed w/advanced degrees, %	⊙	11.7	66	
5.2	**Innovation linkages**		**6.8**	**126**	◇
5.2.1	University–industry R&D collaboration†		6.0	127	○◇
5.2.2	State of cluster development†		21.3	110	
5.2.3	GERD financed by abroad, % GDP	⊙	0.0	80	
5.2.4	Joint venture/strategic alliance deals/bn PPP$ GDP		0.0	98	
5.2.5	Patent families/bn PPP$ GDP		0.1	50	●◆
5.3	**Knowledge absorption**		**24.2**	**110**	
5.3.1	Intellectual property payments, % total trade		0.1	96	
5.3.2	High-tech imports, % total trade		8.3	62	
5.3.3	ICT services imports, % total trade		0.5	110	
5.3.4	FDI net inflows, % GDP		0.8	104	
5.3.5	Research talent, % in businesses		n/a	n/a	
	Knowledge and technology outputs		**13.9**	**96**	
6.1	**Knowledge creation**		**11.5**	**75**	
6.1.1	Patents by origin/bn PPP$ GDP		2.4	30	●◆
6.1.2	PCT patents by origin/bn PPP$ GDP		0.0	101	○◇
6.1.3	Utility models by origin/bn PPP$ GDP		0.4	36	●
6.1.4	Scientific and technical articles/bn PPP$ GDP		7.7	88	
6.1.5	Citable documents H-index		4.1	116	
6.2	**Knowledge impact**		**12.7**	**125**	◇
6.2.1	Labor productivity growth, %		−0.0	96	
6.2.2	Unicorn valuation, % GDP		0.0	48	○◇
6.2.3	Software spending, % GDP		0.1	96	
6.2.4	High-tech manufacturing, %		1.8	110	○◇
6.3	**Knowledge diffusion**		**17.4**	**86**	
6.3.1	Intellectual property receipts, % total trade		0.0	75	
6.3.2	Production and export complexity		55.8	54	●
6.3.3	High-tech exports, % total trade		1.9	61	●
6.3.4	ICT services exports, % total trade		0.3	112	
6.3.5	ISO 9001 quality/bn PPP$ GDP		0.3	126	○
	Creative outputs		**7.0**	**116**	
7.1	**Intangible assets**		**4.5**	**120**	◇
7.1.1	Intangible asset intensity, top 15, %		n/a	n/a	
7.1.2	Trademarks by origin/bn PPP$ GDP		14.0	102	
7.1.3	Global brand value, top 5,000, % GDP		0.0	74	○◇
7.1.4	Industrial designs by origin/bn PPP$ GDP		0.2	107	
7.2	**Creative goods and services**		**1.7**	**[107]**	
7.2.1	Cultural and creative services exports, % total trade		n/a	n/a	
7.2.2	National feature films/mn pop. 15–69		n/a	n/a	
7.2.3	Entertainment and media market/th pop. 15–69		n/a	n/a	
7.2.4	Creative goods exports, % total trade		0.2	89	
7.3	**Online creativity**		**17.1**	**85**	
7.3.1	Generic top-level domains (TLDs)/th pop. 15–69		0.2	116	
7.3.2	Country-code TLDs/th pop. 15–69		0.8	95	
7.3.3	GitHub commits/mn pop. 15–69		7.0	62	
7.3.4	Mobile app creation/bn PPP$ GDP		60.4	81	

NOTES: ● indicates a strength; ○ a weakness; ◆ an income group strength; ◇ an income group weakness; * an index; † a survey question. ⊙ is used when the available economy data are older than the base year; see appendices for details, including the year of the data, at wipo.int/gii-ranking. Square brackets [ ] indicate that the data minimum coverage (DMC) requirements were not met at the sub-pillar or pillar level.

GII 2023 rank

Lao People's Democratic Republic **110**

Output rank	Input rank	Income	Region	Population (mn)	GDP, PPP$ (bn)	GDP per capita, PPP$
120	100	Lower middle	SEAO	7.5	68.6	9,166

	Institutions		Score/ Value	Rank	
	Institutions		**40.8**	**95**	
1.1	**Institutional environment**		**39.0**	**80**	
1.1.1	Operational stability for businesses*		58.3	49	● ◆
1.1.2	Government effectiveness*		19.7	105	
1.2	**Regulatory environment**		**34.1**	**126**	
1.2.1	Regulatory quality*		19.1	120	
1.2.2	Rule of law*		20.9	105	
1.2.3	Cost of redundancy dismissal		34.2	123	
1.3	**Business environment**		**49.4**	**[56]**	
1.3.1	Policies for doing business†		49.4	61	
1.3.2	Entrepreneurship policies and culture†		n/a	n/a	

	Human capital and research		Score/ Value	Rank	
	Human capital and research		**15.1**	**115**	
2.1	**Education**		**29.1**	**122**	
2.1.1	Expenditure on education, % GDP		1.9	121	◇
2.1.2	Government funding/pupil, secondary, % GDP/cap	⊙	12.6	84	
2.1.3	School life expectancy, years		10.1	104	◇
2.1.4	PISA scales in reading, maths and science		n/a	n/a	
2.1.5	Pupil–teacher ratio, secondary		16.8	85	
2.2	**Tertiary education**		**16.1**	**99**	
2.2.1	Tertiary enrolment, % gross		13.0	108	
2.2.2	Graduates in science and engineering, %	⊙	23.1	54	
2.2.3	Tertiary inbound mobility, %		0.6	99	
2.3	**Research and development (R&D)**		**0.0**	**[119]**	
2.3.1	Researchers, FTE/mn pop.		n/a	n/a	
2.3.2	Gross expenditure on R&D, % GDP		n/a	n/a	
2.3.3	Global corporate R&D investors, top 3, mn USD		0.0	40	○ ◇
2.3.4	QS university ranking, top 3*		0.0	71	○ ◇

	Infrastructure		Score/ Value	Rank	
	Infrastructure		**23.8**	**109**	
3.1	**Information and communication technologies (ICTs)**		**36.1**	**112**	
3.1.1	ICT access*		49.3	109	
3.1.2	ICT use*		48.0	104	
3.1.3	Government's online service*		22.7	128	○ ◇
3.1.4	E-participation*		24.4	114	
3.2	**General infrastructure**		**20.8**	**89**	
3.2.1	Electricity output, GWh/mn pop.	⊙	5,493.4	41	● ◆
3.2.2	Logistics performance*		13.6	103	
3.2.3	Gross capital formation, % GDP		n/a	n/a	
3.3	**Ecological sustainability**		**14.6**	**103**	
3.3.1	GDP/unit of energy use		9.8	70	
3.3.2	Environmental performance*		20.0	107	
3.3.3	ISO 14001 environment/bn PPP$ GDP		0.3	107	

	Market sophistication		Score/ Value	Rank	
	Market sophistication		**34.9**	**[65]**	
4.1	**Credit**		**9.8**	**[112]**	
4.1.1	Finance for startups and scaleups†		n/a	n/a	
4.1.2	Domestic credit to private sector, % GDP		n/a	n/a	
4.1.3	Loans from microfinance institutions, % GDP		0.8	31	
4.2	**Investment**		**n/a**	**[n/a]**	
4.2.1	Market capitalization, % GDP		n/a	n/a	
4.2.2	Venture capital (VC) investors, deals/bn PPP$ GDP		n/a	n/a	
4.2.3	VC recipients, deals/bn PPP$ GDP		n/a	n/a	
4.2.4	VC received, value, % GDP		n/a	n/a	
4.3	**Trade, diversification and market scale**		**60.0**	**55**	●
4.3.1	Applied tariff rate, weighted avg., %		1.0	11	● ◆
4.3.2	Domestic industry diversification	⊙	84.8	65	
4.3.3	Domestic market scale, bn PPP$		68.6	99	

	Business sophistication		Score/ Value	Rank	
	Business sophistication		**21.2**	**102**	
5.1	**Knowledge workers**		**18.3**	**[105]**	
5.1.1	Knowledge-intensive employment, %	⊙	13.6	96	
5.1.2	Firms offering formal training, %	⊙	24.4	66	
5.1.3	GERD performed by business, % GDP		n/a	n/a	
5.1.4	GERD financed by business, %		n/a	n/a	
5.1.5	Females employed w/advanced degrees, %	⊙	3.8	97	
5.2	**Innovation linkages**		**24.2**	**57**	●
5.2.1	University–industry R&D collaboration†		47.6	56	●
5.2.2	State of cluster development†		46.5	53	●
5.2.3	GERD financed by abroad, % GDP		n/a	n/a	
5.2.4	Joint venture/strategic alliance deals/bn PPP$ GDP		0.0	108	
5.2.5	Patent families/bn PPP$ GDP		0.0	95	○ ◇
5.3	**Knowledge absorption**		**21.3**	**123**	
5.3.1	Intellectual property payments, % total trade	⊙	0.0	118	○ ◇
5.3.2	High-tech imports, % total trade		3.7	128	
5.3.3	ICT services imports, % total trade	⊙	0.6	104	
5.3.4	FDI net inflows, % GDP		4.9	22	●
5.3.5	Research talent, % in businesses		n/a	n/a	

	Knowledge and technology outputs		Score/ Value	Rank	
	Knowledge and technology outputs		**13.9**	**97**	
6.1	**Knowledge creation**		**2.0**	**124**	◇
6.1.1	Patents by origin/bn PPP$ GDP	⊙	0.0	128	
6.1.2	PCT patents by origin/bn PPP$ GDP		0.0	94	
6.1.3	Utility models by origin/bn PPP$ GDP	⊙	0.0	69	
6.1.4	Scientific and technical articles/bn PPP$ GDP		3.1	116	
6.1.5	Citable documents H-index		3.9	117	
6.2	**Knowledge impact**		**22.4**	**93**	
6.2.1	Labor productivity growth, %		1.6	44	●
6.2.2	Unicorn valuation, % GDP		0.0	48	○ ◇
6.2.3	Software spending, % GDP		0.3	46	●
6.2.4	High-tech manufacturing, %	⊙	4.7	103	◇
6.3	**Knowledge diffusion**		**17.1**	**88**	
6.3.1	Intellectual property receipts, % total trade	⊙	0.0	114	○ ◇
6.3.2	Production and export complexity		42.3	88	
6.3.3	High-tech exports, % total trade		3.1	46	●
6.3.4	ICT services exports, % total trade	⊙	0.6	97	
6.3.5	ISO 9001 quality/bn PPP$ GDP		1.0	110	

	Creative outputs		Score/ Value	Rank	
	Creative outputs		**5.1**	**124**	◇
7.1	**Intangible assets**		**0.7**	**131**	○ ◇
7.1.1	Intangible asset intensity, top 15, %		n/a	n/a	
7.1.2	Trademarks by origin/bn PPP$ GDP	⊙	4.5	125	○
7.1.3	Global brand value, top 5,000, % GDP		0.0	74	○ ◇
7.1.4	Industrial designs by origin/bn PPP$ GDP	⊙	0.0	120	○ ◇
7.2	**Creative goods and services**		**17.2**	**[54]**	
7.2.1	Cultural and creative services exports, % total trade		n/a	n/a	
7.2.2	National feature films/mn pop. 15–69		n/a	n/a	
7.2.3	Entertainment and media market/th pop. 15–69		n/a	n/a	
7.2.4	Creative goods exports, % total trade		1.5	36	●
7.3	**Online creativity**		**1.6**	**126**	◇
7.3.1	Generic top-level domains (TLDs)/th pop. 15–69		2.1	83	
7.3.2	Country-code TLDs/th pop. 15–69		2.4	67	
7.3.3	GitHub commits/mn pop. 15–69		0.5	121	
7.3.4	Mobile app creation/bn PPP$ GDP		n/a	n/a	

NOTES: ● indicates a strength; ○ a weakness; ◆ an income group strength; ◇ an income group weakness; * an index; † a survey question. ⊙ is used when the available economy data are older than the base year; see appendices for details, including the year of the data, at wipo.int/gii-ranking. Square brackets [ ] indicate that the data minimum coverage (DMC) requirements were not met at the sub-pillar or pillar level.

GII 2023 rank

Latvia **37**

Output rank	Input rank	Income	Region	Population (mn)	GDP, PPP$ (bn)	GDP per capita, PPP$
39	38	High	EUR	1.9	72.0	38,124

		Score/Value	Rank	
	Institutions	**62.8**	**39**	
1.1	**Institutional environment**	**66.5**	**33**	
1.1.1	Operational stability for businesses*	72.2	22	
1.1.2	Government effectiveness*	60.8	35	
1.2	**Regulatory environment**	**80.6**	**28**	
1.2.1	Regulatory quality*	73.9	25	
1.2.2	Rule of law*	68.5	28	
1.2.3	Cost of redundancy dismissal	13.0	41	
1.3	**Business environment**	**41.2**	**80**	
1.3.1	Policies for doing business†	37.1	95	○◇
1.3.2	Entrepreneurship policies and culture†	45.4	40	
	Human capital and research	**37.4**	**43**	
2.1	**Education**	**58.7**	**41**	
2.1.1	Expenditure on education, % GDP ⊙	4.4	57	
2.1.2	Government funding/pupil, secondary, % GDP/cap	22.2	40	
2.1.3	School life expectancy, years	16.2	34	
2.1.4	PISA scales in reading, maths and science	487.4	28	
2.1.5	Pupil–teacher ratio, secondary	9.0	21	
2.2	**Tertiary education**	**41.8**	**30**	
2.2.1	Tertiary enrolment, % gross	94.5	8	●
2.2.2	Graduates in science and engineering, %	19.3	80	○
2.2.3	Tertiary inbound mobility, %	12.8	17	●
2.3	**Research and development (R&D)**	**11.7**	**56**	◇
2.3.1	Researchers, FTE/mn pop.	2,403.6	35	
2.3.2	Gross expenditure on R&D, % GDP	0.7	51	
2.3.3	Global corporate R&D investors, top 3, mn USD	0.0	40	○◇
2.3.4	QS university ranking, top 3*	9.7	67	◇
	Infrastructure	**54.5**	**33**	
3.1	**Information and communication technologies (ICTs)**	**83.0**	**27**	
3.1.1	ICT access*	87.6	36	
3.1.2	ICT use*	91.7	17	●
3.1.3	Government's online service*	79.4	35	
3.1.4	E-participation*	73.3	29	
3.2	**General infrastructure**	**33.9**	**44**	
3.2.1	Electricity output, GWh/mn pop.	3,106.7	64	◇
3.2.2	Logistics performance*	63.6	33	
3.2.3	Gross capital formation, % GDP	25.5	49	
3.3	**Ecological sustainability**	**46.8**	**25**	
3.3.1	GDP/unit of energy use	12.5	39	
3.3.2	Environmental performance*	71.5	15	●
3.3.3	ISO 14001 environment/bn PPP$ GDP	4.9	21	
	Market sophistication	**36.0**	**61**	
4.1	**Credit**	**34.9**	**53**	
4.1.1	Finance for startups and scaleups†	58.7	34	
4.1.2	Domestic credit to private sector, % GDP	33.5	91	○◇
4.1.3	Loans from microfinance institutions, % GDP	n/a	n/a	
4.2	**Investment**	**12.4**	**50**	
4.2.1	Market capitalization, % GDP	n/a	n/a	
4.2.2	Venture capital (VC) investors, deals/bn PPP$ GDP	0.1	35	
4.2.3	VC recipients, deals/bn PPP$ GDP	0.1	35	
4.2.4	VC received, value, % GDP	0.0	54	
4.3	**Trade, diversification and market scale**	**60.6**	**52**	
4.3.1	Applied tariff rate, weighted avg., %	1.5	20	
4.3.2	Domestic industry diversification	90.0	48	
4.3.3	Domestic market scale, bn PPP$	72.0	96	○

		Score/Value	Rank	
	Business sophistication	**38.1**	**37**	
5.1	**Knowledge workers**	**52.5**	**26**	
5.1.1	Knowledge-intensive employment, %	44.7	23	
5.1.2	Firms offering formal training, %	52.9	17	
5.1.3	GERD performed by business, % GDP	0.2	51	
5.1.4	GERD financed by business, %	27.0	62	
5.1.5	Females employed w/advanced degrees, %	27.1	12	●
5.2	**Innovation linkages**	**27.4**	**50**	
5.2.1	University–industry R&D collaboration†	42.8	68	
5.2.2	State of cluster development†	41.4	65	
5.2.3	GERD financed by abroad, % GDP	0.2	17	
5.2.4	Joint venture/strategic alliance deals/bn PPP$ GDP	0.0	71	
5.2.5	Patent families/bn PPP$ GDP	0.5	34	
5.3	**Knowledge absorption**	**34.3**	**61**	
5.3.1	Intellectual property payments, % total trade	0.2	91	○◇
5.3.2	High-tech imports, % total trade	13.1	20	●
5.3.3	ICT services imports, % total trade	1.5	58	
5.3.4	FDI net inflows, % GDP	5.1	18	●
5.3.5	Research talent, % in businesses	25.5	51	
	Knowledge and technology outputs	**28.0**	**49**	
6.1	**Knowledge creation**	**21.2**	**52**	
6.1.1	Patents by origin/bn PPP$ GDP	1.9	36	
6.1.2	PCT patents by origin/bn PPP$ GDP	0.6	29	
6.1.3	Utility models by origin/bn PPP$ GDP	n/a	n/a	
6.1.4	Scientific and technical articles/bn PPP$ GDP	18.0	41	
6.1.5	Citable documents H-index	9.8	80	◇
6.2	**Knowledge impact**	**23.9**	**81**	◇
6.2.1	Labor productivity growth, %	2.3	27	◆
6.2.2	Unicorn valuation, % GDP	0.0	48	○◇
6.2.3	Software spending, % GDP	0.1	91	○◇
6.2.4	High-tech manufacturing, %	18.0	66	◇
6.3	**Knowledge diffusion**	**39.0**	**36**	
6.3.1	Intellectual property receipts, % total trade	0.1	63	
6.3.2	Production and export complexity	67.4	35	
6.3.3	High-tech exports, % total trade	7.7	25	
6.3.4	ICT services exports, % total trade	4.5	22	
6.3.5	ISO 9001 quality/bn PPP$ GDP	13.1	20	
	Creative outputs	**39.4**	**31**	
7.1	**Intangible assets**	**28.1**	**72**	
7.1.1	Intangible asset intensity, top 15, % ⊙	−18.7	73	○◇
7.1.2	Trademarks by origin/bn PPP$ GDP	47.4	49	
7.1.3	Global brand value, top 5,000, % GDP	0.0	74	○◇
7.1.4	Industrial designs by origin/bn PPP$ GDP	2.6	38	
7.2	**Creative goods and services**	**62.2**	**1**	●◆
7.2.1	Cultural and creative services exports, % total trade	2.3	10	●
7.2.2	National feature films/mn pop. 15–69	15.5	1	●◆
7.2.3	Entertainment and media market/th pop. 15–69	n/a	n/a	
7.2.4	Creative goods exports, % total trade	3.4	17	●
7.3	**Online creativity**	**39.2**	**31**	
7.3.1	Generic top-level domains (TLDs)/th pop. 15–69	12.0	41	
7.3.2	Country-code TLDs/th pop. 15–69	32.9	22	
7.3.3	GitHub commits/mn pop. 15–69	35.9	29	
7.3.4	Mobile app creation/bn PPP$ GDP	76.0	19	

NOTES: ● indicates a strength; ○ a weakness; ◆ an income group strength; ◇ an income group weakness; * an index; † a survey question. ⊙ is used when the available economy data are older than the base year; see appendices for details, including the year of the data, at wipo.int/gii-ranking. Square brackets [ ] indicate that the data minimum coverage (DMC) requirements were not met at the sub-pillar or pillar level.

GII 2023 rank

Lebanon

92

Output rank	Input rank	Income	Region	Population (mn)	GDP, PPP$ (bn)	GDP per capita, PPP$
95	86	Lower middle	NAWA	5.5	NA	NA

			Score/ Value	Rank	
	Institutions		**29.6**	**125**	○
1.1	**Institutional environment**		**0.6**	**132**	○◇
1.1.1	Operational stability for businesses*		0.0	132	○◇
1.1.2	Government effectiveness*		1.2	131	○◇
1.2	**Regulatory environment**		**56.2**	**86**	
1.2.1	Regulatory quality*		19.2	119	
1.2.2	Rule of law*		8.3	122	○◇
1.2.3	Cost of redundancy dismissal		8.7	20	●◆
1.3	**Business environment**		**31.9**	**95**	
1.3.1	Policies for doing business†	⊙	11.4	125	○◇
1.3.2	Entrepreneurship policies and culture†	⊙	52.3	30	

			Score/ Value	Rank	
	Human capital and research		**29.9**	**72**	◆
2.1	**Education**		**31.2**	**118**	
2.1.1	Expenditure on education, % GDP	⊙	2.4	114	
2.1.2	Government funding/pupil, secondary, % GDP/cap	⊙	6.1	98	
2.1.3	School life expectancy, years		n/a	n/a	
2.1.4	PISA scales in reading, maths and science		376.8	73	○
2.1.5	Pupil–teacher ratio, secondary	⊙	7.7	6	●◆
2.2	**Tertiary education**		**44.2**	**22**	●◆
2.2.1	Tertiary enrolment, % gross		n/a	n/a	
2.2.2	Graduates in science and engineering, %		28.1	27	●
2.2.3	Tertiary inbound mobility, %		12.4	18	●◆
2.3	**Research and development (R&D)**		**14.2**	**[50]**	
2.3.1	Researchers, FTE/mn pop.		n/a	n/a	
2.3.2	Gross expenditure on R&D, % GDP		n/a	n/a	
2.3.3	Global corporate R&D investors, top 3, mn USD		0.0	40	○◇
2.3.4	QS university ranking, top 3*		28.5	43	◆

			Score/ Value	Rank	
	Infrastructure		**29.3**	**96**	
3.1	**Information and communication technologies (ICTs)**		**51.4**	**96**	
3.1.1	ICT access*		71.9	87	
3.1.2	ICT use*		58.8	94	
3.1.3	Government's online service*		36.5	114	
3.1.4	E-participation*		38.4	90	
3.2	**General infrastructure**		**13.5**	**[112]**	
3.2.1	Electricity output, GWh/mn pop.	⊙	2,669.6	69	◆
3.2.2	Logistics performance*		n/a	n/a	
3.2.3	Gross capital formation, % GDP		n/a	n/a	
3.3	**Ecological sustainability**		**23.1**	**70**	◆
3.3.1	GDP/unit of energy use		10.3	62	
3.3.2	Environmental performance*		22.5	102	
3.3.3	ISO 14001 environment/bn PPP$ GDP		n/a	n/a	

			Score/ Value	Rank	
	Market sophistication		**39.6**	**46**	
4.1	**Credit**		**57.0**	**22**	●◆
4.1.1	Finance for startups and scaleups†	⊙	74.0	14	●◆
4.1.2	Domestic credit to private sector, % GDP	⊙	106.6	25	●◆
4.1.3	Loans from microfinance institutions, % GDP		n/a	n/a	
4.2	**Investment**		**7.4**	**62**	
4.2.1	Market capitalization, % GDP		17.9	62	
4.2.2	Venture capital (VC) investors, deals/bn PPP$ GDP	⊙	0.2	30	◆
4.2.3	VC recipients, deals/bn PPP$ GDP	⊙	0.0	49	
4.2.4	VC received, value, % GDP	⊙	0.0	71	
4.3	**Trade, diversification and market scale**		**54.5**	**78**	
4.3.1	Applied tariff rate, weighted avg., %		2.8	70	◆
4.3.2	Domestic industry diversification	⊙	80.2	75	
4.3.3	Domestic market scale, bn PPP$	⊙	77.7	92	

			Score/ Value	Rank	
	Business sophistication		**25.7**	**76**	
5.1	**Knowledge workers**		**35.8**	**[58]**	
5.1.1	Knowledge-intensive employment, %	⊙	27.5	52	◆
5.1.2	Firms offering formal training, %		20.8	77	
5.1.3	GERD performed by business, % GDP		n/a	n/a	
5.1.4	GERD financed by business, %		n/a	n/a	
5.1.5	Females employed w/advanced degrees, %	⊙	14.6	51	◆
5.2	**Innovation linkages**		**17.1**	**89**	
5.2.1	University–industry R&D collaboration†	⊙	35.2	86	
5.2.2	State of cluster development†	⊙	28.1	99	
5.2.3	GERD financed by abroad, % GDP		n/a	n/a	
5.2.4	Joint venture/strategic alliance deals/bn PPP$ GDP	⊙	0.0	84	
5.2.5	Patent families/bn PPP$ GDP		0.0	73	
5.3	**Knowledge absorption**		**24.4**	**108**	
5.3.1	Intellectual property payments, % total trade	⊙	0.1	105	
5.3.2	High-tech imports, % total trade		5.1	113	
5.3.3	ICT services imports, % total trade	⊙	0.9	89	
5.3.4	FDI net inflows, % GDP		3.8	35	●
5.3.5	Research talent, % in businesses		n/a	n/a	

			Score/ Value	Rank	
	Knowledge and technology outputs		**17.3**	**86**	
6.1	**Knowledge creation**		**29.5**	**[33]**	
6.1.1	Patents by origin/bn PPP$ GDP	⊙	1.1	56	
6.1.2	PCT patents by origin/bn PPP$ GDP		n/a	n/a	
6.1.3	Utility models by origin/bn PPP$ GDP		n/a	n/a	
6.1.4	Scientific and technical articles/bn PPP$ GDP	⊙	29.4	24	●◆
6.1.5	Citable documents H-index		13.7	61	
6.2	**Knowledge impact**		**0.8**	**132**	○◇
6.2.1	Labor productivity growth, %		−4.9	131	○◇
6.2.2	Unicorn valuation, % GDP		0.0	48	○◇
6.2.3	Software spending, % GDP		0.0	113	◇
6.2.4	High-tech manufacturing, %		n/a	n/a	
6.3	**Knowledge diffusion**		**21.6**	**68**	
6.3.1	Intellectual property receipts, % total trade	⊙	0.1	55	
6.3.2	Production and export complexity		59.4	47	◆
6.3.3	High-tech exports, % total trade		0.4	94	
6.3.4	ICT services exports, % total trade	⊙	2.0	58	
6.3.5	ISO 9001 quality/bn PPP$ GDP		n/a	n/a	

			Score/ Value	Rank	
	Creative outputs		**13.8**	**96**	
7.1	**Intangible assets**		**3.8**	**[122]**	
7.1.1	Intangible asset intensity, top 15, %		n/a	n/a	
7.1.2	Trademarks by origin/bn PPP$ GDP	⊙	12.7	105	
7.1.3	Global brand value, top 5,000, % GDP		0.0	74	○◇
7.1.4	Industrial designs by origin/bn PPP$ GDP		n/a	n/a	
7.2	**Creative goods and services**		**24.4**	**43**	◆
7.2.1	Cultural and creative services exports, % total trade		2.7	7	●◆
7.2.2	National feature films/mn pop. 15–69		4.3	29	◆
7.2.3	Entertainment and media market/th pop. 15–69	⊙	0.5	56	
7.2.4	Creative goods exports, % total trade		1.3	39	
7.3	**Online creativity**		**23.0**	**57**	◆
7.3.1	Generic top-level domains (TLDs)/th pop. 15–69		8.8	44	◆
7.3.2	Country-code TLDs/th pop. 15–69		0.3	107	
7.3.3	GitHub commits/mn pop. 15–69		8.2	56	◆
7.3.4	Mobile app creation/bn PPP$ GDP	⊙	74.8	25	●◆

NOTES: ● indicates a strength; ○ a weakness; ◆ an income group strength; ◇ an income group weakness; * an index; † a survey question. ⊙ is used when the available economy data are older than the base year; see appendices for details, including the year of the data, at wipo.int/gii-ranking. Square brackets [ ] indicate that the data minimum coverage (DMC) requirements were not met at the sub-pillar or pillar level.

Lithuania

GII 2023 rank

34

Output rank	Input rank	Income	Region	Population (mn)	GDP, PPP$ (bn)	GDP per capita, PPP$
37	32	High	EUR	2.8	130.7	46,159

		Score/ Value	Rank
	Institutions	**73.5**	**19**
1.1	**Institutional environment**	**70.5**	**22**
1.1.1	Operational stability for businesses*	75.0	17
1.1.2	Government effectiveness*	65.9	30
1.2	**Regulatory environment**	**81.9**	**25**
1.2.1	Regulatory quality*	75.2	23
1.2.2	Rule of law*	72.2	26
1.2.3	Cost of redundancy dismissal	13.0	41
1.3	**Business environment**	**68.1**	**24**
1.3.1	Policies for doing business†	57.3	44
1.3.2	Entrepreneurship policies and culture†	79.0	9 ● ◆
	Human capital and research	**37.4**	**42**
2.1	**Education**	**55.1**	**54**
2.1.1	Expenditure on education, % GDP	⊙ 4.0	73
2.1.2	Government funding/pupil, secondary, % GDP/cap	16.8	69 ○ ◇
2.1.3	School life expectancy, years	16.2	32
2.1.4	PISA scales in reading, maths and science	479.7	32
2.1.5	Pupil–teacher ratio, secondary	8.0	10 ● ◆
2.2	**Tertiary education**	**37.0**	**41**
2.2.1	Tertiary enrolment, % gross	70.8	33
2.2.2	Graduates in science and engineering, %	26.0	38
2.2.3	Tertiary inbound mobility, %	6.2	41
2.3	**Research and development (R&D)**	**20.2**	**43**
2.3.1	Researchers, FTE/mn pop.	3,940.7	28
2.3.2	Gross expenditure on R&D, % GDP	1.1	36
2.3.3	Global corporate R&D investors, top 3, mn USD	0.0	40 ○ ◇
2.3.4	QS university ranking, top 3*	20.3	52
	Infrastructure	**51.9**	**43**
3.1	**Information and communication technologies (ICTs)**	**79.5**	**40**
3.1.1	ICT access*	92.8	13 ●
3.1.2	ICT use*	90.0	22
3.1.3	Government's online service*	81.7	28
3.1.4	E-participation*	53.5	67
3.2	**General infrastructure**	**26.3**	**66** ◇
3.2.1	Electricity output, GWh/mn pop.	1,559.0	90 ○ ◇
3.2.2	Logistics performance*	59.1	37
3.2.3	Gross capital formation, % GDP	19.2	103 ○ ◇
3.3	**Ecological sustainability**	**50.0**	**22**
3.3.1	GDP/unit of energy use	13.2	36
3.3.2	Environmental performance*	62.7	30
3.3.3	ISO 14001 environment/bn PPP$ GDP	7.0	13 ● ◆
	Market sophistication	**45.3**	**34**
4.1	**Credit**	**45.3**	**35**
4.1.1	Finance for startups and scaleups†	78.0	10 ● ◆
4.1.2	Domestic credit to private sector, % GDP	37.4	88 ○ ◇
4.1.3	Loans from microfinance institutions, % GDP	n/a	n/a
4.2	**Investment**	**28.1**	**25**
4.2.1	Market capitalization, % GDP	n/a	n/a
4.2.2	Venture capital (VC) investors, deals/bn PPP$ GDP	0.2	29
4.2.3	VC recipients, deals/bn PPP$ GDP	0.1	15
4.2.4	VC received, value, % GDP	0.0	23
4.3	**Trade, diversification and market scale**	**62.6**	**49**
4.3.1	Applied tariff rate, weighted avg., %	1.5	20
4.3.2	Domestic industry diversification	94.6	31
4.3.3	Domestic market scale, bn PPP$	130.7	81

		Score/ Value	Rank
	Business sophistication	**39.3**	**35**
5.1	**Knowledge workers**	**51.7**	**27**
5.1.1	Knowledge-intensive employment, %	46.6	19
5.1.2	Firms offering formal training, %	27.5	60 ○
5.1.3	GERD performed by business, % GDP	0.5	37
5.1.4	GERD financed by business, %	37.3	51
5.1.5	Females employed w/advanced degrees, %	30.8	1 ● ◆
5.2	**Innovation linkages**	**35.4**	**34**
5.2.1	University–industry R&D collaboration†	63.9	29
5.2.2	State of cluster development†	41.1	68
5.2.3	GERD financed by abroad, % GDP	0.4	8 ●
5.2.4	Joint venture/strategic alliance deals/bn PPP$ GDP	0.0	60
5.2.5	Patent families/bn PPP$ GDP	0.4	36
5.3	**Knowledge absorption**	**31.0**	**75** ◇
5.3.1	Intellectual property payments, % total trade	0.2	90 ○ ◇
5.3.2	High-tech imports, % total trade	7.3	80
5.3.3	ICT services imports, % total trade	1.3	69
5.3.4	FDI net inflows, % GDP	6.2	15 ●
5.3.5	Research talent, % in businesses	30.9	42
	Knowledge and technology outputs	**35.3**	**29**
6.1	**Knowledge creation**	**21.6**	**49**
6.1.1	Patents by origin/bn PPP$ GDP	1.3	51
6.1.2	PCT patents by origin/bn PPP$ GDP	0.3	37
6.1.3	Utility models by origin/bn PPP$ GDP	n/a	n/a
6.1.4	Scientific and technical articles/bn PPP$ GDP	23.7	30
6.1.5	Citable documents H-index	13.6	62
6.2	**Knowledge impact**	**49.5**	**17**
6.2.1	Labor productivity growth, %	2.0	33 ◆
6.2.2	Unicorn valuation, % GDP	8.4	1 ● ◆
6.2.3	Software spending, % GDP	0.1	99 ○ ◇
6.2.4	High-tech manufacturing, %	24.5	52
6.3	**Knowledge diffusion**	**34.8**	**43**
6.3.1	Intellectual property receipts, % total trade	0.1	66
6.3.2	Production and export complexity	70.4	29
6.3.3	High-tech exports, % total trade	6.1	31
6.3.4	ICT services exports, % total trade	2.9	45
6.3.5	ISO 9001 quality/bn PPP$ GDP	10.8	27
	Creative outputs	**33.5**	**41**
7.1	**Intangible assets**	**32.4**	**63**
7.1.1	Intangible asset intensity, top 15, %	17.5	67 ○
7.1.2	Trademarks by origin/bn PPP$ GDP	45.8	50
7.1.3	Global brand value, top 5,000, % GDP	0.0	74 ○ ◇
7.1.4	Industrial designs by origin/bn PPP$ GDP	2.7	36
7.2	**Creative goods and services**	**26.6**	**37**
7.2.1	Cultural and creative services exports, % total trade	0.9	33
7.2.2	National feature films/mn pop. 15–69	6.7	14
7.2.3	Entertainment and media market/th pop. 15–69	n/a	n/a
7.2.4	Creative goods exports, % total trade	1.6	33
7.3	**Online creativity**	**42.5**	**28**
7.3.1	Generic top-level domains (TLDs)/th pop. 15–69	15.7	33
7.3.2	Country-code TLDs/th pop. 15–69	34.8	21
7.3.3	GitHub commits/mn pop. 15–69	36.6	28
7.3.4	Mobile app creation/bn PPP$ GDP	82.8	7 ● ◆

NOTES: ● indicates a strength; ○ a weakness; ◆ an income group strength; ◇ an income group weakness; * an index; † a survey question. ⊙ is used when the available economy data are older than the base year; see appendices for details, including the year of the data, at wipo.int/gii-ranking. Square brackets [ ] indicate that the data minimum coverage (DMC) requirements were not met at the sub-pillar or pillar level.

GII 2023 rank

Luxembourg

21

Output rank	Input rank	Income	Region	Population (mn)	GDP, PPP$ (bn)	GDP per capita, PPP$
23	22	High	EUR	0.6	91.1	141,587

		Score/Value	Rank	
	Institutions	**81.6**	**7**	
1.1	**Institutional environment**	**84.1**	**7**	
1.1.1	Operational stability for businesses*	84.0	7	
1.1.2	Government effectiveness*	84.2	7	
1.2	**Regulatory environment**	**82.4**	**23**	
1.2.1	Regulatory quality*	91.8	2	●
1.2.2	Rule of law*	92.1	8	
1.2.3	Cost of redundancy dismissal	21.7	95	○◇
1.3	**Business environment**	**78.3**	**10**	
1.3.1	Policies for doing business†	94.3	3	●◆
1.3.2	Entrepreneurship policies and culture†	62.2	21	
	Human capital and research	**44.4**	**31**	◇
2.1	**Education**	**53.8**	**60**	◇
2.1.1	Expenditure on education, % GDP ⓒ	3.7	81	◇
2.1.2	Government funding/pupil, secondary, % GDP/cap	20.3	50	
2.1.3	School life expectancy, years	14.6	62	◇
2.1.4	PISA scales in reading, maths and science	476.7	35	◇
2.1.5	Pupil–teacher ratio, secondary	7.8	8	◆
2.2	**Tertiary education**	**46.6**	**16**	
2.2.1	Tertiary enrolment, % gross	19.2	101	○◇
2.2.2	Graduates in science and engineering, %	19.2	81	○
2.2.3	Tertiary inbound mobility, %	48.4	1	●◆
2.3	**Research and development (R&D)**	**32.8**	**34**	◇
2.3.1	Researchers, FTE/mn pop.	5,051.0	17	
2.3.2	Gross expenditure on R&D, % GDP	1.0	39	◇
2.3.3	Global corporate R&D investors, top 3, mn USD	60.6	22	
2.3.4	QS university ranking, top 3*	0.0	71	○◇
	Infrastructure	**55.6**	**31**	◇
3.1	**Information and communication technologies (ICTs)**	**87.0**	**15**	
3.1.1	ICT access*	99.7	2	●◆
3.1.2	ICT use*	92.6	15	
3.1.3	Government's online service*	81.4	29	
3.1.4	E-participation*	74.4	25	
3.2	**General infrastructure**	**29.9**	**56**	◇
3.2.1	Electricity output, GWh/mn pop.	2,074.9	80	◇
3.2.2	Logistics performance*	68.2	25	◇
3.2.3	Gross capital formation, % GDP	18.6	106	○◇
3.3	**Ecological sustainability**	**49.8**	**23**	
3.3.1	GDP/unit of energy use	20.0	8	
3.3.2	Environmental performance*	90.5	6	
3.3.3	ISO 14001 environment/bn PPP$ GDP	0.9	68	
	Market sophistication	**45.2**	**35**	◇
4.1	**Credit**	**44.2**	**38**	
4.1.1	Finance for startups and scaleups†	49.2	48	◇
4.1.2	Domestic credit to private sector, % GDP	104.9	27	
4.1.3	Loans from microfinance institutions, % GDP	n/a	n/a	
4.2	**Investment**	**45.3**	**13**	
4.2.1	Market capitalization, % GDP	67.6	25	
4.2.2	Venture capital (VC) investors, deals/bn PPP$ GDP	1.9	2	●◆
4.2.3	VC recipients, deals/bn PPP$ GDP	0.1	26	
4.2.4	VC received, value, % GDP	0.0	21	
4.3	**Trade, diversification and market scale**	**46.1**	**95**	○◇
4.3.1	Applied tariff rate, weighted avg., %	1.5	20	
4.3.2	Domestic industry diversification	n/a	n/a	
4.3.3	Domestic market scale, bn PPP$	91.1	89	○

		Score/Value	Rank	
	Business sophistication	**63.8**	**7**	
5.1	**Knowledge workers**	**70.2**	**6**	
5.1.1	Knowledge-intensive employment, %	64.1	1	●◆
5.1.2	Firms offering formal training, %	66.1	4	◆
5.1.3	GERD performed by business, % GDP	0.5	40	◇
5.1.4	GERD financed by business, % ⓒ	51.3	25	
5.1.5	Females employed w/advanced degrees, %	27.6	11	
5.2	**Innovation linkages**	**54.6**	**16**	
5.2.1	University–industry R&D collaboration†	76.8	16	
5.2.2	State of cluster development†	63.9	33	
5.2.3	GERD financed by abroad, % GDP ⓒ	0.0	50	◇
5.2.4	Joint venture/strategic alliance deals/bn PPP$ GDP	0.1	13	
5.2.5	Patent families/bn PPP$ GDP	3.7	10	
5.3	**Knowledge absorption**	**66.7**	**3**	●◆
5.3.1	Intellectual property payments, % total trade	4.0	1	●◆
5.3.2	High-tech imports, % total trade	1.7	132	○◇
5.3.3	ICT services imports, % total trade	4.9	1	●◆
5.3.4	FDI net inflows, % GDP	48.7	2	●◆
5.3.5	Research talent, % in businesses	31.6	40	◇
	Knowledge and technology outputs	**31.9**	**38**	◇
6.1	**Knowledge creation**	**44.1**	**19**	
6.1.1	Patents by origin/bn PPP$ GDP	6.5	14	
6.1.2	PCT patents by origin/bn PPP$ GDP	3.4	8	
6.1.3	Utility models by origin/bn PPP$ GDP	n/a	n/a	
6.1.4	Scientific and technical articles/bn PPP$ GDP	16.6	44	◇
6.1.5	Citable documents H-index	12.7	65	◇
6.2	**Knowledge impact**	**30.8**	**54**	◇
6.2.1	Labor productivity growth, %	−1.2	119	○◇
6.2.2	Unicorn valuation, % GDP	2.4	15	
6.2.3	Software spending, % GDP	0.2	78	◇
6.2.4	High-tech manufacturing, %	n/a	n/a	
6.3	**Knowledge diffusion**	**20.9**	**71**	◇
6.3.1	Intellectual property receipts, % total trade	1.5	17	
6.3.2	Production and export complexity	n/a	n/a	
6.3.3	High-tech exports, % total trade	0.5	88	○◇
6.3.4	ICT services exports, % total trade	3.3	37	
6.3.5	ISO 9001 quality/bn PPP$ GDP	1.9	87	◇
	Creative outputs	**54.2**	**11**	
7.1	**Intangible assets**	**53.1**	**17**	
7.1.1	Intangible asset intensity, top 15, %	71.6	18	
7.1.2	Trademarks by origin/bn PPP$ GDP	55.6	42	
7.1.3	Global brand value, top 5,000, % GDP	11.6	14	
7.1.4	Industrial designs by origin/bn PPP$ GDP	3.8	26	
7.2	**Creative goods and services**	**38.2**	**15**	
7.2.1	Cultural and creative services exports, % total trade	5.6	1	●◆
7.2.2	National feature films/mn pop. 15–69	2.1	45	◇
7.2.3	Entertainment and media market/th pop. 15–69	n/a	n/a	
7.2.4	Creative goods exports, % total trade	0.1	97	○
7.3	**Online creativity**	**72.5**	**5**	
7.3.1	Generic top-level domains (TLDs)/th pop. 15–69	97.1	4	●◆
7.3.2	Country-code TLDs/th pop. 15–69	70.7	8	
7.3.3	GitHub commits/mn pop. 15–69	48.3	21	
7.3.4	Mobile app creation/bn PPP$ GDP	73.7	35	

NOTES: ● indicates a strength; ○ a weakness; ◆ an income group strength; ◇ an income group weakness; * an index; † a survey question. ⓒ is used when the available economy data are older than the base year; see appendices for details, including the year of the data, at wipo.int/gii-ranking. Square brackets [ ] indicate that the data minimum coverage (DMC) requirements were not met at the sub-pillar or pillar level.

GII 2023 rank

Madagascar

107

Output rank	Input rank	Income	Region	Population (mn)	GDP, PPP$ (bn)	GDP per capita, PPP$
82	125	Low	SSA	29.6	51.8	1,790

			Score/ Value	Rank	
	Institutions		**31.2**	**121**	
1.1	**Institutional environment**		**23.0**	**119**	
1.1.1	Operational stability for businesses*		36.8	104	
1.1.2	Government effectiveness*		9.1	126	
1.2	**Regulatory environment**		**52.2**	**94**	
1.2.1	Regulatory quality*		20.8	116	
1.2.2	Rule of law*		14.3	113	
1.2.3	Cost of redundancy dismissal		14.7	58	●
1.3	**Business environment**		**18.3**	**123**	◇
1.3.1	Policies for doing business†	⊙	22.8	117	◇
1.3.2	Entrepreneurship policies and culture†	⊙	13.8	75	
	Human capital and research		**19.8**	**102**	
2.1	**Education**		**38.1**	**[104]**	
2.1.1	Expenditure on education, % GDP		3.2	101	
2.1.2	Government funding/pupil, secondary, % GDP/cap		n/a	n/a	
2.1.3	School life expectancy, years	⊙	10.2	103	
2.1.4	PISA scales in reading, maths and science		n/a	n/a	
2.1.5	Pupil–teacher ratio, secondary	⊙	18.1	92	
2.2	**Tertiary education**		**21.3**	**87**	◆
2.2.1	Tertiary enrolment, % gross		5.5	124	○
2.2.2	Graduates in science and engineering, %		29.1	22	●◆
2.2.3	Tertiary inbound mobility, %		1.9	77	
2.3	**Research and development (R&D)**		**0.1**	**117**	
2.3.1	Researchers, FTE/mn pop.	⊙	34.0	98	
2.3.2	Gross expenditure on R&D, % GDP	⊙	0.0	112	○◇
2.3.3	Global corporate R&D investors, top 3, mn USD		0.0	40	○◇
2.3.4	QS university ranking, top 3*		0.0	71	○◇
	Infrastructure		**12.5**	**131**	○◇
3.1	**Information and communication technologies (ICTs)**		**22.4**	**127**	
3.1.1	ICT access*		15.0	127	
3.1.2	ICT use*		19.6	125	
3.1.3	Government's online service*		28.3	126	
3.1.4	E-participation*		26.7	106	
3.2	**General infrastructure**		**7.2**	**128**	
3.2.1	Electricity output, GWh/mn pop.	⊙	60.7	125	○
3.2.2	Logistics performance*		9.1	106	○◇
3.2.3	Gross capital formation, % GDP		19.4	102	
3.3	**Ecological sustainability**		**8.0**	**132**	○◇
3.3.1	GDP/unit of energy use		4.7	119	
3.3.2	Environmental performance*		15.4	124	◇
3.3.3	ISO 14001 environment/bn PPP$ GDP		0.2	114	
	Market sophistication		**20.0**	**113**	
4.1	**Credit**		**12.7**	**107**	
4.1.1	Finance for startups and scaleups†	⊙	23.6	76	
4.1.2	Domestic credit to private sector, % GDP		16.4	115	
4.1.3	Loans from microfinance institutions, % GDP		0.9	28	●
4.2	**Investment**		**n/a**	**[n/a]**	
4.2.1	Market capitalization, % GDP		n/a	n/a	
4.2.2	Venture capital (VC) investors, deals/bn PPP$ GDP		n/a	n/a	
4.2.3	VC recipients, deals/bn PPP$ GDP		n/a	n/a	
4.2.4	VC received, value, % GDP		n/a	n/a	
4.3	**Trade, diversification and market scale**		**27.2**	**119**	
4.3.1	Applied tariff rate, weighted avg., %		7.2	103	
4.3.2	Domestic industry diversification		n/a	n/a	
4.3.3	Domestic market scale, bn PPP$		51.8	105	

			Score/ Value	Rank	
	Business sophistication		**16.2**	**123**	
5.1	**Knowledge workers**		**5.0**	**[129]**	
5.1.1	Knowledge-intensive employment, %	⊙	3.7	123	
5.1.2	Firms offering formal training, %	⊙	12.7	92	
5.1.3	GERD performed by business, % GDP		n/a	n/a	
5.1.4	GERD financed by business, %		n/a	n/a	
5.1.5	Females employed w/advanced degrees, %	⊙	1.9	111	
5.2	**Innovation linkages**		**11.8**	**109**	
5.2.1	University–industry R&D collaboration†	⊙	20.4	116	◇
5.2.2	State of cluster development†	⊙	21.9	109	
5.2.3	GERD financed by abroad, % GDP		n/a	n/a	
5.2.4	Joint venture/strategic alliance deals/bn PPP$ GDP	⊙	0.0	76	●
5.2.5	Patent families/bn PPP$ GDP		0.0	95	○◇
5.3	**Knowledge absorption**		**31.9**	**71**	●◆
5.3.1	Intellectual property payments, % total trade		0.3	80	◆
5.3.2	High-tech imports, % total trade		6.0	104	
5.3.3	ICT services imports, % total trade		2.0	37	●
5.3.4	FDI net inflows, % GDP		2.9	52	●
5.3.5	Research talent, % in businesses		n/a	n/a	
	Knowledge and technology outputs		**10.4**	**121**	
6.1	**Knowledge creation**		**4.7**	**116**	
6.1.1	Patents by origin/bn PPP$ GDP		0.1	107	
6.1.2	PCT patents by origin/bn PPP$ GDP		0.0	89	◆
6.1.3	Utility models by origin/bn PPP$ GDP		n/a	n/a	
6.1.4	Scientific and technical articles/bn PPP$ GDP		6.2	100	
6.1.5	Citable documents H-index		4.3	111	
6.2	**Knowledge impact**		**12.7**	**124**	
6.2.1	Labor productivity growth, %		−0.9	116	
6.2.2	Unicorn valuation, % GDP		0.0	48	○◇
6.2.3	Software spending, % GDP		0.0	116	
6.2.4	High-tech manufacturing, %		n/a	n/a	
6.3	**Knowledge diffusion**		**13.9**	**94**	◆
6.3.1	Intellectual property receipts, % total trade		0.1	67	●◆
6.3.2	Production and export complexity		35.5	101	
6.3.3	High-tech exports, % total trade		0.1	119	
6.3.4	ICT services exports, % total trade		3.5	36	●◆
6.3.5	ISO 9001 quality/bn PPP$ GDP		1.4	98	◆
	Creative outputs		**26.0**	**[62]**	
7.1	**Intangible assets**		**50.7**	**[23]**	
7.1.1	Intangible asset intensity, top 15, %		n/a	n/a	
7.1.2	Trademarks by origin/bn PPP$ GDP		63.9	33	●◆
7.1.3	Global brand value, top 5,000, % GDP		n/a	n/a	
7.1.4	Industrial designs by origin/bn PPP$ GDP		7.1	15	●◆
7.2	**Creative goods and services**		**2.2**	**[102]**	
7.2.1	Cultural and creative services exports, % total trade		0.1	82	
7.2.2	National feature films/mn pop. 15–69		n/a	n/a	
7.2.3	Entertainment and media market/th pop. 15–69		n/a	n/a	
7.2.4	Creative goods exports, % total trade		0.2	83	◆
7.3	**Online creativity**		**0.2**	**130**	○◇
7.3.1	Generic top-level domains (TLDs)/th pop. 15–69		0.1	123	
7.3.2	Country-code TLDs/th pop. 15–69		0.1	125	
7.3.3	GitHub commits/mn pop. 15–69		0.6	120	
7.3.4	Mobile app creation/bn PPP$ GDP		0.0	124	○◇

NOTES: ● indicates a strength; ○ a weakness; ◆ an income group strength; ◇ an income group weakness; * an index; † a survey question. ⊙ is used when the available economy data are older than the base year; see appendices for details, including the year of the data, at wipo.int/gii-ranking. Square brackets [ ] indicate that the data minimum coverage (DMC) requirements were not met at the sub-pillar or pillar level.

GII 2023 rank

Malaysia

36

Output rank	Input rank	Income	Region	Population (mn)	GDP, PPP$ (bn)	GDP per capita, PPP$
46	30	Upper middle	SEAO	33.9	1,096.5	33,113

			Score/ Value	Rank	
	Institutions		**68.7**	**29**	◆
1.1	**Institutional environment**		**69.6**	**24**	◆
1.1.1	Operational stability for businesses*		75.0	17	◆
1.1.2	Government effectiveness*		64.1	31	◆
1.2	**Regulatory environment**		**63.5**	**65**	
1.2.1	Regulatory quality*		60.8	43	◆
1.2.2	Rule of law*		56.1	40	◆
1.2.3	Cost of redundancy dismissal		23.9	104	○
1.3	**Business environment**		**72.9**	**20**	◆
1.3.1	Policies for doing business†		66.3	30	◆
1.3.2	Entrepreneurship policies and culture†	⊙	79.5	8	●◆
	Human capital and research		**44.3**	**32**	◆
2.1	**Education**		**48.2**	**72**	
2.1.1	Expenditure on education, % GDP		4.3	60	
2.1.2	Government funding/pupil, secondary, % GDP/cap		20.6	48	
2.1.3	School life expectancy, years		13.3	80	○
2.1.4	PISA scales in reading, maths and science		430.9	48	
2.1.5	Pupil–teacher ratio, secondary		10.9	41	
2.2	**Tertiary education**		**48.8**	**11**	●◆
2.2.1	Tertiary enrolment, % gross		41.4	77	
2.2.2	Graduates in science and engineering, %		43.5	1	●◆
2.2.3	Tertiary inbound mobility, %		8.1	31	◆
2.3	**Research and development (R&D)**		**35.9**	**31**	◆
2.3.1	Researchers, FTE/mn pop.	⊙	2,184.7	39	◆
2.3.2	Gross expenditure on R&D, % GDP	⊙	1.0	43	
2.3.3	Global corporate R&D investors, top 3, mn USD		44.2	38	◆
2.3.4	QS university ranking, top 3*		59.7	14	●◆
	Infrastructure		**46.5**	**51**	
3.1	**Information and communication technologies (ICTs)**		**79.2**	**41**	
3.1.1	ICT access*		91.7	17	●◆
3.1.2	ICT use*		84.0	45	◆
3.1.3	Government's online service*		73.8	53	
3.1.4	E-participation*		67.4	47	
3.2	**General infrastructure**		**37.5**	**37**	◆
3.2.1	Electricity output, GWh/mn pop.	⊙	5,640.8	37	◆
3.2.2	Logistics performance*		68.2	25	◆
3.2.3	Gross capital formation, % GDP		21.4	86	○
3.3	**Ecological sustainability**		**22.9**	**71**	
3.3.1	GDP/unit of energy use		9.3	78	○
3.3.2	Environmental performance*		27.3	93	○◇
3.3.3	ISO 14001 environment/bn PPP$ GDP		2.7	33	
	Market sophistication		**53.2**	**18**	●◆
4.1	**Credit**		**72.3**	**4**	●◆
4.1.1	Finance for startups and scaleups†	⊙	93.9	2	●◆
4.1.2	Domestic credit to private sector, % GDP		133.9	16	●◆
4.1.3	Loans from microfinance institutions, % GDP		n/a	n/a	
4.2	**Investment**		**22.7**	**31**	
4.2.1	Market capitalization, % GDP		117.0	11	●◆
4.2.2	Venture capital (VC) investors, deals/bn PPP$ GDP		0.1	38	
4.2.3	VC recipients, deals/bn PPP$ GDP		0.1	29	◆
4.2.4	VC received, value, % GDP		0.0	43	
4.3	**Trade, diversification and market scale**		**64.6**	**31**	
4.3.1	Applied tariff rate, weighted avg., %		3.6	79	
4.3.2	Domestic industry diversification		93.7	36	
4.3.3	Domestic market scale, bn PPP$		1,096.5	30	

			Score/ Value	Rank	
	Business sophistication		**38.8**	**36**	◆
5.1	**Knowledge workers**		**34.0**	**62**	
5.1.1	Knowledge-intensive employment, %	⊙	28.2	51	
5.1.2	Firms offering formal training, %		24.0	69	○
5.1.3	GERD performed by business, % GDP	⊙	0.5	41	
5.1.4	GERD financed by business, %	⊙	38.2	46	
5.1.5	Females employed w/advanced degrees, %	⊙	14.7	50	
5.2	**Innovation linkages**		**34.2**	**36**	◆
5.2.1	University–industry R&D collaboration†		62.8	31	◆
5.2.2	State of cluster development†		64.3	31	◆
5.2.3	GERD financed by abroad, % GDP	⊙	0.1	45	
5.2.4	Joint venture/strategic alliance deals/bn PPP$ GDP		0.1	20	◆
5.2.5	Patent families/bn PPP$ GDP		0.2	44	
5.3	**Knowledge absorption**		**48.2**	**27**	◆
5.3.1	Intellectual property payments, % total trade		1.1	33	
5.3.2	High-tech imports, % total trade		29.8	3	●◆
5.3.3	ICT services imports, % total trade		1.8	44	
5.3.4	FDI net inflows, % GDP		2.9	49	
5.3.5	Research talent, % in businesses	⊙	15.8	56	○
	Knowledge and technology outputs		**32.2**	**37**	◆
6.1	**Knowledge creation**		**14.5**	**66**	
6.1.1	Patents by origin/bn PPP$ GDP		0.9	62	
6.1.2	PCT patents by origin/bn PPP$ GDP		0.1	50	
6.1.3	Utility models by origin/bn PPP$ GDP		0.1	52	
6.1.4	Scientific and technical articles/bn PPP$ GDP		14.2	51	
6.1.5	Citable documents H-index		23.5	39	
6.2	**Knowledge impact**		**37.7**	**36**	◆
6.2.1	Labor productivity growth, %		1.3	52	
6.2.2	Unicorn valuation, % GDP		0.4	42	
6.2.3	Software spending, % GDP		0.3	38	◆
6.2.4	High-tech manufacturing, %		46.2	17	◆
6.3	**Knowledge diffusion**		**44.3**	**24**	◆
6.3.1	Intellectual property receipts, % total trade		0.1	54	
6.3.2	Production and export complexity		75.9	24	◆
6.3.3	High-tech exports, % total trade		44.7	1	●◆
6.3.4	ICT services exports, % total trade		1.4	74	
6.3.5	ISO 9001 quality/bn PPP$ GDP		12.1	22	
	Creative outputs		**30.7**	**47**	
7.1	**Intangible assets**		**36.5**	**53**	
7.1.1	Intangible asset intensity, top 15, %		62.7	33	
7.1.2	Trademarks by origin/bn PPP$ GDP		20.7	91	○◇
7.1.3	Global brand value, top 5,000, % GDP		10.2	16	◆
7.1.4	Industrial designs by origin/bn PPP$ GDP		0.5	83	○
7.2	**Creative goods and services**		**29.6**	**31**	◆
7.2.1	Cultural and creative services exports, % total trade		0.3	67	
7.2.2	National feature films/mn pop. 15–69		0.3	75	○
7.2.3	Entertainment and media market/th pop. 15–69		10.7	33	◆
7.2.4	Creative goods exports, % total trade		8.8	1	●◆
7.3	**Online creativity**		**20.3**	**64**	
7.3.1	Generic top-level domains (TLDs)/th pop. 15–69		7.6	50	
7.3.2	Country-code TLDs/th pop. 15–69		3.8	61	
7.3.3	GitHub commits/mn pop. 15–69		6.8	64	
7.3.4	Mobile app creation/bn PPP$ GDP		63.1	74	

NOTES: ● indicates a strength; ○ a weakness; ◆ an income group strength; ◇ an income group weakness; * an index; † a survey question. ⊙ is used when the available economy data are older than the base year; see appendices for details, including the year of the data, at wipo.int/gii-ranking. Square brackets [ ] indicate that the data minimum coverage (DMC) requirements were not met at the sub-pillar or pillar level.

GII 2023 rank

Mali

129

Output rank	Input rank	Income	Region	Population (mn)	GDP, PPP$ (bn)	GDP per capita, PPP$
126	129	Low	SSA	22.6	56.1	2,609

			Score/ Value	Rank	
Institutions			**32.5**	**117**	
1.1	**Institutional environment**		**4.3**	**131**	○◇
1.1.1	Operational stability for businesses*		5.6	131	○◇
1.1.2	Government effectiveness*		3.0	129	◇
1.2	**Regulatory environment**		**54.2**	**89**	
1.2.1	Regulatory quality*		26.0	107	
1.2.2	Rule of law*		13.3	117	
1.2.3	Cost of redundancy dismissal		13.6	50	●
1.3	**Business environment**		**39.0**	**[90]**	
1.3.1	Policies for doing business†		39.0	88	
1.3.2	Entrepreneurship policies and culture†		n/a	n/a	
Human capital and research			**13.7**	**121**	
2.1	**Education**		**39.1**	**102**	
2.1.1	Expenditure on education, % GDP		4.4	58	●
2.1.2	Government funding/pupil, secondary, % GDP/cap	⊙	26.5	15	●
2.1.3	School life expectancy, years	⊙	7.5	112	◇
2.1.4	PISA scales in reading, maths and science		n/a	n/a	
2.1.5	Pupil–teacher ratio, secondary		18.5	94	
2.2	**Tertiary education**		**1.2**	**128**	○
2.2.1	Tertiary enrolment, % gross	⊙	4.9	126	○
2.2.2	Graduates in science and engineering, %		n/a	n/a	
2.2.3	Tertiary inbound mobility, %	⊙	0.9	93	◇
2.3	**Research and development (R&D)**		**0.8**	**103**	
2.3.1	Researchers, FTE/mn pop.		30.3	100	
2.3.2	Gross expenditure on R&D, % GDP		0.2	91	
2.3.3	Global corporate R&D investors, top 3, mn USD		0.0	40	○◇
2.3.4	QS university ranking, top 3*		0.0	71	○◇
Infrastructure			**16.8**	**128**	
3.1	**Information and communication technologies (ICTs)**		**28.1**	**122**	
3.1.1	ICT access*		40.2	118	
3.1.2	ICT use*		16.8	128	
3.1.3	Government's online service*		29.8	124	
3.1.4	E-participation*		25.6	111	
3.2	**General infrastructure**		**13.6**	**111**	
3.2.1	Electricity output, GWh/mn pop.		n/a	n/a	
3.2.2	Logistics performance*		22.7	82	
3.2.3	Gross capital formation, % GDP		14.6	121	
3.3	**Ecological sustainability**		**8.7**	**130**	◇
3.3.1	GDP/unit of energy use		n/a	n/a	
3.3.2	Environmental performance*		16.3	117	◇
3.3.3	ISO 14001 environment/bn PPP$ GDP		0.2	113	
Market sophistication			**12.7**	**126**	
4.1	**Credit**		**13.2**	**105**	
4.1.1	Finance for startups and scaleups†		n/a	n/a	
4.1.2	Domestic credit to private sector, % GDP		26.0	107	
4.1.3	Loans from microfinance institutions, % GDP		1.6	20	●
4.2	**Investment**		**4.4**	**[82]**	
4.2.1	Market capitalization, % GDP		n/a	n/a	
4.2.2	Venture capital (VC) investors, deals/bn PPP$ GDP		n/a	n/a	
4.2.3	VC recipients, deals/bn PPP$ GDP		0.0	68	
4.2.4	VC received, value, % GDP		0.0	76	
4.3	**Trade, diversification and market scale**		**20.7**	**126**	
4.3.1	Applied tariff rate, weighted avg., %		9.2	114	
4.3.2	Domestic industry diversification		n/a	n/a	
4.3.3	Domestic market scale, bn PPP$		56.1	103	

			Score/ Value	Rank	
Business sophistication			**18.2**	**115**	
5.1	**Knowledge workers**		**4.6**	**131**	○◇
5.1.1	Knowledge-intensive employment, %	⊙	3.6	124	
5.1.2	Firms offering formal training, %	⊙	17.7	86	◇
5.1.3	GERD performed by business, % GDP		n/a	n/a	
5.1.4	GERD financed by business, %	⊙	0.8	93	
5.1.5	Females employed w/advanced degrees, %	⊙	0.5	125	
5.2	**Innovation linkages**		**18.8**	**85**	
5.2.1	University–industry R&D collaboration†		32.3	92	
5.2.2	State of cluster development†		30.2	93	
5.2.3	GERD financed by abroad, % GDP	⊙	0.1	29	●
5.2.4	Joint venture/strategic alliance deals/bn PPP$ GDP	⊙	0.0	59	●
5.2.5	Patent families/bn PPP$ GDP		0.0	95	○◇
5.3	**Knowledge absorption**		**31.2**	**74**	◆
5.3.1	Intellectual property payments, % total trade		0.0	118	○◇
5.3.2	High-tech imports, % total trade	⊙	7.2	85	
5.3.3	ICT services imports, % total trade		1.7	49	●
5.3.4	FDI net inflows, % GDP		3.8	34	●
5.3.5	Research talent, % in businesses	⊙	31.4	41	◆
Knowledge and technology outputs			**10.8**	**120**	
6.1	**Knowledge creation**		**4.3**	**117**	
6.1.1	Patents by origin/bn PPP$ GDP		0.2	97	
6.1.2	PCT patents by origin/bn PPP$ GDP		0.0	101	○◇
6.1.3	Utility models by origin/bn PPP$ GDP		n/a	n/a	
6.1.4	Scientific and technical articles/bn PPP$ GDP		4.5	109	
6.1.5	Citable documents H-index		4.9	104	
6.2	**Knowledge impact**		**16.1**	**120**	
6.2.1	Labor productivity growth, %		0.2	90	
6.2.2	Unicorn valuation, % GDP		0.0	48	○◇
6.2.3	Software spending, % GDP		0.0	120	
6.2.4	High-tech manufacturing, %		n/a	n/a	
6.3	**Knowledge diffusion**		**12.0**	**98**	
6.3.1	Intellectual property receipts, % total trade		0.0	114	○◇
6.3.2	Production and export complexity		31.0	112	
6.3.3	High-tech exports, % total trade	⊙	0.2	106	
6.3.4	ICT services exports, % total trade		3.0	42	●◆
6.3.5	ISO 9001 quality/bn PPP$ GDP		0.5	123	
Creative outputs			**3.3**	**128**	
7.1	**Intangible assets**		**3.1**	**123**	
7.1.1	Intangible asset intensity, top 15, %		n/a	n/a	
7.1.2	Trademarks by origin/bn PPP$ GDP		6.6	117	
7.1.3	Global brand value, top 5,000, % GDP		0.0	74	○◇
7.1.4	Industrial designs by origin/bn PPP$ GDP		0.2	103	
7.2	**Creative goods and services**		**4.8**	**[87]**	
7.2.1	Cultural and creative services exports, % total trade	⊙	0.5	56	
7.2.2	National feature films/mn pop. 15–69		n/a	n/a	
7.2.3	Entertainment and media market/th pop. 15–69		n/a	n/a	
7.2.4	Creative goods exports, % total trade	⊙	0.0	118	
7.3	**Online creativity**		**2.1**	**125**	
7.3.1	Generic top-level domains (TLDs)/th pop. 15–69		0.1	122	
7.3.2	Country-code TLDs/th pop. 15–69		5.9	54	●◆
7.3.3	GitHub commits/mn pop. 15–69		0.1	129	
7.3.4	Mobile app creation/bn PPP$ GDP		n/a	n/a	

NOTES: ● indicates a strength; ○ a weakness; ◆ an income group strength; ◇ an income group weakness; * an index; † a survey question. ⊙ is used when the available economy data are older than the base year; see appendices for details, including the year of the data, at wipo.int/gii-ranking. Square brackets [ ] indicate that the data minimum coverage (DMC) requirements were not met at the sub-pillar or pillar level.

GII 2023 rank

Malta

25

Output rank	Input rank	Income	Region	Population (mn)	GDP, PPP$ (bn)	GDP per capita, PPP$
17	27	High	EUR	0.5	29.4	56,338

			Score/Value	Rank	
1	**Institutions**		**64.7**	**34**	◇
1.1	**Institutional environment**		**65.4**	**35**	◇
1.1.1	Operational stability for businesses*		69.4	29	
1.1.2	Government effectiveness*		61.4	34	◇
1.2	**Regulatory environment**		**82.1**	**24**	
1.2.1	Regulatory quality*		63.2	39	◇
1.2.2	Rule of law*		65.0	35	◇
1.2.3	Cost of redundancy dismissal		8.0	1	●
1.3	**Business environment**		**46.7**	**[62]**	
1.3.1	Policies for doing business†		46.7	66	◇
1.3.2	Entrepreneurship policies and culture†		n/a	n/a	
2	**Human capital and research**		**39.6**	**39**	◇
2.1	**Education**		**64.2**	**16**	
2.1.1	Expenditure on education, % GDP	⏲	5.0	42	
2.1.2	Government funding/pupil, secondary, % GDP/cap		31.1	8	◆
2.1.3	School life expectancy, years		17.2	17	
2.1.4	PISA scales in reading, maths and science		458.8	42	◇
2.1.5	Pupil–teacher ratio, secondary		6.8	2	●◆
2.2	**Tertiary education**		**35.8**	**44**	
2.2.1	Tertiary enrolment, % gross		71.5	31	
2.2.2	Graduates in science and engineering, %		17.2	92	○◇
2.2.3	Tertiary inbound mobility, %		14.2	14	
2.3	**Research and development (R&D)**		**18.7**	**46**	◇
2.3.1	Researchers, FTE/mn pop.		2,059.7	41	◇
2.3.2	Gross expenditure on R&D, % GDP		0.6	55	◇
2.3.3	Global corporate R&D investors, top 3, mn USD		42.2	39	◇
2.3.4	QS university ranking, top 3*		0.0	71	○◇
3	**Infrastructure**		**59.7**	**17**	
3.1	**Information and communication technologies (ICTs)**		**85.5**	**19**	
3.1.1	ICT access*		92.3	15	
3.1.2	ICT use*		86.8	30	◇
3.1.3	Government's online service*		87.3	18	
3.1.4	E-participation*		75.6	22	
3.2	**General infrastructure**		**30.3**	**53**	◇
3.2.1	Electricity output, GWh/mn pop.		4,274.7	53	◇
3.2.2	Logistics performance*		54.5	42	◇
3.2.3	Gross capital formation, % GDP		20.8	92	○
3.3	**Ecological sustainability**		**63.3**	**1**	**●◆**
3.3.1	GDP/unit of energy use		28.6	3	●◆
3.3.2	Environmental performance*		95.4	4	●◆
3.3.3	ISO 14001 environment/bn PPP$ GDP		2.2	39	
4	**Market sophistication**		**42.7**	**43**	◇
4.1	**Credit**		**30.2**	**[65]**	
4.1.1	Finance for startups and scaleups†		n/a	n/a	
4.1.2	Domestic credit to private sector, % GDP		82.0	41	
4.1.3	Loans from microfinance institutions, % GDP		n/a	n/a	
4.2	**Investment**		**38.7**	**16**	
4.2.1	Market capitalization, % GDP		33.6	44	◇
4.2.2	Venture capital (VC) investors, deals/bn PPP$ GDP		1.1	7	◆
4.2.3	VC recipients, deals/bn PPP$ GDP		0.1	32	
4.2.4	VC received, value, % GDP		0.0	13	
4.3	**Trade, diversification and market scale**		**59.3**	**59**	
4.3.1	Applied tariff rate, weighted avg., %		1.5	20	
4.3.2	Domestic industry diversification	⏲	87.1	61	
4.3.3	Domestic market scale, bn PPP$		29.4	126	○

			Score/Value	Rank	
5	**Business sophistication**		**53.1**	**21**	
5.1	**Knowledge workers**		**54.3**	**24**	◇
5.1.1	Knowledge-intensive employment, %		45.5	21	
5.1.2	Firms offering formal training, %		49.9	20	
5.1.3	GERD performed by business, % GDP		0.4	45	◇
5.1.4	GERD financed by business, %		60.2	14	
5.1.5	Females employed w/advanced degrees, %		17.2	42	◇
5.2	**Innovation linkages**		**48.1**	**22**	
5.2.1	University-industry R&D collaboration†		40.2	72	◇
5.2.2	State of cluster development†		42.5	61	◇
5.2.3	GERD financed by abroad, % GDP		0.1	47	
5.2.4	Joint venture/strategic alliance deals/bn PPP$ GDP		0.3	1	●◆
5.2.5	Patent families/bn PPP$ GDP		2.5	16	
5.3	**Knowledge absorption**		**57.0**	**6**	**●**
5.3.1	Intellectual property payments, % total trade		6.5	1	●◆
5.3.2	High-tech imports, % total trade		7.9	72	
5.3.3	ICT services imports, % total trade		1.1	84	○◇
5.3.4	FDI net inflows, % GDP		26.8	4	●◆
5.3.5	Research talent, % in businesses		47.7	28	
6	**Knowledge and technology outputs**		**33.2**	**36**	◇
6.1	**Knowledge creation**		**27.7**	**35**	◇
6.1.1	Patents by origin/bn PPP$ GDP		2.4	31	
6.1.2	PCT patents by origin/bn PPP$ GDP		1.6	19	
6.1.3	Utility models by origin/bn PPP$ GDP		n/a	n/a	
6.1.4	Scientific and technical articles/bn PPP$ GDP		17.7	42	◇
6.1.5	Citable documents H-index		7.6	88	○◇
6.2	**Knowledge impact**		**30.1**	**56**	◇
6.2.1	Labor productivity growth, %		−0.1	101	○
6.2.2	Unicorn valuation, % GDP		0.0	48	○◇
6.2.3	Software spending, % GDP		0.3	30	
6.2.4	High-tech manufacturing, %	⏲	36.2	32	
6.3	**Knowledge diffusion**		**41.8**	**31**	
6.3.1	Intellectual property receipts, % total trade		4.2	1	●◆
6.3.2	Production and export complexity		n/a	n/a	
6.3.3	High-tech exports, % total trade		3.7	43	
6.3.4	ICT services exports, % total trade		0.5	103	○
6.3.5	ISO 9001 quality/bn PPP$ GDP		8.9	31	
7	**Creative outputs**		**59.2**	**4**	**●◆**
7.1	**Intangible assets**		**72.2**	**4**	**●◆**
7.1.1	Intangible asset intensity, top 15, %		64.6	28	
7.1.2	Trademarks by origin/bn PPP$ GDP		149.6	1	●◆
7.1.3	Global brand value, top 5,000, % GDP		5.2	32	
7.1.4	Industrial designs by origin/bn PPP$ GDP		18.1	5	●◆
7.2	**Creative goods and services**		**39.0**	**12**	
7.2.1	Cultural and creative services exports, % total trade		14.3	1	●◆
7.2.2	National feature films/mn pop. 15–69		7.8	10	
7.2.3	Entertainment and media market/th pop. 15–69		4.1	45	○◇
7.2.4	Creative goods exports, % total trade		0.2	84	○
7.3	**Online creativity**		**53.3**	**19**	
7.3.1	Generic top-level domains (TLDs)/th pop. 15–69		88.1	6	●◆
7.3.2	Country-code TLDs/th pop. 15–69		14.0	34	◇
7.3.3	GitHub commits/mn pop. 15–69		35.7	30	◇
7.3.4	Mobile app creation/bn PPP$ GDP		75.4	23	

NOTES: ● indicates a strength; ○ a weakness; ◆ an income group strength; ◇ an income group weakness; * an index; † a survey question. ⏲ is used when the available economy data are older than the base year; see appendices for details, including the year of the data, at wipo.int/gii-ranking. Square brackets [ ] indicate that the data minimum coverage (DMC) requirements were not met at the sub-pillar or pillar level.

GII 2023 rank

Mauritania

127

Output rank	Input rank	Income	Region	Population (mn)	GDP, PPP$ (bn)	GDP per capita, PPP$
129	122	Lower middle	SSA	4.7	30.0	6,925

			Score/ Value	Rank	
	Institutions		**43.5**	**89**	
1.1	**Institutional environment**		**29.1**	**102**	
1.1.1	Operational stability for businesses*		41.7	87	
1.1.2	Government effectiveness*		16.5	114	
1.2	**Regulatory environment**		**56.3**	**85**	●
1.2.1	Regulatory quality*		14.7	127	◇
1.2.2	Rule of law*		20.1	108	
1.2.3	Cost of redundancy dismissal		10.5	33	●
1.3	**Business environment**		**45.2**	**[69]**	
1.3.1	Policies for doing business†	⊙	45.2	74	●
1.3.2	Entrepreneurship policies and culture†		n/a	n/a	

			Score/ Value	Rank	
	Human capital and research		**14.2**	**119**	
2.1	**Education**		**16.3**	**131**	◇
2.1.1	Expenditure on education, % GDP		1.7	123	◇
2.1.2	Government funding/pupil, secondary, % GDP/cap		8.6	93	
2.1.3	School life expectancy, years		8.7	111	◇
2.1.4	PISA scales in reading, maths and science		n/a	n/a	
2.1.5	Pupil–teacher ratio, secondary	⊙	28.8	118	◇
2.2	**Tertiary education**		**26.2**	**77**	●
2.2.1	Tertiary enrolment, % gross		5.9	123	◇
2.2.2	Graduates in science and engineering, %		34.6	10	●◆
2.2.3	Tertiary inbound mobility, %		1.4	82	
2.3	**Research and development (R&D)**		**0.0**	**119**	○◇
2.3.1	Researchers, FTE/mn pop.		n/a	n/a	
2.3.2	Gross expenditure on R&D, % GDP	⊙	0.0	113	○◇
2.3.3	Global corporate R&D investors, top 3, mn USD		0.0	40	○◇
2.3.4	QS university ranking, top 3*		0.0	71	○◇

			Score/ Value	Rank	
	Infrastructure		**18.5**	**124**	◇
3.1	**Information and communication technologies (ICTs)**		**19.2**	**129**	◇
3.1.1	ICT access*		30.4	122	◇
3.1.2	ICT use*		46.5	107	
3.1.3	Government's online service*		0.0	131	○◇
3.1.4	E-participation*		0.0	131	○◇
3.2	**General infrastructure**		**28.1**	**61**	●
3.2.1	Electricity output, GWh/mn pop.		n/a	n/a	
3.2.2	Logistics performance*		9.1	106	
3.2.3	Gross capital formation, % GDP		40.6	7	●◆
3.3	**Ecological sustainability**		**8.1**	**131**	◇
3.3.1	GDP/unit of energy use		n/a	n/a	
3.3.2	Environmental performance*		15.6	123	
3.3.3	ISO 14001 environment/bn PPP$ GDP		0.1	121	

			Score/ Value	Rank	
	Market sophistication		**8.7**	**[130]**	
4.1	**Credit**		**6.6**	**[122]**	
4.1.1	Finance for startups and scaleups†		n/a	n/a	
4.1.2	Domestic credit to private sector, % GDP	⊙	22.2	113	
4.1.3	Loans from microfinance institutions, % GDP		n/a	n/a	
4.2	**Investment**		**n/a**	**[n/a]**	
4.2.1	Market capitalization, % GDP		n/a	n/a	
4.2.2	Venture capital (VC) investors, deals/bn PPP$ GDP		n/a	n/a	
4.2.3	VC recipients, deals/bn PPP$ GDP		n/a	n/a	
4.2.4	VC received, value, % GDP		n/a	n/a	
4.3	**Trade, diversification and market scale**		**10.8**	**130**	◇
4.3.1	Applied tariff rate, weighted avg., %		12.2	129	◇
4.3.2	Domestic industry diversification		n/a	n/a	
4.3.3	Domestic market scale, bn PPP$		30.0	125	

			Score/ Value	Rank	
	Business sophistication		**20.2**	**108**	
5.1	**Knowledge workers**		**23.3**	**[88]**	
5.1.1	Knowledge-intensive employment, %		n/a	n/a	
5.1.2	Firms offering formal training, %	⊙	52.7	18	●◆
5.1.3	GERD performed by business, % GDP		n/a	n/a	
5.1.4	GERD financed by business, %	⊙	0.0	98	○◇
5.1.5	Females employed w/advanced degrees, %	⊙	0.7	124	
5.2	**Innovation linkages**		**14.0**	**103**	
5.2.1	University–industry R&D collaboration†	⊙	53.1	48	●
5.2.2	State of cluster development†	⊙	12.7	124	◇
5.2.3	GERD financed by abroad, % GDP	⊙	0.0	96	○◇
5.2.4	Joint venture/strategic alliance deals/bn PPP$ GDP		0.0	85	
5.2.5	Patent families/bn PPP$ GDP		0.0	95	○◇
5.3	**Knowledge absorption**		**23.5**	**112**	
5.3.1	Intellectual property payments, % total trade		0.0	108	
5.3.2	High-tech imports, % total trade		7.4	79	●
5.3.3	ICT services imports, % total trade		0.4	113	
5.3.4	FDI net inflows, % GDP		3.6	38	●
5.3.5	Research talent, % in businesses		n/a	n/a	

			Score/ Value	Rank	
	Knowledge and technology outputs		**11.0**	**115**	
6.1	**Knowledge creation**		**0.8**	**131**	◇
6.1.1	Patents by origin/bn PPP$ GDP		0.1	115	
6.1.2	PCT patents by origin/bn PPP$ GDP		0.0	101	○◇
6.1.3	Utility models by origin/bn PPP$ GDP		0.0	75	○◇
6.1.4	Scientific and technical articles/bn PPP$ GDP		1.5	127	
6.1.5	Citable documents H-index		0.6	131	◇
6.2	**Knowledge impact**		**26.3**	**67**	●
6.2.1	Labor productivity growth, %		0.4	85	●
6.2.2	Unicorn valuation, % GDP		0.0	48	○◇
6.2.3	Software spending, % GDP		0.3	33	●
6.2.4	High-tech manufacturing, %		n/a	n/a	
6.3	**Knowledge diffusion**		**6.0**	**123**	
6.3.1	Intellectual property receipts, % total trade		0.0	111	
6.3.2	Production and export complexity		25.9	115	◇
6.3.3	High-tech exports, % total trade		0.0	126	
6.3.4	ICT services exports, % total trade		0.4	107	
6.3.5	ISO 9001 quality/bn PPP$ GDP		0.3	127	

			Score/ Value	Rank	
	Creative outputs		**1.0**	**[131]**	
7.1	**Intangible assets**		**1.3**	**[130]**	
7.1.1	Intangible asset intensity, top 15, %		n/a	n/a	
7.1.2	Trademarks by origin/bn PPP$ GDP		5.2	121	
7.1.3	Global brand value, top 5,000, % GDP		n/a	n/a	
7.1.4	Industrial designs by origin/bn PPP$ GDP		0.0	120	○◇
7.2	**Creative goods and services**		**1.2**	**[113]**	
7.2.1	Cultural and creative services exports, % total trade		0.1	80	
7.2.2	National feature films/mn pop. 15–69		n/a	n/a	
7.2.3	Entertainment and media market/th pop. 15–69		n/a	n/a	
7.2.4	Creative goods exports, % total trade		0.0	132	○◇
7.3	**Online creativity**		**0.2**	**131**	◇
7.3.1	Generic top-level domains (TLDs)/th pop. 15–69		0.2	119	
7.3.2	Country-code TLDs/th pop. 15–69		0.1	121	
7.3.3	GitHub commits/mn pop. 15–69		0.2	127	
7.3.4	Mobile app creation/bn PPP$ GDP		n/a	n/a	

NOTES: ● indicates a strength; ○ a weakness; ◆ an income group strength; ◇ an income group weakness; * an index; † a survey question. ⊙ is used when the available economy data are older than the base year; see appendices for details, including the year of the data, at wipo.int/gii-ranking. Square brackets [ ] indicate that the data minimum coverage (DMC) requirements were not met at the sub-pillar or pillar level.

Mauritius

GII 2023 rank

57

Output rank	Input rank	Income	Region	Population (mn)	GDP, PPP$ (bn)	GDP per capita, PPP$
72	40	Upper middle	SSA	1.3	32.0	25,372

		Score/ Value	Rank	
	Institutions	**70.3**	**26**	●◆
1.1	**Institutional environment**	**71.8**	**21**	●◆
1.1.1	Operational stability for businesses*	83.3	9	●◆
1.1.2	Government effectiveness*	60.2	36	◆
1.2	**Regulatory environment**	**83.5**	**19**	●◆
1.2.1	Regulatory quality*	72.4	27	●◆
1.2.2	Rule of law*	65.3	34	◆
1.2.3	Cost of redundancy dismissal	8.9	23	●◆
1.3	**Business environment**	**55.7**	**[46]**	
1.3.1	Policies for doing business†	55.7	50	
1.3.2	Entrepreneurship policies and culture†	n/a	n/a	
	Human capital and research	**31.3**	**64**	
2.1	**Education**	**60.6**	**34**	
2.1.1	Expenditure on education, % GDP	4.7	48	
2.1.2	Government funding/pupil, secondary, % GDP/cap	31.8	7	●◆
2.1.3	School life expectancy, years	14.9	55	
2.1.4	PISA scales in reading, maths and science	n/a	n/a	
2.1.5	Pupil–teacher ratio, secondary	10.7	37	
2.2	**Tertiary education**	**30.4**	**66**	
2.2.1	Tertiary enrolment, % gross	45.3	70	
2.2.2	Graduates in science and engineering, %	24.8	46	
2.2.3	Tertiary inbound mobility, %	6.7	36	
2.3	**Research and development (R&D)**	**3.0**	**86**	
2.3.1	Researchers, FTE/mn pop.	568.0	67	
2.3.2	Gross expenditure on R&D, % GDP	0.4	69	
2.3.3	Global corporate R&D investors, top 3, mn USD	0.0	40	○◇
2.3.4	QS university ranking, top 3*	0.0	71	○◇
	Infrastructure	**37.6**	**74**	
3.1	**Information and communication technologies (ICTs)**	**64.8**	**77**	
3.1.1	ICT access*	84.8	51	
3.1.2	ICT use*	74.9	62	
3.1.3	Government's online service*	58.9	77	
3.1.4	E-participation*	40.7	88	
3.2	**General infrastructure**	**14.8**	**107**	◇
3.2.1	Electricity output, GWh/mn pop.	⊙ 2,274.9	78	
3.2.2	Logistics performance*	18.2	89	○◇
3.2.3	Gross capital formation, % GDP	20.9	88	
3.3	**Ecological sustainability**	**33.2**	**42**	
3.3.1	GDP/unit of energy use	18.3	11	●◆
3.3.2	Environmental performance*	43.9	58	
3.3.3	ISO 14001 environment/bn PPP$ GDP	1.1	61	
	Market sophistication	**51.6**	**24**	●◆
4.1	**Credit**	**34.1**	**[55]**	
4.1.1	Finance for startups and scaleups†	n/a	n/a	
4.1.2	Domestic credit to private sector, % GDP	91.9	33	
4.1.3	Loans from microfinance institutions, % GDP	n/a	n/a	
4.2	**Investment**	**63.6**	**8**	●◆
4.2.1	Market capitalization, % GDP	60.2	29	
4.2.2	Venture capital (VC) investors, deals/bn PPP$ GDP	2.2	1	●◆
4.2.3	VC recipients, deals/bn PPP$ GDP	0.1	21	◆
4.2.4	VC received, value, % GDP	0.0	5	●◆
4.3	**Trade, diversification and market scale**	**57.0**	**72**	
4.3.1	Applied tariff rate, weighted avg., %	0.9	10	●
4.3.2	Domestic industry diversification	76.5	84	◇
4.3.3	Domestic market scale, bn PPP$	32.0	123	○

		Score/ Value	Rank	
	Business sophistication	**22.9**	**91**	
5.1	**Knowledge workers**	**17.1**	**109**	◇
5.1.1	Knowledge-intensive employment, %	⊙ 23.2	63	
5.1.2	Firms offering formal training, %	n/a	n/a	
5.1.3	GERD performed by business, % GDP	⊙ 0.0	79	○
5.1.4	GERD financed by business, %	⊙ 4.1	83	◇
5.1.5	Females employed w/advanced degrees, %	⊙ 9.2	79	
5.2	**Innovation linkages**	**20.1**	**71**	
5.2.1	University–industry R&D collaboration†	33.8	88	
5.2.2	State of cluster development†	46.0	54	
5.2.3	GERD financed by abroad, % GDP	⊙ 0.0	84	○
5.2.4	Joint venture/strategic alliance deals/bn PPP$ GDP	0.0	48	
5.2.5	Patent families/bn PPP$ GDP	0.5	33	◆
5.3	**Knowledge absorption**	**31.5**	**73**	
5.3.1	Intellectual property payments, % total trade	0.3	88	
5.3.2	High-tech imports, % total trade	6.9	87	
5.3.3	ICT services imports, % total trade	3.2	14	●◆
5.3.4	FDI net inflows, % GDP	2.4	64	
5.3.5	Research talent, % in businesses	⊙ 4.4	70	
	Knowledge and technology outputs	**15.0**	**90**	
6.1	**Knowledge creation**	**6.7**	**[101]**	
6.1.1	Patents by origin/bn PPP$ GDP	0.2	98	
6.1.2	PCT patents by origin/bn PPP$ GDP	n/a	n/a	
6.1.3	Utility models by origin/bn PPP$ GDP	n/a	n/a	
6.1.4	Scientific and technical articles/bn PPP$ GDP	6.4	98	
6.1.5	Citable documents H-index	4.2	113	○
6.2	**Knowledge impact**	**16.6**	**119**	○◇
6.2.1	Labor productivity growth, %	0.7	74	
6.2.2	Unicorn valuation, % GDP	0.0	48	○◇
6.2.3	Software spending, % GDP	0.1	83	
6.2.4	High-tech manufacturing, %	3.5	107	○◇
6.3	**Knowledge diffusion**	**21.6**	**69**	
6.3.1	Intellectual property receipts, % total trade	0.0	83	
6.3.2	Production and export complexity	51.0	65	
6.3.3	High-tech exports, % total trade	0.6	84	
6.3.4	ICT services exports, % total trade	3.3	38	
6.3.5	ISO 9001 quality/bn PPP$ GDP	7.2	38	
	Creative outputs	**27.8**	**57**	
7.1	**Intangible assets**	**38.5**	**48**	
7.1.1	Intangible asset intensity, top 15, %	46.1	56	
7.1.2	Trademarks by origin/bn PPP$ GDP	90.2	17	●
7.1.3	Global brand value, top 5,000, % GDP	0.0	74	○◇
7.1.4	Industrial designs by origin/bn PPP$ GDP	0.9	74	
7.2	**Creative goods and services**	**12.7**	**[62]**	
7.2.1	Cultural and creative services exports, % total trade	0.9	31	
7.2.2	National feature films/mn pop. 15–69	n/a	n/a	
7.2.3	Entertainment and media market/th pop. 15–69	n/a	n/a	
7.2.4	Creative goods exports, % total trade	0.5	62	
7.3	**Online creativity**	**21.5**	**62**	
7.3.1	Generic top-level domains (TLDs)/th pop. 15–69	14.4	35	◆
7.3.2	Country-code TLDs/th pop. 15–69	3.2	64	
7.3.3	GitHub commits/mn pop. 15–69	5.9	69	
7.3.4	Mobile app creation/bn PPP$ GDP	62.3	75	

NOTES: ● indicates a strength; ○ a weakness; ◆ an income group strength; ◇ an income group weakness; * an index; † a survey question. ⊙ is used when the available economy data are older than the base year; see appendices for details, including the year of the data, at wipo.int/gii-ranking. Square brackets [ ] indicate that the data minimum coverage (DMC) requirements were not met at the sub-pillar or pillar level.

GII 2023 rank

Mexico

58

Output rank	Input rank	Income	Region	Population (mn)	GDP, PPP$ (bn)	GDP per capita, PPP$
51	77	Upper middle	LCN	127.5	2,919.9	22,440

		Score/Value	Rank	
	Institutions	**34.8**	**111**	○◇
1.1	**Institutional environment**	**30.0**	**100**	◇
1.1.1	Operational stability for businesses*	31.9	116	○◇
1.1.2	Government effectiveness*	28.1	89	
1.2	**Regulatory environment**	**49.2**	**102**	
1.2.1	Regulatory quality*	36.1	85	
1.2.2	Rule of law*	16.3	109	◇
1.2.3	Cost of redundancy dismissal	22.0	98	
1.3	**Business environment**	**25.0**	**112**	○
1.3.1	Policies for doing business†	19.7	120	○◇
1.3.2	Entrepreneurship policies and culture†	30.3	57	
	Human capital and research	**31.7**	**63**	
2.1	**Education**	**42.8**	**89**	
2.1.1	Expenditure on education, % GDP	⏲ 4.3	62	
2.1.2	Government funding/pupil, secondary, % GDP/cap	12.8	83	○
2.1.3	School life expectancy, years	14.7	60	
2.1.4	PISA scales in reading, maths and science	416.2	57	
2.1.5	Pupil–teacher ratio, secondary	16.0	82	
2.2	**Tertiary education**	**26.2**	**78**	
2.2.1	Tertiary enrolment, % gross	44.8	71	
2.2.2	Graduates in science and engineering, %	25.8	41	
2.2.3	Tertiary inbound mobility, %	0.9	92	○◇
2.3	**Research and development (R&D)**	**26.1**	**38**	◆
2.3.1	Researchers, FTE/mn pop.	⏲ 355.8	77	
2.3.2	Gross expenditure on R&D, % GDP	⏲ 0.3	75	
2.3.3	Global corporate R&D investors, top 3, mn USD	50.4	32	◆
2.3.4	QS university ranking, top 3*	45.1	26	●◆
	Infrastructure	**40.4**	**65**	
3.1	**Information and communication technologies (ICTs)**	**73.2**	**57**	
3.1.1	ICT access*	69.7	90	
3.1.2	ICT use*	70.5	69	
3.1.3	Government's online service*	80.6	31	
3.1.4	E-participation*	72.1	32	
3.2	**General infrastructure**	**21.3**	**84**	
3.2.1	Electricity output, GWh/mn pop.	2,566.2	73	
3.2.2	Logistics performance*	36.4	65	
3.2.3	Gross capital formation, % GDP	20.8	91	
3.3	**Ecological sustainability**	**26.6**	**58**	
3.3.1	GDP/unit of energy use	12.2	47	
3.3.2	Environmental performance*	45.1	57	
3.3.3	ISO 14001 environment/bn PPP$ GDP	0.8	75	
	Market sophistication	**37.2**	**57**	
4.1	**Credit**	**20.8**	**90**	
4.1.1	Finance for startups and scaleups†	39.2	59	
4.1.2	Domestic credit to private sector, % GDP	38.1	85	
4.1.3	Loans from microfinance institutions, % GDP	0.9	29	
4.2	**Investment**	**8.8**	**58**	
4.2.1	Market capitalization, % GDP	33.6	45	
4.2.2	Venture capital (VC) investors, deals/bn PPP$ GDP	0.0	79	○
4.2.3	VC recipients, deals/bn PPP$ GDP	0.0	79	
4.2.4	VC received, value, % GDP	0.0	40	
4.3	**Trade, diversification and market scale**	**81.9**	**12**	●◆
4.3.1	Applied tariff rate, weighted avg., %	⏲ 1.2	13	●
4.3.2	Domestic industry diversification	90.8	45	
4.3.3	Domestic market scale, bn PPP$	2,919.9	13	●◆

		Score/Value	Rank	
	Business sophistication	**25.4**	**79**	
5.1	**Knowledge workers**	**21.2**	**94**	◇
5.1.1	Knowledge-intensive employment, %	20.0	75	
5.1.2	Firms offering formal training, %	n/a	n/a	
5.1.3	GERD performed by business, % GDP	⏲ 0.1	66	
5.1.4	GERD financed by business, %	17.8	69	
5.1.5	Females employed w/advanced degrees, %	10.4	74	
5.2	**Innovation linkages**	**19.0**	**80**	
5.2.1	University–industry R&D collaboration†	37.9	80	
5.2.2	State of cluster development†	52.9	42	
5.2.3	GERD financed by abroad, % GDP	0.0	81	
5.2.4	Joint venture/strategic alliance deals/bn PPP$ GDP	0.0	100	
5.2.5	Patent families/bn PPP$ GDP	0.0	67	
5.3	**Knowledge absorption**	**35.8**	**56**	
5.3.1	Intellectual property payments, % total trade	0.1	104	○◇
5.3.2	High-tech imports, % total trade	17.9	11	●◆
5.3.3	ICT services imports, % total trade	0.1	131	○◇
5.3.4	FDI net inflows, % GDP	2.6	60	
5.3.5	Research talent, % in businesses	⏲ 47.2	29	◆
	Knowledge and technology outputs	**24.7**	**57**	
6.1	**Knowledge creation**	**11.2**	**78**	
6.1.1	Patents by origin/bn PPP$ GDP	0.4	83	
6.1.2	PCT patents by origin/bn PPP$ GDP	0.1	67	
6.1.3	Utility models by origin/bn PPP$ GDP	0.2	40	
6.1.4	Scientific and technical articles/bn PPP$ GDP	5.9	102	
6.1.5	Citable documents H-index	29.7	33	◆
6.2	**Knowledge impact**	**31.3**	**51**	
6.2.1	Labor productivity growth, %	−1.8	123	○◇
6.2.2	Unicorn valuation, % GDP	1.3	31	●◆
6.2.3	Software spending, % GDP	0.2	76	
6.2.4	High-tech manufacturing, %	46.3	16	●◆
6.3	**Knowledge diffusion**	**31.5**	**51**	
6.3.1	Intellectual property receipts, % total trade	0.0	102	◇
6.3.2	Production and export complexity	78.0	20	●◆
6.3.3	High-tech exports, % total trade	14.2	9	●◆
6.3.4	ICT services exports, % total trade	0.0	131	○◇
6.3.5	ISO 9001 quality/bn PPP$ GDP	3.1	72	
	Creative outputs	**31.7**	**45**	
7.1	**Intangible assets**	**38.2**	**50**	
7.1.1	Intangible asset intensity, top 15, %	72.4	15	●
7.1.2	Trademarks by origin/bn PPP$ GDP	53.2	44	
7.1.3	Global brand value, top 5,000, % GDP	4.9	34	
7.1.4	Industrial designs by origin/bn PPP$ GDP	0.5	84	
7.2	**Creative goods and services**	**31.7**	**25**	●◆
7.2.1	Cultural and creative services exports, % total trade	0.0	110	○◇
7.2.2	National feature films/mn pop. 15–69	2.9	39	
7.2.3	Entertainment and media market/th pop. 15–69	8.2	36	
7.2.4	Creative goods exports, % total trade	10.1	1	●◆
7.3	**Online creativity**	**18.9**	**72**	
7.3.1	Generic top-level domains (TLDs)/th pop. 15–69	3.0	70	
7.3.2	Country-code TLDs/th pop. 15–69	4.4	58	
7.3.3	GitHub commits/mn pop. 15–69	3.9	81	
7.3.4	Mobile app creation/bn PPP$ GDP	64.1	69	

NOTES: ● indicates a strength; ○ a weakness; ◆ an income group strength; ◇ an income group weakness; * an index; † a survey question. ⏲ is used when the available economy data are older than the base year; see appendices for details, including the year of the data, at wipo.int/gii-ranking. Square brackets [ ] indicate that the data minimum coverage (DMC) requirements were not met at the sub-pillar or pillar level.

GII 2023 rank

Mongolia **68**

Output rank	Input rank	Income	Region	Population (mn)	GDP, PPP$ (bn)	GDP per capita, PPP$
60	79	Lower middle	SEAO	3.4	47.1	13,611

			Score/ Value	Rank	
Institutions			**46.0**	**80**	
1.1	**Institutional environment**		**41.1**	**75**	
1.1.1	Operational stability for businesses*		58.3	49	◆
1.1.2	Government effectiveness*		23.8	99	
1.2	**Regulatory environment**		**66.8**	**52**	◆
1.2.1	Regulatory quality*		36.7	84	
1.2.2	Rule of law*		33.1	75	
1.2.3	Cost of redundancy dismissal		8.7	18	●◆
1.3	**Business environment**		**30.2**	**[101]**	
1.3.1	Policies for doing business†		30.2	107	
1.3.2	Entrepreneurship policies and culture†		n/a	n/a	
Human capital and research			**31.2**	**65**	◆
2.1	**Education**		**67.3**	**[13]**	
2.1.1	Expenditure on education, % GDP		6.5	12	●◆
2.1.2	Government funding/pupil, secondary, % GDP/cap		n/a	n/a	
2.1.3	School life expectancy, years	⏲	15.0	54	◆
2.1.4	PISA scales in reading, maths and science		n/a	n/a	
2.1.5	Pupil–teacher ratio, secondary	⏲	13.3	63	
2.2	**Tertiary education**		**25.0**	**80**	
2.2.1	Tertiary enrolment, % gross		69.4	40	◆
2.2.2	Graduates in science and engineering, %		18.7	84	
2.2.3	Tertiary inbound mobility, %		1.0	88	
2.3	**Research and development (R&D)**		**1.4**	**97**	
2.3.1	Researchers, FTE/mn pop.	⏲	331.0	79	
2.3.2	Gross expenditure on R&D, % GDP	⏲	0.1	98	
2.3.3	Global corporate R&D investors, top 3, mn USD		0.0	40	○◇
2.3.4	QS university ranking, top 3*		0.0	71	○◇
Infrastructure			**36.0**	**81**	◆
3.1	**Information and communication technologies (ICTs)**		**69.7**	**68**	◆
3.1.1	ICT access*		84.7	52	◆
3.1.2	ICT use*		76.0	59	◆
3.1.3	Government's online service*		58.7	78	
3.1.4	E-participation*		59.3	57	◆
3.2	**General infrastructure**		**26.3**	**65**	
3.2.1	Electricity output, GWh/mn pop.	⏲	2,010.4	82	
3.2.2	Logistics performance*		18.2	89	
3.2.3	Gross capital formation, % GDP		42.8	4	●◆
3.3	**Ecological sustainability**		**11.9**	**119**	
3.3.1	GDP/unit of energy use		6.1	106	
3.3.2	Environmental performance*		18.1	113	
3.3.3	ISO 14001 environment/bn PPP$ GDP		0.8	71	
Market sophistication			**23.7**	**101**	
4.1	**Credit**		**10.9**	**109**	
4.1.1	Finance for startups and scaleups†		n/a	n/a	
4.1.2	Domestic credit to private sector, % GDP		45.8	78	
4.1.3	Loans from microfinance institutions, % GDP		0.5	38	
4.2	**Investment**		**n/a**	**[n/a]**	
4.2.1	Market capitalization, % GDP		n/a	n/a	
4.2.2	Venture capital (VC) investors, deals/bn PPP$ GDP		n/a	n/a	
4.2.3	VC recipients, deals/bn PPP$ GDP		n/a	n/a	
4.2.4	VC received, value, % GDP		n/a	n/a	
4.3	**Trade, diversification and market scale**		**36.5**	**111**	
4.3.1	Applied tariff rate, weighted avg., %		5.3	93	
4.3.2	Domestic industry diversification		42.8	107	○◇
4.3.3	Domestic market scale, bn PPP$		47.1	111	

			Score/ Value	Rank	
Business sophistication			**27.9**	**67**	
5.1	**Knowledge workers**		**43.1**	**43**	◆
5.1.1	Knowledge-intensive employment, %	⏲	26.8	53	◆
5.1.2	Firms offering formal training, %		66.2	3	●◆
5.1.3	GERD performed by business, % GDP	⏲	0.0	85	○
5.1.4	GERD financed by business, %	⏲	8.1	77	
5.1.5	Females employed w/advanced degrees, %	⏲	23.9	23	●◆
5.2	**Innovation linkages**		**9.1**	**121**	◇
5.2.1	University–industry R&D collaboration†		21.7	114	
5.2.2	State of cluster development†		17.5	116	
5.2.3	GERD financed by abroad, % GDP	⏲	0.0	83	
5.2.4	Joint venture/strategic alliance deals/bn PPP$ GDP		0.0	74	
5.2.5	Patent families/bn PPP$ GDP		0.0	95	○◇
5.3	**Knowledge absorption**		**31.7**	**72**	
5.3.1	Intellectual property payments, % total trade		0.3	83	
5.3.2	High-tech imports, % total trade		5.9	105	
5.3.3	ICT services imports, % total trade		1.4	64	
5.3.4	FDI net inflows, % GDP		14.8	7	●◆
5.3.5	Research talent, % in businesses		n/a	n/a	
Knowledge and technology outputs			**15.8**	**88**	
6.1	**Knowledge creation**		**31.2**	**31**	◆
6.1.1	Patents by origin/bn PPP$ GDP		2.5	29	●◆
6.1.2	PCT patents by origin/bn PPP$ GDP		0.1	69	
6.1.3	Utility models by origin/bn PPP$ GDP		4.0	1	●◆
6.1.4	Scientific and technical articles/bn PPP$ GDP		11.0	70	
6.1.5	Citable documents H-index		4.6	107	
6.2	**Knowledge impact**		**5.3**	**130**	○◇
6.2.1	Labor productivity growth, %		n/a	n/a	
6.2.2	Unicorn valuation, % GDP		0.0	48	○◇
6.2.3	Software spending, % GDP		0.1	82	
6.2.4	High-tech manufacturing, %		3.8	106	○◇
6.3	**Knowledge diffusion**		**10.8**	**105**	
6.3.1	Intellectual property receipts, % total trade		0.0	85	
6.3.2	Production and export complexity		32.6	106	
6.3.3	High-tech exports, % total trade		0.3	100	
6.3.4	ICT services exports, % total trade		0.3	110	
6.3.5	ISO 9001 quality/bn PPP$ GDP		4.7	57	◆
Creative outputs			**33.7**	**40**	◆
7.1	**Intangible assets**		**58.3**	**10**	●◆
7.1.1	Intangible asset intensity, top 15, %	⏲	−42.5	77	○◇
7.1.2	Trademarks by origin/bn PPP$ GDP		445.2	1	●◆
7.1.3	Global brand value, top 5,000, % GDP		0.0	74	○◇
7.1.4	Industrial designs by origin/bn PPP$ GDP		32.4	1	●◆
7.2	**Creative goods and services**		**1.5**	**[109]**	
7.2.1	Cultural and creative services exports, % total trade	⏲	0.1	76	
7.2.2	National feature films/mn pop. 15–69		n/a	n/a	
7.2.3	Entertainment and media market/th pop. 15–69		n/a	n/a	
7.2.4	Creative goods exports, % total trade		0.0	129	○
7.3	**Online creativity**		**16.4**	**89**	
7.3.1	Generic top-level domains (TLDs)/th pop. 15–69		0.7	103	
7.3.2	Country-code TLDs/th pop. 15–69		2.9	65	◆
7.3.3	GitHub commits/mn pop. 15–69		5.2	71	
7.3.4	Mobile app creation/bn PPP$ GDP		57.0	90	

NOTES: ● indicates a strength; ○ a weakness; ◆ an income group strength; ◇ an income group weakness; * an index; † a survey question. ⏲ is used when the available economy data are older than the base year; see appendices for details, including the year of the data, at wipo.int/gii-ranking. Square brackets [ ] indicate that the data minimum coverage (DMC) requirements were not met at the sub-pillar or pillar level.

Montenegro

GII 2023 rank

75

Output rank	Input rank	Income	Region	Population (mn)	GDP, PPP$ (bn)	GDP per capita, PPP$
83	62	Upper middle	EUR	0.6	16.2	26,032

			Score/ Value	Rank	
	Institutions		**45.4**	**82**	
1.1	**Institutional environment**		**44.8**	**67**	
1.1.1	Operational stability for businesses*		52.8	65	
1.1.2	Government effectiveness*		36.9	69	
1.2	**Regulatory environment**		**69.6**	**44**	
1.2.1	Regulatory quality*		53.3	51	
1.2.2	Rule of law*		38.0	64	
1.2.3	Cost of redundancy dismissal		11.2	36	●
1.3	**Business environment**		**21.8**	**[116]**	
1.3.1	Policies for doing business†		21.8	118	○ ◇
1.3.2	Entrepreneurship policies and culture†		n/a	n/a	
	Human capital and research		**32.4**	**62**	
2.1	**Education**		**59.4**	**[39]**	
2.1.1	Expenditure on education, % GDP		n/a	n/a	
2.1.2	Government funding/pupil, secondary, % GDP/cap		n/a	n/a	
2.1.3	School life expectancy, years		15.2	46	
2.1.4	PISA scales in reading, maths and science		421.9	55	
2.1.5	Pupil–teacher ratio, secondary		12.9	60	
2.2	**Tertiary education**		**34.2**	**52**	
2.2.1	Tertiary enrolment, % gross		55.6	59	
2.2.2	Graduates in science and engineering, %	⊙	20.5	69	
2.2.3	Tertiary inbound mobility, %		n/a	n/a	
2.3	**Research and development (R&D)**		**3.5**	**84**	
2.3.1	Researchers, FTE/mn pop.	⊙	753.8	60	
2.3.2	Gross expenditure on R&D, % GDP	⊙	0.4	70	
2.3.3	Global corporate R&D investors, top 3, mn USD		0.0	40	○ ◇
2.3.4	QS university ranking, top 3*		0.0	71	○ ◇
	Infrastructure		**44.2**	**56**	
3.1	**Information and communication technologies (ICTs)**		**67.0**	**73**	
3.1.1	ICT access*		89.2	26	●
3.1.2	ICT use*		82.9	51	
3.1.3	Government's online service*		50.6	90	
3.1.4	E-participation*		45.3	81	
3.2	**General infrastructure**		**27.1**	**63**	
3.2.1	Electricity output, GWh/mn pop.	⊙	5,442.8	43	◆
3.2.2	Logistics performance*		31.8	71	
3.2.3	Gross capital formation, % GDP		25.3	51	
3.3	**Ecological sustainability**		**38.5**	**35**	●
3.3.1	GDP/unit of energy use		9.9	68	
3.3.2	Environmental performance*		47.5	49	
3.3.3	ISO 14001 environment/bn PPP$ GDP		5.8	16	●
	Market sophistication		**37.8**	**54**	
4.1	**Credit**		**18.6**	**96**	
4.1.1	Finance for startups and scaleups†		n/a	n/a	
4.1.2	Domestic credit to private sector, % GDP		60.0	60	
4.1.3	Loans from microfinance institutions, % GDP		1.3	21	
4.2	**Investment**		**n/a**	**[n/a]**	
4.2.1	Market capitalization, % GDP		n/a	n/a	
4.2.2	Venture capital (VC) investors, deals/bn PPP$ GDP		n/a	n/a	
4.2.3	VC recipients, deals/bn PPP$ GDP		n/a	n/a	
4.2.4	VC received, value, % GDP		n/a	n/a	
4.3	**Trade, diversification and market scale**		**56.9**	**73**	
4.3.1	Applied tariff rate, weighted avg., %		2.6	67	
4.3.2	Domestic industry diversification	⊙	87.3	60	
4.3.3	Domestic market scale, bn PPP$		16.2	130	○

			Score/ Value	Rank	
	Business sophistication		**28.1**	**66**	
5.1	**Knowledge workers**		**35.4**	**60**	
5.1.1	Knowledge-intensive employment, %	⊙	36.7	38	◆
5.1.2	Firms offering formal training, %		15.8	91	○ ◇
5.1.3	GERD performed by business, % GDP	⊙	0.2	55	
5.1.4	GERD financed by business, %	⊙	37.8	49	
5.1.5	Females employed w/advanced degrees, %	⊙	18.2	38	
5.2	**Innovation linkages**		**15.4**	**96**	
5.2.1	University–industry R&D collaboration†		36.5	81	
5.2.2	State of cluster development†		19.7	113	◇
5.2.3	GERD financed by abroad, % GDP	⊙	0.0	53	
5.2.4	Joint venture/strategic alliance deals/bn PPP$ GDP	⊙	0.0	30	● ◆
5.2.5	Patent families/bn PPP$ GDP		0.0	95	○ ◇
5.3	**Knowledge absorption**		**33.5**	**64**	
5.3.1	Intellectual property payments, % total trade		0.2	92	◇
5.3.2	High-tech imports, % total trade		6.5	96	
5.3.3	ICT services imports, % total trade		2.9	19	● ◆
5.3.4	FDI net inflows, % GDP		10.2	10	● ◆
5.3.5	Research talent, % in businesses	⊙	12.6	58	
	Knowledge and technology outputs		**18.8**	**80**	
6.1	**Knowledge creation**		**15.4**	**64**	
6.1.1	Patents by origin/bn PPP$ GDP	⊙	0.4	84	
6.1.2	PCT patents by origin/bn PPP$ GDP		0.2	38	
6.1.3	Utility models by origin/bn PPP$ GDP		n/a	n/a	
6.1.4	Scientific and technical articles/bn PPP$ GDP		23.0	31	● ◆
6.1.5	Citable documents H-index		2.5	122	○
6.2	**Knowledge impact**		**23.7**	**85**	
6.2.1	Labor productivity growth, %		1.4	48	
6.2.2	Unicorn valuation, % GDP		0.0	48	○ ◇
6.2.3	Software spending, % GDP		0.3	48	
6.2.4	High-tech manufacturing, %	⊙	10.3	90	
6.3	**Knowledge diffusion**		**17.4**	**87**	
6.3.1	Intellectual property receipts, % total trade		0.0	84	
6.3.2	Production and export complexity		n/a	n/a	
6.3.3	High-tech exports, % total trade		0.4	92	
6.3.4	ICT services exports, % total trade		4.0	27	●
6.3.5	ISO 9001 quality/bn PPP$ GDP		10.9	26	●
	Creative outputs		**17.2**	**85**	
7.1	**Intangible assets**		**5.3**	**118**	◇
7.1.1	Intangible asset intensity, top 15, %		−181.4	79	○ ◇
7.1.2	Trademarks by origin/bn PPP$ GDP	⊙	29.6	79	
7.1.3	Global brand value, top 5,000, % GDP		0.0	74	○ ◇
7.1.4	Industrial designs by origin/bn PPP$ GDP	⊙	0.1	114	
7.2	**Creative goods and services**		**9.8**	**[67]**	
7.2.1	Cultural and creative services exports, % total trade		0.9	36	
7.2.2	National feature films/mn pop. 15–69		n/a	n/a	
7.2.3	Entertainment and media market/th pop. 15–69		n/a	n/a	
7.2.4	Creative goods exports, % total trade		0.1	93	
7.3	**Online creativity**		**48.5**	**27**	● ◆
7.3.1	Generic top-level domains (TLDs)/th pop. 15–69		1.7	92	
7.3.2	Country-code TLDs/th pop. 15–69		100.0	1	● ◆
7.3.3	GitHub commits/mn pop. 15–69		27.1	37	◆
7.3.4	Mobile app creation/bn PPP$ GDP		65.0	65	

NOTES: ● indicates a strength; ○ a weakness; ◆ an income group strength; ◇ an income group weakness; * an index; † a survey question. ⊙ is used when the available economy data are older than the base year; see appendices for details, including the year of the data, at wipo.int/gii-ranking. Square brackets [ ] indicate that the data minimum coverage (DMC) requirements were not met at the sub-pillar or pillar level.

Morocco

GII 2023 rank

70

Output rank	Input rank	Income	Region	Population (mn)	GDP, PPP$ (bn)	GDP per capita, PPP$
55	90	Lower middle	NAWA	37.5	359.7	9,808

			Score/ Value	Rank	
	Institutions		**45.3**	**83**	
1.1	**Institutional environment**		**39.7**	**78**	
1.1.1	Operational stability for businesses*		44.4	82	
1.1.2	Government effectiveness*		34.9	74	
1.2	**Regulatory environment**		**55.2**	**87**	
1.2.1	Regulatory quality*		38.9	80	◆
1.2.2	Rule of law*		32.3	78	
1.2.3	Cost of redundancy dismissal		20.7	90	
1.3	**Business environment**		**41.1**	**82**	
1.3.1	Policies for doing business†		63.1	34	●◆
1.3.2	Entrepreneurship policies and culture†		19.1	70	
	Human capital and research		**25.6**	**86**	
2.1	**Education**		**43.4**	**[86]**	
2.1.1	Expenditure on education, % GDP		n/a	n/a	
2.1.2	Government funding/pupil, secondary, % GDP/cap		n/a	n/a	
2.1.3	School life expectancy, years		14.2	69	◆
2.1.4	PISA scales in reading, maths and science		367.9	75	○
2.1.5	Pupil–teacher ratio, secondary		20.6	99	
2.2	**Tertiary education**		**29.7**	**68**	
2.2.1	Tertiary enrolment, % gross		43.4	74	
2.2.2	Graduates in science and engineering, %		28.9	24	●
2.2.3	Tertiary inbound mobility, %		1.9	79	
2.3	**Research and development (R&D)**		**3.7**	**82**	
2.3.1	Researchers, FTE/mn pop.	⊙	1,073.5	51	◆
2.3.2	Gross expenditure on R&D, % GDP		n/a	n/a	
2.3.3	Global corporate R&D investors, top 3, mn USD		0.0	40	○◇
2.3.4	QS university ranking, top 3*		0.0	71	○◇
	Infrastructure		**30.0**	**94**	
3.1	**Information and communication technologies (ICTs)**		**56.0**	**88**	
3.1.1	ICT access*		86.7	42	●◆
3.1.2	ICT use*		70.0	72	◆
3.1.3	Government's online service*		41.7	105	
3.1.4	E-participation*		25.6	111	○
3.2	**General infrastructure**		**17.1**	**101**	
3.2.1	Electricity output, GWh/mn pop.		1,129.2	94	
3.2.2	Logistics performance*		n/a	n/a	
3.2.3	Gross capital formation, % GDP		29.3	26	●
3.3	**Ecological sustainability**		**17.1**	**98**	
3.3.1	GDP/unit of energy use		12.3	42	
3.3.2	Environmental performance*		16.1	118	○
3.3.3	ISO 14001 environment/bn PPP$ GDP		0.8	73	
	Market sophistication		**30.7**	**80**	
4.1	**Credit**		**25.1**	**78**	
4.1.1	Finance for startups and scaleups†		33.4	63	
4.1.2	Domestic credit to private sector, % GDP		91.0	34	●◆
4.1.3	Loans from microfinance institutions, % GDP		0.7	35	
4.2	**Investment**		**7.6**	**60**	
4.2.1	Market capitalization, % GDP		50.9	35	
4.2.2	Venture capital (VC) investors, deals/bn PPP$ GDP		0.0	65	
4.2.3	VC recipients, deals/bn PPP$ GDP		0.0	64	
4.2.4	VC received, value, % GDP		0.0	86	○
4.3	**Trade, diversification and market scale**		**59.5**	**58**	
4.3.1	Applied tariff rate, weighted avg., %		3.6	80	
4.3.2	Domestic industry diversification	⊙	94.2	33	●
4.3.3	Domestic market scale, bn PPP$		359.7	54	

			Score/ Value	Rank	
	Business sophistication		**20.4**	**107**	
5.1	**Knowledge workers**		**20.2**	**[98]**	
5.1.1	Knowledge-intensive employment, %	⊙	8.1	111	○
5.1.2	Firms offering formal training, %		35.7	45	
5.1.3	GERD performed by business, % GDP		n/a	n/a	
5.1.4	GERD financed by business, %		n/a	n/a	
5.1.5	Females employed w/advanced degrees, %	⊙	3.0	102	
5.2	**Innovation linkages**		**16.3**	**93**	
5.2.1	University–industry R&D collaboration†		28.8	99	
5.2.2	State of cluster development†		32.7	88	
5.2.3	GERD financed by abroad, % GDP		n/a	n/a	
5.2.4	Joint venture/strategic alliance deals/bn PPP$ GDP		0.0	103	
5.2.5	Patent families/bn PPP$ GDP		0.0	71	
5.3	**Knowledge absorption**		**24.8**	**105**	
5.3.1	Intellectual property payments, % total trade		0.3	81	
5.3.2	High-tech imports, % total trade		8.1	68	
5.3.3	ICT services imports, % total trade		1.2	75	
5.3.4	FDI net inflows, % GDP		1.3	93	
5.3.5	Research talent, % in businesses	⊙	7.0	64	
	Knowledge and technology outputs		**23.0**	**65**	
6.1	**Knowledge creation**		**13.1**	**69**	
6.1.1	Patents by origin/bn PPP$ GDP		0.8	69	
6.1.2	PCT patents by origin/bn PPP$ GDP		0.1	58	◆
6.1.3	Utility models by origin/bn PPP$ GDP		n/a	n/a	
6.1.4	Scientific and technical articles/bn PPP$ GDP		13.0	60	
6.1.5	Citable documents H-index		11.6	69	
6.2	**Knowledge impact**		**33.2**	**46**	
6.2.1	Labor productivity growth, %		1.3	53	
6.2.2	Unicorn valuation, % GDP		0.0	48	○◇
6.2.3	Software spending, % GDP		0.2	61	
6.2.4	High-tech manufacturing, %	⊙	42.8	23	●◆
6.3	**Knowledge diffusion**		**22.7**	**63**	
6.3.1	Intellectual property receipts, % total trade		0.0	86	
6.3.2	Production and export complexity		45.6	79	
6.3.3	High-tech exports, % total trade		2.1	57	
6.3.4	ICT services exports, % total trade		3.7	30	●
6.3.5	ISO 9001 quality/bn PPP$ GDP		3.6	68	
	Creative outputs		**29.8**	**55**	◆
7.1	**Intangible assets**		**49.2**	**28**	●◆
7.1.1	Intangible asset intensity, top 15, %		61.6	35	
7.1.2	Trademarks by origin/bn PPP$ GDP		61.3	38	●
7.1.3	Global brand value, top 5,000, % GDP		1.3	50	
7.1.4	Industrial designs by origin/bn PPP$ GDP		9.6	10	●◆
7.2	**Creative goods and services**		**2.9**	**98**	
7.2.1	Cultural and creative services exports, % total trade		0.4	59	
7.2.2	National feature films/mn pop. 15–69		0.3	76	○
7.2.3	Entertainment and media market/th pop. 15–69		0.1	59	○◇
7.2.4	Creative goods exports, % total trade		0.1	91	
7.3	**Online creativity**		**17.8**	**80**	
7.3.1	Generic top-level domains (TLDs)/th pop. 15–69		1.8	90	
7.3.2	Country-code TLDs/th pop. 15–69		1.3	84	
7.3.3	GitHub commits/mn pop. 15–69		2.9	91	
7.3.4	Mobile app creation/bn PPP$ GDP		65.1	64	

NOTES: ● indicates a strength; ○ a weakness; ◆ an income group strength; ◇ an income group weakness; * an index; † a survey question. ⊙ is used when the available economy data are older than the base year; see appendices for details, including the year of the data, at wipo.int/gii-ranking. Square brackets [ ] indicate that the data minimum coverage (DMC) requirements were not met at the sub-pillar or pillar level.

Mozambique

GII 2023 rank

126

Output rank	Input rank	Income	Region	Population (mn)	GDP, PPP$ (bn)	GDP per capita, PPP$
124	128	Low	SSA	33.0	48.0	1,457

			Score/Value	Rank	
	Institutions		**22.9**	**129**	◇
1.1	**Institutional environment**		**21.7**	**121**	
1.1.1	Operational stability for businesses*		27.8	120	
1.1.2	Government effectiveness*		15.6	116	
1.2	**Regulatory environment**		**28.6**	**127**	◇
1.2.1	Regulatory quality*		21.9	115	
1.2.2	Rule of law*		9.4	120	
1.2.3	Cost of redundancy dismissal		37.5	126	◇
1.3	**Business environment**		**18.3**	**122**	◇
1.3.1	Policies for doing business†	⊙	36.6	96	
1.3.2	Entrepreneurship policies and culture†	⊙	0.0	85	○◇
	Human capital and research		**14.8**	**116**	
2.1	**Education**		**41.5**	**97**	
2.1.1	Expenditure on education, % GDP		6.9	8	●◆
2.1.2	Government funding/pupil, secondary, % GDP/cap	⊙	39.6	2	
2.1.3	School life expectancy, years	⊙	10.0	105	
2.1.4	PISA scales in reading, maths and science		n/a	n/a	
2.1.5	Pupil–teacher ratio, secondary		45.2	125	○◇
2.2	**Tertiary education**		**1.5**	**127**	
2.2.1	Tertiary enrolment, % gross	⊙	7.3	119	
2.2.2	Graduates in science and engineering, %	⊙	9.6	110	◇
2.2.3	Tertiary inbound mobility, %	⊙	0.4	104	◇
2.3	**Research and development (R&D)**		**1.4**	**95**	
2.3.1	Researchers, FTE/mn pop.	⊙	43.0	96	
2.3.2	Gross expenditure on R&D, % GDP	⊙	0.3	74	
2.3.3	Global corporate R&D investors, top 3, mn USD		0.0	40	○◇
2.3.4	QS university ranking, top 3*		0.0	71	○◇
	Infrastructure		**27.2**	**103**	◆
3.1	**Information and communication technologies (ICTs)**		**20.1**	**128**	
3.1.1	ICT access*		16.3	126	
3.1.2	ICT use*		17.9	126	
3.1.3	Government's online service*		28.9	125	
3.1.4	E-participation*		17.4	125	◇
3.2	**General infrastructure**		**51.5**	**15**	●◆
3.2.1	Electricity output, GWh/mn pop.	⊙	608.9	106	◆
3.2.2	Logistics performance*		n/a	n/a	
3.2.3	Gross capital formation, % GDP		73.1	1	●◆
3.3	**Ecological sustainability**		**9.9**	**127**	
3.3.1	GDP/unit of energy use		3.6	123	◇
3.3.2	Environmental performance*		21.7	104	
3.3.3	ISO 14001 environment/bn PPP$ GDP		0.5	81	◆
	Market sophistication		**14.4**	**122**	
4.1	**Credit**		**2.5**	**129**	
4.1.1	Finance for startups and scaleups†	⊙	0.0	85	○◇
4.1.2	Domestic credit to private sector, % GDP		24.2	111	
4.1.3	Loans from microfinance institutions, % GDP		0.0	57	
4.2	**Investment**		**3.7**	**[88]**	
4.2.1	Market capitalization, % GDP		n/a	n/a	
4.2.2	Venture capital (VC) investors, deals/bn PPP$ GDP		n/a	n/a	
4.2.3	VC recipients, deals/bn PPP$ GDP	⊙	0.0	72	
4.2.4	VC received, value, % GDP	⊙	0.0	81	
4.3	**Trade, diversification and market scale**		**37.1**	**110**	
4.3.1	Applied tariff rate, weighted avg., %		4.1	86	◆
4.3.2	Domestic industry diversification		n/a	n/a	
4.3.3	Domestic market scale, bn PPP$		48.0	108	

			Score/Value	Rank	
	Business sophistication		**14.7**	**129**	
5.1	**Knowledge workers**		**4.8**	**130**	◇
5.1.1	Knowledge-intensive employment, %	⊙	3.9	122	
5.1.2	Firms offering formal training, %	⊙	20.7	79	
5.1.3	GERD performed by business, % GDP	⊙	0.0	91	
5.1.4	GERD financed by business, %	⊙	0.5	95	
5.1.5	Females employed w/advanced degrees, %	⊙	0.7	121	
5.2	**Innovation linkages**		**13.1**	**107**	
5.2.1	University–industry R&D collaboration†	⊙	23.5	107	
5.2.2	State of cluster development†	⊙	13.3	123	◇
5.2.3	GERD financed by abroad, % GDP	⊙	0.1	32	●
5.2.4	Joint venture/strategic alliance deals/bn PPP$ GDP		0.0	56	●
5.2.5	Patent families/bn PPP$ GDP		0.0	95	○◇
5.3	**Knowledge absorption**		**26.3**	**99**	
5.3.1	Intellectual property payments, % total trade		0.0	118	○◇
5.3.2	High-tech imports, % total trade		5.6	107	
5.3.3	ICT services imports, % total trade		1.6	54	●
5.3.4	FDI net inflows, % GDP		26.1	5	●◆
5.3.5	Research talent, % in businesses	⊙	0.3	84	
	Knowledge and technology outputs		**9.5**	**127**	
6.1	**Knowledge creation**		**7.6**	**94**	
6.1.1	Patents by origin/bn PPP$ GDP		0.7	70	●◆
6.1.2	PCT patents by origin/bn PPP$ GDP		0.0	101	○◇
6.1.3	Utility models by origin/bn PPP$ GDP		0.1	59	
6.1.4	Scientific and technical articles/bn PPP$ GDP		9.8	76	
6.1.5	Citable documents H-index		5.6	96	
6.2	**Knowledge impact**		**13.1**	**123**	
6.2.1	Labor productivity growth, %		−0.8	114	
6.2.2	Unicorn valuation, % GDP		0.0	48	○◇
6.2.3	Software spending, % GDP		0.0	117	
6.2.4	High-tech manufacturing, %		n/a	n/a	
6.3	**Knowledge diffusion**		**7.9**	**119**	
6.3.1	Intellectual property receipts, % total trade		0.0	114	○◇
6.3.2	Production and export complexity		32.1	110	
6.3.3	High-tech exports, % total trade		0.1	120	
6.3.4	ICT services exports, % total trade		0.2	119	
6.3.5	ISO 9001 quality/bn PPP$ GDP		1.5	95	◆
	Creative outputs		**7.2**	**115**	
7.1	**Intangible assets**		**13.6**	**101**	
7.1.1	Intangible asset intensity, top 15, %		n/a	n/a	
7.1.2	Trademarks by origin/bn PPP$ GDP		34.7	67	●
7.1.3	Global brand value, top 5,000, % GDP		0.0	74	○◇
7.1.4	Industrial designs by origin/bn PPP$ GDP		0.9	71	●
7.2	**Creative goods and services**		**0.5**	**[124]**	
7.2.1	Cultural and creative services exports, % total trade		n/a	n/a	
7.2.2	National feature films/mn pop. 15–69		n/a	n/a	
7.2.3	Entertainment and media market/th pop. 15–69		n/a	n/a	
7.2.4	Creative goods exports, % total trade		0.0	112	
7.3	**Online creativity**		**1.3**	**127**	
7.3.1	Generic top-level domains (TLDs)/th pop. 15–69		0.0	129	
7.3.2	Country-code TLDs/th pop. 15–69		0.2	112	
7.3.3	GitHub commits/mn pop. 15–69		0.2	125	
7.3.4	Mobile app creation/bn PPP$ GDP		4.6	123	◇

NOTES: ● indicates a strength; ○ a weakness; ◆ an income group strength; ◇ an income group weakness; * an index; † a survey question. ⊙ is used when the available economy data are older than the base year; see appendices for details, including the year of the data, at wipo.int/gii-ranking. Square brackets [ ] indicate that the data minimum coverage (DMC) requirements were not met at the sub-pillar or pillar level.

GII 2023 rank

Namibia

96

Output rank	Input rank	Income	Region	Population (mn)	GDP, PPP$ (bn)	GDP per capita, PPP$
111	80	Upper middle	SSA	2.6	28.0	10,791

			Score/ Value	Rank	
1	**Institutions**		**56.3**	**50**	●
1.1	**Institutional environment**		**47.0**	**60**	
1.1.1	Operational stability for businesses*		55.6	56	
1.1.2	Government effectiveness*		38.4	64	
1.2	**Regulatory environment**		**71.4**	**41**	●◆
1.2.1	Regulatory quality*		42.0	73	
1.2.2	Rule of law*		50.3	48	●◆
1.2.3	Cost of redundancy dismissal		9.7	28	●◆
1.3	**Business environment**		**50.4**	**[53]**	
1.3.1	Policies for doing business†		50.4	60	
1.3.2	Entrepreneurship policies and culture†		n/a	n/a	
2	**Human capital and research**		**28.2**	**76**	
2.1	**Education**		**74.7**	**[2]**	
2.1.1	Expenditure on education, % GDP		9.5	1	●◆
2.1.2	Government funding/pupil, secondary, % GDP/cap		n/a	n/a	
2.1.3	School life expectancy, years		n/a	n/a	
2.1.4	PISA scales in reading, maths and science		n/a	n/a	
2.1.5	Pupil–teacher ratio, secondary	⊙	25.9	112	◇
2.2	**Tertiary education**		**8.0**	**115**	◇
2.2.1	Tertiary enrolment, % gross		27.3	89	◇
2.2.2	Graduates in science and engineering, %		8.9	112	○◇
2.2.3	Tertiary inbound mobility, %		3.2	62	
2.3	**Research and development (R&D)**		**1.9**	**91**	
2.3.1	Researchers, FTE/mn pop.	⊙	149.5	86	
2.3.2	Gross expenditure on R&D, % GDP	⊙	0.3	71	
2.3.3	Global corporate R&D investors, top 3, mn USD		0.0	40	○◇
2.3.4	QS university ranking, top 3*		0.0	71	○◇
3	**Infrastructure**		**28.7**	**100**	◇
3.1	**Information and communication technologies (ICTs)**		**41.6**	**108**	◇
3.1.1	ICT access*		54.4	102	◇
3.1.2	ICT use*		51.3	102	◇
3.1.3	Government's online service*		37.2	113	◇
3.1.4	E-participation*		23.3	115	○◇
3.2	**General infrastructure**		**15.2**	**106**	
3.2.1	Electricity output, GWh/mn pop.	⊙	771.3	103	◇
3.2.2	Logistics performance*		36.4	65	
3.2.3	Gross capital formation, % GDP		15.1	118	○◇
3.3	**Ecological sustainability**		**29.4**	**56**	
3.3.1	GDP/unit of energy use		11.8	49	
3.3.2	Environmental performance*		54.2	37	●◆
3.3.3	ISO 14001 environment/bn PPP$ GDP		0.8	72	
4	**Market sophistication**		**29.0**	**[84]**	
4.1	**Credit**		**26.6**	**[74]**	
4.1.1	Finance for startups and scaleups†		n/a	n/a	
4.1.2	Domestic credit to private sector, % GDP		72.8	49	●
4.1.3	Loans from microfinance institutions, % GDP		n/a	n/a	
4.2	**Investment**		**7.0**	**[66]**	
4.2.1	Market capitalization, % GDP		18.8	60	
4.2.2	Venture capital (VC) investors, deals/bn PPP$ GDP		n/a	n/a	
4.2.3	VC recipients, deals/bn PPP$ GDP		n/a	n/a	
4.2.4	VC received, value, % GDP		n/a	n/a	
4.3	**Trade, diversification and market scale**		**53.3**	**80**	
4.3.1	Applied tariff rate, weighted avg., %		1.3	14	●
4.3.2	Domestic industry diversification	⊙	67.5	97	
4.3.3	Domestic market scale, bn PPP$		28.0	127	○

			Score/ Value	Rank	
5	**Business sophistication**		**21.6**	**99**	◇
5.1	**Knowledge workers**		**18.0**	**106**	◇
5.1.1	Knowledge-intensive employment, %	⊙	18.1	79	
5.1.2	Firms offering formal training, %	⊙	25.4	65	
5.1.3	GERD performed by business, % GDP	⊙	0.0	75	
5.1.4	GERD financed by business, %	⊙	11.1	73	
5.1.5	Females employed w/advanced degrees, %	⊙	7.4	88	◇
5.2	**Innovation linkages**		**21.9**	**65**	
5.2.1	University-industry R&D collaboration†		47.8	54	
5.2.2	State of cluster development†		38.0	77	
5.2.3	GERD financed by abroad, % GDP	⊙	0.1	46	
5.2.4	Joint venture/strategic alliance deals/bn PPP$ GDP		0.0	39	●
5.2.5	Patent families/bn PPP$ GDP		0.1	54	
5.3	**Knowledge absorption**		**25.1**	**103**	◇
5.3.1	Intellectual property payments, % total trade		0.0	110	◇
5.3.2	High-tech imports, % total trade	⊙	7.3	81	
5.3.3	ICT services imports, % total trade		1.8	42	●
5.3.4	FDI net inflows, % GDP		0.8	102	◇
5.3.5	Research talent, % in businesses	⊙	6.9	65	
6	**Knowledge and technology outputs**		**10.1**	**123**	○◇
6.1	**Knowledge creation**		**8.2**	**91**	
6.1.1	Patents by origin/bn PPP$ GDP	⊙	0.4	88	
6.1.2	PCT patents by origin/bn PPP$ GDP		0.1	52	
6.1.3	Utility models by origin/bn PPP$ GDP	⊙	0.2	41	
6.1.4	Scientific and technical articles/bn PPP$ GDP		10.9	71	
6.1.5	Citable documents H-index		4.7	106	
6.2	**Knowledge impact**		**9.4**	**128**	○◇
6.2.1	Labor productivity growth, %		–2.1	127	○◇
6.2.2	Unicorn valuation, % GDP		0.0	48	○◇
6.2.3	Software spending, % GDP		0.1	92	
6.2.4	High-tech manufacturing, %	⊙	4.7	102	
6.3	**Knowledge diffusion**		**12.8**	**95**	◇
6.3.1	Intellectual property receipts, % total trade		0.0	77	
6.3.2	Production and export complexity		41.4	91	
6.3.3	High-tech exports, % total trade	⊙	0.7	80	
6.3.4	ICT services exports, % total trade		0.4	105	
6.3.5	ISO 9001 quality/bn PPP$ GDP		1.9	89	
7	**Creative outputs**		**11.5**	**104**	◇
7.1	**Intangible assets**		**11.2**	**105**	◇
7.1.1	Intangible asset intensity, top 15, %		n/a	n/a	
7.1.2	Trademarks by origin/bn PPP$ GDP	⊙	14.4	101	◇
7.1.3	Global brand value, top 5,000, % GDP		0.0	74	○◇
7.1.4	Industrial designs by origin/bn PPP$ GDP	⊙	1.4	55	
7.2	**Creative goods and services**		**1.9**	**[105]**	
7.2.1	Cultural and creative services exports, % total trade		0.1	91	
7.2.2	National feature films/mn pop. 15–69		n/a	n/a	
7.2.3	Entertainment and media market/th pop. 15–69		n/a	n/a	
7.2.4	Creative goods exports, % total trade	⊙	0.2	78	
7.3	**Online creativity**		**21.5**	**61**	
7.3.1	Generic top-level domains (TLDs)/th pop. 15–69		10.0	42	●
7.3.2	Country-code TLDs/th pop. 15–69		0.9	94	
7.3.3	GitHub commits/mn pop. 15–69		2.0	100	
7.3.4	Mobile app creation/bn PPP$ GDP		73.2	39	●

NOTES: ● indicates a strength; ○ a weakness; ◆ an income group strength; ◇ an income group weakness; * an index; † a survey question. ⊙ is used when the available economy data are older than the base year; see appendices for details, including the year of the data, at wipo.int/gii-ranking. Square brackets [ ] indicate that the data minimum coverage (DMC) requirements were not met at the sub-pillar or pillar level.

Nepal

GII 2023 rank

108

Output rank	Input rank	Income	Region	Population (mn)	GDP, PPP$ (bn)	GDP per capita, PPP$
103	106	Lower middle	CSA	30.5	141.2	4,677

Institutions

			Score/Value	Rank	
	Institutions		**33.0**	**114**	
1.1	**Institutional environment**		**24.7**	**114**	
1.1.1	Operational stability for businesses*		36.8	104	
1.1.2	Government effectiveness*		12.7	122	
1.2	**Regulatory environment**		**44.0**	**113**	
1.2.1	Regulatory quality*		26.1	105	
1.2.2	Rule of law*		26.1	92	
1.2.3	Cost of redundancy dismissal		27.2	109	
1.3	**Business environment**		**30.2**	**[100]**	
1.3.1	Policies for doing business†		30.2	106	
1.3.2	Entrepreneurship policies and culture†		n/a	n/a	

Human capital and research

			Score/Value	Rank	
	Human capital and research		**13.0**	**[123]**	
2.1	**Education**		**30.2**	**120**	
2.1.1	Expenditure on education, % GDP		4.0	69	
2.1.2	Government funding/pupil, secondary, % GDP/cap	⊙	9.4	92	
2.1.3	School life expectancy, years		12.9	84	
2.1.4	PISA scales in reading, maths and science		n/a	n/a	
2.1.5	Pupil–teacher ratio, secondary		30.4	121	○◇
2.2	**Tertiary education**		**8.9**	**[113]**	
2.2.1	Tertiary enrolment, % gross		17.4	103	
2.2.2	Graduates in science and engineering, %		n/a	n/a	
2.2.3	Tertiary inbound mobility, %		n/a	n/a	
2.3	**Research and development (R&D)**		**0.0**	**[119]**	
2.3.1	Researchers, FTE/mn pop.		n/a	n/a	
2.3.2	Gross expenditure on R&D, % GDP		n/a	n/a	
2.3.3	Global corporate R&D investors, top 3, mn USD		0.0	40	○◇
2.3.4	QS university ranking, top 3*		0.0	71	○◇

Infrastructure

			Score/Value	Rank	
	Infrastructure		**23.6**	**110**	
3.1	**Information and communication technologies (ICTs)**		**35.2**	**117**	
3.1.1	ICT access*		43.8	116	
3.1.2	ICT use*		34.7	113	◇
3.1.3	Government's online service*		40.2	109	
3.1.4	E-participation*		22.1	120	
3.2	**General infrastructure**		**25.4**	**72**	
3.2.1	Electricity output, GWh/mn pop.	⊙	213.5	117	
3.2.2	Logistics performance*		n/a	n/a	
3.2.3	Gross capital formation, % GDP		42.3	5	●◆
3.3	**Ecological sustainability**		**10.3**	**126**	○◇
3.3.1	GDP/unit of energy use		6.6	103	
3.3.2	Environmental performance*		15.9	120	
3.3.3	ISO 14001 environment/bn PPP$ GDP		0.3	100	

Market sophistication

			Score/Value	Rank	
	Market sophistication		**35.3**	**63**	●
4.1	**Credit**		**66.4**	**7**	●◆
4.1.1	Finance for startups and scaleups†		n/a	n/a	
4.1.2	Domestic credit to private sector, % GDP		88.4	36	●◆
4.1.3	Loans from microfinance institutions, % GDP		8.5	1	●◆
4.2	**Investment**		**1.0**	**[108]**	
4.2.1	Market capitalization, % GDP		n/a	n/a	
4.2.2	Venture capital (VC) investors, deals/bn PPP$ GDP		n/a	n/a	
4.2.3	VC recipients, deals/bn PPP$ GDP	⊙	0.0	91	
4.2.4	VC received, value, % GDP	⊙	0.0	94	
4.3	**Trade, diversification and market scale**		**38.5**	**107**	
4.3.1	Applied tariff rate, weighted avg., %		11.6	125	○◇
4.3.2	Domestic industry diversification		87.6	58	●
4.3.3	Domestic market scale, bn PPP$		141.2	79	

Business sophistication

			Score/Value	Rank	
	Business sophistication		**23.2**	**[89]**	
5.1	**Knowledge workers**		**20.9**	**[96]**	
5.1.1	Knowledge-intensive employment, %	⊙	13.2	98	
5.1.2	Firms offering formal training, %	⊙	31.9	53	
5.1.3	GERD performed by business, % GDP		n/a	n/a	
5.1.4	GERD financed by business, %		n/a	n/a	
5.1.5	Females employed w/advanced degrees, %	⊙	2.9	103	
5.2	**Innovation linkages**		**14.1**	**102**	
5.2.1	University–industry R&D collaboration†		26.2	104	
5.2.2	State of cluster development†		25.7	104	
5.2.3	GERD financed by abroad, % GDP		n/a	n/a	
5.2.4	Joint venture/strategic alliance deals/bn PPP$ GDP		0.0	83	
5.2.5	Patent families/bn PPP$ GDP		0.0	95	○◇
5.3	**Knowledge absorption**		**34.5**	**[59]**	
5.3.1	Intellectual property payments, % total trade		n/a	n/a	
5.3.2	High-tech imports, % total trade		13.6	18	●
5.3.3	ICT services imports, % total trade		0.2	129	○◇
5.3.4	FDI net inflows, % GDP		0.5	113	
5.3.5	Research talent, % in businesses		n/a	n/a	

Knowledge and technology outputs

			Score/Value	Rank	
	Knowledge and technology outputs		**11.8**	**[110]**	
6.1	**Knowledge creation**		**11.4**	**[76]**	
6.1.1	Patents by origin/bn PPP$ GDP	⊙	0.2	101	
6.1.2	PCT patents by origin/bn PPP$ GDP		n/a	n/a	
6.1.3	Utility models by origin/bn PPP$ GDP		n/a	n/a	
6.1.4	Scientific and technical articles/bn PPP$ GDP		11.4	69	●
6.1.5	Citable documents H-index		8.3	86	
6.2	**Knowledge impact**		**18.1**	**113**	
6.2.1	Labor productivity growth, %		1.8	38	●
6.2.2	Unicorn valuation, % GDP		0.0	48	○◇
6.2.3	Software spending, % GDP		0.0	121	○◇
6.2.4	High-tech manufacturing, %		9.2	94	
6.3	**Knowledge diffusion**		**5.9**	**[124]**	
6.3.1	Intellectual property receipts, % total trade		n/a	n/a	
6.3.2	Production and export complexity		n/a	n/a	
6.3.3	High-tech exports, % total trade		0.1	124	○
6.3.4	ICT services exports, % total trade		1.3	75	
6.3.5	ISO 9001 quality/bn PPP$ GDP		2.5	82	

Creative outputs

			Score/Value	Rank	
	Creative outputs		**12.4**	**101**	
7.1	**Intangible assets**		**10.1**	**107**	
7.1.1	Intangible asset intensity, top 15, %		n/a	n/a	
7.1.2	Trademarks by origin/bn PPP$ GDP	⊙	40.7	56	●
7.1.3	Global brand value, top 5,000, % GDP		0.0	74	○◇
7.1.4	Industrial designs by origin/bn PPP$ GDP	⊙	0.2	109	
7.2	**Creative goods and services**		**10.0**	**[66]**	
7.2.1	Cultural and creative services exports, % total trade		n/a	n/a	
7.2.2	National feature films/mn pop. 15–69	⊙	2.6	42	●◆
7.2.3	Entertainment and media market/th pop. 15–69		n/a	n/a	
7.2.4	Creative goods exports, % total trade		0.3	71	
7.3	**Online creativity**		**19.1**	**70**	
7.3.1	Generic top-level domains (TLDs)/th pop. 15–69		0.6	109	
7.3.2	Country-code TLDs/th pop. 15–69		1.4	82	
7.3.3	GitHub commits/mn pop. 15–69		3.7	83	
7.3.4	Mobile app creation/bn PPP$ GDP		70.8	51	●

NOTES: ● indicates a strength; ○ a weakness; ◆ an income group strength; ◇ an income group weakness; * an index; † a survey question. ⊙ is used when the available economy data are older than the base year; see appendices for details, including the year of the data, at wipo.int/gii-ranking. Square brackets [ ] indicate that the data minimum coverage (DMC) requirements were not met at the sub-pillar or pillar level.

GII 2023 rank

Netherlands (Kingdom of the) 7

Output rank	Input rank	Income	Region	Population (mn)	GDP, PPP$ (bn)	GDP per capita, PPP$
5	10	High	EUR	17.6	1,226.7	69,715

		Score/ Value	Rank
	Institutions	**82.3**	**6 ●**
1.1	**Institutional environment**	**79.2**	**12**
1.1.1	Operational stability for businesses*	72.9	20
1.1.2	Government effectiveness*	85.5	6 ●
1.2	**Regulatory environment**	**86.8**	**15**
1.2.1	Regulatory quality*	87.6	7
1.2.2	Rule of law*	90.7	10
1.2.3	Cost of redundancy dismissal	15.9	65 ○
1.3	**Business environment**	**80.8**	**5 ●◆**
1.3.1	Policies for doing business†	77.7	13
1.3.2	Entrepreneurship policies and culture†	83.9	4 ●◆
	Human capital and research	**55.7**	**13**
2.1	**Education**	**62.9**	**19**
2.1.1	Expenditure on education, % GDP ⊙	5.2	34
2.1.2	Government funding/pupil, secondary, % GDP/cap	22.1	41 ○
2.1.3	School life expectancy, years	18.9	8
2.1.4	PISA scales in reading, maths and science	502.5	15
2.1.5	Pupil–teacher ratio, secondary	13.9	70 ○◇
2.2	**Tertiary education**	**41.3**	**32**
2.2.1	Tertiary enrolment, % gross	92.0	11
2.2.2	Graduates in science and engineering, %	18.8	82 ○◇
2.2.3	Tertiary inbound mobility, %	13.3	16
2.3	**Research and development (R&D)**	**63.0**	**11**
2.3.1	Researchers, FTE/mn pop.	6,069.3	10
2.3.2	Gross expenditure on R&D, % GDP	2.3	15
2.3.3	Global corporate R&D investors, top 3, mn USD	82.0	8
2.3.4	QS university ranking, top 3*	66.7	13
	Infrastructure	**60.2**	**14**
3.1	**Information and communication technologies (ICTs)**	**92.1**	**8**
3.1.1	ICT access*	91.3	19
3.1.2	ICT use*	91.4	18
3.1.3	Government's online service*	89.2	11
3.1.4	E-participation*	96.5	5 ●◆
3.2	**General infrastructure**	**47.3**	**24**
3.2.1	Electricity output, GWh/mn pop.	6,930.9	28
3.2.2	Logistics performance*	90.9	3 ●◆
3.2.3	Gross capital formation, % GDP	21.4	87 ○
3.3	**Ecological sustainability**	**41.3**	**29**
3.3.1	GDP/unit of energy use	13.3	35
3.3.2	Environmental performance*	74.1	11
3.3.3	ISO 14001 environment/bn PPP$ GDP	2.2	41
	Market sophistication	**55.6**	**15**
4.1	**Credit**	**63.1**	**13**
4.1.1	Finance for startups and scaleups†	88.4	3 ●◆
4.1.2	Domestic credit to private sector, % GDP	101.3	28
4.1.3	Loans from microfinance institutions, % GDP	n/a	n/a
4.2	**Investment**	**33.5**	**19**
4.2.1	Market capitalization, % GDP ⊙	109.9	12
4.2.2	Venture capital (VC) investors, deals/bn PPP$ GDP	0.4	16
4.2.3	VC recipients, deals/bn PPP$ GDP	0.1	23
4.2.4	VC received, value, % GDP	0.0	20
4.3	**Trade, diversification and market scale**	**70.1**	**20**
4.3.1	Applied tariff rate, weighted avg., %	1.5	20 ○
4.3.2	Domestic industry diversification	93.7	37
4.3.3	Domestic market scale, bn PPP$	1,226.7	27

		Score/ Value	Rank
	Business sophistication	**62.3**	**8**
5.1	**Knowledge workers**	**65.8**	**13**
5.1.1	Knowledge-intensive employment, %	53.6	4 ●
5.1.2	Firms offering formal training, %	54.1	14
5.1.3	GERD performed by business, % GDP	1.5	16
5.1.4	GERD financed by business, %	56.9	18
5.1.5	Females employed w/advanced degrees, %	23.2	24
5.2	**Innovation linkages**	**65.5**	**7**
5.2.1	University–industry R&D collaboration†	87.9	4 ●
5.2.2	State of cluster development†	83.9	6
5.2.3	GERD financed by abroad, % GDP	0.2	14
5.2.4	Joint venture/strategic alliance deals/bn PPP$ GDP	0.1	22
5.2.5	Patent families/bn PPP$ GDP	4.4	9
5.3	**Knowledge absorption**	**55.6**	**10**
5.3.1	Intellectual property payments, % total trade	6.1	1 ●◆
5.3.2	High-tech imports, % total trade	12.0	21
5.3.3	ICT services imports, % total trade	2.9	21
5.3.4	FDI net inflows, % GDP	–13.2	132 ○◇
5.3.5	Research talent, % in businesses	70.2	6
	Knowledge and technology outputs	**58.8**	**8**
6.1	**Knowledge creation**	**66.7**	**4 ●**
6.1.1	Patents by origin/bn PPP$ GDP	7.9	10
6.1.2	PCT patents by origin/bn PPP$ GDP	3.3	9
6.1.3	Utility models by origin/bn PPP$ GDP	n/a	n/a
6.1.4	Scientific and technical articles/bn PPP$ GDP	31.7	17
6.1.5	Citable documents H-index	70.2	6 ●
6.2	**Knowledge impact**	**50.9**	**14**
6.2.1	Labor productivity growth, %	–0.1	104 ○
6.2.2	Unicorn valuation, % GDP	2.2	16
6.2.3	Software spending, % GDP	0.7	11
6.2.4	High-tech manufacturing, %	47.4	15
6.3	**Knowledge diffusion**	**58.9**	**7**
6.3.1	Intellectual property receipts, % total trade	6.5	1 ●◆
6.3.2	Production and export complexity	73.2	28
6.3.3	High-tech exports, % total trade	11.8	14
6.3.4	ICT services exports, % total trade	4.2	25
6.3.5	ISO 9001 quality/bn PPP$ GDP	8.4	32
	Creative outputs	**56.3**	**9**
7.1	**Intangible assets**	**50.7**	**24**
7.1.1	Intangible asset intensity, top 15, %	80.5	6
7.1.2	Trademarks by origin/bn PPP$ GDP	49.7	46 ○
7.1.3	Global brand value, top 5,000, % GDP	9.1	21
7.1.4	Industrial designs by origin/bn PPP$ GDP	3.6	27
7.2	**Creative goods and services**	**36.6**	**19**
7.2.1	Cultural and creative services exports, % total trade	1.8	14
7.2.2	National feature films/mn pop. 15–69	3.1	38 ○
7.2.3	Entertainment and media market/th pop. 15–69	49.8	18
7.2.4	Creative goods exports, % total trade	3.5	16
7.3	**Online creativity**	**87.2**	**1 ●◆**
7.3.1	Generic top-level domains (TLDs)/th pop. 15–69	92.4	5 ●◆
7.3.2	Country-code TLDs/th pop. 15–69	100.0	1 ●◆
7.3.3	GitHub commits/mn pop. 15–69	82.8	4 ●
7.3.4	Mobile app creation/bn PPP$ GDP	73.7	34

NOTES: ● indicates a strength; ○ a weakness; ◆ an income group strength; ◇ an income group weakness; * an index; † a survey question. ⊙ is used when the available economy data are older than the base year; see appendices for details, including the year of the data, at wipo.int/gii-ranking. Square brackets [ ] indicate that the data minimum coverage (DMC) requirements were not met at the sub-pillar or pillar level.

GII 2023 rank

New Zealand

27

Output rank	Input rank	Income	Region	Population (mn)	GDP, PPP$ (bn)	GDP per capita, PPP$
31	24	High	SEAO	5.2	261.0	50,851

			Score/ Value	Rank
Institutions			**78.5**	**12**
1.1	**Institutional environment**		**83.9**	**9 ●◆**
1.1.1	Operational stability for businesses*		93.8	2 ●◆
1.1.2	Government effectiveness*		74.0	20
1.2	**Regulatory environment**		**95.5**	**3 ●◆**
1.2.1	Regulatory quality*		89.0	6 ●◆
1.2.2	Rule of law*		93.0	5 ●◆
1.2.3	Cost of redundancy dismissal		8.0	1 ●◆
1.3	**Business environment**		**56.2**	**[44]**
1.3.1	Policies for doing business†		56.2	47
1.3.2	Entrepreneurship policies and culture†		n/a	n/a
Human capital and research			**51.1**	**21**
2.1	**Education**		**61.4**	**27**
2.1.1	Expenditure on education, % GDP	⊙	5.2	32
2.1.2	Government funding/pupil, secondary, % GDP/cap		14.8	75 ○◇
2.1.3	School life expectancy, years		20.3	2 ●◆
2.1.4	PISA scales in reading, maths and science		502.9	13
2.1.5	Pupil–teacher ratio, secondary		14.6	74 ○◇
2.2	**Tertiary education**		**46.8**	**15**
2.2.1	Tertiary enrolment, % gross		79.9	25
2.2.2	Graduates in science and engineering, %		23.6	52
2.2.3	Tertiary inbound mobility, %		17.5	11
2.3	**Research and development (R&D)**		**45.2**	**22**
2.3.1	Researchers, FTE/mn pop.	⊙	5,585.9	12
2.3.2	Gross expenditure on R&D, % GDP	⊙	1.4	31
2.3.3	Global corporate R&D investors, top 3, mn USD		49.9	33
2.3.4	QS university ranking, top 3*		47.8	24
Infrastructure			**56.1**	**29**
3.1	**Information and communication technologies (ICTs)**		**91.3**	**10 ●**
3.1.1	ICT access*		87.6	37
3.1.2	ICT use*		87.0	29
3.1.3	Government's online service*		95.3	6 ●◆
3.1.4	E-participation*		95.3	6 ●◆
3.2	**General infrastructure**		**44.1**	**26**
3.2.1	Electricity output, GWh/mn pop.		8,519.3	17
3.2.2	Logistics performance*		68.2	25
3.2.3	Gross capital formation, % GDP		24.5	61
3.3	**Ecological sustainability**		**32.9**	**43**
3.3.1	GDP/unit of energy use		9.9	69 ○
3.3.2	Environmental performance*		64.1	26
3.3.3	ISO 14001 environment/bn PPP$ GDP		1.6	54
Market sophistication			**46.7**	**31**
4.1	**Credit**		**61.2**	**[17]**
4.1.1	Finance for startups and scaleups†		n/a	n/a
4.1.2	Domestic credit to private sector, % GDP		160.5	9 ●◆
4.1.3	Loans from microfinance institutions, % GDP		n/a	n/a
4.2	**Investment**		**20.2**	**35**
4.2.1	Market capitalization, % GDP		51.2	34
4.2.2	Venture capital (VC) investors, deals/bn PPP$ GDP		0.2	26
4.2.3	VC recipients, deals/bn PPP$ GDP		0.1	16
4.2.4	VC received, value, % GDP		0.0	52 ○
4.3	**Trade, diversification and market scale**		**58.6**	**65 ○**
4.3.1	Applied tariff rate, weighted avg., %		0.8	9 ●
4.3.2	Domestic industry diversification		75.8	85 ○
4.3.3	Domestic market scale, bn PPP$		261.0	61

			Score/ Value	Rank
Business sophistication			**45.7**	**29**
5.1	**Knowledge workers**		**49.6**	**[32]**
5.1.1	Knowledge-intensive employment, %		n/a	n/a
5.1.2	Firms offering formal training, %		n/a	n/a
5.1.3	GERD performed by business, % GDP	⊙	0.9	27
5.1.4	GERD financed by business, %	⊙	49.9	30
5.1.5	Females employed w/advanced degrees, %	⊙	21.5	27
5.2	**Innovation linkages**		**36.9**	**31**
5.2.1	University–industry R&D collaboration†		56.2	42
5.2.2	State of cluster development†		50.1	45
5.2.3	GERD financed by abroad, % GDP	⊙	0.1	31
5.2.4	Joint venture/strategic alliance deals/bn PPP$ GDP		0.1	21
5.2.5	Patent families/bn PPP$ GDP		1.3	25
5.3	**Knowledge absorption**		**50.5**	**18**
5.3.1	Intellectual property payments, % total trade		1.7	19
5.3.2	High-tech imports, % total trade		11.0	26
5.3.3	ICT services imports, % total trade		3.6	10 ●◆
5.3.4	FDI net inflows, % GDP		1.7	81 ○
5.3.5	Research talent, % in businesses	⊙	35.7	36
Knowledge and technology outputs			**31.8**	**39**
6.1	**Knowledge creation**		**40.1**	**24**
6.1.1	Patents by origin/bn PPP$ GDP		1.4	48
6.1.2	PCT patents by origin/bn PPP$ GDP		1.3	21
6.1.3	Utility models by origin/bn PPP$ GDP		n/a	n/a
6.1.4	Scientific and technical articles/bn PPP$ GDP		36.6	11 ●
6.1.5	Citable documents H-index		35.8	27
6.2	**Knowledge impact**		**24.1**	**78 ○◇**
6.2.1	Labor productivity growth, %		1.1	61
6.2.2	Unicorn valuation, % GDP		0.0	48 ○◇
6.2.3	Software spending, % GDP		0.2	55
6.2.4	High-tech manufacturing, %		16.1	74 ○◇
6.3	**Knowledge diffusion**		**31.1**	**52**
6.3.1	Intellectual property receipts, % total trade		1.7	15
6.3.2	Production and export complexity		56.0	53
6.3.3	High-tech exports, % total trade		1.8	64 ○
6.3.4	ICT services exports, % total trade		1.9	61
6.3.5	ISO 9001 quality/bn PPP$ GDP		4.4	58
Creative outputs			**43.3**	**28**
7.1	**Intangible assets**		**46.7**	**34**
7.1.1	Intangible asset intensity, top 15, %		58.4	39
7.1.2	Trademarks by origin/bn PPP$ GDP		101.1	12 ◆
7.1.3	Global brand value, top 5,000, % GDP		3.5	40
7.1.4	Industrial designs by origin/bn PPP$ GDP		1.3	59
7.2	**Creative goods and services**		**24.9**	**40**
7.2.1	Cultural and creative services exports, % total trade		0.7	43
7.2.2	National feature films/mn pop. 15–69		4.2	32
7.2.3	Entertainment and media market/th pop. 15–69		54.6	13
7.2.4	Creative goods exports, % total trade		0.4	65 ○
7.3	**Online creativity**		**54.8**	**18**
7.3.1	Generic top-level domains (TLDs)/th pop. 15–69		34.5	20
7.3.2	Country-code TLDs/th pop. 15–69		61.1	15
7.3.3	GitHub commits/mn pop. 15–69		53.1	19
7.3.4	Mobile app creation/bn PPP$ GDP		70.7	52

NOTES: ● indicates a strength; ○ a weakness; ◆ an income group strength; ◇ an income group weakness; * an index; † a survey question. ⊙ is used when the available economy data are older than the base year; see appendices for details, including the year of the data, at wipo.int/gii-ranking. Square brackets [ ] indicate that the data minimum coverage (DMC) requirements were not met at the sub-pillar or pillar level.

Nicaragua

GII 2023 rank

115

Output rank	Input rank	Income	Region	Population (mn)	GDP, PPP$ (bn)	GDP per capita, PPP$
118	110	Lower middle	LCN	6.9	47.3	7,154

			Score/ Value	Rank	
	Institutions		**25.2**	**127**	◇
1.1	**Institutional environment**		**23.3**	**117**	
1.1.1	Operational stability for businesses*		33.3	114	
1.1.2	Government effectiveness*		13.2	120	
1.2	**Regulatory environment**		**48.2**	**105**	
1.2.1	Regulatory quality*		20.4	117	
1.2.2	Rule of law*		0.0	132	○◇
1.2.3	Cost of redundancy dismissal		14.9	60	●
1.3	**Business environment**		**4.2**	**[131]**	
1.3.1	Policies for doing business†	⊙	4.2	128	○◇
1.3.2	Entrepreneurship policies and culture†		n/a	n/a	
	Human capital and research		**14.0**	**[120]**	
2.1	**Education**		**31.3**	**[117]**	
2.1.1	Expenditure on education, % GDP		4.1	67	
2.1.2	Government funding/pupil, secondary, % GDP/cap		n/a	n/a	
2.1.3	School life expectancy, years		n/a	n/a	
2.1.4	PISA scales in reading, maths and science		n/a	n/a	
2.1.5	Pupil–teacher ratio, secondary		n/a	n/a	
2.2	**Tertiary education**		**10.0**	**[112]**	
2.2.1	Tertiary enrolment, % gross	⊙	19.1	102	
2.2.2	Graduates in science and engineering, %		n/a	n/a	
2.2.3	Tertiary inbound mobility, %		n/a	n/a	
2.3	**Research and development (R&D)**		**0.6**	**108**	
2.3.1	Researchers, FTE/mn pop.		n/a	n/a	
2.3.2	Gross expenditure on R&D, % GDP	⊙	0.1	103	
2.3.3	Global corporate R&D investors, top 3, mn USD		0.0	40	○◇
2.3.4	QS university ranking, top 3*		0.0	71	○◇
	Infrastructure		**23.2**	**113**	
3.1	**Information and communication technologies (ICTs)**		**38.8**	**109**	
3.1.1	ICT access*		44.2	114	
3.1.2	ICT use*		44.9	108	
3.1.3	Government's online service*		42.6	104	
3.1.4	E-participation*		23.3	115	
3.2	**General infrastructure**		**13.6**	**110**	
3.2.1	Electricity output, GWh/mn pop.	⊙	572.1	108	
3.2.2	Logistics performance*		18.2	89	
3.2.3	Gross capital formation, % GDP		24.1	67	●
3.3	**Ecological sustainability**		**17.1**	**97**	
3.3.1	GDP/unit of energy use		8.5	85	
3.3.2	Environmental performance*		31.9	82	
3.3.3	ISO 14001 environment/bn PPP$ GDP		0.2	117	
	Market sophistication		**37.0**	**58**	●
4.1	**Credit**		**21.3**	**89**	
4.1.1	Finance for startups and scaleups†		n/a	n/a	
4.1.2	Domestic credit to private sector, % GDP		30.1	96	
4.1.3	Loans from microfinance institutions, % GDP		2.8	13	●
4.2	**Investment**		**n/a**	**[n/a]**	
4.2.1	Market capitalization, % GDP		n/a	n/a	
4.2.2	Venture capital (VC) investors, deals/bn PPP$ GDP		n/a	n/a	
4.2.3	VC recipients, deals/bn PPP$ GDP		n/a	n/a	
4.2.4	VC received, value, % GDP		n/a	n/a	
4.3	**Trade, diversification and market scale**		**52.8**	**82**	
4.3.1	Applied tariff rate, weighted avg., %		1.8	57	●◆
4.3.2	Domestic industry diversification		69.3	96	
4.3.3	Domestic market scale, bn PPP$		47.3	109	

			Score/ Value	Rank	
	Business sophistication		**21.8**	**97**	
5.1	**Knowledge workers**		**37.5**	**[53]**	
5.1.1	Knowledge-intensive employment, %	⊙	13.8	94	
5.1.2	Firms offering formal training, %	⊙	57.3	11	●◆
5.1.3	GERD performed by business, % GDP		n/a	n/a	
5.1.4	GERD financed by business, %		n/a	n/a	
5.1.5	Females employed w/advanced degrees, %	⊙	6.1	90	
5.2	**Innovation linkages**		**3.4**	**129**	◇
5.2.1	University–industry R&D collaboration†	⊙	2.9	128	○◇
5.2.2	State of cluster development†	⊙	4.5	127	◇
5.2.3	GERD financed by abroad, % GDP		n/a	n/a	
5.2.4	Joint venture/strategic alliance deals/bn PPP$ GDP		0.0	67	●
5.2.5	Patent families/bn PPP$ GDP		0.0	95	○◇
5.3	**Knowledge absorption**		**24.3**	**109**	
5.3.1	Intellectual property payments, % total trade		0.0	112	◇
5.3.2	High-tech imports, % total trade		8.0	69	●
5.3.3	ICT services imports, % total trade		0.4	122	
5.3.4	FDI net inflows, % GDP		6.2	14	●◆
5.3.5	Research talent, % in businesses		n/a	n/a	
	Knowledge and technology outputs		**10.2**	**122**	
6.1	**Knowledge creation**		**1.7**	**126**	◇
6.1.1	Patents by origin/bn PPP$ GDP	⊙	0.0	124	
6.1.2	PCT patents by origin/bn PPP$ GDP		0.0	101	○◇
6.1.3	Utility models by origin/bn PPP$ GDP		n/a	n/a	
6.1.4	Scientific and technical articles/bn PPP$ GDP		1.9	125	
6.1.5	Citable documents H-index		3.5	119	
6.2	**Knowledge impact**		**15.0**	**122**	
6.2.1	Labor productivity growth, %		−0.6	110	
6.2.2	Unicorn valuation, % GDP		0.0	48	○◇
6.2.3	Software spending, % GDP		0.1	103	
6.2.4	High-tech manufacturing, %		14.4	79	
6.3	**Knowledge diffusion**		**13.9**	**93**	
6.3.1	Intellectual property receipts, % total trade		0.0	114	○◇
6.3.2	Production and export complexity		35.7	100	
6.3.3	High-tech exports, % total trade		0.4	93	
6.3.4	ICT services exports, % total trade		3.1	41	●
6.3.5	ISO 9001 quality/bn PPP$ GDP		0.7	114	
	Creative outputs		**8.7**	**111**	
7.1	**Intangible assets**		**8.9**	**109**	
7.1.1	Intangible asset intensity, top 15, %		n/a	n/a	
7.1.2	Trademarks by origin/bn PPP$ GDP	⊙	41.0	55	
7.1.3	Global brand value, top 5,000, % GDP		0.0	74	○◇
7.1.4	Industrial designs by origin/bn PPP$ GDP	⊙	0.0	120	
7.2	**Creative goods and services**		**9.4**	**[69]**	
7.2.1	Cultural and creative services exports, % total trade		n/a	n/a	
7.2.2	National feature films/mn pop. 15–69		n/a	n/a	
7.2.3	Entertainment and media market/th pop. 15–69		n/a	n/a	
7.2.4	Creative goods exports, % total trade		0.8	52	●
7.3	**Online creativity**		**7.7**	**119**	◇
7.3.1	Generic top-level domains (TLDs)/th pop. 15–69		3.0	72	
7.3.2	Country-code TLDs/th pop. 15–69		0.3	109	
7.3.3	GitHub commits/mn pop. 15–69		1.6	106	
7.3.4	Mobile app creation/bn PPP$ GDP	⊙	26.1	120	◇

NOTES: ● indicates a strength; ○ a weakness; ◆ an income group strength; ◇ an income group weakness; * an index; † a survey question. ⊙ is used when the available economy data are older than the base year; see appendices for details, including the year of the data, at wipo.int/gii-ranking. Square brackets [ ] indicate that the data minimum coverage (DMC) requirements were not met at the sub-pillar or pillar level.

Niger

GII 2023 rank

131

Output rank	Input rank	Income	Region	Population (mn)	GDP, PPP$ (bn)	GDP per capita, PPP$
131	124	Low	SSA	26.2	37.6	1,443

	Institutions		Score/Value	Rank	
	Institutions		**40.9**	**94**	
1.1	**Institutional environment**		**25.2**	**112**	
1.1.1	Operational stability for businesses*		30.6	117	
1.1.2	Government effectiveness*		19.8	104	
1.2	**Regulatory environment**		**56.7**	**82**	●
1.2.1	Regulatory quality*		22.8	114	
1.2.2	Rule of law*		27.9	87	
1.2.3	Cost of redundancy dismissal		14.0	54	●
1.3	**Business environment**		**n/a**	**[n/a]**	
1.3.1	Policies for doing business†		n/a	n/a	
1.3.2	Entrepreneurship policies and culture†		n/a	n/a	

	Human capital and research		Score/Value	Rank	
	Human capital and research		**9.0**	**130**	◇
2.1	**Education**		**19.1**	**129**	◇
2.1.1	Expenditure on education, % GDP	⊙	3.5	93	
2.1.2	Government funding/pupil, secondary, % GDP/cap	⊙	11.8	87	◇
2.1.3	School life expectancy, years	⊙	6.4	113	○◇
2.1.4	PISA scales in reading, maths and science		n/a	n/a	
2.1.5	Pupil–teacher ratio, secondary	⊙	29.7	120	
2.2	**Tertiary education**		**8.0**	**114**	
2.2.1	Tertiary enrolment, % gross		4.4	127	○◇
2.2.2	Graduates in science and engineering, %	⊙	12.3	104	◇
2.2.3	Tertiary inbound mobility, %	⊙	5.4	46	●◆
2.3	**Research and development (R&D)**		**0.0**	**118**	
2.3.1	Researchers, FTE/mn pop.	⊙	26.5	102	
2.3.2	Gross expenditure on R&D, % GDP		n/a	n/a	
2.3.3	Global corporate R&D investors, top 3, mn USD		0.0	40	○◇
2.3.4	QS university ranking, top 3*		0.0	71	○◇

	Infrastructure		Score/Value	Rank	
	Infrastructure		**17.7**	**125**	
3.1	**Information and communication technologies (ICTs)**		**17.1**	**131**	◇
3.1.1	ICT access*		0.0	132	○◇
3.1.2	ICT use*		12.7	130	
3.1.3	Government's online service*		32.6	119	
3.1.4	E-participation*		23.3	115	
3.2	**General infrastructure**		**19.1**	**95**	
3.2.1	Electricity output, GWh/mn pop.	⊙	26.4	126	○◇
3.2.2	Logistics performance*		n/a	n/a	
3.2.3	Gross capital formation, % GDP		35.3	12	●
3.3	**Ecological sustainability**		**17.0**	**99**	◆
3.3.1	GDP/unit of energy use		8.5	84	◆
3.3.2	Environmental performance*		31.9	82	●◆
3.3.3	ISO 14001 environment/bn PPP$ GDP		0.1	124	

	Market sophistication		Score/Value	Rank	
	Market sophistication		**15.8**	**120**	
4.1	**Credit**		**3.2**	**127**	
4.1.1	Finance for startups and scaleups†		n/a	n/a	
4.1.2	Domestic credit to private sector, % GDP		11.7	127	◇
4.1.3	Loans from microfinance institutions, % GDP		0.3	43	
4.2	**Investment**		**6.3**	**[69]**	
4.2.1	Market capitalization, % GDP		n/a	n/a	
4.2.2	Venture capital (VC) investors, deals/bn PPP$ GDP		n/a	n/a	
4.2.3	VC recipients, deals/bn PPP$ GDP	⊙	0.0	44	●
4.2.4	VC received, value, % GDP	⊙	0.0	95	
4.3	**Trade, diversification and market scale**		**38.1**	**108**	
4.3.1	Applied tariff rate, weighted avg., %		8.1	105	
4.3.2	Domestic industry diversification	⊙	65.6	99	
4.3.3	Domestic market scale, bn PPP$		37.6	120	

	Business sophistication		Score/Value	Rank	
	Business sophistication		**17.8**	**[116]**	
5.1	**Knowledge workers**		**17.4**	**[108]**	
5.1.1	Knowledge-intensive employment, %	⊙	15.3	87	◆
5.1.2	Firms offering formal training, %	⊙	27.5	60	●
5.1.3	GERD performed by business, % GDP		n/a	n/a	
5.1.4	GERD financed by business, %		n/a	n/a	
5.1.5	Females employed w/advanced degrees, %	⊙	0.7	123	
5.2	**Innovation linkages**		**1.8**	**[130]**	
5.2.1	University–industry R&D collaboration†		n/a	n/a	
5.2.2	State of cluster development†		n/a	n/a	
5.2.3	GERD financed by abroad, % GDP		n/a	n/a	
5.2.4	Joint venture/strategic alliance deals/bn PPP$ GDP	⊙	0.0	90	
5.2.5	Patent families/bn PPP$ GDP		0.0	95	○◇
5.3	**Knowledge absorption**		**34.4**	**60**	●◆
5.3.1	Intellectual property payments, % total trade		0.0	118	○◇
5.3.2	High-tech imports, % total trade		7.2	84	●
5.3.3	ICT services imports, % total trade		2.6	26	●◆
5.3.4	FDI net inflows, % GDP		4.1	30	●
5.3.5	Research talent, % in businesses		n/a	n/a	

	Knowledge and technology outputs		Score/Value	Rank	
	Knowledge and technology outputs		**9.0**	**129**	
6.1	**Knowledge creation**		**2.6**	**123**	
6.1.1	Patents by origin/bn PPP$ GDP		0.1	109	
6.1.2	PCT patents by origin/bn PPP$ GDP		0.0	101	○◇
6.1.3	Utility models by origin/bn PPP$ GDP		0.0	75	○◇
6.1.4	Scientific and technical articles/bn PPP$ GDP		4.0	113	◇
6.1.5	Citable documents H-index		3.4	120	
6.2	**Knowledge impact**		**20.5**	**101**	
6.2.1	Labor productivity growth, %		1.9	36	●
6.2.2	Unicorn valuation, % GDP		0.0	48	○◇
6.2.3	Software spending, % GDP		0.0	119	
6.2.4	High-tech manufacturing, %	⊙	15.8	75	
6.3	**Knowledge diffusion**		**3.9**	**127**	◇
6.3.1	Intellectual property receipts, % total trade		0.0	109	
6.3.2	Production and export complexity		n/a	n/a	
6.3.3	High-tech exports, % total trade		0.5	89	◆
6.3.4	ICT services exports, % total trade		0.7	94	
6.3.5	ISO 9001 quality/bn PPP$ GDP		0.2	130	◇

	Creative outputs		Score/Value	Rank	
	Creative outputs		**0.2**	**[132]**	
7.1	**Intangible assets**		**0.0**	**[132]**	
7.1.1	Intangible asset intensity, top 15, %		n/a	n/a	
7.1.2	Trademarks by origin/bn PPP$ GDP		1.4	128	○◇
7.1.3	Global brand value, top 5,000, % GDP		n/a	n/a	
7.1.4	Industrial designs by origin/bn PPP$ GDP		0.0	120	○◇
7.2	**Creative goods and services**		**0.5**	**[123]**	
7.2.1	Cultural and creative services exports, % total trade		0.0	92	
7.2.2	National feature films/mn pop. 15–69		n/a	n/a	
7.2.3	Entertainment and media market/th pop. 15–69		n/a	n/a	
7.2.4	Creative goods exports, % total trade		0.0	125	
7.3	**Online creativity**		**0.3**	**128**	◇
7.3.1	Generic top-level domains (TLDs)/th pop. 15–69		0.9	100	◆
7.3.2	Country-code TLDs/th pop. 15–69		0.0	130	
7.3.3	GitHub commits/mn pop. 15–69		0.0	132	○◇
7.3.4	Mobile app creation/bn PPP$ GDP		n/a	n/a	

NOTES: ● indicates a strength; ○ a weakness; ◆ an income group strength; ◇ an income group weakness; * an index; † a survey question. ⊙ is used when the available economy data are older than the base year; see appendices for details, including the year of the data, at wipo.int/gii-ranking. Square brackets [ ] indicate that the data minimum coverage (DMC) requirements were not met at the sub-pillar or pillar level.

Nigeria

GII 2023 rank **109**

Output rank	Input rank	Income	Region	Population (mn)	GDP, PPP$ (bn)	GDP per capita, PPP$
98	**116**	**Lower middle**	**SSA**	**218.5**	**1,275.3**	**5,884**

Code	Indicator		Score/ Value	Rank	
1	**Institutions**		**32.9**	**115**	
1.1	**Institutional environment**		**13.0**	**129**	○◇
1.1.1	Operational stability for businesses*		16.7	128	○◇
1.1.2	Government effectiveness*		9.3	125	○◇
1.2	**Regulatory environment**		**58.1**	**79**	
1.2.1	Regulatory quality*		17.9	124	
1.2.2	Rule of law*		14.7	112	
1.2.3	Cost of redundancy dismissal		8.0	1	●◆
1.3	**Business environment**		**27.6**	**[106]**	
1.3.1	Policies for doing business†		27.6	110	
1.3.2	Entrepreneurship policies and culture†		n/a	n/a	
2	**Human capital and research**		**27.8**	**[80]**	
2.1	**Education**		**78.1**	**[1]**	
2.1.1	Expenditure on education, % GDP		n/a	n/a	
2.1.2	Government funding/pupil, secondary, % GDP/cap		n/a	n/a	
2.1.3	School life expectancy, years		n/a	n/a	
2.1.4	PISA scales in reading, maths and science		n/a	n/a	
2.1.5	Pupil–teacher ratio, secondary	⏱	14.7	75	
2.2	**Tertiary education**		**5.3**	**[120]**	
2.2.1	Tertiary enrolment, % gross	⏱	12.1	110	
2.2.2	Graduates in science and engineering, %		n/a	n/a	
2.2.3	Tertiary inbound mobility, %		n/a	n/a	
2.3	**Research and development (R&D)**		**0.0**	**[119]**	
2.3.1	Researchers, FTE/mn pop.		n/a	n/a	
2.3.2	Gross expenditure on R&D, % GDP		n/a	n/a	
2.3.3	Global corporate R&D investors, top 3, mn USD		0.0	40	○◇
2.3.4	QS university ranking, top 3*		0.0	71	○◇
3	**Infrastructure**		**18.7**	**123**	◇
3.1	**Information and communication technologies (ICTs)**		**35.7**	**115**	
3.1.1	ICT access*		37.0	119	◇
3.1.2	ICT use*		29.4	117	◇
3.1.3	Government's online service*		47.5	95	
3.1.4	E-participation*		29.1	105	
3.2	**General infrastructure**		**11.1**	**120**	
3.2.1	Electricity output, GWh/mn pop.	⏱	157.3	118	
3.2.2	Logistics performance*		22.7	82	
3.2.3	Gross capital formation, % GDP		17.9	113	◇
3.3	**Ecological sustainability**		**9.4**	**129**	○◇
3.3.1	GDP/unit of energy use		6.3	105	
3.3.2	Environmental performance*		15.9	120	
3.3.3	ISO 14001 environment/bn PPP$ GDP		0.1	127	○
4	**Market sophistication**		**12.4**	**127**	○◇
4.1	**Credit**		**4.5**	**125**	○◇
4.1.1	Finance for startups and scaleups†		n/a	n/a	
4.1.2	Domestic credit to private sector, % GDP		12.1	126	○◇
4.1.3	Loans from microfinance institutions, % GDP		0.5	36	
4.2	**Investment**		**9.0**	**57**	●
4.2.1	Market capitalization, % GDP		10.1	72	
4.2.2	Venture capital (VC) investors, deals/bn PPP$ GDP		0.0	56	
4.2.3	VC recipients, deals/bn PPP$ GDP		0.1	38	●
4.2.4	VC received, value, % GDP		0.0	46	●
4.3	**Trade, diversification and market scale**		**23.7**	**122**	◇
4.3.1	Applied tariff rate, weighted avg., %		12.4	131	○◇
4.3.2	Domestic industry diversification		n/a	n/a	
4.3.3	Domestic market scale, bn PPP$		1,275.3	26	●

Code	Indicator		Score/ Value	Rank	
5	**Business sophistication**		**24.5**	**82**	
5.1	**Knowledge workers**		**37.0**	**[55]**	
5.1.1	Knowledge-intensive employment, %	⏱	38.1	35	●◆
5.1.2	Firms offering formal training, %	⏱	30.7	55	●
5.1.3	GERD performed by business, % GDP		n/a	n/a	
5.1.4	GERD financed by business, %		n/a	n/a	
5.1.5	Females employed w/advanced degrees, %	⏱	5.8	91	
5.2	**Innovation linkages**		**11.5**	**111**	
5.2.1	University–industry R&D collaboration†		12.9	122	◇
5.2.2	State of cluster development†		29.2	96	
5.2.3	GERD financed by abroad, % GDP		n/a	n/a	
5.2.4	Joint venture/strategic alliance deals/bn PPP$ GDP		0.0	86	
5.2.5	Patent families/bn PPP$ GDP		0.0	94	
5.3	**Knowledge absorption**		**24.9**	**104**	
5.3.1	Intellectual property payments, % total trade		0.4	77	
5.3.2	High-tech imports, % total trade		6.5	97	
5.3.3	ICT services imports, % total trade		0.6	100	
5.3.4	FDI net inflows, % GDP		0.6	111	
5.3.5	Research talent, % in businesses		n/a	n/a	
6	**Knowledge and technology outputs**		**9.9**	**124**	
6.1	**Knowledge creation**		**7.4**	**97**	
6.1.1	Patents by origin/bn PPP$ GDP	⏱	0.4	86	
6.1.2	PCT patents by origin/bn PPP$ GDP		0.0	98	
6.1.3	Utility models by origin/bn PPP$ GDP		n/a	n/a	
6.1.4	Scientific and technical articles/bn PPP$ GDP		4.8	107	
6.1.5	Citable documents H-index		13.8	60	●
6.2	**Knowledge impact**		**17.1**	**115**	
6.2.1	Labor productivity growth, %		–1.1	118	
6.2.2	Unicorn valuation, % GDP		0.3	43	●
6.2.3	Software spending, % GDP		0.1	88	
6.2.4	High-tech manufacturing, %		n/a	n/a	
6.3	**Knowledge diffusion**		**5.3**	**125**	○◇
6.3.1	Intellectual property receipts, % total trade		0.0	114	○◇
6.3.2	Production and export complexity		16.2	118	○◇
6.3.3	High-tech exports, % total trade		0.4	96	
6.3.4	ICT services exports, % total trade		0.2	116	
6.3.5	ISO 9001 quality/bn PPP$ GDP		0.4	124	○
7	**Creative outputs**		**17.3**	**84**	
7.1	**Intangible assets**		**26.0**	**78**	
7.1.1	Intangible asset intensity, top 15, %		47.5	52	
7.1.2	Trademarks by origin/bn PPP$ GDP	⏱	10.5	111	
7.1.3	Global brand value, top 5,000, % GDP		0.4	65	●
7.1.4	Industrial designs by origin/bn PPP$ GDP	⏱	1.0	70	●
7.2	**Creative goods and services**		**1.2**	**[115]**	
7.2.1	Cultural and creative services exports, % total trade		n/a	n/a	
7.2.2	National feature films/mn pop. 15–69		n/a	n/a	
7.2.3	Entertainment and media market/th pop. 15–69		1.6	53	
7.2.4	Creative goods exports, % total trade		0.1	103	
7.3	**Online creativity**		**15.9**	**91**	
7.3.1	Generic top-level domains (TLDs)/th pop. 15–69		0.5	111	
7.3.2	Country-code TLDs/th pop. 15–69		0.4	100	
7.3.3	GitHub commits/mn pop. 15–69		3.9	79	
7.3.4	Mobile app creation/bn PPP$ GDP		58.9	86	

NOTES: ● indicates a strength; ○ a weakness; ◆ an income group strength; ◇ an income group weakness; * an index; † a survey question. ⏱ is used when the available economy data are older than the base year; see appendices for details, including the year of the data, at wipo.int/gii-ranking. Square brackets [ ] indicate that the data minimum coverage (DMC) requirements were not met at the sub-pillar or pillar level.

GII 2023 rank

North Macedonia

54

Output rank	Input rank	Income	Region	Population (mn)	GDP, PPP$ (bn)	GDP per capita, PPP$
58	49	Upper middle	EUR	2.1	40.9	19,783

			Score/ Value	Rank	
	Institutions		**47.2**	**75**	
1.1	**Institutional environment**		**46.4**	**64**	
1.1.1	Operational stability for businesses*		58.3	49	
1.1.2	Government effectiveness*		34.4	76	
1.2	**Regulatory environment**		**66.2**	**54**	
1.2.1	Regulatory quality*		52.9	52	
1.2.2	Rule of law*		37.5	65	
1.2.3	Cost of redundancy dismissal		14.4	57	
1.3	**Business environment**		**29.0**	**103**	
1.3.1	Policies for doing business†		24.7	116	○
1.3.2	Entrepreneurship policies and culture†	⊙	33.3	55	
	Human capital and research		**28.1**	**78**	
2.1	**Education**		**56.2**	**[53]**	
2.1.1	Expenditure on education, % GDP		n/a	n/a	
2.1.2	Government funding/pupil, secondary, % GDP/cap		n/a	n/a	
2.1.3	School life expectancy, years		13.2	81	
2.1.4	PISA scales in reading, maths and science		400.1	67	○
2.1.5	Pupil–teacher ratio, secondary		8.1	11	●◆
2.2	**Tertiary education**		**24.4**	**81**	
2.2.1	Tertiary enrolment, % gross		43.0	75	
2.2.2	Graduates in science and engineering, %		20.6	67	
2.2.3	Tertiary inbound mobility, %		5.0	48	
2.3	**Research and development (R&D)**		**3.6**	**83**	
2.3.1	Researchers, FTE/mn pop.		752.8	61	
2.3.2	Gross expenditure on R&D, % GDP		0.4	67	
2.3.3	Global corporate R&D investors, top 3, mn USD		0.0	40	○◇
2.3.4	QS university ranking, top 3*		0.0	71	○◇
	Infrastructure		**53.3**	**40**	**●◆**
3.1	**Information and communication technologies (ICTs)**		**69.6**	**69**	
3.1.1	ICT access*		72.7	85	
3.1.2	ICT use*		70.1	71	
3.1.3	Government's online service*		67.1	65	
3.1.4	E-participation*		68.6	43	
3.2	**General infrastructure**		**29.5**	**57**	
3.2.1	Electricity output, GWh/mn pop.		2,663.4	70	
3.2.2	Logistics performance*		45.5	56	
3.2.3	Gross capital formation, % GDP		n/a	n/a	
3.3	**Ecological sustainability**		**60.7**	**3**	**●◆**
3.3.1	GDP/unit of energy use		11.6	52	
3.3.2	Environmental performance*		60.0	32	●◆
3.3.3	ISO 14001 environment/bn PPP$ GDP		12.0	3	●◆
	Market sophistication		**47.1**	**30**	**●◆**
4.1	**Credit**		**34.1**	**54**	
4.1.1	Finance for startups and scaleups†	⊙	48.4	49	
4.1.2	Domestic credit to private sector, % GDP		55.7	65	
4.1.3	Loans from microfinance institutions, % GDP		n/a	n/a	
4.2	**Investment**		**n/a**	**[n/a]**	
4.2.1	Market capitalization, % GDP		n/a	n/a	
4.2.2	Venture capital (VC) investors, deals/bn PPP$ GDP		n/a	n/a	
4.2.3	VC recipients, deals/bn PPP$ GDP		n/a	n/a	
4.2.4	VC received, value, % GDP		n/a	n/a	
4.3	**Trade, diversification and market scale**		**60.1**	**54**	
4.3.1	Applied tariff rate, weighted avg., %		1.7	55	
4.3.2	Domestic industry diversification	⊙	90.8	44	
4.3.3	Domestic market scale, bn PPP$		40.9	117	○

			Score/ Value	Rank	
	Business sophistication		**29.2**	**60**	
5.1	**Knowledge workers**		**36.3**	**57**	
5.1.1	Knowledge-intensive employment, %		33.2	44	◆
5.1.2	Firms offering formal training, %		39.0	36	
5.1.3	GERD performed by business, % GDP	⊙	0.1	62	
5.1.4	GERD financed by business, %		22.3	64	
5.1.5	Females employed w/advanced degrees, %		17.0	43	
5.2	**Innovation linkages**		**13.4**	**106**	
5.2.1	University–industry R&D collaboration†		23.2	110	○◇
5.2.2	State of cluster development†		27.1	100	
5.2.3	GERD financed by abroad, % GDP		0.0	61	
5.2.4	Joint venture/strategic alliance deals/bn PPP$ GDP		n/a	n/a	
5.2.5	Patent families/bn PPP$ GDP		0.0	95	○◇
5.3	**Knowledge absorption**		**37.9**	**51**	
5.3.1	Intellectual property payments, % total trade		1.9	15	●◆
5.3.2	High-tech imports, % total trade		6.6	93	
5.3.3	ICT services imports, % total trade		1.3	66	
5.3.4	FDI net inflows, % GDP		3.2	44	
5.3.5	Research talent, % in businesses	⊙	27.9	45	
	Knowledge and technology outputs		**26.6**	**53**	
6.1	**Knowledge creation**		**12.6**	**71**	
6.1.1	Patents by origin/bn PPP$ GDP		1.3	52	
6.1.2	PCT patents by origin/bn PPP$ GDP		0.1	60	
6.1.3	Utility models by origin/bn PPP$ GDP		n/a	n/a	
6.1.4	Scientific and technical articles/bn PPP$ GDP		11.8	67	
6.1.5	Citable documents H-index		6.7	91	
6.2	**Knowledge impact**		**32.4**	**47**	
6.2.1	Labor productivity growth, %	⊙	1.3	57	
6.2.2	Unicorn valuation, % GDP		0.0	48	○◇
6.2.3	Software spending, % GDP		0.1	87	
6.2.4	High-tech manufacturing, %	⊙	49.8	11	●◆
6.3	**Knowledge diffusion**		**34.9**	**42**	
6.3.1	Intellectual property receipts, % total trade		0.1	48	
6.3.2	Production and export complexity		54.1	57	
6.3.3	High-tech exports, % total trade		2.7	50	
6.3.4	ICT services exports, % total trade		3.8	29	●
6.3.5	ISO 9001 quality/bn PPP$ GDP		19.9	13	●◆
	Creative outputs		**23.5**	**69**	
7.1	**Intangible assets**		**27.0**	**76**	
7.1.1	Intangible asset intensity, top 15, %		–26.7	75	○
7.1.2	Trademarks by origin/bn PPP$ GDP		57.4	40	●
7.1.3	Global brand value, top 5,000, % GDP		0.0	74	○◇
7.1.4	Industrial designs by origin/bn PPP$ GDP		1.8	44	
7.2	**Creative goods and services**		**17.1**	**55**	
7.2.1	Cultural and creative services exports, % total trade		1.1	26	●◆
7.2.2	National feature films/mn pop. 15–69		4.5	25	●◆
7.2.3	Entertainment and media market/th pop. 15–69		n/a	n/a	
7.2.4	Creative goods exports, % total trade		0.1	98	
7.3	**Online creativity**		**23.0**	**58**	
7.3.1	Generic top-level domains (TLDs)/th pop. 15–69		7.7	49	
7.3.2	Country-code TLDs/th pop. 15–69		5.7	55	
7.3.3	GitHub commits/mn pop. 15–69		9.1	55	
7.3.4	Mobile app creation/bn PPP$ GDP		69.5	56	

NOTES: ● indicates a strength; ○ a weakness; ◆ an income group strength; ◇ an income group weakness; * an index; † a survey question. ⊙ is used when the available economy data are older than the base year; see appendices for details, including the year of the data, at wipo.int/gii-ranking. Square brackets [ ] indicate that the data minimum coverage (DMC) requirements were not met at the sub-pillar or pillar level.

Norway

GII 2023 rank

19

Output rank	Input rank	Income	Region	Population (mn)	GDP, PPP$ (bn)	GDP per capita, PPP$
28	15	High	EUR	5.4	425.6	78,128

		Score/ Value	Rank
	Institutions	**85.1**	**4 ●◆**
1.1	**Institutional environment**	**86.8**	**3 ●◆**
1.1.1	Operational stability for businesses*	86.1	5 ●◆
1.1.2	Government effectiveness*	87.5	5 ●
1.2	**Regulatory environment**	**94.7**	**4 ●**
1.2.1	Regulatory quality*	84.5	10
1.2.2	Rule of law*	96.8	2 ●◆
1.2.3	Cost of redundancy dismissal	8.7	20
1.3	**Business environment**	**73.7**	**18**
1.3.1	Policies for doing business† ⏲	75.3	18
1.3.2	Entrepreneurship policies and culture†	72.2	14
	Human capital and research	**53.2**	**19**
2.1	**Education**	**73.4**	**3 ●◆**
2.1.1	Expenditure on education, % GDP ⏲	7.9	4 ●◆
2.1.2	Government funding/pupil, secondary, % GDP/cap	26.6	14
2.1.3	School life expectancy, years	18.2	12
2.1.4	PISA scales in reading, maths and science	496.9	22
2.1.5	Pupil-teacher ratio, secondary	8.7	20 ◆
2.2	**Tertiary education**	**33.9**	**54**
2.2.1	Tertiary enrolment, % gross	84.4	18
2.2.2	Graduates in science and engineering, %	21.2	64 ○
2.2.3	Tertiary inbound mobility, %	4.4	54
2.3	**Research and development (R&D)**	**52.4**	**19**
2.3.1	Researchers, FTE/mn pop.	7,140.3	6 ●
2.3.2	Gross expenditure on R&D, % GDP	1.9	20
2.3.3	Global corporate R&D investors, top 3, mn USD	56.2	27
2.3.4	QS university ranking, top 3*	44.7	28
	Infrastructure	**63.2**	**7 ●**
3.1	**Information and communication technologies (ICTs)**	**82.7**	**29**
3.1.1	ICT access*	88.4	32
3.1.2	ICT use*	95.9	8
3.1.3	Government's online service*	78.0	39 ◇
3.1.4	E-participation*	68.6	43
3.2	**General infrastructure**	**64.3**	**4 ●◆**
3.2.1	Electricity output, GWh/mn pop.	29,134.6	1 ●◆
3.2.2	Logistics performance*	72.7	18
3.2.3	Gross capital formation, % GDP	24.2	64 ○
3.3	**Ecological sustainability**	**42.7**	**27**
3.3.1	GDP/unit of energy use	11.4	55
3.3.2	Environmental performance*	68.5	20
3.3.3	ISO 14001 environment/bn PPP$ GDP	4.2	23
	Market sophistication	**47.5**	**29**
4.1	**Credit**	**64.6**	**12**
4.1.1	Finance for startups and scaleups†	65.8	25
4.1.2	Domestic credit to private sector, % GDP	166.0	6 ●
4.1.3	Loans from microfinance institutions, % GDP	n/a	n/a
4.2	**Investment**	**19.1**	**37 ◇**
4.2.1	Market capitalization, % GDP ⏲	68.8	24
4.2.2	Venture capital (VC) investors, deals/bn PPP$ GDP	0.2	28
4.2.3	VC recipients, deals/bn PPP$ GDP	0.1	34
4.2.4	VC received, value, % GDP	0.0	39 ◇
4.3	**Trade, diversification and market scale**	**58.9**	**62**
4.3.1	Applied tariff rate, weighted avg., %	2.8	69 ○◇
4.3.2	Domestic industry diversification	85.8	62 ○
4.3.3	Domestic market scale, bn PPP$	425.6	50

		Score/ Value	Rank
	Business sophistication	**52.5**	**22 ◇**
5.1	**Knowledge workers**	**61.5**	**19**
5.1.1	Knowledge-intensive employment, %	52.3	5 ●
5.1.2	Firms offering formal training, %	n/a	n/a
5.1.3	GERD performed by business, % GDP	1.0	21
5.1.4	GERD financed by business, %	44.5	36 ◇
5.1.5	Females employed w/advanced degrees, %	27.6	10
5.2	**Innovation linkages**	**52.9**	**17**
5.2.1	University-industry R&D collaboration† ⏲	72.6	22
5.2.2	State of cluster development† ⏲	75.9	17
5.2.3	GERD financed by abroad, % GDP	0.2	24
5.2.4	Joint venture/strategic alliance deals/bn PPP$ GDP	0.1	14
5.2.5	Patent families/bn PPP$ GDP	1.8	21
5.3	**Knowledge absorption**	**43.2**	**35 ◇**
5.3.1	Intellectual property payments, % total trade	0.5	72 ○◇
5.3.2	High-tech imports, % total trade	6.8	89 ○
5.3.3	ICT services imports, % total trade	3.1	15
5.3.4	FDI net inflows, % GDP	1.9	74 ○
5.3.5	Research talent, % in businesses	51.0	24
	Knowledge and technology outputs	**37.5**	**28 ◇**
6.1	**Knowledge creation**	**49.7**	**15**
6.1.1	Patents by origin/bn PPP$ GDP	4.1	21
6.1.2	PCT patents by origin/bn PPP$ GDP	1.9	16
6.1.3	Utility models by origin/bn PPP$ GDP	n/a	n/a
6.1.4	Scientific and technical articles/bn PPP$ GDP	36.3	12
6.1.5	Citable documents H-index	42.6	21
6.2	**Knowledge impact**	**34.6**	**42 ◇**
6.2.1	Labor productivity growth, %	0.2	92 ○
6.2.2	Unicorn valuation, % GDP	0.9	35 ◇
6.2.3	Software spending, % GDP	0.6	18
6.2.4	High-tech manufacturing, %	17.7	69 ○◇
6.3	**Knowledge diffusion**	**28.0**	**56 ◇**
6.3.1	Intellectual property receipts, % total trade	0.3	39 ◇
6.3.2	Production and export complexity	67.1	37 ◇
6.3.3	High-tech exports, % total trade	2.8	49
6.3.4	ICT services exports, % total trade	1.6	67 ○
6.3.5	ISO 9001 quality/bn PPP$ GDP	7.1	39
	Creative outputs	**44.7**	**23**
7.1	**Intangible assets**	**38.7**	**47 ◇**
7.1.1	Intangible asset intensity, top 15, %	64.1	31
7.1.2	Trademarks by origin/bn PPP$ GDP	30.8	76 ○
7.1.3	Global brand value, top 5,000, % GDP	7.5	28
7.1.4	Industrial designs by origin/bn PPP$ GDP	1.2	62
7.2	**Creative goods and services**	**31.5**	**26**
7.2.1	Cultural and creative services exports, % total trade	0.6	48
7.2.2	National feature films/mn pop. 15–69	5.0	22
7.2.3	Entertainment and media market/th pop. 15–69	75.7	4 ●
7.2.4	Creative goods exports, % total trade	0.5	63
7.3	**Online creativity**	**69.9**	**7 ●**
7.3.1	Generic top-level domains (TLDs)/th pop. 15–69	57.9	13
7.3.2	Country-code TLDs/th pop. 15–69	65.5	12
7.3.3	GitHub commits/mn pop. 15–69	82.0	5 ●
7.3.4	Mobile app creation/bn PPP$ GDP	74.1	32

NOTES: ● indicates a strength; ○ a weakness; ◆ an income group strength; ◇ an income group weakness; * an index; † a survey question. ⏲ is used when the available economy data are older than the base year; see appendices for details, including the year of the data, at wipo.int/gii-ranking. Square brackets [ ] indicate that the data minimum coverage (DMC) requirements were not met at the sub-pillar or pillar level.

Oman

GII 2023 rank

69

Output rank	Input rank	Income	Region	Population (mn)	GDP, PPP$ (bn)	GDP per capita, PPP$
78	65	High	NAWA	4.6	190.5	41,150

			Score/ Value	Rank	
	Institutions		**51.9**	**62**	◇
1.1	**Institutional environment**		**47.0**	**61**	◇
1.1.1	Operational stability for businesses*		60.4	46	
1.1.2	Government effectiveness*		33.5	78	◇
1.2	**Regulatory environment**		**51.1**	**96**	◇
1.2.1	Regulatory quality*		50.7	54	◇
1.2.2	Rule of law*		51.6	47	◇
1.2.3	Cost of redundancy dismissal		n/a	n/a	
1.3	**Business environment**		**57.6**	**39**	
1.3.1	Policies for doing business†	⊙	74.8	19	●
1.3.2	Entrepreneurship policies and culture†		40.5	48	
	Human capital and research		**34.2**	**52**	◇
2.1	**Education**		**56.3**	**52**	
2.1.1	Expenditure on education, % GDP	⊙	4.4	59	
2.1.2	Government funding/pupil, secondary, % GDP/cap		28.5	9	● ◆
2.1.3	School life expectancy, years		14.6	63	◇
2.1.4	PISA scales in reading, maths and science		n/a	n/a	
2.1.5	Pupil–teacher ratio, secondary		12.2	54	
2.2	**Tertiary education**		**41.9**	**27**	●
2.2.1	Tertiary enrolment, % gross		47.4	69	◇
2.2.2	Graduates in science and engineering, %		39.5	2	● ◆
2.2.3	Tertiary inbound mobility, %		3.1	63	
2.3	**Research and development (R&D)**		**4.4**	**79**	◇
2.3.1	Researchers, FTE/mn pop.		284.4	80	◇
2.3.2	Gross expenditure on R&D, % GDP		0.3	77	◇
2.3.3	Global corporate R&D investors, top 3, mn USD		0.0	40	○ ◇
2.3.4	QS university ranking, top 3*		9.9	65	◇
	Infrastructure		**42.5**	**61**	◇
3.1	**Information and communication technologies (ICTs)**		**76.3**	**46**	
3.1.1	ICT access*		91.7	16	●
3.1.2	ICT use*		76.6	58	◇
3.1.3	Government's online service*		71.5	58	
3.1.4	E-participation*		65.1	50	
3.2	**General infrastructure**		**37.0**	**38**	
3.2.1	Electricity output, GWh/mn pop.	⊙	7,474.1	24	●
3.2.2	Logistics performance*		54.5	42	
3.2.3	Gross capital formation, % GDP		23.2	71	
3.3	**Ecological sustainability**		**14.2**	**107**	◇
3.3.1	GDP/unit of energy use		5.3	116	○ ◇
3.3.2	Environmental performance*		20.0	107	◇
3.3.3	ISO 14001 environment/bn PPP$ GDP		1.7	53	
	Market sophistication		**33.3**	**74**	
4.1	**Credit**		**36.0**	**49**	
4.1.1	Finance for startups and scaleups†		43.9	55	◇
4.1.2	Domestic credit to private sector, % GDP		76.6	44	
4.1.3	Loans from microfinance institutions, % GDP		n/a	n/a	
4.2	**Investment**		**3.6**	**89**	◇
4.2.1	Market capitalization, % GDP		20.6	58	
4.2.2	Venture capital (VC) investors, deals/bn PPP$ GDP		0.1	46	
4.2.3	VC recipients, deals/bn PPP$ GDP		0.0	92	○ ◇
4.2.4	VC received, value, % GDP		0.0	91	○ ◇
4.3	**Trade, diversification and market scale**		**60.3**	**53**	
4.3.1	Applied tariff rate, weighted avg., %		1.7	54	
4.3.2	Domestic industry diversification	⊙	87.8	57	
4.3.3	Domestic market scale, bn PPP$		190.5	71	

			Score/ Value	Rank	
	Business sophistication		**22.3**	**95**	◇
5.1	**Knowledge workers**		**16.1**	**111**	◇
5.1.1	Knowledge-intensive employment, %	⊙	15.9	85	◇
5.1.2	Firms offering formal training, %		n/a	n/a	
5.1.3	GERD performed by business, % GDP	⊙	0.1	65	◇
5.1.4	GERD financed by business, %	⊙	31.8	56	
5.1.5	Females employed w/advanced degrees, %	⊙	0.9	119	○ ◇
5.2	**Innovation linkages**		**27.9**	**46**	
5.2.1	University–industry R&D collaboration†	⊙	54.4	43	
5.2.2	State of cluster development†	⊙	71.4	21	●
5.2.3	GERD financed by abroad, % GDP	⊙	0.0	86	○ ◇
5.2.4	Joint venture/strategic alliance deals/bn PPP$ GDP		0.0	37	
5.2.5	Patent families/bn PPP$ GDP		0.0	87	
5.3	**Knowledge absorption**		**23.0**	**115**	○ ◇
5.3.1	Intellectual property payments, % total trade		n/a	n/a	
5.3.2	High-tech imports, % total trade		5.0	116	○
5.3.3	ICT services imports, % total trade		0.7	97	◇
5.3.4	FDI net inflows, % GDP		4.4	27	●
5.3.5	Research talent, % in businesses	⊙	0.3	83	○ ◇
	Knowledge and technology outputs		**20.9**	**75**	◇
6.1	**Knowledge creation**		**14.7**	**65**	◇
6.1.1	Patents by origin/bn PPP$ GDP		3.2	23	●
6.1.2	PCT patents by origin/bn PPP$ GDP		0.0	77	◇
6.1.3	Utility models by origin/bn PPP$ GDP		n/a	n/a	
6.1.4	Scientific and technical articles/bn PPP$ GDP		8.6	82	◇
6.1.5	Citable documents H-index		8.7	85	◇
6.2	**Knowledge impact**		**23.8**	**83**	◇
6.2.1	Labor productivity growth, %		2.9	19	● ◆
6.2.2	Unicorn valuation, % GDP		0.0	48	○ ◇
6.2.3	Software spending, % GDP		0.0	105	◇
6.2.4	High-tech manufacturing, %	⊙	17.0	72	◇
6.3	**Knowledge diffusion**		**24.1**	**59**	◇
6.3.1	Intellectual property receipts, % total trade		n/a	n/a	
6.3.2	Production and export complexity		46.9	78	◇
6.3.3	High-tech exports, % total trade		2.2	56	
6.3.4	ICT services exports, % total trade		1.2	80	
6.3.5	ISO 9001 quality/bn PPP$ GDP		3.8	64	
	Creative outputs		**19.2**	**79**	◇
7.1	**Intangible assets**		**27.2**	**75**	
7.1.1	Intangible asset intensity, top 15, %		34.0	66	
7.1.2	Trademarks by origin/bn PPP$ GDP	⊙	49.8	45	
7.1.3	Global brand value, top 5,000, % GDP		0.7	60	
7.1.4	Industrial designs by origin/bn PPP$ GDP		0.1	113	○ ◇
7.2	**Creative goods and services**		**2.9**	**[99]**	
7.2.1	Cultural and creative services exports, % total trade		n/a	n/a	
7.2.2	National feature films/mn pop. 15–69		n/a	n/a	
7.2.3	Entertainment and media market/th pop. 15–69		3.0	50	◇
7.2.4	Creative goods exports, % total trade		0.2	74	
7.3	**Online creativity**		**19.5**	**68**	◇
7.3.1	Generic top-level domains (TLDs)/th pop. 15–69		2.3	78	◇
7.3.2	Country-code TLDs/th pop. 15–69		0.4	103	◇
7.3.3	GitHub commits/mn pop. 15–69		1.3	112	◇
7.3.4	Mobile app creation/bn PPP$ GDP		74.2	31	●

NOTES: ● indicates a strength; ○ a weakness; ◆ an income group strength; ◇ an income group weakness; * an index; † a survey question. ⊙ is used when the available economy data are older than the base year; see appendices for details, including the year of the data, at wipo.int/gii-ranking. Square brackets [ ] indicate that the data minimum coverage (DMC) requirements were not met at the sub-pillar or pillar level.

Pakistan

GII 2023 rank

88

Output rank	Input rank	Income	Region	Population (mn)	GDP, PPP$ (bn)	GDP per capita, PPP$
68	113	Lower middle	CSA	235.8	1,512.5	6,662

			Score/ Value	Rank	
	Institutions		**33.7**	**113**	
1.1	**Institutional environment**		**28.1**	**105**	
1.1.1	Operational stability for businesses*		30.6	117	
1.1.2	Government effectiveness*		25.6	93	
1.2	**Regulatory environment**		**42.0**	**116**	
1.2.1	Regulatory quality*		23.1	113	
1.2.2	Rule of law*		21.1	104	
1.2.3	Cost of redundancy dismissal		27.2	109	
1.3	**Business environment**		**31.1**	**98**	
1.3.1	Policies for doing business†		53.5	55	
1.3.2	Entrepreneurship policies and culture†	⊙	8.6	80	○◇
	Human capital and research		**14.8**	**117**	
2.1	**Education**		**29.6**	**121**	
2.1.1	Expenditure on education, % GDP		2.1	117	○◇
2.1.2	Government funding/pupil, secondary, % GDP/cap	⊙	17.1	65	
2.1.3	School life expectancy, years	⊙	8.7	110	○◇
2.1.4	PISA scales in reading, maths and science		n/a	n/a	
2.1.5	Pupil-teacher ratio, secondary	⊙	17.0	86	
2.2	**Tertiary education**		**5.4**	**[119]**	
2.2.1	Tertiary enrolment, % gross	⊙	12.2	109	
2.2.2	Graduates in science and engineering, %		n/a	n/a	
2.2.3	Tertiary inbound mobility, %		n/a	n/a	
2.3	**Research and development (R&D)**		**9.5**	**62**	
2.3.1	Researchers, FTE/mn pop.		422.8	73	
2.3.2	Gross expenditure on R&D, % GDP		0.2	95	
2.3.3	Global corporate R&D investors, top 3, mn USD		0.0	40	○◇
2.3.4	QS university ranking, top 3*		30.8	42	●◆
	Infrastructure		**19.7**	**120**	◇
3.1	**Information and communication technologies (ICTs)**		**41.8**	**107**	
3.1.1	ICT access*		45.4	113	
3.1.2	ICT use*		35.1	112	◇
3.1.3	Government's online service*		52.0	88	
3.1.4	E-participation*		34.9	96	
3.2	**General infrastructure**		**4.2**	**132**	○◇
3.2.1	Electricity output, GWh/mn pop.	⊙	601.3	107	
3.2.2	Logistics performance*		n/a	n/a	
3.2.3	Gross capital formation, % GDP		15.1	119	○◇
3.3	**Ecological sustainability**		**13.2**	**113**	
3.3.1	GDP/unit of energy use		10.8	58	
3.3.2	Environmental performance*		9.7	128	○◇
3.3.3	ISO 14001 environment/bn PPP$ GDP		0.7	77	
	Market sophistication		**24.7**	**97**	
4.1	**Credit**		**13.7**	**103**	
4.1.1	Finance for startups and scaleups†	⊙	28.9	72	
4.1.2	Domestic credit to private sector, % GDP		15.0	119	○
4.1.3	Loans from microfinance institutions, % GDP		0.7	34	
4.2	**Investment**		**4.6**	**81**	
4.2.1	Market capitalization, % GDP		n/a	n/a	
4.2.2	Venture capital (VC) investors, deals/bn PPP$ GDP		0.0	85	
4.2.3	VC recipients, deals/bn PPP$ GDP		0.0	73	
4.2.4	VC received, value, % GDP		0.0	61	
4.3	**Trade, diversification and market scale**		**55.9**	**75**	
4.3.1	Applied tariff rate, weighted avg., %		8.7	110	
4.3.2	Domestic industry diversification	⊙	91.4	43	
4.3.3	Domestic market scale, bn PPP$		1,512.5	22	●

			Score/ Value	Rank	
	Business sophistication		**26.6**	**72**	
5.1	**Knowledge workers**		**19.0**	**[101]**	
5.1.1	Knowledge-intensive employment, %	⊙	11.4	102	
5.1.2	Firms offering formal training, %	⊙	32.0	50	
5.1.3	GERD performed by business, % GDP		n/a	n/a	
5.1.4	GERD financed by business, %		n/a	n/a	
5.1.5	Females employed w/advanced degrees, %	⊙	2.0	109	
5.2	**Innovation linkages**		**25.0**	**54**	◆
5.2.1	University-industry R&D collaboration†		59.2	35	●◆
5.2.2	State of cluster development†		55.2	39	●◆
5.2.3	GERD financed by abroad, % GDP	⊙	0.0	87	
5.2.4	Joint venture/strategic alliance deals/bn PPP$ GDP		0.0	50	◆
5.2.5	Patent families/bn PPP$ GDP		0.0	89	
5.3	**Knowledge absorption**		**35.8**	**57**	◆
5.3.1	Intellectual property payments, % total trade		0.5	74	
5.3.2	High-tech imports, % total trade		16.2	14	●◆
5.3.3	ICT services imports, % total trade		1.1	81	
5.3.4	FDI net inflows, % GDP		0.7	108	
5.3.5	Research talent, % in businesses		n/a	n/a	
	Knowledge and technology outputs		**21.9**	**69**	
6.1	**Knowledge creation**		**19.2**	**[57]**	
6.1.1	Patents by origin/bn PPP$ GDP		0.3	89	
6.1.2	PCT patents by origin/bn PPP$ GDP		n/a	n/a	
6.1.3	Utility models by origin/bn PPP$ GDP		n/a	n/a	
6.1.4	Scientific and technical articles/bn PPP$ GDP		16.5	45	●
6.1.5	Citable documents H-index		19.5	43	●◆
6.2	**Knowledge impact**		**27.3**	**63**	
6.2.1	Labor productivity growth, %	⊙	0.9	70	
6.2.2	Unicorn valuation, % GDP		0.0	48	○◇
6.2.3	Software spending, % GDP		0.3	31	●
6.2.4	High-tech manufacturing, %	⊙	21.1	60	
6.3	**Knowledge diffusion**		**19.3**	**79**	
6.3.1	Intellectual property receipts, % total trade		0.0	87	
6.3.2	Production and export complexity		42.4	87	
6.3.3	High-tech exports, % total trade		0.7	82	
6.3.4	ICT services exports, % total trade		4.4	23	●
6.3.5	ISO 9001 quality/bn PPP$ GDP		2.4	83	
	Creative outputs		**23.5**	**70**	
7.1	**Intangible assets**		**36.6**	**52**	
7.1.1	Intangible asset intensity, top 15, %		53.8	44	
7.1.2	Trademarks by origin/bn PPP$ GDP		32.4	72	
7.1.3	Global brand value, top 5,000, % GDP		n/a	n/a	
7.1.4	Industrial designs by origin/bn PPP$ GDP		0.3	92	
7.2	**Creative goods and services**		**0.8**	**117**	
7.2.1	Cultural and creative services exports, % total trade		0.1	81	
7.2.2	National feature films/mn pop. 15–69		0.0	81	○◇
7.2.3	Entertainment and media market/th pop. 15–69		0.0	61	○◇
7.2.4	Creative goods exports, % total trade		0.1	110	
7.3	**Online creativity**		**20.0**	**65**	
7.3.1	Generic top-level domains (TLDs)/th pop. 15–69		0.6	107	
7.3.2	Country-code TLDs/th pop. 15–69		0.2	111	
7.3.3	GitHub commits/mn pop. 15–69		1.4	108	
7.3.4	Mobile app creation/bn PPP$ GDP		77.6	13	●◆

NOTES: ● indicates a strength; ○ a weakness; ◆ an income group strength; ◇ an income group weakness; * an index; † a survey question. ⊙ is used when the available economy data are older than the base year; see appendices for details, including the year of the data, at wipo.int/gii-ranking. Square brackets [ ] indicate that the data minimum coverage (DMC) requirements were not met at the sub-pillar or pillar level.

GII 2023 rank

Panama

84

Output rank	Input rank	Income	Region	Population (mn)	GDP, PPP$ (bn)	GDP per capita, PPP$
75	93	High	LCN	4.4	159.9	36,370

Code	Indicator	Score/ Value	Rank	
1	**Institutions**	**47.0**	**77**	◇
1.1	**Institutional environment**	**47.7**	**58**	●◇
1.1.1	Operational stability for businesses*	54.2	62	◇
1.1.2	Government effectiveness*	41.1	61	◇
1.2	**Regulatory environment**	**59.9**	**73**	◇
1.2.1	Regulatory quality*	47.1	61	◇
1.2.2	Rule of law*	32.5	77	◇
1.2.3	Cost of redundancy dismissal	18.1	78	
1.3	**Business environment**	**33.4**	**93**	◇
1.3.1	Policies for doing business†	37.9	93	◇
1.3.2	Entrepreneurship policies and culture†	28.9	59	
2	**Human capital and research**	**19.1**	**103**	◇
2.1	**Education**	**40.2**	**99**	◇
2.1.1	Expenditure on education, % GDP	3.5	91	◇
2.1.2	Government funding/pupil, secondary, % GDP/cap	n/a	n/a	
2.1.3	School life expectancy, years	⊙ 12.9	83	◇
2.1.4	PISA scales in reading, maths and science	364.8	76	○◇
2.1.5	Pupil–teacher ratio, secondary	⊙ 13.6	67	
2.2	**Tertiary education**	**16.4**	**98**	◇
2.2.1	Tertiary enrolment, % gross	44.4	72	◇
2.2.2	Graduates in science and engineering, %	13.7	102	◇
2.2.3	Tertiary inbound mobility, %	3.1	64	
2.3	**Research and development (R&D)**	**0.8**	**104**	◇
2.3.1	Researchers, FTE/mn pop.	⊙ 39.1	97	
2.3.2	Gross expenditure on R&D, % GDP	0.2	93	◇
2.3.3	Global corporate R&D investors, top 3, mn USD	0.0	40	○◇
2.3.4	QS university ranking, top 3*	0.0	71	○◇
3	**Infrastructure**	**45.0**	**55**	●◇
3.1	**Information and communication technologies (ICTs)**	**63.3**	**79**	◇
3.1.1	ICT access*	77.9	79	◇
3.1.2	ICT use*	61.4	90	◇
3.1.3	Government's online service*	64.0	71	◇
3.1.4	E-participation*	50.0	75	◇
3.2	**General infrastructure**	**31.7**	**51**	●◇
3.2.1	Electricity output, GWh/mn pop.	⊙ 2,533.0	74	◇
3.2.2	Logistics performance*	45.5	56	◇
3.2.3	Gross capital formation, % GDP	34.3	14	●◆
3.3	**Ecological sustainability**	**40.1**	**31**	●
3.3.1	GDP/unit of energy use	24.5	5	●◆
3.3.2	Environmental performance*	53.6	40	●
3.3.3	ISO 14001 environment/bn PPP$ GDP	0.2	111	◇
4	**Market sophistication**	**23.5**	**102**	◇
4.1	**Credit**	**31.4**	**61**	
4.1.1	Finance for startups and scaleups†	23.2	77	◇
4.1.2	Domestic credit to private sector, % GDP	105.9	26	●
4.1.3	Loans from microfinance institutions, % GDP	n/a	n/a	
4.2	**Investment**	**4.3**	**83**	◇
4.2.1	Market capitalization, % GDP	25.2	52	
4.2.2	Venture capital (VC) investors, deals/bn PPP$ GDP	0.0	86	
4.2.3	VC recipients, deals/bn PPP$ GDP	0.0	87	
4.2.4	VC received, value, % GDP	0.0	68	
4.3	**Trade, diversification and market scale**	**34.9**	**113**	◇
4.3.1	Applied tariff rate, weighted avg., %	5.8	95	◇
4.3.2	Domestic industry diversification	38.8	108	○◇
4.3.3	Domestic market scale, bn PPP$	159.9	76	

Code	Indicator	Score/ Value	Rank	
5	**Business sophistication**	**16.2**	**124**	○◇
5.1	**Knowledge workers**	**12.8**	**114**	◇
5.1.1	Knowledge-intensive employment, %	10.9	103	◇
5.1.2	Firms offering formal training, %	n/a	n/a	
5.1.3	GERD performed by business, % GDP	⊙ 0.0	92	○◇
5.1.4	GERD financed by business, %	1.1	91	○◇
5.1.5	Females employed w/advanced degrees, %	11.3	68	◇
5.2	**Innovation linkages**	**13.6**	**105**	◇
5.2.1	University–industry R&D collaboration†	23.5	108	◇
5.2.2	State of cluster development†	29.5	95	◇
5.2.3	GERD financed by abroad, % GDP	0.1	44	●
5.2.4	Joint venture/strategic alliance deals/bn PPP$ GDP	0.0	102	◇
5.2.5	Patent families/bn PPP$ GDP	0.1	58	●
5.3	**Knowledge absorption**	**22.3**	**118**	◇
5.3.1	Intellectual property payments, % total trade	0.5	70	
5.3.2	High-tech imports, % total trade	3.8	127	○◇
5.3.3	ICT services imports, % total trade	0.4	121	○◇
5.3.4	FDI net inflows, % GDP	1.6	85	
5.3.5	Research talent, % in businesses	n/a	n/a	
6	**Knowledge and technology outputs**	**17.1**	**87**	◇
6.1	**Knowledge creation**	**4.9**	**114**	◇
6.1.1	Patents by origin/bn PPP$ GDP	0.3	92	◇
6.1.2	PCT patents by origin/bn PPP$ GDP	0.1	74	◇
6.1.3	Utility models by origin/bn PPP$ GDP	0.0	68	◇
6.1.4	Scientific and technical articles/bn PPP$ GDP	3.4	114	◇
6.1.5	Citable documents H-index	12.0	67	
6.2	**Knowledge impact**	**18.1**	**114**	◇
6.2.1	Labor productivity growth, %	0.4	84	
6.2.2	Unicorn valuation, % GDP	0.0	48	○◇
6.2.3	Software spending, % GDP	0.2	77	
6.2.4	High-tech manufacturing, %	7.6	96	◇
6.3	**Knowledge diffusion**	**28.4**	**55**	●
6.3.1	Intellectual property receipts, % total trade	0.0	76	
6.3.2	Production and export complexity	65.7	40	●
6.3.3	High-tech exports, % total trade	⊙ 9.4	19	●
6.3.4	ICT services exports, % total trade	1.2	79	
6.3.5	ISO 9001 quality/bn PPP$ GDP	1.9	88	◇
7	**Creative outputs**	**23.9**	**67**	◇
7.1	**Intangible assets**	**20.0**	**85**	◇
7.1.1	Intangible asset intensity, top 15, %	2.5	69	◇
7.1.2	Trademarks by origin/bn PPP$ GDP	34.5	69	
7.1.3	Global brand value, top 5,000, % GDP	0.4	67	◇
7.1.4	Industrial designs by origin/bn PPP$ GDP	0.0	118	○◇
7.2	**Creative goods and services**	**28.3**	**[32]**	
7.2.1	Cultural and creative services exports, % total trade	0.2	69	
7.2.2	National feature films/mn pop. 15–69	n/a	n/a	
7.2.3	Entertainment and media market/th pop. 15–69	n/a	n/a	
7.2.4	Creative goods exports, % total trade	⊙ 4.5	14	●◆
7.3	**Online creativity**	**27.2**	**46**	●
7.3.1	Generic top-level domains (TLDs)/th pop. 15–69	37.4	19	●
7.3.2	Country-code TLDs/th pop. 15–69	1.4	77	◇
7.3.3	GitHub commits/mn pop. 15–69	3.4	86	◇
7.3.4	Mobile app creation/bn PPP$ GDP	66.6	62	

NOTES: ● indicates a strength; ○ a weakness; ◆ an income group strength; ◇ an income group weakness; * an index; † a survey question. ⊙ is used when the available economy data are older than the base year; see appendices for details, including the year of the data, at wipo.int/gii-ranking. Square brackets [ ] indicate that the data minimum coverage (DMC) requirements were not met at the sub-pillar or pillar level.

Paraguay

GII 2023 rank

98

Output rank	Input rank	Income	Region	Population (mn)	GDP, PPP$ (bn)	GDP per capita, PPP$
92	101	Upper middle	LCN	6.8	108.3	14,528

			Score/ Value	Rank	
	Institutions		**33.9**	**112**	◇
1.1	**Institutional environment**		**32.0**	**97**	
1.1.1	Operational stability for businesses*		44.4	82	
1.1.2	Government effectiveness*		19.5	107	◇
1.2	**Regulatory environment**		**43.8**	**114**	◇
1.2.1	Regulatory quality*		36.7	83	
1.2.2	Rule of law*		23.4	96	
1.2.3	Cost of redundancy dismissal		29.4	117	◇
1.3	**Business environment**		**25.8**	**108**	
1.3.1	Policies for doing business†		37.4	94	
1.3.2	Entrepreneurship policies and culture†	⊙	14.1	74	◇

			Score/ Value	Rank	
	Human capital and research		**10.1**	**[129]**	
2.1	**Education**		**19.2**	**[127]**	
2.1.1	Expenditure on education, % GDP		3.5	94	
2.1.2	Government funding/pupil, secondary, % GDP/cap		12.6	85	
2.1.3	School life expectancy, years		n/a	n/a	
2.1.4	PISA scales in reading, maths and science		n/a	n/a	
2.1.5	Pupil–teacher ratio, secondary		n/a	n/a	
2.2	**Tertiary education**		**n/a**	**[n/a]**	
2.2.1	Tertiary enrolment, % gross		n/a	n/a	
2.2.2	Graduates in science and engineering, %		n/a	n/a	
2.2.3	Tertiary inbound mobility, %		n/a	n/a	
2.3	**Research and development (R&D)**		**1.0**	**100**	
2.3.1	Researchers, FTE/mn pop.	⊙	129.8	87	◇
2.3.2	Gross expenditure on R&D, % GDP	⊙	0.2	96	
2.3.3	Global corporate R&D investors, top 3, mn USD		0.0	40	○◇
2.3.4	QS university ranking, top 3*		0.0	71	○◇

			Score/ Value	Rank	
	Infrastructure		**35.4**	**83**	
3.1	**Information and communication technologies (ICTs)**		**57.9**	**86**	
3.1.1	ICT access*		65.4	93	◇
3.1.2	ICT use*		59.6	93	
3.1.3	Government's online service*		56.4	84	
3.1.4	E-participation*		50.0	75	
3.2	**General infrastructure**		**25.2**	**73**	●
3.2.1	Electricity output, GWh/mn pop.		5,524.9	39	●◆
3.2.2	Logistics performance*		27.3	76	
3.2.3	Gross capital formation, % GDP		24.2	62	●
3.3	**Ecological sustainability**		**23.2**	**69**	●
3.3.1	GDP/unit of energy use		12.2	43	●
3.3.2	Environmental performance*		37.3	69	●
3.3.3	ISO 14001 environment/bn PPP$ GDP		0.4	92	

			Score/ Value	Rank	
	Market sophistication		**31.6**	**79**	
4.1	**Credit**		**12.5**	**108**	◇
4.1.1	Finance for startups and scaleups†	⊙	7.5	84	○◇
4.1.2	Domestic credit to private sector, % GDP		50.0	73	●
4.1.3	Loans from microfinance institutions, % GDP		n/a	n/a	
4.2	**Investment**		**n/a**	**[n/a]**	
4.2.1	Market capitalization, % GDP		n/a	n/a	
4.2.2	Venture capital (VC) investors, deals/bn PPP$ GDP		n/a	n/a	
4.2.3	VC recipients, deals/bn PPP$ GDP		n/a	n/a	
4.2.4	VC received, value, % GDP		n/a	n/a	
4.3	**Trade, diversification and market scale**		**50.6**	**84**	
4.3.1	Applied tariff rate, weighted avg., %		4.0	84	
4.3.2	Domestic industry diversification	⊙	75.7	86	
4.3.3	Domestic market scale, bn PPP$		108.3	86	

			Score/ Value	Rank	
	Business sophistication		**23.3**	**87**	
5.1	**Knowledge workers**		**29.7**	**71**	●
5.1.1	Knowledge-intensive employment, %		20.6	74	
5.1.2	Firms offering formal training, %	⊙	46.4	23	●
5.1.3	GERD performed by business, % GDP		n/a	n/a	
5.1.4	GERD financed by business, %		0.2	96	○◇
5.1.5	Females employed w/advanced degrees, %	⊙	9.5	78	
5.2	**Innovation linkages**		**9.2**	**120**	◇
5.2.1	University–industry R&D collaboration†		11.6	125	○◇
5.2.2	State of cluster development†		22.2	108	◇
5.2.3	GERD financed by abroad, % GDP		0.0	65	
5.2.4	Joint venture/strategic alliance deals/bn PPP$ GDP		n/a	n/a	
5.2.5	Patent families/bn PPP$ GDP		0.0	88	
5.3	**Knowledge absorption**		**31.0**	**76**	
5.3.1	Intellectual property payments, % total trade		0.1	97	◇
5.3.2	High-tech imports, % total trade		19.4	8	●◆
5.3.3	ICT services imports, % total trade		0.0	132	○◇
5.3.4	FDI net inflows, % GDP		0.6	110	◇
5.3.5	Research talent, % in businesses		n/a	n/a	

			Score/ Value	Rank	
	Knowledge and technology outputs		**12.3**	**109**	◇
6.1	**Knowledge creation**		**3.0**	**121**	
6.1.1	Patents by origin/bn PPP$ GDP	⊙	0.2	105	
6.1.2	PCT patents by origin/bn PPP$ GDP		n/a	n/a	
6.1.3	Utility models by origin/bn PPP$ GDP	⊙	0.1	60	
6.1.4	Scientific and technical articles/bn PPP$ GDP		2.3	121	◇
6.1.5	Citable documents H-index		3.8	118	
6.2	**Knowledge impact**		**16.0**	**121**	◇
6.2.1	Labor productivity growth, %		−0.1	103	
6.2.2	Unicorn valuation, % GDP		0.0	48	○◇
6.2.3	Software spending, % GDP		0.0	110	◇
6.2.4	High-tech manufacturing, %	⊙	15.0	77	
6.3	**Knowledge diffusion**		**17.8**	**83**	
6.3.1	Intellectual property receipts, % total trade		n/a	n/a	
6.3.2	Production and export complexity		45.0	83	
6.3.3	High-tech exports, % total trade		0.8	77	
6.3.4	ICT services exports, % total trade		0.1	127	○
6.3.5	ISO 9001 quality/bn PPP$ GDP		4.2	61	●

			Score/ Value	Rank	
	Creative outputs		**19.7**	**76**	
7.1	**Intangible assets**		**32.0**	**64**	●
7.1.1	Intangible asset intensity, top 15, %		n/a	n/a	
7.1.2	Trademarks by origin/bn PPP$ GDP	⊙	131.9	6	●◆
7.1.3	Global brand value, top 5,000, % GDP		0.0	74	○◇
7.1.4	Industrial designs by origin/bn PPP$ GDP	⊙	0.3	96	
7.2	**Creative goods and services**		**0.6**	**[119]**	
7.2.1	Cultural and creative services exports, % total trade		0.0	107	○◇
7.2.2	National feature films/mn pop. 15–69		n/a	n/a	
7.2.3	Entertainment and media market/th pop. 15–69		n/a	n/a	
7.2.4	Creative goods exports, % total trade		0.1	95	
7.3	**Online creativity**		**14.3**	**102**	
7.3.1	Generic top-level domains (TLDs)/th pop. 15–69		1.9	86	
7.3.2	Country-code TLDs/th pop. 15–69		1.7	75	●
7.3.3	GitHub commits/mn pop. 15–69		2.4	96	
7.3.4	Mobile app creation/bn PPP$ GDP		51.3	100	

NOTES: ● indicates a strength; ○ a weakness; ◆ an income group strength; ◇ an income group weakness; * an index; † a survey question. ⊙ is used when the available economy data are older than the base year; see appendices for details, including the year of the data, at wipo.int/gii-ranking. Square brackets [ ] indicate that the data minimum coverage (DMC) requirements were not met at the sub-pillar or pillar level.

Peru

GII 2023 rank

76

Output rank	Input rank	Income	Region	Population (mn)	GDP, PPP$ (bn)	GDP per capita, PPP$
84	60	Upper middle	LCN	34.0	521.8	15,273

			Score/ Value	Rank	
	Institutions		**45.9**	**81**	
1.1	**Institutional environment**		**34.9**	**93**	
1.1.1	Operational stability for businesses*		40.3	94	
1.1.2	Government effectiveness*		29.5	88	
1.2	**Regulatory environment**		**63.8**	**64**	
1.2.1	Regulatory quality*		44.2	68	
1.2.2	Rule of law*		24.6	94	
1.2.3	Cost of redundancy dismissal		11.4	37	●
1.3	**Business environment**		**38.9**	**91**	
1.3.1	Policies for doing business†		32.4	101	
1.3.2	Entrepreneurship policies and culture†	⊙	45.3	41	
	Human capital and research		**34.7**	**50**	
2.1	**Education**		**43.5**	**85**	
2.1.1	Expenditure on education, % GDP		4.0	72	
2.1.2	Government funding/pupil, secondary, % GDP/cap		15.5	73	
2.1.3	School life expectancy, years	⊙	15.0	53	
2.1.4	PISA scales in reading, maths and science		401.5	66	
2.1.5	Pupil–teacher ratio, secondary		13.9	69	
2.2	**Tertiary education**		**52.6**	**7**	●◆
2.2.1	Tertiary enrolment, % gross	⊙	70.7	34	●
2.2.2	Graduates in science and engineering, %	⊙	29.6	21	●◆
2.2.3	Tertiary inbound mobility, %		n/a	n/a	
2.3	**Research and development (R&D)**		**8.0**	**67**	
2.3.1	Researchers, FTE/mn pop.		n/a	n/a	
2.3.2	Gross expenditure on R&D, % GDP	⊙	0.2	92	
2.3.3	Global corporate R&D investors, top 3, mn USD		0.0	40	○◇
2.3.4	QS university ranking, top 3*		21.1	50	
	Infrastructure		**41.4**	**63**	
3.1	**Information and communication technologies (ICTs)**		**69.9**	**66**	
3.1.1	ICT access*		64.4	94	◇
3.1.2	ICT use*		60.7	92	
3.1.3	Government's online service*		79.0	37	●
3.1.4	E-participation*		75.6	22	●
3.2	**General infrastructure**		**23.8**	**78**	
3.2.1	Electricity output, GWh/mn pop.		1,742.6	88	
3.2.2	Logistics performance*		40.9	60	
3.2.3	Gross capital formation, % GDP		25.2	52	
3.3	**Ecological sustainability**		**30.5**	**51**	
3.3.1	GDP/unit of energy use		16.3	19	●◆
3.3.2	Environmental performance*		35.4	74	
3.3.3	ISO 14001 environment/bn PPP$ GDP		1.9	49	
	Market sophistication		**37.9**	**52**	
4.1	**Credit**		**44.8**	**36**	●◆
4.1.1	Finance for startups and scaleups†	⊙	44.3	54	
4.1.2	Domestic credit to private sector, % GDP		55.2	66	
4.1.3	Loans from microfinance institutions, % GDP		6.0	5	●◆
4.2	**Investment**		**4.9**	**78**	
4.2.1	Market capitalization, % GDP		42.8	39	
4.2.2	Venture capital (VC) investors, deals/bn PPP$ GDP		0.0	88	○
4.2.3	VC recipients, deals/bn PPP$ GDP		0.0	93	○
4.2.4	VC received, value, % GDP		0.0	77	
4.3	**Trade, diversification and market scale**		**64.0**	**34**	●
4.3.1	Applied tariff rate, weighted avg., %		0.7	6	●◆
4.3.2	Domestic industry diversification		85.1	64	
4.3.3	Domestic market scale, bn PPP$		521.8	45	

			Score/ Value	Rank	
	Business sophistication		**31.0**	**52**	
5.1	**Knowledge workers**		**48.4**	**[33]**	
5.1.1	Knowledge-intensive employment, %		14.9	89	◇
5.1.2	Firms offering formal training, %	⊙	65.9	5	●◆
5.1.3	GERD performed by business, % GDP		n/a	n/a	
5.1.4	GERD financed by business, %		n/a	n/a	
5.1.5	Females employed w/advanced degrees, %		11.5	67	
5.2	**Innovation linkages**		**11.6**	**110**	◇
5.2.1	University–industry R&D collaboration†		19.8	119	○◇
5.2.2	State of cluster development†		25.4	106	
5.2.3	GERD financed by abroad, % GDP		n/a	n/a	
5.2.4	Joint venture/strategic alliance deals/bn PPP$ GDP		0.0	125	○
5.2.5	Patent families/bn PPP$ GDP		0.0	79	
5.3	**Knowledge absorption**		**32.9**	**69**	
5.3.1	Intellectual property payments, % total trade		0.7	53	
5.3.2	High-tech imports, % total trade		9.2	46	
5.3.3	ICT services imports, % total trade		1.2	71	
5.3.4	FDI net inflows, % GDP		1.9	75	
5.3.5	Research talent, % in businesses		n/a	n/a	
	Knowledge and technology outputs		**13.6**	**101**	
6.1	**Knowledge creation**		**8.1**	**93**	
6.1.1	Patents by origin/bn PPP$ GDP		0.2	102	
6.1.2	PCT patents by origin/bn PPP$ GDP		0.1	70	
6.1.3	Utility models by origin/bn PPP$ GDP		0.4	35	
6.1.4	Scientific and technical articles/bn PPP$ GDP		4.8	106	
6.1.5	Citable documents H-index		15.0	56	
6.2	**Knowledge impact**		**21.6**	**94**	
6.2.1	Labor productivity growth, %		0.6	75	
6.2.2	Unicorn valuation, % GDP		0.0	48	○◇
6.2.3	Software spending, % GDP		0.2	63	
6.2.4	High-tech manufacturing, %		12.4	84	
6.3	**Knowledge diffusion**		**11.1**	**101**	◇
6.3.1	Intellectual property receipts, % total trade		0.1	68	
6.3.2	Production and export complexity		35.1	102	○◇
6.3.3	High-tech exports, % total trade		0.4	95	
6.3.4	ICT services exports, % total trade		0.2	120	○
6.3.5	ISO 9001 quality/bn PPP$ GDP		3.8	66	
	Creative outputs		**20.9**	**74**	
7.1	**Intangible assets**		**31.3**	**67**	
7.1.1	Intangible asset intensity, top 15, %		44.9	58	
7.1.2	Trademarks by origin/bn PPP$ GDP		62.3	35	●
7.1.3	Global brand value, top 5,000, % GDP		0.7	58	
7.1.4	Industrial designs by origin/bn PPP$ GDP		0.2	106	○
7.2	**Creative goods and services**		**3.1**	**95**	
7.2.1	Cultural and creative services exports, % total trade		n/a	n/a	
7.2.2	National feature films/mn pop. 15–69		0.1	80	○◇
7.2.3	Entertainment and media market/th pop. 15–69		6.2	39	
7.2.4	Creative goods exports, % total trade		0.2	73	
7.3	**Online creativity**		**17.8**	**78**	
7.3.1	Generic top-level domains (TLDs)/th pop. 15–69		5.7	54	
7.3.2	Country-code TLDs/th pop. 15–69		1.8	74	
7.3.3	GitHub commits/mn pop. 15–69		4.7	72	
7.3.4	Mobile app creation/bn PPP$ GDP		59.0	85	

NOTES: ● indicates a strength; ○ a weakness; ◆ an income group strength; ◇ an income group weakness; * an index; † a survey question. ⊙ is used when the available economy data are older than the base year; see appendices for details, including the year of the data, at wipo.int/gii-ranking. Square brackets [ ] indicate that the data minimum coverage (DMC) requirements were not met at the sub-pillar or pillar level.

Philippines

GII 2023 rank

56

Output rank	Input rank	Income	Region	Population (mn)	GDP, PPP$ (bn)	GDP per capita, PPP$
52	69	Lower middle	SEAO	115.6	1,154.9	10,344

		Score/Value	Rank	
	Institutions	**46.3**	**79**	
1.1	**Institutional environment**	**39.8**	**77**	
1.1.1	Operational stability for businesses*	41.0	93	
1.1.2	Government effectiveness*	38.7	62	◆
1.2	**Regulatory environment**	**47.0**	**108**	○
1.2.1	Regulatory quality*	44.1	69	◆
1.2.2	Rule of law*	20.9	106	○
1.2.3	Cost of redundancy dismissal	27.4	114	○
1.3	**Business environment**	**52.0**	**51**	
1.3.1	Policies for doing business†	41.9	81	
1.3.2	Entrepreneurship policies and culture† ⊙	62.0	22	
	Human capital and research	**25.3**	**88**	
2.1	**Education**	**33.2**	**115**	○
2.1.1	Expenditure on education, % GDP	3.9	79	
2.1.2	Government funding/pupil, secondary, % GDP/cap	n/a	n/a	
2.1.3	School life expectancy, years	13.1	82	
2.1.4	PISA scales in reading, maths and science	349.7	78	○
2.1.5	Pupil–teacher ratio, secondary	24.6	109	○
2.2	**Tertiary education**	**35.7**	**45**	◆
2.2.1	Tertiary enrolment, % gross	35.5	82	
2.2.2	Graduates in science and engineering, %	26.3	37	
2.2.3	Tertiary inbound mobility, %	n/a	n/a	
2.3	**Research and development (R&D)**	**6.9**	**70**	
2.3.1	Researchers, FTE/mn pop. ⊙	173.6	84	○
2.3.2	Gross expenditure on R&D, % GDP ⊙	0.3	73	
2.3.3	Global corporate R&D investors, top 3, mn USD	0.0	40	○◇
2.3.4	QS university ranking, top 3*	20.4	51	◆
	Infrastructure	**33.6**	**86**	
3.1	**Information and communication technologies (ICTs)**	**53.6**	**94**	
3.1.1	ICT access*	53.5	103	
3.1.2	ICT use*	54.1	100	
3.1.3	Government's online service*	59.1	76	
3.1.4	E-participation*	47.7	79	
3.2	**General infrastructure**	**26.9**	**64**	
3.2.1	Electricity output, GWh/mn pop. ⊙	928.6	99	
3.2.2	Logistics performance*	54.5	42	◆
3.2.3	Gross capital formation, % GDP	25.0	55	
3.3	**Ecological sustainability**	**20.4**	**80**	
3.3.1	GDP/unit of energy use	14.8	26	●◆
3.3.2	Environmental performance*	16.9	116	○
3.3.3	ISO 14001 environment/bn PPP$ GDP	1.0	64	◆
	Market sophistication	**37.7**	**55**	
4.1	**Credit**	**33.3**	**58**	
4.1.1	Finance for startups and scaleups† ⊙	81.2	7	
4.1.2	Domestic credit to private sector, % GDP	52.0	71	
4.1.3	Loans from microfinance institutions, % GDP	0.0	53	○
4.2	**Investment**	**12.1**	**51**	
4.2.1	Market capitalization, % GDP	74.3	23	
4.2.2	Venture capital (VC) investors, deals/bn PPP$ GDP	0.0	61	
4.2.3	VC recipients, deals/bn PPP$ GDP	0.0	74	
4.2.4	VC received, value, % GDP	0.0	47	
4.3	**Trade, diversification and market scale**	**67.8**	**23**	●◆
4.3.1	Applied tariff rate, weighted avg., %	1.7	52	◆
4.3.2	Domestic industry diversification	89.3	51	
4.3.3	Domestic market scale, bn PPP$	1,154.9	29	●

		Score/Value	Rank	
	Business sophistication	**37.9**	**38**	◆
5.1	**Knowledge workers**	**38.1**	**51**	◆
5.1.1	Knowledge-intensive employment, % ⊙	17.5	83	
5.1.2	Firms offering formal training, % ⊙	59.8	8	●◆
5.1.3	GERD performed by business, % GDP ⊙	0.1	68	
5.1.4	GERD financed by business, % ⊙	38.0	48	
5.1.5	Females employed w/advanced degrees, % ⊙	12.3	62	
5.2	**Innovation linkages**	**19.2**	**79**	
5.2.1	University–industry R&D collaboration†	46.8	57	
5.2.2	State of cluster development†	41.2	67	
5.2.3	GERD financed by abroad, % GDP ⊙	0.0	89	○
5.2.4	Joint venture/strategic alliance deals/bn PPP$ GDP	0.0	61	
5.2.5	Patent families/bn PPP$ GDP	0.0	84	
5.3	**Knowledge absorption**	**56.4**	**8**	●◆
5.3.1	Intellectual property payments, % total trade	0.6	60	
5.3.2	High-tech imports, % total trade	31.3	1	●◆
5.3.3	ICT services imports, % total trade	2.0	38	◆
5.3.4	FDI net inflows, % GDP	2.4	62	
5.3.5	Research talent, % in businesses ⊙	51.8	23	
	Knowledge and technology outputs	**29.9**	**46**	◆
6.1	**Knowledge creation**	**14.3**	**67**	
6.1.1	Patents by origin/bn PPP$ GDP	0.5	81	
6.1.2	PCT patents by origin/bn PPP$ GDP	0.0	82	
6.1.3	Utility models by origin/bn PPP$ GDP	1.7	9	●
6.1.4	Scientific and technical articles/bn PPP$ GDP	2.0	124	○
6.1.5	Citable documents H-index	15.3	55	
6.2	**Knowledge impact**	**31.6**	**50**	
6.2.1	Labor productivity growth, %	0.5	80	
6.2.2	Unicorn valuation, % GDP	0.2	44	
6.2.3	Software spending, % GDP	0.2	57	
6.2.4	High-tech manufacturing, %	40.3	26	●◆
6.3	**Knowledge diffusion**	**43.9**	**25**	●◆
6.3.1	Intellectual property receipts, % total trade	0.0	82	
6.3.2	Production and export complexity	70.1	30	◆
6.3.3	High-tech exports, % total trade	35.6	2	●◆
6.3.4	ICT services exports, % total trade	5.9	18	●◆
6.3.5	ISO 9001 quality/bn PPP$ GDP	3.7	67	
	Creative outputs	**26.4**	**60**	◆
7.1	**Intangible assets**	**33.3**	**60**	
7.1.1	Intangible asset intensity, top 15, %	57.0	41	
7.1.2	Trademarks by origin/bn PPP$ GDP	34.5	68	
7.1.3	Global brand value, top 5,000, % GDP	3.9	38	◆
7.1.4	Industrial designs by origin/bn PPP$ GDP	0.7	78	
7.2	**Creative goods and services**	**20.3**	**49**	◆
7.2.1	Cultural and creative services exports, % total trade	0.1	85	
7.2.2	National feature films/mn pop. 15–69	1.1	59	
7.2.3	Entertainment and media market/th pop. 15–69	4.2	44	◆
7.2.4	Creative goods exports, % total trade	5.8	10	●◆
7.3	**Online creativity**	**18.7**	**74**	
7.3.1	Generic top-level domains (TLDs)/th pop. 15–69	1.2	93	
7.3.2	Country-code TLDs/th pop. 15–69	0.4	101	
7.3.3	GitHub commits/mn pop. 15–69	3.1	88	
7.3.4	Mobile app creation/bn PPP$ GDP	70.2	55	

NOTES: ● indicates a strength; ○ a weakness; ◆ an income group strength; ◇ an income group weakness; * an index; † a survey question. ⊙ is used when the available economy data are older than the base year; see appendices for details, including the year of the data, at wipo.int/gii-ranking. Square brackets [ ] indicate that the data minimum coverage (DMC) requirements were not met at the sub-pillar or pillar level.

Poland

GII 2023 rank

41

Output rank	Input rank	Income	Region	Population (mn)	GDP, PPP$ (bn)	GDP per capita, PPP$
36	50	High	EUR	39.9	1,599.0	42,466

		Score/Value	Rank	
	Institutions	**47.1**	**76**	◇
1.1	**Institutional environment**	**53.0**	**50**	◇
1.1.1	Operational stability for businesses*	61.1	43	
1.1.2	Government effectiveness*	44.8	52	◇
1.2	**Regulatory environment**	**68.5**	**47**	
1.2.1	Regulatory quality*	63.9	37	
1.2.2	Rule of law*	52.7	45	◇
1.2.3	Cost of redundancy dismissal	18.8	80	
1.3	**Business environment**	**19.9**	**119**	○◇
1.3.1	Policies for doing business†	18.9	121	○◇
1.3.2	Entrepreneurship policies and culture†	21.0	68	○◇

		Score/Value	Rank	
	Human capital and research	**37.7**	**40**	
2.1	**Education**	**60.2**	**36**	
2.1.1	Expenditure on education, % GDP ⊙	4.7	47	
2.1.2	Government funding/pupil, secondary, % GDP/cap	21.2	46	
2.1.3	School life expectancy, years	16.1	36	
2.1.4	PISA scales in reading, maths and science	512.8	9	●
2.1.5	Pupil–teacher ratio, secondary	10.4	34	
2.2	**Tertiary education**	**29.1**	**70**	◇
2.2.1	Tertiary enrolment, % gross	70.5	36	
2.2.2	Graduates in science and engineering, %	19.4	78	
2.2.3	Tertiary inbound mobility, %	4.5	53	
2.3	**Research and development (R&D)**	**23.7**	**40**	
2.3.1	Researchers, FTE/mn pop.	3,584.8	29	
2.3.2	Gross expenditure on R&D, % GDP	1.4	29	
2.3.3	Global corporate R&D investors, top 3, mn USD	0.0	40	○◇
2.3.4	QS university ranking, top 3*	32.2	40	

		Score/Value	Rank	
	Infrastructure	**48.5**	**47**	◇
3.1	**Information and communication technologies (ICTs)**	**76.9**	**45**	
3.1.1	ICT access*	86.0	47	
3.1.2	ICT use*	80.4	57	◇
3.1.3	Government's online service*	77.1	43	
3.1.4	E-participation*	64.0	51	
3.2	**General infrastructure**	**36.3**	**39**	
3.2.1	Electricity output, GWh/mn pop.	4,681.6	49	
3.2.2	Logistics performance*	68.2	25	
3.2.3	Gross capital formation, % GDP	22.2	80	
3.3	**Ecological sustainability**	**32.2**	**45**	
3.3.1	GDP/unit of energy use	11.7	51	
3.3.2	Environmental performance*	53.7	39	
3.3.3	ISO 14001 environment/bn PPP$ GDP	2.0	47	

		Score/Value	Rank	
	Market sophistication	**34.5**	**67**	
4.1	**Credit**	**24.7**	**79**	◇
4.1.1	Finance for startups and scaleups†	54.3	40	
4.1.2	Domestic credit to private sector, % GDP	49.8	74	
4.1.3	Loans from microfinance institutions, % GDP	0.2	48	○
4.2	**Investment**	**5.0**	**76**	◇
4.2.1	Market capitalization, % GDP	27.4	49	
4.2.2	Venture capital (VC) investors, deals/bn PPP$ GDP	0.0	69	○
4.2.3	VC recipients, deals/bn PPP$ GDP	0.0	77	○
4.2.4	VC received, value, % GDP	0.0	74	○◇
4.3	**Trade, diversification and market scale**	**73.8**	**17**	●
4.3.1	Applied tariff rate, weighted avg., %	1.5	20	
4.3.2	Domestic industry diversification	96.7	22	●
4.3.3	Domestic market scale, bn PPP$	1,599.0	21	●

		Score/Value	Rank	
	Business sophistication	**36.7**	**41**	
5.1	**Knowledge workers**	**47.6**	**35**	
5.1.1	Knowledge-intensive employment, %	41.5	28	
5.1.2	Firms offering formal training, %	21.7	75	○◇
5.1.3	GERD performed by business, % GDP	0.9	26	
5.1.4	GERD financed by business, %	50.6	26	
5.1.5	Females employed w/advanced degrees, %	22.6	26	●
5.2	**Innovation linkages**	**18.8**	**84**	◇
5.2.1	University–industry R&D collaboration†	29.3	97	○◇
5.2.2	State of cluster development†	37.9	78	◇
5.2.3	GERD financed by abroad, % GDP	0.1	37	
5.2.4	Joint venture/strategic alliance deals/bn PPP$ GDP	0.0	78	
5.2.5	Patent families/bn PPP$ GDP	0.3	40	
5.3	**Knowledge absorption**	**43.6**	**34**	
5.3.1	Intellectual property payments, % total trade	1.1	32	
5.3.2	High-tech imports, % total trade	9.4	45	
5.3.3	ICT services imports, % total trade	1.7	47	
5.3.4	FDI net inflows, % GDP	3.9	33	
5.3.5	Research talent, % in businesses	53.1	21	

		Score/Value	Rank	
	Knowledge and technology outputs	**31.6**	**40**	
6.1	**Knowledge creation**	**25.3**	**39**	
6.1.1	Patents by origin/bn PPP$ GDP	2.7	26	●
6.1.2	PCT patents by origin/bn PPP$ GDP	0.2	39	
6.1.3	Utility models by origin/bn PPP$ GDP	0.5	33	
6.1.4	Scientific and technical articles/bn PPP$ GDP	20.8	34	
6.1.5	Citable documents H-index	37.0	26	●
6.2	**Knowledge impact**	**34.5**	**43**	
6.2.1	Labor productivity growth, %	3.3	11	●◆
6.2.2	Unicorn valuation, % GDP	0.0	48	○◇
6.2.3	Software spending, % GDP	0.3	40	
6.2.4	High-tech manufacturing, %	27.5	46	
6.3	**Knowledge diffusion**	**35.0**	**40**	
6.3.1	Intellectual property receipts, % total trade	0.3	35	
6.3.2	Production and export complexity	73.8	26	
6.3.3	High-tech exports, % total trade	6.0	32	
6.3.4	ICT services exports, % total trade	2.9	44	
6.3.5	ISO 9001 quality/bn PPP$ GDP	7.4	35	

		Score/Value	Rank	
	Creative outputs	**37.6**	**35**	
7.1	**Intangible assets**	**45.8**	**35**	
7.1.1	Intangible asset intensity, top 15, %	72.1	16	●
7.1.2	Trademarks by origin/bn PPP$ GDP	36.5	63	
7.1.3	Global brand value, top 5,000, % GDP	4.4	36	
7.1.4	Industrial designs by origin/bn PPP$ GDP	5.7	19	●
7.2	**Creative goods and services**	**24.1**	**44**	
7.2.1	Cultural and creative services exports, % total trade	1.0	29	
7.2.2	National feature films/mn pop. 15–69	1.9	48	◇
7.2.3	Entertainment and media market/th pop. 15–69	11.7	31	◇
7.2.4	Creative goods exports, % total trade	4.5	13	●◆
7.3	**Online creativity**	**34.8**	**34**	
7.3.1	Generic top-level domains (TLDs)/th pop. 15–69	7.9	47	
7.3.2	Country-code TLDs/th pop. 15–69	25.6	27	●
7.3.3	GitHub commits/mn pop. 15–69	32.3	33	
7.3.4	Mobile app creation/bn PPP$ GDP	73.2	38	

NOTES: ● indicates a strength; ○ a weakness; ◆ an income group strength; ◇ an income group weakness; * an index; † a survey question. ⊙ is used when the available economy data are older than the base year; see appendices for details, including the year of the data, at wipo.int/gii-ranking. Square brackets [ ] indicate that the data minimum coverage (DMC) requirements were not met at the sub-pillar or pillar level.

GII 2023 rank

Portugal

30

Output rank	Input rank	Income	Region	Population (mn)	GDP, PPP$ (bn)	GDP per capita, PPP$
29	31	High	EUR	10.3	432.1	42,067

			Score/Value	Rank
Institutions			**64.3**	**35**
1.1	**Institutional environment**		**69.6**	**25**
1.1.1	Operational stability for businesses*		75.0	17 ●
1.1.2	Government effectiveness*		64.1	32
1.2	**Regulatory environment**		**74.6**	**35**
1.2.1	Regulatory quality*		61.2	41
1.2.2	Rule of law*		72.9	23
1.2.3	Cost of redundancy dismissal		17.0	69 ○
1.3	**Business environment**		**48.6**	**59 ○**
1.3.1	Policies for doing business†		45.4	72 ○
1.3.2	Entrepreneurship policies and culture†	⏲	51.8	32
Human capital and research			**49.5**	**23**
2.1	**Education**		**63.7**	**17 ●**
2.1.1	Expenditure on education, % GDP	⏲	4.6	50
2.1.2	Government funding/pupil, secondary, % GDP/cap		28.5	11 ●◆
2.1.3	School life expectancy, years		17.0	19
2.1.4	PISA scales in reading, maths and science		492.0	26
2.1.5	Pupil-teacher ratio, secondary		8.5	18 ●
2.2	**Tertiary education**		**43.4**	**25**
2.2.1	Tertiary enrolment, % gross		70.4	37
2.2.2	Graduates in science and engineering, %		27.8	30
2.2.3	Tertiary inbound mobility, %		11.6	22
2.3	**Research and development (R&D)**		**41.5**	**26**
2.3.1	Researchers, FTE/mn pop.		5,473.3	15 ●
2.3.2	Gross expenditure on R&D, % GDP		1.7	23
2.3.3	Global corporate R&D investors, top 3, mn USD		45.7	37
2.3.4	QS university ranking, top 3*		33.4	38
Infrastructure			**50.8**	**45**
3.1	**Information and communication technologies (ICTs)**		**80.9**	**37**
3.1.1	ICT access*		88.6	30
3.1.2	ICT use*		85.4	39
3.1.3	Government's online service*		77.4	40
3.1.4	E-participation*		72.1	32
3.2	**General infrastructure**		**32.6**	**47**
3.2.1	Electricity output, GWh/mn pop.		4,771.7	47
3.2.2	Logistics performance*		59.1	37
3.2.3	Gross capital formation, % GDP		20.6	95 ○
3.3	**Ecological sustainability**		**39.0**	**34**
3.3.1	GDP/unit of energy use		16.6	18 ●
3.3.2	Environmental performance*		53.4	41
3.3.3	ISO 14001 environment/bn PPP$ GDP		2.8	32
Market sophistication			**43.4**	**42**
4.1	**Credit**		**52.6**	**25**
4.1.1	Finance for startups and scaleups†	⏲	67.5	20
4.1.2	Domestic credit to private sector, % GDP		101.0	29
4.1.3	Loans from microfinance institutions, % GDP		n/a	n/a
4.2	**Investment**		**11.0**	**52 ○**
4.2.1	Market capitalization, % GDP	⏲	29.1	47 ○
4.2.2	Venture capital (VC) investors, deals/bn PPP$ GDP		0.1	32
4.2.3	VC recipients, deals/bn PPP$ GDP		0.1	40
4.2.4	VC received, value, % GDP		0.0	53 ○
4.3	**Trade, diversification and market scale**		**66.5**	**26**
4.3.1	Applied tariff rate, weighted avg., %		1.5	20
4.3.2	Domestic industry diversification		100.0	1 ●
4.3.3	Domestic market scale, bn PPP$		432.1	49

		Score/Value	Rank
Business sophistication		**39.8**	**34**
5.1	**Knowledge workers**	**49.8**	**30**
5.1.1	Knowledge-intensive employment, %	41.9	26
5.1.2	Firms offering formal training, %	29.0	59 ○
5.1.3	GERD performed by business, % GDP	1.0	22
5.1.4	GERD financed by business, %	52.2	24
5.1.5	Females employed w/advanced degrees, %	21.2	29
5.2	**Innovation linkages**	**29.7**	**40**
5.2.1	University-industry R&D collaboration†	61.0	34
5.2.2	State of cluster development†	46.7	52
5.2.3	GERD financed by abroad, % GDP	0.1	35
5.2.4	Joint venture/strategic alliance deals/bn PPP$ GDP	0.0	45
5.2.5	Patent families/bn PPP$ GDP	0.6	30
5.3	**Knowledge absorption**	**39.8**	**46**
5.3.1	Intellectual property payments, % total trade	0.9	40
5.3.2	High-tech imports, % total trade	9.1	51
5.3.3	ICT services imports, % total trade	1.7	48
5.3.4	FDI net inflows, % GDP	3.0	46
5.3.5	Research talent, % in businesses	44.0	32
Knowledge and technology outputs		**34.4**	**32**
6.1	**Knowledge creation**	**31.9**	**30**
6.1.1	Patents by origin/bn PPP$ GDP	2.6	27
6.1.2	PCT patents by origin/bn PPP$ GDP	0.5	32
6.1.3	Utility models by origin/bn PPP$ GDP	0.2	48 ○
6.1.4	Scientific and technical articles/bn PPP$ GDP	40.2	8 ●◆
6.1.5	Citable documents H-index	33.9	30
6.2	**Knowledge impact**	**37.9**	**35**
6.2.1	Labor productivity growth, %	0.8	73 ○
6.2.2	Unicorn valuation, % GDP	0.0	48 ○◇
6.2.3	Software spending, % GDP	0.7	6 ●◆
6.2.4	High-tech manufacturing, %	29.4	41
6.3	**Knowledge diffusion**	**33.5**	**45**
6.3.1	Intellectual property receipts, % total trade	0.1	47
6.3.2	Production and export complexity	68.4	34
6.3.3	High-tech exports, % total trade	3.3	44
6.3.4	ICT services exports, % total trade	3.6	32
6.3.5	ISO 9001 quality/bn PPP$ GDP	11.1	24
Creative outputs		**46.0**	**19 ●**
7.1	**Intangible assets**	**55.2**	**16 ●**
7.1.1	Intangible asset intensity, top 15, %	67.9	22
7.1.2	Trademarks by origin/bn PPP$ GDP	97.8	14 ●◆
7.1.3	Global brand value, top 5,000, % GDP	4.9	33
7.1.4	Industrial designs by origin/bn PPP$ GDP	4.9	22
7.2	**Creative goods and services**	**23.1**	**45**
7.2.1	Cultural and creative services exports, % total trade	0.6	46 ○
7.2.2	National feature films/mn pop. 15–69	4.4	26
7.2.3	Entertainment and media market/th pop. 15–69	33.1	22
7.2.4	Creative goods exports, % total trade	1.5	34
7.3	**Online creativity**	**50.5**	**25**
7.3.1	Generic top-level domains (TLDs)/th pop. 15–69	22.5	29
7.3.2	Country-code TLDs/th pop. 15–69	66.9	11 ●◆
7.3.3	GitHub commits/mn pop. 15–69	41.0	25
7.3.4	Mobile app creation/bn PPP$ GDP	71.4	45

NOTES: ● indicates a strength; ○ a weakness; ◆ an income group strength; ◇ an income group weakness; * an index; † a survey question. ⏲ is used when the available economy data are older than the base year; see appendices for details, including the year of the data, at wipo.int/gii-ranking. Square brackets [ ] indicate that the data minimum coverage (DMC) requirements were not met at the sub-pillar or pillar level.

GII 2023 rank

Qatar

50

Output rank	Input rank	Income	Region	Population (mn)	GDP, PPP$ (bn)	GDP per capita, PPP$
70	39	High	NAWA	2.7	303.6	113,675

			Score/ Value	Rank	
	Institutions		**71.6**	**23**	●
1.1	**Institutional environment**		**67.4**	**31**	
1.1.1	Operational stability for businesses*		67.4	35	
1.1.2	Government effectiveness*		67.5	28	
1.2	**Regulatory environment**		**67.8**	**50**	
1.2.1	Regulatory quality*		64.5	34	
1.2.2	Rule of law*		66.9	30	
1.2.3	Cost of redundancy dismissal		23.2	101	◇
1.3	**Business environment**		**79.7**	**6**	● ◆
1.3.1	Policies for doing business†		79.4	9	●
1.3.2	Entrepreneurship policies and culture†		80.0	7	● ◆
	Human capital and research		**33.8**	**54**	◇
2.1	**Education**		**45.0**	**82**	◇
2.1.1	Expenditure on education, % GDP	⊙	3.2	99	◇
2.1.2	Government funding/pupil, secondary, % GDP/cap		n/a	n/a	
2.1.3	School life expectancy, years		12.8	85	◇
2.1.4	PISA scales in reading, maths and science		413.5	60	◇
2.1.5	Pupil–teacher ratio, secondary		12.5	57	
2.2	**Tertiary education**		**47.5**	**14**	●
2.2.1	Tertiary enrolment, % gross		25.0	93	◇
2.2.2	Graduates in science and engineering, %		18.7	83	
2.2.3	Tertiary inbound mobility, %		37.6	1	● ◆
2.3	**Research and development (R&D)**		**8.9**	**64**	◇
2.3.1	Researchers, FTE/mn pop.		902.6	53	◇
2.3.2	Gross expenditure on R&D, % GDP		0.7	52	
2.3.3	Global corporate R&D investors, top 3, mn USD		0.0	40	○ ◇
2.3.4	QS university ranking, top 3*		14.4	60	
	Infrastructure		**53.4**	**39**	
3.1	**Information and communication technologies (ICTs)**		**67.2**	**72**	◇
3.1.1	ICT access*		93.2	12	●
3.1.2	ICT use*		82.5	52	
3.1.3	Government's online service*		56.8	83	◇
3.1.4	E-participation*		36.0	93	◇
3.2	**General infrastructure**		**75.4**	**1**	● ◆
3.2.1	Electricity output, GWh/mn pop.	⊙	17,098.2	5	● ◆
3.2.2	Logistics performance*		63.6	33	
3.2.3	Gross capital formation, % GDP		n/a	n/a	
3.3	**Ecological sustainability**		**17.5**	**94**	◇
3.3.1	GDP/unit of energy use		5.7	111	◇
3.3.2	Environmental performance*		23.9	99	◇
3.3.3	ISO 14001 environment/bn PPP$ GDP		2.4	36	
	Market sophistication		**40.7**	**44**	
4.1	**Credit**		**57.5**	**20**	●
4.1.1	Finance for startups and scaleups†		62.3	28	
4.1.2	Domestic credit to private sector, % GDP		138.9	14	●
4.1.3	Loans from microfinance institutions, % GDP		n/a	n/a	
4.2	**Investment**		**10.3**	**55**	
4.2.1	Market capitalization, % GDP		98.2	16	
4.2.2	Venture capital (VC) investors, deals/bn PPP$ GDP		0.1	50	
4.2.3	VC recipients, deals/bn PPP$ GDP		0.0	99	○ ◇
4.2.4	VC received, value, % GDP		0.0	100	○ ◇
4.3	**Trade, diversification and market scale**		**54.5**	**77**	
4.3.1	Applied tariff rate, weighted avg., %		3.5	78	◇
4.3.2	Domestic industry diversification	⊙	80.1	76	
4.3.3	Domestic market scale, bn PPP$		303.6	60	

			Score/ Value	Rank	
	Business sophistication		**26.6**	**73**	◇
5.1	**Knowledge workers**		**15.2**	**112**	◇
5.1.1	Knowledge-intensive employment, %	⊙	21.9	69	◇
5.1.2	Firms offering formal training, %		n/a	n/a	
5.1.3	GERD performed by business, % GDP	⊙	0.1	67	◇
5.1.4	GERD financed by business, %	⊙	9.3	75	◇
5.1.5	Females employed w/advanced degrees, %	⊙	5.3	93	◇
5.2	**Innovation linkages**		**35.6**	**33**	
5.2.1	University–industry R&D collaboration†		82.8	10	●
5.2.2	State of cluster development†		76.8	16	●
5.2.3	GERD financed by abroad, % GDP	⊙	0.0	90	○ ◇
5.2.4	Joint venture/strategic alliance deals/bn PPP$ GDP		0.0	29	
5.2.5	Patent families/bn PPP$ GDP		0.0	72	
5.3	**Knowledge absorption**		**29.1**	**82**	◇
5.3.1	Intellectual property payments, % total trade	⊙	0.0	118	
5.3.2	High-tech imports, % total trade		6.0	102	
5.3.3	ICT services imports, % total trade		2.7	25	●
5.3.4	FDI net inflows, % GDP		−1.3	126	○
5.3.5	Research talent, % in businesses	⊙	16.1	55	◇
	Knowledge and technology outputs		**18.4**	**82**	◇
6.1	**Knowledge creation**		**9.4**	**83**	◇
6.1.1	Patents by origin/bn PPP$ GDP		0.2	103	◇
6.1.2	PCT patents by origin/bn PPP$ GDP		0.1	61	
6.1.3	Utility models by origin/bn PPP$ GDP		n/a	n/a	
6.1.4	Scientific and technical articles/bn PPP$ GDP		10.1	72	◇
6.1.5	Citable documents H-index		12.7	65	
6.2	**Knowledge impact**		**31.1**	**52**	
6.2.1	Labor productivity growth, %		0.3	87	
6.2.2	Unicorn valuation, % GDP		0.0	48	○ ◇
6.2.3	Software spending, % GDP		0.3	37	
6.2.4	High-tech manufacturing, %	⊙	37.7	30	
6.3	**Knowledge diffusion**		**14.6**	**92**	◇
6.3.1	Intellectual property receipts, % total trade	⊙	0.0	114	
6.3.2	Production and export complexity		48.8	70	◇
6.3.3	High-tech exports, % total trade		0.2	103	◇
6.3.4	ICT services exports, % total trade		1.1	84	
6.3.5	ISO 9001 quality/bn PPP$ GDP		3.9	63	
	Creative outputs		**24.7**	**65**	◇
7.1	**Intangible assets**		**38.3**	**49**	
7.1.1	Intangible asset intensity, top 15, %		48.0	50	
7.1.2	Trademarks by origin/bn PPP$ GDP		5.6	119	○ ◇
7.1.3	Global brand value, top 5,000, % GDP		9.4	19	●
7.1.4	Industrial designs by origin/bn PPP$ GDP		n/a	n/a	
7.2	**Creative goods and services**		**4.3**	**89**	◇
7.2.1	Cultural and creative services exports, % total trade		0.2	75	
7.2.2	National feature films/mn pop. 15–69		n/a	n/a	
7.2.3	Entertainment and media market/th pop. 15–69		9.9	34	◇
7.2.4	Creative goods exports, % total trade		0.0	131	○
7.3	**Online creativity**		**17.8**	**81**	◇
7.3.1	Generic top-level domains (TLDs)/th pop. 15–69		4.2	60	◇
7.3.2	Country-code TLDs/th pop. 15–69		2.8	66	◇
7.3.3	GitHub commits/mn pop. 15–69		3.4	85	◇
7.3.4	Mobile app creation/bn PPP$ GDP		60.5	80	◇

NOTES: ● indicates a strength; ○ a weakness; ◆ an income group strength; ◇ an income group weakness; * an index; † a survey question. ⊙ is used when the available economy data are older than the base year; see appendices for details, including the year of the data, at wipo.int/gii-ranking. Square brackets [ ] indicate that the data minimum coverage (DMC) requirements were not met at the sub-pillar or pillar level.

GII 2023 rank

Republic of Korea **10**

Output rank	Input rank	Income	Region	Population (mn)	GDP, PPP$ (bn)	GDP per capita, PPP$
7	12	High	SEAO	51.8	2,765.8	53,574

		Score/ Value	Rank	
	Institutions	**66.7**	**32**	◇
1.1	**Institutional environment**	**73.9**	**19**	
1.1.1	Operational stability for businesses*	72.2	22	
1.1.2	Government effectiveness*	75.6	16	
1.2	**Regulatory environment**	**66.6**	**53**	◇
1.2.1	Regulatory quality*	70.6	28	
1.2.2	Rule of law*	72.7	24	
1.2.3	Cost of redundancy dismissal	27.4	111	○◇
1.3	**Business environment**	**59.5**	**34**	
1.3.1	Policies for doing business†	52.0	58	◇
1.3.2	Entrepreneurship policies and culture†	67.1	17	
	Human capital and research	**66.9**	**1**	●◆
2.1	**Education**	**67.3**	**12**	
2.1.1	Expenditure on education, % GDP	⊙ 4.7	46	
2.1.2	Government funding/pupil, secondary, % GDP/cap	36.3	3	●◆
2.1.3	School life expectancy, years	16.6	26	
2.1.4	PISA scales in reading, maths and science	519.7	6	
2.1.5	Pupil–teacher ratio, secondary	11.8	52	
2.2	**Tertiary education**	**46.0**	**17**	
2.2.1	Tertiary enrolment, % gross	102.5	4	●◆
2.2.2	Graduates in science and engineering, %	30.2	18	◆
2.2.3	Tertiary inbound mobility, %	3.7	58	○◇
2.3	**Research and development (R&D)**	**87.3**	**1**	●◆
2.3.1	Researchers, FTE/mn pop.	9,097.1	2	●◆
2.3.2	Gross expenditure on R&D, % GDP	4.9	2	●◆
2.3.3	Global corporate R&D investors, top 3, mn USD	88.8	5	
2.3.4	QS university ranking, top 3*	77.4	10	
	Infrastructure	**60.6**	**11**	
3.1	**Information and communication technologies (ICTs)**	**95.7**	**1**	●◆
3.1.1	ICT access*	92.4	14	
3.1.2	ICT use*	98.1	4	●◆
3.1.3	Government's online service*	98.1	3	●◆
3.1.4	E-participation*	94.2	9	
3.2	**General infrastructure**	**56.5**	**10**	
3.2.1	Electricity output, GWh/mn pop.	11,597.6	12	
3.2.2	Logistics performance*	77.3	16	
3.2.3	Gross capital formation, % GDP	32.1	18	◆
3.3	**Ecological sustainability**	**29.7**	**55**	◇
3.3.1	GDP/unit of energy use	7.7	90	○
3.3.2	Environmental performance*	47.5	49	◇
3.3.3	ISO 14001 environment/bn PPP$ GDP	3.3	28	
	Market sophistication	**52.0**	**23**	
4.1	**Credit**	**64.7**	**11**	
4.1.1	Finance for startups and scaleups†	66.7	23	
4.1.2	Domestic credit to private sector, % GDP	164.1	7	
4.1.3	Loans from microfinance institutions, % GDP	n/a	n/a	
4.2	**Investment**	**17.4**	**42**	◇
4.2.1	Market capitalization, % GDP	101.4	15	
4.2.2	Venture capital (VC) investors, deals/bn PPP$ GDP	0.1	34	◇
4.2.3	VC recipients, deals/bn PPP$ GDP	0.0	63	○◇
4.2.4	VC received, value, % GDP	0.0	41	◇
4.3	**Trade, diversification and market scale**	**73.9**	**16**	
4.3.1	Applied tariff rate, weighted avg., %	5.5	94	○◇
4.3.2	Domestic industry diversification	⊙ 97.8	12	
4.3.3	Domestic market scale, bn PPP$	2,765.8	14	

		Score/ Value	Rank	
	Business sophistication	**60.9**	**9**	
5.1	**Knowledge workers**	**75.1**	**3**	●◆
5.1.1	Knowledge-intensive employment, %	39.6	31	◇
5.1.2	Firms offering formal training, %	n/a	n/a	
5.1.3	GERD performed by business, % GDP	3.9	2	●◆
5.1.4	GERD financed by business, %	76.1	4	◆
5.1.5	Females employed w/advanced degrees, %	21.4	28	
5.2	**Innovation linkages**	**52.0**	**19**	
5.2.1	University–industry R&D collaboration†	72.8	21	
5.2.2	State of cluster development†	70.4	22	
5.2.3	GERD financed by abroad, % GDP	0.0	69	○◇
5.2.4	Joint venture/strategic alliance deals/bn PPP$ GDP	0.0	32	◇
5.2.5	Patent families/bn PPP$ GDP	12.5	1	●◆
5.3	**Knowledge absorption**	**55.6**	**11**	
5.3.1	Intellectual property payments, % total trade	1.6	21	
5.3.2	High-tech imports, % total trade	17.2	13	
5.3.3	ICT services imports, % total trade	1.2	74	○◇
5.3.4	FDI net inflows, % GDP	0.7	106	○
5.3.5	Research talent, % in businesses	82.9	1	●◆
	Knowledge and technology outputs	**53.3**	**11**	
6.1	**Knowledge creation**	**66.1**	**5**	
6.1.1	Patents by origin/bn PPP$ GDP	74.0	1	●◆
6.1.2	PCT patents by origin/bn PPP$ GDP	8.0	1	●◆
6.1.3	Utility models by origin/bn PPP$ GDP	1.4	14	
6.1.4	Scientific and technical articles/bn PPP$ GDP	24.5	29	
6.1.5	Citable documents H-index	46.5	17	
6.2	**Knowledge impact**	**45.0**	**22**	
6.2.1	Labor productivity growth, %	1.2	58	
6.2.2	Unicorn valuation, % GDP	1.8	24	
6.2.3	Software spending, % GDP	0.2	65	○◇
6.2.4	High-tech manufacturing, %	⊙ 56.2	7	
6.3	**Knowledge diffusion**	**48.8**	**19**	
6.3.1	Intellectual property receipts, % total trade	1.2	20	
6.3.2	Production and export complexity	93.4	4	◆
6.3.3	High-tech exports, % total trade	27.9	6	◆
6.3.4	ICT services exports, % total trade	1.6	68	○
6.3.5	ISO 9001 quality/bn PPP$ GDP	7.0	41	
	Creative outputs	**58.2**	**5**	
7.1	**Intangible assets**	**79.4**	**2**	●◆
7.1.1	Intangible asset intensity, top 15, %	63.4	32	
7.1.2	Trademarks by origin/bn PPP$ GDP	119.0	7	◆
7.1.3	Global brand value, top 5,000, % GDP	16.8	6	
7.1.4	Industrial designs by origin/bn PPP$ GDP	24.3	3	●◆
7.2	**Creative goods and services**	**39.2**	**11**	
7.2.1	Cultural and creative services exports, % total trade	0.7	42	
7.2.2	National feature films/mn pop. 15–69	5.0	23	
7.2.3	Entertainment and media market/th pop. 15–69	50.8	16	
7.2.4	Creative goods exports, % total trade	5.0	12	◆
7.3	**Online creativity**	**34.9**	**33**	◇
7.3.1	Generic top-level domains (TLDs)/th pop. 15–69	9.5	43	◇
7.3.2	Country-code TLDs/th pop. 15–69	8.0	44	◇
7.3.3	GitHub commits/mn pop. 15–69	45.5	24	
7.3.4	Mobile app creation/bn PPP$ GDP	76.6	15	

NOTES: ● indicates a strength; ○ a weakness; ◆ an income group strength; ◇ an income group weakness; * an index; † a survey question. ⊙ is used when the available economy data are older than the base year; see appendices for details, including the year of the data, at wipo.int/gii-ranking. Square brackets [ ] indicate that the data minimum coverage (DMC) requirements were not met at the sub-pillar or pillar level.

GII 2023 rank

Republic of Moldova **60**

Output rank	Input rank	Income	Region	Population (mn)	GDP, PPP$ (bn)	GDP per capita, PPP$
50	81	Upper middle	EUR	3.3	41.9	16,483

			Score/ Value	Rank	
	Institutions		**39.4**	**96**	
1.1	**Institutional environment**		**36.4**	**87**	
1.1.1	Operational stability for businesses*		47.2	75	
1.1.2	Government effectiveness*		25.6	94	
1.2	**Regulatory environment**		**52.6**	**92**	
1.2.1	Regulatory quality*		42.5	72	
1.2.2	Rule of law*		30.0	82	
1.2.3	Cost of redundancy dismissal		23.7	102	
1.3	**Business environment**		**29.3**	**[102]**	
1.3.1	Policies for doing business†	⊙	29.3	108	○
1.3.2	Entrepreneurship policies and culture†		n/a	n/a	
	Human capital and research		**30.5**	**67**	
2.1	**Education**		**54.1**	**57**	
2.1.1	Expenditure on education, % GDP		5.8	20	●
2.1.2	Government funding/pupil, secondary, % GDP/cap		21.6	43	
2.1.3	School life expectancy, years		14.8	57	
2.1.4	PISA scales in reading, maths and science		424.4	51	
2.1.5	Pupil–teacher ratio, secondary		10.9	40	
2.2	**Tertiary education**		**34.4**	**51**	
2.2.1	Tertiary enrolment, % gross		62.7	51	
2.2.2	Graduates in science and engineering, %		25.0	45	
2.2.3	Tertiary inbound mobility, %		6.5	39	
2.3	**Research and development (R&D)**		**3.0**	**87**	
2.3.1	Researchers, FTE/mn pop.		788.1	58	
2.3.2	Gross expenditure on R&D, % GDP		0.2	85	
2.3.3	Global corporate R&D investors, top 3, mn USD		0.0	40	○◇
2.3.4	QS university ranking, top 3*		0.0	71	○◇
	Infrastructure		**37.3**	**75**	
3.1	**Information and communication technologies (ICTs)**		**73.4**	**55**	
3.1.1	ICT access*		84.2	57	
3.1.2	ICT use*		70.7	68	
3.1.3	Government's online service*		71.0	60	
3.1.4	E-participation*		67.4	47	
3.2	**General infrastructure**		**19.5**	**91**	
3.2.1	Electricity output, GWh/mn pop.		2,587.4	71	
3.2.2	Logistics performance*		18.2	89	○◇
3.2.3	Gross capital formation, % GDP		28.4	30	●
3.3	**Ecological sustainability**		**19.1**	**83**	
3.3.1	GDP/unit of energy use		7.3	94	
3.3.2	Environmental performance*		40.3	62	
3.3.3	ISO 14001 environment/bn PPP$ GDP		0.3	101	
	Market sophistication		**32.4**	**76**	
4.1	**Credit**		**32.2**	**60**	
4.1.1	Finance for startups and scaleups†		n/a	n/a	
4.1.2	Domestic credit to private sector, % GDP		27.9	102	
4.1.3	Loans from microfinance institutions, % GDP		4.7	7	●◆
4.2	**Investment**		**7.3**	**[63]**	
4.2.1	Market capitalization, % GDP		n/a	n/a	
4.2.2	Venture capital (VC) investors, deals/bn PPP$ GDP		n/a	n/a	
4.2.3	VC recipients, deals/bn PPP$ GDP	⊙	0.0	62	
4.2.4	VC received, value, % GDP	⊙	0.0	60	
4.3	**Trade, diversification and market scale**		**57.8**	**67**	
4.3.1	Applied tariff rate, weighted avg., %		1.3	14	●
4.3.2	Domestic industry diversification		80.8	71	
4.3.3	Domestic market scale, bn PPP$		41.9	116	○

			Score/ Value	Rank	
	Business sophistication		**21.3**	**101**	◇
5.1	**Knowledge workers**		**25.1**	**77**	
5.1.1	Knowledge-intensive employment, %		17.7	82	
5.1.2	Firms offering formal training, %		38.1	38	
5.1.3	GERD performed by business, % GDP	⊙	0.0	74	○
5.1.4	GERD financed by business, %	⊙	15.5	72	
5.1.5	Females employed w/advanced degrees, %		10.9	70	
5.2	**Innovation linkages**		**10.7**	**116**	○◇
5.2.1	University–industry R&D collaboration†	⊙	25.9	105	○
5.2.2	State of cluster development†	⊙	14.4	121	○◇
5.2.3	GERD financed by abroad, % GDP	⊙	0.0	72	
5.2.4	Joint venture/strategic alliance deals/bn PPP$ GDP		0.0	55	
5.2.5	Patent families/bn PPP$ GDP		0.1	51	
5.3	**Knowledge absorption**		**27.9**	**89**	
5.3.1	Intellectual property payments, % total trade		0.7	57	
5.3.2	High-tech imports, % total trade		8.4	61	
5.3.3	ICT services imports, % total trade		1.4	62	
5.3.4	FDI net inflows, % GDP		2.8	54	
5.3.5	Research talent, % in businesses	⊙	6.2	67	
	Knowledge and technology outputs		**23.8**	**60**	
6.1	**Knowledge creation**		**23.1**	**46**	
6.1.1	Patents by origin/bn PPP$ GDP		1.6	43	
6.1.2	PCT patents by origin/bn PPP$ GDP		0.1	62	
6.1.3	Utility models by origin/bn PPP$ GDP		2.9	5	●◆
6.1.4	Scientific and technical articles/bn PPP$ GDP		6.0	101	
6.1.5	Citable documents H-index		5.6	96	
6.2	**Knowledge impact**		**23.7**	**86**	
6.2.1	Labor productivity growth, %		2.2	28	●
6.2.2	Unicorn valuation, % GDP		0.0	48	○◇
6.2.3	Software spending, % GDP		0.1	93	
6.2.4	High-tech manufacturing, %		19.0	64	
6.3	**Knowledge diffusion**		**24.7**	**58**	
6.3.1	Intellectual property receipts, % total trade		0.0	72	
6.3.2	Production and export complexity		51.7	62	
6.3.3	High-tech exports, % total trade		0.7	83	
6.3.4	ICT services exports, % total trade		6.6	13	●◆
6.3.5	ISO 9001 quality/bn PPP$ GDP		2.5	80	
	Creative outputs		**33.2**	**42**	◆
7.1	**Intangible assets**		**49.8**	**27**	●◆
7.1.1	Intangible asset intensity, top 15, %		n/a	n/a	
7.1.2	Trademarks by origin/bn PPP$ GDP		101.6	11	●◆
7.1.3	Global brand value, top 5,000, % GDP		0.0	74	○◇
7.1.4	Industrial designs by origin/bn PPP$ GDP		16.7	6	●◆
7.2	**Creative goods and services**		**9.3**	**[70]**	
7.2.1	Cultural and creative services exports, % total trade		0.9	38	
7.2.2	National feature films/mn pop. 15–69		n/a	n/a	
7.2.3	Entertainment and media market/th pop. 15–69		n/a	n/a	
7.2.4	Creative goods exports, % total trade		0.1	102	
7.3	**Online creativity**		**23.8**	**55**	
7.3.1	Generic top-level domains (TLDs)/th pop. 15–69		3.0	71	
7.3.2	Country-code TLDs/th pop. 15–69		3.9	60	
7.3.3	GitHub commits/mn pop. 15–69		10.9	54	
7.3.4	Mobile app creation/bn PPP$ GDP		77.2	14	●◆

NOTES: ● indicates a strength; ○ a weakness; ◆ an income group strength; ◇ an income group weakness; * an index; † a survey question. ⊙ is used when the available economy data are older than the base year; see appendices for details, including the year of the data, at wipo.int/gii-ranking. Square brackets [ ] indicate that the data minimum coverage (DMC) requirements were not met at the sub-pillar or pillar level.

Romania

GII 2023 rank

47

Output rank	Input rank	Income	Region	Population (mn)	GDP, PPP$ (bn)	GDP per capita, PPP$
47	55	High	EUR	19.7	731.5	38,097

		Score/Value	Rank	
	Institutions	**47.6**	**74**	◇
1.1	**Institutional environment**	**44.4**	**70**	◇
1.1.1	Operational stability for businesses*	55.6	56	◇
1.1.2	Government effectiveness*	33.2	79	◇
1.2	**Regulatory environment**	**75.4**	**33**	
1.2.1	Regulatory quality*	50.1	55	◇
1.2.2	Rule of law*	51.7	46	◇
1.2.3	Cost of redundancy dismissal	8.0	1	● ◆
1.3	**Business environment**	**22.9**	**115**	○ ◇
1.3.1	Policies for doing business†	32.2	102	◇
1.3.2	Entrepreneurship policies and culture†	13.7	76	○ ◇
	Human capital and research	**29.1**	**75**	◇
2.1	**Education**	**46.8**	**77**	◇
2.1.1	Expenditure on education, % GDP ⊙	3.6	87	
2.1.2	Government funding/pupil, secondary, % GDP/cap	20.0	54	
2.1.3	School life expectancy, years	14.3	68	◇
2.1.4	PISA scales in reading, maths and science	427.8	49	◇
2.1.5	Pupil–teacher ratio, secondary	11.7	50	
2.2	**Tertiary education**	**35.8**	**43**	
2.2.1	Tertiary enrolment, % gross	53.2	66	
2.2.2	Graduates in science and engineering, %	29.1	23	
2.2.3	Tertiary inbound mobility, %	6.0	42	
2.3	**Research and development (R&D)**	**4.6**	**77**	◇
2.3.1	Researchers, FTE/mn pop.	995.4	52	◇
2.3.2	Gross expenditure on R&D, % GDP	0.5	61	◇
2.3.3	Global corporate R&D investors, top 3, mn USD	0.0	40	○ ◇
2.3.4	QS university ranking, top 3*	0.0	71	○ ◇
	Infrastructure	**54.5**	**34**	
3.1	**Information and communication technologies (ICTs)**	**74.0**	**53**	
3.1.1	ICT access*	86.0	46	
3.1.2	ICT use*	83.5	49	
3.1.3	Government's online service*	64.8	69	◇
3.1.4	E-participation*	61.6	54	
3.2	**General infrastructure**	**30.6**	**52**	◇
3.2.1	Electricity output, GWh/mn pop.	3,082.9	65	◇
3.2.2	Logistics performance*	50.0	50	◇
3.2.3	Gross capital formation, % GDP	27.8	33	
3.3	**Ecological sustainability**	**58.9**	**6**	● ◆
3.3.1	GDP/unit of energy use	15.7	21	●
3.3.2	Environmental performance*	62.9	29	
3.3.3	ISO 14001 environment/bn PPP$ GDP	9.5	8	● ◆
	Market sophistication	**32.8**	**75**	
4.1	**Credit**	**28.4**	**68**	◇
4.1.1	Finance for startups and scaleups†	39.3	58	◇
4.1.2	Domestic credit to private sector, % GDP	25.8	108	○ ◇
4.1.3	Loans from microfinance institutions, % GDP	3.2	11	●
4.2	**Investment**	**2.5**	**98**	○ ◇
4.2.1	Market capitalization, % GDP	9.7	73	○ ◇
4.2.2	Venture capital (VC) investors, deals/bn PPP$ GDP	0.0	76	○
4.2.3	VC recipients, deals/bn PPP$ GDP	0.0	84	○
4.2.4	VC received, value, % GDP	0.0	87	○ ◇
4.3	**Trade, diversification and market scale**	**67.5**	**25**	
4.3.1	Applied tariff rate, weighted avg., %	1.5	20	
4.3.2	Domestic industry diversification	96.5	23	
4.3.3	Domestic market scale, bn PPP$	731.5	35	

		Score/Value	Rank	
	Business sophistication	**32.1**	**51**	
5.1	**Knowledge workers**	**35.6**	**59**	
5.1.1	Knowledge-intensive employment, %	28.2	50	◇
5.1.2	Firms offering formal training, %	20.5	80	○ ◇
5.1.3	GERD performed by business, % GDP	0.3	48	
5.1.4	GERD financed by business, %	55.6	21	
5.1.5	Females employed w/advanced degrees, %	13.3	57	◇
5.2	**Innovation linkages**	**17.9**	**86**	◇
5.2.1	University–industry R&D collaboration†	38.2	79	◇
5.2.2	State of cluster development†	38.1	76	◇
5.2.3	GERD financed by abroad, % GDP	0.1	49	
5.2.4	Joint venture/strategic alliance deals/bn PPP$ GDP	0.0	87	
5.2.5	Patent families/bn PPP$ GDP	0.0	66	
5.3	**Knowledge absorption**	**42.7**	**37**	
5.3.1	Intellectual property payments, % total trade	0.9	43	
5.3.2	High-tech imports, % total trade	10.1	35	
5.3.3	ICT services imports, % total trade	2.9	18	●
5.3.4	FDI net inflows, % GDP	2.8	53	
5.3.5	Research talent, % in businesses	33.1	39	
	Knowledge and technology outputs	**33.3**	**35**	
6.1	**Knowledge creation**	**13.5**	**68**	◇
6.1.1	Patents by origin/bn PPP$ GDP	1.2	53	
6.1.2	PCT patents by origin/bn PPP$ GDP	0.1	73	◇
6.1.3	Utility models by origin/bn PPP$ GDP	0.1	57	
6.1.4	Scientific and technical articles/bn PPP$ GDP	13.6	55	
6.1.5	Citable documents H-index	19.8	42	
6.2	**Knowledge impact**	**39.6**	**31**	
6.2.1	Labor productivity growth, %	3.3	10	● ◆
6.2.2	Unicorn valuation, % GDP	0.0	48	○ ◇
6.2.3	Software spending, % GDP	0.3	43	
6.2.4	High-tech manufacturing, %	43.8	21	
6.3	**Knowledge diffusion**	**46.9**	**21**	●
6.3.1	Intellectual property receipts, % total trade	0.1	58	
6.3.2	Production and export complexity	79.2	19	●
6.3.3	High-tech exports, % total trade	6.5	28	
6.3.4	ICT services exports, % total trade	6.7	12	●
6.3.5	ISO 9001 quality/bn PPP$ GDP	18.3	15	● ◆
	Creative outputs	**26.9**	**58**	
7.1	**Intangible assets**	**32.4**	**62**	
7.1.1	Intangible asset intensity, top 15, %	49.7	49	
7.1.2	Trademarks by origin/bn PPP$ GDP	38.3	61	
7.1.3	Global brand value, top 5,000, % GDP	1.5	49	
7.1.4	Industrial designs by origin/bn PPP$ GDP	1.1	65	
7.2	**Creative goods and services**	**15.5**	**57**	
7.2.1	Cultural and creative services exports, % total trade	1.8	12	●
7.2.2	National feature films/mn pop. 15–69	1.3	55	◇
7.2.3	Entertainment and media market/th pop. 15–69	7.8	38	◇
7.2.4	Creative goods exports, % total trade	0.8	50	
7.3	**Online creativity**	**27.3**	**45**	
7.3.1	Generic top-level domains (TLDs)/th pop. 15–69	5.7	53	
7.3.2	Country-code TLDs/th pop. 15–69	13.7	36	
7.3.3	GitHub commits/mn pop. 15–69	19.1	45	
7.3.4	Mobile app creation/bn PPP$ GDP	70.5	53	

NOTES: ● indicates a strength; ○ a weakness; ◆ an income group strength; ◇ an income group weakness; * an index; † a survey question. ⊙ is used when the available economy data are older than the base year; see appendices for details, including the year of the data, at wipo.int/gii-ranking. Square brackets [ ] indicate that the data minimum coverage (DMC) requirements were not met at the sub-pillar or pillar level.

GII 2023 rank

Russian Federation 51

Output rank	Input rank	Income	Region	Population (mn)	GDP, PPP$ (bn)	GDP per capita, PPP$
53	58	Upper middle	EUR	144.7	4,649.7	31,967

			Score/ Value	Rank	
Institutions			**34.9**	**110**	○◇
1.1	**Institutional environment**		**25.3**	**111**	○◇
1.1.1	Operational stability for businesses*		18.8	124	○◇
1.1.2	Government effectiveness*		31.9	83	
1.2	**Regulatory environment**		**51.4**	**95**	
1.2.1	Regulatory quality*		28.4	101	◇
1.2.2	Rule of law*		14.2	114	○◇
1.2.3	Cost of redundancy dismissal		17.3	73	
1.3	**Business environment**		**27.9**	**105**	
1.3.1	Policies for doing business†	⊙	39.1	87	
1.3.2	Entrepreneurship policies and culture†	⊙	16.8	71	○◇
Human capital and research			**47.2**	**26**	◆
2.1	**Education**		**57.0**	**50**	
2.1.1	Expenditure on education, % GDP	⊙	3.5	90	
2.1.2	Government funding/pupil, secondary, % GDP/cap		n/a	n/a	
2.1.3	School life expectancy, years	⊙	15.8	43	
2.1.4	PISA scales in reading, maths and science		481.3	31	◆
2.1.5	Pupil–teacher ratio, secondary	⊙	13.7	68	
2.2	**Tertiary education**		**45.9**	**20**	●◆
2.2.1	Tertiary enrolment, % gross	⊙	86.4	16	●◆
2.2.2	Graduates in science and engineering, %		32.6	13	●◆
2.2.3	Tertiary inbound mobility, %	⊙	5.0	49	
2.3	**Research and development (R&D)**		**38.7**	**27**	◆
2.3.1	Researchers, FTE/mn pop.	⊙	2,711.9	33	◆
2.3.2	Gross expenditure on R&D, % GDP	⊙	1.1	37	◆
2.3.3	Global corporate R&D investors, top 3, mn USD		58.0	26	◆
2.3.4	QS university ranking, top 3*		49.0	21	●◆
Infrastructure			**38.0**	**72**	
3.1	**Information and communication technologies (ICTs)**		**74.8**	**49**	
3.1.1	ICT access*		82.8	63	
3.1.2	ICT use*		86.3	32	◆
3.1.3	Government's online service*		70.9	61	
3.1.4	E-participation*		59.3	57	
3.2	**General infrastructure**		**25.8**	**69**	
3.2.1	Electricity output, GWh/mn pop.		8,060.6	19	●◆
3.2.2	Logistics performance*		22.7	82	
3.2.3	Gross capital formation, % GDP		20.1	97	
3.3	**Ecological sustainability**		**13.4**	**111**	○◇
3.3.1	GDP/unit of energy use		4.7	120	○◇
3.3.2	Environmental performance*		31.5	84	
3.3.3	ISO 14001 environment/bn PPP$ GDP		0.2	110	○
Market sophistication			**37.7**	**56**	
4.1	**Credit**		**18.6**	**97**	
4.1.1	Finance for startups and scaleups†	⊙	30.6	70	
4.1.2	Domestic credit to private sector, % GDP		59.7	61	
4.1.3	Loans from microfinance institutions, % GDP	⊙	0.3	45	
4.2	**Investment**		**4.7**	**80**	
4.2.1	Market capitalization, % GDP		42.7	40	
4.2.2	Venture capital (VC) investors, deals/bn PPP$ GDP		0.0	82	○
4.2.3	VC recipients, deals/bn PPP$ GDP		0.0	100	○◇
4.2.4	VC received, value, % GDP		0.0	80	
4.3	**Trade, diversification and market scale**		**89.8**	**7**	●◆
4.3.1	Applied tariff rate, weighted avg., %		4.1	85	
4.3.2	Domestic industry diversification		95.7	26	
4.3.3	Domestic market scale, bn PPP$		4,649.7	1	●◆

			Score/ Value	Rank	
Business sophistication			**34.7**	**44**	
5.1	**Knowledge workers**		**41.8**	**44**	
5.1.1	Knowledge-intensive employment, %	⊙	45.5	22	●◆
5.1.2	Firms offering formal training, %		11.8	94	○◇
5.1.3	GERD performed by business, % GDP	⊙	0.6	35	
5.1.4	GERD financed by business, %		29.2	60	
5.1.5	Females employed w/advanced degrees, %	⊙	26.1	16	●◆
5.2	**Innovation linkages**		**19.7**	**76**	
5.2.1	University–industry R&D collaboration†	⊙	45.7	60	
5.2.2	State of cluster development†	⊙	43.1	60	
5.2.3	GERD financed by abroad, % GDP		0.0	63	
5.2.4	Joint venture/strategic alliance deals/bn PPP$ GDP		0.0	94	
5.2.5	Patent families/bn PPP$ GDP		0.2	45	
5.3	**Knowledge absorption**		**42.7**	**36**	
5.3.1	Intellectual property payments, % total trade		1.7	18	●◆
5.3.2	High-tech imports, % total trade		8.6	56	
5.3.3	ICT services imports, % total trade		1.4	61	
5.3.4	FDI net inflows, % GDP		1.6	84	
5.3.5	Research talent, % in businesses	⊙	46.5	30	◆
Knowledge and technology outputs			**26.4**	**54**	
6.1	**Knowledge creation**		**29.5**	**32**	◆
6.1.1	Patents by origin/bn PPP$ GDP		4.5	18	●◆
6.1.2	PCT patents by origin/bn PPP$ GDP		0.2	48	
6.1.3	Utility models by origin/bn PPP$ GDP		2.0	8	●◆
6.1.4	Scientific and technical articles/bn PPP$ GDP		8.5	83	
6.1.5	Citable documents H-index		38.1	25	◆
6.2	**Knowledge impact**		**27.7**	**60**	
6.2.1	Labor productivity growth, %		1.3	56	
6.2.2	Unicorn valuation, % GDP		0.0	48	○◇
6.2.3	Software spending, % GDP		0.2	73	
6.2.4	High-tech manufacturing, %		29.0	43	
6.3	**Knowledge diffusion**		**22.0**	**65**	
6.3.1	Intellectual property receipts, % total trade		0.3	37	◆
6.3.2	Production and export complexity		56.7	51	
6.3.3	High-tech exports, % total trade		2.3	55	
6.3.4	ICT services exports, % total trade		1.6	69	
6.3.5	ISO 9001 quality/bn PPP$ GDP		1.0	109	○
Creative outputs			**29.9**	**53**	
7.1	**Intangible assets**		**41.0**	**40**	
7.1.1	Intangible asset intensity, top 15, %		51.5	47	
7.1.2	Trademarks by origin/bn PPP$ GDP		72.9	23	
7.1.3	Global brand value, top 5,000, % GDP		3.3	42	
7.1.4	Industrial designs by origin/bn PPP$ GDP		1.4	56	
7.2	**Creative goods and services**		**10.9**	**64**	
7.2.1	Cultural and creative services exports, % total trade		1.0	30	
7.2.2	National feature films/mn pop. 15–69		1.4	53	
7.2.3	Entertainment and media market/th pop. 15–69		n/a	n/a	
7.2.4	Creative goods exports, % total trade		0.4	67	
7.3	**Online creativity**		**26.4**	**48**	
7.3.1	Generic top-level domains (TLDs)/th pop. 15–69		3.8	62	
7.3.2	Country-code TLDs/th pop. 15–69		13.9	35	
7.3.3	GitHub commits/mn pop. 15–69		13.7	50	
7.3.4	Mobile app creation/bn PPP$ GDP		74.4	30	

NOTES: ● indicates a strength; ○ a weakness; ◆ an income group strength; ◇ an income group weakness; * an index; † a survey question. ⊙ is used when the available economy data are older than the base year; see appendices for details, including the year of the data, at wipo.int/gii-ranking. Square brackets [ ] indicate that the data minimum coverage (DMC) requirements were not met at the sub-pillar or pillar level.

Rwanda

GII 2023 rank

103

Output rank	Input rank	Income	Region	Population (mn)	GDP, PPP$ (bn)	GDP per capita, PPP$
113	85	Low	SSA	13.8	37.6	2,836

		Score/ Value	Rank
	Institutions	**65.4**	**33 ●◆**
1.1	**Institutional environment**	**53.9**	**47 ◆**
1.1.1	Operational stability for businesses*	63.9	39 ●◆
1.1.2	Government effectiveness*	44.0	55 ◆
1.2	**Regulatory environment**	**63.2**	**66**
1.2.1	Regulatory quality*	43.9	70 ◆
1.2.2	Rule of law*	45.6	56 ◆
1.2.3	Cost of redundancy dismissal	17.3	70
1.3	**Business environment**	**79.1**	**[8]**
1.3.1	Policies for doing business†	79.1	11 ●◆
1.3.2	Entrepreneurship policies and culture†	n/a	n/a
	Human capital and research	**22.6**	**94 ◆**
2.1	**Education**	**37.7**	**106**
2.1.1	Expenditure on education, % GDP	4.0	70
2.1.2	Government funding/pupil, secondary, % GDP/cap	24.8	22 ●
2.1.3	School life expectancy, years ⊙	11.2	97
2.1.4	PISA scales in reading, maths and science	n/a	n/a
2.1.5	Pupil–teacher ratio, secondary	27.4	116 ○
2.2	**Tertiary education**	**26.6**	**75 ◆**
2.2.1	Tertiary enrolment, % gross	7.3	120 ○
2.2.2	Graduates in science and engineering, %	32.1	15 ●◆
2.2.3	Tertiary inbound mobility, %	4.2	55
2.3	**Research and development (R&D)**	**3.5**	**85 ◆**
2.3.1	Researchers, FTE/mn pop. ⊙	58.8	94
2.3.2	Gross expenditure on R&D, % GDP ⊙	0.8	48 ◆
2.3.3	Global corporate R&D investors, top 3, mn USD	0.0	40 ○◇
2.3.4	QS university ranking, top 3*	0.0	71 ○◇
	Infrastructure	**27.9**	**101 ◆**
3.1	**Information and communication technologies (ICTs)**	**53.7**	**93 ◆**
3.1.1	ICT access*	44.1	115 ◆
3.1.2	ICT use*	30.6	115 ◆
3.1.3	Government's online service*	77.2	41 ●◆
3.1.4	E-participation*	62.8	53 ◆
3.2	**General infrastructure**	**18.3**	**99**
3.2.1	Electricity output, GWh/mn pop. ⊙	67.2	124 ○
3.2.2	Logistics performance*	31.8	71 ◆
3.2.3	Gross capital formation, % GDP	25.8	46
3.3	**Ecological sustainability**	**11.6**	**121**
3.3.1	GDP/unit of energy use	5.5	112
3.3.2	Environmental performance*	23.6	100
3.3.3	ISO 14001 environment/bn PPP$ GDP	0.2	109
	Market sophistication	**18.6**	**115**
4.1	**Credit**	**8.1**	**118**
4.1.1	Finance for startups and scaleups†	n/a	n/a
4.1.2	Domestic credit to private sector, % GDP	25.0	110
4.1.3	Loans from microfinance institutions, % GDP	0.7	33
4.2	**Investment**	**18.0**	**39 ◆**
4.2.1	Market capitalization, % GDP ⊙	31.0	46
4.2.2	Venture capital (VC) investors, deals/bn PPP$ GDP	n/a	n/a
4.2.3	VC recipients, deals/bn PPP$ GDP	0.1	20 ●◆
4.2.4	VC received, value, % GDP	0.0	57 ◆
4.3	**Trade, diversification and market scale**	**29.7**	**116**
4.3.1	Applied tariff rate, weighted avg., %	10.2	119
4.3.2	Domestic industry diversification	54.4	103 ○
4.3.3	Domestic market scale, bn PPP$	37.6	121

		Score/ Value	Rank
	Business sophistication	**20.0**	**109 ◆**
5.1	**Knowledge workers**	**12.1**	**115**
5.1.1	Knowledge-intensive employment, % ⊙	6.5	116
5.1.2	Firms offering formal training, %	35.9	43 ◆
5.1.3	GERD performed by business, % GDP ⊙	0.0	73 ◆
5.1.4	GERD financed by business, % ⊙	0.6	94 ○
5.1.5	Females employed w/advanced degrees, % ⊙	3.3	100 ◆
5.2	**Innovation linkages**	**24.9**	**55 ◆**
5.2.1	University–industry R&D collaboration†	35.9	82
5.2.2	State of cluster development†	39.5	72 ◆
5.2.3	GERD financed by abroad, % GDP ⊙	0.2	18 ●◆
5.2.4	Joint venture/strategic alliance deals/bn PPP$ GDP	0.0	34 ●◆
5.2.5	Patent families/bn PPP$ GDP	0.0	95 ○◇
5.3	**Knowledge absorption**	**23.0**	**114**
5.3.1	Intellectual property payments, % total trade	0.0	115
5.3.2	High-tech imports, % total trade	10.9	28 ●◆
5.3.3	ICT services imports, % total trade	0.7	95
5.3.4	FDI net inflows, % GDP	2.0	71
5.3.5	Research talent, % in businesses ⊙	5.6	68
	Knowledge and technology outputs	**13.6**	**100**
6.1	**Knowledge creation**	**8.2**	**92**
6.1.1	Patents by origin/bn PPP$ GDP	0.5	82 ◆
6.1.2	PCT patents by origin/bn PPP$ GDP	0.0	101 ○◇
6.1.3	Utility models by origin/bn PPP$ GDP	0.1	61
6.1.4	Scientific and technical articles/bn PPP$ GDP	14.0	53 ◆
6.1.5	Citable documents H-index	4.2	113
6.2	**Knowledge impact**	**27.7**	**61 ◆**
6.2.1	Labor productivity growth, %	6.0	2 ●◆
6.2.2	Unicorn valuation, % GDP	0.0	48 ○◇
6.2.3	Software spending, % GDP	0.0	106
6.2.4	High-tech manufacturing, %	7.3	97
6.3	**Knowledge diffusion**	**5.1**	**126 ○**
6.3.1	Intellectual property receipts, % total trade	0.0	92
6.3.2	Production and export complexity	n/a	n/a
6.3.3	High-tech exports, % total trade	0.6	87 ◆
6.3.4	ICT services exports, % total trade	1.0	88
6.3.5	ISO 9001 quality/bn PPP$ GDP	0.5	118
	Creative outputs	**6.9**	**117**
7.1	**Intangible assets**	**7.0**	**114**
7.1.1	Intangible asset intensity, top 15, %	n/a	n/a
7.1.2	Trademarks by origin/bn PPP$ GDP	20.6	92
7.1.3	Global brand value, top 5,000, % GDP	0.0	74 ○◇
7.1.4	Industrial designs by origin/bn PPP$ GDP	0.3	95
7.2	**Creative goods and services**	**1.5**	**[110]**
7.2.1	Cultural and creative services exports, % total trade	0.0	99
7.2.2	National feature films/mn pop. 15–69	n/a	n/a
7.2.3	Entertainment and media market/th pop. 15–69	n/a	n/a
7.2.4	Creative goods exports, % total trade	0.2	75 ◆
7.3	**Online creativity**	**12.2**	**109 ◆**
7.3.1	Generic top-level domains (TLDs)/th pop. 15–69	0.2	121
7.3.2	Country-code TLDs/th pop. 15–69	0.2	115
7.3.3	GitHub commits/mn pop. 15–69	2.7	93 ◆
7.3.4	Mobile app creation/bn PPP$ GDP	45.7	108

NOTES: ● indicates a strength; ○ a weakness; ◆ an income group strength; ◇ an income group weakness; * an index; † a survey question. ⊙ is used when the available economy data are older than the base year; see appendices for details, including the year of the data, at wipo.int/gii-ranking. Square brackets [ ] indicate that the data minimum coverage (DMC) requirements were not met at the sub-pillar or pillar level.

GII 2023 rank

Saudi Arabia

48

Output rank	Input rank	Income	Region	Population (mn)	GDP, PPP$ (bn)	GDP per capita, PPP$
67	37	High	NAWA	36.4	2,018.3	55,802

		Score/ Value	Rank	
	Institutions	**59.2**	**45**	
1.1	**Institutional environment**	**44.3**	**71**	◇
1.1.1	Operational stability for businesses*	38.2	100	◇
1.1.2	Government effectiveness*	50.4	46	◇
1.2	**Regulatory environment**	**58.7**	**78**	◇
1.2.1	Regulatory quality*	50.8	53	◇
1.2.2	Rule of law*	46.5	54	◇
1.2.3	Cost of redundancy dismissal	23.7	103	○ ◇
1.3	**Business environment**	**74.6**	**15**	●
1.3.1	Policies for doing business†	75.4	16	●
1.3.2	Entrepreneurship policies and culture†	73.7	11	● ◆

		Score/ Value	Rank	
	Human capital and research	**40.6**	**35**	
2.1	**Education**	**56.4**	**[51]**	
2.1.1	Expenditure on education, % GDP	n/a	n/a	
2.1.2	Government funding/pupil, secondary, % GDP/cap	n/a	n/a	
2.1.3	School life expectancy, years	16.2	33	
2.1.4	PISA scales in reading, maths and science	386.2	71	○ ◇
2.1.5	Pupil–teacher ratio, secondary	13.5	65	
2.2	**Tertiary education**	**32.1**	**61**	
2.2.1	Tertiary enrolment, % gross	71.4	32	
2.2.2	Graduates in science and engineering, %	22.8	56	
2.2.3	Tertiary inbound mobility, %	4.0	56	
2.3	**Research and development (R&D)**	**33.2**	**33**	
2.3.1	Researchers, FTE/mn pop.	700.6	62	◇
2.3.2	Gross expenditure on R&D, % GDP	0.5	63	◇
2.3.3	Global corporate R&D investors, top 3, mn USD	68.2	16	●
2.3.4	QS university ranking, top 3*	49.3	20	●

		Score/ Value	Rank	
	Infrastructure	**48.3**	**48**	◇
3.1	**Information and communication technologies (ICTs)**	**85.2**	**20**	●
3.1.1	ICT access*	96.4	7	● ◆
3.1.2	ICT use*	95.3	10	●
3.1.3	Government's online service*	80.3	32	
3.1.4	E-participation*	68.6	43	
3.2	**General infrastructure**	**43.9**	**28**	
3.2.1	Electricity output, GWh/mn pop.	⊙ 11,349.5	13	●
3.2.2	Logistics performance*	59.1	37	
3.2.3	Gross capital formation, % GDP	20.8	90	
3.3	**Ecological sustainability**	**16.0**	**101**	○ ◇
3.3.1	GDP/unit of energy use	6.7	102	○
3.3.2	Environmental performance*	32.2	81	◇
3.3.3	ISO 14001 environment/bn PPP$ GDP	0.4	94	◇

		Score/ Value	Rank	
	Market sophistication	**47.5**	**28**	
4.1	**Credit**	**44.7**	**37**	
4.1.1	Finance for startups and scaleups†	70.3	18	
4.1.2	Domestic credit to private sector, % GDP	⊙ 54.0	69	
4.1.3	Loans from microfinance institutions, % GDP	n/a	n/a	
4.2	**Investment**	**33.1**	**20**	
4.2.1	Market capitalization, % GDP	235.2	4	● ◆
4.2.2	Venture capital (VC) investors, deals/bn PPP$ GDP	0.1	51	
4.2.3	VC recipients, deals/bn PPP$ GDP	0.0	80	○
4.2.4	VC received, value, % GDP	0.0	22	
4.3	**Trade, diversification and market scale**	**64.8**	**30**	
4.3.1	Applied tariff rate, weighted avg., %	4.2	87	◇
4.3.2	Domestic industry diversification	78.5	81	
4.3.3	Domestic market scale, bn PPP$	2,018.3	17	●

		Score/ Value	Rank	
	Business sophistication	**34.4**	**[45]**	
5.1	**Knowledge workers**	**n/a**	**[n/a]**	
5.1.1	Knowledge-intensive employment, %	n/a	n/a	
5.1.2	Firms offering formal training, %	n/a	n/a	
5.1.3	GERD performed by business, % GDP	n/a	n/a	
5.1.4	GERD financed by business, %	n/a	n/a	
5.1.5	Females employed w/advanced degrees, %	n/a	n/a	
5.2	**Innovation linkages**	**38.5**	**29**	
5.2.1	University–industry R&D collaboration†	53.9	45	
5.2.2	State of cluster development†	82.9	8	● ◆
5.2.3	GERD financed by abroad, % GDP	n/a	n/a	
5.2.4	Joint venture/strategic alliance deals/bn PPP$ GDP	0.0	54	
5.2.5	Patent families/bn PPP$ GDP	0.4	35	
5.3	**Knowledge absorption**	**30.3**	**[79]**	
5.3.1	Intellectual property payments, % total trade	n/a	n/a	
5.3.2	High-tech imports, % total trade	7.5	74	
5.3.3	ICT services imports, % total trade	0.5	111	○ ◇
5.3.4	FDI net inflows, % GDP	1.2	96	
5.3.5	Research talent, % in businesses	n/a	n/a	

		Score/ Value	Rank	
	Knowledge and technology outputs	**22.0**	**68**	◇
6.1	**Knowledge creation**	**21.5**	**51**	
6.1.1	Patents by origin/bn PPP$ GDP	0.8	64	
6.1.2	PCT patents by origin/bn PPP$ GDP	0.2	42	
6.1.3	Utility models by origin/bn PPP$ GDP	n/a	n/a	
6.1.4	Scientific and technical articles/bn PPP$ GDP	20.0	38	
6.1.5	Citable documents H-index	27.3	37	
6.2	**Knowledge impact**	**22.4**	**92**	◇
6.2.1	Labor productivity growth, %	−1.9	126	○ ◇
6.2.2	Unicorn valuation, % GDP	0.0	48	○ ◇
6.2.3	Software spending, % GDP	0.3	35	
6.2.4	High-tech manufacturing, %	26.3	47	
6.3	**Knowledge diffusion**	**22.0**	**66**	◇
6.3.1	Intellectual property receipts, % total trade	n/a	n/a	
6.3.2	Production and export complexity	65.4	42	
6.3.3	High-tech exports, % total trade	0.8	76	◇
6.3.4	ICT services exports, % total trade	0.6	98	
6.3.5	ISO 9001 quality/bn PPP$ GDP	1.3	99	◇

		Score/ Value	Rank	
	Creative outputs	**24.1**	**66**	◇
7.1	**Intangible assets**	**35.4**	**54**	
7.1.1	Intangible asset intensity, top 15, %	65.1	27	
7.1.2	Trademarks by origin/bn PPP$ GDP	13.9	103	○ ◇
7.1.3	Global brand value, top 5,000, % GDP	9.9	18	
7.1.4	Industrial designs by origin/bn PPP$ GDP	0.5	82	◇
7.2	**Creative goods and services**	**7.9**	**75**	◇
7.2.1	Cultural and creative services exports, % total trade	0.0	97	○ ◇
7.2.2	National feature films/mn pop. 15–69	n/a	n/a	
7.2.3	Entertainment and media market/th pop. 15–69	18.8	28	
7.2.4	Creative goods exports, % total trade	0.4	66	
7.3	**Online creativity**	**17.5**	**82**	◇
7.3.1	Generic top-level domains (TLDs)/th pop. 15–69	3.0	69	◇
7.3.2	Country-code TLDs/th pop. 15–69	1.0	91	◇
7.3.3	GitHub commits/mn pop. 15–69	1.8	101	○ ◇
7.3.4	Mobile app creation/bn PPP$ GDP	64.2	68	

NOTES: ● indicates a strength; ○ a weakness; ◆ an income group strength; ◇ an income group weakness; * an index; † a survey question. ⊙ is used when the available economy data are older than the base year; see appendices for details, including the year of the data, at wipo.int/gii-ranking. Square brackets [ ] indicate that the data minimum coverage (DMC) requirements were not met at the sub-pillar or pillar level.

Senegal

GII 2023 rank

93

Output rank	Input rank	Income	Region	Population (mn)	GDP, PPP$ (bn)	GDP per capita, PPP$
93	95	Lower middle	SSA	17.3	72.7	4,113

		Score/Value	Rank
	Institutions	**52.0**	**59 ◆**
1.1	**Institutional environment**	**48.4**	**57 ◆**
1.1.1	Operational stability for businesses*	58.3	49 ◆
1.1.2	Government effectiveness*	38.4	65 ◆
1.2	**Regulatory environment**	**59.0**	**76**
1.2.1	Regulatory quality*	34.0	88
1.2.2	Rule of law*	29.0	85
1.2.3	Cost of redundancy dismissal	14.8	59
1.3	**Business environment**	**48.6**	**58**
1.3.1	Policies for doing business†	43.2	76
1.3.2	Entrepreneurship policies and culture†	⊙ 54.0	27
	Human capital and research	**18.1**	**107**
2.1	**Education**	**38.2**	**103**
2.1.1	Expenditure on education, % GDP	5.6	23 ●
2.1.2	Government funding/pupil, secondary, % GDP/cap	⊙ 20.2	52
2.1.3	School life expectancy, years	9.0	108 ○◇
2.1.4	PISA scales in reading, maths and science	n/a	n/a
2.1.5	Pupil–teacher ratio, secondary	24.5	108
2.2	**Tertiary education**	**12.1**	**107**
2.2.1	Tertiary enrolment, % gross	15.6	104
2.2.2	Graduates in science and engineering, %	n/a	n/a
2.2.3	Tertiary inbound mobility, %	6.3	40 ●
2.3	**Research and development (R&D)**	**4.0**	**80**
2.3.1	Researchers, FTE/mn pop.	⊙ 564.3	68
2.3.2	Gross expenditure on R&D, % GDP	⊙ 0.6	56
2.3.3	Global corporate R&D investors, top 3, mn USD	0.0	40 ○◇
2.3.4	QS university ranking, top 3*	0.0	71 ○◇
	Infrastructure	**29.2**	**98**
3.1	**Information and communication technologies (ICTs)**	**45.0**	**106**
3.1.1	ICT access*	48.1	111
3.1.2	ICT use*	55.4	98
3.1.3	Government's online service*	44.0	100
3.1.4	E-participation*	32.6	100
3.2	**General infrastructure**	**24.0**	**77**
3.2.1	Electricity output, GWh/mn pop.	⊙ 346.4	114 ○
3.2.2	Logistics performance*	n/a	n/a
3.2.3	Gross capital formation, % GDP	40.2	8 ●◆
3.3	**Ecological sustainability**	**18.8**	**86**
3.3.1	GDP/unit of energy use	12.0	48
3.3.2	Environmental performance*	25.4	98
3.3.3	ISO 14001 environment/bn PPP$ GDP	0.3	97
	Market sophistication	**30.7**	**81**
4.1	**Credit**	**30.2**	**66**
4.1.1	Finance for startups and scaleups†	⊙ 42.9	56
4.1.2	Domestic credit to private sector, % GDP	29.4	98
4.1.3	Loans from microfinance institutions, % GDP	3.3	10 ●
4.2	**Investment**	**20.9**	**34 ●**
4.2.1	Market capitalization, % GDP	n/a	n/a
4.2.2	Venture capital (VC) investors, deals/bn PPP$ GDP	0.1	45 ◆
4.2.3	VC recipients, deals/bn PPP$ GDP	0.1	37 ●◆
4.2.4	VC received, value, % GDP	0.0	19 ●◆
4.3	**Trade, diversification and market scale**	**40.9**	**101**
4.3.1	Applied tariff rate, weighted avg., %	9.1	112
4.3.2	Domestic industry diversification	⊙ 80.0	77
4.3.3	Domestic market scale, bn PPP$	72.7	95

		Score/Value	Rank
	Business sophistication	**16.5**	**122 ○◇**
5.1	**Knowledge workers**	**5.7**	**126 ○◇**
5.1.1	Knowledge-intensive employment, %	⊙ 4.6	119 ○◇
5.1.2	Firms offering formal training, %	⊙ 17.4	87 ○◇
5.1.3	GERD performed by business, % GDP	n/a	n/a
5.1.4	GERD financed by business, %	⊙ 2.1	88 ◇
5.1.5	Females employed w/advanced degrees, %	⊙ 1.0	117 ○
5.2	**Innovation linkages**	**16.4**	**92**
5.2.1	University–industry R&D collaboration†	45.1	62
5.2.2	State of cluster development†	25.4	105
5.2.3	GERD financed by abroad, % GDP	⊙ 0.0	51 ◆
5.2.4	Joint venture/strategic alliance deals/bn PPP$ GDP	0.0	97
5.2.5	Patent families/bn PPP$ GDP	0.0	70
5.3	**Knowledge absorption**	**27.3**	**90**
5.3.1	Intellectual property payments, % total trade	0.1	98
5.3.2	High-tech imports, % total trade	5.0	115
5.3.3	ICT services imports, % total trade	1.3	68
5.3.4	FDI net inflows, % GDP	6.7	13 ●◆
5.3.5	Research talent, % in businesses	n/a	n/a
	Knowledge and technology outputs	**23.1**	**63**
6.1	**Knowledge creation**	**6.0**	**107**
6.1.1	Patents by origin/bn PPP$ GDP	0.5	77
6.1.2	PCT patents by origin/bn PPP$ GDP	0.0	101 ○◇
6.1.3	Utility models by origin/bn PPP$ GDP	0.0	75 ○◇
6.1.4	Scientific and technical articles/bn PPP$ GDP	7.6	90
6.1.5	Citable documents H-index	6.2	93
6.2	**Knowledge impact**	**51.0**	**13 ●◆**
6.2.1	Labor productivity growth, %	0.9	69
6.2.2	Unicorn valuation, % GDP	5.7	1 ●◆
6.2.3	Software spending, % GDP	0.3	54
6.2.4	High-tech manufacturing, %	⊙ 22.1	59
6.3	**Knowledge diffusion**	**12.3**	**97**
6.3.1	Intellectual property receipts, % total trade	0.1	64
6.3.2	Production and export complexity	38.9	95
6.3.3	High-tech exports, % total trade	0.3	97
6.3.4	ICT services exports, % total trade	1.4	72
6.3.5	ISO 9001 quality/bn PPP$ GDP	1.2	102
	Creative outputs	**8.5**	**113**
7.1	**Intangible assets**	**7.0**	**113**
7.1.1	Intangible asset intensity, top 15, %	n/a	n/a
7.1.2	Trademarks by origin/bn PPP$ GDP	11.1	110
7.1.3	Global brand value, top 5,000, % GDP	1.5	48
7.1.4	Industrial designs by origin/bn PPP$ GDP	0.4	89
7.2	**Creative goods and services**	**10.4**	**[65]**
7.2.1	Cultural and creative services exports, % total trade	0.9	32 ●
7.2.2	National feature films/mn pop. 15–69	n/a	n/a
7.2.3	Entertainment and media market/th pop. 15–69	n/a	n/a
7.2.4	Creative goods exports, % total trade	0.2	85
7.3	**Online creativity**	**9.4**	**117**
7.3.1	Generic top-level domains (TLDs)/th pop. 15–69	1.1	96
7.3.2	Country-code TLDs/th pop. 15–69	0.2	110
7.3.3	GitHub commits/mn pop. 15–69	0.9	114
7.3.4	Mobile app creation/bn PPP$ GDP	35.4	116 ○◇

NOTES: ● indicates a strength; ○ a weakness; ◆ an income group strength; ◇ an income group weakness; * an index; † a survey question. ⊙ is used when the available economy data are older than the base year; see appendices for details, including the year of the data, at wipo.int/gii-ranking. Square brackets [ ] indicate that the data minimum coverage (DMC) requirements were not met at the sub-pillar or pillar level.

Serbia

GII 2023 rank

53

Output rank	Input rank	Income	Region	Population (mn)	GDP, PPP$ (bn)	GDP per capita, PPP$
64	41	Upper middle	EUR	7.2	164.8	24,084

		Score/ Value	Rank	
	Institutions	**53.2**	**57**	
1.1	**Institutional environment**	**45.1**	**66**	
1.1.1	Operational stability for businesses*	52.1	69	
1.1.2	Government effectiveness*	38.1	66	
1.2	**Regulatory environment**	**70.1**	**43**	
1.2.1	Regulatory quality*	43.5	71	
1.2.2	Rule of law*	37.0	68	
1.2.3	Cost of redundancy dismissal	8.0	1	● ◆
1.3	**Business environment**	**44.3**	**72**	
1.3.1	Policies for doing business†	46.0	68	
1.3.2	Entrepreneurship policies and culture†	42.5	45	

		Score/ Value	Rank	
	Human capital and research	**34.7**	**51**	
2.1	**Education**	**54.9**	**55**	
2.1.1	Expenditure on education, % GDP ⊙	3.6	85	
2.1.2	Government funding/pupil, secondary, % GDP/cap	n/a	n/a	
2.1.3	School life expectancy, years	14.4	66	
2.1.4	PISA scales in reading, maths and science	442.5	44	
2.1.5	Pupil–teacher ratio, secondary	7.6	5	● ◆
2.2	**Tertiary education**	**39.1**	**36**	
2.2.1	Tertiary enrolment, % gross	69.2	42	
2.2.2	Graduates in science and engineering, %	30.1	20	◆
2.2.3	Tertiary inbound mobility, %	4.5	52	
2.3	**Research and development (R&D)**	**10.1**	**60**	
2.3.1	Researchers, FTE/mn pop.	2,206.8	38	◆
2.3.2	Gross expenditure on R&D, % GDP	1.0	40	
2.3.3	Global corporate R&D investors, top 3, mn USD	0.0	40	○ ◇
2.3.4	QS university ranking, top 3*	0.0	71	○ ◇

		Score/ Value	Rank	
	Infrastructure	**54.4**	**35**	◆
3.1	**Information and communication technologies (ICTs)**	**83.3**	**26**	◆
3.1.1	ICT access*	87.4	39	
3.1.2	ICT use*	81.8	54	
3.1.3	Government's online service*	83.6	26	◆
3.1.4	E-participation*	80.2	15	● ◆
3.2	**General infrastructure**	**28.2**	**60**	
3.2.1	Electricity output, GWh/mn pop.	5,482.2	42	◆
3.2.2	Logistics performance*	31.8	71	
3.2.3	Gross capital formation, % GDP	27.0	38	
3.3	**Ecological sustainability**	**51.7**	**20**	◆
3.3.1	GDP/unit of energy use	7.6	91	
3.3.2	Environmental performance*	42.4	59	
3.3.3	ISO 14001 environment/bn PPP$ GDP	12.3	2	● ◆

		Score/ Value	Rank	
	Market sophistication	**43.7**	**41**	
4.1	**Credit**	**23.7**	**82**	
4.1.1	Finance for startups and scaleups†	31.6	66	○
4.1.2	Domestic credit to private sector, % GDP	45.5	79	
4.1.3	Loans from microfinance institutions, % GDP	n/a	n/a	
4.2	**Investment**	**n/a**	**[n/a]**	
4.2.1	Market capitalization, % GDP	n/a	n/a	
4.2.2	Venture capital (VC) investors, deals/bn PPP$ GDP	n/a	n/a	
4.2.3	VC recipients, deals/bn PPP$ GDP	n/a	n/a	
4.2.4	VC received, value, % GDP	n/a	n/a	
4.3	**Trade, diversification and market scale**	**63.6**	**37**	
4.3.1	Applied tariff rate, weighted avg., % ⊙	1.4	19	
4.3.2	Domestic industry diversification	96.7	21	◆
4.3.3	Domestic market scale, bn PPP$	164.8	75	

		Score/ Value	Rank	
	Business sophistication	**27.8**	**68**	
5.1	**Knowledge workers**	**29.7**	**70**	
5.1.1	Knowledge-intensive employment, % ⊙	28.3	49	
5.1.2	Firms offering formal training, %	38.3	37	
5.1.3	GERD performed by business, % GDP	0.4	42	
5.1.4	GERD financed by business, %	2.1	87	○ ◇
5.1.5	Females employed w/advanced degrees, % ⊙	15.2	49	
5.2	**Innovation linkages**	**20.4**	**69**	
5.2.1	University–industry R&D collaboration†	44.5	65	
5.2.2	State of cluster development†	38.2	75	
5.2.3	GERD financed by abroad, % GDP	0.1	40	
5.2.4	Joint venture/strategic alliance deals/bn PPP$ GDP	0.0	92	○
5.2.5	Patent families/bn PPP$ GDP	0.1	61	
5.3	**Knowledge absorption**	**33.1**	**67**	
5.3.1	Intellectual property payments, % total trade	1.2	28	
5.3.2	High-tech imports, % total trade	6.8	90	
5.3.3	ICT services imports, % total trade	1.8	45	
5.3.4	FDI net inflows, % GDP	7.4	11	● ◆
5.3.5	Research talent, % in businesses	10.5	61	○

		Score/ Value	Rank	
	Knowledge and technology outputs	**31.4**	**41**	
6.1	**Knowledge creation**	**24.5**	**41**	
6.1.1	Patents by origin/bn PPP$ GDP	1.1	57	
6.1.2	PCT patents by origin/bn PPP$ GDP	0.2	49	
6.1.3	Utility models by origin/bn PPP$ GDP	0.7	27	
6.1.4	Scientific and technical articles/bn PPP$ GDP	33.8	14	● ◆
6.1.5	Citable documents H-index	16.8	52	
6.2	**Knowledge impact**	**26.4**	**66**	
6.2.1	Labor productivity growth, %	3.1	14	●
6.2.2	Unicorn valuation, % GDP	0.0	48	○ ◇
6.2.3	Software spending, % GDP	0.0	112	○ ◇
6.2.4	High-tech manufacturing, %	24.3	54	
6.3	**Knowledge diffusion**	**43.4**	**27**	◆
6.3.1	Intellectual property receipts, % total trade	0.3	36	◆
6.3.2	Production and export complexity	67.0	38	
6.3.3	High-tech exports, % total trade	2.5	51	
6.3.4	ICT services exports, % total trade	6.0	17	● ◆
6.3.5	ISO 9001 quality/bn PPP$ GDP	23.6	5	● ◆

		Score/ Value	Rank	
	Creative outputs	**15.6**	**92**	
7.1	**Intangible assets**	**8.7**	**110**	○ ◇
7.1.1	Intangible asset intensity, top 15, %	−110.4	79	○ ◇
7.1.2	Trademarks by origin/bn PPP$ GDP	25.8	82	
7.1.3	Global brand value, top 5,000, % GDP	0.0	74	○ ◇
7.1.4	Industrial designs by origin/bn PPP$ GDP	0.9	72	
7.2	**Creative goods and services**	**19.1**	**51**	
7.2.1	Cultural and creative services exports, % total trade	1.8	13	● ◆
7.2.2	National feature films/mn pop. 15–69	2.3	44	
7.2.3	Entertainment and media market/th pop. 15–69	n/a	n/a	
7.2.4	Creative goods exports, % total trade	0.5	61	
7.3	**Online creativity**	**25.7**	**49**	
7.3.1	Generic top-level domains (TLDs)/th pop. 15–69	2.1	82	
7.3.2	Country-code TLDs/th pop. 15–69	7.4	46	
7.3.3	GitHub commits/mn pop. 15–69	19.0	46	◆
7.3.4	Mobile app creation/bn PPP$ GDP	74.6	28	

NOTES: ● indicates a strength; ○ a weakness; ◆ an income group strength; ◇ an income group weakness; * an index; † a survey question. ⊙ is used when the available economy data are older than the base year; see appendices for details, including the year of the data, at wipo.int/gii-ranking. Square brackets [ ] indicate that the data minimum coverage (DMC) requirements were not met at the sub-pillar or pillar level.

Singapore

GII 2023 rank

5

Output rank	Input rank	Income	Region	Population (mn)	GDP, PPP$ (bn)	GDP per capita, PPP$
12	1	High	SEAO	6.0	701.0	131,426

			Score/ Value	Rank	
	Institutions		**98.4**	**1**	●◆
1.1	**Institutional environment**		**100.0**	**1**	●◆
1.1.1	Operational stability for businesses*		100.0	1	●◆
1.1.2	Government effectiveness*		100.0	1	●◆
1.2	**Regulatory environment**		**98.5**	**1**	●◆
1.2.1	Regulatory quality*		100.0	1	●◆
1.2.2	Rule of law*		94.1	4	
1.2.3	Cost of redundancy dismissal		8.0	1	●
1.3	**Business environment**		**96.7**	**[1]**	
1.3.1	Policies for doing business†		96.7	2	●◆
1.3.2	Entrepreneurship policies and culture†		n/a	n/a	
	Human capital and research		**63.2**	**2**	●◆
2.1	**Education**		**58.2**	**46**	
2.1.1	Expenditure on education, % GDP		2.5	113	○◇
2.1.2	Government funding/pupil, secondary, % GDP/cap		20.6	49	○
2.1.3	School life expectancy, years		16.6	25	
2.1.4	PISA scales in reading, maths and science		556.5	2	●◆
2.1.5	Pupil–teacher ratio, secondary		11.5	45	
2.2	**Tertiary education**		**69.8**	**2**	●◆
2.2.1	Tertiary enrolment, % gross		93.1	9	
2.2.2	Graduates in science and engineering, %		36.3	6	◆
2.2.3	Tertiary inbound mobility, %		n/a	n/a	
2.3	**Research and development (R&D)**		**61.5**	**14**	
2.3.1	Researchers, FTE/mn pop.	⊙	7,488.4	5	
2.3.2	Gross expenditure on R&D, % GDP	⊙	2.2	16	
2.3.3	Global corporate R&D investors, top 3, mn USD		60.2	23	
2.3.4	QS university ranking, top 3*		68.6	12	
	Infrastructure		**63.1**	**8**	
3.1	**Information and communication technologies (ICTs)**		**94.5**	**5**	◆
3.1.1	ICT access*		100.0	1	●◆
3.1.2	ICT use*		84.7	40	◇
3.1.3	Government's online service*		95.8	5	◆
3.1.4	E-participation*		97.7	3	●◆
3.2	**General infrastructure**		**57.2**	**9**	
3.2.1	Electricity output, GWh/mn pop.		10,295.2	15	
3.2.2	Logistics performance*		100.0	1	●◆
3.2.3	Gross capital formation, % GDP		23.6	69	○
3.3	**Ecological sustainability**		**37.6**	**37**	
3.3.1	GDP/unit of energy use		16.3	20	
3.3.2	Environmental performance*		54.2	37	
3.3.3	ISO 14001 environment/bn PPP$ GDP		2.2	40	
	Market sophistication		**67.4**	**6**	
4.1	**Credit**		**49.4**	**[29]**	
4.1.1	Finance for startups and scaleups†		n/a	n/a	
4.1.2	Domestic credit to private sector, % GDP		130.6	17	
4.1.3	Loans from microfinance institutions, % GDP		n/a	n/a	
4.2	**Investment**		**89.8**	**1**	●◆
4.2.1	Market capitalization, % GDP		185.7	6	◆
4.2.2	Venture capital (VC) investors, deals/bn PPP$ GDP		1.9	3	●◆
4.2.3	VC recipients, deals/bn PPP$ GDP		0.9	1	●◆
4.2.4	VC received, value, % GDP		0.0	1	●◆
4.3	**Trade, diversification and market scale**		**63.0**	**45**	
4.3.1	Applied tariff rate, weighted avg., %		0.0	3	●◆
4.3.2	Domestic industry diversification		74.2	88	○◇
4.3.3	Domestic market scale, bn PPP$		701.0	37	

			Score/ Value	Rank	
	Business sophistication		**69.4**	**3**	●◆
5.1	**Knowledge workers**		**72.3**	**5**	
5.1.1	Knowledge-intensive employment, %	⊙	59.9	2	●◆
5.1.2	Firms offering formal training, %		n/a	n/a	
5.1.3	GERD performed by business, % GDP	⊙	1.4	18	
5.1.4	GERD financed by business, %		58.3	16	
5.1.5	Females employed w/advanced degrees, %	⊙	29.6	3	●◆
5.2	**Innovation linkages**		**61.6**	**12**	
5.2.1	University–industry R&D collaboration†		85.5	8	
5.2.2	State of cluster development†		80.8	11	
5.2.3	GERD financed by abroad, % GDP		0.1	38	○
5.2.4	Joint venture/strategic alliance deals/bn PPP$ GDP		0.2	6	
5.2.5	Patent families/bn PPP$ GDP		2.6	14	
5.3	**Knowledge absorption**		**74.4**	**1**	●◆
5.3.1	Intellectual property payments, % total trade		2.6	9	
5.3.2	High-tech imports, % total trade		24.3	5	◆
5.3.3	ICT services imports, % total trade		4.0	9	
5.3.4	FDI net inflows, % GDP		26.0	6	◆
5.3.5	Research talent, % in businesses	⊙	54.2	19	
	Knowledge and technology outputs		**55.3**	**10**	
6.1	**Knowledge creation**		**44.1**	**20**	
6.1.1	Patents by origin/bn PPP$ GDP		3.2	24	
6.1.2	PCT patents by origin/bn PPP$ GDP		2.5	11	
6.1.3	Utility models by origin/bn PPP$ GDP		n/a	n/a	
6.1.4	Scientific and technical articles/bn PPP$ GDP		21.0	33	
6.1.5	Citable documents H-index		40.0	22	
6.2	**Knowledge impact**		**69.2**	**2**	●◆
6.2.1	Labor productivity growth, %		2.1	31	◆
6.2.2	Unicorn valuation, % GDP		5.1	8	◆
6.2.3	Software spending, % GDP		0.2	59	○◇
6.2.4	High-tech manufacturing, %		78.5	1	●◆
6.3	**Knowledge diffusion**		**52.6**	**13**	
6.3.1	Intellectual property receipts, % total trade		1.6	16	
6.3.2	Production and export complexity		91.8	5	
6.3.3	High-tech exports, % total trade		28.6	4	◆
6.3.4	ICT services exports, % total trade		2.8	46	
6.3.5	ISO 9001 quality/bn PPP$ GDP		6.9	42	
	Creative outputs		**46.0**	**18**	
7.1	**Intangible assets**		**39.9**	**41**	◇
7.1.1	Intangible asset intensity, top 15, %		42.4	59	○◇
7.1.2	Trademarks by origin/bn PPP$ GDP		23.7	87	○◇
7.1.3	Global brand value, top 5,000, % GDP		13.5	11	
7.1.4	Industrial designs by origin/bn PPP$ GDP		1.1	66	○◇
7.2	**Creative goods and services**		**47.2**	**6**	◆
7.2.1	Cultural and creative services exports, % total trade		4.9	1	●◆
7.2.2	National feature films/mn pop. 15–69		0.8	62	○◇
7.2.3	Entertainment and media market/th pop. 15–69		42.1	20	
7.2.4	Creative goods exports, % total trade		3.6	15	
7.3	**Online creativity**		**56.9**	**16**	
7.3.1	Generic top-level domains (TLDs)/th pop. 15–69		29.8	23	
7.3.2	Country-code TLDs/th pop. 15–69		12.3	39	◇
7.3.3	GitHub commits/mn pop. 15–69		100.0	1	●◆
7.3.4	Mobile app creation/bn PPP$ GDP		85.5	4	◆

NOTES: ● indicates a strength; ○ a weakness; ◆ an income group strength; ◇ an income group weakness; * an index; † a survey question. ⊙ is used when the available economy data are older than the base year; see appendices for details, including the year of the data, at wipo.int/gii-ranking. Square brackets [ ] indicate that the data minimum coverage (DMC) requirements were not met at the sub-pillar or pillar level.

Slovakia

GII 2023 rank

45

Output rank	Input rank	Income	Region	Population (mn)	GDP, PPP$ (bn)	GDP per capita, PPP$
45	51	High	EUR	5.6	211.1	38,620

			Score/ Value	Rank	
	Institutions		**49.9**	**65**	◇
1.1	**Institutional environment**		**61.1**	**41**	
1.1.1	Operational stability for businesses*		70.8	27	
1.1.2	Government effectiveness*		51.4	45	
1.2	**Regulatory environment**		**70.6**	**42**	
1.2.1	Regulatory quality*		64.8	33	
1.2.2	Rule of law*		60.4	38	
1.2.3	Cost of redundancy dismissal		18.8	82	
1.3	**Business environment**		**17.9**	**124**	○◇
1.3.1	Policies for doing business†		28.2	109	○◇
1.3.2	Entrepreneurship policies and culture†		7.6	81	○◇
	Human capital and research		**33.9**	**53**	◇
2.1	**Education**		**53.5**	**61**	
2.1.1	Expenditure on education, % GDP	©	4.3	61	
2.1.2	Government funding/pupil, secondary, % GDP/cap		21.7	42	
2.1.3	School life expectancy, years		14.6	65	◇
2.1.4	PISA scales in reading, maths and science		469.4	38	
2.1.5	Pupil–teacher ratio, secondary		11.1	42	
2.2	**Tertiary education**		**31.7**	**62**	
2.2.1	Tertiary enrolment, % gross		47.6	68	◇
2.2.2	Graduates in science and engineering, %		22.2	60	
2.2.3	Tertiary inbound mobility, %		10.3	25	
2.3	**Research and development (R&D)**		**16.7**	**47**	
2.3.1	Researchers, FTE/mn pop.		3,220.0	31	
2.3.2	Gross expenditure on R&D, % GDP		0.9	44	
2.3.3	Global corporate R&D investors, top 3, mn USD		0.0	40	○◇
2.3.4	QS university ranking, top 3*		16.8	58	
	Infrastructure		**53.2**	**41**	
3.1	**Information and communication technologies (ICTs)**		**71.7**	**61**	◇
3.1.1	ICT access*		87.9	35	
3.1.2	ICT use*		83.7	46	
3.1.3	Government's online service*		69.7	62	
3.1.4	E-participation*		45.3	81	◇
3.2	**General infrastructure**		**32.0**	**50**	
3.2.1	Electricity output, GWh/mn pop.		5,397.2	44	
3.2.2	Logistics performance*		54.5	42	
3.2.3	Gross capital formation, % GDP		20.5	96	
3.3	**Ecological sustainability**		**55.8**	**11**	●◆
3.3.1	GDP/unit of energy use		10.1	64	
3.3.2	Environmental performance*		69.7	18	●
3.3.3	ISO 14001 environment/bn PPP$ GDP		9.5	7	●◆
	Market sophistication		**33.5**	**72**	
4.1	**Credit**		**38.6**	**43**	
4.1.1	Finance for startups and scaleups†		53.3	42	
4.1.2	Domestic credit to private sector, % GDP		66.2	56	
4.1.3	Loans from microfinance institutions, % GDP		n/a	n/a	
4.2	**Investment**		**2.7**	**95**	○◇
4.2.1	Market capitalization, % GDP	©	5.6	74	
4.2.2	Venture capital (VC) investors, deals/bn PPP$ GDP		0.0	58	
4.2.3	VC recipients, deals/bn PPP$ GDP		0.0	82	○
4.2.4	VC received, value, % GDP		0.0	83	○◇
4.3	**Trade, diversification and market scale**		**59.2**	**60**	
4.3.1	Applied tariff rate, weighted avg., %		1.5	20	
4.3.2	Domestic industry diversification		82.8	69	
4.3.3	Domestic market scale, bn PPP$		211.1	67	

		Score/ Value	Rank	
	Business sophistication	**33.4**	**47**	
5.1	**Knowledge workers**	**47.5**	**37**	
5.1.1	Knowledge-intensive employment, %	38.3	34	
5.1.2	Firms offering formal training, %	43.3	28	
5.1.3	GERD performed by business, % GDP	0.5	38	
5.1.4	GERD financed by business, %	43.7	38	
5.1.5	Females employed w/advanced degrees, %	18.8	36	
5.2	**Innovation linkages**	**18.9**	**82**	◇
5.2.1	University–industry R&D collaboration†	28.2	101	○◇
5.2.2	State of cluster development†	38.6	74	◇
5.2.3	GERD financed by abroad, % GDP	0.1	30	
5.2.4	Joint venture/strategic alliance deals/bn PPP$ GDP	0.0	93	
5.2.5	Patent families/bn PPP$ GDP	0.2	48	
5.3	**Knowledge absorption**	**33.9**	**63**	
5.3.1	Intellectual property payments, % total trade	0.7	54	
5.3.2	High-tech imports, % total trade	11.4	23	●
5.3.3	ICT services imports, % total trade	1.2	70	
5.3.4	FDI net inflows, % GDP	0.6	109	○
5.3.5	Research talent, % in businesses	27.2	47	
	Knowledge and technology outputs	**34.7**	**31**	
6.1	**Knowledge creation**	**22.1**	**48**	
6.1.1	Patents by origin/bn PPP$ GDP	1.0	58	
6.1.2	PCT patents by origin/bn PPP$ GDP	0.2	46	
6.1.3	Utility models by origin/bn PPP$ GDP	1.3	18	◆
6.1.4	Scientific and technical articles/bn PPP$ GDP	20.4	36	
6.1.5	Citable documents H-index	17.3	50	
6.2	**Knowledge impact**	**39.7**	**30**	
6.2.1	Labor productivity growth, %	1.1	60	
6.2.2	Unicorn valuation, % GDP	0.0	48	○◇
6.2.3	Software spending, % GDP	0.3	49	
6.2.4	High-tech manufacturing, %	61.4	3	●◆
6.3	**Knowledge diffusion**	**42.3**	**28**	
6.3.1	Intellectual property receipts, % total trade	0.0	71	
6.3.2	Production and export complexity	82.5	13	●
6.3.3	High-tech exports, % total trade	7.9	24	●
6.3.4	ICT services exports, % total trade	1.8	62	
6.3.5	ISO 9001 quality/bn PPP$ GDP	21.2	9	●◆
	Creative outputs	**28.6**	**56**	
7.1	**Intangible assets**	**19.2**	**87**	◇
7.1.1	Intangible asset intensity, top 15, %	−175.0	79	○◇
7.1.2	Trademarks by origin/bn PPP$ GDP	61.7	36	
7.1.3	Global brand value, top 5,000, % GDP	0.2	72	◇
7.1.4	Industrial designs by origin/bn PPP$ GDP	2.5	39	
7.2	**Creative goods and services**	**43.2**	**10**	●
7.2.1	Cultural and creative services exports, % total trade	0.3	63	
7.2.2	National feature films/mn pop. 15–69	6.5	15	●
7.2.3	Entertainment and media market/th pop. 15–69	n/a	n/a	
7.2.4	Creative goods exports, % total trade	6.9	8	●◆
7.3	**Online creativity**	**32.6**	**37**	
7.3.1	Generic top-level domains (TLDs)/th pop. 15–69	3.7	63	◇
7.3.2	Country-code TLDs/th pop. 15–69	32.6	23	●
7.3.3	GitHub commits/mn pop. 15–69	22.4	40	
7.3.4	Mobile app creation/bn PPP$ GDP	71.9	44	

NOTES: ● indicates a strength; ○ a weakness; ◆ an income group strength; ◇ an income group weakness; * an index; † a survey question. © is used when the available economy data are older than the base year; see appendices for details, including the year of the data, at wipo.int/gii-ranking. Square brackets [ ] indicate that the data minimum coverage (DMC) requirements were not met at the sub-pillar or pillar level.

GII 2023 rank

Slovenia

33

Output rank	Input rank	Income	Region	Population (mn)	GDP, PPP$ (bn)	GDP per capita, PPP$
38	29	High	EUR	2.1	105.5	49,968

			Score/ Value	Rank	
	Institutions		**63.3**	**38**	
1.1	**Institutional environment**		**69.4**	**26**	
1.1.1	Operational stability for businesses*		69.4	29	
1.1.2	Government effectiveness*		69.3	26	
1.2	**Regulatory environment**		**80.8**	**26**	
1.2.1	Regulatory quality*		63.8	38	
1.2.2	Rule of law*		69.9	27	
1.2.3	Cost of redundancy dismissal		10.7	35	
1.3	**Business environment**		**39.8**	**86**	○
1.3.1	Policies for doing business†		46.3	67	
1.3.2	Entrepreneurship policies and culture†		33.3	54	○
	Human capital and research		**47.6**	**25**	
2.1	**Education**		**61.2**	**29**	
2.1.1	Expenditure on education, % GDP	⊙	4.9	43	
2.1.2	Government funding/pupil, secondary, % GDP/cap		23.2	32	
2.1.3	School life expectancy, years		17.7	15	
2.1.4	PISA scales in reading, maths and science		503.7	11	
2.1.5	Pupil–teacher ratio, secondary		14.1	72	◇
2.2	**Tertiary education**		**43.0**	**26**	
2.2.1	Tertiary enrolment, % gross		79.9	24	
2.2.2	Graduates in science and engineering, %		28.6	25	
2.2.3	Tertiary inbound mobility, %		7.8	33	
2.3	**Research and development (R&D)**		**38.6**	**28**	
2.3.1	Researchers, FTE/mn pop.		5,252.6	16	
2.3.2	Gross expenditure on R&D, % GDP		2.1	18	
2.3.3	Global corporate R&D investors, top 3, mn USD		50.9	31	
2.3.4	QS university ranking, top 3*		10.8	63	
	Infrastructure		**58.6**	**20**	
3.1	**Information and communication technologies (ICTs)**		**84.9**	**22**	
3.1.1	ICT access*		93.9	11	●
3.1.2	ICT use*		85.9	35	
3.1.3	Government's online service*		85.3	22	
3.1.4	E-participation*		74.4	25	
3.2	**General infrastructure**		**38.2**	**35**	
3.2.1	Electricity output, GWh/mn pop.		7,400.4	25	
3.2.2	Logistics performance*		54.5	42	
3.2.3	Gross capital formation, % GDP		25.6	48	
3.3	**Ecological sustainability**		**52.8**	**16**	
3.3.1	GDP/unit of energy use		12.2	44	
3.3.2	Environmental performance*		82.0	7	●◆
3.3.3	ISO 14001 environment/bn PPP$ GDP		6.0	15	●
	Market sophistication		**34.5**	**68**	
4.1	**Credit**		**35.1**	**52**	
4.1.1	Finance for startups and scaleups†		55.3	38	
4.1.2	Domestic credit to private sector, % GDP		43.3	80	○◇
4.1.3	Loans from microfinance institutions, % GDP		n/a	n/a	
4.2	**Investment**		**4.8**	**79**	○◇
4.2.1	Market capitalization, % GDP		14.6	65	○
4.2.2	Venture capital (VC) investors, deals/bn PPP$ GDP		0.0	70	○
4.2.3	VC recipients, deals/bn PPP$ GDP		0.0	53	
4.2.4	VC received, value, % GDP		0.0	72	○◇
4.3	**Trade, diversification and market scale**		**63.6**	**38**	
4.3.1	Applied tariff rate, weighted avg., %		1.5	20	
4.3.2	Domestic industry diversification		98.2	9	●
4.3.3	Domestic market scale, bn PPP$		105.5	87	○

			Score/ Value	Rank	
	Business sophistication		**47.6**	**26**	
5.1	**Knowledge workers**		**60.4**	**20**	
5.1.1	Knowledge-intensive employment, %		46.7	18	
5.1.2	Firms offering formal training, %		44.0	26	
5.1.3	GERD performed by business, % GDP		1.6	15	
5.1.4	GERD financed by business, %		49.5	31	
5.1.5	Females employed w/advanced degrees, %		25.7	17	
5.2	**Innovation linkages**		**42.4**	**28**	
5.2.1	University–industry R&D collaboration†		50.2	51	
5.2.2	State of cluster development†		40.3	70	
5.2.3	GERD financed by abroad, % GDP		0.5	4	●◆
5.2.4	Joint venture/strategic alliance deals/bn PPP$ GDP		0.0	49	
5.2.5	Patent families/bn PPP$ GDP		1.2	26	
5.3	**Knowledge absorption**		**40.0**	**44**	
5.3.1	Intellectual property payments, % total trade		0.6	63	
5.3.2	High-tech imports, % total trade		6.5	98	○
5.3.3	ICT services imports, % total trade		1.6	55	
5.3.4	FDI net inflows, % GDP		2.8	55	
5.3.5	Research talent, % in businesses		59.9	16	
	Knowledge and technology outputs		**37.7**	**27**	
6.1	**Knowledge creation**		**42.3**	**22**	
6.1.1	Patents by origin/bn PPP$ GDP	⊙	4.4	19	
6.1.2	PCT patents by origin/bn PPP$ GDP		1.1	25	
6.1.3	Utility models by origin/bn PPP$ GDP		n/a	n/a	
6.1.4	Scientific and technical articles/bn PPP$ GDP		41.7	6	●◆
6.1.5	Citable documents H-index		19.5	45	
6.2	**Knowledge impact**		**29.6**	**58**	
6.2.1	Labor productivity growth, %		1.6	41	
6.2.2	Unicorn valuation, % GDP		0.0	48	○◇
6.2.3	Software spending, % GDP		0.1	95	○◇
6.2.4	High-tech manufacturing, %		42.0	25	
6.3	**Knowledge diffusion**		**41.4**	**32**	
6.3.1	Intellectual property receipts, % total trade		0.2	44	
6.3.2	Production and export complexity		84.8	11	●
6.3.3	High-tech exports, % total trade		5.0	38	
6.3.4	ICT services exports, % total trade		1.8	63	
6.3.5	ISO 9001 quality/bn PPP$ GDP		21.1	10	●◆
	Creative outputs		**30.6**	**48**	
7.1	**Intangible assets**		**20.8**	**83**	○◇
7.1.1	Intangible asset intensity, top 15, %		−164.6	79	○◇
7.1.2	Trademarks by origin/bn PPP$ GDP	⊙	68.1	27	
7.1.3	Global brand value, top 5,000, % GDP		0.5	64	
7.1.4	Industrial designs by origin/bn PPP$ GDP	⊙	2.7	37	
7.2	**Creative goods and services**		**38.3**	**14**	●
7.2.1	Cultural and creative services exports, % total trade		1.0	27	
7.2.2	National feature films/mn pop. 15–69		11.3	5	●◆
7.2.3	Entertainment and media market/th pop. 15–69		n/a	n/a	
7.2.4	Creative goods exports, % total trade		1.8	28	
7.3	**Online creativity**		**42.3**	**29**	
7.3.1	Generic top-level domains (TLDs)/th pop. 15–69		23.4	27	
7.3.2	Country-code TLDs/th pop. 15–69		29.7	24	
7.3.3	GitHub commits/mn pop. 15–69		37.0	27	
7.3.4	Mobile app creation/bn PPP$ GDP		79.1	11	●

NOTES: ● indicates a strength; ○ a weakness; ◆ an income group strength; ◇ an income group weakness; * an index; † a survey question. ⊙ is used when the available economy data are older than the base year; see appendices for details, including the year of the data, at wipo.int/gii-ranking. Square brackets [ ] indicate that the data minimum coverage (DMC) requirements were not met at the sub-pillar or pillar level.

South Africa

GII 2023 rank

59

Output rank	Input rank	Income	Region	Population (mn)	GDP, PPP$ (bn)	GDP per capita, PPP$
57	71	Upper middle	SSA	59.9	949.8	15,556

			Score/ Value	Rank	
	Institutions		**43.7**	**88**	
1.1	**Institutional environment**		**37.6**	**84**	
1.1.1	Operational stability for businesses*		38.9	96	○
1.1.2	Government effectiveness*		36.3	72	
1.2	**Regulatory environment**		**69.6**	**45**	
1.2.1	Regulatory quality*		40.2	75	
1.2.2	Rule of law*		43.5	58	
1.2.3	Cost of redundancy dismissal		9.3	25	● ◆
1.3	**Business environment**		**24.1**	**113**	○
1.3.1	Policies for doing business†		35.3	100	○
1.3.2	Entrepreneurship policies and culture†		12.8	77	○ ◇
	Human capital and research		**25.8**	**84**	
2.1	**Education**		**49.9**	**69**	
2.1.1	Expenditure on education, % GDP		6.6	11	● ◆
2.1.2	Government funding/pupil, secondary, % GDP/cap		25.1	20	●
2.1.3	School life expectancy, years		13.4	79	
2.1.4	PISA scales in reading, maths and science		n/a	n/a	
2.1.5	Pupil–teacher ratio, secondary		27.2	115	○ ◇
2.2	**Tertiary education**		**15.3**	**102**	○ ◇
2.2.1	Tertiary enrolment, % gross		24.2	95	◇
2.2.2	Graduates in science and engineering, %		17.4	91	○
2.2.3	Tertiary inbound mobility, %		3.0	65	
2.3	**Research and development (R&D)**		**12.2**	**53**	
2.3.1	Researchers, FTE/mn pop.	⊙	494.5	71	
2.3.2	Gross expenditure on R&D, % GDP	⊙	0.7	53	
2.3.3	Global corporate R&D investors, top 3, mn USD		0.0	40	○ ◇
2.3.4	QS university ranking, top 3*		31.8	41	
	Infrastructure		**39.3**	**68**	
3.1	**Information and communication technologies (ICTs)**		**68.8**	**70**	
3.1.1	ICT access*		82.3	67	
3.1.2	ICT use*		62.6	88	
3.1.3	Government's online service*		72.2	55	
3.1.4	E-participation*		58.1	61	
3.2	**General infrastructure**		**32.1**	**49**	
3.2.1	Electricity output, GWh/mn pop.		3,987.7	55	
3.2.2	Logistics performance*		72.7	18	● ◆
3.2.3	Gross capital formation, % GDP		13.8	125	○ ◇
3.3	**Ecological sustainability**		**16.9**	**100**	○ ◇
3.3.1	GDP/unit of energy use		5.9	108	○ ◇
3.3.2	Environmental performance*		31.0	86	
3.3.3	ISO 14001 environment/bn PPP$ GDP		1.2	60	
	Market sophistication		**40.4**	**45**	
4.1	**Credit**		**30.9**	**64**	
4.1.1	Finance for startups and scaleups†		36.8	60	
4.1.2	Domestic credit to private sector, % GDP		111.2	22	● ◆
4.1.3	Loans from microfinance institutions, % GDP		1.2	24	
4.2	**Investment**		**32.6**	**22**	● ◆
4.2.1	Market capitalization, % GDP		265.8	1	● ◆
4.2.2	Venture capital (VC) investors, deals/bn PPP$ GDP		0.1	40	
4.2.3	VC recipients, deals/bn PPP$ GDP		0.1	41	
4.2.4	VC received, value, % GDP		0.0	55	
4.3	**Trade, diversification and market scale**		**57.7**	**68**	
4.3.1	Applied tariff rate, weighted avg., %		4.4	88	
4.3.2	Domestic industry diversification	⊙	81.2	70	
4.3.3	Domestic market scale, bn PPP$		949.8	32	

			Score/ Value	Rank	
	Business sophistication		**29.0**	**61**	
5.1	**Knowledge workers**		**20.4**	**97**	◇
5.1.1	Knowledge-intensive employment, %		22.3	67	
5.1.2	Firms offering formal training, %		7.9	95	○ ◇
5.1.3	GERD performed by business, % GDP	⊙	0.2	52	
5.1.4	GERD financed by business, %	⊙	27.1	61	
5.1.5	Females employed w/advanced degrees, %		10.0	75	
5.2	**Innovation linkages**		**28.1**	**45**	
5.2.1	University–industry R&D collaboration†		58.7	36	◆
5.2.2	State of cluster development†		48.0	48	
5.2.3	GERD financed by abroad, % GDP	⊙	0.1	39	
5.2.4	Joint venture/strategic alliance deals/bn PPP$ GDP		0.0	31	◆
5.2.5	Patent families/bn PPP$ GDP		0.2	42	
5.3	**Knowledge absorption**		**38.6**	**49**	
5.3.1	Intellectual property payments, % total trade		1.3	27	●
5.3.2	High-tech imports, % total trade		9.2	49	
5.3.3	ICT services imports, % total trade		2.7	22	● ◆
5.3.4	FDI net inflows, % GDP		4.0	31	
5.3.5	Research talent, % in businesses	⊙	11.4	59	
	Knowledge and technology outputs		**25.0**	**56**	
6.1	**Knowledge creation**		**23.5**	**45**	
6.1.1	Patents by origin/bn PPP$ GDP		2.1	34	
6.1.2	PCT patents by origin/bn PPP$ GDP		0.2	40	
6.1.3	Utility models by origin/bn PPP$ GDP		n/a	n/a	
6.1.4	Scientific and technical articles/bn PPP$ GDP		15.8	46	
6.1.5	Citable documents H-index		31.8	31	◆
6.2	**Knowledge impact**		**31.9**	**49**	
6.2.1	Labor productivity growth, %		1.3	55	
6.2.2	Unicorn valuation, % GDP		0.6	37	
6.2.3	Software spending, % GDP		0.3	28	● ◆
6.2.4	High-tech manufacturing, %	⊙	23.4	56	
6.3	**Knowledge diffusion**		**19.8**	**75**	
6.3.1	Intellectual property receipts, % total trade		0.1	49	
6.3.2	Production and export complexity		49.4	69	
6.3.3	High-tech exports, % total trade		2.1	59	
6.3.4	ICT services exports, % total trade		0.7	95	
6.3.5	ISO 9001 quality/bn PPP$ GDP		4.4	59	
	Creative outputs		**25.3**	**63**	
7.1	**Intangible assets**		**37.4**	**51**	
7.1.1	Intangible asset intensity, top 15, %		58.4	40	
7.1.2	Trademarks by origin/bn PPP$ GDP		29.7	78	
7.1.3	Global brand value, top 5,000, % GDP		8.4	22	● ◆
7.1.4	Industrial designs by origin/bn PPP$ GDP		0.8	75	
7.2	**Creative goods and services**		**6.7**	**77**	
7.2.1	Cultural and creative services exports, % total trade		0.3	66	
7.2.2	National feature films/mn pop. 15–69		0.8	65	○
7.2.3	Entertainment and media market/th pop. 15–69		8.2	37	
7.2.4	Creative goods exports, % total trade		0.7	55	
7.3	**Online creativity**		**19.7**	**67**	
7.3.1	Generic top-level domains (TLDs)/th pop. 15–69		3.4	65	
7.3.2	Country-code TLDs/th pop. 15–69		10.0	41	
7.3.3	GitHub commits/mn pop. 15–69		4.5	73	
7.3.4	Mobile app creation/bn PPP$ GDP		61.0	78	

NOTES: ● indicates a strength; ○ a weakness; ◆ an income group strength; ◇ an income group weakness; * an index; † a survey question. ⊙ is used when the available economy data are older than the base year; see appendices for details, including the year of the data, at wipo.int/gii-ranking. Square brackets [ ] indicate that the data minimum coverage (DMC) requirements were not met at the sub-pillar or pillar level.

Spain

GII 2023 rank

29

Output rank	Input rank	Income	Region	Population (mn)	GDP, PPP$ (bn)	GDP per capita, PPP$
26	28	High	EUR	47.6	2,216.0	46,551

		Score/Value	Rank
	Institutions	**59.2**	**46**
1.1	**Institutional environment**	**62.3**	**38**
1.1.1	Operational stability for businesses*	61.8	41
1.1.2	Government effectiveness*	62.9	33
1.2	**Regulatory environment**	**72.8**	**38**
1.2.1	Regulatory quality*	63.1	40
1.2.2	Rule of law*	65.4	33
1.2.3	Cost of redundancy dismissal	17.4	75 ○
1.3	**Business environment**	**42.4**	**77** ○
1.3.1	Policies for doing business†	38.1	91 ○◇
1.3.2	Entrepreneurship policies and culture†	46.6	39
	Human capital and research	**45.6**	**27**
2.1	**Education**	**58.0**	**47**
2.1.1	Expenditure on education, % GDP	⊙ 4.2	63 ○
2.1.2	Government funding/pupil, secondary, % GDP/cap	19.1	58 ○
2.1.3	School life expectancy, years	18.1	14 ●
2.1.4	PISA scales in reading, maths and science	482.3	29
2.1.5	Pupil–teacher ratio, secondary	11.2	44
2.2	**Tertiary education**	**35.6**	**46**
2.2.1	Tertiary enrolment, % gross	96.0	6 ●◆
2.2.2	Graduates in science and engineering, %	20.8	65 ○
2.2.3	Tertiary inbound mobility, %	3.8	57 ○
2.3	**Research and development (R&D)**	**43.3**	**24**
2.3.1	Researchers, FTE/mn pop.	3,256.3	30
2.3.2	Gross expenditure on R&D, % GDP	1.4	30
2.3.3	Global corporate R&D investors, top 3, mn USD	68.8	15 ●
2.3.4	QS university ranking, top 3*	45.1	25
	Infrastructure	**59.7**	**16** ●
3.1	**Information and communication technologies (ICTs)**	**84.0**	**24**
3.1.1	ICT access*	87.6	38
3.1.2	ICT use*	90.1	21
3.1.3	Government's online service*	84.1	25
3.1.4	E-participation*	74.4	25
3.2	**General infrastructure**	**42.9**	**29**
3.2.1	Electricity output, GWh/mn pop.	5,724.2	35
3.2.2	Logistics performance*	81.8	13
3.2.3	Gross capital formation, % GDP	22.7	74 ○
3.3	**Ecological sustainability**	**52.2**	**19**
3.3.1	GDP/unit of energy use	14.6	28
3.3.2	Environmental performance*	63.9	27
3.3.3	ISO 14001 environment/bn PPP$ GDP	7.2	11 ●◆
	Market sophistication	**46.0**	**33**
4.1	**Credit**	**45.5**	**34**
4.1.1	Finance for startups and scaleups†	50.1	45 ○
4.1.2	Domestic credit to private sector, % GDP	108.9	23
4.1.3	Loans from microfinance institutions, % GDP	n/a	n/a
4.2	**Investment**	**15.3**	**45**
4.2.1	Market capitalization, % GDP	55.8	32
4.2.2	Venture capital (VC) investors, deals/bn PPP$ GDP	0.1	41
4.2.3	VC recipients, deals/bn PPP$ GDP	0.1	39
4.2.4	VC received, value, % GDP	0.0	37
4.3	**Trade, diversification and market scale**	**77.1**	**14** ●
4.3.1	Applied tariff rate, weighted avg., %	1.5	20
4.3.2	Domestic industry diversification	93.3	38
4.3.3	Domestic market scale, bn PPP$	2,216.0	16 ●

		Score/Value	Rank
	Business sophistication	**42.8**	**32**
5.1	**Knowledge workers**	**56.6**	**23**
5.1.1	Knowledge-intensive employment, %	35.7	39
5.1.2	Firms offering formal training, %	55.2	13 ●
5.1.3	GERD performed by business, % GDP	0.8	30
5.1.4	GERD financed by business, %	49.2	33
5.1.5	Females employed w/advanced degrees, %	24.9	20
5.2	**Innovation linkages**	**29.4**	**41**
5.2.1	University–industry R&D collaboration†	42.0	70 ○
5.2.2	State of cluster development†	64.1	32
5.2.3	GERD financed by abroad, % GDP	0.1	34
5.2.4	Joint venture/strategic alliance deals/bn PPP$ GDP	0.0	35
5.2.5	Patent families/bn PPP$ GDP	0.5	31
5.3	**Knowledge absorption**	**42.3**	**38**
5.3.1	Intellectual property payments, % total trade	1.3	26
5.3.2	High-tech imports, % total trade	8.5	57
5.3.3	ICT services imports, % total trade	2.2	31
5.3.4	FDI net inflows, % GDP	2.6	61
5.3.5	Research talent, % in businesses	39.2	35
	Knowledge and technology outputs	**39.4**	**24**
6.1	**Knowledge creation**	**38.6**	**25**
6.1.1	Patents by origin/bn PPP$ GDP	1.6	42
6.1.2	PCT patents by origin/bn PPP$ GDP	0.7	28
6.1.3	Utility models by origin/bn PPP$ GDP	1.5	13 ◆
6.1.4	Scientific and technical articles/bn PPP$ GDP	28.1	25
6.1.5	Citable documents H-index	61.8	12 ●
6.2	**Knowledge impact**	**39.3**	**32**
6.2.1	Labor productivity growth, %	−0.5	107 ○◇
6.2.2	Unicorn valuation, % GDP	0.5	39
6.2.3	Software spending, % GDP	0.7	12 ●◆
6.2.4	High-tech manufacturing, %	37.1	31
6.3	**Knowledge diffusion**	**40.3**	**34**
6.3.1	Intellectual property receipts, % total trade	0.8	24
6.3.2	Production and export complexity	68.6	33
6.3.3	High-tech exports, % total trade	5.1	37
6.3.4	ICT services exports, % total trade	3.0	43
6.3.5	ISO 9001 quality/bn PPP$ GDP	15.9	18
	Creative outputs	**43.0**	**29**
7.1	**Intangible assets**	**52.4**	**20**
7.1.1	Intangible asset intensity, top 15, %	64.5	29
7.1.2	Trademarks by origin/bn PPP$ GDP	49.4	47
7.1.3	Global brand value, top 5,000, % GDP	8.2	24
7.1.4	Industrial designs by origin/bn PPP$ GDP	7.7	14 ●◆
7.2	**Creative goods and services**	**28.0**	**34**
7.2.1	Cultural and creative services exports, % total trade	1.0	28
7.2.2	National feature films/mn pop. 15–69	8.1	8 ●
7.2.3	Entertainment and media market/th pop. 15–69	29.8	24
7.2.4	Creative goods exports, % total trade	0.8	51
7.3	**Online creativity**	**39.4**	**30**
7.3.1	Generic top-level domains (TLDs)/th pop. 15–69	32.2	22
7.3.2	Country-code TLDs/th pop. 15–69	17.4	31
7.3.3	GitHub commits/mn pop. 15–69	33.9	32
7.3.4	Mobile app creation/bn PPP$ GDP	73.9	33

NOTES: ● indicates a strength; ○ a weakness; ◆ an income group strength; ◇ an income group weakness; * an index; † a survey question. ⊙ is used when the available economy data are older than the base year; see appendices for details, including the year of the data, at wipo.int/gii-ranking. Square brackets [ ] indicate that the data minimum coverage (DMC) requirements were not met at the sub-pillar or pillar level.

Sri Lanka

GII 2023 rank **90**

Output rank	Input rank	Income	Region	Population (mn)	GDP, PPP$ (bn)	GDP per capita, PPP$
79	103	Lower middle	CSA	21.8	318.7	14,230

			Score/ Value	Rank
Institutions			**30.8**	**124**
1.1	**Institutional environment**		**34.9**	**92**
1.1.1	Operational stability for businesses*		35.4	110
1.1.2	Government effectiveness*		34.5	75
1.2	**Regulatory environment**		**18.3**	**131** ○◇
1.2.1	Regulatory quality*		32.5	92
1.2.2	Rule of law*		40.8	61 ◆
1.2.3	Cost of redundancy dismissal		58.5	130 ○◇
1.3	**Business environment**		**39.2**	**[89]**
1.3.1	Policies for doing business†		39.2	86
1.3.2	Entrepreneurship policies and culture†		n/a	n/a
Human capital and research			**17.3**	**110**
2.1	**Education**		**32.2**	**116**
2.1.1	Expenditure on education, % GDP	⊙	2.0	120 ○◇
2.1.2	Government funding/pupil, secondary, % GDP/cap	⊙	6.3	97 ○◇
2.1.3	School life expectancy, years	⊙	14.1	71
2.1.4	PISA scales in reading, maths and science		n/a	n/a
2.1.5	Pupil–teacher ratio, secondary		17.7	89
2.2	**Tertiary education**		**18.9**	**93**
2.2.1	Tertiary enrolment, % gross		22.2	97
2.2.2	Graduates in science and engineering, %		24.1	48
2.2.3	Tertiary inbound mobility, %		0.4	105 ○
2.3	**Research and development (R&D)**		**0.7**	**105**
2.3.1	Researchers, FTE/mn pop.	⊙	105.6	89
2.3.2	Gross expenditure on R&D, % GDP	⊙	0.1	101
2.3.3	Global corporate R&D investors, top 3, mn USD		0.0	40 ○◇
2.3.4	QS university ranking, top 3*		0.0	71 ○◇
Infrastructure			**35.5**	**82** ◆
3.1	**Information and communication technologies (ICTs)**		**55.7**	**89**
3.1.1	ICT access*		71.4	88
3.1.2	ICT use*		65.7	83
3.1.3	Government's online service*		51.9	89
3.1.4	E-participation*		33.7	97
3.2	**General infrastructure**		**18.8**	**96**
3.2.1	Electricity output, GWh/mn pop.	⊙	710.8	104
3.2.2	Logistics performance*		31.8	71
3.2.3	Gross capital formation, % GDP		24.7	58
3.3	**Ecological sustainability**		**32.1**	**46** ●◆
3.3.1	GDP/unit of energy use		23.6	6 ●◆
3.3.2	Environmental performance*		26.8	94
3.3.3	ISO 14001 environment/bn PPP$ GDP		0.9	66
Market sophistication			**22.4**	**106**
4.1	**Credit**		**16.4**	**[98]**
4.1.1	Finance for startups and scaleups†		n/a	n/a
4.1.2	Domestic credit to private sector, % GDP	⊙	47.0	76
4.1.3	Loans from microfinance institutions, % GDP		n/a	n/a
4.2	**Investment**		**2.0**	**102**
4.2.1	Market capitalization, % GDP		17.6	63
4.2.2	Venture capital (VC) investors, deals/bn PPP$ GDP		0.0	92 ○◇
4.2.3	VC recipients, deals/bn PPP$ GDP		0.0	94
4.2.4	VC received, value, % GDP		0.0	97 ○
4.3	**Trade, diversification and market scale**		**48.8**	**89**
4.3.1	Applied tariff rate, weighted avg., %		6.3	100
4.3.2	Domestic industry diversification	⊙	80.4	74
4.3.3	Domestic market scale, bn PPP$		318.7	58

			Score/ Value	Rank
Business sophistication			**26.9**	**71**
5.1	**Knowledge workers**		**23.4**	**86**
5.1.1	Knowledge-intensive employment, %	⊙	21.7	70
5.1.2	Firms offering formal training, %		n/a	n/a
5.1.3	GERD performed by business, % GDP	⊙	0.1	71
5.1.4	GERD financed by business, %	⊙	40.3	42 ●
5.1.5	Females employed w/advanced degrees, %	⊙	3.7	99
5.2	**Innovation linkages**		**23.3**	**61**
5.2.1	University–industry R&D collaboration†		52.9	49 ●
5.2.2	State of cluster development†		49.5	46 ●
5.2.3	GERD financed by abroad, % GDP	⊙	0.0	75
5.2.4	Joint venture/strategic alliance deals/bn PPP$ GDP		0.0	40 ●◆
5.2.5	Patent families/bn PPP$ GDP		0.0	77
5.3	**Knowledge absorption**		**34.0**	**62**
5.3.1	Intellectual property payments, % total trade		n/a	n/a
5.3.2	High-tech imports, % total trade		11.3	24 ●
5.3.3	ICT services imports, % total trade		0.9	91
5.3.4	FDI net inflows, % GDP		0.7	107
5.3.5	Research talent, % in businesses	⊙	20.0	53
Knowledge and technology outputs			**21.5**	**71**
6.1	**Knowledge creation**		**8.7**	**88**
6.1.1	Patents by origin/bn PPP$ GDP		0.8	66
6.1.2	PCT patents by origin/bn PPP$ GDP		0.1	71
6.1.3	Utility models by origin/bn PPP$ GDP		n/a	n/a
6.1.4	Scientific and technical articles/bn PPP$ GDP		4.7	108
6.1.5	Citable documents H-index		11.2	70
6.2	**Knowledge impact**		**24.7**	**75**
6.2.1	Labor productivity growth, %		−0.6	112
6.2.2	Unicorn valuation, % GDP		0.0	48 ○◇
6.2.3	Software spending, % GDP		0.5	20 ●◆
6.2.4	High-tech manufacturing, %	⊙	7.9	95
6.3	**Knowledge diffusion**		**31.1**	**53** ●◆
6.3.1	Intellectual property receipts, % total trade		n/a	n/a
6.3.2	Production and export complexity		48.5	71
6.3.3	High-tech exports, % total trade		0.7	78
6.3.4	ICT services exports, % total trade		6.6	14 ●◆
6.3.5	ISO 9001 quality/bn PPP$ GDP		4.1	62 ◆
Creative outputs			**18.6**	**83**
7.1	**Intangible assets**		**24.4**	**79**
7.1.1	Intangible asset intensity, top 15, %		46.6	54
7.1.2	Trademarks by origin/bn PPP$ GDP		19.4	94
7.1.3	Global brand value, top 5,000, % GDP		0.0	74 ○◇
7.1.4	Industrial designs by origin/bn PPP$ GDP		0.3	93
7.2	**Creative goods and services**		**7.8**	**[76]**
7.2.1	Cultural and creative services exports, % total trade		n/a	n/a
7.2.2	National feature films/mn pop. 15–69		n/a	n/a
7.2.3	Entertainment and media market/th pop. 15–69		n/a	n/a
7.2.4	Creative goods exports, % total trade		0.7	56 ●
7.3	**Online creativity**		**17.8**	**79**
7.3.1	Generic top-level domains (TLDs)/th pop. 15–69		0.8	102
7.3.2	Country-code TLDs/th pop. 15–69		1.1	89
7.3.3	GitHub commits/mn pop. 15–69		12.1	51 ●◆
7.3.4	Mobile app creation/bn PPP$ GDP		57.1	89

NOTES: ● indicates a strength; ○ a weakness; ◆ an income group strength; ◇ an income group weakness; * an index; † a survey question. ⊙ is used when the available economy data are older than the base year; see appendices for details, including the year of the data, at wipo.int/gii-ranking. Square brackets [ ] indicate that the data minimum coverage (DMC) requirements were not met at the sub-pillar or pillar level.

GII 2023 rank

Sweden 2

Output rank	Input rank	Income	Region	Population (mn)	GDP, PPP$ (bn)	GDP per capita, PPP$
3	4	High	EUR	10.5	684.5	63,877

		Score/Value	Rank
	Institutions	**74.3**	**18**
1.1	**Institutional environment**	**80.1**	**10**
1.1.1	Operational stability for businesses*	77.8	10
1.1.2	Government effectiveness*	82.4	8
1.2	**Regulatory environment**	**88.1**	**14**
1.2.1	Regulatory quality*	87.6	8
1.2.2	Rule of law*	90.5	11
1.2.3	Cost of redundancy dismissal	14.4	56 ○
1.3	**Business environment**	**54.8**	**48 ○◇**
1.3.1	Policies for doing business†	66.5	29
1.3.2	Entrepreneurship policies and culture†	43.1	43 ○◇
	Human capital and research	**62.7**	**3 ●◆**
2.1	**Education**	**71.8**	**4 ●◆**
2.1.1	Expenditure on education, % GDP ⓒ	7.6	5 ●◆
2.1.2	Government funding/pupil, secondary, % GDP/cap	23.8	27
2.1.3	School life expectancy, years	19.7	4 ●◆
2.1.4	PISA scales in reading, maths and science	502.5	14
2.1.5	Pupil-teacher ratio, secondary	12.5	56 ○
2.2	**Tertiary education**	**41.8**	**28**
2.2.1	Tertiary enrolment, % gross	84.5	17
2.2.2	Graduates in science and engineering, %	27.0	33
2.2.3	Tertiary inbound mobility, %	7.0	35 ○
2.3	**Research and development (R&D)**	**74.4**	**3 ●**
2.3.1	Researchers, FTE/mn pop.	9,640.3	1 ●◆
2.3.2	Gross expenditure on R&D, % GDP	3.3	4 ●
2.3.3	Global corporate R&D investors, top 3, mn USD	77.7	10
2.3.4	QS university ranking, top 3*	59.7	15
	Infrastructure	**67.6**	**2 ●◆**
3.1	**Information and communication technologies (ICTs)**	**86.7**	**16**
3.1.1	ICT access*	89.2	27
3.1.2	ICT use*	96.5	6
3.1.3	Government's online service*	89.0	13
3.1.4	E-participation*	72.1	32
3.2	**General infrastructure**	**64.8**	**3 ●◆**
3.2.1	Electricity output, GWh/mn pop.	16,179.7	7 ◆
3.2.2	Logistics performance*	86.4	7
3.2.3	Gross capital formation, % GDP	27.5	34
3.3	**Ecological sustainability**	**51.4**	**21**
3.3.1	GDP/unit of energy use	11.4	54 ○
3.3.2	Environmental performance*	91.2	5 ●◆
3.3.3	ISO 14001 environment/bn PPP$ GDP	4.6	22
	Market sophistication	**59.9**	**10**
4.1	**Credit**	**62.2**	**16**
4.1.1	Finance for startups and scaleups†	72.1	15
4.1.2	Domestic credit to private sector, % GDP	137.8	15
4.1.3	Loans from microfinance institutions, % GDP	n/a	n/a
4.2	**Investment**	**49.6**	**12**
4.2.1	Market capitalization, % GDP	n/a	n/a
4.2.2	Venture capital (VC) investors, deals/bn PPP$ GDP	0.4	15
4.2.3	VC recipients, deals/bn PPP$ GDP	0.2	11
4.2.4	VC received, value, % GDP	0.0	7
4.3	**Trade, diversification and market scale**	**67.9**	**22**
4.3.1	Applied tariff rate, weighted avg., %	1.5	20 ○
4.3.2	Domestic industry diversification	98.5	8
4.3.3	Domestic market scale, bn PPP$	684.5	38

		Score/Value	Rank
	Business sophistication	**75.8**	**1 ●◆**
5.1	**Knowledge workers**	**77.7**	**1 ●◆**
5.1.1	Knowledge-intensive employment, %	57.1	3 ●◆
5.1.2	Firms offering formal training, %	61.9	7
5.1.3	GERD performed by business, % GDP	2.4	6
5.1.4	GERD financed by business, % ⓒ	62.4	13
5.1.5	Females employed w/advanced degrees, %	28.7	5 ●
5.2	**Innovation linkages**	**77.0**	**2 ●◆**
5.2.1	University-industry R&D collaboration†	82.1	11
5.2.2	State of cluster development†	78.5	13
5.2.3	GERD financed by abroad, % GDP ⓒ	0.3	11
5.2.4	Joint venture/strategic alliance deals/bn PPP$ GDP	0.2	4 ●
5.2.5	Patent families/bn PPP$ GDP	7.0	1 ●◆
5.3	**Knowledge absorption**	**72.7**	**2 ●◆**
5.3.1	Intellectual property payments, % total trade	3.5	6 ◆
5.3.2	High-tech imports, % total trade	8.8	54 ○
5.3.3	ICT services imports, % total trade	4.5	6 ◆
5.3.4	FDI net inflows, % GDP	4.9	21
5.3.5	Research talent, % in businesses	77.6	4 ◆
	Knowledge and technology outputs	**63.4**	**3 ●◆**
6.1	**Knowledge creation**	**74.3**	**2 ●◆**
6.1.1	Patents by origin/bn PPP$ GDP	10.8	8
6.1.2	PCT patents by origin/bn PPP$ GDP	6.5	1 ●◆
6.1.3	Utility models by origin/bn PPP$ GDP	n/a	n/a
6.1.4	Scientific and technical articles/bn PPP$ GDP	41.3	7 ◆
6.1.5	Citable documents H-index	59.3	13
6.2	**Knowledge impact**	**57.1**	**6**
6.2.1	Labor productivity growth, %	1.0	63 ○
6.2.2	Unicorn valuation, % GDP	3.5	13
6.2.3	Software spending, % GDP	0.6	19
6.2.4	High-tech manufacturing, %	47.4	14
6.3	**Knowledge diffusion**	**58.9**	**8**
6.3.1	Intellectual property receipts, % total trade	3.4	7 ◆
6.3.2	Production and export complexity	85.9	8
6.3.3	High-tech exports, % total trade	6.8	27
6.3.4	ICT services exports, % total trade	6.2	16
6.3.5	ISO 9001 quality/bn PPP$ GDP	5.1	53 ○
	Creative outputs	**57.3**	**8**
7.1	**Intangible assets**	**56.9**	**12**
7.1.1	Intangible asset intensity, top 15, %	79.4	7
7.1.2	Trademarks by origin/bn PPP$ GDP	44.7	52 ○
7.1.3	Global brand value, top 5,000, % GDP	17.8	5 ●
7.1.4	Industrial designs by origin/bn PPP$ GDP	3.3	30
7.2	**Creative goods and services**	**48.6**	**4 ●◆**
7.2.1	Cultural and creative services exports, % total trade	3.3	4 ●◆
7.2.2	National feature films/mn pop. 15–69	7.0	12
7.2.3	Entertainment and media market/th pop. 15–69	61.5	10
7.2.4	Creative goods exports, % total trade	1.8	29
7.3	**Online creativity**	**66.7**	**11**
7.3.1	Generic top-level domains (TLDs)/th pop. 15–69	47.6	17
7.3.2	Country-code TLDs/th pop. 15–69	61.8	14
7.3.3	GitHub commits/mn pop. 15–69	77.2	8
7.3.4	Mobile app creation/bn PPP$ GDP	80.3	10

NOTES: ● indicates a strength; ○ a weakness; ◆ an income group strength; ◇ an income group weakness; * an index; † a survey question. ⓒ is used when the available economy data are older than the base year; see appendices for details, including the year of the data, at wipo.int/gii-ranking. Square brackets [ ] indicate that the data minimum coverage (DMC) requirements were not met at the sub-pillar or pillar level.

GII 2023 rank

Switzerland 1

Output rank	Input rank	Income	Region	Population (mn)	GDP, PPP$ (bn)	GDP per capita, PPP$
1	3	High	EUR	8.7	737.8	84,469

		Score/Value	Rank
	Institutions	**87.3**	**2 ●◆**
1.1	**Institutional environment**	**85.3**	**4**
1.1.1	Operational stability for businesses*	77.8	10
1.1.2	Government effectiveness*	92.8	2 ●◆
1.2	**Regulatory environment**	**92.8**	**5**
1.2.1	Regulatory quality*	87.1	9
1.2.2	Rule of law*	92.7	6
1.2.3	Cost of redundancy dismissal	10.1	31
1.3	**Business environment**	**83.8**	**3 ●◆**
1.3.1	Policies for doing business†	100.0	1 ●◆
1.3.2	Entrepreneurship policies and culture†	67.7	15
	Human capital and research	**59.8**	**6**
2.1	**Education**	**61.9**	**25**
2.1.1	Expenditure on education, % GDP	⊙ 5.1	38
2.1.2	Government funding/pupil, secondary, % GDP/cap	⊙ 22.9	34 ○
2.1.3	School life expectancy, years	16.6	23
2.1.4	PISA scales in reading, maths and science	498.2	21
2.1.5	Pupil–teacher ratio, secondary	9.7	27
2.2	**Tertiary education**	**45.6**	**21**
2.2.1	Tertiary enrolment, % gross	65.3	47 ○
2.2.2	Graduates in science and engineering, %	25.2	44 ○
2.2.3	Tertiary inbound mobility, %	18.1	9
2.3	**Research and development (R&D)**	**71.8**	**4**
2.3.1	Researchers, FTE/mn pop.	⊙ 5,562.4	13
2.3.2	Gross expenditure on R&D, % GDP	⊙ 3.2	7
2.3.3	Global corporate R&D investors, top 3, mn USD	89.0	4
2.3.4	QS university ranking, top 3*	83.2	5
	Infrastructure	**64.3**	**4**
3.1	**Information and communication technologies (ICTs)**	**83.7**	**25**
3.1.1	ICT access*	90.9	21
3.1.2	ICT use*	100.0	1 ●◆
3.1.3	Government's online service*	74.3	49 ○◇
3.1.4	E-participation*	69.8	41
3.2	**General infrastructure**	**50.5**	**16**
3.2.1	Electricity output, GWh/mn pop.	7,196.8	26
3.2.2	Logistics performance*	90.9	3 ●◆
3.2.3	Gross capital formation, % GDP	26.5	42
3.3	**Ecological sustainability**	**58.7**	**7 ◆**
3.3.1	GDP/unit of energy use	26.5	4 ◆
3.3.2	Environmental performance*	79.7	9
3.3.3	ISO 14001 environment/bn PPP$ GDP	3.3	29
	Market sophistication	**64.4**	**7**
4.1	**Credit**	**70.1**	**5**
4.1.1	Finance for startups and scaleups†	75.1	12
4.1.2	Domestic credit to private sector, % GDP	⊙ 170.4	5
4.1.3	Loans from microfinance institutions, % GDP	n/a	n/a
4.2	**Investment**	**59.5**	**10**
4.2.1	Market capitalization, % GDP	241.1	3 ●◆
4.2.2	Venture capital (VC) investors, deals/bn PPP$ GDP	0.7	9
4.2.3	VC recipients, deals/bn PPP$ GDP	0.3	8
4.2.4	VC received, value, % GDP	0.0	24
4.3	**Trade, diversification and market scale**	**63.7**	**36**
4.3.1	Applied tariff rate, weighted avg., %	1.4	18
4.3.2	Domestic industry diversification	⊙ 84.1	66 ○
4.3.3	Domestic market scale, bn PPP$	737.8	34

		Score/Value	Rank
	Business sophistication	**65.5**	**5**
5.1	**Knowledge workers**	**67.1**	**9**
5.1.1	Knowledge-intensive employment, %	50.9	10
5.1.2	Firms offering formal training, %	n/a	n/a
5.1.3	GERD performed by business, % GDP	⊙ 2.2	8
5.1.4	GERD financed by business, %	⊙ 64.7	7
5.1.5	Females employed w/advanced degrees, %	20.7	31
5.2	**Innovation linkages**	**76.8**	**3 ●◆**
5.2.1	University–industry R&D collaboration†	99.4	3 ●◆
5.2.2	State of cluster development†	91.3	3 ●◆
5.2.3	GERD financed by abroad, % GDP	⊙ 0.2	21
5.2.4	Joint venture/strategic alliance deals/bn PPP$ GDP	0.2	9
5.2.5	Patent families/bn PPP$ GDP	8.6	1 ●◆
5.3	**Knowledge absorption**	**52.6**	**13**
5.3.1	Intellectual property payments, % total trade	5.5	1 ●◆
5.3.2	High-tech imports, % total trade	5.2	112 ○
5.3.3	ICT services imports, % total trade	3.3	13
5.3.4	FDI net inflows, % GDP	−10.8	131 ○◇
5.3.5	Research talent, % in businesses	⊙ 48.3	27
	Knowledge and technology outputs	**65.3**	**1 ●◆**
6.1	**Knowledge creation**	**78.7**	**1 ●◆**
6.1.1	Patents by origin/bn PPP$ GDP	14.4	4
6.1.2	PCT patents by origin/bn PPP$ GDP	7.3	1 ●◆
6.1.3	Utility models by origin/bn PPP$ GDP	n/a	n/a
6.1.4	Scientific and technical articles/bn PPP$ GDP	43.3	3 ●◆
6.1.5	Citable documents H-index	66.2	10
6.2	**Knowledge impact**	**56.9**	**7**
6.2.1	Labor productivity growth, %	0.9	68 ○
6.2.2	Unicorn valuation, % GDP	1.5	28
6.2.3	Software spending, % GDP	0.7	9
6.2.4	High-tech manufacturing, %	⊙ 67.3	2 ●◆
6.3	**Knowledge diffusion**	**60.4**	**4**
6.3.1	Intellectual property receipts, % total trade	6.0	1 ●◆
6.3.2	Production and export complexity	97.4	2 ●◆
6.3.3	High-tech exports, % total trade	7.4	26
6.3.4	ICT services exports, % total trade	2.6	49 ○
6.3.5	ISO 9001 quality/bn PPP$ GDP	11.0	25
	Creative outputs	**68.5**	**1 ●◆**
7.1	**Intangible assets**	**67.5**	**6 ◆**
7.1.1	Intangible asset intensity, top 15, %	76.2	10
7.1.2	Trademarks by origin/bn PPP$ GDP	68.9	25
7.1.3	Global brand value, top 5,000, % GDP	22.6	2 ●◆
7.1.4	Industrial designs by origin/bn PPP$ GDP	5.0	21
7.2	**Creative goods and services**	**53.0**	**2 ●◆**
7.2.1	Cultural and creative services exports, % total trade	0.7	44 ○
7.2.2	National feature films/mn pop. 15–69	11.7	4 ◆
7.2.3	Entertainment and media market/th pop. 15–69	91.0	2 ●◆
7.2.4	Creative goods exports, % total trade	2.8	19
7.3	**Online creativity**	**86.1**	**2 ●◆**
7.3.1	Generic top-level domains (TLDs)/th pop. 15–69	68.4	10
7.3.2	Country-code TLDs/th pop. 15–69	100.0	1 ●◆
7.3.3	GitHub commits/mn pop. 15–69	100.0	1 ●◆
7.3.4	Mobile app creation/bn PPP$ GDP	75.9	20

NOTES: ● indicates a strength; ○ a weakness; ◆ an income group strength; ◇ an income group weakness; * an index; † a survey question. ⊙ is used when the available economy data are older than the base year; see appendices for details, including the year of the data, at wipo.int/gii-ranking. Square brackets [ ] indicate that the data minimum coverage (DMC) requirements were not met at the sub-pillar or pillar level.

GII 2023 rank

Tajikistan **111**

Output rank	Input rank	Income	Region	Population (mn)	GDP, PPP$ (bn)	GDP per capita, PPP$
107	109	Lower middle	CSA	10.0	47.2	4,803

			Score/ Value	Rank	
	Institutions		**41.3**	**90**	
1.1	**Institutional environment**		**26.9**	**107**	
1.1.1	Operational stability for businesses*		33.3	114	
1.1.2	Government effectiveness*		20.4	102	
1.2	**Regulatory environment**		**40.9**	**119**	
1.2.1	Regulatory quality*		12.9	128	◇
1.2.2	Rule of law*		5.0	129	◇
1.2.3	Cost of redundancy dismissal		21.7	96	
1.3	**Business environment**		**56.1**	**[45]**	
1.3.1	Policies for doing business†	⊙	56.1	49	●
1.3.2	Entrepreneurship policies and culture†		n/a	n/a	
	Human capital and research		**20.8**	**99**	
2.1	**Education**		**42.4**	**[90]**	
2.1.1	Expenditure on education, % GDP		5.7	21	●
2.1.2	Government funding/pupil, secondary, % GDP/cap		n/a	n/a	
2.1.3	School life expectancy, years	⊙	11.4	95	
2.1.4	PISA scales in reading, maths and science		n/a	n/a	
2.1.5	Pupil–teacher ratio, secondary		n/a	n/a	
2.2	**Tertiary education**		**19.4**	**92**	
2.2.1	Tertiary enrolment, % gross	⊙	31.3	87	
2.2.2	Graduates in science and engineering, %	⊙	22.0	61	●
2.2.3	Tertiary inbound mobility, %	⊙	0.8	94	
2.3	**Research and development (R&D)**		**0.5**	**110**	
2.3.1	Researchers, FTE/mn pop.		n/a	n/a	
2.3.2	Gross expenditure on R&D, % GDP	⊙	0.1	105	
2.3.3	Global corporate R&D investors, top 3, mn USD		0.0	40	○◇
2.3.4	QS university ranking, top 3*		0.0	71	○◇
	Infrastructure		**19.5**	**122**	◇
3.1	**Information and communication technologies (ICTs)**		**29.6**	**120**	◇
3.1.1	ICT access*		49.1	110	
3.1.2	ICT use*		12.7	129	◇
3.1.3	Government's online service*		33.3	117	
3.1.4	E-participation*		23.3	115	
3.2	**General infrastructure**		**11.3**	**119**	
3.2.1	Electricity output, GWh/mn pop.	⊙	2,107.4	79	
3.2.2	Logistics performance*		18.2	89	
3.2.3	Gross capital formation, % GDP		14.9	120	◇
3.3	**Ecological sustainability**		**17.5**	**93**	
3.3.1	GDP/unit of energy use		9.5	75	●
3.3.2	Environmental performance*		30.8	87	
3.3.3	ISO 14001 environment/bn PPP$ GDP		0.1	130	○
	Market sophistication		**24.8**	**94**	
4.1	**Credit**		**16.3**	**99**	
4.1.1	Finance for startups and scaleups†		n/a	n/a	
4.1.2	Domestic credit to private sector, % GDP		13.0	124	
4.1.3	Loans from microfinance institutions, % GDP		2.5	16	●
4.2	**Investment**		**6.0**	**[70]**	
4.2.1	Market capitalization, % GDP		n/a	n/a	
4.2.2	Venture capital (VC) investors, deals/bn PPP$ GDP		n/a	n/a	
4.2.3	VC recipients, deals/bn PPP$ GDP		0.0	58	●
4.2.4	VC received, value, % GDP		0.0	69	
4.3	**Trade, diversification and market scale**		**52.0**	**83**	
4.3.1	Applied tariff rate, weighted avg., %		3.9	82	
4.3.2	Domestic industry diversification	⊙	80.5	73	
4.3.3	Domestic market scale, bn PPP$		47.2	110	

			Score/ Value	Rank	
	Business sophistication		**19.7**	**110**	
5.1	**Knowledge workers**		**25.2**	**[76]**	
5.1.1	Knowledge-intensive employment, %		n/a	n/a	
5.1.2	Firms offering formal training, %		24.3	67	
5.1.3	GERD performed by business, % GDP		n/a	n/a	
5.1.4	GERD financed by business, %		n/a	n/a	
5.1.5	Females employed w/advanced degrees, %		n/a	n/a	
5.2	**Innovation linkages**		**10.6**	**118**	
5.2.1	University–industry R&D collaboration†	⊙	31.0	95	
5.2.2	State of cluster development†	⊙	16.3	119	
5.2.3	GERD financed by abroad, % GDP	⊙	0.0	96	○◇
5.2.4	Joint venture/strategic alliance deals/bn PPP$ GDP	⊙	0.0	73	●
5.2.5	Patent families/bn PPP$ GDP		0.0	95	○◇
5.3	**Knowledge absorption**		**23.3**	**113**	
5.3.1	Intellectual property payments, % total trade		0.0	116	◇
5.3.2	High-tech imports, % total trade		8.5	58	●
5.3.3	ICT services imports, % total trade		0.4	117	
5.3.4	FDI net inflows, % GDP		1.6	83	
5.3.5	Research talent, % in businesses		n/a	n/a	
	Knowledge and technology outputs		**17.5**	**85**	
6.1	**Knowledge creation**		**19.4**	**55**	●
6.1.1	Patents by origin/bn PPP$ GDP	⊙	0.1	110	
6.1.2	PCT patents by origin/bn PPP$ GDP		0.0	101	○◇
6.1.3	Utility models by origin/bn PPP$ GDP	⊙	3.6	4	
6.1.4	Scientific and technical articles/bn PPP$ GDP		2.2	122	
6.1.5	Citable documents H-index		1.3	128	◇
6.2	**Knowledge impact**		**24.9**	**74**	●
6.2.1	Labor productivity growth, %		5.3	5	●◆
6.2.2	Unicorn valuation, % GDP		0.0	48	○◇
6.2.3	Software spending, % GDP		0.1	101	
6.2.4	High-tech manufacturing, %	⊙	2.6	109	◇
6.3	**Knowledge diffusion**		**8.2**	**115**	
6.3.1	Intellectual property receipts, % total trade		0.0	103	
6.3.2	Production and export complexity		39.7	93	
6.3.3	High-tech exports, % total trade		0.0	129	
6.3.4	ICT services exports, % total trade		0.1	123	
6.3.5	ISO 9001 quality/bn PPP$ GDP		0.1	131	○◇
	Creative outputs		**5.3**	**123**	◇
7.1	**Intangible assets**		**2.7**	**126**	◇
7.1.1	Intangible asset intensity, top 15, %		n/a	n/a	
7.1.2	Trademarks by origin/bn PPP$ GDP	⊙	13.2	104	
7.1.3	Global brand value, top 5,000, % GDP		0.0	74	○◇
7.1.4	Industrial designs by origin/bn PPP$ GDP	⊙	0.0	120	
7.2	**Creative goods and services**		**0.6**	**[121]**	
7.2.1	Cultural and creative services exports, % total trade		0.0	108	
7.2.2	National feature films/mn pop. 15–69		n/a	n/a	
7.2.3	Entertainment and media market/th pop. 15–69		n/a	n/a	
7.2.4	Creative goods exports, % total trade		0.1	99	
7.3	**Online creativity**		**15.3**	**95**	
7.3.1	Generic top-level domains (TLDs)/th pop. 15–69		0.1	124	
7.3.2	Country-code TLDs/th pop. 15–69		0.3	106	
7.3.3	GitHub commits/mn pop. 15–69		0.4	122	
7.3.4	Mobile app creation/bn PPP$ GDP		60.3	82	

NOTES: ● indicates a strength; ○ a weakness; ◆ an income group strength; ◇ an income group weakness; * an index; † a survey question. ⊙ is used when the available economy data are older than the base year; see appendices for details, including the year of the data, at wipo.int/gii-ranking. Square brackets [ ] indicate that the data minimum coverage (DMC) requirements were not met at the sub-pillar or pillar level.

GII 2023 rank

Thailand 43

Output rank	Input rank	Income	Region	Population (mn)	GDP, PPP$ (bn)	GDP per capita, PPP$
43	44	Upper middle	SEAO	71.7	1,479.6	21,114

			Score/ Value	Rank	
Institutions			**44.7**	**85**	
1.1	**Institutional environment**		**46.9**	**62**	
1.1.1	Operational stability for businesses*		50.0	71	
1.1.2	Government effectiveness*		43.7	57	
1.2	**Regulatory environment**		**44.2**	**112**	○ ◇
1.2.1	Regulatory quality*		44.5	65	
1.2.2	Rule of law*		43.1	59	
1.2.3	Cost of redundancy dismissal		36.0	124	○ ◇
1.3	**Business environment**		**43.1**	**73**	
1.3.1	Policies for doing business†		36.6	97	
1.3.2	Entrepreneurship policies and culture†	⊝	49.6	36	
Human capital and research			**29.2**	**74**	
2.1	**Education**		**39.6**	**100**	
2.1.1	Expenditure on education, % GDP		3.0	107	○ ◇
2.1.2	Government funding/pupil, secondary, % GDP/cap	⊝	18.4	60	
2.1.3	School life expectancy, years	⊝	15.4	45	
2.1.4	PISA scales in reading, maths and science		412.4	61	
2.1.5	Pupil–teacher ratio, secondary		22.0	104	○ ◇
2.2	**Tertiary education**		**28.3**	**72**	
2.2.1	Tertiary enrolment, % gross		44.0	73	
2.2.2	Graduates in science and engineering, %	⊝	27.9	29	
2.2.3	Tertiary inbound mobility, %	⊝	1.3	84	
2.3	**Research and development (R&D)**		**19.7**	**45**	
2.3.1	Researchers, FTE/mn pop.	⊝	2,069.9	40	◆
2.3.2	Gross expenditure on R&D, % GDP	⊝	1.3	32	◆
2.3.3	Global corporate R&D investors, top 3, mn USD		0.0	40	○ ◇
2.3.4	QS university ranking, top 3*		33.5	37	
Infrastructure			**47.4**	**49**	
3.1	**Information and communication technologies (ICTs)**		**81.5**	**33**	◆
3.1.1	ICT access*		88.9	29	
3.1.2	ICT use*		83.7	47	◆
3.1.3	Government's online service*		75.3	47	
3.1.4	E-participation*		77.9	18	● ◆
3.2	**General infrastructure**		**35.1**	**41**	◆
3.2.1	Electricity output, GWh/mn pop.		2,671.7	68	
3.2.2	Logistics performance*		63.6	33	◆
3.2.3	Gross capital formation, % GDP		29.1	27	
3.3	**Ecological sustainability**		**25.7**	**63**	
3.3.1	GDP/unit of energy use		8.8	82	
3.3.2	Environmental performance*		32.5	80	
3.3.3	ISO 14001 environment/bn PPP$ GDP		3.3	30	
Market sophistication			**52.7**	**22**	◆
4.1	**Credit**		**65.2**	**9**	● ◆
4.1.1	Finance for startups and scaleups†	⊝	69.3	19	◆
4.1.2	Domestic credit to private sector, % GDP		160.4	10	● ◆
4.1.3	Loans from microfinance institutions, % GDP		n/a	n/a	
4.2	**Investment**		**24.2**	**29**	
4.2.1	Market capitalization, % GDP		104.0	14	
4.2.2	Venture capital (VC) investors, deals/bn PPP$ GDP		0.1	31	
4.2.3	VC recipients, deals/bn PPP$ GDP		0.1	19	◆
4.2.4	VC received, value, % GDP		0.0	45	
4.3	**Trade, diversification and market scale**		**68.7**	**21**	
4.3.1	Applied tariff rate, weighted avg., %	⊝	3.5	77	
4.3.2	Domestic industry diversification	⊝	97.2	15	● ◆
4.3.3	Domestic market scale, bn PPP$		1,479.6	23	

			Score/ Value	Rank	
Business sophistication			**35.8**	**43**	
5.1	**Knowledge workers**		**36.7**	**56**	
5.1.1	Knowledge-intensive employment, %	⊝	13.7	95	◇
5.1.2	Firms offering formal training, %	⊝	18.0	85	○
5.1.3	GERD performed by business, % GDP	⊝	0.8	31	◆
5.1.4	GERD financed by business, %	⊝	80.8	1	● ◆
5.1.5	Females employed w/advanced degrees, %	⊝	10.6	72	
5.2	**Innovation linkages**		**22.2**	**64**	
5.2.1	University–industry R&D collaboration†		53.7	46	
5.2.2	State of cluster development†		44.7	56	
5.2.3	GERD financed by abroad, % GDP	⊝	0.0	79	○
5.2.4	Joint venture/strategic alliance deals/bn PPP$ GDP		0.0	51	
5.2.5	Patent families/bn PPP$ GDP		0.1	62	
5.3	**Knowledge absorption**		**48.7**	**24**	◆
5.3.1	Intellectual property payments, % total trade		1.8	16	● ◆
5.3.2	High-tech imports, % total trade		18.0	10	● ◆
5.3.3	ICT services imports, % total trade		0.4	116	○ ◇
5.3.4	FDI net inflows, % GDP		1.0	98	
5.3.5	Research talent, % in businesses	⊝	60.8	12	● ◆
Knowledge and technology outputs			**31.3**	**42**	
6.1	**Knowledge creation**		**24.2**	**42**	
6.1.1	Patents by origin/bn PPP$ GDP		0.6	71	
6.1.2	PCT patents by origin/bn PPP$ GDP		0.1	57	
6.1.3	Utility models by origin/bn PPP$ GDP		2.7	6	● ◆
6.1.4	Scientific and technical articles/bn PPP$ GDP		9.4	78	
6.1.5	Citable documents H-index		21.1	41	
6.2	**Knowledge impact**		**33.9**	**45**	
6.2.1	Labor productivity growth, %		−0.1	99	
6.2.2	Unicorn valuation, % GDP		0.6	38	
6.2.3	Software spending, % GDP		0.3	52	
6.2.4	High-tech manufacturing, %	⊝	44.0	20	◆
6.3	**Knowledge diffusion**		**35.8**	**38**	
6.3.1	Intellectual property receipts, % total trade		0.1	61	
6.3.2	Production and export complexity		75.7	25	◆
6.3.3	High-tech exports, % total trade		16.7	8	● ◆
6.3.4	ICT services exports, % total trade		0.1	128	○
6.3.5	ISO 9001 quality/bn PPP$ GDP		9.5	30	
Creative outputs			**33.1**	**44**	◆
7.1	**Intangible assets**		**42.5**	**37**	
7.1.1	Intangible asset intensity, top 15, %		66.5	26	
7.1.2	Trademarks by origin/bn PPP$ GDP		24.9	84	
7.1.3	Global brand value, top 5,000, % GDP		7.4	30	◆
7.1.4	Industrial designs by origin/bn PPP$ GDP		3.2	32	
7.2	**Creative goods and services**		**28.0**	**33**	◆
7.2.1	Cultural and creative services exports, % total trade		0.0	96	○
7.2.2	National feature films/mn pop. 15–69		0.4	72	○
7.2.3	Entertainment and media market/th pop. 15–69		9.2	35	
7.2.4	Creative goods exports, % total trade		8.5	1	● ◆
7.3	**Online creativity**		**19.4**	**69**	
7.3.1	Generic top-level domains (TLDs)/th pop. 15–69		6.1	52	
7.3.2	Country-code TLDs/th pop. 15–69		0.4	102	
7.3.3	GitHub commits/mn pop. 15–69		4.0	77	
7.3.4	Mobile app creation/bn PPP$ GDP		67.2	61	

NOTES: ● indicates a strength; ○ a weakness; ◆ an income group strength; ◇ an income group weakness; * an index; † a survey question. ⊝ is used when the available economy data are older than the base year; see appendices for details, including the year of the data, at wipo.int/gii-ranking. Square brackets [ ] indicate that the data minimum coverage (DMC) requirements were not met at the sub-pillar or pillar level.

Togo

114

Output rank	Input rank	Income	Region	Population (mn)	GDP, PPP$ (bn)	GDP per capita, PPP$
105	120	Low	SSA	8.8	22.8	2,619

		Score/ Value	Rank	
	Institutions	**37.5**	**102**	
1.1	**Institutional environment**	**31.0**	**99**	
1.1.1	Operational stability for businesses*	43.1	85	●
1.1.2	Government effectiveness*	18.9	110	
1.2	**Regulatory environment**	**56.4**	**84**	●
1.2.1	Regulatory quality*	25.7	109	
1.2.2	Rule of law*	23.3	97	
1.2.3	Cost of redundancy dismissal	13.9	52	●
1.3	**Business environment**	**25.0**	**[111]**	
1.3.1	Policies for doing business†	n/a	n/a	
1.3.2	Entrepreneurship policies and culture†	25.0	67	
	Human capital and research	**16.8**	**[111]**	
2.1	**Education**	**41.5**	**[94]**	
2.1.1	Expenditure on education, % GDP	4.2	66	●
2.1.2	Government funding/pupil, secondary, % GDP/cap	n/a	n/a	
2.1.3	School life expectancy, years ⊙	12.7	87	◆
2.1.4	PISA scales in reading, maths and science	n/a	n/a	
2.1.5	Pupil-teacher ratio, secondary	25.9	111	
2.2	**Tertiary education**	**7.5**	**[116]**	
2.2.1	Tertiary enrolment, % gross	15.4	105	◆
2.2.2	Graduates in science and engineering, %	n/a	n/a	
2.2.3	Tertiary inbound mobility, %	n/a	n/a	
2.3	**Research and development (R&D)**	**1.2**	**98**	
2.3.1	Researchers, FTE/mn pop.	45.2	95	
2.3.2	Gross expenditure on R&D, % GDP ⊙	0.3	82	
2.3.3	Global corporate R&D investors, top 3, mn USD	0.0	40	○◇
2.3.4	QS university ranking, top 3*	0.0	71	○◇
	Infrastructure	**20.8**	**117**	
3.1	**Information and communication technologies (ICTs)**	**36.0**	**113**	
3.1.1	ICT access*	41.0	117	
3.1.2	ICT use*	28.4	118	◆
3.1.3	Government's online service*	37.4	112	
3.1.4	E-participation*	37.2	91	
3.2	**General infrastructure**	**14.3**	**108**	
3.2.1	Electricity output, GWh/mn pop. ⊙	84.6	122	○
3.2.2	Logistics performance*	18.2	89	
3.2.3	Gross capital formation, % GDP	26.7	40	●
3.3	**Ecological sustainability**	**12.0**	**118**	
3.3.1	GDP/unit of energy use	4.7	117	
3.3.2	Environmental performance*	25.6	97	
3.3.3	ISO 14001 environment/bn PPP$ GDP	0.4	90	◆
	Market sophistication	**21.1**	**111**	◆
4.1	**Credit**	**27.6**	**71**	●◆
4.1.1	Finance for startups and scaleups†	17.8	80	
4.1.2	Domestic credit to private sector, % GDP	26.6	105	◆
4.1.3	Loans from microfinance institutions, % GDP	4.8	6	●◆
4.2	**Investment**	**n/a**	**[n/a]**	
4.2.1	Market capitalization, % GDP	n/a	n/a	
4.2.2	Venture capital (VC) investors, deals/bn PPP$ GDP	n/a	n/a	
4.2.3	VC recipients, deals/bn PPP$ GDP	n/a	n/a	
4.2.4	VC received, value, % GDP	n/a	n/a	
4.3	**Trade, diversification and market scale**	**14.7**	**128**	○◇
4.3.1	Applied tariff rate, weighted avg., %	11.0	122	
4.3.2	Domestic industry diversification	n/a	n/a	
4.3.3	Domestic market scale, bn PPP$	22.8	129	○

		Score/ Value	Rank	
	Business sophistication	**14.4**	**[131]**	
5.1	**Knowledge workers**	**20.1**	**[99]**	
5.1.1	Knowledge-intensive employment, % ⊙	14.1	91	◆
5.1.2	Firms offering formal training, % ⊙	33.7	49	●
5.1.3	GERD performed by business, % GDP	n/a	n/a	
5.1.4	GERD financed by business, %	n/a	n/a	
5.1.5	Females employed w/advanced degrees, % ⊙	0.9	118	
5.2	**Innovation linkages**	**1.2**	**[131]**	
5.2.1	University-industry R&D collaboration†	n/a	n/a	
5.2.2	State of cluster development†	n/a	n/a	
5.2.3	GERD financed by abroad, % GDP ⊙	0.0	68	
5.2.4	Joint venture/strategic alliance deals/bn PPP$ GDP	n/a	n/a	
5.2.5	Patent families/bn PPP$ GDP	0.0	95	○◇
5.3	**Knowledge absorption**	**21.8**	**121**	
5.3.1	Intellectual property payments, % total trade	0.0	118	○◇
5.3.2	High-tech imports, % total trade	5.3	110	
5.3.3	ICT services imports, % total trade	0.6	102	◇
5.3.4	FDI net inflows, % GDP	1.8	78	●
5.3.5	Research talent, % in businesses	n/a	n/a	
	Knowledge and technology outputs	**12.4**	**108**	
6.1	**Knowledge creation**	**3.6**	**119**	
6.1.1	Patents by origin/bn PPP$ GDP	0.1	111	
6.1.2	PCT patents by origin/bn PPP$ GDP	0.0	101	○◇
6.1.3	Utility models by origin/bn PPP$ GDP	0.0	75	○◇
6.1.4	Scientific and technical articles/bn PPP$ GDP	7.7	87	
6.1.5	Citable documents H-index	1.5	127	◇
6.2	**Knowledge impact**	**22.5**	**90**	
6.2.1	Labor productivity growth, %	1.8	39	●
6.2.2	Unicorn valuation, % GDP	0.0	48	○◇
6.2.3	Software spending, % GDP	0.1	94	◆
6.2.4	High-tech manufacturing, %	n/a	n/a	
6.3	**Knowledge diffusion**	**11.1**	**102**	
6.3.1	Intellectual property receipts, % total trade	0.0	113	
6.3.2	Production and export complexity	36.1	99	
6.3.3	High-tech exports, % total trade	0.1	115	
6.3.4	ICT services exports, % total trade	1.7	66	●
6.3.5	ISO 9001 quality/bn PPP$ GDP	1.5	94	◆
	Creative outputs	**11.1**	**105**	
7.1	**Intangible assets**	**6.2**	**117**	
7.1.1	Intangible asset intensity, top 15, %	n/a	n/a	
7.1.2	Trademarks by origin/bn PPP$ GDP	19.7	93	
7.1.3	Global brand value, top 5,000, % GDP	0.0	74	○◇
7.1.4	Industrial designs by origin/bn PPP$ GDP	0.2	101	
7.2	**Creative goods and services**	**17.4**	**[53]**	
7.2.1	Cultural and creative services exports, % total trade	1.7	17	●◆
7.2.2	National feature films/mn pop. 15–69	n/a	n/a	
7.2.3	Entertainment and media market/th pop. 15–69	n/a	n/a	
7.2.4	Creative goods exports, % total trade	0.0	117	
7.3	**Online creativity**	**14.8**	**98**	◆
7.3.1	Generic top-level domains (TLDs)/th pop. 15–69	0.6	104	◆
7.3.2	Country-code TLDs/th pop. 15–69	0.1	119	
7.3.3	GitHub commits/mn pop. 15–69	0.7	118	
7.3.4	Mobile app creation/bn PPP$ GDP	57.6	88	◆

NOTES: ● indicates a strength; ○ a weakness; ◆ an income group strength; ◇ an income group weakness; * an index; † a survey question. ⊙ is used when the available economy data are older than the base year; see appendices for details, including the year of the data, at wipo.int/gii-ranking. Square brackets [ ] indicate that the data minimum coverage (DMC) requirements were not met at the sub-pillar or pillar level.

GII 2023 rank

Trinidad and Tobago **102**

Output rank	Input rank	Income	Region	Population (mn)	GDP, PPP$ (bn)	GDP per capita, PPP$
108	92	High	LCN	1.5	42.1	29,797

			Score/ Value	Rank	
	Institutions		**49.2**	**68**	◇
1.1	**Institutional environment**		**48.8**	**56**	●◇
1.1.1	Operational stability for businesses*		55.6	56	●◇
1.1.2	Government effectiveness*		42.1	60	●◇
1.2	**Regulatory environment**		**56.5**	**83**	◇
1.2.1	Regulatory quality*		39.9	78	◇
1.2.2	Rule of law*		35.7	71	◇
1.2.3	Cost of redundancy dismissal		20.5	89	
1.3	**Business environment**		**42.2**	**[78]**	
1.3.1	Policies for doing business†		42.2	80	◇
1.3.2	Entrepreneurship policies and culture†		n/a	n/a	
	Human capital and research		**36.2**	**45**	●
2.1	**Education**		**39.2**	**101**	◇
2.1.1	Expenditure on education, % GDP		3.0	106	◇
2.1.2	Government funding/pupil, secondary, % GDP/cap		13.9	78	◇
2.1.3	School life expectancy, years		n/a	n/a	
2.1.4	PISA scales in reading, maths and science	⊙	423.0	54	◇
2.1.5	Pupil–teacher ratio, secondary		12.1	53	●
2.2	**Tertiary education**		**67.7**	**[3]**	
2.2.1	Tertiary enrolment, % gross		n/a	n/a	
2.2.2	Graduates in science and engineering, %		32.3	14	●◆
2.2.3	Tertiary inbound mobility, %		n/a	n/a	
2.3	**Research and development (R&D)**		**1.9**	**93**	◇
2.3.1	Researchers, FTE/mn pop.	⊙	638.8	63	◇
2.3.2	Gross expenditure on R&D, % GDP	⊙	0.1	108	○◇
2.3.3	Global corporate R&D investors, top 3, mn USD		0.0	40	○◇
2.3.4	QS university ranking, top 3*		0.0	71	○◇
	Infrastructure		**32.4**	**88**	◇
3.1	**Information and communication technologies (ICTs)**		**53.9**	**91**	◇
3.1.1	ICT access*		84.4	55	●
3.1.2	ICT use*		65.5	84	◇
3.1.3	Government's online service*		43.5	103	◇
3.1.4	E-participation*		22.1	120	◇
3.2	**General infrastructure**		**25.9**	**68**	◇
3.2.1	Electricity output, GWh/mn pop.	⊙	6,590.4	30	●
3.2.2	Logistics performance*		18.2	89	◇
3.2.3	Gross capital formation, % GDP		n/a	n/a	
3.3	**Ecological sustainability**		**17.4**	**95**	◇
3.3.1	GDP/unit of energy use		2.2	126	○◇
3.3.2	Environmental performance*		49.0	47	●
3.3.3	ISO 14001 environment/bn PPP$ GDP		0.5	86	◇
	Market sophistication		**13.9**	**[124]**	
4.1	**Credit**		**16.0**	**[100]**	
4.1.1	Finance for startups and scaleups†		n/a	n/a	
4.1.2	Domestic credit to private sector, % GDP		46.1	77	◇
4.1.3	Loans from microfinance institutions, % GDP		n/a	n/a	
4.2	**Investment**		**3.2**	**[91]**	
4.2.1	Market capitalization, % GDP		n/a	n/a	
4.2.2	Venture capital (VC) investors, deals/bn PPP$ GDP		0.1	54	
4.2.3	VC recipients, deals/bn PPP$ GDP		n/a	n/a	
4.2.4	VC received, value, % GDP		n/a	n/a	
4.3	**Trade, diversification and market scale**		**22.5**	**125**	○◇
4.3.1	Applied tariff rate, weighted avg., %	⊙	8.6	109	
4.3.2	Domestic industry diversification		n/a	n/a	
4.3.3	Domestic market scale, bn PPP$		42.1	115	

			Score/ Value	Rank	
	Business sophistication		**19.2**	**113**	◇
5.1	**Knowledge workers**		**23.7**	**83**	◇
5.1.1	Knowledge-intensive employment, %	⊙	31.9	47	●
5.1.2	Firms offering formal training, %		n/a	n/a	
5.1.3	GERD performed by business, % GDP	⊙	0.0	84	◇
5.1.4	GERD financed by business, %		4.6	81	◇
5.1.5	Females employed w/advanced degrees, %	⊙	12.8	60	
5.2	**Innovation linkages**		**13.8**	**104**	◇
5.2.1	University–industry R&D collaboration†		22.8	111	◇
5.2.2	State of cluster development†		31.6	89	◇
5.2.3	GERD financed by abroad, % GDP		0.0	77	◇
5.2.4	Joint venture/strategic alliance deals/bn PPP$ GDP		0.0	33	●
5.2.5	Patent families/bn PPP$ GDP		0.0	95	○◇
5.3	**Knowledge absorption**		**20.0**	**130**	○◇
5.3.1	Intellectual property payments, % total trade		0.5	67	
5.3.2	High-tech imports, % total trade		5.5	108	
5.3.3	ICT services imports, % total trade		0.6	103	◇
5.3.4	FDI net inflows, % GDP		0.4	116	
5.3.5	Research talent, % in businesses	⊙	1.4	78	○◇
	Knowledge and technology outputs		**13.4**	**103**	◇
6.1	**Knowledge creation**		**3.8**	**118**	◇
6.1.1	Patents by origin/bn PPP$ GDP		0.1	122	◇
6.1.2	PCT patents by origin/bn PPP$ GDP		0.1	63	
6.1.3	Utility models by origin/bn PPP$ GDP		0.0	67	◇
6.1.4	Scientific and technical articles/bn PPP$ GDP		5.6	104	◇
6.1.5	Citable documents H-index		4.6	108	◇
6.2	**Knowledge impact**		**20.4**	**[102]**	
6.2.1	Labor productivity growth, %		−0.4	106	◇
6.2.2	Unicorn valuation, % GDP		0.0	48	○◇
6.2.3	Software spending, % GDP		n/a	n/a	
6.2.4	High-tech manufacturing, %		n/a	n/a	
6.3	**Knowledge diffusion**		**15.9**	**91**	◇
6.3.1	Intellectual property receipts, % total trade		0.0	94	
6.3.2	Production and export complexity		55.3	55	◇
6.3.3	High-tech exports, % total trade		1.0	73	◇
6.3.4	ICT services exports, % total trade		0.1	124	○◇
6.3.5	ISO 9001 quality/bn PPP$ GDP		2.1	86	◇
	Creative outputs		**9.2**	**109**	◇
7.1	**Intangible assets**		**12.3**	**104**	◇
7.1.1	Intangible asset intensity, top 15, %		n/a	n/a	
7.1.2	Trademarks by origin/bn PPP$ GDP		17.5	97	◇
7.1.3	Global brand value, top 5,000, % GDP		0.0	74	○◇
7.1.4	Industrial designs by origin/bn PPP$ GDP		1.5	52	●
7.2	**Creative goods and services**		**1.2**	**[114]**	
7.2.1	Cultural and creative services exports, % total trade		n/a	n/a	
7.2.2	National feature films/mn pop. 15–69		n/a	n/a	
7.2.3	Entertainment and media market/th pop. 15–69		n/a	n/a	
7.2.4	Creative goods exports, % total trade		0.1	94	
7.3	**Online creativity**		**10.8**	**113**	◇
7.3.1	Generic top-level domains (TLDs)/th pop. 15–69		4.4	59	●◇
7.3.2	Country-code TLDs/th pop. 15–69		1.0	90	◇
7.3.3	GitHub commits/mn pop. 15–69		4.2	75	◇
7.3.4	Mobile app creation/bn PPP$ GDP		33.7	118	○◇

NOTES: ● indicates a strength; ○ a weakness; ◆ an income group strength; ◇ an income group weakness; * an index; † a survey question. ⊙ is used when the available economy data are older than the base year; see appendices for details, including the year of the data, at wipo.int/gii-ranking. Square brackets [ ] indicate that the data minimum coverage (DMC) requirements were not met at the sub-pillar or pillar level.

Tunisia

GII 2023 rank

79

Output rank	Input rank	Income	Region	Population (mn)	GDP, PPP$ (bn)	GDP per capita, PPP$
61	96	Lower middle	NAWA	12.4	151.5	12,490

	Institutions		Score/Value	Rank	
	Institutions		**36.2**	**107**	
1.1	**Institutional environment**		**34.8**	**94**	
1.1.1	Operational stability for businesses*		37.5	101	
1.1.2	Government effectiveness*		32.1	82	
1.2	**Regulatory environment**		**55.2**	**88**	
1.2.1	Regulatory quality*		32.0	93	
1.2.2	Rule of law*		42.5	60	◆
1.2.3	Cost of redundancy dismissal		21.6	94	
1.3	**Business environment**		**18.6**	**121**	○◇
1.3.1	Policies for doing business†		26.5	111	
1.3.2	Entrepreneurship policies and culture†		10.6	78	○◇

	Human capital and research		Score/Value	Rank	
	Human capital and research		**36.1**	**46**	◆
2.1	**Education**		**62.9**	**20**	●◆
2.1.1	Expenditure on education, % GDP	⊙	6.2	16	
2.1.2	Government funding/pupil, secondary, % GDP/cap	⊙	51.1	1	●◆
2.1.3	School life expectancy, years	⊙	15.1	50	◆
2.1.4	PISA scales in reading, maths and science	⊙	371.4	74	○
2.1.5	Pupil–teacher ratio, secondary		13.3	61	
2.2	**Tertiary education**		**37.9**	**38**	●◆
2.2.1	Tertiary enrolment, % gross		37.5	80	
2.2.2	Graduates in science and engineering, %		37.9	5	●◆
2.2.3	Tertiary inbound mobility, %		2.9	68	
2.3	**Research and development (R&D)**		**7.5**	**69**	
2.3.1	Researchers, FTE/mn pop.		1,621.6	47	◆
2.3.2	Gross expenditure on R&D, % GDP	⊙	0.7	49	◆
2.3.3	Global corporate R&D investors, top 3, mn USD		0.0	40	○◇
2.3.4	QS university ranking, top 3*		0.0	71	○◇

	Infrastructure		Score/Value	Rank	
	Infrastructure		**32.3**	**89**	
3.1	**Information and communication technologies (ICTs)**		**63.0**	**80**	◆
3.1.1	ICT access*		74.9	82	
3.1.2	ICT use*		67.4	77	
3.1.3	Government's online service*		56.1	85	
3.1.4	E-participation*		53.5	67	◆
3.2	**General infrastructure**		**7.9**	**127**	○◇
3.2.1	Electricity output, GWh/mn pop.	⊙	1,830.1	85	
3.2.2	Logistics performance*		n/a	n/a	
3.2.3	Gross capital formation, % GDP		15.9	117	○◇
3.3	**Ecological sustainability**		**26.1**	**61**	◆
3.3.1	GDP/unit of energy use		11.0	57	
3.3.2	Environmental performance*		36.9	72	◆
3.3.3	ISO 14001 environment/bn PPP$ GDP		2.0	44	●◆

	Market sophistication		Score/Value	Rank	
	Market sophistication		**24.2**	**98**	
4.1	**Credit**		**23.5**	**83**	
4.1.1	Finance for startups and scaleups†		27.3	74	◇
4.1.2	Domestic credit to private sector, % GDP	⊙	81.7	42	●◆
4.1.3	Loans from microfinance institutions, % GDP		1.1	25	
4.2	**Investment**		**5.5**	**72**	
4.2.1	Market capitalization, % GDP		20.0	59	
4.2.2	Venture capital (VC) investors, deals/bn PPP$ GDP		0.0	55	
4.2.3	VC recipients, deals/bn PPP$ GDP		0.0	48	
4.2.4	VC received, value, % GDP		0.0	85	
4.3	**Trade, diversification and market scale**		**43.7**	**99**	
4.3.1	Applied tariff rate, weighted avg., %	⊙	9.3	116	
4.3.2	Domestic industry diversification	⊙	88.3	55	
4.3.3	Domestic market scale, bn PPP$		151.5	77	

	Business sophistication		Score/Value	Rank	
	Business sophistication		**16.8**	**119**	◇
5.1	**Knowledge workers**		**18.5**	**103**	
5.1.1	Knowledge-intensive employment, %	⊙	15.9	86	
5.1.2	Firms offering formal training, %		19.1	83	
5.1.3	GERD performed by business, % GDP	⊙	0.1	60	
5.1.4	GERD financed by business, %	⊙	18.9	68	
5.1.5	Females employed w/advanced degrees, %	⊙	8.8	80	
5.2	**Innovation linkages**		**11.5**	**112**	
5.2.1	University–industry R&D collaboration†		23.4	109	
5.2.2	State of cluster development†		22.9	107	
5.2.3	GERD financed by abroad, % GDP	⊙	0.0	58	
5.2.4	Joint venture/strategic alliance deals/bn PPP$ GDP		0.0	63	
5.2.5	Patent families/bn PPP$ GDP		0.0	78	
5.3	**Knowledge absorption**		**20.3**	**129**	○◇
5.3.1	Intellectual property payments, % total trade		0.1	101	
5.3.2	High-tech imports, % total trade		8.7	55	
5.3.3	ICT services imports, % total trade		0.4	120	○
5.3.4	FDI net inflows, % GDP		1.5	89	
5.3.5	Research talent, % in businesses	⊙	5.2	69	

	Knowledge and technology outputs		Score/Value	Rank	
	Knowledge and technology outputs		**27.1**	**50**	◆
6.1	**Knowledge creation**		**26.2**	**37**	●◆
6.1.1	Patents by origin/bn PPP$ GDP	⊙	1.3	50	
6.1.2	PCT patents by origin/bn PPP$ GDP		0.0	76	
6.1.3	Utility models by origin/bn PPP$ GDP		n/a	n/a	
6.1.4	Scientific and technical articles/bn PPP$ GDP		36.8	10	●◆
6.1.5	Citable documents H-index		11.9	68	
6.2	**Knowledge impact**		**26.7**	**65**	
6.2.1	Labor productivity growth, %		0.2	91	
6.2.2	Unicorn valuation, % GDP		0.0	48	○◇
6.2.3	Software spending, % GDP		0.3	36	●
6.2.4	High-tech manufacturing, %	⊙	24.3	53	
6.3	**Knowledge diffusion**		**28.4**	**54**	◆
6.3.1	Intellectual property receipts, % total trade		0.1	56	
6.3.2	Production and export complexity		62.1	44	◆
6.3.3	High-tech exports, % total trade		4.5	40	●◆
6.3.4	ICT services exports, % total trade		1.5	71	
6.3.5	ISO 9001 quality/bn PPP$ GDP		8.2	33	●◆

	Creative outputs		Score/Value	Rank	
	Creative outputs		**22.3**	**72**	
7.1	**Intangible assets**		**33.1**	**61**	
7.1.1	Intangible asset intensity, top 15, %		37.4	63	
7.1.2	Trademarks by origin/bn PPP$ GDP		n/a	n/a	
7.1.3	Global brand value, top 5,000, % GDP		0.0	74	○◇
7.1.4	Industrial designs by origin/bn PPP$ GDP	⊙	1.6	50	
7.2	**Creative goods and services**		**6.4**	**81**	
7.2.1	Cultural and creative services exports, % total trade	⊙	0.0	103	○
7.2.2	National feature films/mn pop. 15–69		1.8	50	
7.2.3	Entertainment and media market/th pop. 15–69		0.1	60	○◇
7.2.4	Creative goods exports, % total trade		1.2	41	●
7.3	**Online creativity**		**16.5**	**88**	
7.3.1	Generic top-level domains (TLDs)/th pop. 15–69		3.1	68	◆
7.3.2	Country-code TLDs/th pop. 15–69		1.9	72	
7.3.3	GitHub commits/mn pop. 15–69		6.3	65	
7.3.4	Mobile app creation/bn PPP$ GDP		54.8	96	

NOTES: ● indicates a strength; ○ a weakness; ◆ an income group strength; ◇ an income group weakness; * an index; † a survey question. ⊙ is used when the available economy data are older than the base year; see appendices for details, including the year of the data, at wipo.int/gii-ranking. Square brackets [ ] indicate that the data minimum coverage (DMC) requirements were not met at the sub-pillar or pillar level.

GII 2023 rank

Türkiye **39**

Output rank	Input rank	Income	Region	Population (mn)	GDP, PPP$ (bn)	GDP per capita, PPP$
32	52	Upper middle	NAWA	85.3	3,321.0	38,759

			Score/Value	Rank	
	Institutions		**36.5**	**105**	○
1.1	**Institutional environment**		**37.0**	**85**	
1.1.1	Operational stability for businesses*		39.6	95	○
1.1.2	Government effectiveness*		34.4	77	
1.2	**Regulatory environment**		**45.3**	**110**	○◇
1.2.1	Regulatory quality*		40.0	77	
1.2.2	Rule of law*		27.5	88	
1.2.3	Cost of redundancy dismissal		29.8	118	○◇
1.3	**Business environment**		**27.2**	**107**	○
1.3.1	Policies for doing business†		25.5	114	○
1.3.2	Entrepreneurship policies and culture†	⊘	28.9	60	
	Human capital and research		**37.5**	**41**	
2.1	**Education**		**50.7**	**67**	
2.1.1	Expenditure on education, % GDP	⊘	3.4	96	○
2.1.2	Government funding/pupil, secondary, % GDP/cap		14.6	76	○
2.1.3	School life expectancy, years		18.5	11	●◆
2.1.4	PISA scales in reading, maths and science		462.5	41	
2.1.5	Pupil–teacher ratio, secondary		15.1	76	
2.2	**Tertiary education**		**33.7**	**56**	
2.2.1	Tertiary enrolment, % gross		117.1	2	●◆
2.2.2	Graduates in science and engineering, %		15.2	100	○
2.2.3	Tertiary inbound mobility, %		2.3	74	
2.3	**Research and development (R&D)**		**28.1**	**37**	◆
2.3.1	Researchers, FTE/mn pop.		2,007.0	42	◆
2.3.2	Gross expenditure on R&D, % GDP		1.1	35	◆
2.3.3	Global corporate R&D investors, top 3, mn USD		47.2	35	◆
2.3.4	QS university ranking, top 3*		24.4	45	
	Infrastructure		**46.7**	**50**	
3.1	**Information and communication technologies (ICTs)**		**80.5**	**39**	◆
3.1.1	ICT access*		83.8	59	
3.1.2	ICT use*		75.8	60	
3.1.3	Government's online service*		84.5	24	◆
3.1.4	E-participation*		77.9	18	◆
3.2	**General infrastructure**		**38.5**	**34**	◆
3.2.1	Electricity output, GWh/mn pop.		3,939.4	56	
3.2.2	Logistics performance*		59.1	37	◆
3.2.3	Gross capital formation, % GDP		34.2	15	●◆
3.3	**Ecological sustainability**		**21.1**	**77**	
3.3.1	GDP/unit of energy use		16.7	17	◆
3.3.2	Environmental performance*		12.5	127	○◇
3.3.3	ISO 14001 environment/bn PPP$ GDP		1.1	62	
	Market sophistication		**45.1**	**36**	
4.1	**Credit**		**41.4**	**39**	
4.1.1	Finance for startups and scaleups†	⊘	55.3	37	
4.1.2	Domestic credit to private sector, % GDP		75.2	46	
4.1.3	Loans from microfinance institutions, % GDP		n/a	n/a	
4.2	**Investment**		**9.6**	**56**	
4.2.1	Market capitalization, % GDP		25.5	51	
4.2.2	Venture capital (VC) investors, deals/bn PPP$ GDP		0.0	74	○
4.2.3	VC recipients, deals/bn PPP$ GDP		0.0	70	
4.2.4	VC received, value, % GDP		0.0	34	
4.3	**Trade, diversification and market scale**		**84.1**	**11**	●◆
4.3.1	Applied tariff rate, weighted avg., %		2.8	71	
4.3.2	Domestic industry diversification		99.4	4	●◆
4.3.3	Domestic market scale, bn PPP$		3,321.0	11	●◆

			Score/Value	Rank	
	Business sophistication		**33.5**	**46**	
5.1	**Knowledge workers**		**39.8**	**48**	
5.1.1	Knowledge-intensive employment, %	⊘	23.9	59	
5.1.2	Firms offering formal training, %		30.7	55	
5.1.3	GERD performed by business, % GDP		0.8	32	◆
5.1.4	GERD financed by business, %		62.4	12	●◆
5.1.5	Females employed w/advanced degrees, %	⊘	11.3	69	
5.2	**Innovation linkages**		**19.0**	**81**	
5.2.1	University–industry R&D collaboration†		39.4	76	
5.2.2	State of cluster development†		44.4	57	
5.2.3	GERD financed by abroad, % GDP		0.0	60	
5.2.4	Joint venture/strategic alliance deals/bn PPP$ GDP		0.0	114	○
5.2.5	Patent families/bn PPP$ GDP		0.3	39	
5.3	**Knowledge absorption**		**41.9**	**39**	
5.3.1	Intellectual property payments, % total trade		1.0	39	
5.3.2	High-tech imports, % total trade		8.2	66	
5.3.3	ICT services imports, % total trade		1.0	87	
5.3.4	FDI net inflows, % GDP		1.3	94	○
5.3.5	Research talent, % in businesses		66.9	7	●◆
	Knowledge and technology outputs		**31.1**	**44**	
6.1	**Knowledge creation**		**27.4**	**36**	
6.1.1	Patents by origin/bn PPP$ GDP		3.0	25	◆
6.1.2	PCT patents by origin/bn PPP$ GDP		0.5	31	
6.1.3	Utility models by origin/bn PPP$ GDP		1.5	11	●
6.1.4	Scientific and technical articles/bn PPP$ GDP		12.4	63	
6.1.5	Citable documents H-index		29.7	33	◆
6.2	**Knowledge impact**		**43.7**	**23**	◆
6.2.1	Labor productivity growth, %		2.6	21	
6.2.2	Unicorn valuation, % GDP		1.4	30	◆
6.2.3	Software spending, % GDP		0.5	23	◆
6.2.4	High-tech manufacturing, %		30.0	36	
6.3	**Knowledge diffusion**		**22.4**	**64**	
6.3.1	Intellectual property receipts, % total trade		0.1	60	
6.3.2	Production and export complexity		65.7	41	
6.3.3	High-tech exports, % total trade		2.0	60	
6.3.4	ICT services exports, % total trade		0.9	89	
6.3.5	ISO 9001 quality/bn PPP$ GDP		3.2	71	
	Creative outputs		**43.6**	**27**	◆
7.1	**Intangible assets**		**68.0**	**5**	●◆
7.1.1	Intangible asset intensity, top 15, %		75.0	12	
7.1.2	Trademarks by origin/bn PPP$ GDP		133.8	5	●◆
7.1.3	Global brand value, top 5,000, % GDP		1.3	51	
7.1.4	Industrial designs by origin/bn PPP$ GDP		20.1	4	●◆
7.2	**Creative goods and services**		**13.9**	**61**	
7.2.1	Cultural and creative services exports, % total trade		0.2	71	
7.2.2	National feature films/mn pop. 15–69		1.3	56	
7.2.3	Entertainment and media market/th pop. 15–69		4.6	43	
7.2.4	Creative goods exports, % total trade		3.3	18	
7.3	**Online creativity**		**24.4**	**53**	
7.3.1	Generic top-level domains (TLDs)/th pop. 15–69		12.4	40	◆
7.3.2	Country-code TLDs/th pop. 15–69		2.2	70	
7.3.3	GitHub commits/mn pop. 15–69		7.0	63	
7.3.4	Mobile app creation/bn PPP$ GDP		76.0	18	

NOTES: ● indicates a strength; ○ a weakness; ◆ an income group strength; ◇ an income group weakness; * an index; † a survey question. ⊘ is used when the available economy data are older than the base year; see appendices for details, including the year of the data, at wipo.int/gii-ranking. Square brackets [ ] indicate that the data minimum coverage (DMC) requirements were not met at the sub-pillar or pillar level.

GII 2023 rank

121

Uganda

Output rank	Input rank	Income	Region	Population (mn)	GDP, PPP$ (bn)	GDP per capita, PPP$
121	117	Low	SSA	47.2	132.0	3,018

			Score/ Value	Rank
	Institutions		**50.5**	**64 ●◆**
1.1	**Institutional environment**		**29.9**	**101**
1.1.1	Operational stability for businesses*		38.9	96
1.1.2	Government effectiveness*		21.0	101
1.2	**Regulatory environment**		**64.1**	**63 ●◆**
1.2.1	Regulatory quality*		29.7	98
1.2.2	Rule of law*		29.4	84
1.2.3	Cost of redundancy dismissal		8.7	20 ●
1.3	**Business environment**		**57.4**	**[41]**
1.3.1	Policies for doing business†	⊙	57.4	43 ●
1.3.2	Entrepreneurship policies and culture†		n/a	n/a
	Human capital and research		**12.8**	**[124]**
2.1	**Education**		**37.3**	**[107]**
2.1.1	Expenditure on education, % GDP		2.6	112 ◇
2.1.2	Government funding/pupil, secondary, % GDP/cap		n/a	n/a
2.1.3	School life expectancy, years		n/a	n/a
2.1.4	PISA scales in reading, maths and science		n/a	n/a
2.1.5	Pupil–teacher ratio, secondary	⊙	20.5	98
2.2	**Tertiary education**		**0.5**	**[129]**
2.2.1	Tertiary enrolment, % gross	⊙	5.1	125 ○
2.2.2	Graduates in science and engineering, %		n/a	n/a
2.2.3	Tertiary inbound mobility, %		n/a	n/a
2.3	**Research and development (R&D)**		**0.6**	**107**
2.3.1	Researchers, FTE/mn pop.	⊙	27.8	101
2.3.2	Gross expenditure on R&D, % GDP	⊙	0.1	97
2.3.3	Global corporate R&D investors, top 3, mn USD		0.0	40 ○◇
2.3.4	QS university ranking, top 3*		0.0	71 ○◇
	Infrastructure		**21.0**	**116**
3.1	**Information and communication technologies (ICTs)**		**35.4**	**116**
3.1.1	ICT access*		30.4	123
3.1.2	ICT use*		25.2	120
3.1.3	Government's online service*		46.6	98
3.1.4	E-participation*		39.5	89
3.2	**General infrastructure**		**13.4**	**113**
3.2.1	Electricity output, GWh/mn pop.	⊙	97.3	121 ○
3.2.2	Logistics performance*		n/a	n/a
3.2.3	Gross capital formation, % GDP		28.0	31 ●
3.3	**Ecological sustainability**		**14.2**	**106**
3.3.1	GDP/unit of energy use		5.8	109
3.3.2	Environmental performance*		28.6	89
3.3.3	ISO 14001 environment/bn PPP$ GDP		0.5	87 ◆
	Market sophistication		**11.9**	**128 ○**
4.1	**Credit**		**3.4**	**126 ○**
4.1.1	Finance for startups and scaleups†		n/a	n/a
4.1.2	Domestic credit to private sector, % GDP		14.2	121
4.1.3	Loans from microfinance institutions, % GDP		0.3	46
4.2	**Investment**		**7.2**	**65**
4.2.1	Market capitalization, % GDP		n/a	n/a
4.2.2	Venture capital (VC) investors, deals/bn PPP$ GDP	⊙	0.0	89 ◆
4.2.3	VC recipients, deals/bn PPP$ GDP		0.1	42 ●
4.2.4	VC received, value, % GDP		0.0	62 ◆
4.3	**Trade, diversification and market scale**		**25.2**	**121**
4.3.1	Applied tariff rate, weighted avg., %		8.1	106
4.3.2	Domestic industry diversification		n/a	n/a
4.3.3	Domestic market scale, bn PPP$		132.0	80

			Score/ Value	Rank
	Business sophistication		**17.0**	**118**
5.1	**Knowledge workers**		**11.7**	**117**
5.1.1	Knowledge-intensive employment, %	⊙	4.5	120 ○
5.1.2	Firms offering formal training, %	⊙	34.7	47
5.1.3	GERD performed by business, % GDP	⊙	0.0	87
5.1.4	GERD financed by business, %	⊙	3.4	85
5.1.5	Females employed w/advanced degrees, %	⊙	3.3	101 ◆
5.2	**Innovation linkages**		**17.0**	**90**
5.2.1	University–industry R&D collaboration†	⊙	39.6	74
5.2.2	State of cluster development†	⊙	30.9	92
5.2.3	GERD financed by abroad, % GDP	⊙	0.1	43
5.2.4	Joint venture/strategic alliance deals/bn PPP$ GDP	⊙	0.0	113 ◇
5.2.5	Patent families/bn PPP$ GDP		0.0	95 ○◇
5.3	**Knowledge absorption**		**22.5**	**117**
5.3.1	Intellectual property payments, % total trade		0.1	100
5.3.2	High-tech imports, % total trade	⊙	6.6	95
5.3.3	ICT services imports, % total trade		1.2	73
5.3.4	FDI net inflows, % GDP		2.9	50 ●
5.3.5	Research talent, % in businesses	⊙	4.0	72
	Knowledge and technology outputs		**12.8**	**105**
6.1	**Knowledge creation**		**8.8**	**87**
6.1.1	Patents by origin/bn PPP$ GDP	⊙	0.1	106
6.1.2	PCT patents by origin/bn PPP$ GDP		0.0	93 ◆
6.1.3	Utility models by origin/bn PPP$ GDP	⊙	0.2	44 ●
6.1.4	Scientific and technical articles/bn PPP$ GDP		13.6	56 ●◆
6.1.5	Citable documents H-index		10.3	76 ◆
6.2	**Knowledge impact**		**17.0**	**117**
6.2.1	Labor productivity growth, %		0.6	77
6.2.2	Unicorn valuation, % GDP		0.0	48 ○◇
6.2.3	Software spending, % GDP		0.0	126 ○
6.2.4	High-tech manufacturing, %		n/a	n/a
6.3	**Knowledge diffusion**		**12.6**	**96 ◆**
6.3.1	Intellectual property receipts, % total trade		0.1	52 ●◆
6.3.2	Production and export complexity		42.7	86 ◆
6.3.3	High-tech exports, % total trade	⊙	0.2	113
6.3.4	ICT services exports, % total trade		1.3	77
6.3.5	ISO 9001 quality/bn PPP$ GDP		1.4	96 ◆
	Creative outputs		**5.8**	**122**
7.1	**Intangible assets**		**6.4**	**116**
7.1.1	Intangible asset intensity, top 15, %		n/a	n/a
7.1.2	Trademarks by origin/bn PPP$ GDP	⊙	14.7	100
7.1.3	Global brand value, top 5,000, % GDP		0.0	74 ○◇
7.1.4	Industrial designs by origin/bn PPP$ GDP	⊙	0.4	86
7.2	**Creative goods and services**		**0.6**	**[120]**
7.2.1	Cultural and creative services exports, % total trade		0.0	94
7.2.2	National feature films/mn pop. 15–69		n/a	n/a
7.2.3	Entertainment and media market/th pop. 15–69		n/a	n/a
7.2.4	Creative goods exports, % total trade	⊙	0.1	105
7.3	**Online creativity**		**10.1**	**114**
7.3.1	Generic top-level domains (TLDs)/th pop. 15–69		0.2	117
7.3.2	Country-code TLDs/th pop. 15–69		0.1	122
7.3.3	GitHub commits/mn pop. 15–69		1.3	110
7.3.4	Mobile app creation/bn PPP$ GDP		38.8	114

NOTES: ● indicates a strength; ○ a weakness; ◆ an income group strength; ◇ an income group weakness; * an index; † a survey question. ⊙ is used when the available economy data are older than the base year; see appendices for details, including the year of the data, at wipo.int/gii-ranking. Square brackets [ ] indicate that the data minimum coverage (DMC) requirements were not met at the sub-pillar or pillar level.

GII 2023 rank

Ukraine

55

Output rank	Input rank	Income	Region	Population (mn)	GDP, PPP$ (bn)	GDP per capita, PPP$
42	78	Lower middle	EUR	39.7	NA	NA

			Score/ Value	Rank	
	Institutions		**38.4**	**100**	
1.1	**Institutional environment**		**17.2**	**126**	○◇
1.1.1	Operational stability for businesses*		9.0	130	○◇
1.1.2	Government effectiveness*		25.5	95	
1.2	**Regulatory environment**		**58.9**	**77**	
1.2.1	Regulatory quality*		34.9	87	
1.2.2	Rule of law*		20.4	107	
1.2.3	Cost of redundancy dismissal		13.0	41	
1.3	**Business environment**		**39.2**	**[88]**	
1.3.1	Policies for doing business†		39.2	85	
1.3.2	Entrepreneurship policies and culture†		n/a	n/a	
	Human capital and research		**35.6**	**47**	◆
2.1	**Education**		**60.9**	**31**	◆
2.1.1	Expenditure on education, % GDP		5.6	24	
2.1.2	Government funding/pupil, secondary, % GDP/cap		28.5	10	●◆
2.1.3	School life expectancy, years	⊙	14.9	56	
2.1.4	PISA scales in reading, maths and science		462.7	40	◆
2.1.5	Pupil–teacher ratio, secondary		8.3	14	●◆
2.2	**Tertiary education**		**38.2**	**37**	◆
2.2.1	Tertiary enrolment, % gross	⊙	82.7	21	
2.2.2	Graduates in science and engineering, %		25.7	43	
2.2.3	Tertiary inbound mobility, %		4.9	50	
2.3	**Research and development (R&D)**		**7.8**	**68**	
2.3.1	Researchers, FTE/mn pop.		587.5	66	
2.3.2	Gross expenditure on R&D, % GDP		0.3	76	
2.3.3	Global corporate R&D investors, top 3, mn USD		0.0	40	○◇
2.3.4	QS university ranking, top 3*		20.1	53	◆
	Infrastructure		**36.9**	**77**	◆
3.1	**Information and communication technologies (ICTs)**		**72.6**	**59**	◆
3.1.1	ICT access*		82.2	68	◆
3.1.2	ICT use*		69.6	73	◆
3.1.3	Government's online service*		79.5	34	◆
3.1.4	E-participation*		59.3	57	◆
3.2	**General infrastructure**		**16.3**	**105**	
3.2.1	Electricity output, GWh/mn pop.		3,604.0	60	◆
3.2.2	Logistics performance*		27.3	76	
3.2.3	Gross capital formation, % GDP	⊙	13.8	124	○◇
3.3	**Ecological sustainability**		**21.9**	**74**	◆
3.3.1	GDP/unit of energy use		5.4	115	○◇
3.3.2	Environmental performance*		52.0	43	◆
3.3.3	ISO 14001 environment/bn PPP$ GDP		0.6	79	
	Market sophistication		**23.2**	**104**	
4.1	**Credit**		**4.9**	**124**	○◇
4.1.1	Finance for startups and scaleups†		n/a	n/a	
4.1.2	Domestic credit to private sector, % GDP		28.2	101	
4.1.3	Loans from microfinance institutions, % GDP		0.1	52	○
4.2	**Investment**		**1.2**	**107**	○
4.2.1	Market capitalization, % GDP	⊙	4.3	75	○
4.2.2	Venture capital (VC) investors, deals/bn PPP$ GDP	⊙	0.0	67	
4.2.3	VC recipients, deals/bn PPP$ GDP	⊙	0.0	97	○◇
4.2.4	VC received, value, % GDP	⊙	0.0	90	○
4.3	**Trade, diversification and market scale**		**63.5**	**40**	◆
4.3.1	Applied tariff rate, weighted avg., %		1.7	52	◆
4.3.2	Domestic industry diversification		88.7	54	
4.3.3	Domestic market scale, bn PPP$	⊙	588.4	43	

			Score/ Value	Rank	
	Business sophistication		**32.4**	**48**	◆
5.1	**Knowledge workers**		**44.6**	**42**	◆
5.1.1	Knowledge-intensive employment, %	⊙	37.9	36	◆
5.1.2	Firms offering formal training, %		24.3	67	
5.1.3	GERD performed by business, % GDP	⊙	0.3	49	◆
5.1.4	GERD financed by business, %	⊙	30.5	58	
5.1.5	Females employed w/advanced degrees, %	⊙	30.0	2	●◆
5.2	**Innovation linkages**		**19.4**	**77**	
5.2.1	University–industry R&D collaboration†		44.7	63	
5.2.2	State of cluster development†		30.0	94	
5.2.3	GERD financed by abroad, % GDP	⊙	0.1	36	◆
5.2.4	Joint venture/strategic alliance deals/bn PPP$ GDP	⊙	0.0	109	
5.2.5	Patent families/bn PPP$ GDP		0.2	47	◆
5.3	**Knowledge absorption**		**33.2**	**66**	
5.3.1	Intellectual property payments, % total trade		0.9	45	◆
5.3.2	High-tech imports, % total trade		9.2	48	
5.3.3	ICT services imports, % total trade		1.1	77	
5.3.4	FDI net inflows, % GDP		2.6	57	
5.3.5	Research talent, % in businesses	⊙	27.3	46	
	Knowledge and technology outputs		**30.0**	**45**	◆
6.1	**Knowledge creation**		**32.9**	**28**	◆
6.1.1	Patents by origin/bn PPP$ GDP		2.2	33	◆
6.1.2	PCT patents by origin/bn PPP$ GDP	⊙	0.2	44	◆
6.1.3	Utility models by origin/bn PPP$ GDP		7.4	1	●◆
6.1.4	Scientific and technical articles/bn PPP$ GDP	⊙	8.2	85	
6.1.5	Citable documents H-index		17.0	51	
6.2	**Knowledge impact**		**25.3**	**71**	
6.2.1	Labor productivity growth, %		−3.4	129	○◇
6.2.2	Unicorn valuation, % GDP		0.0	48	○◇
6.2.3	Software spending, % GDP		0.7	4	●◆
6.2.4	High-tech manufacturing, %		18.8	65	
6.3	**Knowledge diffusion**		**31.8**	**48**	◆
6.3.1	Intellectual property receipts, % total trade		0.1	57	
6.3.2	Production and export complexity		58.5	49	◆
6.3.3	High-tech exports, % total trade		1.6	66	
6.3.4	ICT services exports, % total trade		8.6	6	●◆
6.3.5	ISO 9001 quality/bn PPP$ GDP		2.5	79	
	Creative outputs		**34.6**	**37**	◆
7.1	**Intangible assets**		**52.4**	**[19]**	
7.1.1	Intangible asset intensity, top 15, %		n/a	n/a	
7.1.2	Trademarks by origin/bn PPP$ GDP		75.1	22	●◆
7.1.3	Global brand value, top 5,000, % GDP		n/a	n/a	
7.1.4	Industrial designs by origin/bn PPP$ GDP		6.0	16	●◆
7.2	**Creative goods and services**		**6.0**	**82**	
7.2.1	Cultural and creative services exports, % total trade		0.6	49	
7.2.2	National feature films/mn pop. 15–69		0.8	66	
7.2.3	Entertainment and media market/th pop. 15–69		n/a	n/a	
7.2.4	Creative goods exports, % total trade		0.2	86	
7.3	**Online creativity**		**27.6**	**44**	◆
7.3.1	Generic top-level domains (TLDs)/th pop. 15–69		5.7	55	◆
7.3.2	Country-code TLDs/th pop. 15–69		6.1	53	◆
7.3.3	GitHub commits/mn pop. 15–69		20.8	43	◆
7.3.4	Mobile app creation/bn PPP$ GDP	⊙	78.0	12	●◆

NOTES: ● indicates a strength; ○ a weakness; ◆ an income group strength; ◇ an income group weakness; * an index; † a survey question. ⊙ is used when the available economy data are older than the base year; see appendices for details, including the year of the data, at wipo.int/gii-ranking. Square brackets [ ] indicate that the data minimum coverage (DMC) requirements were not met at the sub-pillar or pillar level.

GII 2023 rank

United Arab Emirates **32**

Output rank	Input rank	Income	Region	Population (mn)	GDP, PPP$ (bn)	GDP per capita, PPP$
54	19	High	NAWA	9.4	814.7	77,272

		Score/ Value	Rank	
	Institutions	**80.8**	**10**	
1.1	**Institutional environment**	**67.5**	**30**	
1.1.1	Operational stability for businesses*	59.7	47	
1.1.2	Government effectiveness*	75.4	18	
1.2	**Regulatory environment**	**83.1**	**21**	
1.2.1	Regulatory quality*	68.4	30	
1.2.2	Rule of law*	64.0	36	
1.2.3	Cost of redundancy dismissal	8.0	1	●◆
1.3	**Business environment**	**91.7**	**2**	●◆
1.3.1	Policies for doing business†	83.3	5	●◆
1.3.2	Entrepreneurship policies and culture†	100.0	1	●◆
	Human capital and research	**54.3**	**16**	
2.1	**Education**	**54.5**	**56**	
2.1.1	Expenditure on education, % GDP	3.9	77	○
2.1.2	Government funding/pupil, secondary, % GDP/cap	25.6	17	
2.1.3	School life expectancy, years	16.0	38	
2.1.4	PISA scales in reading, maths and science	433.5	47	◇
2.1.5	Pupil–teacher ratio, secondary	8.5	16	
2.2	**Tertiary education**	**71.2**	**1**	●◆
2.2.1	Tertiary enrolment, % gross	55.3	61	
2.2.2	Graduates in science and engineering, %	36.2	7	●◆
2.2.3	Tertiary inbound mobility, %	70.3	1	●◆
2.3	**Research and development (R&D)**	**37.3**	**29**	
2.3.1	Researchers, FTE/mn pop.	2,488.8	34	
2.3.2	Gross expenditure on R&D, % GDP	1.5	26	
2.3.3	Global corporate R&D investors, top 3, mn USD	59.4	24	
2.3.4	QS university ranking, top 3*	37.5	34	
	Infrastructure	**59.8**	**15**	
3.1	**Information and communication technologies (ICTs)**	**89.0**	**14**	
3.1.1	ICT access*	97.9	4	●◆
3.1.2	ICT use*	91.1	20	
3.1.3	Government's online service*	89.1	12	
3.1.4	E-participation*	77.9	18	
3.2	**General infrastructure**	**58.4**	**8**	●◆
3.2.1	Electricity output, GWh/mn pop.	⏲ 13,883.7	8	●◆
3.2.2	Logistics performance*	86.4	7	◆
3.2.3	Gross capital formation, % GDP	22.9	73	
3.3	**Ecological sustainability**	**32.0**	**47**	
3.3.1	GDP/unit of energy use	7.6	92	○
3.3.2	Environmental performance*	56.8	34	
3.3.3	ISO 14001 environment/bn PPP$ GDP	3.0	31	
	Market sophistication	**50.3**	**25**	
4.1	**Credit**	**54.4**	**24**	
4.1.1	Finance for startups and scaleups†	75.1	13	
4.1.2	Domestic credit to private sector, % GDP	90.8	35	
4.1.3	Loans from microfinance institutions, % GDP	n/a	n/a	
4.2	**Investment**	**32.1**	**23**	
4.2.1	Market capitalization, % GDP	65.9	27	
4.2.2	Venture capital (VC) investors, deals/bn PPP$ GDP	0.3	18	
4.2.3	VC recipients, deals/bn PPP$ GDP	0.1	30	
4.2.4	VC received, value, % GDP	0.0	12	
4.3	**Trade, diversification and market scale**	**64.4**	**33**	
4.3.1	Applied tariff rate, weighted avg., %	3.3	75	
4.3.2	Domestic industry diversification	96.8	20	
4.3.3	Domestic market scale, bn PPP$	814.7	33	

		Score/ Value	Rank	
	Business sophistication	**51.6**	**23**	
5.1	**Knowledge workers**	**49.9**	**29**	
5.1.1	Knowledge-intensive employment, %	⏲ 35.1	42	
5.1.2	Firms offering formal training, %	n/a	n/a	
5.1.3	GERD performed by business, % GDP	⏲ 0.8	33	
5.1.4	GERD financed by business, %	⏲ 74.3	5	
5.1.5	Females employed w/advanced degrees, %	⏲ 12.2	63	◇
5.2	**Innovation linkages**	**56.3**	**15**	
5.2.1	University–industry R&D collaboration†	73.1	20	
5.2.2	State of cluster development†	86.7	4	●◆
5.2.3	GERD financed by abroad, % GDP	n/a	n/a	
5.2.4	Joint venture/strategic alliance deals/bn PPP$ GDP	0.2	8	●◆
5.2.5	Patent families/bn PPP$ GDP	0.1	55	
5.3	**Knowledge absorption**	**48.6**	**25**	
5.3.1	Intellectual property payments, % total trade	0.7	58	
5.3.2	High-tech imports, % total trade	14.3	17	
5.3.3	ICT services imports, % total trade	1.1	78	
5.3.4	FDI net inflows, % GDP	5.0	20	
5.3.5	Research talent, % in businesses	⏲ 77.9	3	●◆
	Knowledge and technology outputs	**23.9**	**59**	◇
6.1	**Knowledge creation**	**7.4**	**96**	○◇
6.1.1	Patents by origin/bn PPP$ GDP	0.1	112	○◇
6.1.2	PCT patents by origin/bn PPP$ GDP	0.1	54	
6.1.3	Utility models by origin/bn PPP$ GDP	⏲ 0.0	72	○◇
6.1.4	Scientific and technical articles/bn PPP$ GDP	9.0	80	○◇
6.1.5	Citable documents H-index	14.7	58	
6.2	**Knowledge impact**	**32.4**	**48**	
6.2.1	Labor productivity growth, %	1.0	64	
6.2.2	Unicorn valuation, % GDP	1.0	34	
6.2.3	Software spending, % GDP	0.2	60	
6.2.4	High-tech manufacturing, %	29.3	42	
6.3	**Knowledge diffusion**	**31.9**	**47**	
6.3.1	Intellectual property receipts, % total trade	1.0	22	
6.3.2	Production and export complexity	37.1	98	○◇
6.3.3	High-tech exports, % total trade	10.6	16	
6.3.4	ICT services exports, % total trade	2.0	59	
6.3.5	ISO 9001 quality/bn PPP$ GDP	6.2	46	
	Creative outputs	**30.3**	**50**	
7.1	**Intangible assets**	**34.6**	**55**	
7.1.1	Intangible asset intensity, top 15, %	60.3	37	
7.1.2	Trademarks by origin/bn PPP$ GDP	11.4	109	○◇
7.1.3	Global brand value, top 5,000, % GDP	12.1	12	
7.1.4	Industrial designs by origin/bn PPP$ GDP	0.1	110	○◇
7.2	**Creative goods and services**	**24.9**	**41**	
7.2.1	Cultural and creative services exports, % total trade	0.1	78	○
7.2.2	National feature films/mn pop. 15–69	1.4	54	○◇
7.2.3	Entertainment and media market/th pop. 15–69	22.3	27	
7.2.4	Creative goods exports, % total trade	5.6	11	◆
7.3	**Online creativity**	**27.1**	**47**	
7.3.1	Generic top-level domains (TLDs)/th pop. 15–69	13.1	36	
7.3.2	Country-code TLDs/th pop. 15–69	8.2	43	
7.3.3	GitHub commits/mn pop. 15–69	12.0	52	◇
7.3.4	Mobile app creation/bn PPP$ GDP	75.0	24	

NOTES: ● indicates a strength; ○ a weakness; ◆ an income group strength; ◇ an income group weakness; * an index; † a survey question. ⏲ is used when the available economy data are older than the base year; see appendices for details, including the year of the data, at wipo.int/gii-ranking. Square brackets [ ] indicate that the data minimum coverage (DMC) requirements were not met at the sub-pillar or pillar level.

GII 2023 rank

United Kingdom 4

Output rank	Input rank	Income	Region	Population (mn)	GDP, PPP$ (bn)	GDP per capita, PPP$
2	6	High	EUR	67.5	3,776.0	55,862

		Score/Value	Rank
	Institutions	**70.9**	**24**
1.1	**Institutional environment**	**66.9**	**32** ◇
1.1.1	Operational stability for businesses*	61.8	41 ◇
1.1.2	Government effectiveness*	72.1	24
1.2	**Regulatory environment**	**89.1**	**12**
1.2.1	Regulatory quality*	80.1	17
1.2.2	Rule of law*	81.5	19
1.2.3	Cost of redundancy dismissal	9.3	25
1.3	**Business environment**	**56.5**	**43**
1.3.1	Policies for doing business†	65.8	32
1.3.2	Entrepreneurship policies and culture†	47.3	38 ○◇

		Score/Value	Rank
	Human capital and research	**58.9**	**8**
2.1	**Education**	**59.6**	**38**
2.1.1	Expenditure on education, % GDP ⊙	5.2	27
2.1.2	Government funding/pupil, secondary, % GDP/cap	22.3	38 ○
2.1.3	School life expectancy, years	17.3	16
2.1.4	PISA scales in reading, maths and science	503.5	12
2.1.5	Pupil–teacher ratio, secondary	17.3	87 ○◇
2.2	**Tertiary education**	**46.0**	**18**
2.2.1	Tertiary enrolment, % gross	69.5	38
2.2.2	Graduates in science and engineering, %	22.8	57 ○
2.2.3	Tertiary inbound mobility, %	20.1	7
2.3	**Research and development (R&D)**	**71.3**	**6** ●
2.3.1	Researchers, FTE/mn pop. ⊙	4,683.8	20
2.3.2	Gross expenditure on R&D, % GDP ⊙	2.9	11
2.3.3	Global corporate R&D investors, top 3, mn USD	84.6	7 ●
2.3.4	QS university ranking, top 3*	99.4	2 ●◆

		Score/Value	Rank
	Infrastructure	**63.7**	**6** ●
3.1	**Information and communication technologies (ICTs)**	**94.2**	**6** ●◆
3.1.1	ICT access*	94.4	10
3.1.2	ICT use*	99.5	3 ●◆
3.1.3	Government's online service*	87.4	17
3.1.4	E-participation*	95.3	6
3.2	**General infrastructure**	**35.0**	**42** ◇
3.2.1	Electricity output, GWh/mn pop.	4,560.7	50 ○◇
3.2.2	Logistics performance*	72.7	18
3.2.3	Gross capital formation, % GDP	17.4	114 ○◇
3.3	**Ecological sustainability**	**61.9**	**2** ●◆
3.3.1	GDP/unit of energy use	17.9	12
3.3.2	Environmental performance*	99.7	2 ●◆
3.3.3	ISO 14001 environment/bn PPP$ GDP	5.1	20

		Score/Value	Rank
	Market sophistication	**69.3**	**3** ●◆
4.1	**Credit**	**60.2**	**18**
4.1.1	Finance for startups and scaleups†	64.8	27
4.1.2	Domestic credit to private sector, % GDP	146.6	11
4.1.3	Loans from microfinance institutions, % GDP	n/a	n/a
4.2	**Investment**	**57.4**	**11**
4.2.1	Market capitalization, % GDP ⊙	126.6	9
4.2.2	Venture capital (VC) investors, deals/bn PPP$ GDP	0.6	11
4.2.3	VC recipients, deals/bn PPP$ GDP	0.3	7
4.2.4	VC received, value, % GDP	0.0	8
4.3	**Trade, diversification and market scale**	**90.1**	**6** ●◆
4.3.1	Applied tariff rate, weighted avg., %	1.3	16
4.3.2	Domestic industry diversification	97.5	14
4.3.3	Domestic market scale, bn PPP$	3,776.0	9 ◆

		Score/Value	Rank
	Business sophistication	**58.4**	**13**
5.1	**Knowledge workers**	**67.1**	**10**
5.1.1	Knowledge-intensive employment, % ⊙	50.6	11
5.1.2	Firms offering formal training, %	n/a	n/a
5.1.3	GERD performed by business, % GDP	2.1	10
5.1.4	GERD financed by business, %	57.5	17
5.1.5	Females employed w/advanced degrees, % ⊙	24.1	22
5.2	**Innovation linkages**	**62.4**	**11**
5.2.1	University–industry R&D collaboration†	82.0	12
5.2.2	State of cluster development†	77.7	14
5.2.3	GERD financed by abroad, % GDP	0.3	9
5.2.4	Joint venture/strategic alliance deals/bn PPP$ GDP	0.2	10
5.2.5	Patent families/bn PPP$ GDP	1.9	20
5.3	**Knowledge absorption**	**45.7**	**30**
5.3.1	Intellectual property payments, % total trade	2.0	13
5.3.2	High-tech imports, % total trade	10.0	36
5.3.3	ICT services imports, % total trade	1.8	40
5.3.4	FDI net inflows, % GDP	1.9	76 ○
5.3.5	Research talent, % in businesses ⊙	41.8	34 ○◇

		Score/Value	Rank
	Knowledge and technology outputs	**61.4**	**7** ●◆
6.1	**Knowledge creation**	**60.6**	**9**
6.1.1	Patents by origin/bn PPP$ GDP	5.1	16
6.1.2	PCT patents by origin/bn PPP$ GDP	1.5	20
6.1.3	Utility models by origin/bn PPP$ GDP	n/a	n/a
6.1.4	Scientific and technical articles/bn PPP$ GDP	32.0	16
6.1.5	Citable documents H-index	100.0	1 ●◆
6.2	**Knowledge impact**	**65.4**	**4** ●◆
6.2.1	Labor productivity growth, %	0.3	86 ○
6.2.2	Unicorn valuation, % GDP	5.2	7 ●◆
6.2.3	Software spending, % GDP	0.7	2 ●◆
6.2.4	High-tech manufacturing, %	42.9	22
6.3	**Knowledge diffusion**	**58.0**	**9**
6.3.1	Intellectual property receipts, % total trade	2.9	9
6.3.2	Production and export complexity	84.8	10
6.3.3	High-tech exports, % total trade	8.1	22
6.3.4	ICT services exports, % total trade	4.8	20
6.3.5	ISO 9001 quality/bn PPP$ GDP	11.7	23

		Score/Value	Rank
	Creative outputs	**60.0**	**2** ●◆
7.1	**Intangible assets**	**63.4**	**8**
7.1.1	Intangible asset intensity, top 15, %	85.2	4 ●◆
7.1.2	Trademarks by origin/bn PPP$ GDP	65.7	30
7.1.3	Global brand value, top 5,000, % GDP	14.1	10
7.1.4	Industrial designs by origin/bn PPP$ GDP	8.3	13
7.2	**Creative goods and services**	**45.0**	**9**
7.2.1	Cultural and creative services exports, % total trade	3.1	6 ●
7.2.2	National feature films/mn pop. 15–69	3.4	36 ○
7.2.3	Entertainment and media market/th pop. 15–69	70.9	6
7.2.4	Creative goods exports, % total trade	2.1	25
7.3	**Online creativity**	**68.1**	**9**
7.3.1	Generic top-level domains (TLDs)/th pop. 15–69	70.5	9
7.3.2	Country-code TLDs/th pop. 15–69	70.9	7 ●
7.3.3	GitHub commits/mn pop. 15–69	55.3	17
7.3.4	Mobile app creation/bn PPP$ GDP	75.5	22

NOTES: ● indicates a strength; ○ a weakness; ◆ an income group strength; ◇ an income group weakness; * an index; † a survey question. ⊙ is used when the available economy data are older than the base year; see appendices for details, including the year of the data, at wipo.int/gii-ranking. Square brackets [ ] indicate that the data minimum coverage (DMC) requirements were not met at the sub-pillar or pillar level.

GII 2023 rank

United Republic of Tanzania 113

Output rank	Input rank	Income	Region	Population (mn)	GDP, PPP$ (bn)	GDP per capita, PPP$
123	105	Lower middle	SSA	65.5	207.6	3,374

			Score/ Value	Rank	
Institutions			**47.8**	**73**	●
1.1	**Institutional environment**		**28.4**	**103**	
1.1.1	Operational stability for businesses*		37.5	101	
1.1.2	Government effectiveness*		19.3	109	
1.2	**Regulatory environment**		**61.2**	**69**	●◆
1.2.1	Regulatory quality*		25.8	108	
1.2.2	Rule of law*		24.4	95	
1.2.3	Cost of redundancy dismissal		9.3	25	●◆
1.3	**Business environment**		**53.7**	**[50]**	
1.3.1	Policies for doing business†		53.7	54	●
1.3.2	Entrepreneurship policies and culture†		n/a	n/a	
Human capital and research			**11.0**	**126**	◇
2.1	**Education**		**28.7**	**123**	
2.1.1	Expenditure on education, % GDP		3.4	95	
2.1.2	Government funding/pupil, secondary, % GDP/cap	⏲	15.2	74	
2.1.3	School life expectancy, years		8.7	109	◇
2.1.4	PISA scales in reading, maths and science		n/a	n/a	
2.1.5	Pupil–teacher ratio, secondary		23.3	107	
2.2	**Tertiary education**		**2.0**	**125**	◇
2.2.1	Tertiary enrolment, % gross		7.8	118	◇
2.2.2	Graduates in science and engineering, %	⏲	9.5	111	○◇
2.2.3	Tertiary inbound mobility, %		n/a	n/a	
2.3	**Research and development (R&D)**		**2.3**	**89**	
2.3.1	Researchers, FTE/mn pop.	⏲	19.2	104	
2.3.2	Gross expenditure on R&D, % GDP	⏲	0.5	60	
2.3.3	Global corporate R&D investors, top 3, mn USD		0.0	40	○◇
2.3.4	QS university ranking, top 3*		0.0	71	○◇
Infrastructure			**21.4**	**115**	
3.1	**Information and communication technologies (ICTs)**		**29.2**	**121**	◇
3.1.1	ICT access*		22.2	125	◇
3.1.2	ICT use*		27.6	119	◇
3.1.3	Government's online service*		41.4	107	
3.1.4	E-participation*		25.6	111	
3.2	**General infrastructure**		**21.3**	**85**	
3.2.1	Electricity output, GWh/mn pop.	⏲	133.1	120	
3.2.2	Logistics performance*		n/a	n/a	
3.2.3	Gross capital formation, % GDP		37.6	10	●◆
3.3	**Ecological sustainability**		**13.6**	**109**	
3.3.1	GDP/unit of energy use		6.7	101	
3.3.2	Environmental performance*		25.9	96	
3.3.3	ISO 14001 environment/bn PPP$ GDP		0.3	105	
Market sophistication			**30.3**	**83**	
4.1	**Credit**		**51.5**	**26**	●◆
4.1.1	Finance for startups and scaleups†		n/a	n/a	
4.1.2	Domestic credit to private sector, % GDP		13.2	123	
4.1.3	Loans from microfinance institutions, % GDP	⏲	14.5	1	
4.2	**Investment**		**3.8**	**87**	
4.2.1	Market capitalization, % GDP		10.4	71	
4.2.2	Venture capital (VC) investors, deals/bn PPP$ GDP		0.0	91	◇
4.2.3	VC recipients, deals/bn PPP$ GDP		0.0	69	
4.2.4	VC received, value, % GDP		0.0	67	
4.3	**Trade, diversification and market scale**		**35.6**	**112**	
4.3.1	Applied tariff rate, weighted avg., %		8.9	111	
4.3.2	Domestic industry diversification	⏲	60.2	101	
4.3.3	Domestic market scale, bn PPP$		207.6	68	●

			Score/ Value	Rank	
Business sophistication			**20.5**	**105**	
5.1	**Knowledge workers**		**11.9**	**[116]**	
5.1.1	Knowledge-intensive employment, %	⏲	3.2	125	○◇
5.1.2	Firms offering formal training, %	⏲	30.7	55	
5.1.3	GERD performed by business, % GDP		n/a	n/a	
5.1.4	GERD financed by business, %		n/a	n/a	
5.1.5	Females employed w/advanced degrees, %	⏲	0.2	127	○◇
5.2	**Innovation linkages**		**28.6**	**44**	●◆
5.2.1	University–industry R&D collaboration†		58.6	37	●◆
5.2.2	State of cluster development†		52.4	44	●
5.2.3	GERD financed by abroad, % GDP		n/a	n/a	
5.2.4	Joint venture/strategic alliance deals/bn PPP$ GDP		0.0	95	
5.2.5	Patent families/bn PPP$ GDP		0.0	95	○◇
5.3	**Knowledge absorption**		**21.1**	**126**	
5.3.1	Intellectual property payments, % total trade		0.0	107	
5.3.2	High-tech imports, % total trade		6.8	92	
5.3.3	ICT services imports, % total trade		0.2	126	◇
5.3.4	FDI net inflows, % GDP		1.5	90	
5.3.5	Research talent, % in businesses		n/a	n/a	
Knowledge and technology outputs			**10.9**	**119**	
6.1	**Knowledge creation**		**4.9**	**115**	
6.1.1	Patents by origin/bn PPP$ GDP	⏲	0.0	131	
6.1.2	PCT patents by origin/bn PPP$ GDP		0.0	101	○◇
6.1.3	Utility models by origin/bn PPP$ GDP	⏲	0.0	73	
6.1.4	Scientific and technical articles/bn PPP$ GDP		7.7	89	
6.1.5	Citable documents H-index		9.9	79	
6.2	**Knowledge impact**		**19.7**	**106**	
6.2.1	Labor productivity growth, %		2.9	17	●
6.2.2	Unicorn valuation, % GDP		0.0	48	○◇
6.2.3	Software spending, % GDP		0.0	129	○◇
6.2.4	High-tech manufacturing, %	⏲	6.9	98	
6.3	**Knowledge diffusion**		**8.2**	**117**	
6.3.1	Intellectual property receipts, % total trade		0.0	110	
6.3.2	Production and export complexity		32.5	107	
6.3.3	High-tech exports, % total trade		0.2	105	
6.3.4	ICT services exports, % total trade		0.2	117	
6.3.5	ISO 9001 quality/bn PPP$ GDP		0.6	116	
Creative outputs			**6.3**	**[120]**	
7.1	**Intangible assets**		**6.8**	**[115]**	
7.1.1	Intangible asset intensity, top 15, %		n/a	n/a	
7.1.2	Trademarks by origin/bn PPP$ GDP	⏲	11.5	108	
7.1.3	Global brand value, top 5,000, % GDP		n/a	n/a	
7.1.4	Industrial designs by origin/bn PPP$ GDP		n/a	n/a	
7.2	**Creative goods and services**		**0.6**	**[118]**	
7.2.1	Cultural and creative services exports, % total trade		n/a	n/a	
7.2.2	National feature films/mn pop. 15–69		n/a	n/a	
7.2.3	Entertainment and media market/th pop. 15–69		n/a	n/a	
7.2.4	Creative goods exports, % total trade		0.1	107	
7.3	**Online creativity**		**11.1**	**112**	
7.3.1	Generic top-level domains (TLDs)/th pop. 15–69		0.2	120	
7.3.2	Country-code TLDs/th pop. 15–69		0.2	114	
7.3.3	GitHub commits/mn pop. 15–69		0.3	124	
7.3.4	Mobile app creation/bn PPP$ GDP		43.7	110	

NOTES: ● indicates a strength; ○ a weakness; ◆ an income group strength; ◇ an income group weakness; * an index; † a survey question. ⏲ is used when the available economy data are older than the base year; see appendices for details, including the year of the data, at wipo.int/gii-ranking. Square brackets [ ] indicate that the data minimum coverage (DMC) requirements were not met at the sub-pillar or pillar level.

GII 2023 rank

United States of America 3

Output rank	Input rank	Income	Region	Population (mn)	GDP, PPP$ (bn)	GDP per capita, PPP$
4	2	High	NAC	338.3	25,035.2	75,180

		Score/ Value	Rank
Institutions		**77.4**	**16**
1.1	**Institutional environment**	**69.1**	**27**
1.1.1	Operational stability for businesses*	64.6	37
1.1.2	Government effectiveness*	73.6	21
1.2	**Regulatory environment**	**90.2**	**11**
1.2.1	Regulatory quality*	79.8	18
1.2.2	Rule of law*	81.2	20
1.2.3	Cost of redundancy dismissal	8.0	1 ●
1.3	**Business environment**	**72.7**	**21**
1.3.1	Policies for doing business†	81.4	7
1.3.2	Entrepreneurship policies and culture†	64.0	18

		Score/ Value	Rank
Human capital and research		**56.5**	**12**
2.1	**Education**	**58.3**	**45**
2.1.1	Expenditure on education, % GDP	⊙ 5.0	41
2.1.2	Government funding/pupil, secondary, % GDP/cap	22.6	36
2.1.3	School life expectancy, years	16.3	31
2.1.4	PISA scales in reading, maths and science	495.3	24
2.1.5	Pupil–teacher ratio, secondary	14.5	73 ○◇
2.2	**Tertiary education**	**34.1**	**53**
2.2.1	Tertiary enrolment, % gross	87.6	14
2.2.2	Graduates in science and engineering, %	20.1	70 ○
2.2.3	Tertiary inbound mobility, %	5.1	47
2.3	**Research and development (R&D)**	**77.2**	**2 ●◆**
2.3.1	Researchers, FTE/mn pop.	⊙ 4,500.5	24
2.3.2	Gross expenditure on R&D, % GDP	3.5	3 ●
2.3.3	Global corporate R&D investors, top 3, mn USD	100.0	1 ●◆
2.3.4	QS university ranking, top 3*	100.0	1 ●◆

		Score/ Value	Rank
Infrastructure		**56.7**	**25**
3.1	**Information and communication technologies (ICTs)**	**90.6**	**11**
3.1.1	ICT access*	84.4	56
3.1.2	ICT use*	95.0	11
3.1.3	Government's online service*	92.3	9
3.1.4	E-participation*	90.7	10
3.2	**General infrastructure**	**53.7**	**12**
3.2.1	Electricity output, GWh/mn pop.	13,154.8	9
3.2.2	Logistics performance*	77.3	16
3.2.3	Gross capital formation, % GDP	22.0	81 ○
3.3	**Ecological sustainability**	**25.8**	**62 ◇**
3.3.1	GDP/unit of energy use	9.7	73 ○
3.3.2	Environmental performance*	54.6	36
3.3.3	ISO 14001 environment/bn PPP$ GDP	0.2	116 ○◇

		Score/ Value	Rank
Market sophistication		**82.9**	**1 ●◆**
4.1	**Credit**	**83.5**	**2 ●◆**
4.1.1	Finance for startups and scaleups†	83.9	6 ◆
4.1.2	Domestic credit to private sector, % GDP	216.2	2 ●◆
4.1.3	Loans from microfinance institutions, % GDP	n/a	n/a
4.2	**Investment**	**68.8**	**4 ◆**
4.2.1	Market capitalization, % GDP	166.7	7
4.2.2	Venture capital (VC) investors, deals/bn PPP$ GDP	0.4	13
4.2.3	VC recipients, deals/bn PPP$ GDP	0.3	6 ◆
4.2.4	VC received, value, % GDP	0.0	1 ●◆
4.3	**Trade, diversification and market scale**	**96.3**	**1 ●◆**
4.3.1	Applied tariff rate, weighted avg., %	1.5	49
4.3.2	Domestic industry diversification	98.7	6
4.3.3	Domestic market scale, bn PPP$	25,035.2	1 ●◆

		Score/ Value	Rank
Business sophistication		**69.9**	**2 ●◆**
5.1	**Knowledge workers**	**76.8**	**2 ●◆**
5.1.1	Knowledge-intensive employment, %	51.5	9
5.1.2	Firms offering formal training, %	n/a	n/a
5.1.3	GERD performed by business, % GDP	2.7	3 ●
5.1.4	GERD financed by business, %	67.9	6
5.1.5	Females employed w/advanced degrees, %	27.9	9
5.2	**Innovation linkages**	**75.8**	**4 ◆**
5.2.1	University–industry R&D collaboration†	99.9	2 ●◆
5.2.2	State of cluster development†	100.0	1 ●◆
5.2.3	GERD financed by abroad, % GDP	0.2	15
5.2.4	Joint venture/strategic alliance deals/bn PPP$ GDP	0.2	5
5.2.5	Patent families/bn PPP$ GDP	3.3	12
5.3	**Knowledge absorption**	**57.2**	**5**
5.3.1	Intellectual property payments, % total trade	1.6	20
5.3.2	High-tech imports, % total trade	18.5	9 ◆
5.3.3	ICT services imports, % total trade	1.5	60
5.3.4	FDI net inflows, % GDP	1.4	91 ○
5.3.5	Research talent, % in businesses	⊙ 80.4	2 ●◆

		Score/ Value	Rank
Knowledge and technology outputs		**63.7**	**2 ●◆**
6.1	**Knowledge creation**	**61.2**	**8**
6.1.1	Patents by origin/bn PPP$ GDP	11.4	7
6.1.2	PCT patents by origin/bn PPP$ GDP	2.4	13
6.1.3	Utility models by origin/bn PPP$ GDP	n/a	n/a
6.1.4	Scientific and technical articles/bn PPP$ GDP	14.1	52 ◇
6.1.5	Citable documents H-index	100.0	1 ●◆
6.2	**Knowledge impact**	**77.6**	**1 ●◆**
6.2.1	Labor productivity growth, %	1.4	50
6.2.2	Unicorn valuation, % GDP	7.8	1 ●◆
6.2.3	Software spending, % GDP	1.0	1 ●◆
6.2.4	High-tech manufacturing, %	42.4	24
6.3	**Knowledge diffusion**	**52.5**	**14**
6.3.1	Intellectual property receipts, % total trade	4.4	1 ●◆
6.3.2	Production and export complexity	83.4	12
6.3.3	High-tech exports, % total trade	9.2	20
6.3.4	ICT services exports, % total trade	2.0	57
6.3.5	ISO 9001 quality/bn PPP$ GDP	1.1	104 ○◇

		Score/ Value	Rank
Creative outputs		**53.0**	**12**
7.1	**Intangible assets**	**52.2**	**21**
7.1.1	Intangible asset intensity, top 15, %	93.4	1 ●◆
7.1.2	Trademarks by origin/bn PPP$ GDP	24.0	86 ○◇
7.1.3	Global brand value, top 5,000, % GDP	20.6	3 ●◆
7.1.4	Industrial designs by origin/bn PPP$ GDP	1.0	69 ○◇
7.2	**Creative goods and services**	**47.3**	**5 ◆**
7.2.1	Cultural and creative services exports, % total trade	1.6	19
7.2.2	National feature films/mn pop. 15–69	4.0	34
7.2.3	Entertainment and media market/th pop. 15–69	100.0	1 ●◆
7.2.4	Creative goods exports, % total trade	2.7	20
7.3	**Online creativity**	**60.4**	**13**
7.3.1	Generic top-level domains (TLDs)/th pop. 15–69	100.0	1 ●◆
7.3.2	Country-code TLDs/th pop. 15–69	2.3	68 ○◇
7.3.3	GitHub commits/mn pop. 15–69	63.7	11
7.3.4	Mobile app creation/bn PPP$ GDP	75.7	21

NOTES: ● indicates a strength; ○ a weakness; ◆ an income group strength; ◇ an income group weakness; * an index; † a survey question. ⊙ is used when the available economy data are older than the base year; see appendices for details, including the year of the data, at wipo.int/gii-ranking. Square brackets [ ] indicate that the data minimum coverage (DMC) requirements were not met at the sub-pillar or pillar level.

GII 2023 rank

Uruguay

63

Output rank	Input rank	Income	Region	Population (mn)	GDP, PPP$ (bn)	GDP per capita, PPP$
73	**56**	**High**	**LCN**	**3.4**	**96.8**	**27,233**

			Score/ Value	Rank	
	Institutions		**67.5**	**31**	
1.1	**Institutional environment**		**68.9**	**28**	
1.1.1	Operational stability for businesses*		77.8	10	●
1.1.2	Government effectiveness*		59.9	38	
1.2	**Regulatory environment**		**67.8**	**49**	
1.2.1	Regulatory quality*		60.9	42	
1.2.2	Rule of law*		61.2	37	
1.2.3	Cost of redundancy dismissal		20.8	91	
1.3	**Business environment**		**65.9**	**27**	
1.3.1	Policies for doing business†		89.3	4	● ◆
1.3.2	Entrepreneurship policies and culture†		42.5	44	
	Human capital and research		**26.7**	**83**	◇
2.1	**Education**		**48.0**	**73**	◇
2.1.1	Expenditure on education, % GDP		4.5	55	
2.1.2	Government funding/pupil, secondary, % GDP/cap		14.5	77	◇
2.1.3	School life expectancy, years		16.8	21	●
2.1.4	PISA scales in reading, maths and science		423.5	52	◇
2.1.5	Pupil–teacher ratio, secondary		15.1	77	◇
2.2	**Tertiary education**		**22.4**	**84**	◇
2.2.1	Tertiary enrolment, % gross		67.9	46	
2.2.2	Graduates in science and engineering, %		15.2	99	○ ◇
2.2.3	Tertiary inbound mobility, %		2.1	76	◇
2.3	**Research and development (R&D)**		**9.7**	**61**	◇
2.3.1	Researchers, FTE/mn pop.		795.4	57	◇
2.3.2	Gross expenditure on R&D, % GDP	⊙	0.4	64	◇
2.3.3	Global corporate R&D investors, top 3, mn USD		0.0	40	○ ◇
2.3.4	QS university ranking, top 3*		22.8	48	
	Infrastructure		**43.9**	**57**	◇
3.1	**Information and communication technologies (ICTs)**		**74.8**	**51**	
3.1.1	ICT access*		79.3	74	◇
3.1.2	ICT use*		88.0	25	●
3.1.3	Government's online service*		73.9	52	
3.1.4	E-participation*		58.1	61	
3.2	**General infrastructure**		**24.9**	**75**	◇
3.2.1	Electricity output, GWh/mn pop.		4,545.2	51	
3.2.2	Logistics performance*		40.9	60	◇
3.2.3	Gross capital formation, % GDP		18.4	108	○ ◇
3.3	**Ecological sustainability**		**31.9**	**48**	
3.3.1	GDP/unit of energy use		14.1	31	
3.3.2	Environmental performance*		31.4	85	◇
3.3.3	ISO 14001 environment/bn PPP$ GDP		3.8	26	●
	Market sophistication		**28.1**	**86**	◇
4.1	**Credit**		**19.1**	**93**	◇
4.1.1	Finance for startups and scaleups†		29.4	71	○ ◇
4.1.2	Domestic credit to private sector, % GDP		27.9	103	◇
4.1.3	Loans from microfinance institutions, % GDP		n/a	n/a	
4.2	**Investment**		**17.9**	**40**	
4.2.1	Market capitalization, % GDP		n/a	n/a	
4.2.2	Venture capital (VC) investors, deals/bn PPP$ GDP		0.3	17	●
4.2.3	VC recipients, deals/bn PPP$ GDP		0.0	66	
4.2.4	VC received, value, % GDP		0.0	31	
4.3	**Trade, diversification and market scale**		**47.3**	**92**	◇
4.3.1	Applied tariff rate, weighted avg., %		5.3	92	◇
4.3.2	Domestic industry diversification	⊙	74.0	89	
4.3.3	Domestic market scale, bn PPP$		96.8	88	

			Score/ Value	Rank	
	Business sophistication		**29.2**	**59**	◇
5.1	**Knowledge workers**		**29.2**	**73**	◇
5.1.1	Knowledge-intensive employment, %		24.7	56	◇
5.1.2	Firms offering formal training, %	⊙	53.3	16	●
5.1.3	GERD performed by business, % GDP	⊙	0.1	59	◇
5.1.4	GERD financed by business, %		4.2	82	○ ◇
5.1.5	Females employed w/advanced degrees, %		10.4	73	◇
5.2	**Innovation linkages**		**18.8**	**83**	◇
5.2.1	University–industry R&D collaboration†		43.5	67	
5.2.2	State of cluster development†		37.8	79	◇
5.2.3	GERD financed by abroad, % GDP		0.0	57	
5.2.4	Joint venture/strategic alliance deals/bn PPP$ GDP		0.0	72	
5.2.5	Patent families/bn PPP$ GDP		0.1	52	
5.3	**Knowledge absorption**		**39.6**	**47**	
5.3.1	Intellectual property payments, % total trade		0.9	42	
5.3.2	High-tech imports, % total trade		6.6	94	
5.3.3	ICT services imports, % total trade		4.6	5	● ◆
5.3.4	FDI net inflows, % GDP		3.2	43	
5.3.5	Research talent, % in businesses		0.8	80	○ ◇
	Knowledge and technology outputs		**22.8**	**66**	◇
6.1	**Knowledge creation**		**11.8**	**74**	◇
6.1.1	Patents by origin/bn PPP$ GDP	⊙	0.3	90	◇
6.1.2	PCT patents by origin/bn PPP$ GDP		n/a	n/a	
6.1.3	Utility models by origin/bn PPP$ GDP	⊙	0.3	38	
6.1.4	Scientific and technical articles/bn PPP$ GDP		12.0	65	◇
6.1.5	Citable documents H-index		10.7	73	◇
6.2	**Knowledge impact**		**21.4**	**96**	◇
6.2.1	Labor productivity growth, %		0.5	79	
6.2.2	Unicorn valuation, % GDP		0.0	48	○ ◇
6.2.3	Software spending, % GDP		0.2	71	
6.2.4	High-tech manufacturing, %	⊙	15.0	78	
6.3	**Knowledge diffusion**		**35.2**	**39**	
6.3.1	Intellectual property receipts, % total trade		0.2	46	
6.3.2	Production and export complexity		51.1	64	◇
6.3.3	High-tech exports, % total trade		0.8	75	◇
6.3.4	ICT services exports, % total trade		7.9	7	● ◆
6.3.5	ISO 9001 quality/bn PPP$ GDP		16.6	17	●
	Creative outputs		**19.2**	**78**	◇
7.1	**Intangible assets**		**17.1**	**93**	◇
7.1.1	Intangible asset intensity, top 15, %		n/a	n/a	
7.1.2	Trademarks by origin/bn PPP$ GDP		56.3	41	
7.1.3	Global brand value, top 5,000, % GDP		0.0	74	○ ◇
7.1.4	Industrial designs by origin/bn PPP$ GDP	⊙	0.7	79	
7.2	**Creative goods and services**		**14.6**	**59**	◇
7.2.1	Cultural and creative services exports, % total trade		0.8	40	
7.2.2	National feature films/mn pop. 15–69		4.2	31	
7.2.3	Entertainment and media market/th pop. 15–69		n/a	n/a	
7.2.4	Creative goods exports, % total trade		0.0	113	○
7.3	**Online creativity**		**27.8**	**43**	
7.3.1	Generic top-level domains (TLDs)/th pop. 15–69		7.6	51	
7.3.2	Country-code TLDs/th pop. 15–69		12.3	38	
7.3.3	GitHub commits/mn pop. 15–69		20.7	44	
7.3.4	Mobile app creation/bn PPP$ GDP		70.8	49	

NOTES: ● indicates a strength; ○ a weakness; ◆ an income group strength; ◇ an income group weakness; * an index; † a survey question. ⊙ is used when the available economy data are older than the base year; see appendices for details, including the year of the data, at wipo.int/gii-ranking. Square brackets [ ] indicate that the data minimum coverage (DMC) requirements were not met at the sub-pillar or pillar level.

Uzbekistan

GII 2023 rank

82

Output rank	Input rank	Income	Region	Population (mn)	GDP, PPP$ (bn)	GDP per capita, PPP$
88	72	Lower middle	CSA	34.6	334.3	9,478

			Score/Value	Rank	
	Institutions		**54.7**	**55**	◆
1.1	**Institutional environment**		**40.0**	**76**	
1.1.1	Operational stability for businesses*		48.6	74	
1.1.2	Government effectiveness*		31.3	84	
1.2	**Regulatory environment**		**51.0**	**97**	
1.2.1	Regulatory quality*		27.0	104	
1.2.2	Rule of law*		13.8	115	
1.2.3	Cost of redundancy dismissal		17.3	73	
1.3	**Business environment**		**73.3**	**[19]**	
1.3.1	Policies for doing business†	⏲	73.3	23	●◆
1.3.2	Entrepreneurship policies and culture†		n/a	n/a	
	Human capital and research		**25.2**	**89**	
2.1	**Education**		**46.4**	**78**	
2.1.1	Expenditure on education, % GDP		4.6	52	
2.1.2	Government funding/pupil, secondary, % GDP/cap		13.9	79	
2.1.3	School life expectancy, years		12.1	93	
2.1.4	PISA scales in reading, maths and science		n/a	n/a	
2.1.5	Pupil–teacher ratio, secondary		9.8	28	●◆
2.2	**Tertiary education**		**27.4**	**74**	
2.2.1	Tertiary enrolment, % gross		21.2	99	
2.2.2	Graduates in science and engineering, %		32.8	12	●◆
2.2.3	Tertiary inbound mobility, %		0.7	97	
2.3	**Research and development (R&D)**		**1.9**	**92**	
2.3.1	Researchers, FTE/mn pop.		523.4	69	
2.3.2	Gross expenditure on R&D, % GDP		0.1	99	
2.3.3	Global corporate R&D investors, top 3, mn USD		0.0	40	○◇
2.3.4	QS university ranking, top 3*		0.0	71	○◇
	Infrastructure		**37.9**	**73**	◆
3.1	**Information and communication technologies (ICTs)**		**71.4**	**63**	◆
3.1.1	ICT access*		79.1	75	◆
3.1.2	ICT use*		74.5	63	◆
3.1.3	Government's online service*		71.7	57	◆
3.1.4	E-participation*		60.5	55	◆
3.2	**General infrastructure**		**27.3**	**62**	
3.2.1	Electricity output, GWh/mn pop.	⏲	1,942.6	83	
3.2.2	Logistics performance*		22.7	82	
3.2.3	Gross capital formation, % GDP		42.1	6	●◆
3.3	**Ecological sustainability**		**15.1**	**102**	
3.3.1	GDP/unit of energy use		5.8	110	◇
3.3.2	Environmental performance*		32.7	79	
3.3.3	ISO 14001 environment/bn PPP$ GDP		0.3	99	
	Market sophistication		**33.9**	**69**	
4.1	**Credit**		**7.0**	**121**	○
4.1.1	Finance for startups and scaleups†		n/a	n/a	
4.1.2	Domestic credit to private sector, % GDP		35.7	90	
4.1.3	Loans from microfinance institutions, % GDP		0.2	49	
4.2	**Investment**		**n/a**	**[n/a]**	
4.2.1	Market capitalization, % GDP		n/a	n/a	
4.2.2	Venture capital (VC) investors, deals/bn PPP$ GDP		n/a	n/a	
4.2.3	VC recipients, deals/bn PPP$ GDP		n/a	n/a	
4.2.4	VC received, value, % GDP		n/a	n/a	
4.3	**Trade, diversification and market scale**		**60.8**	**51**	
4.3.1	Applied tariff rate, weighted avg., %		2.6	68	◆
4.3.2	Domestic industry diversification		92.4	42	
4.3.3	Domestic market scale, bn PPP$		334.3	56	

			Score/Value	Rank	
	Business sophistication		**25.5**	**78**	
5.1	**Knowledge workers**		**23.3**	**87**	
5.1.1	Knowledge-intensive employment, %		n/a	n/a	
5.1.2	Firms offering formal training, %		16.9	88	○◇
5.1.3	GERD performed by business, % GDP	⏲	0.1	69	
5.1.4	GERD financed by business, %	⏲	42.4	40	◆
5.1.5	Females employed w/advanced degrees, %	⏲	8.1	84	
5.2	**Innovation linkages**		**26.3**	**51**	◆
5.2.1	University–industry R&D collaboration†	⏲	62.4	32	●◆
5.2.2	State of cluster development†	⏲	66.1	29	●◆
5.2.3	GERD financed by abroad, % GDP	⏲	0.0	92	○
5.2.4	Joint venture/strategic alliance deals/bn PPP$ GDP		0.0	96	
5.2.5	Patent families/bn PPP$ GDP		0.0	95	○◇
5.3	**Knowledge absorption**		**27.0**	**92**	
5.3.1	Intellectual property payments, % total trade		0.5	75	
5.3.2	High-tech imports, % total trade		10.9	27	●
5.3.3	ICT services imports, % total trade		0.6	101	
5.3.4	FDI net inflows, % GDP		3.3	41	●
5.3.5	Research talent, % in businesses	⏲	12.9	57	
	Knowledge and technology outputs		**19.3**	**78**	
6.1	**Knowledge creation**		**12.4**	**72**	
6.1.1	Patents by origin/bn PPP$ GDP		1.4	47	
6.1.2	PCT patents by origin/bn PPP$ GDP		0.0	99	
6.1.3	Utility models by origin/bn PPP$ GDP		1.3	17	●
6.1.4	Scientific and technical articles/bn PPP$ GDP		2.8	117	○
6.1.5	Citable documents H-index		4.1	115	
6.2	**Knowledge impact**		**33.9**	**44**	
6.2.1	Labor productivity growth, %		5.0	6	●◆
6.2.2	Unicorn valuation, % GDP		0.0	48	○◇
6.2.3	Software spending, % GDP		0.2	80	
6.2.4	High-tech manufacturing, %		24.8	51	
6.3	**Knowledge diffusion**		**11.6**	**100**	
6.3.1	Intellectual property receipts, % total trade		0.0	104	
6.3.2	Production and export complexity		47.2	77	
6.3.3	High-tech exports, % total trade		0.1	122	○
6.3.4	ICT services exports, % total trade		0.8	92	
6.3.5	ISO 9001 quality/bn PPP$ GDP		1.2	103	
	Creative outputs		**14.6**	**93**	
7.1	**Intangible assets**		**19.5**	**[86]**	
7.1.1	Intangible asset intensity, top 15, %		n/a	n/a	
7.1.2	Trademarks by origin/bn PPP$ GDP		35.3	65	
7.1.3	Global brand value, top 5,000, % GDP		n/a	n/a	
7.1.4	Industrial designs by origin/bn PPP$ GDP		0.8	77	
7.2	**Creative goods and services**		**3.0**	**96**	
7.2.1	Cultural and creative services exports, % total trade		0.1	88	
7.2.2	National feature films/mn pop. 15–69		0.4	73	○
7.2.3	Entertainment and media market/th pop. 15–69		3.2	49	◆
7.2.4	Creative goods exports, % total trade		0.4	64	
7.3	**Online creativity**		**16.2**	**90**	
7.3.1	Generic top-level domains (TLDs)/th pop. 15–69		0.0	132	○◇
7.3.2	Country-code TLDs/th pop. 15–69		1.4	78	
7.3.3	GitHub commits/mn pop. 15–69		2.6	94	
7.3.4	Mobile app creation/bn PPP$ GDP		60.8	79	

NOTES: ● indicates a strength; ○ a weakness; ◆ an income group strength; ◇ an income group weakness; * an index; † a survey question. ⏲ is used when the available economy data are older than the base year; see appendices for details, including the year of the data, at wipo.int/gii-ranking. Square brackets [ ] indicate that the data minimum coverage (DMC) requirements were not met at the sub-pillar or pillar level.

Viet Nam

GII 2023 rank **46**

Output rank	Input rank	Income	Region	Population (mn)	GDP, PPP$ (bn)	GDP per capita, PPP$
40	57	Lower middle	SEAO	98.2	1,299.7	13,075

			Score/Value	Rank	
	Institutions		**55.1**	**54**	◆
1.1	**Institutional environment**		**53.8**	**48**	◆
1.1.1	Operational stability for businesses*		63.2	40	◆
1.1.2	Government effectiveness*		44.4	54	◆
1.2	**Regulatory environment**		**50.4**	**98**	
1.2.1	Regulatory quality*		31.8	94	
1.2.2	Rule of law*		35.4	72	◆
1.2.3	Cost of redundancy dismissal		24.6	105	○
1.3	**Business environment**		**61.2**	**31**	◆
1.3.1	Policies for doing business†		62.0	36	◆
1.3.2	Entrepreneurship policies and culture†	⊙	60.4	24	

			Score/Value	Rank	
	Human capital and research		**29.9**	**71**	◆
2.1	**Education**		**49.3**	**[70]**	
2.1.1	Expenditure on education, % GDP		3.0	108	○
2.1.2	Government funding/pupil, secondary, % GDP/cap		n/a	n/a	
2.1.3	School life expectancy, years		n/a	n/a	
2.1.4	PISA scales in reading, maths and science	⊙	502.0	16	◆
2.1.5	Pupil-teacher ratio, secondary		20.6	100	○
2.2	**Tertiary education**		**20.5**	**89**	
2.2.1	Tertiary enrolment, % gross		35.4	83	
2.2.2	Graduates in science and engineering, %	⊙	22.7	59	
2.2.3	Tertiary inbound mobility, %		0.4	103	○
2.3	**Research and development (R&D)**		**19.9**	**44**	◆
2.3.1	Researchers, FTE/mn pop.	⊙	756.7	59	
2.3.2	Gross expenditure on R&D, % GDP	⊙	0.4	66	
2.3.3	Global corporate R&D investors, top 3, mn USD		52.3	29	◆
2.3.4	QS university ranking, top 3*		12.4	61	

			Score/Value	Rank	
	Infrastructure		**38.9**	**70**	◆
3.1	**Information and communication technologies (ICTs)**		**68.4**	**71**	◆
3.1.1	ICT access*		87.2	40	◆
3.1.2	ICT use*		72.8	67	◆
3.1.3	Government's online service*		61.1	75	
3.1.4	E-participation*		52.3	71	◆
3.2	**General infrastructure**		**34.8**	**43**	◆
3.2.1	Electricity output, GWh/mn pop.	⊙	2,466.8	75	
3.2.2	Logistics performance*		54.5	42	◆
3.2.3	Gross capital formation, % GDP		34.7	13	●
3.3	**Ecological sustainability**		**13.4**	**110**	○
3.3.1	GDP/unit of energy use		9.7	72	
3.3.2	Environmental performance*		2.0	130	○◇
3.3.3	ISO 14001 environment/bn PPP$ GDP		2.1	43	◆

			Score/Value	Rank	
	Market sophistication		**38.2**	**49**	
4.1	**Credit**		**31.3**	**62**	
4.1.1	Finance for startups and scaleups†	⊙	49.4	47	
4.1.2	Domestic credit to private sector, % GDP		115.5	21	●◆
4.1.3	Loans from microfinance institutions, % GDP		0.1	51	○
4.2	**Investment**		**10.8**	**53**	
4.2.1	Market capitalization, % GDP		47.1	36	
4.2.2	Venture capital (VC) investors, deals/bn PPP$ GDP		0.0	60	
4.2.3	VC recipients, deals/bn PPP$ GDP		0.0	47	
4.2.4	VC received, value, % GDP		0.0	48	
4.3	**Trade, diversification and market scale**		**72.6**	**19**	●◆
4.3.1	Applied tariff rate, weighted avg., %		1.3	17	●◆
4.3.2	Domestic industry diversification	⊙	98.7	7	●◆
4.3.3	Domestic market scale, bn PPP$		1,299.7	25	

			Score/Value	Rank	
	Business sophistication		**32.2**	**49**	◆
5.1	**Knowledge workers**		**28.2**	**75**	
5.1.1	Knowledge-intensive employment, %		7.8	112	○
5.1.2	Firms offering formal training, %	⊙	22.2	71	
5.1.3	GERD performed by business, % GDP	⊙	0.4	47	◆
5.1.4	GERD financed by business, %	⊙	64.1	9	●◆
5.1.5	Females employed w/advanced degrees, %		7.5	87	
5.2	**Innovation linkages**		**28.6**	**43**	◆
5.2.1	University-industry R&D collaboration†		65.3	27	◆
5.2.2	State of cluster development†		68.8	26	◆
5.2.3	GERD financed by abroad, % GDP	⊙	0.0	59	
5.2.4	Joint venture/strategic alliance deals/bn PPP$ GDP		0.0	81	
5.2.5	Patent families/bn PPP$ GDP		0.0	69	
5.3	**Knowledge absorption**		**39.8**	**45**	◆
5.3.1	Intellectual property payments, % total trade	⊙	0.3	85	
5.3.2	High-tech imports, % total trade		29.5	4	●◆
5.3.3	ICT services imports, % total trade	⊙	0.2	127	
5.3.4	FDI net inflows, % GDP		4.6	24	
5.3.5	Research talent, % in businesses	⊙	24.1	52	

			Score/Value	Rank	
	Knowledge and technology outputs		**28.7**	**48**	◆
6.1	**Knowledge creation**		**9.9**	**80**	
6.1.1	Patents by origin/bn PPP$ GDP		0.9	60	
6.1.2	PCT patents by origin/bn PPP$ GDP		0.0	88	
6.1.3	Utility models by origin/bn PPP$ GDP		0.3	39	
6.1.4	Scientific and technical articles/bn PPP$ GDP		6.5	97	
6.1.5	Citable documents H-index		14.2	59	
6.2	**Knowledge impact**		**43.0**	**24**	◆
6.2.1	Labor productivity growth, %		5.3	4	●◆
6.2.2	Unicorn valuation, % GDP		1.1	33	
6.2.3	Software spending, % GDP		0.2	64	
6.2.4	High-tech manufacturing, %	⊙	29.9	38	◆
6.3	**Knowledge diffusion**		**33.4**	**46**	◆
6.3.1	Intellectual property receipts, % total trade	⊙	0.0	95	
6.3.2	Production and export complexity		56.2	52	◆
6.3.3	High-tech exports, % total trade		35.1	3	●◆
6.3.4	ICT services exports, % total trade	⊙	0.3	115	
6.3.5	ISO 9001 quality/bn PPP$ GDP		5.6	50	◆

			Score/Value	Rank	
	Creative outputs		**37.3**	**36**	◆
7.1	**Intangible assets**		**47.1**	**32**	◆
7.1.1	Intangible asset intensity, top 15, %		59.3	38	
7.1.2	Trademarks by origin/bn PPP$ GDP		68.3	26	◆
7.1.3	Global brand value, top 5,000, % GDP		8.4	23	◆
7.1.4	Industrial designs by origin/bn PPP$ GDP		1.9	43	
7.2	**Creative goods and services**		**31.2**	**29**	◆
7.2.1	Cultural and creative services exports, % total trade		0.1	87	
7.2.2	National feature films/mn pop. 15–69		0.3	77	○
7.2.3	Entertainment and media market/th pop. 15–69		n/a	n/a	
7.2.4	Creative goods exports, % total trade		7.7	7	●◆
7.3	**Online creativity**		**23.9**	**54**	◆
7.3.1	Generic top-level domains (TLDs)/th pop. 15–69		2.9	73	
7.3.2	Country-code TLDs/th pop. 15–69		2.2	71	
7.3.3	GitHub commits/mn pop. 15–69		7.9	58	◆
7.3.4	Mobile app creation/bn PPP$ GDP		82.6	8	●◆

NOTES: ● indicates a strength; ○ a weakness; ◆ an income group strength; ◇ an income group weakness; * an index; † a survey question. ⊙ is used when the available economy data are older than the base year; see appendices for details, including the year of the data, at wipo.int/gii-ranking. Square brackets [ ] indicate that the data minimum coverage (DMC) requirements were not met at the sub-pillar or pillar level.

GII 2023 rank

Zambia

118

Output rank	Input rank	Income	Region	Population (mn)	GDP, PPP$ (bn)	GDP per capita, PPP$
122	111	Low	SSA	20.0	76.3	3,808

			Score/Value	Rank	
	Institutions		**31.3**	**119**	
1.1	**Institutional environment**		**28.3**	**104**	
1.1.1	Operational stability for businesses*		42.4	86	
1.1.2	Government effectiveness*		14.2	119	
1.2	**Regulatory environment**		**20.4**	**130**	○◇
1.2.1	Regulatory quality*		27.8	102	
1.2.2	Rule of law*		22.3	99	
1.2.3	Cost of redundancy dismissal		50.6	128	○◇
1.3	**Business environment**		**45.4**	**[68]**	
1.3.1	Policies for doing business†		45.4	73	●
1.3.2	Entrepreneurship policies and culture†		n/a	n/a	
	Human capital and research		**22.7**	**[93]**	
2.1	**Education**		**45.3**	**[80]**	
2.1.1	Expenditure on education, % GDP	⊙	3.9	74	
2.1.2	Government funding/pupil, secondary, % GDP/cap		n/a	n/a	
2.1.3	School life expectancy, years		n/a	n/a	
2.1.4	PISA scales in reading, maths and science		n/a	n/a	
2.1.5	Pupil–teacher ratio, secondary	⊙	21.1	103	
2.2	**Tertiary education**		**n/a**	**[n/a]**	
2.2.1	Tertiary enrolment, % gross		n/a	n/a	
2.2.2	Graduates in science and engineering, %		n/a	n/a	
2.2.3	Tertiary inbound mobility, %		n/a	n/a	
2.3	**Research and development (R&D)**		**0.0**	**[119]**	
2.3.1	Researchers, FTE/mn pop.		n/a	n/a	
2.3.2	Gross expenditure on R&D, % GDP		n/a	n/a	
2.3.3	Global corporate R&D investors, top 3, mn USD		0.0	40	○◇
2.3.4	QS university ranking, top 3*		0.0	71	○◇
	Infrastructure		**23.5**	**111**	
3.1	**Information and communication technologies (ICTs)**		**37.7**	**111**	
3.1.1	ICT access*		52.3	105	◆
3.1.2	ICT use*		24.1	121	
3.1.3	Government's online service*		38.3	111	
3.1.4	E-participation*		36.0	93	
3.2	**General infrastructure**		**18.3**	**97**	
3.2.1	Electricity output, GWh/mn pop.		932.3	98	◆
3.2.2	Logistics performance*		n/a	n/a	
3.2.3	Gross capital formation, % GDP		31.5	21	●
3.3	**Ecological sustainability**		**14.6**	**104**	◆
3.3.1	GDP/unit of energy use		5.5	113	
3.3.2	Environmental performance*		33.1	78	●◆
3.3.3	ISO 14001 environment/bn PPP$ GDP		0.2	118	
	Market sophistication		**21.7**	**110**	◆
4.1	**Credit**		**9.7**	**113**	
4.1.1	Finance for startups and scaleups†		n/a	n/a	
4.1.2	Domestic credit to private sector, % GDP		15.2	118	
4.1.3	Loans from microfinance institutions, % GDP		1.3	22	●
4.2	**Investment**		**5.9**	**[71]**	
4.2.1	Market capitalization, % GDP		n/a	n/a	
4.2.2	Venture capital (VC) investors, deals/bn PPP$ GDP		n/a	n/a	
4.2.3	VC recipients, deals/bn PPP$ GDP		0.0	57	●
4.2.4	VC received, value, % GDP		0.0	70	
4.3	**Trade, diversification and market scale**		**49.6**	**87**	◆
4.3.1	Applied tariff rate, weighted avg., %		4.8	89	◆
4.3.2	Domestic industry diversification	⊙	78.4	82	
4.3.3	Domestic market scale, bn PPP$		76.3	93	

			Score/Value	Rank	
	Business sophistication		**21.7**	**98**	◆
5.1	**Knowledge workers**		**22.8**	**[90]**	
5.1.1	Knowledge-intensive employment, %	⊙	10.6	106	
5.1.2	Firms offering formal training, %		36.6	42	●◆
5.1.3	GERD performed by business, % GDP		n/a	n/a	
5.1.4	GERD financed by business, %		n/a	n/a	
5.1.5	Females employed w/advanced degrees, %	⊙	3.8	98	◆
5.2	**Innovation linkages**		**21.0**	**67**	●◆
5.2.1	University–industry R&D collaboration†		38.6	77	
5.2.2	State of cluster development†		38.8	73	●◆
5.2.3	GERD financed by abroad, % GDP		n/a	n/a	
5.2.4	Joint venture/strategic alliance deals/bn PPP$ GDP		0.0	65	●
5.2.5	Patent families/bn PPP$ GDP		0.0	95	○◇
5.3	**Knowledge absorption**		**21.2**	**125**	○
5.3.1	Intellectual property payments, % total trade		0.3	86	◆
5.3.2	High-tech imports, % total trade		4.2	123	○◇
5.3.3	ICT services imports, % total trade		0.5	109	◇
5.3.4	FDI net inflows, % GDP		−0.0	122	○
5.3.5	Research talent, % in businesses		n/a	n/a	
	Knowledge and technology outputs		**8.7**	**130**	○
6.1	**Knowledge creation**		**6.8**	**100**	
6.1.1	Patents by origin/bn PPP$ GDP	⊙	0.3	93	
6.1.2	PCT patents by origin/bn PPP$ GDP		0.0	101	○◇
6.1.3	Utility models by origin/bn PPP$ GDP		n/a	n/a	
6.1.4	Scientific and technical articles/bn PPP$ GDP		8.2	84	
6.1.5	Citable documents H-index		6.8	90	
6.2	**Knowledge impact**		**11.3**	**127**	○◇
6.2.1	Labor productivity growth, %		−1.3	120	◇
6.2.2	Unicorn valuation, % GDP		0.0	48	○◇
6.2.3	Software spending, % GDP		0.0	118	
6.2.4	High-tech manufacturing, %	⊙	10.1	91	
6.3	**Knowledge diffusion**		**8.1**	**118**	
6.3.1	Intellectual property receipts, % total trade		0.0	100	
6.3.2	Production and export complexity		34.5	103	
6.3.3	High-tech exports, % total trade		0.1	116	
6.3.4	ICT services exports, % total trade		0.3	113	
6.3.5	ISO 9001 quality/bn PPP$ GDP		0.5	119	
	Creative outputs		**8.7**	**112**	
7.1	**Intangible assets**		**16.9**	**94**	
7.1.1	Intangible asset intensity, top 15, %		n/a	n/a	
7.1.2	Trademarks by origin/bn PPP$ GDP	⊙	31.4	74	●
7.1.3	Global brand value, top 5,000, % GDP		0.0	74	○◇
7.1.4	Industrial designs by origin/bn PPP$ GDP	⊙	2.0	41	●
7.2	**Creative goods and services**		**0.5**	**[122]**	
7.2.1	Cultural and creative services exports, % total trade		n/a	n/a	
7.2.2	National feature films/mn pop. 15–69		n/a	n/a	
7.2.3	Entertainment and media market/th pop. 15–69		n/a	n/a	
7.2.4	Creative goods exports, % total trade		0.0	111	
7.3	**Online creativity**		**0.3**	**129**	○◇
7.3.1	Generic top-level domains (TLDs)/th pop. 15–69		0.1	125	○
7.3.2	Country-code TLDs/th pop. 15–69		0.1	118	
7.3.3	GitHub commits/mn pop. 15–69		0.6	119	
7.3.4	Mobile app creation/bn PPP$ GDP		n/a	n/a	

NOTES: ● indicates a strength; ○ a weakness; ◆ an income group strength; ◇ an income group weakness; * an index; † a survey question. ⊙ is used when the available economy data are older than the base year; see appendices for details, including the year of the data, at wipo.int/gii-ranking. Square brackets [ ] indicate that the data minimum coverage (DMC) requirements were not met at the sub-pillar or pillar level.

Zimbabwe

GII 2023 rank

117

Output rank	Input rank	Income	Region	Population (mn)	GDP, PPP$ (bn)	GDP per capita, PPP$
97	127	Lower middle	SSA	16.3	40.4	2,555

			Score/Value	Rank	
1	**Institutions**		**21.3**	**130**	○◇
1.1	**Institutional environment**		**8.5**	**130**	○◇
1.1.1	Operational stability for businesses*		14.6	129	◇
1.1.2	Government effectiveness*		2.4	130	○◇
1.2	**Regulatory environment**		**35.2**	**125**	
1.2.1	Regulatory quality*		6.5	131	○◇
1.2.2	Rule of law*		2.8	130	○◇
1.2.3	Cost of redundancy dismissal		25.3	106	
1.3	**Business environment**		**20.2**	**[117]**	
1.3.1	Policies for doing business†	⊙	20.2	119	◇
1.3.2	Entrepreneurship policies and culture†		n/a	n/a	
2	**Human capital and research**		**18.5**	**104**	
2.1	**Education**		**33.6**	**114**	
2.1.1	Expenditure on education, % GDP	⊙	2.1	119	◇
2.1.2	Government funding/pupil, secondary, % GDP/cap	⊙	22.6	35	
2.1.3	School life expectancy, years	⊙	11.4	96	
2.1.4	PISA scales in reading, maths and science		n/a	n/a	
2.1.5	Pupil–teacher ratio, secondary	⊙	22.5	106	
2.2	**Tertiary education**		**21.9**	**86**	
2.2.1	Tertiary enrolment, % gross	⊙	8.9	117	◇
2.2.2	Graduates in science and engineering, %	⊙	30.2	17	●
2.2.3	Tertiary inbound mobility, %	⊙	0.5	100	
2.3	**Research and development (R&D)**		**0.0**	**[119]**	
2.3.1	Researchers, FTE/mn pop.		n/a	n/a	
2.3.2	Gross expenditure on R&D, % GDP		n/a	n/a	
2.3.3	Global corporate R&D investors, top 3, mn USD		0.0	40	○◇
2.3.4	QS university ranking, top 3*		0.0	71	○◇
3	**Infrastructure**		**20.4**	**119**	◇
3.1	**Information and communication technologies (ICTs)**		**33.4**	**118**	◇
3.1.1	ICT access*		46.8	112	
3.1.2	ICT use*		33.9	114	◇
3.1.3	Government's online service*		32.0	120	
3.1.4	E-participation*		20.9	122	
3.2	**General infrastructure**		**10.2**	**123**	
3.2.1	Electricity output, GWh/mn pop.	⊙	451.5	112	
3.2.2	Logistics performance*		18.2	89	
3.2.3	Gross capital formation, % GDP		n/a	n/a	
3.3	**Ecological sustainability**		**17.6**	**92**	
3.3.1	GDP/unit of energy use		3.5	124	○◇
3.3.2	Environmental performance*		46.3	54	●◆
3.3.3	ISO 14001 environment/bn PPP$ GDP		0.4	93	
4	**Market sophistication**		**15.2**	**121**	◇
4.1	**Credit**		**1.5**	**131**	○◇
4.1.1	Finance for startups and scaleups†		n/a	n/a	
4.1.2	Domestic credit to private sector, % GDP		5.4	129	○◇
4.1.3	Loans from microfinance institutions, % GDP		0.2	47	
4.2	**Investment**		**5.4**	**[73]**	
4.2.1	Market capitalization, % GDP		n/a	n/a	
4.2.2	Venture capital (VC) investors, deals/bn PPP$ GDP		n/a	n/a	
4.2.3	VC recipients, deals/bn PPP$ GDP		0.0	50	●
4.2.4	VC received, value, % GDP		0.0	88	
4.3	**Trade, diversification and market scale**		**38.5**	**106**	
4.3.1	Applied tariff rate, weighted avg., %	⊙	5.0	90	
4.3.2	Domestic industry diversification	⊙	47.2	104	◇
4.3.3	Domestic market scale, bn PPP$		40.4	118	

			Score/Value	Rank	
5	**Business sophistication**		**19.3**	**112**	
5.1	**Knowledge workers**		**23.5**	**[84]**	
5.1.1	Knowledge-intensive employment, %	⊙	9.4	108	
5.1.2	Firms offering formal training, %	⊙	26.4	63	
5.1.3	GERD performed by business, % GDP		n/a	n/a	
5.1.4	GERD financed by business, %		n/a	n/a	
5.1.5	Females employed w/advanced degrees, %	⊙	9.8	76	
5.2	**Innovation linkages**		**7.7**	**125**	◇
5.2.1	University–industry R&D collaboration†	⊙	14.5	121	◇
5.2.2	State of cluster development†	⊙	5.8	126	◇
5.2.3	GERD financed by abroad, % GDP		n/a	n/a	
5.2.4	Joint venture/strategic alliance deals/bn PPP$ GDP		0.0	46	●◆
5.2.5	Patent families/bn PPP$ GDP		0.0	95	○◇
5.3	**Knowledge absorption**		**26.6**	**98**	
5.3.1	Intellectual property payments, % total trade		0.1	106	
5.3.2	High-tech imports, % total trade		8.3	63	●
5.3.3	ICT services imports, % total trade		1.1	83	
5.3.4	FDI net inflows, % GDP		0.8	103	
5.3.5	Research talent, % in businesses		n/a	n/a	
6	**Knowledge and technology outputs**		**11.4**	**113**	
6.1	**Knowledge creation**		**9.1**	**85**	
6.1.1	Patents by origin/bn PPP$ GDP	⊙	0.2	100	
6.1.2	PCT patents by origin/bn PPP$ GDP		0.0	75	
6.1.3	Utility models by origin/bn PPP$ GDP		0.1	55	
6.1.4	Scientific and technical articles/bn PPP$ GDP		15.3	48	●
6.1.5	Citable documents H-index		7.5	89	
6.2	**Knowledge impact**		**17.0**	**118**	
6.2.1	Labor productivity growth, %		−1.8	122	◇
6.2.2	Unicorn valuation, % GDP		0.0	48	○◇
6.2.3	Software spending, % GDP		0.2	70	●
6.2.4	High-tech manufacturing, %	⊙	17.5	70	
6.3	**Knowledge diffusion**		**8.2**	**116**	
6.3.1	Intellectual property receipts, % total trade	⊙	0.0	74	●
6.3.2	Production and export complexity		32.4	108	
6.3.3	High-tech exports, % total trade	⊙	0.2	111	
6.3.4	ICT services exports, % total trade		0.4	106	
6.3.5	ISO 9001 quality/bn PPP$ GDP		0.4	125	
7	**Creative outputs**		**16.9**	**86**	
7.1	**Intangible assets**		**26.8**	**77**	●
7.1.1	Intangible asset intensity, top 15, %		46.5	55	
7.1.2	Trademarks by origin/bn PPP$ GDP	⊙	4.1	126	○
7.1.3	Global brand value, top 5,000, % GDP		0.5	63	●
7.1.4	Industrial designs by origin/bn PPP$ GDP		n/a	n/a	
7.2	**Creative goods and services**		**1.4**	**[111]**	
7.2.1	Cultural and creative services exports, % total trade		n/a	n/a	
7.2.2	National feature films/mn pop. 15–69		0.2	78	
7.2.3	Entertainment and media market/th pop. 15–69		n/a	n/a	
7.2.4	Creative goods exports, % total trade		0.2	88	
7.3	**Online creativity**		**12.3**	**107**	
7.3.1	Generic top-level domains (TLDs)/th pop. 15–69		0.5	113	
7.3.2	Country-code TLDs/th pop. 15–69		1.4	80	
7.3.3	GitHub commits/mn pop. 15–69		0.8	116	
7.3.4	Mobile app creation/bn PPP$ GDP		46.5	106	

NOTES: ● indicates a strength; ○ a weakness; ◆ an income group strength; ◇ an income group weakness; * an index; † a survey question. ⊙ is used when the available economy data are older than the base year; see appendices for details, including the year of the data, at wipo.int/gii-ranking. Square brackets [ ] indicate that the data minimum coverage (DMC) requirements were not met at the sub-pillar or pillar level.

Appendices

Appendix I
Conceptual and measurement framework of the Global Innovation Index

Rationale and origins

The Global Innovation Index (GII) was launched in 2007 with the aim of identifying and determining metrics and methods that could capture a picture of innovation in society that is as complete as possible.

There were several motivations for setting this goal. First, innovation is important for driving economic progress and competitiveness – for both developed and developing economies. Many governments are putting innovation at the center of their growth strategies. Second, the definition of innovation has broadened – it is no longer restricted to research and development (R&D) laboratories and published scientific papers. The concept of innovation has become more general and horizontal in nature, and now includes social, business model and technical aspects. Last, but not least, recognizing and celebrating innovation in emerging markets is critical for inspiring people – especially the next generation of entrepreneurs and innovators.

Now in its 16th edition, the GII helps to create an environment in which these innovation factors are subject to continual evaluation. It provides a key tool for decision-makers and a rich database of detailed metrics, offering a convenient source of information for refining innovation policies.

Measuring innovation outputs and their impact remains a challenging task, hence great emphasis is placed on measuring the climate and infrastructure for innovation and assessing related outcomes.

Although the final results are presented as a ranking, the primary aim of the GII is to improve the "journey" to more accurate methods of measurement, understanding innovation and identifying targeted policies, good practices and other levers that foster innovation. The rich data metrics, at index, sub-index or indicator level, can be used to monitor performance over time and to benchmark developments against economies within the same region or income group classification.

Defining innovation in the GII

The GII adopts a broad definition of innovation, originally elaborated in the *Oslo Manual* developed by the Statistical Office of the European Communities and the Organisation for Economic Co-operation and Development (OECD). In its fourth edition, in 2018, the *Oslo Manual* introduced a more general definition of innovation:[1]

> "An innovation is a new or improved product or process (or combination thereof) that differs significantly from the unit's previous products or processes and that has been made available to potential users (product) or brought into use by the unit (process)."

This update of the *Oslo Manual* also introduced a series of definitions associated with innovation in business activities and for different types of innovation firms. In this context, innovation translates as improvements made to outcomes in the form of either new goods or new services, or any combination of these. While the GII focuses on a more general definition of innovation, it is important to highlight how these specific definitions capture the evolution of the way in which innovation has been perceived and understood over the past two decades.

Economists and policymakers previously focused on R&D-based technological product innovation, largely produced in-house and mainly in manufacturing industries. Innovation of this nature was executed by a highly educated labor force in R&D-intensive companies. The process leading to such innovation was conceptualized as closed, internal and localized. Technological breakthroughs were necessarily "radical" and took place at the "global knowledge frontier." This characterization implied the existence of leading and lagging economies, with low- or middle- income economies only able to play "catch-up."

Today, innovation capability is increasingly seen as the ability to exploit new technological combinations; it embraces the concept of incremental innovation and "innovation without research." Non-R&D innovative expenditure is an important component of reaping the rewards of technological innovation. Interest in understanding how innovation evolves in low- and middle- income economies is increasing, along with an awareness that incremental forms of innovation can impact development.

Furthermore, the process of innovation itself has changed significantly. Investment in innovation-related activity and intangible assets has intensified consistently at the firm, economy and global levels, adding both new innovation actors from outside high-income economies and non-profit actors. The structure of knowledge production activity is more complex, collaborative and geographically dispersed than ever.[2]

A key challenge is to find metrics that capture innovation as it actually happens in the world today. Direct official measures that quantify innovation outputs remain extremely scarce. For example, there are no official statistics on the amount of innovative activity - defined as the number of new products, processes or other innovations - for any given innovation actor, let alone for any given country. Most measurements also struggle to appropriately capture the innovation outputs of a wider spectrum of innovation actors, such as users or the public and services sectors, or more informal means, which are often the drivers of innovation in developing countries.[3]

The GII aims to improve the measurement of innovation in order to provide a more complete picture of innovation ecosystems across the globe. It explores new metrics regularly to reflect the changing nature of innovation and the increasingly sprawling field of new (big data) innovation indicators.

Since its inception, the GII has also made a special effort to cover creativity and creative outputs, taking a fresh view of the previously siloed approach to innovation versus creativity. In the opinion of the GII Editors, innovation and creativity are simply two faces of the same coin.

Interest in applying the GII framework and indicators to develop complementary and mutually reinforcing sub-national innovation indices is also growing among WIPO member states.[4] WIPO has been supporting these exercises since 2022.

Finally, since 2021, when WIPO became the sole editor of the GII, the GII team at WIPO has developed a robust data infrastructure for the GII - led by GII co-editor Lorena Rivera León - increasing the data quality and data quality control, and the robustness and replicability of the GII model (Appendix Box 1).

Appendix Box 1 Building a robust data infrastructure for the Global Innovation Index

To facilitate and permit a comprehensive workflow of the GII model, from data storage to the GII calculations, a new data infrastructure was developed in 2021, after WIPO became solely responsible for the GII. The data infrastructure comprises three parts.

- Data storage - the GII database: All GII data are stored, maintained and managed in the GII database. The database stores all collected data in a structured manner for all WIPO member states (not only the ranked GII economies) and for all indicators (those already included in the GII model and the new ones). It also stores data on outlier analysis (generated by the data quality checks that the GII team carries out after data collection - see below), as well as all the data queries sent to the GII data providers following an outlier analysis.
- The GII repository of collaborative codes: The GII repository of collaborative codes is on GitHub, which is one of the largest code-hosting platforms for version control and collaboration. The GII repository contains eight repositories in the statistical programming language R (R-codes), which are linked to diverse elements of the GII workflow and the GII report, enabling data collection, data calculation and data quality control of all GII indicators.
- The GII R-package for the calculation of the GII model: The GII R-package is a custom-built package of tools, created using R, to calculate the GII model and analyze its results. The structure of the tailor-made GII R-package follows the general COINr R-package, which was

developed by the European Commission Joint Research Centre (JRC) and follows the steps in the OECD/JRC Handbook for constructing composite indicators.[5]

Assuring data quality control is at the center of the GII methodology and processes. Each collected indicator for the GII undergoes a data quality control and data audit process every year. Several data tests and analyses are performed on all collected indicators, including the analysis of means, identification of outliers based on mean and z-scores for both unscaled and scaled data, analysis of rank changes, analysis of missing data and analysis of outdated data. Following these analyses, the GII team goes back to the data providers for any necessary clarification and, when required, the data providers themselves correct the data at the source. These additional exhaustive checks ensure the reliability of all data used in the GII.

This new infrastructure enables a complete workflow that links data storage and data quality control with data analysis (GII rankings and the GII report) in a fully integrated way, increasing the overall robustness of the GII data and model.

The GII conceptual framework

The overall GII ranking is based on two sub-indices that are both equally important in presenting a complete picture of innovation: the Innovation Input Sub-Index and the Innovation Output Sub-Index. Hence, three indices are calculated:

- Innovation Input Sub-Index: Five input pillars capture elements of the economy that enable and facilitate innovative activities. The idea is that the innovation inputs of today - and corresponding efforts to develop the science, innovation and human capital base, and the associated innovation environment - prepare the ground for the innovation outputs of tomorrow.
- Innovation Output Sub-Index: Innovation outputs are the result of innovative activities within the economy. Although the Output Sub-Index includes only two pillars, it carries the same weight as the Input Sub-Index in calculating the overall GII scores. In other words, innovation output pillars and indicators have a disproportionally greater weight compared to innovation inputs.
- The overall GII score is the average of the Input and Output Sub-Indices, from which the GII economy rankings are produced.

Each of the five input and two output pillars is divided into three sub-pillars, each of which is composed of individual indicators - a total of 80 this year (see the Economy profiles section for the Framework of the Global Innovation Index 2023). Each sub-pillar is calculated by taking the weighted average of its individual indicators' scores, which are normalized to again produce *scores* between 0 and 100. Pillar scores are calculated using the weighted average of each pillar's sub-pillar scores.

Adjustments to the GII model in 2023

Appendix Table 1 summarizes the adjustments made to the GII 2023 framework. Three indicators have undergone methodology changes. In addition, there is one new indicator and two indicators have been dropped from the framework. Furthermore, one indicator has shifted its position in the indicator framework, changing sub-pillars. Due to the removal of two indicators, the numbering of two remaining indicators has been adjusted, but without altering their methodology. Lastly, the names of three indicators and one sub-pillar have been modified.

Appendix Table 1 Changes to the GII 2023 framework

	GII 2022	Adjustment		GII 2023
1.1	Political environment	Name changed	1.1	Institutional environment
1.1.1	Political and operational stability*	Name changed	1.1.1	Operational stability for businesses*
1.3.2	Entrepreneurship policies and culture*	Methodology changed	1.3.2	Entrepreneurship policies and culture†
4.1.1	Finance for startups and scaleups*	Methodology changed	4.1.1	Finance for startups and scaleups†
6.2.2	New businesses/th pop. 15–64	Removed		
		New indicator	6.2.2	Unicorn valuation, % GDP
6.2.5	High-tech manufacturing, %	New indicator numbering	6.2.4	High-tech manufacturing, %
6.2.4	ISO 9001 quality certificates/bn PPP$ GDP	Sub-pillar and name changed	6.3.5	ISO 9001 quality/bn PPP$ GDP
7.2.4	Printing and other media, % manufacturing	Removed		
7.2.5	Creative goods exports, % total trade	New indicator numbering	7.2.4	Creative goods exports, % total trade
7.3.3	GitHub commit pushes received/ mn pop. 15–69	Methodology and name changed	7.3.3	GitHub commits/mn pop. 15–69

Source: Global Innovation Index 2023, WIPO.

Notes: Refer to Appendix III: Sources and definitions for a detailed explanation of terminology and acronyms.

Data limitations and treatment

This year, the GII model includes 132 economies, which represent 92.5 percent of the world's population and 97.6 percent of the world's GDP in purchasing power parity current international dollars.

The timeliest possible indicators are used for the GII 2023: from the non-missing data, 3.8 percent are from 2023, 34.7 percent are from 2022, 34.2 percent are from 2021, 15.1 percent are from 2020, 5.1 percent are from 2019, 2.8 percent are from 2018 and the small remainder of 4.2 percent are from earlier years.[6]

The GII 2023 model includes 80 indicators, which fall into three categories:

- quantitative/objective/hard data (64 indicators);
- composite indicators/index data (11 indicators); and
- survey/qualitative/subjective/soft data (5 indicators).

This year, for an economy to feature in the GII 2023, the minimum symmetric data coverage requirement is at least 36 indicators in the Innovation Input Sub-Index (66 percent) and 17 indicators in the Innovation Output Sub-Index (66 percent), with scores for at least two sub-pillars per pillar. In the GII 2023, 132 economies had sufficient data available to be included in the Index. A total of 61 economies did not make it into the GII 2023 due to a lack of available data. For each economy, only the most recent yearly data were considered. As a rule, the GII indicators consider data from as far back as 2013.

Missing values

For the sake of transparency and replicability of results, missing values are not estimated; they are indicated with "n/a" and are not considered in the sub-pillar score. In other words, missing indicators do not translate into a zero for the country in question; the indicator is simply not taken into consideration in the aggregation process.

That said, the audit undertaken by the European Commission's Competence Centre on Composite Indicators and Scoreboards at the Joint Research Centre (JRC-COIN) (see Appendix II) assesses the robustness of the GII modeling choices (no imputation of missing data, fixed predefined weights and arithmetic averages) by imputing missing data, applying random sets of perturbed weights and using geometric averages. Since 2012, based on this assessment, a confidence interval has been provided for each ranking in the GII as well as for the Input and Output Sub-Indices (Appendix II).

Treatment of series with outliers

Potentially problematic indicators with outliers that could polarize results and unduly bias the rankings were treated according to the rules listed below, as per the recommendations of the JRC-COIN. Only hard data indicators were treated (34 out of 64).

First rule: selection
Indicators were classified as problematic if they had:

- an absolute value of skewness greater than 2.25; and
- kurtosis greater than 3.5.[7]

Second rule: treatment
Indicators with between one and five outliers (27 cases) were winsorized; the values distorting the indicator distribution were assigned the next highest value, up to the level where skewness and/or kurtosis had the values specified above.[8]

Indicators with five or more outliers, and for which skewness or kurtosis did not fall within the ranges specified above, were transformed using natural logarithms after multiplication by a given factor *f*.[9] Since only "goods" were affected (i.e., indicators for which higher values indicate better outcomes, as opposed to "bads"), the following formula was used:

$$\ln\left[\frac{(\max \times f - 1)\,(\textit{economy value} - \min)}{\max - \min} + 1\right]$$

where "min" and "max" are the minimum and maximum indicator sample values, respectively.[10]

Normalization

The 80 indicators were then normalized into the [0, 100] range, with higher scores representing better outcomes. Normalization was undertaken according to the min–max method, where the "min" and "max" values were the minimum and maximum indicator sample values, respectively. Following the recommendation of the JRC-COIN, all indicators, including index and survey data, were normalized to a 0–100 range. This normalization ensures that all indicators share the same range, facilitating their individual contribution to the overall index score.

Weights

In 2012, the JRC-COIN and GII team made a joint decision that scaling coefficients of 0.5 or 1.0 should be used instead of importance coefficients. This decision aimed to achieve balanced sub-pillar and pillar scores by considering the underlying components. In other words, the goal was to ensure that indicators and sub-pillars contribute a similar amount of variance to their respective sub-pillars/pillars.

To prevent multicollinearity during the aggregation process, any indicators within a sub-index that exhibited a high correlation, exceeding an absolute correlation of 0.95, were assigned a weight of 0.5. In 2023, two indicators have a weight of 0.5 – 1.2.1 Regulatory quality and 1.2.2 Rule of law – both of which fall within the input sub-pillar 1.2 Regulatory environment. Additionally, two sub-pillars – 7.2 Creative goods and services and 7.3 Online creativity – were also assigned a weight of 0.5.

Strengths and weaknesses

Strengths and weaknesses are calculated for all economies covered in the GII and are presented in the individual economy profiles (see the explanatory section Economy profiles). In simple terms, strengths and weaknesses are the top- and bottom-ranked indicators for each country. In addition, income group strengths and weaknesses are also provided, which are the respective high- and low-performing indicators within income groups.

The methodology for the calculation of strengths and weaknesses is as follows:

- The scores of each indicator are converted to percentile ranks.
- Strengths are defined as the indicators of an economy that have a percentile rank greater than or equal to the 10th percentile rank (across the indicators of that economy). Note that this can result in more than 10 strengths in the event of tied results.
- Weaknesses are defined in an equivalent manner for the bottom 10 indicators.
- If a country has an indicator that ranks equal to or lower than three, it is automatically a strength, regardless of the percentile rank.
- Importantly, although the cut-off value used to define the strengths (i.e., the 10th highest percentile rank) is calculated using only indicator percentile ranks, it is also applied to sub-pillars and pillars.
- In addition, for pillars and sub-pillars that do not meet the Data Minimum Coverage (DMC) criteria, strengths and weaknesses are not signaled. Pillars and sub-pillars that do not meet the DMC show the pillars and sub-pillars in brackets in the economy profiles.
- Income group strengths and weaknesses are somewhat similar to overall strengths and weaknesses but are defined within income groups and use means and standard deviations. The methodology for the calculation of income group strengths and weaknesses is as follows:
  - For a given economy, income group strengths are those scores that are above the income group average plus the standard deviation within the group.
  - For that economy, weaknesses are those scores that are below the income group average minus the standard deviation within the group.
  - The only exceptions to the income group strengths and weaknesses are the top 25 high-income economies, where these strengths and weaknesses are computed within the top 25 group.
  - As the only non-high-income economy in the top 25, China's income group strengths and weaknesses are computed within the non-top 25 group.
- Since, occasionally, the low threshold for weaknesses is below zero, any score of zero is automatically marked as a weakness.
- Finally, as of 2023 and following the recommendation of the audit by the WIPO Internal Oversight Section,[11] strengths and weaknesses are reset, or not signaled, where the data year for a given indicator is older than the indicator mode minus five years. In practice, for the GII 2023, this means that for indicators with a data year mode of 2022, the data year of an economy must be 2017 or later to qualify as a strength or weakness.

Caveats on the year-to-year comparison of rankings

The GII compares the performance of national innovation systems across economies and presents the changes in economy rankings over time.

It is important to note that scores and rankings are not directly comparable between one year and another. Each ranking reflects the relative position of a particular economy based on the conceptual framework, the data coverage and the sample of economies of that specific GII edition, and also reflects changes in the underlying indicators at source and in data availability.

A number of factors influence the year-on-year rankings of an economy:

- the actual performance of the economy in question;
- adjustments made to the GII framework (changes in indicator composition and measurement revisions);
- data updates, the treatment of outliers and missing values; and
- the inclusion or exclusion of economies in the sample.

Additionally, the following characteristics complicate the time-series analysis based on simple GII rankings or scores:

- **Missing values**: The GII produces relative index scores, which means that a missing value for one economy affects the index score of other economies. Because the number of missing values decreases every year, this problem reduces overtime.
- **Reference year**: The data underlying the GII do not refer to a single year but to several years, depending on the latest available year for any given variable. In addition, the

reference years for different variables are not the same for each economy, due to measures to limit the number of missing data points.

- **Scaling factors**: Most GII variables are scaled using either GDP or population, with the intention of enabling cross-economy comparability. However, this implies that year-on-year changes in individual indicators may be driven either by the variable (numerator) or by its scaling factor (denominator).
- **Consistent data collection**: Measuring the change in year-on-year performance relies on the consistent collection of data over time. Changes in the definition of variables or in the data collection process could create movements in the rankings that are unrelated to performance.

A detailed economy study based on the GII database and the economy profile over time, coupled with analytical work on the ground, including that of innovation actors and decision-makers, yields the best results in terms of monitoring an economy's innovation performance, as well as identifying possible avenues for improvement.

Notes

1 OECD and Eurostat (2018).

2 See WIPO (2011–2023) for bi-annual elaborations on the changing nature and geographic dispersion of innovation. See Arundel *et al.* (2021) for an elaboration on the role and measurement of knowledge and technology transfer between innovation actors.

3 On innovation in the informal economy, see Kraemer-Mbula and Wunsch-Vincent (2016).

4 See Box 2 in the main results and WIPO (2023, forthcoming).

5 OECD and EC JRC (2008).

6 The GII is calculated based on 9,403 data points out of a possible 10,560 (132 economies multiplied by 80 indicators), implying that 10.9 percent of data points are missing. The GII 2023 database includes the data year used for each indicator and economy, downloadable at www.wipo.int/global_innovation_index/en/2023. If an indicator for an economy is missing, it is marked as "n/a" in the economy profiles.

7 Based on Groeneveld and Meeden (1984), which sets the criteria of absolute skewness above 1 and kurtosis above 3.5. The skewness criterion was relaxed to accommodate the small sample under consideration (132 economies).

8 The indicators treated using winsorization are: 4.2.1, 5.2.3, 5.2.4, 5.3.2, 6.1.5, 7.2.2 and 7.3.1 (one outlier); 2.2.3, 3.2.1, 5.3.3, 6.1.3, 7.2.1 and 7.3.3 (two outliers); 4.1.3, 4.2.4, 6.3.4, 7.1.2 and 7.3.2 (three outliers); 4.2.3, 5.3.1 and 6.2.2 (four outliers); and 4.3.3, 5.2.5, 6.1.2, 6.3.1 and 7.2.4 (five outliers). Finally, indicator 7.1.1 was winsorized from the bottom of the distribution, on three outlier observations.

9 Indicators 2.3.3, 4.2.2, 5.3.4, 6.1.1, 6.3.3, 7.1.4 and 7.3.4 were treated using log-transformation (factor f of 1).

10 This formula achieves two things: it converts all series into "goods" and scales the series within the range [1, max] so that natural logs are positive, starting at 0, where "min" and "max" are the minimum and maximum indicator sample values. The corresponding formula for "bads" is:

$$\ln\left[\frac{(\max \times f - 1)(\max - \textit{economy value})}{\max - \min} + 1\right]$$

11 IOD Ref: IA 2022-03, April 14, 2023: www.wipo.int/export/sites/www/about-wipo/en/oversight/docs/iaod/audit/audit-gii.pdf.

References

Arundel, A., S. Athreye and S. Wunsch-Vincent (2021). *Harnessing Public Research for Innovation in the 21st Century: An International Assessment of Knowledge Transfer Policies.* Intellectual Property, Innovation and Economic Development series. Geneva and Cambridge: World Intellectual Property Organization and Cambridge University Press.

Groeneveld, R.A. and G. Meeden (1984). Measuring skewness and kurtosis. *The Statistician*, 33(4), 391–399.

Kraemer-Mbula E. and S. Wunsch-Vincent (eds) (2016). *The Informal Economy in Developing Nations: Hidden Engine of Innovation?* Intellectual Property, Innovation and Economic Development series. Cambridge: Cambridge University Press. Available at: www.cambridge.org/core/books/the-informal-economy-in-developing-nations/C7494C6FD7EE4DC86BBADB4A7B87BCE3.

OECD and EC JRC (Organisation for Economic Co-operation and Development and European Commission, Joint Research Centre) (2008). *Handbook on Constructing Composite Indicators: Methodology and User Guide.* Paris: Organisation for Economic Co-operation and Development.

OECD and Eurostat (2018). *Oslo Manual 2018: Guidelines for Collecting, Reporting and Using Data on Innovation* (4th ed.). Paris and Luxembourg: Organisation for Economic Co-operation and Development and Eurostat. Available at: https://doi.org/10.1787/9789264304604-en.

WIPO (2011–2023). *World Intellectual Property Report* (various editions). Geneva: World Intellectual Property Organization. Available at: www.wipo.int/wipr.

WIPO (2023, forthcoming). *Enabling Innovation Measurement at the Sub-National Level: A WIPO Toolkit* (authors: G. de Rassenfosse (EPFL) and S. Wunsch-Vincent (WIPO)). Geneva: WIPO.

Appendix II
Joint Research Centre (JRC) statistical audit of the 2023 Global Innovation Index

Begoña Cabeza Martínez, Jaime Lagüera González, Ana Rita Neves, Panagiotis Ravanos, Michaela Saisana, Oscar Smallenbroek and Carlos Tacao Moura, European Commission, JRC, Ispra, Italy

Conceptual and practical challenges are inevitable when trying to understand and model the fundamentals of innovation at the national level worldwide. Now in its 16th edition, the Global Innovation Index (GII) 2023, considers these conceptual challenges and deals with practical issues relating to data quality and methodological choices.

This appendix summarizes the main conclusions of the audit, conducted for the 13th consecutive year by the European Commission's Competence Centre on Composite Indicators and Scoreboards (COIN) at the Joint Research Centre (JRC), concerning the statistical soundness and assumptions used to arrive at the final index rankings of the GII 2023. The independent statistical assessment of the GII provided by the JRC-COIN guarantees the transparency and reliability of the index for both policymakers and other stakeholders, thus facilitating more accurate priority setting and policy formulation in the innovation field.

As in past GII reports, the JRC-COIN analysis complements the economy rankings with confidence intervals for the GII, the Innovation Input Sub-Index and the Innovation Output Sub-Index, in order to allow a better appreciation of the robustness of these rankings to the choice of computation methodology. Finally, the JRC-COIN analysis also includes an assessment of the added value of the GII and a measure of "distance to the efficiency frontier" of innovation by using data envelopment analysis.

This is a shortened version of the audit. The full audit is available at www.wipo.int/global_innovation_index/en/2023.

Main conclusions

The JRC-COIN analysis suggests that the conceptualized multilevel structure of the GII 2023 – with its 80 indicators, 21 sub-pillars, seven pillars and two sub-indices comprising the overall index – is statistically sound and balanced: that is, each sub-pillar makes a similar contribution to the variation of its respective pillar. The refinements made by the developing team over the years have helped to enhance an already strong statistical coherence within the GII framework, in which the capacity of the 80 indicators to distinguish between economies' performances is maintained at the sub-pillar level or lower in all but four cases.

The decision not to impute missing values, which is common in comparable contexts and justified on the grounds of transparency and replicability, can at times have an undesirable impact on some economies' scores, with the additional negative side-effect that it might encourage economies not to report low data values. The GII team's adoption, in 2016, of a more stringent data coverage threshold (at least 66 percent data availability for each of the input- and output-related indicators) has notably improved confidence in the economy ranking for the GII and the two sub-indices.

Additionally, the GII team's decision, in 2012, to use weights as scaling coefficients during index development constitutes a significant departure from the traditional, yet erroneous, vision of weights as a reflection of indicators' importance in a weighted average. It is hoped that such an approach will be adopted by other developers of composite indicators to avoid situations where bias sneaks in when least expected.

Strong correlations between the GII components are proven not to be a sign of redundancy of information within the GII. For more than 34 percent (up to 70 percent) of the 132 economies included in the GII 2023, the GII ranking and the rankings of any of the seven pillars differ by 10 positions or more. This demonstrates the added value of the GII ranking, which helps to highlight other components of innovation not immediately apparent from a separate analysis of each pillar. At the same time, this finding points to there being value in duly considering the merits of the GII pillars, sub-pillars and their constituent indicators individually. By doing so, economy-specific strengths and bottlenecks in innovation can be identified and serve as an input for evidence-based policymaking.

To test the impact of the GII modeling assumptions, a number of different models were tested in this audit, based on different approaches to imputing of missing data, aggregation at the pillar level and assignment of weights. Using these models, the 90 percent confidence intervals relating to the ranking positions that an economy might have had under different model assumptions were computed. For the vast majority of economies, these intervals are sufficiently narrow to allow meaningful inferences to be drawn: there is a shift of 10 or fewer positions for 89 of the 132 economies. However, it is also true that a few economies experience significant changes in rank with variations in weights and aggregation formula and when imputing missing data. Five economies – Bahrain, Belarus, Botswana, Brunei Darussalam and Zimbabwe – have 90 percent confidence interval widths of more than 20 positions (21, 24, 21, 41 and 21 positions, respectively). Consequently, their GII rankings (67th, 80th, 85th, 87th and 117th, respectively) in the GII classification should be interpreted cautiously and certainly not taken at face value. However, this is a remarkable improvement compared to GII versions up to 2016, when more than 40 economies had confidence interval widths of more than 20 positions. The improvement in the confidence that can be placed in the GII 2023 ranking is the direct result of the decision to adopt a more stringent criterion for an economy's inclusion since 2016, which now requires at least 66 percent data availability within each of the two sub-indices. Some caution is also warranted in regard to the Input Sub-Index for one economy – Brunei Darussalam – which has a 90 percent confidence interval width of more than 20 positions (22). A similar degree of caution is needed in the Output Sub-Index for three economies – Botswana, Côte d'Ivoire and Ghana – which have 90 percent confidence interval widths of more than 20 positions (up to 24 for Ghana). Compared to the GII 2019, the higher data availability in the Output Sub-Index this year has led to a much lower number of countries with very wide intervals (three compared to 13 in the GII 2019 edition), which is a noteworthy improvement.

Although the rankings for a few economies, in the GII 2023 overall or in the two sub-indices, appear to be sensitive to methodological choices, the published rankings for the vast majority can be considered as representative of the plurality of scenarios simulated in this audit. Taking the median rank as the benchmark for an economy's expected rank in the realm of the GII's unavoidable methodological uncertainties, 80 percent of the economies are found to shift fewer than three positions with respect to the median rank in the GII and the Input Sub-Index; however, the percentage for the Output Sub-Index is lower, at 62 percent.

In order to offer full transparency and complete information, Appendix Table 2 reports the GII 2023 Index and Input and Output Sub-Indices' economy ranks together with the simulated 90 percent confidence intervals to allow a better appreciation of the robustness of the results to the choice of weights and aggregation formula and the impact of estimating missing data (where applicable).

All things considered, the present JRC-COIN audit findings confirm that the GII 2023 meets international quality standards for statistical soundness, which indicates that the GII is a reliable benchmarking tool for innovation practices at the economy level around the world.

Finally, the "distance to the efficiency frontier" measure, calculated using data envelopment analysis, can be used both as a measure of efficiency and as a suitable approach to benchmarking economies' multidimensional performance on innovation, without imposing a fixed and common set of weights that may be unfair to a particular economy. The decision made by the GII team to abandon the efficiency ratio (ratio of Output to Input Sub-Index) is particularly laudable. In fact, ratios of composite indicators (Output to Input Sub-Index in this case) come with much higher uncertainty than the sum of the components (Input plus Output Sub-Index, equivalent to the GII). For this reason, developers and users of indices alike need to approach efficiency ratios of this nature with great care. The GII should not be considered as the ultimate and definitive ranking of economies with respect to innovation. On the contrary, the GII best represents an ongoing attempt to find metrics and approaches that capture the richness of innovation more effectively, continuously adapting the GII framework to reflect the improved availability of statistics and the theoretical advances in the field. In any case, the GII should be regarded as a sound attempt, based on the principle of transparency, matured over 16 years of constant refinement, to pave the way for better and more informed innovation policies worldwide.

Appendix Table 2 GII 2023 and Input/Output Sub-Indices: rankings and 90 percent confidence intervals

	GII 2023		Input Sub-Index		Output Sub-Index	
	Rank	Interval	Rank	Interval	Rank	Interval
Switzerland	1	[1, 1]	3	[2, 4]	1	[1, 1]
Sweden	2	[2, 3]	4	[2, 5]	3	[3, 3]
United States	3	[2, 4]	2	[2, 5]	4	[4, 6]
United Kingdom	4	[3, 6]	6	[6, 9]	2	[2, 2]
Singapore	5	[4, 9]	1	[1, 1]	12	[12, 13]
Finland	6	[4, 6]	5	[4, 5]	9	[9, 10]
Netherlands (Kingdom of the)	7	[5, 8]	10	[8, 10]	5	[5, 8]
Germany	8	[7, 10]	13	[13, 15]	6	[5, 6]
Denmark	9	[8, 10]	7	[6, 8]	10	[9, 10]
Republic of Korea	10	[7, 10]	12	[10, 13]	7	[7, 8]
France	11	[11, 13]	17	[14, 21]	11	[11, 11]
China	12	[11, 14]	25	[24, 26]	8	[4, 8]
Japan	13	[13, 15]	11	[11, 12]	14	[13, 16]
Israel	14	[12, 18]	21	[14, 22]	13	[13, 15]
Canada	15	[14, 18]	9	[7, 11]	20	[19, 24]
Estonia	16	[15, 18]	14	[12, 19]	16	[16, 18]
Hong Kong, China	17	[11, 22]	8	[6, 10]	24	[13, 30]
Austria	18	[14, 18]	18	[16, 21]	15	[13, 16]
Norway	19	[19, 25]	15	[14, 20]	28	[26, 29]
Iceland	20	[19, 21]	20	[17, 21]	25	[23, 25]
Luxembourg	21	[18, 24]	22	[16, 23]	23	[21, 27]
Ireland	22	[18, 24]	26	[24, 26]	18	[17, 20]
Belgium	23	[19, 25]	23	[22, 23]	22	[21, 26]
Australia	24	[22, 25]	16	[15, 21]	30	[29, 30]
Malta	25	[20, 26]	27	[27, 27]	17	[14, 20]
Italy	26	[25, 28]	35	[33, 35]	19	[18, 20]
New Zealand	27	[26, 31]	24	[24, 26]	31	[31, 35]
Cyprus	28	[27, 29]	33	[30, 33]	21	[21, 26]
Spain	29	[28, 30]	28	[28, 29]	26	[25, 27]
Portugal	30	[30, 31]	31	[30, 34]	29	[28, 29]
Czech Republic	31	[26, 31]	34	[30, 35]	27	[19, 28]
United Arab Emirates	32	[31, 39]	19	[18, 22]	54	[54, 57]
Slovenia	33	[32, 35]	29	[28, 31]	38	[37, 39]
Lithuania	34	[32, 35]	32	[31, 35]	37	[36, 37]
Hungary	35	[32, 36]	36	[36, 37]	33	[31, 34]
Malaysia	36	[35, 37]	30	[28, 32]	46	[45, 46]
Latvia	37	[37, 40]	38	[37, 38]	39	[38, 40]
Bulgaria	38	[36, 40]	45	[42, 47]	34	[33, 35]
Türkiye	39	[36, 42]	52	[48, 55]	32	[31, 33]
India	40	[37, 43]	46	[44, 51]	35	[32, 37]
Poland	41	[39, 42]	50	[42, 51]	36	[35, 38]
Greece	42	[40, 44]	42	[39, 43]	41	[39, 41]
Thailand	43	[41, 45]	44	[40, 49]	43	[41, 43]
Croatia	44	[42, 44]	43	[41, 45]	44	[41, 44]
Slovakia	45	[44, 46]	51	[46, 51]	45	[45, 48]
Viet Nam	46	[44, 47]	57	[53, 58]	40	[40, 43]
Romania	47	[46, 50]	55	[52, 57]	47	[47, 49]
Saudi Arabia	48	[47, 54]	37	[36, 38]	67	[64, 70]
Brazil	49	[48, 53]	59	[53, 61]	49	[49, 50]
Qatar	50	[49, 65]	39	[39, 40]	70	[69, 79]
Russian Federation	51	[48, 55]	58	[51, 61]	53	[51, 53]
Chile	52	[49, 53]	48	[45, 49]	56	[56, 60]
Serbia	53	[49, 67]	41	[40, 51]	64	[62, 72]
North Macedonia	54	[51, 59]	49	[47, 60]	58	[57, 61]
Ukraine	55	[48, 56]	78	[70, 78]	42	[42, 44]
Philippines	56	[51, 59]	69	[64, 71]	52	[50, 54]
Mauritius	57	[49, 69]	40	[39, 51]	72	[70, 80]
Mexico	58	[54, 63]	77	[73, 77]	51	[51, 54]
South Africa	59	[57, 65]	71	[68, 73]	57	[57, 61]
Republic of Moldova	60	[53, 65]	81	[78, 82]	50	[47, 52]
Indonesia	61	[59, 66]	64	[62, 67]	63	[62, 65]
Iran (Islamic Republic of)	62	[57, 75]	87	[85, 100]	48	[45, 48]
Uruguay	63	[56, 68]	56	[52, 62]	73	[64, 74]
Kuwait	64	[61, 72]	67	[65, 73]	65	[63, 69]
Georgia	65	[56, 70]	54	[52, 60]	77	[66, 77]
Colombia	66	[62, 72]	63	[57, 63]	71	[69, 73]
Bahrain	67	[60, 81]	47	[43, 58]	86	[84, 96]
Mongolia	68	[58, 75]	79	[79, 84]	60	[51, 68]

Appendix Table 2 Continued

	GII 2023		Input Sub-Index		Output Sub-Index	
	Rank	Interval	Rank	Interval	Rank	Interval
Oman	69	[67, 74]	65	[61, 67]	78	[73, 79]
Morocco	70	[64, 76]	90	[86, 91]	55	[55, 58]
Jordan	71	[68, 77]	70	[66, 71]	76	[73, 81]
Armenia	72	[63, 75]	83	[81, 85]	62	[55, 62]
Argentina	73	[65, 79]	84	[80, 87]	59	[58, 65]
Costa Rica	74	[65, 78]	66	[61, 70]	81	[69, 82]
Montenegro	75	[70, 77]	62	[59, 65]	83	[74, 83]
Peru	76	[72, 84]	60	[55, 68]	84	[84, 93]
Bosnia and Herzegovina	77	[73, 86]	75	[72, 79]	80	[80, 86]
Jamaica	78	[72, 82]	82	[77, 86]	69	[65, 74]
Tunisia	79	[71, 83]	96	[89, 96]	61	[59, 63]
Belarus	80	[58, 82]	88	[77, 92]	66	[54, 69]
Kazakhstan	81	[78, 84]	68	[65, 70]	87	[83, 94]
Uzbekistan	82	[78, 84]	72	[71, 76]	88	[82, 90]
Albania	83	[80, 87]	73	[70, 76]	94	[87, 94]
Panama	84	[82, 88]	93	[86, 96]	75	[73, 84]
Botswana	85	[83, 104]	61	[58, 63]	110	[107, 129]
Egypt	86	[82, 92]	99	[94, 100]	74	[73, 76]
Brunei Darussalam	87	[72, 113]	53	[42, 64]	125	[112, 126]
Pakistan	88	[84, 100]	113	[103, 113]	68	[66, 79]
Azerbaijan	89	[85, 96]	76	[71, 78]	104	[101, 107]
Sri Lanka	90	[85, 98]	103	[100, 105]	79	[76, 80]
Cabo Verde	91	[87, 99]	74	[73, 86]	106	[90, 107]
Lebanon	92	[80, 93]	86	[82, 91]	95	[78, 95]
Senegal	93	[88, 99]	95	[92, 99]	93	[85, 97]
Dominican Republic	94	[90, 95]	89	[85, 92]	96	[95, 98]
El Salvador	95	[89, 98]	102	[98, 103]	90	[84, 90]
Namibia	96	[92, 104]	80	[79, 86]	111	[108, 112]
Bolivia (Plurinational State of)	97	[91, 105]	91	[86, 99]	101	[100, 103]
Paraguay	98	[91, 102]	101	[97, 106]	92	[85, 94]
Ghana	99	[90, 110]	107	[105, 114]	85	[84, 108]
Kenya	100	[91, 104]	104	[103, 105]	91	[89, 99]
Cambodia	101	[97, 104]	97	[96, 104]	100	[94, 100]
Trinidad and Tobago	102	[95, 106]	92	[86, 97]	108	[105, 109]
Rwanda	103	[95, 110]	85	[84, 100]	113	[102, 113]
Ecuador	104	[95, 104]	98	[94, 99]	99	[92, 100]
Bangladesh	105	[96, 108]	114	[114, 122]	89	[85, 92]
Kyrgyzstan	106	[100, 108]	94	[87, 96]	112	[106, 112]
Madagascar	107	[101, 120]	125	[121, 128]	82	[81, 98]
Nepal	108	[103, 110]	106	[104, 111]	103	[98, 103]
Nigeria	109	[104, 120]	116	[113, 119]	98	[98, 116]
Lao People's Democratic Republic	110	[106, 117]	100	[100, 103]	120	[109, 123]
Tajikistan	111	[105, 114]	109	[105, 112]	107	[100, 115]
Côte d'Ivoire	112	[108, 122]	112	[107, 119]	102	[102, 125]
United Republic of Tanzania	113	[110, 120]	105	[103, 118]	123	[112, 124]
Togo	114	[111, 117]	120	[116, 120]	105	[105, 112]
Nicaragua	115	[112, 121]	110	[108, 114]	118	[116, 120]
Honduras	116	[109, 118]	115	[106, 116]	114	[111, 117]
Zimbabwe	117	[108, 129]	127	[122, 128]	97	[96, 115]
Zambia	118	[112, 120]	111	[107, 119]	122	[110, 123]
Algeria	119	[110, 121]	118	[106, 119]	116	[110, 121]
Benin	120	[114, 126]	108	[105, 114]	128	[127, 130]
Uganda	121	[115, 122]	117	[115, 122]	121	[118, 121]
Guatemala	122	[110, 122]	121	[117, 122]	115	[104, 117]
Cameroon	123	[120, 124]	123	[120, 125]	117	[116, 121]
Burkina Faso	124	[122, 128]	119	[117, 121]	127	[124, 129]
Ethiopia	125	[121, 127]	130	[130, 131]	109	[101, 119]
Mozambique	126	[123, 131]	128	[124, 131]	124	[122, 129]
Mauritania	127	[124, 130]	122	[122, 126]	129	[127, 130]
Guinea	128	[124, 129]	131	[126, 132]	119	[114, 128]
Mali	129	[125, 129]	129	[124, 129]	126	[123, 126]
Burundi	130	[129, 131]	126	[126, 130]	130	[127, 131]
Niger	131	[125, 132]	124	[124, 128]	131	[122, 132]
Angola	132	[131, 132]	132	[131, 132]	132	[131, 132]

Source: European Commission, Joint Research Centre, 2023.
Notes: Confidence intervals are calculated over 4,000 simulated scenarios combining simulated weights, imputation versus no imputation of missing values, and geometric versus arithmetic average at the pillar level.

Appendix III
Sources and definitions

This appendix complements the economy profiles and the online data tables by providing the title, description, definition and source for each of the 80 indicators included in the Global Innovation Index (GII) this year.

For all 132 economies in the GII in 2023, the most recent values, within the period 2013 to 2023, were used for each indicator.

The year provided next to the indicator description (directly below the indicator title) corresponds to the year when data were most frequently available for economies. When more than one year is considered, the period used is indicated at the end of the indicator's source in parentheses.

Of the 80 indicators, 64 variables are hard data, 11 are composite indicators, marked with an asterisk (*), and five are survey questions from the World Economic Forum's Executive Opinion Survey (three) and from the Global Entrepreneurship Monitor's National Expert Survey (NES) (two), marked with a dagger (†). Instances marked with [a] signal indicators that were assigned half weights and those marked with [b] are indicators where higher scores indicate poorer outcomes, commonly known as "bads." Appendix I presents more details on the computation.

Some indicators are scaled during computation to make them comparable across economies. Indicators are scaled either in relation to other comparable indicators or through division by gross domestic product (GDP) in current US dollars, purchasing power parity GDP in international dollars (PPP$ GDP), population, total trade, etc. In all cases, the scaling factor used was the value that corresponded to the same year of the indicator.

1. Institutions

1.1. Institutional environment

1.1.1. Operational stability for businesses*
Political, legal, operational or security risk index*[b] | 2022

Index that measures the likelihood and severity of political, legal, operational or security risks affecting business operations. Scores are annualized, standardized and aggregated for end Q1, Q2, Q3 and Q4.

Source: S&P Global, Market Intelligence, Country Risk Dataset (www.marketplace.spglobal.com/en/datasets/country-risk-(255)). Data year: 2022.

1.1.2. Government effectiveness*
Government effectiveness index* | 2021

Index that reflects perceptions of the quality of public services, the quality of the civil service and the degree of its independence from political pressures, the quality of policy formulation and implementation, and the credibility of the government's commitment to such policies. Scores are standardized.

Source: World Bank, Worldwide Governance Indicators (http://info.worldbank.org/governance/wgi). Data year: 2021.

1.2. Regulatory environment

1.2.1. Regulatory quality*

Regulatory quality index*[a] | 2021

Index that reflects perceptions of the ability of the government to formulate and implement sound policies and regulations that permit and promote private-sector development. Scores are standardized.

Source: World Bank, Worldwide Governance Indicators (http://info.worldbank.org/governance/wgi). Data year: 2021.

1.2.2. Rule of law*

Rule of law index*[a] | 2021

Index that reflects perceptions of the extent to which agents have confidence in and abide by the rules of society, and in particular the quality of contract enforcement, property rights, the police and the courts, as well as the likelihood of crime and violence. Scores are standardized.

Source: World Bank, Worldwide Governance Indicators (http://info.worldbank.org/governance/wgi). Data year: 2021.

1.2.3. Cost of redundancy dismissal

Sum of notice period and severance pay for redundancy dismissal (salary in weeks, averages for workers with one, five and 10 years of tenure, with a minimum threshold of eight weeks)[b] | 2020

Redundancy costs measure the cost of advance notice requirements and severance payments due when terminating a redundant worker's employment, expressed in weeks of salary. The average value of notice requirements and severance payments applicable to a worker with one year of tenure, a worker with five years and a worker with 10 years are considered. One month is recorded as 4.3 weeks. If the redundancy cost adds up to eight or fewer weeks of salary, a value of eight is assigned but the actual number of weeks is published. If the cost adds up to more than eight weeks of salary, the score is the number of weeks.

Source: World Bank, Employing Workers Project (www.worldbank.org/en/research/employing-workers). Data year: 2020.

1.3. Business environment

1.3.1. Policies for doing business†

The extent to which governments ensure a stable policy environment for doing business† | 2022

Average answer to the survey question: In your country, to what extent does the government ensure a stable policy environment for doing business? [1 = not at all; 7 = to a great extent].

Source: World Economic Forum, Executive Opinion Survey 2022 (www.weforum.org). Data years: 2018–2022.

1.3.2. Entrepreneurship policies and culture†

Entrepreneurship policies and culture index† | 2022

Average perception scores (five-year average) of experts on entrepreneurial policies and entrepreneurial culture (Items B, C and I3 and I4 of the Global Entrepreneurship Monitor (GEM) National Expert Survey (NES)). Experts in different fields (purposive sampling, minimum 36 experts per year) assess conditions for entrepreneurship in their country via statements (0 = completely false; 10 = completely true). Country participation in GEM varies and therefore the number of experts and years on which this item is based differs according to country.

Source: Global Entrepreneurship Monitor (GEM), National Expert Survey (NES) (www.gemconsortium.org/wiki/1142). Data years: 2015–2022.

2. Human capital and research

2.1. Education

2.1.1. Expenditure on education, % GDP

Government expenditure on education (% of GDP) | 2021

Total general (local, regional and central) government expenditure on education (current, capital and transfers), expressed as a percentage of GDP. It includes expenditure funded by transfers from international sources to government.

Source: UNESCO Institute for Statistics (UIS) online database (http://data.uis.unesco.org). Data years: 2013–2022.

2.1.2. Government funding/pupil, secondary, % GDP/cap

Government funding per secondary pupil (% of GDP per capita) | 2019

Average total (current, capital and transfers) general government expenditure per student at secondary level, expressed as a percentage of GDP per capita.

Source: UNESCO Institute for Statistics (UIS) online database (http://data.uis.unesco.org). Data years: 2013–2021.

2.1.3. School life expectancy, years

School life expectancy, primary to tertiary education, both sexes (years) | 2020

Total number of years that a person of school entrance age can expect to spend within the primary to tertiary levels of education. For a child of a given age, the school life expectancy is calculated as the sum of the age-specific enrolment rates for primary to tertiary levels of education. The part of the enrolment that is not distributed by age is divided by the school-age population for the primary to tertiary level of education in which they are enrolled and multiplied by the duration of that level of education. The result is then added to the sum of the age-specific enrolment rates. A relatively high value indicates a greater probability of children spending more years in education and a higher overall retention rate within the education system. It must be noted that the expected number of years does not necessarily coincide with the expected number of grades of education completed due to grade repetition.

Source: UNESCO Institute for Statistics (UIS) online database (http://data.uis.unesco.org). Data years: 2013–2022.

2.1.4. PISA scales in reading, maths and science

PISA scales in reading, mathematics and science | 2018

PISA is the OECD's (Organisation for Economic Co-operation and Development) Programme for International Student Assessment. PISA measures 15-year-olds' ability to use their reading, mathematics and science knowledge skills. Results from PISA indicate the quality and equity of learning outcomes attained around the world. The 2018 PISA survey is the seventh round of the triennial assessment.

The indicator is built using the average of the reading, mathematics and science scores for each country. PISA scores are set in relation to the variation in results observed across all test participants in a country. There is, theoretically, no minimum or maximum score in

PISA; rather, the results are scaled to fit approximately normal distributions, with means around 500 score points and standard deviations around 100 score points.

The 2018 scores for China correspond to the provinces/municipalities of Beijing, Shanghai, Jiangsu and Zhejiang only. The 2018 scores for Azerbaijan correspond only to the capital Baku. The 2018 average scores for Spain are based only on the scores for mathematics and science, as the reading scores were not published by the OECD owing to implausible student response behavior.

Source: OECD Programme for International Student Assessment (PISA) (www.oecd.org/pisa). Data years: 2015–2018.

2.1.5. Pupil–teacher ratio, secondary

Pupil–teacher ratio, secondary[b] | 2020

The number of pupils enrolled in secondary school divided by the number of secondary school teachers (regardless of their teaching assignment). Where the data are missing for the secondary education level as a whole, the ratios for upper-secondary are reported; if these are also missing, the ratios for lower-secondary education are reported instead. A high pupil–teacher ratio suggests that each teacher has to be responsible for a large number of pupils. In other words, the higher the pupil–teacher ratio, the lower the relative access of pupils to teachers.

Source: UNESCO Institute for Statistics (UIS) online database (http://data.uis.unesco.org). Data years: 2013–2022.

2.2. Tertiary education

2.2.1. Tertiary enrolment, % gross

School enrolment, tertiary (% gross) | 2020

The ratio of total tertiary enrolment, regardless of age, to the population of the age group that officially corresponds to the tertiary level of education. Tertiary education, whether or not at an advanced research qualification level, normally requires, as a minimum condition of admission, the successful completion of education at the secondary level. The school enrolment ratio can exceed 100 percent due to grade repetition and the inclusion of under-aged and over-aged students, who are early or late entrants.

Source: UNESCO Institute for Statistics (UIS) online database (http://data.uis.unesco.org). Data years: 2014–2022.

2.2.2. Graduates in science and engineering, %

Graduates from science, technology, engineering and mathematics programs (% of total tertiary graduates) | 2020

The share of all tertiary-level graduates in natural sciences, mathematics, statistics, information and technology, manufacturing, engineering and construction as a percentage of all tertiary-level graduates.

Source: UNESCO Institute for Statistics (UIS) online database (http://data.uis.unesco.org); Eurostat database (https://ec.europa.eu/eurostat/data/database); and OECD, Education at a Glance (https://stats.oecd.org/Index.aspx?DatasetCode=RGRADSTY). Data years: 2015–2022.

2.2.3. Tertiary inbound mobility, %

Tertiary inbound mobility rate (%) | 2020

The number of students from abroad studying in a given country as a percentage of the total tertiary-level enrolment in that country.

Source: UNESCO Institute for Statistics (UIS) online database (http://data.uis.unesco.org). Data years: 2015–2022.

2.3. Research and development (R&D)

2.3.1. Researchers, FTE/mn pop.

Researchers, full-time equivalent (FTE) (per million population)[a] | 2021

Researchers in R&D are professionals engaged in the conception or creation of new knowledge. They conduct research and improve or develop concepts, theories, models, techniques, instrumentation, software or operational methods.

Source: UNESCO Institute for Statistics (UIS) online database (http://data.uis.unesco.org); Eurostat database (https://ec.europa.eu/eurostat/data/database); OECD, Main Science and Technology Indicators (MSTI) database (https://stats.oecd.org/Index.aspx?DataSetCode=MSTI_PUB); and Ibero-American and Inter-American Network of Science and Technology Indicators (RICYT) (www.ricyt.org/en/). Data years: 2013–2021.

2.3.2. Gross expenditure on R&D, % GDP

Gross expenditure on R&D (% of GDP)[a] | 2021

Gross expenditure on R&D (GERD) is the total domestic intramural expenditure on R&D during a given period as a percentage of GDP. "Intramural R&D expenditure" is all expenditure for R&D performed within a statistical unit or sector of the economy during a specific period, regardless of the source of funding.

Source: UNESCO Institute for Statistics (UIS) online database (http://data.uis.unesco.org); Eurostat database (https://ec.europa.eu/eurostat/data/database); OECD, Main Science and Technology Indicators (MSTI) database (https://stats.oecd.org/Index.aspx?DataSetCode=MSTI_PUB); and Ibero-American and Inter-American Network of Science and Technology Indicators (RICYT) (www.ricyt.org/en/). Data years: 2013–2022.

2.3.3. Global corporate R&D investors, top 3, mn USD

Average expenditure of a country's top three global companies on R&D, million USD | 2022

Average expenditure on R&D of the top three global companies. If a country has fewer than three global companies listed, the figure is either the average of the sum of the two companies listed or the total for a single listed company. A score of 0 is given to countries with no listed companies. The data include economies outside the European Union (EU).

Source: The 2022 EU Industrial R&D Investment Scoreboard (https://iri.jrc.ec.europa.eu/scoreboard/2022-eu-industrial-rd-investment-scoreboard). Data year: 2022.

2.3.4. QS university ranking, top 3*

Average score of the top three universities according to the QS world university ranking* | 2022

Average score of the top three universities per country. If fewer than three universities are listed in the QS ranking of the global top 1,000 universities, the sum of the scores of the listed universities is divided by three, thus implying a score of zero for the non-listed universities. The 2023 ranking corresponds to data published in March 2022.

Source: QS Quacquarelli Symonds Ltd, QS World University Rankings, Top Global Universities (www.topuniversities.com/university-rankings/world-university-rankings/2023). Data year: 2022.

3. Infrastructure

3.1. Information and communication technologies (ICTs)

3.1.1. ICT access*

ICT access index* | 2021

The ICT access index is a composite index that assigns weights to four ICT indicators (25 percent each): (1) Percentage of the population covered by mobile networks (at least 3G, at least LTE/WiMax); (2) Mobile cellular telephone subscriptions per 100 inhabitants; (3) International internet bandwidth (bit/s) per internet user; and (4) Percentage of households with internet access.

Source: World Intellectual Property Organization (www.wipo.int); and World Telecommunication/ICT Indicators Database (released January 2023) (www.itu.int/en/ITU-D/Statistics/Pages/publications/wtid.aspx). Data year: 2021.

3.1.2. ICT use*

ICT use index* | 2021

The ICT use index is a composite index that assigns weights to four ICT indicators (25 percent each): (1) Percentage of individuals using the internet; (2) Fixed (wired) broadband internet subscriptions per 100 inhabitants; (3) Active mobile broadband subscriptions per 100 inhabitants; and (4) Mobile broadband internet traffic (gigabytes/subscriptions).

Source: World Intellectual Property Organization (www.wipo.int); and World Telecommunication/ICT Indicators Database (released January 2023) (www.itu.int/en/ITU-D/Statistics/Pages/publications/wtid.aspx). Data year: 2021.

3.1.3. Government's online service*

Government online service index* | 2022

The Online Service Index (OSI) is a component of the E-Government Development Index. The OSI is a composite indicator that assesses how well governments use technology to deliver public services at the national level. It is based on a survey of national websites and e-government policies, with scores normalized to a range of 0 to 1. In the 2022 edition, the OSI is now calculated based on five weighted sub-indices: services provision (45 percent), technology (5 percent), institutional framework (10 percent), content provision (5 percent) and e-participation (35 percent), with the overall score calculated from the normalized values of each sub-index.

Source: Division for Public Institutions and Digital Government (DPIDG) of the United Nations Department of Economic and Social Affairs (UN DESA), E-Government Survey 2022 (https://publicadministration.un.org/egovkb/en-us/Reports/UN-E-Government-Survey-2022). Data year: 2022.

3.1.4. E-participation*

E-Participation Index* | 2022

The E-Participation Index (EPI) is a measure of citizen engagement in public policymaking through e-government programs. It is a supplement to the United Nations E-Government Survey, which assesses how well governments use online services to provide information, interact with stakeholders and engage in decision-making. Scores range from 0 to 1, with higher values indicating greater e-participation. The index questions are periodically updated to reflect changes in e-government trends and technologies. In the 2022 Survey, the e-participation questions were further expanded to reflect current trends and modalities relating to the ways in which governments promote the engagement of their people in public policymaking, implementation and evaluation.

Source: Division for Public Institutions and Digital Government (DPIDG) of the United Nations Department of Economic and Social Affairs (UN DESA), E-Government Survey 2022 (https://publicadministration.un.org/egovkb/en-us/Reports/UN-E-Government-Survey-2022). Data year: 2022.

3.2. General infrastructure

3.2.1. Electricity output, GWh/mn pop.

Electricity output (GWh per million population) | 2021

Electricity production, measured at the terminals of all alternator sets in a station. In addition to hydropower, coal, oil, gas and nuclear power generation, this indicator covers the generation of electricity by means of geothermal, solar, wind, tide and wave energy, as well as that from combustible renewables and waste. Production includes the output of plants that are designed to produce solely electricity, as well as the output of combined heat and power plants. Electricity output in GWh is scaled by population.

Source: International Energy Agency (IEA) World Energy Balances, 2022 edition and April 2023 edition (Population) (www.iea.org/reports/world-energy-balances-overview). Data years: 2020–2021.

3.2.2. Logistics performance*

Logistics Performance Index* | 2023

A multidimensional assessment of logistics performance, the 2023 Logistics Performance Index (LPI) ranks 139 countries, combining data on six core performance components into a single aggregate measure that includes customs performance, infrastructure quality and timeliness of shipments. The data used in the ranking come from a survey of logistics professionals who are asked questions about the foreign countries in which they operate. The LPI's six components are: (1) Customs: the efficiency of customs and border management clearance; (2) Infrastructure: the quality of trade and transport infrastructure; (3) International shipments: the ease of arranging competitively priced shipments; (4) Services quality: the competence and quality of logistics services; (5) Tracking and tracing: the ability to track and trace consignments; and (6) Timeliness: the frequency with which shipments reach consignees within scheduled or expected delivery times.

Source: World Bank, *Connecting to Compete 2023: Trade Logistics in the Global Economy – The Logistics Performance Index and its Indicators* (https://lpi.worldbank.org). Data year: 2023.

3.2.3. Gross capital formation, % GDP

Gross capital formation (% of GDP) | 2022

Gross capital formation is expressed as the ratio of total investment in current local currency to GDP in current local currency. Investment or gross capital formation is measured by the total value of the gross fixed capital formation and changes in inventories and acquisitions less disposals of valuables for a unit or sector, on the basis of the System of National Accounts (SNA) 1993.

Source: International Monetary Fund, World Economic Outlook Database, October 2022 (www.imf.org/en/Publications/WEO/weo-database/2022/October). Data years: 2021–2022.

3.3. Ecological sustainability

3.3.1. GDP/unit of energy use

GDP per total energy supply (per thousand 2015 PPP$ GDP) | 2020

Purchasing power parity gross domestic product (2015 PPP$ GDP) per total energy supply (TES). TES is made up of production + imports – exports – international marine bunkers – international aviation bunkers +/– stock changes. GDP/TES is an indicator of energy productivity.

Source: International Energy Agency (IEA) World Energy Balances, 2022 edition (www.iea.org/reports/world-energy-balances-overview). Data years: 2020–2021.

3.3.2. Environmental performance*

Environmental Performance Index* | 2022

The 2022 Environmental Performance Index (EPI) ranks 180 countries on different categories covering environmental health and ecosystem vitality. These indicators provide a gauge of how close countries are to achieving established environmental policy targets. The EPI offers a scorecard that highlights leaders and laggards in environmental performance and provides practical guidance for countries that aspire to move toward a sustainable future. The index ranges from 0 to 100, with 100 indicating best performance.

Source: Wolf, M.J., Emerson, J.W., Esty, D.C., de Sherbinin, A., Wendling, Z.A., *et al.* (2022). *2022 Environmental Performance Index*. New Haven, CT: Yale Center for Environmental Law & Policy (https://epi.yale.edu). Data year: 2022.

3.3.3. ISO 14001 environment/bn PPP$ GDP

ISO 14001 Environmental management systems – Number of certificates issued (per billion PPP$ GDP) | 2021

ISO 14001 specifies the requirements for an environmental management system that an organization can use to enhance its environmental performance. ISO 14001 is intended for use by an organization that is seeking to manage its environmental responsibilities in a systematic manner that contributes to the environmental pillar of sustainability. ISO 14001 helps an organization to achieve the intended outcomes of its environmental management system, providing value for the environment, the organization itself and interested parties. Consistent with the organization's environmental policy, the intended outcomes of an environmental management system include enhancement of environmental performance, fulfillment of compliance obligations and achievement of environmental objectives. ISO 14001 is applicable to any organization, regardless of size, type or nature, and applies to the environmental aspects of its activities, products and services that the organization determines it can either control or influence from a life-cycle perspective. ISO 14001 does not state specific environmental performance criteria. It can be used in whole or in part to systematically improve environmental management. Claims of conformity to ISO 14001, however, are not acceptable unless all its requirements are incorporated into an organization's environmental management system and fulfilled without exclusion. The data are reported per billion PPP$ GDP.

Source: International Organization for Standardization, ISO Survey of Certifications to Management System Standards, 2021 (www.iso.org/the-iso-survey.html); and International Monetary Fund, World Economic Outlook Database, October 2022 (www.imf.org/en/Publications/WEO/weo-database/2022/October). Data year: 2021.

4. Market sophistication

4.1. Credit

4.1.1. Finance for startups and scaleups†

Finance for startups and scaleups† | 2022

Average perception scores (five-year average) of experts on finance for starting and growing firms (Item A1 of the GEM National Expert Survey). Experts in different fields (purposive sampling, minimum 36 experts per year) assess conditions for entrepreneurship in their country via statements (0 = completely false; 10 = completely true). Country participation in GEM varies and therefore the number of experts and years on which this item is based differs according to country.

Source: Global Entrepreneurship Monitor (GEM), National Expert Survey (NES) (www.gemconsortium.org/wiki/1142). Data years: 2015–2022.

4.1.2. Domestic credit to private sector, % GDP

Domestic credit to private sector (% of GDP) | 2020

Domestic credit to private sector refers to financial resources provided to the private sector by financial corporations, such as through loans, purchases of non-equity securities and trade credits and other accounts receivable, that establish a claim for repayment. For some countries, these claims include credit to public enterprises. The financial corporations include monetary authorities and deposit money banks, as well as other financial corporations where data are available (including corporations that do not allow transferable deposits but do accept such liabilities as time and savings deposits). Examples of other financial corporations are finance and leasing companies, money lenders, insurance corporations, pension funds and foreign exchange companies.

Source: International Monetary Fund, International Financial Statistics and data files (https://data.imf.org); and World Bank and OECD GDP estimates, extracted from the World Bank's World Development Indicators database (https://databank.worldbank.org/source/world-development-indicators). Data years: 2015–2020.

4.1.3. Loans from microfinance institutions, % GDP

Loans from all microfinance institutions (% of GDP) | 2021

Outstanding loans from all microfinance institutions in a country as a percentage of its GDP.

Source: International Monetary Fund, Financial Access Survey (https://data.imf.org/?sk=E5DCAB7E-A5CA-4892-A6EA-598B5463A34C). Data years: 2014–2021.

4.2. Investment

4.2.1. Market capitalization, % GDP

Market capitalization of listed domestic companies (% of GDP, three-year average) | 2020

Market capitalization (also known as "market value") is the share price times the number of shares outstanding (including their several classes) for listed domestic companies. Investment funds, unit trusts and companies whose only business goal is to hold shares of other listed companies are excluded. Data are the average of the end-of-year values for the last three years.

Source: World Federation of Exchanges database (www.world-exchanges.org/our-work/statistics); and extracted from the World Bank's World Development Indicators database (https://databank.worldbank.org/source/world-development-indicators). Data years: 2014–2020.

4.2.2. Venture capital (VC) investors, deals/bn PPP$ GDP

Number of venture capital deals invested in (per billion PPP$ GDP, three-year average) | 2022

Refinitiv data on private equity deals, per deal, with information on the location of the firm investing in a venture capital (VC) deal, among other details. The data extraction corresponds to a query on VC deals between January 1, 2020 and December 31, 2022, with the data aggregated by the location of the investing firm. The data represent the three-year average of 2020–2022 deals invested in and are reported per billion PPP$ GDP.

Source: Refinitiv (a London Stock Exchange Group (LSEG) business) Eikon (private equity screener) accessed April 6, 2023 (https://solutions.refinitiv.com/eikon-trading-software); and International Monetary Fund World Economic Outlook Database, October 2022 (www.imf.org/en/Publications/WEO/weo-database/2022/October). Data years: 2020–2022.

4.2.3. VC recipients, deals/bn PPP$ GDP

Number of venture capital deals received (per billion PPP$ GDP, three-year average) | 2022

Refinitiv data on private equity deals, per deal, with information on the location of the firm receiving the VC investment, among other details. The data extraction corresponds to a query on VC deals between January 1, 2020 and December 31, 2022, with the data aggregated by the location invested in. The data represent the three-year average of 2020–2022 deals received and are reported per billion PPP$ GDP.

Source: Refinitiv (an LSEG business) Eikon (private equity screener) accessed March 24, 2023 (https://solutions.refinitiv.com/eikon-trading-software); and International Monetary Fund, World Economic Outlook Database, October 2022 (www.imf.org/en/Publications/WEO/weo-database/2022/October). Data years: 2020–2022.

4.2.4. VC received, value, % GDP

Total value of venture capital received (% of GDP, three-year average) | 2022

Refinitiv data on the monetary value of private equity deals, per deal, with information on the location of the firm receiving the VC investment, among other details. The data extraction corresponds to a query on VC deals between January 1, 2020 and December 31, 2022, with the data aggregated by the location invested in. The data represent the three-year average of reported deal value received, in current USD (billions).

Source: Refinitiv (an LSEG business) Eikon (private equity screener) accessed March 24, 2023 (https://solutions.refinitiv.com/eikon-trading-software); and International Monetary Fund, World Economic Outlook Database, October 2022 (www.imf.org/en/Publications/WEO/weo-database/2022/October). Data years: 2020–2022.

4.3. Trade, diversification and market scale

4.3.1. Applied tariff rate, weighted avg., %

Tariff rate, applied, weighted average, all products (%)[b] | 2020

Weighted average applied tariff is the average of effectively applied rates weighted by the product import shares corresponding to each partner country. Data are classified using the Harmonized System of trade at the six- or eight-digit level. Tariff line data were matched to Standard International Trade Classification (SITC) Revision 3 codes to define commodity groups and import weights. As far as possible, specific rates have been converted to their ad valorem equivalent rates and have been included in the calculation of weighted average tariffs. Effectively applied tariff rates at the six- and eight-digit product level are averaged for products in each commodity group. When the effectively applied rate is unavailable, the most favored nation rate is used instead. Data extracted from the World Bank's World Development Indicators database.

Source: World Bank, based on data from United Nations Conference on Trade and Development's Trade Analysis Information System (TRAINS) database and the World Trade Organization's Integrated Database (IDB) and Consolidated Tariff Schedules (CTS) database (http://data.worldbank.org). Data years: 2013–2020.

4.3.2. Domestic industry diversification

Domestic industry diversification (based on manufacturing output)[b] | 2020

The Herfindahl-Hirschman Index (HHI) for a country's industry is defined as the sum of the squared shares of subsectors in total manufacturing output. The HHI is a measure of concentration and can help to determine the extent to which a country's industrial system is diversified across different industrial subsectors (or, conversely, concentrated in a few industrial subsectors). A country with a perfectly diversified industrial system will have an index close to zero, whereas a country that is active in only one industrial subsector will have a value of one (least diversified).

Source: United Nations Industrial Development Organization (UNIDO), Industrial Statistics Database, two-digit level of the International Standard Industrial Classification (ISIC) Revision 3 (INDSTAT 2 2022), Enhancing the Quality of Industrial Policies (EQuIP) Tool 4: Diversification - Domestic and Export Dimensions, 2015 (http://stat.unido.org). Data years: 2013–2021.

4.3.3. Domestic market scale, bn PPP$
Domestic market scale as measured by GDP, bn PPP$ | 2022

The domestic market size is measured by GDP based on the PPP valuation of country GDP, in current international dollars (billions).

Source: International Monetary Fund, World Economic Outlook Database, October 2022 (www.imf.org/en/Publications/WEO/weo-database/2022/October). Data years: 2020–2022.

5. Business sophistication

5.1. Knowledge workers

5.1.1. Knowledge-intensive employment, %
Employment in knowledge-intensive services (% of workforce, 15+ years old) | 2022

Sum of people in categories 1 to 3 as a percentage of total people employed, according to the International Standard Classification of Occupations (ISCO). Categories included in ISCO-08 are: 1 Managers; 2 Professionals; 3 Technicians and associate professionals. Where ISCO-08 data were not available, ISCO-88 data were used. Categories included in ISCO-88 are: 1 Legislators, senior officials and managers; 2 Professionals; 3 Technicians and associate professionals.

Source: International Labour Organization (ILO), ILOSTAT Database of Labour Statistics (https://ilostat.ilo.org). Data years: 2014–2022.

5.1.2. Firms offering formal training, %
Firms offering formal training (% of firms) | 2019

The percentage of firms offering formal training programs for their permanent, full-time employees in the sample of firms in the World Bank's Enterprise Survey in each country. Data for Bangladesh, India, Iraq and Madagascar, published in 2022, and data covering the COVID-19 period are not being used after discussions with the Enterprise Survey World Bank staff.

Source: World Bank Enterprise Surveys (www.enterprisesurveys.org). Data years: 2013–2021.

5.1.3. GERD performed by business, % GDP
GERD performed by business enterprises (% of GDP) | 2021

Gross expenditure on R&D performed by business enterprises as a percentage of GDP. For the definition of GERD, see indicator 2.3.2.

Source: UNESCO Institute for Statistics (UIS) online database (http://data.uis.unesco.org); Eurostat database (https://ec.europa.eu/eurostat/data/database); OECD, Main Science and Technology Indicators (MSTI) database (https://stats.oecd.org/Index.aspx?DataSetCode=MSTI_PUB); and Ibero-American and Inter-American Network of Science and Technology Indicators (RICYT) (www.ricyt.org/en/). Data years: 2013–2022.

5.1.4. GERD financed by business, %

GERD financed by business enterprises (% of GERD) | 2020

Gross expenditure on R&D financed by business enterprises as a percentage of total gross expenditure on R&D. For the definition of GERD, see indicator 2.3.2.

Source: UNESCO Institute for Statistics (UIS) online database (http://data.uis.unesco.org); Eurostat database (https://ec.europa.eu/eurostat/data/database); OECD, Main Science and Technology Indicators (MSTI) database (https://stats.oecd.org/Index.aspx?DataSetCode=MSTI_PUB); and Ibero-American and Inter-American Network of Science and Technology Indicators (RICYT) (www.ricyt.org/en/). Data years: 2013–2022.

5.1.5. Females employed w/advanced degrees, %

Females employed with advanced degrees (% total employed, 25+ years old) | 2022

The percentage of females employed with advanced degrees out of total employed. The employed comprise all persons of working age who, during a specified brief period, were in one of the following categories: (1) paid employment; or (2) self-employment. Data are disaggregated by level of education, which refers to the highest level of education completed, classified according to the International Standard Classification of Education (ISCE). Data for Canada are based on Table 14-10-0020-01 of the country's Labour Force Survey estimates.

Source: International Labour Organization, ILOSTAT Database of Labour Statistics (https://ilostat.ilo.org); and Statistics Canada, Table 14-10-0020-01 Unemployment rate, participation rate and employment rate by educational attainment, annual (www150.statcan.gc.ca/t1/tbl1/en/tv.action?pid=1410002001). Data years: 2013–2022.

5.2. Innovation linkages

5.2.1. University–industry R&D collaboration†

The extent to which businesses and universities collaborate on R&D† | 2022

Average answer to the survey question: In your country, to what extent do businesses and universities collaborate on research and development (R&D)? [1 = not at all; 7 = to a great extent].

Source: World Economic Forum, Executive Opinion Survey 2022 (www.weforum.org). Data years: 2018–2022.

5.2.2. State of cluster development†

How widespread clusters are† | 2022

Average answer to the survey question: In your country, how widespread are well-developed and deep clusters (geographic concentrations of firms, suppliers, producers of related products and services, and specialized institutions in a particular field)? [1 = nonexistent; 7 = widespread in many fields].

Source: World Economic Forum, Executive Opinion Survey 2022 (www.weforum.org). Data years: 2018–2022.

5.2.3. GERD financed by abroad, % GDP

GERD financed by abroad (% of GDP) | 2020

Percentage of gross expenditure on R&D financed by abroad (billions, national currency) – that is, with foreign financing as a percentage of GDP (billions, national currency). For the definition of GERD, see indicator 2.3.2.

Source: UNESCO Institute for Statistics (UIS) online database (http://data.uis.unesco.org); Eurostat database (https://ec.europa.eu/eurostat/data/database); OECD, Main Science and Technology Indicators (MSTI) database (https://stats.oecd.org/Index.aspx?DataSetCode=MSTI_PUB); and Ibero-American and Inter-American Network of Science and Technology Indicators (RICYT) (www.ricyt.org/en/). Data years: 2013–2022.

5.2.4. Joint venture/strategic alliance deals/bn PPP$ GDP

Number of joint venture/strategic alliance deals, fractional counting (per billion PPP$ GDP, three-year average) | 2022

Refinitiv's data on joint ventures/strategic alliances, per deal, with details on the country of origin of partner firms, among others. The data extraction corresponds to a query on joint venture/strategic alliance deals between January 1, 2020 and December 31, 2022. The nation of each company participating in a deal (n companies per deal) is allocated, per deal, a score equivalent to $1/n$ (with the effect that all country scores add up to the total number of deals). The data are reported per billion PPP$ GDP.

Source: Refinitiv (an LSEG business) SDC Platinum database (www.refinitiv.com/en/financial-data/deals-data/joint-venture-deals); and International Monetary Fund World Economic Outlook Database, October 2022 (www.imf.org/en/Publications/WEO/weo-database/2022/October). Data years: 2020–2022.

5.2.5. Patent families/bn PPP$ GDP

Number of patent families filed in at least two offices (per billion PPP$ GDP) | 2019

A patent family is a set of interrelated patent applications filed in one or more countries or jurisdictions to protect the same invention. Patent families containing applications filed in at least two different offices is a subset of patent families where protection of the same invention is sought in at least two different countries. In this report, "patent families data" refers to patent families containing applications filed in at least two intellectual property (IP) offices; the data are scaled by PPP$ GDP (billions). A patent is a set of exclusive rights granted by law to applicants for inventions that are new, non-obvious and industrially applicable. A patent is valid for a limited period of time (generally 20 years) and within a defined territory. The patent system is designed to encourage innovation by providing innovators with time-limited exclusive legal rights, thus enabling them to reap the rewards of their innovative activity.

Source: World Intellectual Property Organization, Intellectual Property Statistics (www.wipo.int/ipstats); and International Monetary Fund, World Economic Outlook Database, October 2022 (www.imf.org/en/Publications/WEO/weo-database/2022/October). Data year: 2019.

5.3. Knowledge absorption

5.3.1. Intellectual property payments, % total trade

Charges for use of intellectual property, i.e., payments (% of total trade, three-year average) | 2021

Charges for the use of intellectual property not included elsewhere, i.e., payments (% of total trade), average of three most recent years or most recent year. Value is calculated according to the Extended Balance of Payments Services Classification EBOPS 2010 – that is, code SH: Charges for the use of intellectual property not included elsewhere, as a percentage of total trade. Total trade is defined as the sum of total imports of code G goods and code SOX commercial services (excluding government goods and services not included elsewhere) plus total exports of code G goods and code SOX commercial services (excluding government goods and services not included elsewhere), divided by 2. According to the sixth edition (2009) of the International Monetary Fund's *Balance of Payments and International Investment Position Manual*, the item "Goods" covers general merchandise, net exports of goods under merchanting and non-monetary gold. The "commercial services" category is defined as being equal to "services" minus "government goods and services not included elsewhere." Receipts are between residents and non-residents for the use of proprietary rights (such as patents, trademarks, copyrights, industrial processes and designs, including trade secrets and franchises), and for licenses to reproduce or distribute (or both) intellectual property embodied in produced originals or prototypes (such as copyrights on books and manuscripts, computer software, cinematographic works and sound recordings) and related rights (such as for live performances and television, cable or satellite broadcast).

Source: World Trade Organization and United Nations Conference on Trade and Development, Trade in Commercial Services database (www.wto.org/english/thewto_e/coher_e/wto_unctad_e.htm). Data years: 2014–2021.

5.3.2. High-tech imports, % total trade
High-tech imports (% of total trade) | 2021

High-technology imports as a percentage of total trade. High-technology exports and imports contain technical products with a high intensity of R&D, defined by the Eurostat classification, which is based on Standard International Trade Classification (SITC) Revision 4 and the OECD definition (see http://ec.europa.eu/eurostat/cache/metadata/Annexes/htec_esms_an5.pdf). Commodities belong to the following sectors: aerospace; computers and office machines; electronics - telecommunications; pharmacy; scientific instruments; electrical machinery; chemistry; non-electrical machinery; and armament.

Source: United Nations Comtrade Database (http://comtrade.un.org); and World Trade Organization and United Nations Conference on Trade and Development (www.wto.org/english/thewto_e/coher_e/wto_unctad_e.htm). Data years: 2015–2021.

5.3.3. ICT services imports, % total trade
Telecommunications, computer and information services imports (% of total trade) | 2021

Telecommunications, computer and information services imports as a percentage of total trade according to the OECD's Extended Balance of Payments Services Classification EBOPS 2010, coded SI: Telecommunications, computer, and information services. Values are based on the classification of the sixth (2009) edition of the International Monetary Fund's *Balance of Payments and International Investment Position Manual* and Balance of Payments database. For the definition of total trade, see indicator 5.3.1.

Source: World Trade Organization and United Nations Conference on Trade and Development, Trade in Commercial Services database (www.wto.org/english/thewto_e/coher_e/wto_unctad_e.htm). Data years: 2014–2021.

5.3.4. FDI net inflows, % GDP
Foreign direct investment (FDI) net inflows (% of GDP, three-year average) | 2021

FDI net inflow is the average of the most recent three years of net inflows of investment to acquire a lasting management interest (10 percent or more of voting stock) in an enterprise operating in an economy other than that of the investor. It is the sum of equity capital, reinvestment of earnings, other long-term capital and short-term capital as shown in the balance of payments. This data series shows net inflows (new investment inflows less disinvestment) in the reporting economy from foreign investors, and is divided by GDP. Data extracted from the World Bank's World Development Indicators database.

Source: International Monetary Fund, International Financial Statistics and Balance of Payments databases (https://data.imf.org); World Bank, International Debt Statistics (www.worldbank.org/en/programs/debt-statistics); and OECD GDP estimates (https://data.oecd.org). Data years: 2020–2021.

5.3.5. Research talent, % in businesses
Researchers in business enterprise (%) | 2021

Researchers in the business enterprise sector, measured in full-time equivalence (FTE), refers to researchers as professionals engaged in the conception or creation of new knowledge, products, processes, methods and systems, as well as in the management of these projects, broken down by the sectors in which they are employed (business enterprise, government, higher education and private non-profit organizations). In the context of R&D statistics, the business enterprise sector includes all firms, organizations and institutions whose primary activity is the market production of goods or services (other than higher education) for sale to the general public at an economically significant price, and the mainly private non-profit institutions serving them; the core of this sector is made up of private enterprises.

Source: UNESCO Institute for Statistics (UIS) online database (http://data.uis.unesco.org); Eurostat database (https://ec.europa.eu/eurostat/data/database); OECD, Main Science and Technology Indicators (MSTI) database (https://stats.oecd.org/Index.aspx?DataSetCode=MSTI_PUB); and Ibero-American and Inter-American Network of Science and Technology Indicators (RICYT) (www.ricyt.org/en/). Data years: 2013–2021.

6. Knowledge and technology outputs

6.1. Knowledge creation

6.1.1. Patents by origin/bn PPP$ GDP

Number of resident patent applications filed at a given national or regional patent office (per billion PPP$ GDP) | 2021

The definition of a patent can be found in the description of indicator 5.2.5. A resident patent application refers to an application filed with an IP office for or on behalf of the first-named applicant's country of residence. For example, an application filed with the Japan Patent Office by a resident of Japan is to be considered a resident application for Japan. Similarly, an application filed with the European Patent Office (EPO) by an applicant who resides in any of the EPO member states (for example, Germany) is considered to be a resident application for that member state (Germany). Data are scaled by PPP$ GDP (billions).

Source: World Intellectual Property Organization, Intellectual Property Statistics (www.wipo.int/ipstats); and International Monetary Fund, World Economic Outlook Database, October 2022 (www.imf.org/en/Publications/WEO/weo-database/2022/October). Data years: 2014–2021.

6.1.2. PCT patents by origin/bn PPP$ GDP

Number of Patent Cooperation Treaty (PCT) applications (per billion PPP$ GDP) | 2022

A PCT application refers to an international patent application filed through the WIPO-administered Patent Cooperation Treaty. The PCT system makes it possible to seek patent protection for an invention simultaneously in a number of countries by filing a single international patent application. The origin of PCT applications is defined by the residence of the first-named applicant. Data are available only for those economies that are PCT Contracting States (157 to date). Data are scaled by PPP$ GDP (billions).

Source: World Intellectual Property Organization, Intellectual Property Statistics (www.wipo.int/ipstats); and International Monetary Fund, World Economic Outlook Database, October 2022 (www.imf.org/en/Publications/WEO/weo-database/2022/October). Data years: 2021–2022.

6.1.3. Utility models by origin/bn PPP$ GDP

Number of resident utility model applications filed at the national patent office (per billion PPP$ GDP) | 2021

A utility model (UM) is a special form of patent right. The terms and conditions for granting a UM are slightly different from those for patents and include a shorter term of protection and less stringent patentability requirements. A resident UM application refers to an application filed with an IP office for or on behalf of the first-named applicant's country of residence. For example, an application filed with the IP office of Germany by a resident of

Germany is considered a resident application for Germany. Data are scaled by PPP$ GDP (billions).

Source: World Intellectual Property Organization, Intellectual Property Statistics (www.wipo.int/ipstats); and International Monetary Fund, World Economic Outlook Database, October 2022 (www.imf.org/en/Publications/WEO/weo-database/2022/October). Data years: 2015–2021.

6.1.4. Scientific and technical articles/bn PPP$ GDP

Number of scientific and technical journal articles (per billion PPP$ GDP) | 2022

The number of articles published in the fields of science and technology. This encompasses 182 different research categories belonging to research areas including engineering, chemistry, physics, environmental sciences, computer science, mathematics, biochemistry, molecular biology, oncology, agriculture, cell biology and many more. Article counts are taken from a set of journals covered by the Science Citation Index Expanded (SCIE) and the Social Sciences Citation Index (SSCI). Articles are classified by year of publication and assigned to each economy on the basis of the institutional address(es) listed in the article.

Articles are counted on a count basis (rather than a fractional basis) – that is, for articles with collaborating institutions from multiple economies, each economy receives credit on the basis of its participating institutions. The data are reported per billion PPP$ GDP.

Source: Clarivate, Web of Science, accessed March 21, 2023 (https://clarivate.com/webofsciencegroup/solutions/web-of-science); and International Monetary Fund, World Economic Outlook Database, October 2022 (www.imf.org/en/Publications/WEO/weo-database/2022/October). Data years: 2020–2022.

6.1.5. Citable documents H-index

The H-index is the economy's number of published articles (H) that have received at least H citations | 2022

The H-index expresses the journal's number of articles (H) that have received at least H citations. It quantifies both journal scientific productivity and scientific impact, and is also applicable to scientists, journals, and so on. The H-index is tabulated from the number of citations received in subsequent years by articles published in a given year, divided by the number of articles published that year.

Source: SCImago, SJR – SCImago Journal & Country Rank, retrieved May 2022 (www.scimagojr.com). Data year: 2022.

6.2. Knowledge impact

6.2.1. Labor productivity growth, %

Growth rate of GDP per person employed (%, five-year average) | 2022

Growth rate of real GDP per person employed, average of five most recent available years (2017–2021). Growth of GDP per person engaged provides a measure of labor productivity (defined as output per unit of labor input). GDP per person employed is GDP divided by total employment in the economy.

Source: The Conference Board Total Economy Database™, April 2023 (www.conference-board.org/data/economydatabase). Data years: 2020–2022.

6.2.2. Unicorn valuation, % GDP

Combined valuation of a country's unicorns (% of GDP) | 2023

Total valuation of all unicorns in a country as a percentage of GDP. A unicorn company is a private company with a valuation over USD 1 billion. Unicorn companies worldwide number 1,207 as of April 7, 2023.

Source: CBInsights, Tracker – The Complete List of Unicorn Companies (www.cbinsights.com/research-unicorn-companies); and International Monetary Fund World Economic Outlook Database, October 2022 (www.imf.org/en/Publications/WEO/weo-database/2022/October). Data year: 2023.

6.2.3. Software spending, % GDP

Total computer software spending (% of GDP) | 2022

Computer software spending includes the total value of purchased or leased packaged software, such as operating systems, database systems, programming tools, utilities and applications. It excludes expenditures for internal software development and outsourced custom software development. The data are a combination of actual figures and estimates. Data are reported as a percentage of GDP.

Source: S&P Global, Market Intelligence (www.marketplace.spglobal.com/en/datasets). Data year: 2022.

6.2.4. High-tech manufacturing, %

High-tech and medium-high-tech manufacturing (% of total manufacturing output) | 2020

High-technology and medium-high-technology output as a percentage of total manufacturing output, on the basis of the OECD classification of Technology Intensity Definition (www.oecd.org/sti/ind/48350231.pdf), itself based on International Standard Industrial Classification (ISIC) Revision 4 and Revision 3, and using data from the INDSTAT 2 and INDSTAT 4 databases of the United Nations Industrial Development Organization (UNIDO).

Source: United Nations Industrial Development Organization (UNIDO), Industrial Statistics Database INDSTAT 2 2023 and INDSTAT 4 2023 (https://stat.unido.org). Data years: 2013–2021.

6.3. Knowledge diffusion

6.3.1. Intellectual property receipts, % total trade

Charges for use of intellectual property, i.e., receipts (% total trade, three-year average) | 2021

Charges for the use of intellectual property not included elsewhere, i.e., receipts (% of total trade), average of three most recent years or most recent year. Value is calculated according to the Extended Balance of Payments Services Classification EBOPS 2010 – that is, code SH: Charges for the use of intellectual property not included elsewhere, as a percentage of total trade. Receipts are between residents and non-residents for the use of proprietary rights (such as patents, trademarks, copyrights, industrial processes and designs, including trade secrets and franchises), and for licenses to reproduce or distribute (or both) intellectual property embodied in produced originals or prototypes (such as copyrights on books and manuscripts, computer software, cinematographic works and sound recordings) and related rights (such as for live performances and television, cable, or satellite broadcast). Values are based on the classification of the sixth (2009) edition of the International Monetary Fund's *Balance of Payments and International Investment Position Manual* and Balance of Payments database. For the definition of total trade, see indicator 5.3.1.

Source: World Trade Organization and United Nations Conference on Trade and Development, Trade in Commercial Services database (www.wto.org/english/thewto_e/coher_e/wto_unctad_e.htm). Data years: 2014–2021.

6.3.2. Production and export complexity

The Economic Complexity Index | 2020

The Economic Complexity Index is a ranking of countries based on the diversity and complexity of their export basket. High-complexity countries are home to a range of sophisticated, specialized capabilities and are therefore able to produce a highly diversified set of complex products. Determining the economic complexity of a country is not solely dependent on a country's productive knowledge. Information about how many capabilities the country has is contained not only in the absolute number of products that it makes, but also in the ubiquity of those products (the number of countries that import those products) and in the sophistication and diversity of the products that those other countries make. Economic complexity expresses the diversity and sophistication of the productive capabilities embedded in the exports of each country.

Source: The Atlas of Economic Complexity, Growth Lab at Harvard University (https://atlas.cid.harvard.edu). Data year: 2020.

6.3.3. High-tech exports, % total trade
High-tech exports (% of total trade) | 2021

High-technology exports as a percentage of total trade. See indicator 5.3.2 for details. Data for Hong Kong, China are corrected for re-exports using data from the Trade Data Monitor.

Source: United Nations Comtrade Database (http://comtrade.un.org); World Trade Organization and United Nations Conference on Trade and Development (www.wto.org/english/thewto_e/coher_e/wto_unctad_e.htm); and Trade Data Monitor (www.tradedatamonitor.com). Data years: 2015–2021.

6.3.4. ICT services exports, % total trade
Telecommunications, computer and information services exports (% of total trade) | 2021

Telecommunications, computer and information services exports as a percentage of total trade according to the Extended Balance of Payments Services Classification EBOPS 2010, coded SI: Telecommunications, computer, and information services. Values are based on the classification of the sixth (2009) edition of the International Monetary Fund's *Balance of Payments and International Investment Position Manual* and Balance of Payments database. For the definition of total trade, see indicator 5.3.1.

Source: World Trade Organization and United Nations Conference on Trade and Development, Trade in Commercial Services database (www.wto.org/english/thewto_e/coher_e/wto_unctad_e.htm). Data years: 2014–2021.

6.3.5. ISO 9001 quality/bn PPP$ GDP
ISO 9001 Quality management systems – number of certificates issued (per billion PPP$ GDP) | 2021

ISO 9001 specifies requirements for a quality management system when an organization needs to demonstrate its ability to provide products and services that meet both customer and applicable statutory and regulatory requirements. It aims to enhance customer satisfaction through the effective application of the system, including processes for improving the system and ensuring conformity to customer and applicable statutory and regulatory requirements. All the requirements of ISO 9001 are generic and intended to be applicable to any organization, regardless of type or size, or the products and services it provides. The data are reported per billion PPP$ GDP.

Source: International Organization for Standardization (ISO) Survey 2021 (www.iso.org/the-iso-survey.html); and International Monetary Fund, World Economic Outlook Database, October 2022 (www.imf.org/en/Publications/WEO/weo-database/2022/October). Data year: 2021.

7. Creative outputs

7.1. Intangible assets

7.1.1. Intangible asset intensity, top 15, %

Intangible asset value as a percentage of the firm's total value, average of the top 15 firms | 2022

The data cover a global list of firms for which intangible asset value and total firm value are observed. Only the top 15 firms of each economy are considered, ranked by intangible assets in absolute terms (in USD). Countries with fewer than 15 firms are not considered. For each firm, the intangible asset value is divided by the firm's total value before computing the arithmetic mean across the top 15 firms for each economy.

Source: Brand Finance Global Intangible Finance Tracker (GIFT™) (https://brandirectory.com/reports/gift-2022). Data years: 2021–2022.

7.1.2. Trademarks by origin/bn PPP$ GDP

Number of classes in resident trademark applications issued at a given national or regional office (per billion PPP$ GDP) | 2021

A trademark is a sign used by the owner of certain products or provider of certain services to distinguish them from the products or services of other companies. A trademark can consist of words or a combination of words and other elements, such as slogans, names, logos, figures and images, letters, numbers, sounds and moving images. The procedures for registering trademarks are governed by the legislation and procedures of national and regional IP offices. Trademark rights are limited to the jurisdiction of the IP office that registers the trademark. Trademarks can be registered by filing an application at the relevant national or regional office(s) or by filing an international application through the Madrid System. A resident trademark application refers to an application filed with an IP office for or on behalf of the first-named applicant's country of residence. For example, an application filed with the Japan Patent Office by a resident of Japan is considered to be a resident application for Japan. Similarly, an application filed with the Office for Harmonization in the Internal Market (OHIM) by an applicant who resides in any of the EU member states, such as France, is considered to be a resident application for that member state (France). This indicator is based on class count – the total number of goods and services classes specified in resident trademark applications. Data are scaled by PPP$ GDP (billions).

Source: World Intellectual Property Organization, Intellectual Property Statistics (www.wipo.int/ipstats); and International Monetary Fund, World Economic Outlook Database, October 2022 (www.imf.org/en/Publications/WEO/weo-database/2022/October). Data years: 2013–2021.

7.1.3. Global brand value, top 5,000, % GDP

Global brand value of the top 5,000 brands (% of GDP) | 2023

Sum of global brand values, top 5,000 as a percentage of GDP. Brand Finance calculates brand value using the royalty relief methodology, which determines the value that a company would be willing to pay to license its brand if it did not own it. The methodology is compliant with industry standards set in ISO 10668. This approach involves estimating the future revenue attributable to a brand and calculating a royalty rate that would be charged for the use of the brand. Brand Finance's study is based on publicly available information on the largest brands in the world. This indicator assesses the economy's brands in the top 5,000 global brand database and produces the sum of the brand values corresponding to that economy. This sum is then scaled by GDP. A score of 0 is assigned where there are no brands in the country that make the top 5,000 ranking. A score of "n/a" is assigned where Brand Finance has been unable to determine if there are brands from the country that would rank within the top 5,000, because of data availability limitations.

Source: Brand Finance database (https://brandirectory.com); and International Monetary Fund, World Economic Outlook Database, October 2022 (www.imf.org/en/Publications/WEO/weo-database/2022/October). Data year: 2023.

7.1.4. Industrial designs by origin/bn PPP$ GDP

Number of designs contained in resident industrial design applications filed at a given national or regional office (per billion PPP$ GDP) | 2021

An industrial design is a set of exclusive rights granted by law to applicants to protect the ornamental or aesthetic aspect of their products. An industrial design is valid for a limited period of time and within a defined territory. A resident industrial design application refers to an application filed with the IP office for or on behalf of the applicant's country of residence. For example, an application filed with the Japan Patent Office by a resident of Japan is considered to be a resident application for Japan. Similarly, an application filed with the Office for Harmonization in the Internal Market (OHIM) by an applicant who resides in any of the OHIM member states, such as Italy, is considered to be a resident application for that member state (Italy). This indicator is based on design count – the total number of designs contained in the resident industrial design applications. Data are scaled by PPP$ GDP (billions).

Source: World Intellectual Property Organization, Intellectual Property Statistics (www.wipo.int/ipstats); and International Monetary Fund, World Economic Outlook Database, October 2022 (www.imf.org/en/Publications/WEO/weo-database/2022/October). Data years: 2014–2021.

7.2. Creative goods and services

7.2.1. Cultural and creative services exports, % total trade

Cultural and creative services exports (% of total trade) | 2021

Creative services exports as a percentage of total exports according to the Extended Balance of Payments Services Classification EBOPS 2010 – that is, EBOPS code SI3: Information services; code SJ22: Advertising, market research, and public opinion polling services; code SK1: Audio-visual and related services; and code SK23: Heritage and recreational services as a percentage of total trade. Values are based on the classification of the sixth (2009) edition of the International Monetary Fund's *Balance of Payments and International Investment Position Manual* and Balance of Payments database. See indicator 5.3.1 for the full definition of total trade.

Source: World Trade Organization and United Nations Conference on Trade and Development, Trade in Commercial Services database (www.wto.org/english/thewto_e/coher_e/wto_unctad_e.htm). Data years: 2014–2021.

7.2.2. National feature films/mn pop. 15–69

Number of national feature films produced (per million population, 15–69 years old) | 2021

A feature film is defined as a film with a running time of 60 minutes or longer. It includes works of fiction, animation and documentaries. It is intended for commercial exhibition in cinemas. Feature films produced exclusively for television broadcasting, as well as newsreels and advertising films, are excluded. Country of origin for co-productions is attributed to the majority producer. Data are reported per million population aged 15–69 years old.

Source: OMDIA (https://omdia.tech.informa.com/products/cinema-and-movies-intelligence-service); and United Nations Department of Economic and Social Affairs, Population Division, World Population Prospects 2022 (https://population.un.org/wpp). Data years: 2015–2021.

7.2.3. Entertainment and media market/th pop. 15–69

Global entertainment and media market (per thousand population, 15–69 years old) | 2022

The Global Entertainment & Media Outlook is a comprehensive source of global analyses and five-year forecasts of consumer and advertising spending across different territories and entertainment and media segments.

The figures for Algeria, Bahrain, the Islamic Republic of Iran, Jordan, Kuwait, Lebanon, Malta, Morocco, Oman, Qatar, Tunisia and Yemen were estimated from a total corresponding to Middle East and North Africa (MENA) countries using a breakdown of total GDP (current USD) for the above-mentioned countries to define referential percentages.

Source: PwC, Global Entertainment and Media Outlook, 2022–2026 (www.pwc.com/outlook); United Nations Department of Economic and Social Affairs, Population Division, World Population Prospects 2022 (https://population.un.org/wpp); and International Monetary Fund, World Economic Outlook Database, October 2022 (www.imf.org/en/Publications/WEO/weo-database/2022/October). Data years: 2020–2022.

7.2.4. Creative goods exports, % total trade

Creative goods exports (% of total trade) | 2021

Total value of creative goods exports (current USD) as a percentage of total trade. Creative goods exports based on the 2009 UNESCO Framework for Cultural Statistics, Table 3, International trade of cultural goods and services defined with the Harmonized System (HS) 2007 codes; World Trade Organization and United Nations Conference on Trade and Development, Trade in Commercial Services database, itself based on the sixth (2009) edition of the International Monetary Fund's *Balance of Payments and International Investment Position Manual* and Balance of Payments database. For the definition of total trade, see indicator 5.3.1.

Source: United Nations Comtrade Database (http://comtrade.un.org); and World Trade Organization and United Nations Conference on Trade and Development (www.wto.org/english/thewto_e/coher_e/wto_unctad_e.htm). Data years: 2015–2021.

7.3. Online creativity

7.3.1. Generic top-level domains (TLDs)/th pop. 15–69

Generic top-level domains (TLDs) (per thousand population, 15–69 years old) | 2022

A generic top-level domain (TLD) is one of the categories of TLDs maintained by the Internet Assigned Numbers Authority (IANA) for use on the internet. Generic TLDs can be unrestricted (.com, .info, .net and .org) or restricted – that is, used on the basis of fulfilling eligibility criteria (.biz, .name and .pro). Of these, the statistic covers the five generic domains .biz, .info, .org, .net and .com. Generic domains .name and .pro, and sponsored domains (.arpa, .aero, .asia, .cat, .coop, .edu, .gov, .int, .jobs, .mil, .museum, .tel and .travel) are not included. Neither are country-code top-level domains (refer to indicator 7.3.2). The statistic represents the total number of registered domains (i.e., net totals as of December 2021, existing domains + new registrations – expired domains). Data are collected on the basis of a 4 percent random sample of the total population of domains drawn from the root zone files (a complete listing of active domains) for each TLD. The geographic location of a domain is determined by the registration address for the domain name registrant that is returned from a whois query. These registration data are parsed by country and postal code and then aggregated to the required geographic levels, such as county, city or economy. The original hard data were scaled by thousand population, 15–69 years old. For confidentiality reasons, only normalized values are reported; while relative positions are preserved, magnitudes are not.

Source: ZookNIC Inc (www.zooknic.com); and United Nations Department of Economic and Social Affairs, Population Division, World Population Prospects 2022 (https://population.un.org/wpp). Data year: 2022.

7.3.2. Country-code TLDs/th pop. 15–69

Country-code top-level domains (TLDs) (per thousand population, 15–69 years old) | 2022

A country-code top-level domain (TLD) is one of the categories of TLDs maintained by the Internet Assigned Numbers Authority (IANA) for use on the internet. Country-code TLDs are two-letter domains especially designated for a particular economy, country or autonomous territory. The statistic represents the total number of registered domains (i.e., net totals as of December 2021, existing domains + new registrations – expired domains). Data are collected from the registry responsible for each country-code TLD and represent the total number of domain registrations in the country-code TLD. Each country-code TLD is assigned to the country with which it is associated rather than based on the registration address of the registrant. ZookNIC reports that, for the country-code TLDs it covers, 85–100 percent of domains are registered in the same country; the only exceptions are the country-code TLDs that have been licensed for worldwide commercial use. Data are reported per thousand population, 15–69 years old. For confidentiality reasons, only normalized values are reported; while relative positions are preserved, magnitudes are not.

Source: ZookNIC Inc (www.zooknic.com); and United Nations Department of Economic and Social Affairs, Population Division, World Population Prospects 2022 (https://population.un.org/wpp). Data year: 2022.

7.3.3. GitHub commits/mn pop. 15–69

GitHub commit pushes received and sent (per million population, 15–69 years old) | 2022

GitHub is the world's largest host of source code and a commit is the term used for a change on this platform. One or more commits can be saved (or pushed) to projects (or repositories). Thus, "GitHub commit pushes received and sent" refers to the sum of the number of batched changes received and sent by projects on GitHub that are publicly available within a specific economy. Automated activity resulting in non-productive commits is excluded.

Source: GitHub (https://github.com); and United Nations Department of Economic and Social Affairs, Population Division, World Population Prospects 2022 (https://population.un.org/wpp). Data year: 2022.

7.3.4. Mobile app creation/bn PPP$ GDP

Global downloads of mobile apps (per billion PPP$ GDP, two-year average) | 2022

Global downloads of mobile apps, by origin of the headquarters of the developer/firm, scaled by PPP$ GDP (billions). Global downloads are compiled by data.ia, public data sources and the company's proprietary forecast model based on data from Google Play Store and iOS App Store in each country. Since data for China are not available for Google Play Store and only for iOS App Store, data from China are treated as missing and classified as "n/a."

Source: data.ia (formerly App Annie) (www.data.ai/en/); and International Monetary Fund, World Economic Outlook Database, October 2022 (www.imf.org/en/Publications/WEO/weo-database/2022/October). Data years: 2020–2022.

Appendix IV Global Innovation Index science and technology cluster methodology

Since 2016, the Global Innovation Index (GII) has sought to identify science and technology (S&T) clusters using a bottom-up approach. This approach disregards administrative or political borders and instead pinpoints those geographical areas that show a high density of inventors and scientific authors. The resulting clusters often encompass several municipal districts, sub-federal states and sometimes even two or more countries. Two innovation metrics are employed in the compilation of the top 100 GII S&T clusters worldwide: location of inventors listed on published patent applications and authors listed on published scientific articles.

For patents, this method relies on applications under WIPO's Patent Cooperation Treaty (PCT). PCT patents offer a useful basis for analyzing patents globally. The PCT system applies a single set of procedural rules and collects information based on uniform filing standards. This reduces potential biases that could arise from using data collected from multiple national sources. The patents selected were published over the most recent five-year period available, between 2018 and 2022, to minimize the effects of volatility that can occur between years.[1]

To widen the range of innovation included, scientific publications from the Web of Science's Science Citation Index Expanded (SCIE) are incorporated. The SCIE provides detailed coverage of the world's most impactful academic journals. For the analysis presented here, science and technology fields are the focus, while articles from the fields of social sciences and humanities are disregarded. In addition, scientific publications are limited solely to articles of original research. This excludes other published items, such as meeting abstracts, conference summaries or paper briefs. As with PCT filings, the most recent five-year period according to data availability was also used for the SCIE – publication years 2017 to 2021.

The WIPO PCT patent data set consists of approximately 1.3 million patent applications published between 2018 and 2022, containing 3.9 million inventor addresses. For the SCIE, the data set comprises 7.6 million articles published between 2017 and 2021, containing 25.1 million listed author addresses.

The process for geocoding of addresses for this report is as follows. PCT inventor addresses were geocoded using the Environmental Systems Research Institute (ESRI) ArcGIS World Geocoder service.[2] In cases where the ESRI address matches proved either ambiguous or insufficiently accurate, the city name in the address string was extracted and matched using records in the city-level data set from the GeoNames Gazetteer database.[3] This latter database gives the geolocation of cities around the globe and contains 48,000 geocoded cities. This same city-matching approach was applied to all SCIE author addresses.

Overall, 97.6 percent of inventor addresses were geocoded at either the city level or a more accurate level, while 95.7 percent of scientific author addresses were geocoded at the city level. Appendix Table 5 provides a summary of the geocoding results for the top 20 countries, which together account for the majority of inventor and scientific author addresses. As shown in the table, the coverage of geocoded PCT inventor addresses across all 20 countries is typically above 98 percent, only falling below 98 percent in one instance. Coverage of scientific author addresses is also high, above 90% in all but one instance. All of the 20 countries had at least 95 percent of their PCT applications and Scientific articles contain at least one inventor or author with a geocoded address, only falling below 95 percent in one instance.

Addresses were clustered by applying the density-based spatial clustering of applications with noise (DBSCAN) algorithm. This algorithm requires predefined radius and density parameters. As in previous years, a radius of 15 km and a density of 4,500 listed inventors/authors was applied. Equal weight was given to inventors and authors by expressing data points as a share of total inventor and author addresses, respectively. Given that the number of scientific articles far exceeds the number of patents, cluster identification based on the raw data points would have resulted in clusters shaped predominantly by the scientific author landscape.

The result was an initial list of 248 clusters. After review, neighboring clusters were merged if the edge of one cluster was within 3–5 km of another and where the co-author/co-inventor relationships were higher than for any other relationship with any other cluster or non-cluster points. A total of 22 clusters met these criteria, with mergers reducing the overall number of clusters identified to 237.[4]

The remaining 237 clusters were then ranked by counting the number of patents and scientific articles in a given cluster. Numbers were aggregated using fractional counting, in which counts reflect the share of a patent's inventors and an article's authors present in a particular cluster. In addition, mirroring the equal weighting approach described above, fractional counts are relative to the total numbers of patents and scientific articles.

To produce an intensity ranking, the European Commission's Global Human Settlement Layer (GHSL) population distribution data were matched geographically to the top 100 clusters identified in the overall ranking.[5] Just as with inventor/author geocoded locations, these population data allowed us to define the total population of a cluster using a bottom-up approach. We chose to define a cluster's area as all the space within 0.05 degrees of each inventor/author location. Overlaying the resultant cluster polygons on top of the population data and aggregating all points which lay within each polygon gave a total population estimate for each cluster.[6] The clusters were then ranked by dividing the total S&T share by population.

Appendix Table 3 Top 100 S&T clusters, 2023

Rank	Cluster name	Economy	PCT applications	Scientific publications	Share total PCT filings (%)	Share of total pubs (%)	Total	Previous rank[a]	Rank change[a]
1	Tokyo–Yokohama	JP	127,418	115,020	10.1	1.5	11.7	1	0
2	Shenzhen–Hong Kong–Guangzhou	CN/HK	113,482	153,180	9.0	2.1	11.1	2	0
3	Seoul	KR	63,447	133,604	5.1	1.8	6.8	4	1
4	Beijing	CN	38,067	279,485	3.0	3.7	6.8	3	−1
5	Shanghai–Suzhou	CN	32,924	162,635	2.6	2.2	4.8	6	1
6	San Jose–San Francisco, CA	US	47,269	58,575	3.8	0.8	4.6	5	−1
7	Osaka–Kobe–Kyoto	JP	38,413	51,948	3.1	0.7	3.8	7	0
8	Boston–Cambridge, MA	US	18,184	76,378	1.4	1.0	2.5	8	0
9	San Diego, CA	US	23,261	20,928	1.9	0.3	2.1	11	2
10	New York City, NY	US	13,838	74,849	1.1	1.0	2.1	9	−1
11	Nanjing	CN	7,143	113,488	0.6	1.5	2.1	12	1
12	Paris	FR	15,176	61,692	1.2	0.8	2.0	10	−2
13	Wuhan	CN	6,250	89,756	0.5	1.2	1.7	15	2
14	Hangzhou	CN	10,755	62,924	0.9	0.8	1.7	14	0
15	Nagoya	JP	17,736	16,091	1.4	0.2	1.6	13	−2
16	Los Angeles, CA	US	11,556	44,058	0.9	0.6	1.5	16	0
17	Washington, DC–Baltimore, MD	US	5,525	76,039	0.4	1.0	1.5	17	0
18	Daejeon	KR	12,275	25,552	1.0	0.3	1.3	20	2
19	Xi'an	CN	1,786	86,937	0.1	1.2	1.3	21	2
20	London	GB	5,981	59,068	0.5	0.8	1.3	18	−2
21	Seattle, WA	US	11,472	20,322	0.9	0.3	1.2	19	−2
22	Munich	DE	10,248	24,239	0.8	0.3	1.1	22	0
23	Qingdao	CN	7,286	39,745	0.6	0.5	1.1	29	6
24	Chengdu	CN	2,046	67,334	0.2	0.9	1.1	27	3
25	Cologne	DE	7,466	34,286	0.6	0.5	1.1	23	−2
26	Amsterdam–Rotterdam	NL	4,230	52,864	0.3	0.7	1.0	25	−1
27	Taipei–Hsinchu	TW*	3,907	52,752	0.3	0.7	1.0	26	−1
28	Houston, TX	US	8,475	24,636	0.7	0.3	1.0	24	−4
29	Stuttgart	DE	9,342	14,874	0.7	0.2	0.9	28	−1
30	Tel Aviv–Jerusalem	IL	7,268	24,219	0.6	0.3	0.9	31	1
31	Moscow	RU	2,036	55,086	0.2	0.7	0.9	32	1
32	Chicago, IL	US	5,763	32,343	0.5	0.4	0.9	30	−2
33	Singapore	SG/MY	4,861	36,803	0.4	0.5	0.9	35	2
34	Tehran	IR	249	63,113	0.0	0.8	0.9	33	−1
35	Philadelphia, PA	US	5,390	32,309	0.4	0.4	0.9	34	−1
36	Tianjin	CN	1,267	53,680	0.1	0.7	0.8	36	0
37	Changsha	CN	1,149	52,768	0.1	0.7	0.8	39	2
38	Stockholm	SE	6,069	19,984	0.5	0.3	0.8	37	−1
39	Minneapolis, MN	US	6,625	15,375	0.5	0.2	0.7	38	−1
40	Hefei	CN	2,549	38,974	0.2	0.5	0.7	53	13
41	Eindhoven	NL	7,982	5,339	0.6	0.1	0.7	40	−1
42	Melbourne	AU	2,126	40,056	0.2	0.5	0.7	41	−1
43	Berlin	DE	3,624	30,464	0.3	0.4	0.7	42	−1
44	Chongqing	CN	1,651	41,412	0.1	0.6	0.7	49	5
45	Frankfurt am Main	DE	5,410	18,590	0.4	0.2	0.7	43	−2
46	Sydney	AU	2,539	33,695	0.2	0.5	0.7	44	−2
47	Raleigh, NC	US	3,057	30,206	0.2	0.4	0.6	45	−2
48	Madrid	ES	1,580	38,849	0.1	0.5	0.6	46	−2
49	Zürich	CH	3,759	24,437	0.3	0.3	0.6	50	1
50	Milan	IT	2,578	31,077	0.2	0.4	0.6	51	1
51	Brussels–Antwerp	BE	3,079	27,659	0.2	0.4	0.6	48	−3

Appendix Table 3 Continued

Rank	Cluster name	Economy	PCT applications	Scientific publications	Share total PCT filings (%)	Share of total pubs (%)	Total	Previous rank[a]	Rank change[a]
52	Toronto, ON	CA	2,756	28,967	0.2	0.4	0.6	54	2
53	Harbin	CN	251	42,974	0.0	0.6	0.6	55	2
54	Barcelona	ES	2,431	29,851	0.2	0.4	0.6	52	−2
55	Jinan	CN	1,638	34,308	0.1	0.5	0.6	57	2
56	Bengaluru	IN	4,342	15,579	0.3	0.2	0.6	60	4
57	Denver, CO	US	3,084	21,910	0.2	0.3	0.5	59	2
58	Changchun	CN	376	37,310	0.0	0.5	0.5	63	5
59	Istanbul	TR	2,144	26,230	0.2	0.4	0.5	47	−12
60	Montréal, QC	CA	2,235	25,406	0.2	0.3	0.5	58	−2
61	Copenhagen	DK	3,123	18,911	0.2	0.3	0.5	62	1
62	Heidelberg–Mannheim	DE	3,941	13,849	0.3	0.2	0.5	61	−1
63	Shenyang	CN	716	32,840	0.1	0.4	0.5	68	5
64	Delhi	IN	1,111	30,443	0.1	0.4	0.5	65	1
65	Cambridge	GB	3,146	17,751	0.3	0.2	0.5	64	−1
66	Rome	IT	960	29,642	0.1	0.4	0.5	67	1
67	Portland, OR	US	4,769	6,705	0.4	0.1	0.5	56	−11
68	Atlanta, GA	US	1,844	23,550	0.1	0.3	0.5	66	−2
69	Dalian	CN	1,089	27,534	0.1	0.4	0.5	69	0
70	Nuremberg–Erlangen	DE	3,619	9,491	0.3	0.1	0.4	71	1
71	Dallas, TX	US	3,458	10,093	0.3	0.1	0.4	73	2
72	São Paulo	BR	763	25,815	0.1	0.3	0.4	70	−2
73	Helsinki	FI	2,841	13,367	0.2	0.2	0.4	74	1
74	Busan	KR	2,314	16,194	0.2	0.2	0.4	75	1
75	Zhengzhou	CN	740	25,472	0.1	0.3	0.4	82	7
76	Vienna	AT	1,589	20,160	0.1	0.3	0.4	76	0
77	Cincinnati, OH	US	3,460	7,753	0.3	0.1	0.4	72	−5
78	Pittsburgh, PA	US	1,869	17,051	0.1	0.2	0.4	79	1
79	Oxford	GB	1,583	18,437	0.1	0.2	0.4	77	−2
80	Xiamen	CN	1,947	16,127	0.2	0.2	0.4	85	5
81	Ann Arbor, MI	US	1,266	19,984	0.1	0.3	0.4	78	−3
82	Lanzhou	CN	464	23,368	0.0	0.3	0.4	93	11
83	Chennai	IN	1,133	19,367	0.1	0.3	0.4	88	5
84	Mumbai	IN	1,606	16,203	0.1	0.2	0.3	84	0
85	Vancouver, BC	CA	1,586	16,167	0.1	0.2	0.3	83	−2
86	Kanazawa	JP	3,687	3,441	0.3	0.0	0.3	80	−6
87	Ankara	TR	739	20,308	0.1	0.3	0.3	86	−1
88	Lyon	FR	2,123	12,050	0.2	0.2	0.3	81	−7
89	Zhenjiang	CN	928	18,948	0.1	0.3	0.3	104	15
90	Warsaw	PL	446	21,602	0.0	0.3	0.3	89	−1
91	Daegu	KR	1,837	13,061	0.1	0.2	0.3	91	0
92	Austin, TX	US	2,320	9,917	0.2	0.1	0.3	90	−2
93	Wuxi	CN	2,110	10,906	0.2	0.1	0.3	106	13
94	Fuzhou	CN	678	19,405	0.1	0.3	0.3	102	8
95	Ottawa, ON	CA	1,898	11,986	0.2	0.2	0.3	92	−3
96	Phoenix, AZ	US	2,364	9,051	0.2	0.1	0.3	87	−9
97	Basel	CH/DE/FR	2,556	7,774	0.2	0.1	0.3	96	−1
98	Göteborg	SE	2,078	10,329	0.2	0.1	0.3	95	−3
99	Hamburg	DE	1,765	11,479	0.1	0.2	0.3	99	0
100	Brisbane	AU	1,129	15,233	0.1	0.2	0.3	97	−3

Source: WIPO Statistics Database, May 2023.

Notes: [a] This column represents the previous year's rankings, which have been adjusted to align with the updated methodology. The codes given in the tables in this appendix are the ISO alpha-2 country codes, with the following addition: TW* = Taiwan, Province of China.

Appendix Table 4 Ranking of S&T intensity

Rank per capita	Cluster name	Economy	Estimated cluster population	PCT applications per capita[a]	Scientific publications per capita[a]	Total S&T share per capita[a]	Rank change[b]
1	Cambridge	GB	477,995	6,582	37,136	1.02	0
2	San Jose–San Francisco, CA	US	6,262,908	7,547	9,353	0.73	0
3	Oxford	GB	539,483	2,934	34,176	0.69	0
4	Eindhoven	NL	1,031,903	7,735	5,174	0.69	0
5	Boston–Cambridge, MA	US	4,232,444	4,296	18,046	0.58	1
6	Daejeon	KR	2,348,673	5,226	10,879	0.56	−1
7	Ann Arbor, MI	US	659,586	1,920	30,297	0.56	0
8	San Diego, CA	US	3,835,826	6,064	5,456	0.56	0
9	Seattle, WA	US	2,526,151	4,541	8,045	0.47	0
10	Munich	DE	2,767,781	3,702	8,757	0.41	4
11	Kanazawa	JP	881,092	4,184	3,905	0.39	1
12	Raleigh, NC	US	1,772,830	1,724	17,038	0.37	3
13	Göteborg	SE	841,183	2,470	12,279	0.36	3
14	Beijing	CN	19,292,327	1,973	14,487	0.35	4
15	Stockholm	SE	2,159,150	2,811	9,255	0.35	2
16	Helsinki	FI	1,232,664	2,305	10,844	0.33	3
17	Zürich	CH	1,933,135	1,945	12,641	0.32	3
18	Tokyo–Yokohama	JP	36,197,318	3,520	3,178	0.32	3
19	Basel	CH/DE/FR	1,020,380	2,505	7,619	0.30	6
20	Copenhagen	DK	1,670,776	1,869	11,319	0.30	2
21	Nuremberg–Erlangen	DE	1,384,238	2,615	6,857	0.30	2
22	Stuttgart	DE	3,195,495	2,923	4,655	0.30	2
23	Minneapolis, MN	US	2,699,170	2,454	5,696	0.27	3
24	Pittsburgh, PA	US	1,395,595	1,339	12,218	0.27	3
25	Seoul	KR	26,436,274	2,400	5,054	0.26	4
26	Heidelberg–Mannheim	DE	2,003,186	1,968	6,914	0.25	2
27	Ottawa, ON	CA	1,255,368	1,512	9,548	0.25	3
28	Nanjing	CN	8,632,198	827	13,147	0.24	7
29	Hangzhou	CN	7,021,090	1,532	8,962	0.24	4
30	Osaka–Kobe–Kyoto	JP	15,704,848	2,446	3,308	0.24	2
31	Qingdao	CN	4,883,232	1,492	8,139	0.23	7
32	Shenzhen–Hong Kong–Guangzhou	CN/HK	49,538,901	2,291	3,092	0.22	5
33	Washington, DC–Baltimore, MD	US	6,958,796	794	10,927	0.21	3
34	Portland, OR	US	2,258,229	2,112	2,969	0.21	−3
35	Xi'an	CN	6,290,985	284	13,819	0.21	6
36	Cincinnati, OH	US	1,857,103	1,863	4,175	0.20	−2
37	Changsha	CN	3,997,004	288	13,202	0.20	6
38	Wuhan	CN	8,839,629	707	10,154	0.19	8
39	Nagoya	JP	8,964,894	1,978	1,795	0.18	0
40	Paris	FR	11,217,166	1,353	5,500	0.18	2
41	Vancouver, BC	CA	1,920,504	826	8,418	0.18	3
42	Frankfurt am Main	DE	3,813,326	1,419	4,875	0.18	3
43	Lyon	FR	1,874,163	1,133	6,429	0.18	−3
44	Denver, CO	US	3,072,747	1,004	7,130	0.18	5
45	Sydney	AU	3,839,713	661	8,775	0.17	3
46	Philadelphia, PA	US	5,076,519	1,062	6,364	0.17	4
47	Vienna	AT	2,406,439	660	8,377	0.16	5
48	Houston, TX	US	6,128,063	1,383	4,020	0.16	−1
49	Berlin	DE	4,275,066	848	7,126	0.16	2
50	Atlanta, GA	US	2,841,151	649	8,289	0.16	3

Appendix Table 4 Continued

Rank per capita	Cluster name	Economy	Estimated cluster population	PCT applications per capita[a]	Scientific publications per capita[a]	Total S&T share per capita[a]	Rank change[b]
51	Austin, TX	US	1,967,860	1,179	5,039	0.16	3
52	Melbourne	AU	4,529,662	469	8,843	0.16	3
53	Amsterdam–Rotterdam	NL	6,953,571	608	7,602	0.15	3
54	Montréal, QC	CA	3,507,450	637	7,244	0.15	3
55	Changchun	CN	3,624,328	104	10,294	0.15	5
56	Brussels–Antwerp	BE	4,254,045	724	6,502	0.14	2
57	Brisbane	AU	2,049,367	551	7,433	0.14	2
58	Milan	IT	4,470,896	577	6,951	0.14	4
59	Jinan	CN	4,262,386	384	8,049	0.14	8
60	Chengdu	CN	7,789,484	263	8,644	0.14	13
61	Rome	IT	3,501,527	274	8,465	0.14	3
62	Toronto, ON	CA	4,493,449	613	6,446	0.14	1
63	Hefei	CN	5,429,701	469	7,178	0.13	18
64	New York City, NY	US	16,134,372	858	4,639	0.13	1
65	Chicago, IL	US	6,900,333	835	4,687	0.13	−4
66	Harbin	CN	4,649,090	54	9,244	0.13	6
67	Dalian	CN	3,559,819	306	7,735	0.13	8
68	Tehran	IR	6,771,866	37	9,320	0.13	−2
69	Warsaw	PL	2,547,547	175	8,480	0.13	0
70	Lanzhou	CN	2,761,553	168	8,462	0.13	7
71	Tel Aviv–Jerusalem	IL	7,215,450	1,007	3,357	0.13	−3
72	London	GB	10,204,869	586	5,788	0.12	−2
73	Los Angeles, CA	US	12,262,007	942	3,593	0.12	1
74	Shanghai–Suzhou	CN	39,290,672	838	4,139	0.12	8
75	Hamburg	DE	2,435,222	725	4,714	0.12	−4
76	Barcelona	ES	5,060,158	480	5,899	0.12	0
77	Singapore	SG/MY	7,629,733	637	4,824	0.12	1
78	Daegu	KR	2,828,895	650	4,617	0.11	2
79	Cologne	DE	9,636,503	775	3,558	0.11	0
80	Zhenjiang	CN	3,107,637	299	6,097	0.11	n.a.
81	Xiamen	CN	3,575,564	545	4,510	0.10	6
82	Madrid	ES	6,430,213	246	6,042	0.10	2
83	Phoenix, AZ	US	3,160,779	748	2,864	0.10	0
84	Busan	KR	4,108,717	563	3,941	0.10	1
85	Tianjin	CN	8,503,650	149	6,313	0.10	3
86	Dallas, TX	US	4,264,360	811	2,367	0.10	0
87	Taipei–Hsinchu	TW*	11,351,789	344	4,647	0.09	2
88	Shenyang	CN	5,926,243	121	5,541	0.08	2
89	Fuzhou	CN	3,788,203	179	5,123	0.08	n.a.
90	Chongqing	CN	8,587,433	192	4,822	0.08	1
91	Zhengzhou	CN	5,355,743	138	4,756	0.07	2
92	Wuxi	CN	4,557,289	463	2,393	0.07	n.a.
93	Ankara	TR	4,858,391	152	4,180	0.07	−1
94	Moscow	RU	14,055,141	145	3,919	0.06	0
95	Istanbul	TR	12,694,255	169	2,066	0.04	0
96	Bengaluru	IN	14,805,929	293	1,052	0.04	0
97	Chennai	IN	10,687,599	106	1,812	0.03	0
98	São Paulo	BR	18,356,410	42	1,406	0.02	0
99	Delhi	IN	28,458,701	39	1,070	0.02	0
100	Mumbai	IN	21,112,341	76	767	0.02	0

Source: WIPO Statistics Database, May 2023.

Notes: [a] Per capita figures refer to 1,000,000 of population. [b] This column represents the previous year's rankings, which have been adjusted to align with the updated methodology. n.a. indicates not applicable. The codes given in the tables in this appendix are the ISO alpha-2 country codes, with the following addition: TW* = Taiwan, Province of China.

Appendix Table 5 Summary of geocoding results

Country	Scientific publications: Number of addresses	Scientific publications: City-level address accuracy (%)	Scientific publications: Publications covered (%)	PCT applications: Number of addresses	PCT applications: Block-level address accuracy (%)	PCT applications: Sub-city-level address accuracy (%)	PCT applications: City-level address accuracy (%)	PCT applications: Applications covered (%)
China	5,709,166	99.0	99.5	899,931	83.0	0.0	16.9	99.8
United States	6,926,084	97.0	98.3	945,562	96.0	3.7	0.2	99.9
Japan	1,292,914	92.2	95.5	621,999	32.9	23.6	41.4	98.4
Germany	1,512,886	97.6	98.4	272,949	97.3	0.7	1.9	99.9
Republic of Korea	858,760	96.5	98.1	293,886	30.3	0.6	69.0	99.9
United Kingdom	1,541,130	96.9	97.9	87,833	54.8	39.5	5.4	99.7
France	1,137,986	93.3	95.5	107,561	92.6	3.9	2.4	99.1
Italy	1,282,423	95.9	97.3	46,693	93.3	4.8	1.6	99.7
India	899,463	92.4	95.0	48,458	34.7	53.3	11.1	99.4
Canada	973,115	98.3	99.0	47,255	96.9	2.8	0.3	99.8
Spain	972,255	97.5	98.6	27,806	85.2	11.3	2.8	99.7
Netherlands (Kingdom of the)	549,403	97.5	98.6	50,507	85.1	0.3	14.0	99.4
Brazil	742,852	98.5	99.6	10,818	89.3	9.3	1.1	99.7
Australia	941,612	86.2	90.4	21,683	91.1	5.2	3.4	99.8
Switzerland	368,966	90.8	92.5	43,048	92.2	1.3	6.2	99.7
Russian Federation	430,319	99.0	99.2	16,506	94.3	3.9	1.4	99.7
Sweden	324,003	98.0	98.4	46,067	94.9	0.7	4.0	99.6
Türkiye	423,747	96.5	96.6	17,814	59.6	27.8	10.9	98.8
Israel	176,686	92.5	96.8	32,813	70.7	4.1	18.6	96.2
Belgium	270,683	95.6	97.2	19,179	98.2	0.9	0.7	99.8
World Total	**25,138,682**	**95.7**	**98.6**	**3,932,217**	**73.2**	**7.0**	**17.4**	**97.8**

Source: WIPO Statistics Database, May 2023.

Note: This list includes the top 20 countries that account for and ordered by the highest combined shares of patents and scientific articles. PCT inventor addresses were geocoded to the highest level of detail. Due to their much larger volume, scientific author addresses were geocoded to the city level only.

Notes

1 In previous editions, PCT publications years were aligned with SCIE publication years, as SCIE data is available with a one-year lag. This year we decided to change to "most recently available data" in order to more accurately reflect the most recent innovation.

2 ESRI ArcGIS World Geocoder service: www.esri.com/en-us/arcgis/products/arcgis-world-geocoder.

3 GeoNames: http://geonames.org.

4 The mergers involved the following clusters: Aurora with Chicago; Baltimore with Washington DC; Boulder with Denver; Cheonan-si with Seoul; Irvine with Los Angeles; Jerusalem with Tel Aviv; Matsudo with Tokyo–Yokohama; Rotterdam with Amsterdam; Suzhou with Shanghai; Wilmington with Philadelphia; Worcester with Boston–Cambridge, MA.

5 See Schiavina *et al.* (2023).

6 See Bergquist and Fink (2020: 61–63) for a more detailed description of how population data were matched to clusters.

References

Bergquist, K. and C. Fink (2000). The top 100 science and technology clusters. In Dutta, S., B. Lanvin and S. Wunsch-Vincent (eds), *The Global Innovation Index 2000: Who Will Finance Innovation?* Ithaca, NY, Fontainebleau and Geneva: Cornell University, INSEAD and World Intellectual Property Organization. Available at: www.wipo.int/edocs/pubdocs/en/wipo_pub_gii_2020.pdf.

Schiavina M., S. Freire, A. Carioli and K. MacManus (2023). GHS-POP R2023A – GHS population grid multitemporal (1975--2030). Brussels: European Commission, Joint Research Centre (JRC). Available at: http://data.europa.eu/89h/2ff68a52-5b5b-4a22-8f40-c41da8332cfe.

www.ingramcontent.com/pod-product-compliance
Ingram Content Group UK Ltd.
Pitfield, Milton Keynes, MK11 3LW, UK
UKHW052153041026
15590UKWH00007B/2051